P9-ASN-977

DISCARDED
UNIVERSITY OF WINNIPEG
LIBRARY
515 Portage Avenue
Winnipeg, Manitoba R3B 2E9

Queen Anne

1 Queen Anne in 1703, by Edmund Lilly

DA
495
.G73
1980

Edward Gregg

Queen Anne

Routledge & Kegan Paul
London, Boston and Henley

To my parents

First published in 1980
by Routledge & Kegan Paul Ltd
39 Store Street, London WC1E 7DD,
9 Park Street, Boston, Mass. 02108, USA, and
Broadway House, Newtown Road,
Henley-on-Thames, Oxon RG9 1EN
Set in Linocomp Palatino by
Rowland Phototypesetting Ltd
Bury St Edmunds, Suffolk
and printed in Great Britain by
Unwin Brothers Limited,
The Gresham Press, Old Woking, Surrey
Copyright Edward Gregg 1980
No part of this book may be reproduced in
any form without permission from the
publisher, except for the quotation of brief
passages in criticism

British Library Cataloguing in Publication Data

Gregg, Edward

Queen Anne.
1. Anne, Queen of Great Britain
2. Great Britain – Queens – Biography
I. Title
941.06'9'0924   DA495   79-41312

ISBN 0 7100 0400 1

Contents

Illustrations

Acknowledgments

I gratefully acknowledge the gracious permission of Her Majesty the Queen for access to the Royal Archives at Windsor and for permission to reproduce paintings from the Royal Collection; His Royal Highness the Prince of Wales for access to the Chevening papers; His Grace the Duke of Portland, and the Trustees of the British Library, for access to the Portland Loan; His Grace the Duke of Marlborough for the right to quote from the Blenheim archives, as well as the right to reproduce portraits which are on public view at Blenheim Palace; and I also offer my thanks to the Marquess of Bath, the Earl Spencer, and the Earl of Stair for permission to examine manuscripts in their possession.

Many individuals have been generous with their time, advice and specialized knowledge. I must thank Dr G. V. Bennett of New College, Oxford; Dr Derek McKay of the London School of Economics; Dr Stephen Baxter of the University of North Carolina; Dr Hugh Dunthorne of University College, Swansea; and Mr Robert Bergh, who translated Danish texts for me and also generously supplied me with material from his own research work. Those readers who examine the notes will realize the enormous debt which I owe to Professor Henry L. Snyder of the University of Kansas. Above all, I should like to thank Professor Ragnhild M. Hatton of the London School of Economics, for her help, advice, criticism, and encouragement.

The archivists and librarians in the public and private institutions where I have worked have been unfailingly helpful, as have my colleagues at the University of South Carolina, on whom I have called for advice on particular points. Ms Preshema Harris deserves particular thanks for typing the final manuscript. Any errors, of course, remain my own responsibility.

Preface

Queen Anne has often been portrayed as a pasteboard character, a dull, weak, irresolute woman dominated by favourites, her policies determined by the outcome of bedchamber quarrels. This was the view propagated during the queen's life and after her death by Sarah Churchill, Duchess of Marlborough, and it was immortalized in the first of the 'inside' political autobiographies, *The Conduct of the dowager Duchess of Marlborough*, published twenty-eight years after Queen Anne's death. So widely accepted did Sarah's account become that the queen was largely relegated to the background in subsequent studies of the reign, whose treatment of her was either harshly censorious or overly sympathetic, depending upon whether the authors were pro- or anti-Marlborough.

The present work is not an attempt to present a 'life and times' account of the queen; *England under Queen Anne* by G. M. Trevelyan, who pioneered a new interpretation of the queen's role and importance, remains as magisterial today as when it was published forty years ago. It would be equally useless to attempt a 'private life' of a monarch who stood at the centre of the political stage. Instead, the present work is an effort to integrate the public and private aspects of the queen's life in order to present a balanced picture of her, both as a ruler and as a private individual.

The scope of Trevelyan's work did not allow him to deal extensively with the queen, nor was he allowed access to the Blenheim archives. This source was opened to historians after the Second World War and, since the research for the present book was completed, these papers have been acquired by the nation. The Blenheim archives contain the bulk of the queen's extant personal correspondence, which presents a formidable challenge to the professional historian, for she habitually failed to date her letters ('Wednesday, Windsor' is a typical example). I have attempted to place more than 1,000 letters in correct chronological sequence; from these letters, many of which have never before been published, emerges a picture of a woman and a ruler which differs in many points from the traditional image. The queen's reign was dominated by a great international struggle against Louis XIV and by the activities of her potential successors, Hanoverian and Jacobite; consequently, I have drawn extensively from material in foreign archives, particularly from the Archives des Affaires Étrangères in Paris and the Niedersächsisches Staatsarchiv in Hanover, as well as from works published by Continental historians. The dispatches of foreign agents, despite their frequent confusion regarding the English party system, often provide acute perceptions of the problems and personalities of the age. Finally, I have relied heavily on the extensive work and interpretation of other contemporary scholars in the period, particularly J. H. Plumb, Geoffrey Holmes, G. V. Bennett, and Henry Snyder.

The reader will frequently be confronted by the clash between illusion and reality – the illusion produced by an age which vaunted the position of royalty, the reality imposed by common human frailty. Queen Anne's story may confirm Hobbes's observation that life is 'nasty, brutish, and short'; it may also confirm the queen's domination of the age which took her name.

Genealogy

The House of Stuart

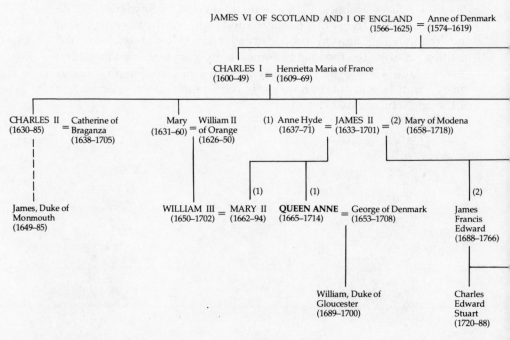

JAMES VI OF SCOTLAND AND I OF ENGLAND = Anne of Denmark
(1566–1625)   (1574–1619)

CHARLES I = Henrietta Maria of France
(1600–49)   (1609–69)

CHARLES II = Catherine of Braganza (1638–1705)
(1630–85)

Mary (1631–60) = William II of Orange (1626–50)

(1) Anne Hyde (1637–71) = JAMES II (1633–1701) = (2) Mary of Modena (1658–1718))

James, Duke of Monmouth (1649–85)

WILLIAM III (1650–1702) = MARY II (1662–94)

(1)

QUEEN ANNE (1665–1714) = George of Denmark (1653–1708)

(1)

(2)

James Francis Edward (1688–1766)

William, Duke of Gloucester (1689–1700)

Charles Edward Stuart (1720–88)

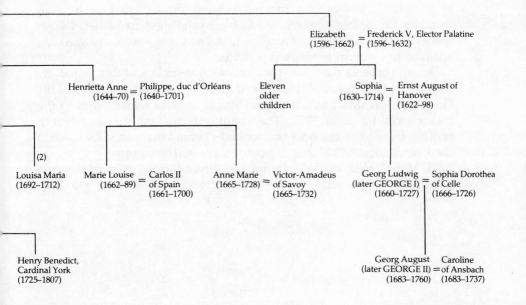

Elizabeth = Frederick V, Elector Palatine
(1596–1662)   (1596–1632)

Henrietta Anne = Philippe, duc d'Orléans   Eleven   Sophia = Ernst August of
(1644–70)   (1640–1701)   older   (1630–1714)   Hanover
                                                   children   (1622–98)

(2)
Louisa Maria   Marie Louise = Carlos II   Anne Marie = Victor-Amadeus   Georg Ludwig = Sophia Dorothea
(1692–1712)   (1662–89)   of Spain   (1665–1728)   of Savoy   (later GEORGE I)   of Celle
                                     (1661–1700)   (1665–1732)   (1660–1727)   (1666–1726)

Henry Benedict,   Georg August   Caroline
Cardinal York   (later GEORGE II) = of Ansbach
(1725–1807)   (1683–1760)   (1683–1737)

Note on Spelling and Dating

In so far as possible, I have attempted to reproduce Queen Anne's letters, and those of her contemporaries, exactly as they were written. For this reason, I have preferred to quote from the original text, whenever available, rather than from modernized, printed versions. In order to make the queen's letters intelligible to the modern reader, I have modernized the punctuation and – in a few cases – have changed her spelling to conform to modern practice.

Dating presents particular problems to any student of this period. By the time of Queen Anne's birth, most European nations had adopted the Gregorian calendar, but Protestant Britain was to remain loyal to the Julian calendar until 1752. The result was that in the seventeenth century the British calendar was ten days behind that generally used on the Continent; in 1700 this difference increased to eleven days.

All dates used in the text are Old Style (OS); for events on the Continent, I have either indicated New Style (NS) or have given both dates.

1

'I have a Good Heart Thank God'

Child of State,
1665–83

Queen Anne was born and bred in a civilization deeply scarred by turmoil and in an age in which the past was a frail and uncertain guide to the future. The history of her dynasty, the house of Stuart, was overshadowed by the century of warfare between Roman Catholicism and Protestantism from which Europe was only just beginning to recover. Her future inheritance, the crowns of England, Scotland, and Ireland, had recently emerged from the most turbulent twenty years in their joint histories. The policies of her grandfather, Charles I, had led him into a civil war against his subjects which culminated with the king's execution in January 1649 and the establishment of a republic under the guidance of Oliver Cromwell. The Stuarts, in exile on the Continent, were only the most prominent losers in this fratricidal conflict; the episcopal Church of England was disestablished and the traditional political predominance of the hereditary upper classes was overthrown.

The new, radical, republican settlement which seemed permanent during the 1650s was, in reality, only held together by the genius of its presiding officer: as soon as Cromwell died, in September 1658, his work began to unravel. By 30 May 1660, the titular king, Charles II, was restored in triumph to his martyred father's throne. The propertied classes rapidly, and relentlessly, re-established their traditional political, social, and economic domination of English life. The Church of England was also restored, armed with new, persecuting statute laws to ensure that its enemies, the Puritan Dissenters, would never again challenge its supremacy. Despite the initial unanimity and jubilation produced by the Restoration, however, the three island kingdoms remained prey to endemic division, and they were a European by-word for political instability.

This instability was due in no small part to the personal tragedies which marred the year of the Restoration for the house of Stuart. When Charles II reclaimed his throne, he was unmarried and without legiti-

1

mate issue, but the succession seemed to be safely provided for by the king's unmarried brothers, James, Duke of York, and Henry, Duke of Gloucester, and by his sisters, Mary, Princess of Orange, and Henrietta Anne. In September 1660, however, the Duke of Gloucester died of smallpox, a scourge which also claimed his elder sister Mary of Orange in December. By the end of the year, the king's only heirs were his brother the Duke of York, his sister the Princess Henrietta, and a nine-year-old nephew, William Henry, Prince of Orange (prospective heir to the stadhoudership of the Dutch republic, an elective office traditional in the house of Orange, but one which had been vacant since his father's death in 1650).

The question of the succession to the throne was complicated in 1660 by the marriage of the heir presumptive to the throne, the Duke of York, to Anne Hyde, who was the only daughter of Sir Edward Hyde, Charles II's chief advisor from 1644 throughout this exile and, from 1657, titular lord chancellor. Such a marriage between a royal personage and the daughter of a respectable but undistinguished country family was deemed unfitting and unwise; by the social mores of the times it was scandalous. James, born in 1633, and Anne Hyde, born in 1637, had first met in Paris in 1656 at the court of Charles I's widow, Henrietta Maria of France, while Mistress Hyde was acting as maid of honour to the Princess of Orange, who was visiting her mother. The duke, as excessively prone as his brother to temptations of the flesh and the prospect of deflowering virgins, was immensely taken with Anne Hyde's charms of body and mind, and over the succeeding three years the romance prospered at intervals, whenever the duke visited the Princess of Orange at The Hague. In later life James rather ungallantly recalled that Anne Hyde 'indeed shew'd both her witt and her vertue in managing the affaire so dexterously, that the Duke, overmaster'd by his passion, at last gave her a promise of marriage some time before the Restoration'; Anne Hyde claimed more precisely that 'The Duke of Yorke haveing solicited me in the way of Marriage near the space of a yeare', she agreed to the so-called 'contract' at Breda on 24 November 1659.[1]

The contract, apparently no more binding than a verbal promise, none the less resulted in conjugal relations and the predictable outcome: by the time of Charles II's triumphant entry into London on 30 May 1660, Anne Hyde was visibly pregnant with a child which had, strictly speaking, been conceived out of wedlock. The result was general embarrassment: by the sexual standards of the time Anne Hyde was eminently suitable as a royal mistress, but by social conventions she was equally unfit to be a royal bride. This was certainly the unanimous opinion of the royal family – and one with which Sir Edward Hyde felt constrained to agree, telling his daughter that he would rather see her dead than disgrace the royal family.[2] The pressure placed on James was intense: as he recalled in his *Memoirs* (with a malicious touch which stressed the unsuitability of the marriage), the king, James's own friends, 'and most especially some of his meniall Servants with a violent Zeal opposed the match'.[3] Some 'gallants' even offered to testify to their own sexual contacts with Mistress Hyde, thereby relieving the duke of the paternity of the expected child. Despite these pressures, James acted with a resolve which did credit to his integrity but underlined two serious defects of his character, his susceptibility to feminine domination and his intractable stubbornness in the face of opposition of any kind: on 3 September 1660, in a hole-and-corner ceremony held in Worcester House, James married Anne Hyde between 10 p.m. and 2 a.m. The only witnesses were James's chaplain, Dr Joseph Crowther, who performed the Church of England ceremony; Thomas Butler, Lord Ossory (the heir of the Stuarts' Irish champion, James Butler, Duke of Ormonde), who gave the bride away; and Ellen Stroud, Anne Hyde's maid.[4] The marriage, which remained secret from the public, came none too soon: exactly seven weeks after the ceremony, on 22 October 1660, Anne Hyde gave birth to a son, named Charles after his uncle the king. The immediate beneficiary of the child's birth was his grandfather, Sir Edward Hyde: twelve days after the birth, he was raised to the peerage as Baron Hyde of Hindon and given a royal grant of £20,000.[5] For the parents and the royal family, however, the birth of a son of questionable legitimacy seems to have been an embarrassment, for the infant's christening was delayed until New Year's Day, 1661, when the king and the child's grandmother the dowager Queen Henrietta Maria stood as godparents.[6] On 18 February 1661, James, Anne Hyde, and the witnesses of their marriage filed formal depositions with the Privy Council attesting to the fact, and Anne Hyde was recognized as Duchess of York, with precedence above all royal ladies except the Queen Mother (another decision which rankled with society); on 20 April 1661 the new Duchess's father was created Earl of Clarendon and given the royal manor of Cornbury. Then on 5 May the firstborn son of the duke and duchess died. Samuel Pepys, who as secretary of the Navy was in close contact with the duke, who was serving as lord high admiral, recorded in his diary: 'I hear tonight that the Duke of Yorkes son is this day dead, which I believe will please everybody; and I hear that the Duke and his Lady themselfs are not much troubled at it.'[7] Despite the removal of the embarrassing child, and the undoubted legitimacy of any subsequent progeny of Anne Hyde, the social stigma of the Hydes' 'low birth' could never be obliterated, particularly in the minds of such Continental relatives of the duke as his first cousin Sophia, Duchess of Hanover, and his nephew William of Orange.[8]

In the ordinary course of events, the children of the Duke of York would have played only minor roles in world events. Charles II had already proved his fertility by siring four bastards before the Restoration (his total was eventually to reach fourteen children by seven mothers);[9] however, his marriage to the Portuguese princess Catherine of Braganza, consummated in May 1662 after diplomatic negotiations which had been supervised by Clarendon, proved barren. Aspiring politicians, envious of the royal bounties which had fallen to Clarendon and his sons, Henry and Lawrence, ascribed the Portuguese marriage to Clarendon's desire to ensure that his grandchildren would wear the English crown, although rumours that the queen was pregnant continued for several years after her marriage.

The Lady Anne was born at St James's Palace in London on Monday, 6 February 1665, at 11.39 p.m.[10] She was preceded into the world by a sister, the Lady Mary (born in April 1662), and a brother, James, Duke of Cambridge (born in July 1663). It is possible that her birth took place before the large entourage customary at royal deliveries, a group which would have included the king and queen; her paternal grandmother, the dowager Queen Henrietta Maria (who was visiting London at the time);[11] and her maternal grandparents, the lord chancellor and the Countess of Clarendon. However, the rapidity of her mother's labour and the absence of any eyewitness accounts suggests that the birth was more private than usual. Even Pepys, normally an avid chronicler of events in the York household, failed to note her birth, an omission which might be due to the universal disappointment that the baby was female. As the king wrote to his younger sister, Henrietta Anne (or Madame, as she was known at the French court, having married Louis XIV's younger brother, Philippe, duc d'Orléans, in 1661):

> I am glad to hear that your indisposition of health is turned into a great belly. I hope you will have better luck with it than the Duchess here had, who was brought to bed, Monday last, of a girl. One part I wish you to have which is that you may have as easy a labour, for she dispatched her business in little more than an hour.[12]

Soon after her birth, the young child was christened in the rites of the Church of England: her godfather was Gilbert Sheldon, Archbishop of Canterbury, and her godmothers were her three-year-old sister, the Lady Mary, and the fourteen-year-old Anne, Duchess of Monmouth (who had been married two years previously to Charles II's eldest bastard).[13] Clarendon described his granddaughter at the age of nine months as 'the best natured and the best humoured childe in the world'.[14]

From the time of her birth and christening, the infant slipped into the obscurity of the nursery at Richmond, the traditional home of royal children since Tudor times, which isolated her from her parents, who resided at St James's Palace.[15] The nursery – not the parents – provided the first food, the first security, the first education for a royal infant: small wonder, then, that Lady Anne, in approved seventeenth-century form, habitually referred to her household as her 'family'. The newborn infant was taken from her natural mother and placed in the arms of Mrs Martha Farthing who, thirty-seven years later when her charge became queen, claimed and received a £300 pension because she had been 'wett nurse and did give sucke to her present Majestie Queene Anne for the space of fifteene monthes or thereabouts'.[16] Mrs Farthing's daughter, Margery, who was roughly the same age as Lady Anne and served in her household throughout her life, was invariably referred to as Lady Anne's 'foster sister'.[17] The immediate household attached to Lady Anne included 'a dresser, three rockers, seamstress, Page of the Back-Stairs and Necessary Woman' (all unnamed), although the infant was undoubtedly also served by her elder sister's 'two dressers, rocker and Laundress'. Over this household presided the governess, Lady Frances Villiers (at £400 per annum), although day-by-day control was exercised by the undergoverness, 'Mistress Mary Kilbert' (at £150 per annum).[18] Very early in life, a royal child learned that faithful servants were to be cherished and valued: most of Lady Anne's menials were to attend her until death or physical infirmity made such service impossible. At the same time, a royal child learned to be wary and guarded, for fear that a servant, whether from indolence, stupidity, or – worst of all – malice, might prove less than trustworthy. The 'family' was the proper foundation for the education of a child of state and the ties of the nursery and household were to prove more binding than those of blood and kinship.

Royal parents in the seventeenth century assumed the roles which became general with the Victorian aristocracy: they were 'Olympian beings who must at all costs be protected from noise, intrusion, worry, interruption – in fact from children, in whom all such hazards are inherent'.[19] Although Lady Anne's father, James, Duke of York, shared his brother's weaknesses of the flesh, in terms of character he was the opposite of the 'Merry Monarch': a Jacobite historian was later to declare that the duke 'seem'd to be the Antipodes of his Brother in temper and Disposition . . . grave, severe, devout'.[20] In his *Memoirs*, written after his children had deserted him and he had been forced into exile, James laid heavy stress on his claim that he had been 'the best of fathers'; even later Protestant historians allowed that James was 'a kind Husband, and an indulgent father',[21] and Pepys once delightedly noted seeing the Duke of York playing with Lady Mary 'like an ordinary private father of a child'.[22] The underlying implication, however, is that James was kind and indulgent on the infrequent occasions when he condescended to take notice of his children. There are, for example, no extant rules and regulations for his children's household comparable to those he drew up in exile for the Prince of Wales: these regulations, composed in 1696, suggest that James was subconsciously attempting to compensate for his negligence of his elder children by excessive supervision of his younger progeny, stressing as they do the strict security which the prince's governor should impose to prevent him from all contacts with whisperers, flatterers, favourites, or secrets in general.[23] Certainly, what indulgence was present in the father–daughter relationship was hedged by the strictest formality and protocol: Lady Anne habitually referred to James as 'the Duke' or 'the King', never as 'my father'. The little evidence available suggests that the Duchess of York, twenty-eight at the time of her second daughter's birth, was even less interested than her husband in their children. She left a shadowy and indistinct impression with Lady Anne, who was six when her mother died: twenty-two years later, she recorded that she had 'seen my Mother's picture, & believe tis a very good one, tho I do not remember enough of her to know whether it is like her or no, but it is very like one the King had, which every body said was so'.[24]

The immediate legacy which Lady Anne inherited from her parents was poor health, a condition which was to prove chronic by the time she reached adulthood. Apart from Lady Mary and Lady Anne, who survived to maturity, the other six children born to the duke and duchess between 1660 and 1671 had an average lifespan of twenty months, a figure which is distorted by the fact that Lady Anne's elder brother James, Duke of Cambridge, lived for three years (11 July 1663–20 June 1666) and her younger brother Edgar, Duke of Cambridge, died within three months of his fourth birthday (14 September 1667–8 June 1671). Lady Anne suffered from 'defluxion' of the eyes, a complaint which also troubled Lady Mary but which appeared inveterate in the younger girl.[25] Four months after Lady Anne's third birthday, in June 1668, a decision was taken to place her under the care of French eye specialists (whose reports do not appear to have survived) and to board her with her grandmother the dowager queen Henrietta Maria at the latter's home at Colombes, outside Paris. On 5 July 1668, Lady Anne and her small entourage landed at Dieppe aboard the royal yacht *Anne*,

6

where they were met by Sir George Bond, one of the Queen Mother's household, who escorted them to Colombes. They arrived on the evening of 9 July.[26]

The medical treatment which Lady Anne received over the next two years was the least important aspect of her residence in France. She was to remain troubled by her eyes for the remainder of her life; forty years later, substantial payments were being made to experts 'for cureing the Queen's Eyes'.[27] As an adult, her perpetual squinting probably accounted in large part for the 'tincture of sourness' or petulance noted by contemporaries. Lady Anne's defective eyes were important in shaping her character. On the one hand, her near-sightedness reinforced her natural desire to lead a 'private' life in a small circle of easily recognized friends, rather than to subject herself to the daily exposure of life in an open court, where it would be mandatory for a royal personage to recognize, identify, and converse with comparative strangers. This, in combination with her other physical disabilities, was to produce an unsocial (not to say anti-social) court life. On the other hand Lady Anne was unwilling to admit to her visual deficiency, thereby reinforcing a natural streak of stubbornness in her character. After Queen Anne's death, the Duchess of Marlborough confided to paper ('The Character of Princes') that Anne's 'positive sticking to any point which she had once affirm'd, or desir'd to be believ'd, was a peculiarity of Temper, which had, from Her infancy, been observ'd in Her'. Sarah's anecdote to support this contention may be partly apocryphal, but if it occurred it undoubtedly happened after Lady Anne's return to England in 1670:

I remember her Sister Queen Mary used to tell a story that shews it [stubbornness] to have been one of Her favourite & deep-rooted perfections. When they were children, walking in the park together, a dispute was started between them, whether something they saw at a great distance were a Man or a Tree; her sister being of the former opinion, & She of the latter. When they came so near that their Eyesight could convince them it was a Man, the Lady Mary said, Now sister, are you satisfied that It is a Man? But Lady Anne, after she saw what it was, turn'd a way, & persisting still in her own Side of the Question, cried out, No, Sister, It is a Tree.[28]

Lady Anne's residence in France for two years not only helped her to learn the French language, but it also reinforced in her that cosmopolitanism which was characteristic of all European royal families during the seventeenth century: as an adult, Lady Anne was to prove much more open and receptive to Continental ideas and individuals than others of noble rank. Among her life-long servants was a French

Huguenot domestic, one La Roche, who was in her household for more than forty years.[29] One of her favourite ladies of the bedchamber, Lady Charlotte Boeverwart, was Dutch, and her husband and many of his servants were Danes. Although Queen Anne's court would not be as cosmopolitan as William III's or George I's, it would compare favourably with those of Charles II and James II.

Most importantly for her future development, between the ages of four and a half and six years, Lady Anne suffered the loss of three crucial maternal figures: the deaths of her grandmother, her aunt, and her mother were to instil a sense of insecurity and uncertainty which she never successfully overcame. Of her stay at Henrietta Maria's château at Colombes, we know virtually nothing. While Henrietta Maria was ill for several months, her death on 30 August 1669 OS was a distinct surprise to the English court.[30] After the death of her grandmother, Lady Anne was transferred to the nursery of her cousins, the daughters of Madame, where her aunt gave her, according to a contemporary witness, 'toutes les attentions possible'.[31] Lady Anne's companions in the nursery were Marie-Louise d'Orléans, born in 1662 and destined to become the first wife of Carlos II of Spain, and Anne-Marie, born in 1669 and later to marry Victor Amadeus, Duke of Savoy. Apparently the attention which Lady Anne received in the nursery produced pleasant feelings: in the last two years of her life, she was to refer with affection to the Duchess of Savoy as the only remaining member of her immediate family.[32] The happy atmosphere made even more traumatic for the young child the unexpected death of Madame on 20 June 1670 OS, only two weeks after her return from England where she had acted as the intermediary for her brother-in-law Louis XIV in signing the secret Treaty of Dover with Charles II. Madame's death, which appears to have been due to a ruptured appendix, was popularly attributed to poison, it being widely alleged that her husband, jealous of his wife's diplomatic prominence, had secured his revenge: so widespread was the rumour that the English resident in Paris accepted it as true.[33] The French court made strenuous efforts, including a formal autopsy, to clear the king's brother from such an imputation and to attribute Madame's death to natural causes.[34] Despite these French avowals, the Duke of York dispatched the treasurer of his household, Sir Allen Apsley, and his master of the robes and his children's governess, Colonel Edward and Lady Frances Villiers, to Paris before the end of June to bring Lady Anne back to England, using the diplomatic but thin excuse that Lady Anne was 'now completely cured of her ailments'.[35] While Sir Allen and the Villierses were *en route* to Paris, Monsieur made his two daughters and his niece the centre-piece of a state occasion: he dressed up his little daughter [Marie-Louise] and her cousin, the Princess Anne, in long trailing mantles of violet velvet and, with his usual ridiculous love of ceremony, insisted that formal visits of condolence should be paid not only to these children, but to his younger daughter, the baby Mlle. de Valois [Anne-Marie] in her nursery.[36]

In an obvious attempt to propitiate Charles II, his new ally, Louis XIV presented the English king's niece with a farewell gift of extraordinary value for a five-year-old: 'two braceletts of Pearle besett with Diamante valued at 10,000 Crowns'. Accompanied by Sir Allen and the Villierses, Lady Anne left Paris on 18 July OS, landing at Rye on 23 July and returning to her parents at St James's a few days later.[37]

Unknown to the five-year-old princess, her parents had taken a step during her absence which was to alter decisively the course of her life: the Duke and Duchess of York had secretly forsaken the Church of England to become Roman Catholic converts. The duke had been interested in, and sympathetic to, Roman Catholicism from his exile during the Interregnum, and one reason for his lack of popularity in England during the 1660s was the suspicion that he had papist leanings.[38] The fall of Clarendon in August 1667, following the unsuccessful conclusion of the second Anglo–Dutch War and Parliament's vote in November 1667 to exile him permanently (he died in Rouen in 1674), had seriously weakened the influence of his son-in-law and his daughter, the duke and duchess. Charles II's new trusted advisors had only their antipathy towards Clarendon in common: although ironically labelled 'the Cabal' from the initial letters of their names (Clifford, Arlington, Buckingham, Ashley Cooper, Lauderdale), only Thomas, Lord Clifford, and Henry Bennett, Lord Arlington, were entrusted with the king's secret. On 25 January 1669, Charles had confided to his brother and the two ministers that he was a Roman Catholic 'at heart' and wished to procure the formal re-establishment of Roman Catholicism as the state religion as an essential part of his scheme to dispense permanently with Parliament and to establish an absolutist regime on the French model in England. By this time, according to James II's *Memoirs*, James himself had already become a secret convert, although he continued to attend Church of England ceremonies for the next seven years.[39] The nature of Charles II's religious view – if any – will be for ever debated: there can be no doubt, however, that James experienced a genuine religious conversion, finding within the Church of Rome's authoritarian system and doctrine spiritual solace and a natural complement to his own authoritarian nature. Inspired as he was by the zeal of a convert, evangelistic and propagandizing, James would

9

never during his tragic career doubt for a moment the divine veracity of the rock upon which he had based his life.

The motive behind the duchess's conversion is more open to specula-tion. Like her parents and her brothers, Anne Hyde had been a devotee of the Church of England. On her own testimony her active interest in the Old Faith began in November 1669, eleven months after her husband's conversion,[40] and may have been inspired in part by the desire to retain her influence with James. She accepted Anglican com-munion for the last time at Christmas, 1669, and thereafter pursued her studies of Roman doctrine while Charles II was busily negotia-ting through Madame an alliance with Louis XIV. The result, the secret Treaty of Dover (May 1670), included the key provision that Louis would provide a French army and financial support when Charles II chose to declare his own conversion and his decision to re-establish formally the Church of Rome in England. Significantly, it was only three months later, in August 1670, that the duchess formally embraced Roman Catholicism, 'tho the world knew it not till she dyd'.[41]

In the courts of Whitehall and St James's, where gossip was the staff of life, neither the religious proclivities of the royal family nor the secret provisions of the Treaty of Dover could remain entirely secret. Even the old Earl of Clarendon, exiled in Rouen, heard of his daughter's con-version and wrote her two letters (published after her death) remarkable for their defence of the Church of England's doctrines and for the absence of any hint that the Duke of York was also a Catholic.[42] The Duchess of York's conversion took place during her eighth and last full pregnancy. On 9 February 1671, three days after lady Anne's sixth birthday, the duchess gave birth to a daughter, Katherine. The duchess, however, never recovered from her labour, rapidly succumbing to an agonizing complaint which was probably cancer of the uterus. Despite the efforts of her brothers, Henry and Lawrence Hyde, to provide her with Anglican priests, the Duchess of York steadfastly refused to accept the sacraments of the Church of England and, when she died on 31 March 1671, her profession of Roman Catholicism was a matter of public knowledge.[43]

It seems unlikely that the effects of the duke and duchess's conversion immediately penetrated the nursery at St James's. For the Lady Anne, her mother was the third figure of feminine authority to die within nineteen months, and this bereavement underlined the uncertainty of the child's future; furthermore, the nursery itself was decimated within the next few months. In June 1671, Lady Anne's four-year-old brother Edgar, Duke of Cambridge, died; in December 1671, the infant Lady

Katherine died, leaving only Lady Mary and Lady Anne as the surviving children of the Duke of York's first marriage.

In the absence of any contemporary commentary, one can only speculate on the effects of this rapid series of deaths on Lady Anne's character development. Undoubtedly, they were responsible in part for reinforcing the princess's natural reserve and self-protectiveness; conversely, the removal of all maternal figures undoubtedly inspired her search for authority, whether in friends or in institutions. However, to Lady Anne, self-protection always outweighed authority. As for friends, Sarah Churchill, who allegedly dominated the princess for twenty-five years, concluded that 'she still kept her heart untouch'd & unposses'd by any one but Her self'.[44] Although Lady Anne was taught to revere the monarchy and the Church, self-preservation was later to induce her to renounce her childhood lessons by modifying the powers of both institutions.

The education of Lady Anne and her elder sister was typical of the late seventeenth century's treatment of women: the Renaissance principle of providing royal princesses as well as princes with formidable linguistic, philosophical, and historical training was as dead as Mary and Elizabeth Tudor, Lady Jane Grey, and Mary, Queen of Scots. The social upheaval caused by the Civil War and the Interregnum contributed to a general decline in educational standards, as did the rustic atmosphere of Charles II's Whitehall, where at 'ye Court they talk there of nothing but horses & dogs'.[45] Against this background, the education of the two princesses was conducted 'avec peu de pompe',[46] stressing domestic accomplishments to the exclusion of almost all literary endeavour: sewing, embroidery, and other domestic skills were taught, while it appears that the princesses gained little more than a smattering of history, geography, or constitutional and legal training. Neither Lady Mary nor Lady Anne ever fully came to grips with the grammatical intricacies of the English language. Although they could sometimes be extremely eloquent in writing, usually their sentences were less than grammatical and their spelling remained phonetic and uncertain, albeit of a higher standard than that of most ladies of their age. Their greatest literary accomplishment was their mastery of French; Lady Anne progressed to the point where she had no difficulty, in later life, in conversing privately with foreign ambassadors[47] and had no hesitation about altering the wording of formal diplomatic letters drafted by Bolingbroke, an acknowledged English master of the French language.[48] Lady Anne also received extensive training in music, for which she displayed a natural aptitude: her family included a 'Dancing Master', a 'Teacher of the Harpsicord', and a 'Guitar Master'. By contrast, her education did little

11

to inspire interest in the theatre – although in December 1674 she and Lady Mary appeared 'all covered with jewels' in John Crowne's *Calisto, or the Chaste Nymphe* before the court.[49] When she was queen, theatricals were presented only infrequently at her court (between 1704 and 1706 there were only four such performances),[50] although her privy purse accounts record frequent payments to Italian performers 'for singing & playing before Her Majesty', as well as ten guineas paid 'to the Woman for Dancing the Doggs before the Queen'.[51] Lady Anne's disinterest in the spoken word was not due to lack of tuition, for her natural speaking ability, improved by training, was one feature of her personality praised by all observers as 'a sort of charm'; rather it reflected the inner uncertainty and fear produced during her earliest childhood. The second Lord Dartmouth, later one of the queen's secretaries of state, recorded that Charles II

> was so pleased with the natural sweetness of her [Lady Anne's] voice,
> that he ordered Mrs. Barry, a famous actress, should teach her to
> speak, which she did with such success, that it was a real pleasure to
> hear her, *though she had a bashfulness that made it very uneasy to herself
> to say much in public.*[52]

This personal reserve was noticed by observers of Anne both as a young girl and as a mature woman. She was habitually taciturn in both personal and business conversations, listening intently but rarely commenting freely outside a circle of trusted friends. In short, the princess learned at an early age to avoid commitment whenever possible. Consequently, she avoided conversations on matters of substance, preferring letters, Sarah Churchill explained, 'where she could make use of a little piece of art, which I know she had often practic'd, of taking notice only of something that was of no consequence, and by pretending to be in haste, never to come to the main point'.[53] Her poor eyesight prevented her from developing the interest in the visual arts which was so pronounced in her elder sister; indeed, virtually all of the major works of painting, sculpture, and architecture completed during Anne's reign were initiated by her predecessors. Except for portraits of friends and interior décor, Lady Anne never displayed great interest in art. On the other hand, outdoor activities – principally gardening and hunting – satisfied Lady Anne's longing for fresh air and provided a high degree of privacy from opportunists. As queen, Anne was to be largely responsible for the expansion of the gardens at Hampton Court and Kensington Palace.[54] Hunting became her principal recreation, and remained so even after she had become an invalid, when she rode in a small chariot pulled by two horses. As a young woman, she attended the fashionable horse-races at Newmarket, going to cockfights between races,[55] and as queen she remained an active patron of the turf, establishing the Royal Ascot race in 1712.[56] In short, through training and inclination, Lady Anne reflected the social and intellectual pursuits characteristic of the English governing classes of the late seventeenth century.

The central part of Lady Anne's education, indeed the only formal preparation which she was to receive for the great role which destiny held in store for her, was in the field of religion. There càn be no question that the Duke of York would have preferred to rear his children as Roman Catholics; according to his Jesuit confessor, in later years James was accustomed to pray that his Protestant daughters, 'who have had the unhappiness to be brought up in another Communion, soon acknowledge their Errors, and open their Eyes to the Truth'.[57] If James did not adequately appreciate the incendiary nature of the secret Treaty of Dover, with its provisions for the formal re-establishment of Roman Catholicism by French arms upon an unwilling English nation, Charles II did; in October 1670, only five months after the treaty had been signed, James complained to the French envoy that he was 'saddened to see his brother's reluctance to declare himself a Catholic'.[58] The wide-spread suspicion of the royal family aroused at Anne Hyde's death by the knowledge of her conversion strengthened Charles II's reluctance to take decisive action, particularly as his foremost ally Louis XIV was principally intent on crushing the Dutch republic rather than catholi-cizing Great Britain; therefore, Charles cautiously prescribed that his two nieces, potential heiresses of the crown, should be reared by tutors from the Church of England. This caution proved well advised. From the moment of the Anglo–French attack on the Dutch republic in 1672, the war was unpopular in England. The stubborn resistance of the Dutch against overwhelming odds and the republic's election of Charles and James's twenty-one-year-old nephew, William III of Orange, as stadhouder to defend the seven provinces, further fuelled the growth of anti-Catholic feeling in England. In 1673, the Cavalier Parliament, dominated by those families whose loyalties were to the Church of England and the house of Stuart, enacted the Test Act, which prescribed that every crown office-holder should swear an oath against the doctrine of transubstantiation, central to the mass. No good Roman Catholic could solemnly deny one of the basic tenets of the Church. The object of the Test Act was to expose secret Roman Catholics in government and in this it was successful: the Duke of York was forced to resign his position as lord high admiral. Simultaneously, a Continental search for a new wife for James was being conducted by Henry, Earl of Peterborough, a search in which all the potential candidates were Roman Catholics.[59] On

13

30 September 1673, Peterborough stood proxy for the Duke of York in a marriage ceremony with Maria Beatrice d'Este, the fifteen-year-old sister of the Duke of Modena. The marriage, arranged with the help of Louis XIV, proved so unpopular in England that Charles II was forced to prorogue Parliament to prevent addresses against its consummation. When news of the proxy ceremony reached London, the Duke of York 'sent his daughter, Lady Mary, word the same night, he had provided a playfellow for her'.[60]

The arrival of the new duchess in London inspired even stronger anti-Catholic agitation among the general public. In February 1674 the House of Lords voted an address to the king praying for the removal of the Ladies Mary and Anne from the household of their father.[61] This action, combined with the success of Parliament in forcing Charles II to retire from the third Anglo–Dutch War, guaranteed that the king would henceforward be forced to rely on staunch Anglicans (now led by Thomas Osborne, Earl of Danby), who were increasingly labelled 'Tories' by their enemies, the 'Whigs'. Therefore, it became impossible for James to prevent the education of his daughters as Protestants and Anglicans if he wished them to remain under his control. Consequently, James became a bitter personal enemy of his daughters' tutor, the Reverend Henry Compton, Bishop of London, whose elevation to the archbishopric of Canterbury James successfully opposed in 1678. In his *Memoirs*, James recorded bitterly that he had told Compton

> that it was much against his will that his Daughters went to Church &
> were bred Protestants; and that the reason why he had not endeavour'd
> to have them instructed in his own Religion, was because he knew if
> he should have attempted it, they would have immediately been quite
> taken from him.[62]

Through no fault of her own, therefore, Lady Anne's new stepmother played only a minor role in shaping Anne's education and personality. Before her marriage, Mary of Modena had decided to become a nun, a vocation to which she was attracted all her life; the political considerations which instead placed her in the arms of a man old enough to be her father were to begin with compensated for by the fact that the pope himself had exhorted her to act as an evangelist for the True Faith in England.[63] This hope proving impossible even within her own household, the new duchess found that 'I cannot yet accustom myself to this state of life [marriage] . . . therefore I cry a great deal and am much afflicted, not being able to rid myself of my melancholy', surely a strange sight for her younger stepdaughter, who was already something of a stoic.[64] By March 1675 it was being reported to Modena that the Duchess of York 'diverts herself with the Princesses, whose conversation is much to her taste and satisfaction'.[65] Although her marriage became a genuine love affair, Mary of Modena was less successful in making friends with her stepdaughters. While there is no hint in Lady Anne's early letters of the antipathy with which she regarded her stepmother after her father became king in 1685, there is also little or no sign of affection. Despite the Duchess of York's best efforts, she remained an Italian, a Roman Catholic and – of increasing importance to the two children of state – the potential mother of male heirs who would block the road to the crown. The duchess's first child, Catherine Laura, was born on 10 January 1675, only hours after she had dined with the princesses.[66] Although the child lived less than nine months (10 January – 3 October 1675), she was succeeded in August 1676 by another girl, Isabella, who survived infancy. The duchess undoubtedly tried to establish rapport with her stepdaughters, but was impeded not only by her nationality, her religion, and the possibility that she might produce male heirs, but also by 'her entire lack of understanding of English society and politics'.[67] The role of the new Duchess of York in the development of Lady Anne's personality was minimal.

In contrast, Henry Compton, Bishop of London, played a leading part in guiding Lady Anne towards what were to be the foci of her personal and political life – an unflagging loyalty to, and devout belief in, the doctrines of the Church of England. Compton, a younger son of the Earl of Northampton, had been present in Charles I's camp at the battle of Edgehill in 1642, and during the Protectorate had remained a devoted royalist and Anglican, entering holy orders in 1666 after a military career.[68] Compton enjoyed a reputation as 'the great patron of converts from Popery'.[69] As the preceptor of Lady Mary and Lady Anne, Compton imbued the two princesses with the unshakeable conviction that the Church of England was the one, true apostolic Church of Christ. The Church of Rome was Antichrist personified, scarred by centuries of the perversion of truth by tradition, and successfully maintained by the limitless villainies of Jesuit priests and their deluded followers. Protestant Dissenters or Nonconformists, of course, were regicides and potential rebels against the house of Stuart; their doctrines, if not heretical, were to be avoided, but their iniquities paled by comparison with those of the papacy. The lessons taught by Compton and his subordinates reflected a profound shift in English public opinion, a change in attitudes which even pervaded the court of Whitehall. In reaction to Puritan domination during the Protectorate, Protestant Nonconformists had been popularly regarded during the 1660s as the major potential enemies to English political stability; by the 1670s, however, anti-

15

Catholicism had become the predominant prejudice of all classes, a position which it was to retain throughout and well beyond Lady Anne's lifetime. This popular hatred of Catholicism was 'in essence . . . political, patriotic, and anti-clerical rather than religious',[70] although Compton provided the spiritual justification for a bias which, in Lady Anne, was to remain crude and basic throughout her life: four days before her death, she proved reluctant to trust a foreign envoy 'because he was a Roman Catholick'.[71] 'God be thanked we were not bred up in that communion', she wrote to her sister in 1686, when she felt herself persecuted because of her religion,

> but are of a Church that is pious and sincere, and conformable in all
> its principles to the Scriptures. Our Church teaches no doctrine but
> what is just, holy, and good, or what is profitable to salvation; and
> the Church of England is, without all doubt, the only true Church.[72]

Such an education could only increase the emotional distance between Lady Anne and her father and stepmother, particularly when the duke (who still publicly attended Anglican services) did what little he could to hinder the Protestant education of his daughters. In January 1676, when Lady Mary was fourteen and Lady Anne was on the eve of her eleventh birthday, Compton decided that they should be confirmed in the Church of England; when the duke refused his permission, Compton went over James's head to the king, who ordered Compton to proceed with the double confirmation service, held on 23 January 1676, 'a victory for the national Protestant feeling and a personal triumph for Compton'.[73] James was not a man to take such an affront lightly or to accept it intelligently: he used it as an excuse to avoid attending Easter communion in March 1676, and thereafter ceased to attend Anglican services altogether.[74] This abstinence from Anglican rites confirmed the deep division of religious beliefs between father and daughters, although personal relations remained harmonious if somewhat remote and superficial.

In the following year, the Duke of York again suffered a signal defeat in plans relating to his daughters, this time at the hands of the lord treasurer, Thomas Osborne, Earl of Danby. The founder of the Tory party which was based on joint loyalty to the crown and to the Church of England, Danby wished to strengthen his own position and that of Charles II by engaging England in an unchallengeable Protestant alliance by marrying James's eldest daughter, Lady Mary, to her first cousin, William Henry, Prince of Orange and stadhouder of the Dutch republic. Such an alliance would necessarily be anti-French, for the republic and Louis XIV were still at war. James, on the other hand, had hoped to marry his eldest daughter to the French dauphin, a marriage which would necessitate Mary's conversion to Catholicism. With ill grace, James was once again forced to bow to his brother's wishes.

The circumstances surrounding her sister's marriage in November 1677 shattered Lady Anne's nursery world. The diary of the princesses' sub-preceptor, Dr Edward Lake, provides a detailed chronology of events. On 5 November, the day after Lady Mary's marriage to the Prince of Orange, Lady Anne fell ill; on 7 November 'The Duchesse of York was safely delivered of a son, to the great joy of the whole court (but the Clarendon party)'; and on 10 November it became apparent that Lady Anne had smallpox and would have to be quarantined, particularly from the Princess of Orange who had never been stricken with this most democratic of seventeenth-century scourges. Although William and Mary did not leave for the republic until 19 November, the two sisters did not meet again before then; indeed, the duke 'commanded that her sister's departure should be conceal'd from her [Lady Anne]; wherefore there was a feigned message sent every morning from the princesse [Mary] to her highnesse [Anne] to know how she did'. On 12 November the pox marks 'appear'd very many, and her highnesse somewhat giddy and very much disordered' and for three days 'Her highnesse continued very ill'. In view of the quarantine Dr Lake was originally ordered (presumably by the duke) to stay away from Lady Anne which, in his own words, 'very much troubled me, and the more because her nurse was a very busy, zealous Roman Catholick, and would probably discompose her if she had an opportunity'. To prevent such proselytizing, Lake appealed to Lady Anne's governess, Lady Frances Villiers, who proved unwilling to intervene and who 'bade me indeed to do as I thought fitt'. Lake then appealed to Compton, who immediately ordered him 'to wait constantly on her highnesse, and to do all suitable offices ministeriall which were incumbent on mee'. The duke highly resented Compton's unprecedented interference in his domestic arrangements but, according to Lake, Lady Anne appreciated it: 'Her Highnesse requested mee not to leave her, but come often to her; recommended to mee her foster sister [Lady Isabella], that I would take care to instruct her in the Protestant religion.'

While Lady Anne was slowly recovering from her bout of smallpox, which left her face permanently pitted,[75] Lady Frances Villiers was struck by the disease and died on 23 November, thereby necessitating a rearrangement in Lady Anne's household. Lady Frances was succeeded by Lady Henrietta Hyde, the wife of Lawrence Hyde, Lady Anne's younger maternal uncle. This arrangement did little to strengthen Lady

17

Anne's ties with her mother's family: she cordially disliked her aunt and dispensed with her services at the first opportunity. The death of Lady Frances Villiers deprived Lady Anne of her one remaining maternal figure, and underlined the chasm between Protestants and Catholics at court: the Duchess of York unwisely repeated to several visitors a dream which she had had, in which 'Lady Frances Villiers appear'd to her, and told her that she was damn'd, and now in the flames of Hell'. When the duchess had incredulously questioned this, Lady Frances had held her hand 'which seemed so extremely hot that it was impossible for the duchess to endure it'. This story, which 'occasion'd a great deal of discourse both at court and in the city', naturally outraged Lady Frances's relatives and Protestants in general.

By 3 December, Lady Anne had recovered sufficiently to visit the Duchess of York in her lodgings, 'the servants all rejoicing to see her highnesse so perfectly recovered'. Unfortunately, she was still carrying the infection and the disease was transmitted to her infant half-brother, Charles Duke of Cambridge, who died on 12 December.[76] After her complete recovery, Lady Anne began attending Anglican services with strict regularity and her Protestant education continued apace; what her training lacked in quality was more than compensated for by youthful zeal. On Easter Sunday, 1678, when she was to receive her first communion, Lake recorded: 'Her highnesse was not (through negligence) instructed how much of the wine to drink, but drank of it twice or thrice, whereat I was much concern'd, lest the duke should have notice of it.'[77]

Although the Princess of Orange and Lady Anne corresponded regularly, letters were inadequate substitutes for the personal companionship which Lady Mary's marriage interrupted. In the autumn of 1678 the Duchess of York received permission from her husband and the king to accompany Lady Anne on a visit to the Princess of Orange at The Hague; their party included the Duchesses of Monmouth and Buckingham, the Countesses of Richmond and Peterborough, and Lady Henrietta Hyde. On 27 September, James notified the Prince of Orange that the royal ladies would travel 'very *incognito*' with 'Lord Ossory for their Governeur'.[78] The expedition lasted for three weeks, the party leaving London on 1 October. When the duchess and Lady Anne returned to London on 24 October, they discovered that one man had altered the entire English political scene and had initiated ten years of terror which were profoundly to affect England's destiny and Lady Anne's life.[79]

Titus Oates, a defrocked Anglican priest turned Roman Catholic, had used his homosexuality as a *laisser-passer* into various English Catholic institutions on the Continent, determined to advance his own interests either with the help of – or at the expense of – his new co-religionists. At the Jesuit retreat at St Omer in the Spanish Netherlands, Oates had acquired through gossip extensive knowledge of the Roman Catholic connections of the Duke of York's household, particularly those of the duchess's secretary, Edward Coleman. Returning to England in the summer of 1678, Oates joined forces with a genuine anti-Catholic fanatic, Israel Tonge, to compose a pamphlet outlining a fictitious 'Popish Plot', in which a gigantic international Jesuit conspiracy was planning to murder Charles II to make way for his brother, to invade England with French and Irish armies, and to extirpate Protestantism by force of arms. Although these charges, which Oates formally laid before the Privy Council on 29 September, appeared fantastic in the aggregate, they contained sufficiently detailed assertions, particularly concerning Coleman, to give the lord treasurer, Danby, pause. Danby ordered Coleman's lodging to be searched and royal officers discovered Coleman's correspondence with Louis XIV's Jesuit confessor, Père La Chaise, which Coleman had attempted to hide. The burden of this correspondence, that Roman Catholics would find an active and sympathetic protector in the Duke of York when he became king, was extremely compromising to James; what caused public hysteria, however, was the discovery on 17 October that Sir Edmund Berry Godfrey, the London magistrate before whom Oates had made a sworn deposition of his charges, had been murdered. Oates and his colleagues, including those opponents of Charles II and Danby who were now called 'Whigs', portrayed Godfrey's murder as the first step in the 'Popish Plot' in order to incite the London mob. Coleman was arrested for high treason, convicted, and executed.

With the execution of Coleman, the opposition to Charles II, Danby, and their followers – the 'Tories' – rallied round the leadership of Anthony Ashley Cooper, Earl of Shaftesbury, the Duke of York's most bitter enemy; Shaftesbury's followers, the Whigs, were unanimously convinced that it was necessary to exclude the Duke of York from the succession to the throne in order to preserve the Protestant religion in England. Whig unity, however, ended when the question of designating an alternative heir was broached: some Whigs favoured James, Duke of Monmouth (the eldest of Charles II's bastards), who would be an excellent puppet for Whig control of the state but whose claims were weakened by his illegitimacy; other Whigs favoured the legitimist pretensions of Princess Mary, or of William and Mary as joint heirs; it was even suggested, albeit without significant results, that Lady Anne should be named heir, as the candidate of national unity, being of

19

undoubted legitimacy and unscarred by marriage to a foreign prince and by residence abroad.

Feeling was strong against the Duke of York, and the Tories were so unenthusiastic in the king's support that in January 1679 he was forced to dismiss Danby and to dissolve the Cavalier Parliament, which had met intermittently for eighteen years. So strong was Whig sentiment throughout the country that the Popish Plot hysteria helped to elect a majority of anti-Yorkist members to the House of Commons in the general election held in February 1679. Hoping to ameliorate this opposition, Charles II decided to remove his controversial brother temporarily from England and from the public eye. The Duke and Duchess of York were formally ordered to retire from England to the Spanish Netherlands, and they sailed from London on 3 March 1679. Until two days before their departure, James and Mary had expected to be accompanied by their two daughters, the Ladies Anne and Isabella;[80] at the last minute, however, the king ordered that the two princesses and their retinues should remain in England, a decision which clearly left Lady Anne desolated: 'the young lady', reported an eyewitness to the royal family's farewell scene, 'cried as much as the rest to part company'.[81]

This initial separation from her father and stepmother just after her fourteenth birthday is crucial to explaining Lady Anne's future relations with her closest relatives. She could hardly have been unaware of the reason for James's forced departure. While she uncritically embraced the standard court description of the Whigs as crypto-Roundheads bent on destroying royal authority, the separation also reinforced the lessons of her youth: the paramount duty of princes was to follow the interests of the state, and the defence of the Protestant religion might require the greatest personal sacrifices.

The Duke of York's departure from England did nothing to mitigate the fury of his enemies, and the new Parliament, which opened on 6 March, rapidly proceeded to the consideration of an Exclusion bill. To prevent its certain passage in the House of Commons, the king prorogued Parliament in May and dissolved it in July; the ensuing general election, however, produced no radical changes in the composition of the Commons, and Charles adopted a new strategy, simply failing to summon Parliament to meet in order to gain time to ride out the storm. Against the background of this new strategy, in early August Charles acceded to James's pleas that his daughters be sent to Brussels 'to help me to beare my banishment with somewhat more pacience'.[82] James, however, agreed that his daughters should return to England before Charles allowed Parliament to meet and Charles decreed that the visit to Brussels should last only 'for a month or two'.[83]

On 20 August 1679 the Ladies Anne and Isabella, with carefully selected servants, left London to sail to the Spanish Netherlands.[84] Lady Anne's joy at her reunion with her parents was quickly ended, however, when her father secretly left Brussels on 29 August to return to England. Charles II had fallen gravely ill at Windsor, and his ministers had summoned James to return to guard against Monmouth's partisans in case they should attempt to seize the throne by force of arms if Charles should die.

During the duke's absence from Brussels, his frightened but resolute daughter ('I have a good heart thank God or els it would have bin down long ago')[85] recorded her impressions in a series of letters to Lady Frances Apsley, the first of her feminine confidantes. Both the friendship and the correspondence are revelatory. Inevitably, Frances (as all of Lady Anne's future friends) was closely connected with the Restoration court. Frances was the daughter of Sir Allen Apsley, comptroller of the Duke of York's household, and his wife was in the duchess's household. The original friendship had been between the Lady Mary and Frances, who were the same age, and had been extended to include the younger Lady Anne. The passionate correspondence between Lady Mary (even after she became Princess of Orange) and Frances Apsley reflected the excesses of the romantic French novels then so popular among educated ladies; Lady Anne, in her correspondence with Frances Apsley, figured as 'Ziphares', a man who pined for a sight of his 'faire Semandra'. Too much can be – and perhaps has been – read into the adolescent romanticism and subconscious sexuality revealed by these letters, particularly in the light of Lady Anne's later close association with the future Duchess of Marlborough. To some extent, the later 'Mrs Morley' and 'Mrs Freeman' correspondence between the queen and the duchess was a repetition of the teen-aged Lady Anne's correspondence with Frances Apsley, a search for a fantasy world in which Lady Anne could shed her exalted rank and correspond with 'faire Semandra' as an equal. More importantly, Lady Anne's choice of the male role in the friendship (as opposed to Lady Mary's female role *vis-à-vis* Frances Apsley) suggests that Lady Anne intended to be the dominant partner in the friendship. Indeed, as we shall see, this intention became an automatic assumption in every close relationship which Lady Anne was to develop in later life. Lack of originality – not a deficiency of innate intelligence and good judgment – was Lady Anne's besetting flaw. She was, of course, subject to being influenced and guided, particularly in matters with which she was unacquainted, but she was no more prone to this than the average prince. In the final analysis, the chief inherent privilege of rank was the right to make the final decision – a privilege to which Lady

21

Anne, despite her attempts to avoid rank in a world of fantasy, was to cling tenaciously throughout her life.

From Lady Anne's own reports, it is obvious that her sojourn in Brussels was intended to be of short duration and that her accommodation in the Prince de Ligne's palace was makeshift: 'my sistter Issabellas lodgings & mine are much better than I expected . . . for our lodgings they weare all one great Room & now are devided with boards into severall'.[86] In her father's absence, her principal social activity was her attendance incognito at the court ball (with 'fyer works and bon fyers') celebrating the marriage of her French cousin, Marie-Louise d'Orléans, to Carlos II of Spain. Her two months in the Spanish Netherlands were her most important exposure to life in a predominantly Roman Catholic country. Neither of her parents made any attempt to convert her and she was carefully guarded not only by the Anglican chaplains who had accompanied her but also by those already in residence to minister to the Yorks' Protestant servants.[87] Nevertheless, Lady Anne saw enough to confirm and harden her strong prejudices against popery: as she reported to Frances Apsley, 'all the fine churches & monasterys you know I must not see so can give you no good account of them, but those things which I must needs see as theire images which are in every shope & corner of the street the more I heare of that Religion, the more I dislike it'.[88] This aversion was to remain constant throughout her life.

When the Duke of York returned to Brussels on 27 September, after the king's recovery from his illness, he had not only procured Monmouth's banishment from England but also Charles II's agreement that James should be transferred to Scotland, thereby strengthening James's hand in the event of a struggle for the succession.[89] The king, however, had ordered that the Ladies Anne and Isabella should return to England, a decision which distressed James, who assured William of Orange 'that I would be glad to be with them as long as I could'.[90] Within five or six days of James's return to Brussels, the entire York entourage was at The Hague to spend a few days with the Prince and Princess of Orange before returning to England; the incredible circumstances under which the Lady Anne was next to meet her sister and brother-in-law nine years later could scarcely have been envisioned in 1679. By 12 October the Yorks' party had crossed the Channel and arrived in London.[91]

Now in her fifteenth year, Lady Anne's reunion with her father, which had lasted for scarcely a month, was brought to an end. On 27 October the duke and duchess started on a journey to Scotland; Lady Anne accompanied them as far as Hatfield, where the party spent the first night, and she returned to Whitehall the next day[92] acutely aware that the aristocracy regarded her father as a pariah: their nominal host at

Hatfield, the Earl of Salisbury, had deliberately absented himself, a pattern which was repeated until the Yorks reached Scotland.[93] The Exclusion crisis was at its height and the Whigs were furious that the king continued to refuse to allow the new Parliament to meet.

Charles had promised his brother that his stay in Scotland would be short, and the duke and duchess were summoned to return to England early in 1680. They arrived in London on 24 February, two weeks after Lady Anne's fifteenth birthday.

In the seventeenth century, a princess who had attained such an advanced age was normally regarded as eminently marriageable. While the Exclusion crisis lasted, however, both the king and the Duke of York obviously wished to defer, if possible, any choice of a husband for Lady Anne. Her marriage might prove to be the trump card in strengthening the royal brothers' tenuous position both at home and abroad. William of Orange, who was struggling to maintain an anti-French diplomatic coalition, was obviously interested in the future of his sister-in-law; Louis XIV equally wanted to ensure that Lady Anne's marriage would not strengthen a Protestant, anti-French alliance. James himself was determined that his wishes would be consulted in Lady Anne's case, as they had not been in that of the Princess of Orange. Louis XIV's envoy in London, Paul de Barillon, even suggested that James (despite his unshakeable determination to maintain the strict hereditary principle) might agree to marry Lady Anne to the Duke of Monmouth (should the Duchess of Monmouth die) and to settle the succession on them jointly in order to spite William.[94] The bitter personal enmity between James and his illegitimate nephew made this suggestion unworkable, but it reflected the fact that neither Charles nor James was willing to undertake serious matrimonial negotiations on Lady Anne's behalf until the Exclusion crisis was resolved.

Against this background, the desultory exploration in 1680 of the prospects for a marriage between Lady Anne and Georg Ludwig, Prince of Hanover, must be examined. After her death in 1714, when Queen Anne was succeeded by the prince as King George I, it was alleged that Lady Anne had bitterly hated her Hanoverian heir because he had spurned her hand in 1680; as one observer commented in 1719, there was talk of a Hanoverian marriage 'at that Time, but more generally since'.[95] A quarter of a century after the event, Ezechial Spanheim, the Prussian envoy in London, recalled that as early as 1678 he had broached the possibility of such a marriage to Sophia, Duchess of Hanover, a granddaughter of James I and a first cousin of Charles II and the Duke of York. Sophia had replied that her son, then a martial youth of eighteen, displayed little interest in any marriage; furthermore,

Sophia herself felt little inclination to ally her eldest son with a daughter of Anne Hyde, 'née d'une famille fort médiocre'.[96] The principal champion of the marriage proposal was Sophia's brother Prince Rupert, once Charles I's leading general during the Civil War but now possessing little political influence in London.

Soon after the Duke of York's return to London in February 1680, it began to be widely rumoured that Lady Anne would marry Georg Ludwig, a scheme sponsored by the Prince of Orange.[97] It soon became known that Georg Ludwig intended to visit London, ostensibly as a part of his Grand Tour. Even before his arrival in December, however, any effective chance for serious matrimonial negotiations was nullified; financial necessity had finally forced Charles II to summon Parliament to meet on 21 October and consequently the Duke and Duchess of York were once again forced to return to Scotland, sailing on 20 October to an exile which was to last for eighteen months. James's departure did little to allay the fury of the Whig majority in the House of Commons at the prospect of a Roman Catholic heir to the throne. The lower house almost immediately passed an Exclusion bill directed against the Duke of York; partisans of the Prince of Orange urged in vain that the Ladies Mary, Anne, and Isabella should be named specifically as Charles II's heirs. Monmouth's supporters prevented any specific designation, arguing that either the king or the Duke of York might yet produce sons.[98] In November, however, the House of Lords threw out the Exclusion bill by a vote of 63 to 30; despite the unpopularity of the Duke of York and of his religion, the aristocracy was not yet ready to endanger the hereditary principle on which Restoration society, and their own power, was based. Having succeeded in temporarily avoiding any adverse resolution of the Exclusion crisis, Charles II promptly dissolved Parliament.

It was during this Parliament that the twenty-year-old Prince of Hanover arrived in London on 8 December 1680. Although the initial half-hour interview between Lady Anne and Georg Ludwig, who were both shy and taciturn, appears to have been difficult, the Modenese envoy, who enjoyed privileged access to the York household, reported that Lady Anne was infatuated with the Hanoverian prince. It seems clear that Charles II and the Duke of York, not the Hanoverian court, vetoed the marriage.[99] Georg Ludwig returned to Hanover in March 1681, without having made a formal proposal during his four-month sojourn in England. The pernicious suggestion made thirty years later by her enemies (including, by then, the Duchess of Marlborough) that Lady Anne had felt rejected, and that it was from the bitterness of a woman scorned that she opposed the Hanoverian succession, is not borne out by the facts. She would have known that the king and her father opposed the match (although Prince Rupert kept up his efforts until 1682),[100] that Georg Ludwig's marriage in 1682 to his first cousin Sophia-Dorothea of Celle was designed to protect Hanoverian territorial interests, and that her own future was subject to the demands of state. The fact that her own marriage of twenty-five years' duration was exceptionally congenial would have obliterated any antipathy towards Georg Ludwig; rather than animosity, her own future comments concerning her first suitor would suggest trust and fond memories of his stay in London.

Apart from the Hanoverian prince's departure, March 1681 proved to be pivotal to Lady Anne's future. On 6 March her half-sister, Lady Isabella, died at the age of five, reinforcing the widespread belief that James and Mary were incapable of conceiving healthy children who could survive the rigours of seventeenth-century childhood. On 21 March, Charles met his third and last Exclusion Parliament at Oxford. Strengthened by a secret promise from Louis XIV that he would provide a large French pension to relieve Charles of the necessity of summoning Parliament, the king shrewdly gave the Whigs enough rope with which to hang themselves. Charles himself proposed an Exclusion scheme whereby the Prince and Princess of Orange would exercise the royal powers as regents during James's lifetime; angrily Shaftesbury and his followers rejected this proposal and, for the first time, supported Monmouth's pretensions openly. Charles dissolved Parliament abruptly on 28 March, and the Whigs fled from Oxford on the same night, fearing for their lives. The Whig reign of terror was at an end; the Tory reign of terror was about to begin.

The nation – and with it, Lady Anne – readily accepted the court's version of these events. The Whigs, in supporting a bastard's claims to supplant not only her father but also her sister and Lady Anne herself, had driven the nation to the verge of civil war. The horrors of the 1640s were all too vividly recalled, and it was not to be doubted that the Whigs aimed at destroying not only the hereditary principle and the independence of the crown, but the social and political dominance of the Church of England as well. From the dissolution of the third Exclusion Parliament, public opinion in England swung violently in favour of the crown, the hereditary principle – and the Duke of York. The growing strength of the royal position was felt by Lady Anne in the summer of 1681, when the king agreed to allow her to join her parents in their Scottish exile. As early as May, the Duke of York had hoped that Lady Anne might be permitted to reside with him,[101] and had appealed to the king through his brother-in-law, Lawrence, Lord Hyde, Hyde's wife (Lady Anne's

governess), and Lady Anne herself.[102] Their solicitation proved successful and Lady Anne embarked for Scotland by sea on 13 July, arriving in
Edinburgh on 19 July for a stay which was to last for ten months.[103]

All indirect evidence suggests that her sojourn in Scotland was one of
the most profound formative experiences of the adolescence of Lady
Anne, who celebrated her seventeenth birthday in Edinburgh. Superficially, her life there was an extension of the social frivolity characteristic of Whitehall, her time spent largely in the company of the duchess
and 'the ladies of quality [who], when the weather is fair, divert themselves on horseback some few miles from Edinburgh with hats and
plumes of feathers on them'.[104] When the weather was inclement,
entertainment was provided by the card game bassett, private theatricals, or by country dancing, in which both the duchess and Lady Anne
enjoyed participating.[105] Nevertheless, Lady Anne was unhappy. 'I
hope', she wrote to Frances Apsley in September 1681, with the wistful
uncertainty common to exiles, 'that we shall be happy in seeing one
anotther tho God & the King onely knowes when.'[106] Her unhappiness
was inspired not only by homesickness for England but also by what she
and the Protestant members of the York household observed in
Edinburgh. As the king's deputy in Scotland, the duke's first goal was to
ensure his own succession to the Scottish crown, which he achieved
through a compliant Parliament. His second goal was to suppress anti-
Stuart activity in the northern kingdom by persecuting fanatic Presby-
terians who refused to conform to the anglicanized, episcopal Church of
Scotland. English Protestants, however unsympathetic to Presbyterianism, were appalled by the barbaric means of torture – including the
boot and the rack – still employed in Scotland and horrified that the
duke himself should attend interrogations conducted with such instru-
ments. Three generations later, the aged Duchess of Marlborough
recalled

> the Duke's arbitrary Proceedings in Scotland . . . for I saw it myself,
> and was much grieved at the Trials of several People that were
> hang'd . . . I have cried at some of these Trials, to see the Cruelty that
> was done to these Men only for their choosing to die rather than tell
> a Lye.[107]

In the intimacy of the ducal court at Holyrood, Lady Anne could
hardly escape such impressions or the conclusion advanced by her
Protestant compatriots that Roman Catholicism could transform her
gentle, well-intentioned father into a persecutor.

Although she was later to refer to the Scots as 'strange people', it was
no accident that Lady Anne would be largely responsible for the union

between the northern and southern kingdoms of Great Britain. Her sojourn in Scotland (which was not to be repeated by another British monarch until George IV) made her realize not only Scotland's immense importance to English security but also the necessity of ameliorating the religious differences between the Protestants of the two kingdoms.

In England, the Tory reaction in favour of the Duke of York continued, and the York household returned by sea to London on 27 May 1682.[108] Apart from the return to more familiar and congenial friends and surroundings, the move from Scotland to England made little difference to Lady Anne's daily life: her time was still largely taken up by hunting, dancing, cards, and devout attendance at Anglican services. Her own position, however, was becoming precarious, for an unmarried princess of seventeen attracted many predators in the court of Charles II. For Lady Anne, 1682 was to be a year of acute embarrassment.

The villain of this melodrama was John Sheffield, Lord Mulgrave, a favourite of Charles II, a bachelor and, at thirty-five, Lady Anne's senior by eighteen years. The nature of Mulgrave's 'soe briske attempts upon the Lady Anne'[109] remains obscure. Mulgrave claimed that his crime was 'only ogling',[110] but all independent accounts agreed that he had written letters 'intimating too near an address to her'.[111] When this correspondence was discovered and Mulgrave was banned from court in November 1682, London gossips concluded that Mulgrave had seduced Lady Anne, 'so far as to spoil her marrying to any body else, and therefore the town has given him the nickname of King John'.[112] Although Mulgrave was temporarily exiled to Tangiers, his later career suggests that his intimacy with Lady Anne was vastly overrated by gossip. He subsequently married three times (his third wife, jokingly called 'the princess', was an illegitimate daughter of the Duke of York and consequently Lady Anne's half-sister) and he held high office under James II, William III (who created him Marquess of Normanby) and Queen Anne (who created him Duke of Buckingham). Mulgrave's success was due to his position in the Tory party, not to any unrequited love which Lady Anne bore for him; indeed, Mulgrave himself in later years left ample testimony that he possessed little personal influence with her.[113] The Mulgrave affair contained serious portents for the future. First, it hastened negotiations for Lady Anne's marriage which, as we shall see in the next chapter, were completed eight months later. Secondly, it underlined – and perhaps contributed to – a growing divergence between Lady Anne and her sister. The Princess of Orange's letter to their mutual friend, Frances Apsley, is revealing: while deploring the fate of 'my pore sister' and conventionally, if unconvincingly, defending Lady Anne ('not but that I believe my sister very innocent'),

27

the Princess of Orange strongly hinted that her sister lacked discretion and good judgment: 'I am so nice upon the point of reputation that it makes me mad she should be exposed to such reports, & now what will not this insolent man say being provokt.'[114] No correspondence between the royal sisters is extant for this period, but it is likely that some hint of her sister's priggish attitude was conveyed to Lady Anne.

Finally, and most importantly, the Mulgrave affair marked the flowering of the friendship between Lady Anne and Sarah Jennings, a friendship which would influence the destiny of Europe. The two women first met as children at play in 1670 or 1671, when Lady Anne was five and Mistress Jennings was ten. In her *Conduct of the dowager Duchess of Marlborough*, published in 1742, Sarah claimed that Lady Anne immediately displayed a marked liking for her and (drawing a large red herring across the tracks) intimated that their acquaintance rapidly progressed to intimate friendship while Lady Anne was still in her nursery.[115] In reality, there is nothing to suggest that their relationship was especially close before 1682 or 1683; indeed, in an earlier, unpublished version of her autobiography, Sarah referred to herself as 'not having been in any degree of favour till after that' (i.e. the Mulgrave affair).[116] In 1710, Sarah referred to 'fourty yeares acquaintance & twenty five yeares very faithfull servise' to the queen,[117] although in her letters to her husband she would date her service to Lady Anne from 1683. Their acquaintance undoubtedly ripened after Sarah began to live regularly at court in 1673; Sarah appeared with Lady Anne in the production of *Calisto* in December 1674,[118] but the crucial age difference between Sarah, who was beginning to attract suitors, and Lady Anne, still a child, would have prevented common interests. As a maid of honour to the Duchess of York, Sarah met John Churchill in 1675. After three years of courtship they were married secretly late in 1677 or early in 1678.[119] One immediate consequence of the marriage was that through her husband Sarah's future *entrée* to the York household and to Lady Anne's circle was firmly established.

Churchill's father, Sir Winston, was a Cavalier who had been impoverished during the Interregnum and rewarded by a series of minor positions after the Restoration. John, the eldest son, had been born in 1650 and had spent his formative years (as had Sarah) in genteel poverty. In 1663, John Churchill entered St Paul's School, but it was closed by the Plague in 1665; at the same time, his elder sister Arabella became the mistress of the Duke of York and John entered his household as a page.[120]

(The fact that Arabella Churchill produced four bastards for the Duke of York made little or no contribution to the ensuing friendship between

Lady Anne and the Churchills. Arabella's children – the eldest of whom, James FitzJames, was later created Duke of Berwick and Maréchal de France – were reared in France as Roman Catholics. Sarah claimed that her husband was 'ashamed' of such connections[121] and that puritanical attitude was undoubtedly shared by Lady Anne; there is no mention of her illegitimate half-brothers and half-sisters in her extant correspondence and she never displayed any interest in them.)

As 'ye only favourite of his master',[122] young Churchill entered the Army in 1667 as an ensign and worked his way up through the ranks under the patronage of the Duke of York. Churchill's family motto was 'Faithfull but Unfortunate', but his whole career was to belie it. He intrigued against every English monarch from James II to George I, while managing to amass the largest private fortune in Europe. He began early. Before his marriage, his affair with Charles II's most noteworthy mistress, Barbara Palmer, Duchess of Cleveland, netted Churchill £10,000 from the grateful duchess's fortune. At the same time, he displayed an extraordinary ability to advance himself at the expense of others, mainly by treating royalty diplomatically. Reporting on a youthful duel in which the twenty-one-year-old Churchill was twice wounded in the arm while running his opponent, the future Lord Herbert of Cherbury, through the thigh, a contemporary witness added 'that Churchill has so spoke of it, that the King and Duke are angry with Herbert. I know not what he [Churchill] has done to justifie himself.'[123] To his political enemies, the mainspring of Churchill's career was his avarice and his desire to establish a dynasty; according to the second Lord Dartmouth, Churchill

> was undoubtedly the most fortunate man that ever lived, having always received the reward, before the merit, and the appearance of having deserved it came afterwards, for which he expected and constantly had a second gratification, till he had procured all the honours and wealth his own country could give him.[124]

To illustrate Churchill's ambition and avarice in no way denigrates the extraordinary abilities which were to elevate him to the foremost position in England and Europe. His military genius, rivalled only by his political and diplomatic skill, was on a level with that of Napoleon. It was early demonstrated but Churchill had little opportunity to exercise it before 1702. Power and influence naturally gravitated to Churchill, who invariably appeared calm, balanced, and judicious. Far-seeing and resolute, Churchill could not be governed by anyone other than the equally remarkable woman who became his wife.

Self-confident from her earliest years, Sarah was never self-contained:

her virtues – her sharp intelligence, her wit, her devotion to the interests of her family (a devotion which became inseparable from the interests of Lady Anne after 1683) – were increasingly marred as the years passed by her chief vice, an all-pervading and ungovernable temper, although even this, combined with extreme old age, did little to dim the physical attractions which made her one of the greatest beauties of her generation. 'I was born with a great avertion to Fools & Tyrants',[125] she once wrote, and for Sarah there were few people who did not eventually fall into one or other categories. Outspokenly convinced of the infallibility of her own opinions, Sarah was not one to shrink from politics, a field conventionally considered alien to women in the seventeenth century; indeed, she actively sought to gain power, on the household and on the national front. In 1716, after Marlborough's debilitating stroke had removed him from political life and he went to Bath to take the waters, one of Sarah's closest friends, Mary, Countess Cowper, recorded in her diary: 'The Schemers flocked thither; for though the Duke could not advise, he could lend his Name and Purse, both which the Duchess governed (a pleasure to her, who loved Power even more than the Duke).'[126]

The friendship between Sarah and Lady Anne appeared strange to those who knew them both and, for us, it is virtually impossible to assess precisely the nature of their relationship, for we possess only one side of their correspondence, the letters of Lady Anne. Were Sarah's responses as passionate, as tender, as full of devotion as the notes which poured forth daily from the princess's pen? We do not know, for Sarah imposed a condition upon Lady Anne (as she did upon her husband) that her letters should be burnt after they had been read. Only after their final and fatal quarrel began did Sarah keep copies of her letters to the queen. Sarah herself attributed the friendship to the mediocre personalities who surrounded Lady Anne: 'her Highness's court was throughout so oddly composed', she recalled in her *Conduct*, 'that I think it would be making myself no great compliment, if I should say, her chusing to spend more of her time with me, than with any of her other servants, did no discredit to her taste'.[127]

For Lady Anne, it was of vital importance that, next to Lord Churchill, she should stand first in Sarah's affections. The theme is repeated over and over again in her letters: 'I hope that next to Lord Churchill', she wrote in 1684, 'I may claim ye first place in your heart' and later, 'I hope ye little corner of your heart that my Lord Churchill has left empty is mine'.[128] One reason for her devotion to Sarah was her conviction that Sarah would never flatter her or tell her a lie. Having grown up in a court where intrigue and back-stabbing were rampant, Lady Anne appreciated Sarah's undoubted honesty and integrity and her letters to Lady Churchill bear out Sarah's contention that frankness was the quality in her which the princess most prized:

> Young as I was, when I first became this high favourite, I laid it down for a maxim, that flattery was falsehood to my trust, and ingratitude to my greatest friend; and that I did not deserve so much favour, if I could not venture the loss of it by speaking the truth, and by preferring the real interest of my mistress before the pleasing her fancy, or the sacrificing to her passion. From this rule I never swerved. And though my temper and my notions in most things were widely different from those of the Princess, yet during a long course of years, she was so far from being displeased with me for openly speaking my sentiments, that she sometimes professed a desire, and even added her command, that it should be always continued, promising never to be offended at it, but to love me the better for my frankness.[129]

Unfortunately, a day was to come when frankness was no longer prized, when the open speaking of sentiments became offensive, when love was dead. But for many years to come, the friendship formed between Lady Anne and Lady Churchill was to influence not only the course of the princess's life, but also the course of English history.

2

'Firm to my Religion'

The Revolution,
1683–9

Serious negotiations for the marriage of the eighteen-year-old Lady
Anne with Prince George of Denmark apparently began early in 1683,
after the Prince of Hanover had married his first cousin. The Anglo–
Danish negotiations were conducted in London under the sponsorship
of Louis XIV, who wished to see the two naval powers in alliance against
the Dutch.[1] This goal accorded well with the Duke of York's desire to
lessen the influence of his son-in-law William of Orange in British
domestic politics.[2] In order to forestall any possible interference by the
Prince of Orange, the negotiations were conducted in the deepest
secrecy by Lady Anne's uncle, Lawrence Hyde, now Earl of Rochester,
and the secretary of state, Robert Spencer, Earl of Sunderland; consequently, 'a match that could have been of the greatest dynastic
significance was huddled through in the most underhand manner'.[3]

Rochester drove a hard financial bargain with the Danes: the Duke of
York would provide the young couple with £5,000 annually, as well as
£40,000 dowry; the remainder of the couple's income would be derived
from the Prince of Denmark's personal estates.[4] Furthermore, Prince
George was to make his permanent home in England and was to take
precedence only as the son of the Duke of York.[5] Faced with these stiff
conditions, Lente, the Danish envoy, privately sounded out Barillon,
Louis XIV's representative in London, on the possibility of substituting
George and Anne in the English succession for William and Mary, but
the French envoy's response was an emphatic negative. Barillon pointed
out to Lente that such a proposal directly contravened hereditary right,
which the king had supported at such great sacrifice throughout the
Popish Plot and the Exclusion crisis. Both Charles and James were
implacably opposed to any alteration in the divinely established succession.[6]

The motives for the English court's haste and secrecy were undoubtedly mixed: the Mulgrave affair pointed up the necessity of

marrying Lady Anne as quickly as possible, while secrecy was necessary in order to forestall any possible opposition to an anti-Orangist alliance. Within two months of the initiation of the Anglo–Danish negotiations verbal agreement had been reached, and the news of the proposed marriage was made public during the first week of May 1683.[7] James was delighted, particularly by the 'consternation' of the Prince of Orange, who had neither been consulted nor even formally notified of the betrothal of his sister-in-law and cousin, and who felt his credit in England diminished by the entrance of another Protestant prince into the royal family.[8] 'My daughter's being married to the Prince of Denmark will now be no news to you', James wrote to the Marquess of Queensberry, 'and I am the better pleased with it because I find the loyal party here do like it, and the Whigs are as much troubled at it.'[9]

The prospective bride's attitude to marriage with her unknown second cousin once removed (Lady Anne was the great-great-grand-daughter of Frederick II of Denmark and Prince George was his great-grandson) is unrecorded; she did, however, reassure Frances Apsley that though 'your Ziphares [Lady Anne] . . . changes his condition yet nothing shall ever alter him from being ye same to his deare Semandra that he ever was'.[10] During the period immediately prior to her marriage, Lady Anne's chief occupation was ensuring that an important new member, Lady Churchill, would be added to her 'family'. Three undated notes from Lady Anne to Sarah, now in the Blenheim archives, suggest that the Duke of York raised some objection to Sarah's appoint-ment, possibly because Rochester (who wished to preserve his wife's position) strongly opposed Lady Churchill's appointment.[11] In the first note, Lady Anne informed Sarah that

tis no trouble to me to obey your Commands but I don't yet know any
more for ye Duke was with me this morning but . . . he did not say
a word to me of ye business . . . assure your self yt whatever lyes in
my power shall not be wanting.[12]

The second note, which suggests that the duke had refused his daughter's initial request, illustrates not only Lady Anne's insecurity but also her desire to soften Sarah's temper:

Oh deare Lady Churchill lett me begg you once more not to beleeve
that I am in fault tho I must Confess you may have some reason to
beleeve it becaus I gave you my word so often yt I would never give
my Consent to any more [i.e. ladies of the bedchamber], I have not
but have said all that was possible for one to say, the only reason that
kept me from telling it to you was becaus I was yet in hopes that I
might prevail with ye Duke & I will try once more, be he never so

33

angry; but oh do not lett this take away your kindness from me, for I assure you tis ye greatest trouble in ye world to me & I am sure you have not a faithfuller friend on earth nor that loves you better then I do, my eyes are full, I canot say a word more but I hope you wil com to me at six aclock.[13]

The third letter, again without date, is an announcement of victory mingled with a gracious allusion to the personal sacrifices which Lady Churchill would have to undertake in her new position as a lady of the bedchamber:

The Duke came just as you weare gon & made no difficultys but has promised me that I shall have you which I asure you is a great Joy to me. I should say a gret deale for your kindnes in ofering it but I am not good at compliments. I will only say that I do take it exstream kindly & shall be ready at any time to do you all ye Service that lyes in my power.[14]

The proposed marriage was welcomed by the Churchills, for it reinforced their position in the Duke of York's favour. Lord Churchill's youngest brother, Charles, had gone to Copenhagen in 1669 to serve as a page of honour to King Christian V and in 1672 had become gentleman of the bedchamber to the King of Denmark's younger brother, Prince George.[15] John Churchill was chosen by Charles II to go to Denmark to bring Prince George to England for his marriage.[16]

The prince's arrival in London on 19 July 1683 produced new difficulties, most of them raised by his closest confidant and secretary Christian Siegfried von Plessen 'who possessed the entire confidence of Prince George'. One of the English demands was that no Danes should remain in Prince George's household, a condition which von Plessen naturally resented. Because no agreement could be reached on this point, the marriage was concluded without a formal contract at ten o'clock on the evening of 28 July (St Anne's Day). The ceremony, which took place in the Chapel Royal of St James's Palace, was small, because the king 'wished neither ceremony nor ostentation';[17] after the ceremony, at which Bishop Compton presided, the king, queen, duke, and duchess 'all supped there together, the Prince and Princess sitting together at the end of the table'.[18] The prince's gifts to his bride were 'a necklace of pearle, valewd at six thousand pound, a rich jewell of diamonds to weare before, and a paire of pendants and bodkin guess'd to be worth fifteen thousand pound, besides a box of massie gold set with diamonds (wherein they were inclosed)'.[19]

Her elder sister had shed bitter tears at the prospect of marrying the Prince of Orange, but Lady Anne apparently accepted her fate stoically.

One contemporary observer said of the bride: 'She is a princesse of a very ingenious and debonaire demeaner, full of goodness in all her aire.'[20] Certainly her groom was more handsome than William III: 'he had the Danish Countenance, blound; a young gentleman of few words, spake French but ill, seemed somewhat heavy; but reported Valient' was the diarist Evelyn's comment.[21] The prince, born in 1653, was twelve years older than his new wife. Trained as a military man, he had made a Grand Tour of Europe during his adolescence, spending eight months in France in 1668–9 and the summer of 1669 in England, where an Italian diplomat had concluded that the prince had a 'well grounded acquaintance with several sciences'.[22] He and his brother King Christian V had achieved widespread acclaim for their valour in the battle of Landskrone in 1677 against Charles XI of Sweden. As a devout Protestant, Prince George was politically acceptable to England and personally acceptable to his wife. The immediate enthusiastic welcome which Prince George received in London ('I think nobody could please better and more universally in one afternoon than he hath done', one newswriter recorded)[23] soon wore off and the general estimate of the prince's abilities was summed up by Charles II in his famous quip, 'I have tried him drunk and I have tried him sober and there is nothing in him.'[24] The king, as he so often did, hit the nail on the head; his judgment was accepted by everyone but the new Princess of Denmark, who was to remain blindly devoted to her husband throughout their married life. The princess's devotion rested securely on the fact that she was the undisputed head of their household; this predominance was quickly established when, through Lord Churchill's influence with the Duke of York, the obstreperous von Plessen was sent back to Denmark to manage Prince George's private estates there.[25] Sarah's brother-in-law Colonel Edward Griffith was appointed the prince's secretary in von Plessen's place.[26]

The newly married couple quickly established a group of intimate friends eventually known as 'the Cockpit circle', so named after the Tudor apartments in the Palace of Whitehall given by Charles II to his niece in June 1684 to serve as her London town house.[27] Most prominent in this circle were, of course, Lord and Lady Churchill and Churchill's younger brothers, George, a captain in the Navy, and Charles, a colonel in the Army; other important members were also drawn from the armed forces. Colonel John Berkeley was the colonel of Princess Anne's Dragoons, and his wife, Barbara Villiers (the eldest daughter of Sir Edward and Lady Frances Villiers, the princess's one-time governess), was one of the princess and Lady Churchill's closest confidantes, later to be placed in charge of the royal nursery. Other friends included Sir Benjamin Bathurst, the comptroller of the Denmarks' household, and his wife, the former Frances Apsley; the princess's bastard cousin the Duke of Grafton and his wife,[28] the young Marquess of Ossory (who succeeded his grandfather as the second Duke of Ormonde in 1688) and the Earl of Drumlanrig (who became Duke of Queensberry in 1695).[29] On the fringes of this circle stood Robert and Anne Spencer, Earl and Countess of Sunderland, intimate friends of the Churchills but naturally suspect to the princess because Sunderland, a secretary of state already earning a reputation as a political turncoat, at one point had supported Exclusion. Jealous of Lady Churchill's friendship with Lady Sunderland, the princess concealed her antipathy towards the older couple under a veil of cordiality, but her suspicion and dislike of the Sunderlands was to deepen and harden during the next reign.

The household of the Denmarks, as distinct from their personal friends, had been composed by the Duke of York to reward those who had supported him during the Exclusion crisis. The Earl of Scarsdale was the prince's gentleman of the bedchamber and Lord Cornbury, the eldest son and heir of the princess's uncle, Henry Hyde, now Earl of Clarendon, served as the prince's master of the horse. Lady Clarendon was made first lady of the bedchamber and groom of the stole to the princess; Lord James Murray, heir to the Marquess of Atholl (and to be created first Duke of Atholl by Queen Anne in 1703), served as the princess's master of the horse. During the first years of her marriage, the princess's time was largely spent in regular attendance at prayers, incessant gambling, and continually writing to 'my deare Lady Churchill', who was frequently absent from court in order to supervise her own growing family at St Albans.

The primary reason for the Princess's marriage, of course, was the production of heirs to the throne; indeed, this became the main object of her life and her repeated failure to bear healthy children was to scar her both physically and emotionally. Three months after the wedding, it was rumoured that the princess was pregnant and by December 1683 the pregnancy had been publicly confirmed.[30] On 12 May 1684, however, the princess was brought to bed of a stillborn daughter in what was to prove the first in a long series of such tragedies. At the time, however, the stillbirth was ascribed to Princess Anne's fall from a horse,[31] and at the end of June she and the prince, accompanied by the Duke and Duchess of York, went to take the spa waters of Tunbridge Wells. The princess remained there in convalescence until mid-August.[32] By the end of the year, she was once again pregnant.

This second pregnancy automatically voided plans which were being laid for the prince and princess to accompany the Duke of York to Scotland early in 1685, where the duke was to preside over the Scottish Parliament.[33] Before the duke departed for Edinburgh, however, Charles II suffered a serious stroke on 2 February 1685, and died four days later. It was the princess's twentieth birthday. In the extensive contemporary accounts of Charles II's death, which drew attention to his deathbed conversion to Roman Catholicism at the hands of a priest whom the Duke of York had secretly brought into his brother's bedchamber, there is no mention of the Prince and Princess of Denmark. What seems certain is that the princess heard, and gave some credence to, rumours that Charles II had been poisoned by Roman Catholics to allow for the accession of her father, a monarch who would more blindly follow their interests; it was Lord Mulgrave who first propagated this rumour in print,[34] and twenty-six years after the event Churchill assured a Hanoverian diplomat that his mistress did indeed believe that her uncle had been murdered by the Jesuits.[35] In her correspondence with Lady Churchill, the princess did not comment directly on the rumour, but when the prince was troubled 'with a gidines in his heade' she mentioned that 'I canot help being frighted at ye least thing ever since ye late King's death'.[36]

The death of Charles II and the peaceful accession of her father as James II changed the political and social position of Princess Anne. Not only did she become heiress presumptive after her sister, the Princess of Orange, but she was also the highest ranking Protestant member of the royal family resident in England and consequently attracted the attention of all Protestants. Furthermore, if the house of Stuart was to be perpetuated, it would be through Princess Anne, now five and a half months pregnant, rather than through William and Mary, whose eight-year marriage had proved barren. This elevated position was responsible for new honours for Prince George and for thinly veiled hostility from William. Three days after the new king's accession, on 9 February, Prince George was summoned to the Privy Council and thereafter he met every Sunday with the 'Conseil du Cabinet' which read dispatches and formulated orders to be sent abroad.[37] These honours were formal but empty, for Prince George had no influence whatsoever on the policies of his father-in-law. More significant for the future was the jealousy of William of Orange, inspired in large measure because the Prince of Denmark, as the son and brother of hereditary monarchs, clearly outranked an elected stadhouder of the Dutch republic. William declined to attend James II's coronation, held on St George's Day (23 April), because the Prince of Denmark would have taken precedence over him; William's special envoy to London and his closest confidant,

Hans Willem Bentinck, told Rochester that the Prince of Orange would never come to England as long as the Prince of Denmark was accorded preferential treatment.[38] In addition, the financial settlement made for the Prince and Princess of Denmark was generous in contrast with the 'contemptible dowry' settled on Princess Mary, who received no income whatsoever from England during her father's reign.[39]

On 1 June 1685, after full-term pregnancy, the Princess of Denmark gave birth to a daughter who survived the immediate rigours of childbirth.[40] The daughter, named Mary, was christened the next day by Henry Compton, Bishop of London, with the Earl of Rochester as godfather and the Princess of Orange and the Duchess of Grafton as godmothers.[41] Lady Mary, however, was never very healthy. Two months after her birth, the princess reported to Lady Churchill: 'I am very sory my girle has any soreness in her eyes, for feare she should take after me in that.'[42] At three months, the young mother recorded, 'She has at this time a scaby face which they tell me will do her a great deale of good.'[43] Nevertheless, the infant's mere existence, and the promise of more children, reinforced the princess's political position and her expectations for the future.

During 1685, a number of causes led to the princess's estrangement from her mother's family, a breach which was never fully healed. Lady Churchill and the Countess of Clarendon (whom Sarah described in her *Conduct* as a 'madwoman') were constantly at odds and there could be no doubt that the princess greatly preferred Sarah: 'I am now all alone with my poor Countess who growes more and more naucious every day', she lamented to Lady Churchill.[44] Nor did the princess take any satisfaction in the services which her aunt rendered. 'Ye Countess went this morning to London but will be bak to moro with my birthday cloths,' she reported to Sarah. 'I wish She had not given herself ye trouble for I am sure they will be much ye worse for her looking after.'[45] When it was rumoured that Clarendon would lose his position as lord privy seal and become instead lord-lieutenant of Ireland and that he and the countess would go to Dublin, the princess was ecstatic. 'I am very glad there is some hopes of ye Irish business and shall pray heartily for theire good Success in it,' she told Sarah.[46] Lady Clarendon's departure from England led to Lady Churchill's elevation to first lady of the bed-chamber and groom of the stole in the princess's household, a position which she was to hold for twenty-five years.

While the princess personally disliked the Countess of Clarendon her reasons for argument with Lord and Lady Rochester were two of the oldest bones of contention in any court, lodgings and pensions. The princess was determined to lay claim to the Round Tower at Windsor,

UNIVERSITY OF WINNIPEG
LIBRARY
515 Portage Avenue
Winnipeg, Manitoba R3B 2E9

which had been assigned to the Duke of York during Charles II's reign, while Lady Rochester, the wife of the new lord treasurer, was bent on expanding her own lodgings at Windsor by acquiring a small building which was adjacent to the Round Tower.[47] As the princess explained to Sarah in August:

Lady Rochester is heare in a very peevish kind of a way tho I think
she has no reason since She is so well provided for at Windsor but She
is not yet contented for I am told She lays claime to that that was ye
Duke's wardrobe which never belonged to ye tower tho it be neare it.

If necessary, the princess was prepared to complain to her father, 'for tho it be but one room I shall think it very hard to have it given her since I am to have all that he had when he was Duke'.[48] An appeal to the king finally proved to be the only way and, a month later, the princess informed Sarah that 'I have got ye better of it which makes her in a very peevish way'.[49]

The princess's dispute over money with Rochester was to prove even more serious and was largely caused by the constant gambling for large sums which was common in her court. 'I am sorry you have so ill luck at dice,' the princess wrote to Sarah in 1686, 'yesterday I won three hundred pounds but have lost almost half of it again this morning.'[50] Furthermore, the income which the Denmarks received from the king was only £30,000 per annum, which was to be supplemented by the 300,000 Rix dollars which Prince George should have received from his estates in Denmark; however, these payments were slow to arrive and incomplete,[51] and by the end of 1685 the prince and princess were seriously in debt. One observer recorded that 'the Princess of Denmark has but thirty thousand pounds a year, which is so exhausted by a great establishment that she is really extreme poor for one of her rank'.[52] The princess asked her uncle, Rochester, to intercede with the king for a special grant to pay off her debts, but Rochester 'excused himself by telling her she knew the King's temper in relation to money matters, and such a proposal might do him hurt, and her no good'. Instead, the princess was forced to turn for help to Sidney, Lord Godolphin, who secured from James II a £16,000 free gift to the prince and princess at Christmas, 1685.[53] Rochester's refusal to help his niece left Princess Anne permanently estranged from him; she made it clear that he possessed no influence with her[54] and complained to her sister that Clarendon 'has not behaved himself so well to me as I think he had reason nor no more has any of that family, which one may think a little extraordinary'.[55]

From the tenor of Sarah's *Conduct*, there can be no doubt that the

Churchills laboured to maintain and increase the princess's aversion to the Hydes, whom the Churchills considered their personal opponents. The Churchills were the chief beneficiaries of the princess's quarrels with her mother's family, and the entry of Godolphin into the Cockpit circle was undoubtedly at their suggestion (although Godolphin also had the advantage of being a first cousin of Colonel Berkeley). Sidney Godolphin, of Cornish gentry, had entered court as a page of honour to Charles II in 1663 and had established an intimate friendship with John Churchill and later with his wife, a friendship which was to endure until Godolphin's death. While Churchill had received military training, Godolphin had undertaken diplomatic assignments and had developed a knowledge of Treasury affairs which was rivalled only by Rochester's. Indeed, the two men were professional rivals, despite their Tory loyalties; during the last years of Charles II's reign, Godolphin had been first lord of the Treasury, but with James's accession to the throne he was superseded by Rochester and relegated to the relatively minor position of vice-chamberlain to the queen. By the time of the Revolution in 1688, Godolphin's friendship with the princess had grown to the point where he entrusted her with the safekeeping of 20,000 gold guineas 'and they were constantly removed with her, wherever she went'.[56]

The princess's estrangement from her family, however important for the future, was overshadowed by the broad sweep of public events in 1685. On 22 May the princess attended the opening of the new Parliament,[57] which proved to be as subservient to royal wishes as Charles II's last three Parliaments had been hostile, thanks to the widespread remodelling of the corporation charters undertaken during the last years of Charles's reign. Hardly had Parliament renewed all grants of taxation which had lapsed on Charles's death than it was prorogued, for news had reached London that the Marquess of Argyll had invaded Scotland, and the Duke of Monmouth had landed at Lyme Regis and was quickly forming an army, mainly composed of peasants and Protestant Dissenters, in the West Country. The proclamation which Monmouth issued claimed that he was the legitimate son of Charles II and therefore king; his uncle was a usurper who had murdered his brother to advance Roman Catholic designs. While Argyll's Scottish rebellion was easily suppressed (he was captured and executed as a traitor), the Monmouth rebellion proved sufficiently serious to warrant James's rapid expansion of the Army in England. He appointed large numbers of Roman Catholics as officers, despite the provisions of the Test Act, which he ignored. After Churchill defeated the rebel army at Sedgemoor on 6 July and captured Monmouth (who was executed on 15 July after fruitlessly lodging appeals for clemency with the king, the queen, and the queen dowager), James embarked on a campaign of suppression in the West Country conducted by Chief Justice George Jeffreys in his infamous 'Bloody Assizes'. The ferocity with which Jeffreys acted both as judge and prosecutor, and the dubious legality of many of his verdicts, appalled even loyalist Tories and Anglicans: the corpses publicly displayed throughout western England ignited memories of the fires of Smithfield during the reign of 'Bloody' Mary Tudor, so graphically portrayed in Foxe's *Book of Martyrs*, a Protestant hagiography which, with the Bible, was found in virtually every literate home in seventeenth-century England.

After the suppression of the Monmouth rebellion, James II enjoyed more power than any previous English monarch. He possessed a large army which he had no intention of disbanding, and a subservient Parliament packed with loyalist Tories; for the time being the Whigs were cowed and quiescent. But James's power was overshadowed by that of Louis XIV who in the 1680s reached the apogee of his long reign. Following the Treaty of Nijmegen in 1678, which ended the French war against the Dutch republic and its allies, Louis had rapidly expanded the power of the French crown by arbitrary means; a series of *réunions* in the western Rhineland placed under French military control key defensive areas of the Holy Roman empire (including, in 1681, the city of Strasbourg). The emperor, Leopold I, was unable to retaliate because his resources had been completely absorbed by the last great Ottoman invasion of south-eastern Europe, which had been secretly encouraged by France. With the exception of France, every Christian nation of Europe – whether Catholic or Protestant – had sent volunteers to relieve the Infidel's siege of Vienna in 1683. The resultant loss of *gloire* for the Most Christian King was compounded by Louis's dispute with the papacy; in an attempt to expand the crown's control over the Gallican Church, Louis claimed the right to nominate French bishops, a claim which brought him into direct conflict with the strongest of seventeenth-century pontiffs, Innocent XI. In October 1685, to retrieve his reputation as the first son of the Church, Louis XIV revoked the Edict of Nantes issued by his grandfather, Henri IV, in 1598 to give freedom of religion in limited areas to French Protestants, the Huguenots. While Louis XIV's aggressive foreign policy enabled William III over the next three years to construct an anti-French alliance composed of the Habsburgs in Vienna and Madrid, the German princes, and the pope, Louis's revocation of the Edict of Nantes and the consequent flood of Huguenot *émigrés* seeking relief from persecution in the Dutch republic, Brandenburg, and England, did more to undermine James II's position in Great Britain than did the illegalities of Judge Jeffreys.

To the English, what was happening in France today might well happen in England tomorrow, for the house of Stuart was inevitably associated with France in the minds of Englishmen; Charles II and James had approved the secret Treaty of Dover; they had acted as Louis's close allies; they had survived the storm of the Exclusion crisis thanks to French gold. As king, James II actually attempted to keep his foreign policy independent of France, seeing himself as the arbiter of Europe, holding the balance between William and Louis. But this was obscured in the public mind by James's absolutist domestic policy and by his evident intention to favour his co-religionists, even at the expense of his erstwhile allies, the Tories and the Church of England. When Parliament reconvened in November 1685, for what proved to be its last session during James II's reign, the king requested that the Test Act, as well as the penal laws against Roman Catholics, be repealed. Even the most sub-servient loyalist balked at removing the statutory barriers against Roman Catholics holding office under the crown, and Parliament was pro-rogued eleven days after it had reassembled. Unable to attain his goals through Parliament, James embarked on a campaign of dubious legality in order to secure civil liberties for his fellow Roman Catholics. His goal, during 1686 and 1687, was limited to establishing toleration for the True Church so firmly that it could not be undone by a Protestant successor in the future; however, to Protestants, the king's constant usage of the term 'to establish' suggested that his ultimate, albeit secret, goal was the formal re-establishment of Roman Catholicism as the national religion.

Nowhere was this suspicion more prevalent than in the household of the Princess of Denmark. As profession of Roman Catholicism in-creasingly became the entrée to high favour at court, the princess re-treated into an ostentatious Protestantism which made her the magnet of a silent opposition to the king's policies. She attended divine service daily in the Chapel Royal at Whitehall, where she was accorded full royal honours.[58] At the end of 1685, the princess's chief religious advisor, Bishop Compton, was removed from the Privy Council, ostensibly for opposing in Parliament the repeal of the Test Act, but 'others said for his being industrious to preserve the Princess Ann of Denmarke in the Protestant religion, whom there were some en-deavours to gain to the Church of Rome'.[59] Although Compton had fallen into royal displeasure, there can be little doubt that he still continued to advise the princess privately.[60] Aware that his daughter might be the potential nucleus of a Protestant opposition, the king kept a close watch on her household;[61] when she tried to replace Lady Clarendon in October 1685 with Anne, Countess of Westmorland,[62] the king insisted that she should take Sunderland's eldest daughter as lady of the bedchamber instead.[63] The princess sullenly complied, but complained to her sister of Lady Anne Spencer that 'one must always be careful both of what one says and does before her, knowing from whence she comes'.[64] She realized full well that 'she was beset with spies'.[65]

While James was high-handed with his daughter in questions concerning her household, thereby incurring her suspicion and hostility, he proved hesitant about raising the matter of religion with her. Undoubtedly, the king wished to secure the conversion of both of his daughters to Roman Catholicism to further his political policies and also to secure the salvation of their souls. Throughout 1686 and 1687, James repeatedly confided to Barillon, the French envoy, that he wished the Princess of Denmark would be converted, but realized that her obstinacy was the main stumbling-block; nevertheless, the king did not lose hope, and he frequently drew a parallel between the princess and her mother, Anne Hyde.[66] The princess's obstinacy was reinforced by that of her husband; Father Petre, the king's Jesuit confessor, writing of Prince George, complained: 'He is a Prince with whom I cannot discourse about religion. Luther was never more earnest than this Prince. . . . He has naturally an aversion to our society [the Jesuits], and this antipathy does much to obstruct the progress of our affair.'[67]

James chose to influence his daughter slowly and indirectly. In April 1686 the king published papers of religious devotion written by Charles II and Anne Hyde, which had allegedly been discovered after their respective deaths and which explained their reasons for turning to the Church of Rome.[68] The king personally gave a printed copy of the papers to the princess, who remained unimpressed; she assured the Princess of Orange that their publication would accomplish little 'if they have no greater influence on other people than they have had on us; and I trust in God they will not'. While Princess Anne did not regard her father's act as open proselytism ('Nobody has yet said anything to me about religion,' she commented in the same letter to the Princess of Orange), she was eager to reinforce her Protestant image in the eyes of her elder sister:

I hope you don't doubt but that I will ever be firm to my religion whatever happens. However since you desire me to write freely on this subject, I must tell you that I abhor the principles of the Church of Rome as much as it is possible for any to do, and I as much value the doctrine of the Church of England. And certainly there is a greatest reason in the world to do so, for the doctrine of the Church of Rome is wicked and dangerous, and directly contrary to the Scriptures, and their ceremonies – most of them – plain, downright idolatry.

43

In terms of bias, determination, and obstinacy, James II was fully matched by his younger daughter. Princess Anne concluded her letter to her sister with words which, with two obvious variations, might have been written by their father: 'I do count it as a very great blessing that I am of the Church of England, and as great a misfortune that the King is not. I pray God his eyes may be opened.'[69]

More alarming than any overtures from the king were the rumours originating from the 'Catholic faction', a mixed group composed of Scottish, Irish, and Jesuit advisors who were widely believed to possess great, if not unlimited, influence with James II. Unwilling to trust their future careers to the benevolence of a Protestant successor, the Catholics at court were bent on securing the formal re-establishment of Roman Catholicism during the king's lifetime and cementing it by securing the succession by a Roman Catholic heir.[70] While Princess Mary was known to be under the domination of the Prince of Orange and would never therefore be a suitable candidate for conversion (despite her father's attempts to lead her to Rome),[71] Princess Anne seemed to those who did not know her to be more promising material. In March 1686, Louis XIV's special envoy, François de Bonrepaux, inspired by the Catholic faction, quietly sounded out the Danish envoy on the possibility of the princess's conversion and her substitution for the Princess of Orange in the succession. According to Bonrepaux's report (but uncorroborated by any other evidence), both the Prince and Princess of Denmark had welcomed such suggestions: 'I know certainly that the Princess . . . wishes to be instructed. I arranged to give her books of controversy, which she welcomed. She appears timid and seldom speaks. Those who know her well say she is intelligent and highly ambitious.'[72] One tactic which the Catholic advisors used to frighten the princess was to circulate the rumour that the king intended to legitimize his Roman Catholic sons by Arabella Churchill, James FitzJames (created Duke of Berwick in March 1681) and the thirteen-year-old Henry FitzJames (1673–1702), who would supersede both Mary and Anne in the succession.[73] It was public knowledge that Innocent XI, sceptical of the permanence of increased liberties for Roman Catholics beyond James II's lifetime, encouraged the king to procure the conversion of the Princess of Denmark.[74] To the Cockpit, such rumours and exhortations seemed to be harbingers of sterner policy on the part of the king, despite his present lenience: 'the King had given the Princess of Denmark some bookes & papers to read that looked towards changing her religion', Sarah recorded in 1704, 'but never came to any harshness . . . tho tis probable that would have gon farther, if hee had not had a prince of walles'.[75] The most important attempts of the Catholic faction to influence the princess were made by

Richard Talbot, Earl of Tyrconnel and Sarah's brother-in-law, during the autumn of 1686, before he returned to Ireland in January 1687 to become lord lieutenant in the place of Clarendon, who was dismissed for maintaining the Anglican ascendency in Ireland. Tyrconnel's suggestions that a Roman Catholic conversion might procure the succession for the princess met with no success either from her or from Sarah. As the latter recorded,

> During her Father's whole Reign, the Princess kept her Court as private
> as could be consistent with her Station. When the designs of that
> Bigotted Unhappy Prince came to be barefaced, no wonder there
> were attempts made to draw His daughter into the measures of that
> Court. Lord Tyroconnel took some pains [with Sarah] to Engage Her,
> if possible, to make use of that great Favour which He knew she
> enjoyed, for this End. But all his Endeavours were in vain. The
> Princess had Chaplains, indeed, put about her, who could say but
> little in defence of their own Religion, or to secure Her against the
> Pretences of Popery, recommended to Her by a King & a Father.[76]

In the midst of the Catholic faction's campaign to procure the princess's conversion, James achieved a considerable legal breakthrough in his campaign to extend civil liberties to Roman Catholics. In July 1686 the high courts ruled in the collusive case of *Gordon v. Holles* that the king possessed the inherent power to dispense with the law – in this case, the Test Act – in individual instances in appointing Roman Catholics to civil or military office under the crown. The king's first action after that judgment was to appoint four Roman Catholics to the Privy Council, an action which inspired one of the princess's rare political comments in her correspondence with Sarah during James II's reign: 'I was very much surprised when I heard of ye four new privy councillours & am very sorry for it for it will give great countenance to those sort of people & me thinks it has a very dismall prospect.'[77] To her sister the princess was more explicit about what she regarded as 'a very dismall prospect':

> I am very sorry the King encouraged the Papists so much; and I think
> it is very much to be feared that the desire the King has to take off the
> Test, and all other laws against them, is only a pretence to bring in
> Popery.[78]

By the beginning of 1687, the Princess of Denmark had made her determination to remain an Anglican crystal clear to all those who had originally feared that she might prove too complaisant to the king; at The Hague, Dr Gilbert Burnet, an Anglican priest of Scottish origin who was serving as William and Mary's advisor on English affairs, recorded that Princess Anne began very early to declare to the bishops and several others that she was resolved never to change, so she seemed to apply herself more to devotion, and to be more serious in receiving the sacrament than formerly, and has ever since that time behaved herself so worthily in all respects that now all people trust as much to her as ever they were afraid of her.[79]

The Princess's personal influence and her own stubbornness were re-inforced by the premature birth of a second, and healthy, daughter, who was delivered only two hours after the princess reached Windsor on 12 May 1686.[80] She was christened Anne Sophia by the Bishop of Durham, and Lady Churchill was one of her godmothers.[81] The king visited his daughter the following day and reported to William III: 'I found both the mother and the girl very well, God be thanked, and though the child be not a big one, yet most are of opinion it is not come before its time.'[82] It was rumoured that the king had been accompanied by a Roman Catholic priest, 'who no sooner the Princes[s] saw but she fell a crying, the King seeing it, told her he came only as a fatherly vissitt and sent the priest away'.[83]

To complete her recovery from childbirth, the princess spent July and August 1686 – her third consecutive summer – at Tunbridge Wells. Her alienation from her mother's family, her increasing estrangement from her own father and stepmother, and the mutuality of interests which, as a young mother, she shared with Sarah ('methinks you should take more care of your self then you do till you are quick for you go up & down as much as if you weare not with Child', the princess wrote to her that summer)[84] led to her increasing dependence upon 'my deare Lady Churchill'. Sincerity and an unwillingness to flatter anybody, particu-larly princes who were so subject to flattery, were the virtues upon which Sarah most prided herself, and during these years, the princess accepted Sarah's self-evaluation without question. 'You refer me to ye Queen & Mrs. Berkley [her daughters' governess]', the princess wrote to Sarah,

> for an account of my youngest girle but I desire another time you
> would tell me what you think your self for I depend more upon your
> Sincerity then I can ever do upon what they or any body can say &
> shall be better satisfied with ye least account you can give me then if
> ye others writt whole volumes.[85]

This dependence upon Lady Churchill, largely based on the fact that Sarah was highly experienced in maternal matters, was to be increased by the first period of prolonged tragedy which struck the princess in the opening months of 1687. On 21 January the princess suffered her first miscarriage,[86] which was generally attributed to 'a jolt in her coach',[87] but which the princess herself blamed on a new French dance, 'the Riggadoon . . . for there is a great deal of jumping in it'.[88] She had hardly begun to recover from the miscarriage when her entire family – Prince George and her two daughters – succumbed to an epidemic of smallpox which swept Whitehall, the disease from which the princess herself had suffered ten years before. The younger daughter, Lady Anne, died on 2 February; after an apparent recovery of strength, the elder daughter, Lady Mary, died on 8 February.[89] 'Both the children were opened; the eldest was all consumed, but the youngest very sound and likely to live.'[90] Throughout this domestic tragedy, the princess exhausted herself in nursing her daughters and her husband. By 15 February, Prince George had sufficiently recovered for the bereaved couple to retire from court to Richmond to mourn their two children. 'The good Princess has taken her chastisement very heavily', wrote Lady Russell:

> the first relief of that sorrow proceeded from the threatening of a greater, the Prince being ill. I never heard any relation more moving than that of seeing them together. Sometimes they wept, sometimes they mourned; in a word, then sat silent, hand in hand; he sick in bed, and she the carefullest nurse to him that can be imagined.[91]

The prince, who had not enjoyed good health since 1685, found that his convalescence was prolonged and his difficulty with breathing was to become chronic: observers spoke of the 'unwholesomeness of his looks', and among the Catholic faction the princess's future remarriage to a Roman Catholic prince was already being considered.[92] No prospect could have been more disagreeable personally and politically to the princess and the suggestion was undoubtedly responsible for the resurrection of an idea which had been broached in the autumn of 1686 and then, because of her pregnancy, dropped: a trip for Prince George of Denmark and a simultaneous visit by the princess to her sister at The Hague.[93] The sequence of events, as related by the princess to her sister and by the king to Barillon, agrees on every point: the night Princess Anne returned from Richmond to court in early March, she asked the king for permission for Prince George to go to Denmark while she visited the Princess of Orange, 'which he granted immediately without any difficulty, but in a few days after he told me I must not go'.[94] The king failed to foresee the consequence of the trip, which the queen, Sunderland, and the Catholic faction were quick to point out: both heirs to the throne would be out of England and such a trip could only serve to unify Mary and Anne and reaffirm their attachment to Protestantism. The princess was outraged by her father's refusal and continued to insist but he stubbornly refused to reconsider her request.[95] The princess's *amour propre* was wounded to the quick by her father's stand: not only did it curtail the privileges attached to her position but it also seemed to be an infringement of the basic liberties of Englishmen, an infringement motivated by Catholic politicians. 'Things are come to that pass now', she warned the Princess of Orange, 'that, if they go on much longer, I believe in a little while no Protestant will be able to live here.'[96] The king's refusal to permit her trip to The Hague resulted in the princess's silent but complete estrangement from her father. After returning to court for Easter (27 March), the prince and princess once again retired to Richmond, claiming that the air there was better for Prince George's health.[97] Thereafter and until the end of James II's reign, they avoided residence at court as much as possible.

There were three important consequences produced by the princess's estrangement from the court. First, the denial of her request for permission to travel to The Hague served to crystallize her hatred for her stepmother, a feeling which had been growing since 1685 when the princess had attributed to Queen Mary's influence her father's slowness in adjusting her financial settlement. In July 1685 the princess had commented sarcastically to Lady Churchill that

> ye Queen sent me by Sr. Ch: Scarbrough [the royal physician] a watch
> with her Picture on it sett with diamonds, for wch present I must
> return her most thankfull acknowledgments but among friends I think
> one may say without being vaine that ye Godess might have showered
> down her fayvours on her poor Vassalls with more liberality.[98]

By early 1686, it was widely known that the princess hated the queen and denigrated her when talking with her own confidantes.[99] Indeed, the queen's court was sparsely attended because of her pride and hauteur,[100] but her Catholic evangelism was the major grudge held against her by society. According to Barillon, the queen had even spoken to Princess Anne of the possibility of conversion, which had only served to anger the princess.[101] The queen, Princess Anne reported to her sister in May 1687,

> is the most hated in the world of [by] all sorts of people; for every-
> body believes that she pressed the King to be more violent than he
> would be of himself; which is not unlikely, for she is a very great
> bigot in her way, and one may see by her that she hates all
> Protestants. . . . She pretends to have a great deal of kindness to me,
> but I doubt it is not real, for I never see proofs of it, but rather the
> contrary.[102]

Second, while her stepmother was emerging as a leader of the Catholic faction and attendance at her court was declining, the princess was becoming the rallying point for Protestant courtiers, particularly after the king issued his first Declaration of Indulgence in April 1687, which suspended all penal laws against Roman Catholics and Protestant Dissenters and extended religious toleration to all Christians despite statute laws to the contrary. Well aware that she was being watched closely by both Protestants and Catholics, the princess attended various London churches to hear the most popular Anglican preachers, often incognito which fooled no one but which could be used to justify her movements to the king.[103] Her presence, along with 'an innumerable crowde of people, & at least 30 of the greatest nobility', was carefully noted when strongly anti-Roman Catholic sermons were preached in the Chapel Royal at Whitehall.[104] She even attended the first sermon preached by Dr John Sharp (who was to become her principal religious advisor in later years) following his restoration to the pulpit[105] after his suspension at the hands of James II's illegal Ecclesiastical Commission for his anti-Catholic sermons. As Barillon noted of the princess in May 1687, 'She affects on every occasion to demonstrate her firmness for the Protestant religion.'[106]

Third, and most importantly, the princess began a correspondence with her sister and brother-in-law which she herself termed treasonable. From late February to the end of May 1687, William III's special envoy to London, Everaard van Weede, Heer Van Dijkveld,[107] was busily surveying English political opinion, both at court and in the country. Dijkveld's confidential reports to the Prince of Orange have never been discovered; we know only that Princess Anne, within two weeks of Dijkveld's arrival in London, authorized Lord Churchill to speak with Dijkveld on her behalf. The tenor of her correspondence with her sister also underwent a change, now revolving largely on Princess Anne's denunciations of the king, the queen, Sunderland ('working with all his might to bring in popery'), and Lady Sunderland ('a flattering, dissembling, false woman'). The princess asked Princess Mary to show her letters only to the Prince of Orange, 'for it is all treason that I have spoke'.[108] On 17 May, Churchill wrote directly to William III, assuring the prince that he remained firm to his religion and making the Princess of Denmark's position explicit:

> The Princess of Denmark having ordered me to discourse with
> Monsieur Dyckvelt, and to let him know her resolutions, so that he
> might let your Highness and the Princess her sister, know, that she
> was resolved, by the assistance of God, to suffer all extremities, even
> to death itself, rather than be brought to change her religion.[109]

The correspondence between Princess Anne and Princess Mary was no longer trusted to the ordinary posts, which were susceptible to delay and to royal censorship: instead, trusted messengers carried letters between the Cockpit and The Hague.[110] When Dijkveld returned to the Dutch republic in June 1687, he carried a cypher of cant names which the two sisters could use to disguise their messages.[111]

The only major difficulty which arose between the two sisters during this period was Princess Mary's distrust of the inordinate influence Lord and Lady Churchill were believed to possess over the Princess of Denmark. On the surface, Princess Mary was cordiality personified, maintaining an irregular correspondence with Lady Churchill in which she stressed the mutuality of their interests: 'I write thus freely to you not as a Stranger,' the Princess of Orange told Sarah in May 1686,

> I cannot think you such nor you look upon me so unlesse you have forgot me, but absence had no such effects upoń me, you will find me much by my own inclination & extreamly upon My Sisters account (for I must esteem those she loves) to be always Your affectionate kind friend, Marie.[112]

Princess Mary's side of the correspondence between the two sisters is not extant, and it is impossible to know exactly what led her (and her husband) to suspect that the Churchills would prove to be opportunists who could not resist conversion to Catholicism if it could advance their material interests. However by the beginning of 1687, Princess Anne felt it necessary to come to their defence, telling her sister that 'nobody in the world has better notions of religion than she [Sarah] does'; as for Lord Churchill, the princess was very positive that 'he will always obey the King in all things that are consistent with religion, yet rather than change that, I dare say, he will lose all his places and all that he has'.[113] Political necessity dictated that William and Mary keep their suspicions of the Churchills quiet, particularly after Dijkveld's mission had established a united front between the Cockpit and The Hague, but the suspicions remained and one day would provoke unforeseen consequences.

James II, well aware of his younger daughter's increased political influence, was also suspicious of the Churchills, believing that the Prince of Orange had bribed Lady Churchill, for whom he believed the princess had 'une passion démésurée', to request permission to visit The Hague.[114] James knew, in general terms, of the increased intimacy between his two daughters, which he found disturbing because it was based on their mutual opposition to his policies,[115] while Louis XIV's special envoy, Bonrepaux, suspected that the Princess of Denmark's principal advisors were working for the Prince of Orange. Churchill, he reported to Versailles in the summer of 1687, 'exerts himself more than anyone for the Prince of Orange. Lord Godolphin, who is in all the secret councils, opposes nothing, but plays the good Protestant and always keeps a back door open for access to the Prince of Orange.'[116] Beyond his general suspicions, however, James had no proof against those who surrounded Princess Anne; he realized full well that they bolstered her Protestant prejudices, but he hesitated to dismiss them.[117]

In April 1687, Prince George procured a formal request from his brother, Christian V of Denmark, that James II allow the prince and princess to visit Copenhagen, but by the time von Plessen arrived in London with the King of Denmark's letter, it was apparent that the princess was again pregnant, her fifth pregnancy in less than four years of marriage.[118] The princess's condition naturally made such a trip inadvisable for her and, on 17 June, the prince departed without her for his first and last visit to his native land after 1683, accompanied by Lords Cornbury and Scarsdale.[119] The princess used her pregnancy as an excuse to isolate herself from the court; she made it known that she intended to reside at Richmond during the prince's absence from England and to give birth at Hampton Court, where her future children could be reared safely away from the coal-polluted air of London which she believed had severely affected the health of her two daughters.[120] Pregnancy, however, could not serve the princess as an excuse to disregard completely her royal duties. During the prince's absence she was placed in a humiliating situation in which she was forced to choose either to break completely and publicly with her father or to lend an indirect endorsement to his policies. This came about when the papal envoy to England, Count Ferdinand d'Adda, who had been in the country informally since January 1686, assumed his formal diplomatic character as a papal nuncio. Protocol dictated that new diplomats should be formally introduced to the king, the queen, and other members of the royal family. Elizabethan statutes, however, made it high treason to recognize or hold any correspondence with representatives of the 'Bishop of Rome'. The Duke of Somerset, who as lord chamberlain was responsible for all ceremonial receptions, refused to introduce d'Adda and was dismissed from his post. Characteristically, after raising as many difficulties as possible, the princess chose the path of caution after delaying the introduction several times. On 10 July the princess received the nuncio as a mark of respect and submission to the king, giving rise to new hopes by the Catholic faction that her conversion might yet be procured.[121] It was also suggested that if the princess produced a son, the succession might be altered to exclude the barren Princess of Orange.[122]

Prince George returned to England on 15 August and, after a token appearance at the court at Windsor, the prince and princess took up residence at Hampton Court on the pretext that the air at Windsor was too cold and piercing for the prince's weak lungs (a strange excuse for a Dane, and one which – after the Revolution – did not prevent Windsor from becoming the favourite residence of the prince and princess). In fact, the princess wished to avoid any prolonged interviews with her father, wherein he might press conversion upon her. Again, the court blamed the advice of Lady Churchill for the princess's absence.[123] When the king and queen returned to London in late September from the progress which they had made through the West Country, the king insisted that his daughter resume her residence at the Cockpit, which she did on 12 October.[124] Ten days later she suffered a miscarriage, producing a stillborn son 'born two months before the time as it was supposed lay dead a full month within her'.[125]

At the very moment the princess suffered this fresh wound to her personal pride and her dynastic ambitions, rumours swept the court that the queen was once again pregnant. Protestants were incredulous: the queen had last produced a child in 1682, a daughter who survived only two months,[126] and in November 1683 she had suffered a miscarriage.[127] From 1683 onwards, the queen had suffered from poor health, leading Barillon to the conclusion that her life would not be of long duration.[128] The Catholic faction, which in the summer of 1687 had despaired of the birth of a Catholic heir,[129] was overjoyed: the miracle of the queen's conception (for such they believed it to be) could only culminate in the birth of a son who would displace the Princesses of Orange and Denmark in the succession and who would naturally be reared as a Roman Catholic. 'At London, this rumour of pregnancy is ridiculed', Barillon reported to Louis XIV on 2 November, 'while at Court, a Prince of Wales is spoken of as though he were ready to come into the world.'[130] By late November the queen was positive that she was pregnant.

Her doctors dated the conception from her return from Bath to Windsor on 6 October, although the queen (correctly) was inclined to date it from early September, when she and the king had spent a few days together at Bath.[131] She accepted, however, the prevailing medical opinion that the child would be delivered in mid-July 1688.[132]

The effect of her stepmother's pregnancy on Princess Anne was devastating. Within ten months, the princess had lost her own two daughters and had suffered two miscarriages, only to be confronted with the possibility that her stepmother might produce a son who would supersede the princess and her sister in the succession. Feminine jealousy combined with religious prejudice formed within Princess Anne an anger which could not be concealed; on 23 December the Tuscan envoy in London reported to his master:

> No words can express the rage of the Princess of Denmark at the Queen's condition, she can dissimulate it to no one; and seeing that the Catholic religion has a prospect of advancement, she affects more than ever, both in public and in private to show herself hostile to it, and [to be] the most zealous of Protestants, with whom she is gaining the greatest power and credit at this conjuncture.[133]

Today, no one doubts that Mary's pregnancy and the birth of James Francis Edward Stuart were genuine. If anything, there was a Protestant plot to discredit the birth, rather than a Catholic plot to foist a suppositious child upon the nation. It is clear that Princess Anne was the major perpetrator, and perhaps the originator, of the calumny that her stepmother's pregnancy was false. Two contradictory accounts of the princess's behaviour during the queen's pregnancy survive. The first, recorded in the princess's own letters to her sister and, in the year of her accession to the throne, repeated to William Lloyd, Bishop of Worcester, and finally published in Bishop Burnet's *History of His Own Time* (on the authority of Prince George), claims that the queen refused to let Princess Anne touch her or to see her undressed. As Lloyd recorded it, the princess assured him that during previous pregnancies, the queen 'would put ye Princesses hand upon her belly, and ask her if she felt how her brother kicks her; but She was never admitted to this office and freedom at ye time of this breeding'.[134] However, later in 1688, under the cross-questioning of her uncle, the Earl of Clarendon, the princess admitted that Queen Mary had never permitted her such liberties even during her previous confinements.[135] In direct contradiction to the princess's account, James II's *Memoirs*[136] claim that the princess had felt the baby stir in his mother's womb; twenty-five years later, Pietro Mellarede, the Savoyard ambassador in London, accepted this story as substantially true.[137] The probability of this account is enhanced by the fact that when James II summoned all witnesses to a public meeting in October 1688 to swear depositions concerning the pregnancy and birth, Princess Anne declined to attend: her own pregnancy, which she alleged as an excuse, did not prevent her famous escape from Whitehall and her hazardous journey to Nottingham in the following month. James II's *Memoirs* claim that the princess avoided this meeting because she would have been called upon to swear that she had felt the queen's child move in the womb, a fact which she could not publicly disown before so many ladies who had seen her place her hand upon her step-mother's abdomen.[138]

The princess expressed her opposition to her father's policy by failing to dismiss from her household a person who had publicly fallen under the royal displeasure. In November 1687 the king issued orders to the lords lieutenant to canvass their jurisdiction to elicit public sentiment among the electors on three questions: (1) would they support the repeal of the Test and Penal Acts, (2) would they vote for candidates support-ing such repeal, and (3) would they live in peace with their neighbours regardless of religion? Seventeen lords lieutenant refused to engage in such unprecedented canvassing; among them was the Earl of Scarsdale, the head of Prince George's household. On 30 November 1687 the king dismissed Scarsdale from his lieutenancy of Derbyshire and deprived him of his regiment.[139] The prince and princess sent Lord Churchill to the king to ask what they should do relative to Scarsdale's position in their household. The king declined to issue positive orders to his children, assuming that they would dismiss Scarsdale of their own accord. The upshot was that the prince and princess did nothing, thereby indirectly endorsing Scarsdale's position on the three questions. Finally, the king issued clear and positive orders to the princess that Scarsdale should be dismissed and replaced by Theophilus Hastings, Earl of Huntingdon, a thoroughgoing Jacobite who was to be one of the six noblemen specifically excluded from the Act of Indemnity passed after the Revolution.[140] Conscious of her position as mistress of a house-hold and aware of her responsibilities to her servants, the princess was naturally infuriated by the king's intervention in her own 'family' and the Scarsdale affair contributed to the growing gulf between the princess and her father. Although the princess had to obey the king's positive commands, the Scarsdale affair strengthened her determination to protect her servants so far as possible in the future.

During the spring of 1688, the princess – who believed herself to be pregnant for the sixth time – was obsessed by the prospect that she and her sister might be deprived of their rights of inheritance. Her corres-pondence with the Princess of Orange repeatedly suggested that the Roman Catholics were fully capable of anything: 'I can't help thinking Mansell's [the king's] wife's great belly is a little suspicious', she wrote to the Princess of Orange on 14 March,

> It is true indeed she is very big, but she looks better than ever she did, which is not usual. Her being so positive it will be a son, and the principles of that religion being such that they will stick at nothing, be it never so wicked, if it will promote their interest, give some cause to fear there may be foul play intended.[141]

54

On 20 March she informed her sister in detail of the queen's alleged refusal to let the princess see her undressed or to give any definite proofs of pregnancy. The princess concluded that 'these things give me so much just cause for suspicion that I believe when she is brought to bed, nobody will be convinced it is her child, except it prove a daughter. For my part, I declare I shall not, except I see the child and she parted.'[142] In reality, however, the princess had no intention whatsoever of attending the queen's lying-in. Should the child prove to be a boy, the princess (who by right of precedence would be nearest to the queen's bed) would be a witness to a genuine birth; should the child prove to be a girl, however, the constitutional position of hereditary right would not change and it would be of no use for the princess to be present.

On 10 April, into the third month of her assumed 'pregnancy' the princess became ill; when her uncle Clarendon inquired after her health, 'She was very cheerful, and said she was pretty well; but the women were apprehensive she would miscarry'.[143] Her illness increased in the following days and on the nights of 14 and 15 April 'she seemed in danger of death'.[144] Finally, at 4 a.m. on 16 April, she suffered a miscarriage. When Clarendon visited her later that day, he recorded that 'The Princess told me, she was as well as could be expected: the rumour among the women was, that she had only had a false conception'.[145] This is the first contemporary suggestion that Princess Anne suffered from pseudocyesis or, in layman's terms, false or hysterical pregnancies in which all the physical symptoms of pregnancy appear in the expectant mother without conception having taken place. It was widely reported that the princess did, indeed, suffer a miscarriage on 16 April, and the evidence of pseudocyesis in this instance is too weak to permit a categorical statement that her pregnancy was false. Indirect evidence, however, suggests that such a conclusion is possible: the register of Westminster Abbey does not list a burial for this child, yet in 1690 the register explicitly states that a child buried in that year was the fourth daughter and the sixth child of the Prince and Princess of Denmark, a calculation which would include their first stillborn daughter in 1684, the two daughters who died in February 1687, the miscarried son in October 1687, and the Duke of Gloucester (born in July 1689), but not the children miscarried in January 1687 and April 1688. Certainly, the political situation in which the princess found herself in the spring of 1688, and her obsessive concern with the question of the succession, makes it highly possible that her pregnancy was indeed false.

Although Hippocrates reported twelve cases of hysterical pregnancy during his own medical career, pseudocyesis is a phenomenon which has received little modern study, and today it is a condition which may escape the initial notice of experienced physicians. In general, it is a psychosomatic condition produced by varying degrees of neurosis, either among women who are desperately anxious to produce children (as was the case with Princess Anne and the majority of women who undergo false pregnancies) or among women who have exaggerated and morbid fears of childbirth. It 'may occur in young and newly married women as well as in those approaching the menopause, but it is frequently found in women who have borne children and are thoroughly familiar with the symptoms of pregnancy'. At the end of the condition, patients manifest neurotic reactive symptoms which are largely depressive in character.[146]

For the first time following labour, the princess had difficulty in recovering physically; on 25 April her uncle Clarendon recorded that she was 'extremely ill . . . a fit of the colic'.[147] There can be no doubt that the princess deliberately used her own physical condition as an excuse to leave London as quickly as possible.[148] At the end of April, a conference of the princess's doctors was called at which her favourite physician, Sir John Lower, 'was urgent' that the princess should partake of the spa waters at Bath; her other physician (and the queen's), Sir Charles Scarborough, opposed the trip 'till the Princess had first prepared her selfe for some time by a course of physick'. The conference ended without reaching a decision. According to the royal apothecary, James St Amand, 'within a few days after, the Princesse declared to Mr. St. Amand that she was not satisfied with the late conference of the Physicians, & would have another', at which Lower was present with two new consultants, while Sir Charles Scarborough was excluded. Not surprisingly, the three physicians unanimously declared that the princess should visit Bath, an opinion which the princess clearly desired.[149] Burnet later claimed that King James urged the princess to go to Bath to regain her health and that, against her own will and the advice of doctors and friends, she agreed to go.[150] The princess herself contradicted this account when she assured Bishop Lloyd of Worcester that she was not sent to Bath, but went voluntarily on the advice of her doctors.[151] According to both Mellarede and James II's *Memoirs*, the princess's physicians represented to the king that a trip to Bath was indispensable to the re-establishment of her health and that the king, always an indulgent father, agreed that she and Prince George could leave London before the queen had been brought to bed.[152] James, of course, had everything to gain by her presence at the birth, Anne nothing whatsoever. Significantly, the princess forsook her favourite spa, Tunbridge Wells, which was much closer to London, for Bath. In commenting on Queen Mary's pregnancy to the Princess of Orange,

Princess Anne had reported that 'it is very odd that the Bath, that all the best doctors thought would do her a great deal of harm, should have had so very good effect so soon'.[153]

The prince and princess left London for Bath on or shortly after 24 May – well into the seventh month of the queen's pregnancy, according to the doctors' calculation.[154] Before their departure, the king had issued his second Declaration of Indulgence, essentially a renewal of the first dispensation but including a new, crucial clause ordering the Declaration to be read on two successive Sundays from every Anglican pulpit in the land. In effect, the king demanded that the Church of England propagandize the very instrument which destroyed Anglican supremacy in the state. On 18 May a crucial conference was held at Lambeth Palace, home of the Archbishop of Canterbury, in which seven leading bishops of the Church agreed to petition the king to remove the offensive clause on the grounds that the dispensing power was illegal and that to require Anglican priests to read the Declaration would, in effect, make them accessories to a crime. The petition, which the seven bishops personally presented to the king the same evening, challenged the very basis of James's absolutism, the *Gordon v. Holles* decision. After some hesitation, during which the Declaration was read in only a handful of churches, the king retaliated by charging the bishops with seditious libel. To stress the head-on conflict between the Church and the State, and the Church's defence of the rule of law, the bishops refused to post bail. They were accordingly sent to the Tower on 8 June, and were popularly regarded as new martyrs for the Church of England.

On Sunday, 10 June, the queen gave birth to a son who appeared to be healthy and who was named James Francis Edward. His half-sister, the Princess of Denmark, was still at Bath. Most Protestants, if they possibly could, avoided the royal bedchamber at St James's Palace; according to Churchill's first biographer, 'The Lord Churchill, among the rest, was summoned to attend, and sent for in a particular Manner . . . but he had received some Intimations before, and was purposely out of the Way.'[155] Protestant ladies at court piously attended divine service on Sunday morning rather than witness an event which would determine the political fate of three kingdoms. Those who could not avoid being present, like Godolphin, in attendance as vice-chamberlain to the queen, took care to stand where they could see nothing.[156] Consequently, the great majority of direct eyewitnesses to the birth were Roman Catholics who – if there was a Catholic plot to foist a supposititious child on the nation – obviously could not be trusted. Before the celebratory fires in the streets of London were cold, the Protestant population was convinced that a newborn child had been smuggled into the queen's bedchamber in a warming pan for hot coals.

The king immediately dispatched Colonel Theophilus Oglethorpe to Bath with news of the birth of his son, telling Oglethorpe 'not only to remit his letter but to give testimony *de visu*'.[157] On 15 June the prince and princess returned to London.[158] The princess was obviously determined to disbelieve the validity of the birth: three months earlier she had declared that, unless she was an eyewitness, she would refuse to believe that the new Prince of Wales was the queen's child.[159] Three days after her return to London, on 18 June, she wrote to her sister: '''tis possible it may be her child; but where one believes it, a thousand do not. For my part, except they do give very plain demonstrations, *which is almost impossible now*, I shall ever be of the number of unbelievers.'[160] The Princess of Orange, less determined than her younger sister to believe that their father and stepmother would lend themselves to a scheme to deprive the two princesses of their rights of succession, sent to Princess Anne a long list of detailed questions concerning the pregnancy and birth, a list to which Princess Anne replied in terms which cast further doubt on the validity of the birth.[161] There can be little doubt of Anne's attitude towards the child and its mother: she constantly referred to the Prince of Wales as 'it'[162] and, after the first complimentary visit, she avoided Mary of Modena.[163] The princess was obstinately determined to regard her half-brother as an imposter and avoided making any careful or thorough investigation into the matter. Among those present at the birth were two of her future ministers, Godolphin and Mulgrave.[164] One eyewitness, Lady Isabella Wentworth, was a Protestant, the mother of one of the future queen's ministers (Thomas, Earl of Strafford) and the aunt of Lady Frances Bathurst. In 1702, Lady Wentworth claimed, 'I am Confident . . . her Majesty . . . cannot disbelieve the Prince's Birth', although she did not cite the reasons for her confidence.[165] Another eyewitness (perhaps discredited by her Roman Catholicism) was Sarah's sister, Frances, Countess of Tyrconnel. Despite the easy availability of reliable witnesses to the fact, the princess maintained a public pretence of doubt throughout her life about the validity of the birth, even with her closest friends and relatives. As late as November 1712, when one of her doctors presented her with reasons for believing the 'warming pan' myth, she received this information 'with chearfullness, and by asking me several Questions about the thing'.[166] Her own personal reputation was too heavily staked on the story: if it was discarded, she would appear either as a fool or (much closer to the truth) as a liar.

Although the princess proclaimed her intention of 'going speedily to

Tunbridge' immediately after her return to London from Bath,[167] she and the prince remained in London for a month, even though, as she complained to her sister,

> it is very uneasy to me to be with people that every moment of one's life one must be dissembling with, and put on a face of joy when one's heart has more cause to ache: and the Papists are all so very insolent that it is insupportable living with them.[168]

They remained in the capital for the trial of the seven bishops, which began in Westminster Hall on 29 June. The Tories, deserted by the king and determined to defend the Church of England, joined with the Whigs in mustering the most outstanding legal talent available in defence of the bishops. On 30 June the jury returned a verdict of not guilty, which was greeted by demonstrations of jubilation throughout London, a marked contrast to the lack of popular enthusiasm which greeted the birth of the Prince of Wales. On the night of 30 June, the 'immortal seven' (the Earls of Danby, Devonshire, Shrewsbury, Bishop Compton, Henry Sidney, Lord Edward Russell, and General Henry Lumley) agreed to invite the Prince of Orange to intervene in English affairs with armed force, if necessary, to re-establish the rule of law under the guidance of a 'free Parliament'.

While the Cockpit circle was separate from the main body of con-spirators against James II, there were important connections between the two groups, and the princess and her advisors learned shortly after 30 June the general details of the invitation to her brother-in-law. Bishop Compton was, of course, the princess's former tutor and religious mentor; Lord Edward Russell had carried secret messages between the princess and her sister at The Hague;[169] as early as March 1688, Princess Anne was in contact with Henry Sidney, who was William's closest English friend and the organizer of the conspiracy;[170] later events made it clear that Danby and Devonshire played important roles in planning the princess's escape from London and in providing for her safety. Publicly, the princess continued to symbolize militant Protestantism. On 8 July, in the Chapel Royal at Whitehall, she and a large congregation heard a sermon preached on the text from Exodus 14: 13 – 'Stand still and behold the salvation of the Lord' – which the preacher 'applied so boldly to the conjuncture of the Church of England, as more could scarce be said to encourage disponders'.[171] Before she left London for Tunbridge Wells on 25 July the princess left orders for the extensive re-furbishment of the Chapel Royal at Whitehall.[172]

The 'Princess's plot' crystallized during the two months which she and Prince George spent at Tunbridge Wells before their return to

London in mid-September 1688. For reasons of their own, the Churchills in later years never publicly discussed their roles in the Revolution and, in her printed *Conduct*, Sarah pretended that her actions and those of the princess were 'a thing sudden and unconcerted'.[173] Unpublished evidence, however, makes it clear that the Churchills, and with them the princess, were resolved to join the Prince of Orange at least three months before he actually invaded England. In an early, unpublished draft of her memoirs, Sarah recalled that 'the attempt of succeeding in the Revolution was subject to such a Train of Hazzards and Accidents, that before the Duke [of Marlborough] entered into the design, he made settlements to secure his Family in case of Misfortunes'.[174] This settlement was made on 27 July 1688.[175] On 4 August, Churchill wrote to William III through Henry Sidney, promising to support the prince against the king:

> Mr. Sidney will lett you know how I intend to behave my selfe; I think
> itt is what I owe to God and my Country, my honor I take leave to
> put into your Royalle hinesses hands, in which I think itt safe, if you
> think ther is anny thing else that I aught to doe, you have but to
> comand me, and I shall pay an intier obedience to itt, being resolved
> to dye in that Relliggion that it has pleased God to give you both the
> will and power to protect.[176]

Conspirators obviously leave as little written evidence as possible, but the financial settlement which Churchill made, his letter to the Prince of Orange, and Burnet's memoirs leave no doubt that during the late summer of 1688 Churchill was co-ordinating the moves which his family and the prince and princess would make with the main body of conspirators against the king.[177] During her stay at Tunbridge, the princess was sought out by leading Protestant political and religious figures, including Sir John Trevor, the speaker in the last Parliament,[178] and Dr John Tillotson, the popular dean of St Paul's, who recorded that 'I left the good Princess very well, and I think much better than ever I saw her'.[179] During her absence from court, the princess left her gentleman usher, Henry Sandys, at Richmond to report to her on the health of the infant Prince of Wales.[180]

On 17 September the prince and princess returned to London and the princess paid a brief courtesy call on the queen, who complained to the Princess of Orange that 'I had been two months without seeing her'.[181] The following day the new Danish envoy in London, Frederick Gersdorff, warned Prince George that the great flotilla being assembled in Dutch ports was destined against England and that it would be necessary for the prince to take the field in support of his father-in-law;

the prince (who could hardly have been surprised at this information) agreed that he would accompany the king as an uncommissioned volunteer. He refused, however, to accept any formal command in the Army, flatly informing Gersdorff that disaffection in the ranks was so rampant that the king could not safely rely upon the Army.[182]

Because of Sarah's reticence on the subject of the Revolution, the most revealing contemporary portrait of the princess which we possess is the diary of her uncle, the Earl of Clarendon, who was in closer contact with his niece in the two months preceding the Prince of Orange's invasion than at any other time in her life. When he paid a courtesy call on the princess on 23 September, she repeatedly admonished him to visit her frequently, undoubtedly desiring to maintain every possible source of news. She was not, however, particularly candid, as her uncle discovered. 'She seems to have a mind to say something; and yet, is upon a reserve and, in effect, says nothing,' he concluded. As they discussed the public news reports of the assembly of the Dutch invasion force (an invasion in which James II still refused to believe), 'she said very drily I know nothing but what the Prince tells me he heard the King say'.[183]

As Clarendon's loyalist sympathies became more pronounced, the princess's caution and reserve increased proportionately. Yet she did make it clear that she was not only opposed to the prospect of any reconciliation between the king and his Tory subjects but that she would actively try to sabotage any attempts to reach such an accord. This intransigence was largely inspired by fears for her own personal safety. When indisputable evidence reached Whitehall on 27 September that the Dutch invasion force was destined against England and hysteria swept the court, it was widely rumoured that, while the king and Prince George opposed the Prince of Orange in the field, the queen, the Prince of Wales, and the Princess of Denmark would be sent to Portsmouth, where they could be evacuated to France in case of need.[184] The Danish envoy lent weight to this rumour, suggesting to the prince that alternative plans should be laid to send the prince and princess to Denmark, a course of action which the prince rejected out of hand.[185] When Clarendon met the princess on 27 September, he urged her to go to the king and advise him to consult with his old friends.

> She answered, she never spoke to the King on business. I said her
> father could not but take it well to see her Royal Higness so concerned
> for him; to which she replied, he had no reason to doubt her con-
> cern. . . . The more I pressed her, the more reserved she was; and
> said she must dress herself, it was almost prayer time.[186]

On subsequent occasions, when Clarendon gave her the same advice, the princess simply made no reply.[187] However, she was not hesitant to

61

offer advice which was harmful to her father's efforts. Through Clarendon, who enjoyed intimate connections with leading churchmen, she expressed the wish that the bishops would retire from London to their own dioceses, 'for, said she, it is plain they can do no good. The king will not hearken to them, and they will but expose themselves by being here.'[188]

Now convinced that William actually intended to invade England yet made desperate by the prospect, James reversed his entire policy. Catholics were dismissed from the lieutenancies and other offices and were replaced by Protestants (when they could be brought to accept the royal offers); the writs for a new Parliament – for which elections the king and Sunderland had planned so carefully – were withdrawn; and Sunderland (who had long since been converted to Catholicism) was dismissed from office. Instead of regaining public support for himself, however, James's new policy suggested only weakness and insincerity. Part of the king's campaign was to dispel the myth that the Prince of Wales had been smuggled into the queen's bedchamber: on 22 October a long list of witnesses swore depositions before the Privy Council attesting to the validity of the prince's birth. Prince George attended this meeting, but the princess excused herself on the grounds that she was pregnant, a rumour which the Cockpit circle had deliberately circulated in September as a useful cover story, but one which Prince George later admitted to Clarendon was false.[189] The 'pregnancy' allowed the princess to avoid a meeting where she might have been called upon to testify to her direct knowledge of the queen's pregnancy. The following morning, when Clarendon waited on her, the princess raised the matter and

> told me I had heard a great deal of fine discourse at council, and made herself very merry with that whole affair. She was dressing, and all her women about her, many of whom put in their jests. I was amazed at this behaviour.[190]

The princess may have felt that she had exceeded the bounds of propriety, for she thereafter avoided speaking privately with her uncle[191] until 31 October, when she attempted to justify her actions by pointing out that the queen's behaviour during her pregnancy was odd, in light of the common rumour that she was not pregnant. Clarendon asked her if she had ever spoken to the king concerning these stories, to which she said no. 'She replied, if she had said anything to the King he would have been angry; and then, God knows what might have happened.' When Clarendon begged her to 'do something that the world might see her Royal Highness was satisfied', the princess again made no reply.[192]

Word of the princess's attitude, and that of her household, had reached the king through other sources. On 1 November, ten days after the depositions had been taken, the entire Privy Council was ordered to wait on the princess to present the evidence to her. Her response was disingenuously misleading: 'My Lords, this was not necessary; for I have so much duty to the King, that his word must be more to me than these depositions.'[193] On 3 November the king lent the princess his own copy of William's Declaration,[194] in which the birth of the Prince of Wales was questioned and which referred to the investigation of a free Parliament (an investigation which was subsequently never undertaken), but the princess still declined to be drawn into any public support for her father.

On 5 November 1688 – the anniversary of the Gunpowder Plot and of his own birth – William III landed at Torbay in Dorsetshire with a force of almost 15,000 soldiers. Word of his arrival reached London on 7 November and, two days later, Clarendon made his penultimate plea to the princess to speak with the king. Once again, she refused, saying 'the King did not love she should meddle in any thing and that the Papists would let him do nothing'. She agreed with Clarendon that she owed a duty to her father, who had never troubled her on the question of religion, 'but she grew uneasy at the discourse' and brought the conversation to a close.[195]

Ironically, it was Clarendon's son and heir, Lord Cornbury, who was the first prominent nobleman to desert the king's service to join the Prince of Orange. Although Cornbury did not carry many troops with him, his position as the princess's first cousin and Prince George's master of the horse made his defection spectacular and cast suspicion on the loyalties of the Cockpit circle. The princess attempted to console her uncle with the thought that 'people were so apprehensive of Popery, that she believed many more of the army would do the same'.[196] She was in a position to know, having already secretly received a letter from William III sent through Lady Churchill.[197]

On 17 November, before the king and Prince George left London for Salisbury, where they expected to confront the Prince of Orange, the king executed a new will which left all of his considerable personal fortune to the queen and to his son, and excluded both his daughters by his first marriage.[198] On 18 November, while her father and husband were still *en route* to join the Army, the princess wrote to her brother-in-law informing him that 'you have my wishes for your good success in this so just an undertaking' and promising that Prince George would leave Salisbury to join the Dutch army 'as soon as his friends thought it proper'. Her own plans were still open: 'I am not yet certain if I shall

63

continue here, or remove into the City; that shall depend on the advice my friends will give me.'[199] The princess's decision was obviously dependent upon what happened when the two armies confronted each other.

On 19 November the king and Prince George reached Salisbury, while William's army was still based on Exeter. Despite James's numerical superiority, he had been gravely disturbed by Cornbury's desertion and by the possibility that others might also leave him. In a long conference on 23 November, which was interrupted by an unstaunchable royal nosebleed, the decision was taken to fall back on London. That evening, according to Gersdorff (who accompanied Prince George), the Duke of Grafton (Charles II's illegitimate son), Lord Churchill, and Colonel Berkeley dined with the king until midnight; the three men then had a long conference with Prince George before deserting to the Prince of Orange on the early morning of 24 November.[200] That morning, confronted by the desertion of his nephew and his protégés, the king seemed incapable of taking the decisive steps necessary to prevent further betrayals. Gersdorff urged the king to arrest Edward Griffith, Prince George's secretary and Sarah's brother-in-law, on the grounds that Griffith was as treacherous as Churchill, yet the king told Prince George that Griffith's arrest must be the prince's own decision. That evening, while the prince and the Duke of Ormonde were dining with the king, Griffith – obviously warned by his master – fled from the royal camp. Later that night, immediately after the prince and Ormonde had left the king, they also defected to the Orangist side. In his Memoirs, James made light of this betrayal, claiming that the loss of one good trooper would have been of more consequence than the desertion of his son-in-law.[201] This, however, was not his reaction on the morning of 25 November, when Gersdorff discovered the prince's defection while the king was at mass and burst into the service while James was kneeling at the altar: Gersdorff reported to Christian V, 'Your Majesty can not imagine the King of England's consternation at this news.'[202] The prince left his father-in-law a letter in which he justified his desertion by religious scruples and revealed how large a part the world-view of united Protestantism played in the councils of the Cockpit:

Whilst the restless spirits of the enemies of the reformed religion,
backed by the cruel zeal and prevailing power of France, justly alarm
and unite all the Protestant princes of Christendom and engage them
in so vast an expense for the support of it, can I act so degenerate and
mean a part as to deny my concurrence to such worthy endeavours
for disabusing of your Majesty by the reinforcement of those laws and

establishment of that government on which alone depends the well-being of your Majesty and of the Protestant religion in Europe?[203]

At long last, the king took decisive action. In the early evening of 25 November, orders were dispatched to London that Lady Churchill should be confined to Tyrconnel's lodgings in St James's Palace 'and none admitted to her except her servants' and that Mrs Berkeley should be confined to her father's house 'with the like strictness'.[204] Both the prince and Lord Churchill had expected that their wives would leave London before they had deserted the Army,[205] but due to some unexplained change in plans the princess and her ladies were still in the Cockpit, where the news of Prince George's desertion and of the king's imminent return to London caused consternation. Sarah later recalled: 'This put the Princess into a great fright. She sent for me, told me her distress, and declared, That rather than see her father, she would jump out a window.'[206] The news, which arrived in advance of the king's orders that she should be placed under house arrest, allowed Sarah time to visit Bishop Compton in Suffolk Street, where he was hiding, and to arrange the details of the princess's escape from Whitehall. That evening, the princess retired to bed as usual, leaving her bedchamber doors locked and orders not to be disturbed. She then dressed again and, accompanied by Lady Churchill and Mrs Berkeley, slipped down the back stairs which had recently been constructed for this very purpose. At one o'clock in the morning of 26 November, she met Bishop Compton and the Earl of Dorset, who were waiting with a carriage. They first stopped at Compton's home in the City and, in the early dawn, left London by way of Epping Forest and Loughton and then proceeded to Copt Hall, Dorset's home; the following day, they travelled through Hertfordshire, reaching Castle Ashby – home of Compton's nephew, the Earl of Northampton – on the evening of 28 November. The party had originally intended to proceed as far north as York, where Danby's *coup d'état* had gained control of the city for the Prince of Orange, but on reaching Castle Ashby they regarded themselves as far enough from London and from James II's forces to relax and dropped the disguise under which they had travelled.[207]

In London, the princess's escape had not been discovered by Mrs Beatrice Danvers, one of her bedchamber women, until eight o'clock in the morning, seven hours after the princess had fled from the Cockpit. The princess had left a letter for the queen, lamenting the separation of the king and the prince, and stating:

I see the general feeling of the nobility and gentry who avow to have
no other end than to prevail with the King to secure their religion,

which they saw so much in danger by the violent counsels of the priests, who to promote their own religion, did not care to what dangers they exposed the King.[208]

The king returned to London the same afternoon and ordered that all the Princess's servants be 'confined to their chambers till they have passed a very strict examination'.[209] The desertion of his younger daughter shook the king to the very core of his being. 'God help me!' he cried. 'Even my children have forsaken me.' One court observer believed that James was so afflicted by the discovery of Princess Anne's desertion that 'it disordered his understanding'.[210] In terms of political effect, Mulgrave later concluded that the desertion of the Army officers meant little compared to the flight of the princess and the relevation of the unity of purpose between the Protestant heirs to the throne.[211] While James publicly attempted to gain time by negotiating with William, his secret intention was to send the queen and the Prince of Wales to safety in France and to follow them himself as soon as possible.

After resting at Castle Ashby for a day, on 30 November the princess and her party proceeded to Leicester and on 1 December reached Nottingham, where

> the mayor and the aldermen treated both her Highness and his Lord-
> ship ye Bishop with two noble banquetts, and all demonstrations of
> respect and joy was shewd, with which her Highness was very well
> pleased and seemed wonderful pleasant and cheerful.[212]

Danby urged the princess to proceed to York or to Scarborough Castle for greater safety, but the princess, Compton, and the Earl of Devonshire, who had joined them in Nottingham and who, with his followers, had assumed responsibility for 'her whole charges till the nation is settled',[213] decided to remain in Nottingham to await instructions from the Prince of Orange.[214] The princess sent to London for her clothes[215] and the king allowed Prince George's servants, with his coach and horses, to rejoin their master.[216] On 3 December the princess notified her comptroller, Sir Benjamin Bathurst, of her whereabouts, adding that 'when I am settled, I will be sure to send for you & ye rest of my Servents'.[217]

Even in the comparative safety of Nottingham, however, there were potential dangers, particularly from Catholic nobles and gentry who were rumoured to be in arms for the king. Neighbouring Protestant nobles, including the Earls of Devonshire, Northampton, Scarsdale, and Chesterfield, rallied to the princess in Nottingham, bringing with them forces numbering between 5,000 and 6,000 horsemen and raising the county militia to protect her. The influx of such large forces into

Nottingham caused unforeseen problems and, with the princess's enthusiastic agreement, it was decided to establish a formal council to deal with them. When the princess informed the Earl of Chesterfield that he had been appointed to the council, he refused to serve, assuring the princess that he would defend her with his life but that as a privy councillor to King James he could not serve her in a similar position. 'I found that her Highness and most of the noblemen were highly displeased with my answer', Chesterfield recorded, 'which was called "a tacit" upbraiding of them with rebellion.' Nevertheless, on 9 December Chesterfield accompanied the princess and her advisors to Leicester, where Bishop Compton and Devonshire proposed that everyone accompanying the princess should sign the association formed to protect the Prince of Orange. Again, Chesterfield raised objections, pointing out that such associations were illegal unless sanctioned by Parliament. 'After my refusing it', Chesterfield continued, 'the Lord Scarsdale, the Lord Ferrars, the Lord Cullen, and above 100 gentlemen refused likewise to sign the paper, which made the Princess extreamly angry.'[218] Her anger proved to be obstinate and enduring, particularly against those from whom she had expected more. She later declared that the prince 'had thoughts of taking back Lord Scarsdale again [into his household], but that he [had] proved so pitiful a wretch, that they would have no more to do with him'.[219] Nevertheless, the princess was capable of maintaining a gracious veneer in public. When her entourage reached Warwick on 14 December they received news that the king had fled abroad, whereupon Chesterfield took his leave 'after my having received many thanks from her Highness'.[220]

On 15 December the princess reached Oxford, where she was to be reunited with her husband. A contemporary observer left a detailed description of her enthusiastic reception in the citadel of Stuart loyalism:

> The Princess of Denmark made a splendid entry into Oxford, Saturday last; Sir John Laneer, with his regiment, meeting her Royal Highness some miles out of town. The Earl of Northampton, with 500 horses, led the van. Her Royal Highness was preceded by the Bishop of London, at the head of a noble troop of gentlemen; his Lordship riding in a purple cloak, martial habit, pistols before him, and his sword drawn; and his cornet had the inscription in gold letters on his standard, *Nolumus Leges Angliae mutari*. The rear was brought up by some militia troops. The Mayor and Aldermen in their formalities met her at the North Gate; and the Vice Chancellor, attended by the heads of the University, in their scarlet gowns, made to her a speech in English; and the Prince received her Royal Highness at Christ Church quadrangle, with all possible demonstrations of love and affection.[221]

At Oxford, where she and the prince were entertained by the university at a cost of £1,000,[222] the princess heard that her father's flight to France had been interrupted on the Kentish coast by over-zealous fishermen and that the king had returned to London, only to be ordered by the Prince of Orange to retire to Rochester; on the morning of 18 December, James left Whitehall and that afternoon William took up residence at St James's. The following day, 19 December, the Prince and Princess of Denmark returned to London, and the Prince of Orange immediately called upon them at the Cockpit.[223] On the night of 22 December, James made a second, successful attempt to flee the country, news of which did not ruffle his younger daughter's cold-blooded equanimity. 'People who were with her', her uncle Clarendon noted, '. . . took notice, that when news came of the King's being gone, she seemed not at all moved, but called for cards, and was as merry as she used to be.'[224] To emphasize their political sympathies, the princess and her ladies dressed themselves in orange.[225]

Hitherto, thanks in equal measure to James's folly and obstinacy and to William's foresight, the Revolution had been carried through successfully. Inevitably, however, the victors immediately began to fall out among themselves. Hardly had James II fled than the old party distinctions between Whig and Tory began to re-emerge with a new ferocity which was to colour public life for the next quarter of a century. Furthermore, the latent tensions and hostility between the Prince of Orange and the Princess of Denmark, which had been submerged by the greater danger to their positions posed by a Roman Catholic heir, soon came to the surface. An *ad hoc* gathering of nobles in London invited the Prince of Orange to assume the civilian and military administration of the country until a Parliament could meet to determine the constitutional situation; on 25 December, William issued writs for elections to a Convention, scheduled for 22 January 1689. If, as the Whigs insisted and the Convention ultimately ruled, James II's flight constituted a *de facto* abdication, there were three possible solutions for determining the succession to the throne. First, the Prince of Wales could be recognized as the heir, with William or Mary as regent. In the event, his very existence was ignored by the Convention, for there was almost no desire to make a serious investigation into the circumstances surrounding his birth, and he was also in the custody of his parents in France. Second, the doctrine of hereditary divine right could be followed, as the Tories urged, with Mary alone being declared queen, and Anne and William in that order succeeding her; this solution was rejected by William, who could not allow his power in Great Britain to be dependent upon the longevity of another person. Finally, as the

Convention ultimately decided, William and Mary were declared joint monarchs, with the administration being vested in William during his lifetime; after any children of William and Mary jointly (an unlikely prospect), Princess Anne and her heirs were to precede those of William by a second wife.

Princess Anne was later to refer to this settlement as her 'abdication' and thought it, in the words of an early biographer, 'a little strange that less ceremony should be required in passing away an interest in three Kingdoms, than the conveyance of a cottage'.[226] Sarah shrewdly attributed William's disdain of his sister-in-law to 'the thought the King [William] had, that the Prince & Princesse had been of more use then ever they were like to be again'.[227] A private conversation which the Prince of Orange had with one of his closest advisors, Lord Halifax, before the Convention assembled deserves to be quoted from Halifax's abbreviated notes, for it fully reveals William's suspicions of the Churchills and his underlying resentment of the fact that Princess Anne possessed a better hereditary claim to the throne than he did.

[William] Said that Ld. Churchill could not governe him nor my lady, the Princesse his wife, as they did the Prince and Princesse of Demark.
   This shewd, 1. that Ld. Ch: was very assuming which hee did not like; 2. it shewd a jealous side of the Princesse, and that side of the house.
   Note, a great jealousie of being thought to bee governed. That apprehension will give uneasinesse to men in great places.
   . . . The foregoing discourse happened upon the occasion of its being said, that Ld. Churchill might perhaps prevayle with the Princesse of Demark to give her consent [i.e. that William might precede her in the succession]. That made the sharpnesse; it seemeth there was not complyance &c.[228]

In order to protect her own position, and that of her children (and she knew that she was once again pregnant), the princess made a tentative effort to construct a party which would support her pretensions to follow Mary directly in the succession. She was forced to rely for support largely on High Tories, such as Clarendon, Scarsdale, Ormonde, Digby, and the Bishops of Ely, Peterborough, Bristol, and Bath and Wells, who for the most part voted against the motion to declare that James II had abdicated and that the throne was vacant.[229] They openly declared that 'the Princess of Denmarke was very sensible what a mistake she had committed to leave her father to come into the Prince, who was now endeavouring to invade her right and to gett priority of succession before her'.[230] Four days before the Convention assembled, the princess assured Clarendon that

> she was sure she had given no occasion to have it said, that she had consented to anything, for nobody had ever spoken to her of such a thing . . . and she would never consent to any thing that should be of prejudice to her or her children,

stressing that she relied upon the 'honest party' (i.e. the Tories) to protect her against the designs of the 'Commonwealth party'.[231]

The Churchills, on the other hand, obviously urged a cautious role, realizing that a settlement favouring William was inevitable because, in Sarah's words, 'except for the Jacobites all the considerable men were for it'. Fearful that the princess's obstinacy would be attributed to her, 'while she was thought to be advis'd by me', Sarah chose to discuss the matter with two prominent Whigs, Lady Rachel Russell and Dr Tillotson, and even took Tillotson to the princess, 'and upon what he said, she took care to put an end to all the disturbance that her pretended friends had solicited her to give in that matter [i.e. William being named as king]'.[232] The princess's agreement to this proposal, however, was less genuine than Sarah cared to recall in retrospect. While the Churchills worked with William's supporters, the princess continued to encourage the Tories to support her pretensions until the cause was proved hopeless. In order to avoid public commitment on the crucial question of whether James II had abdicated, Churchill retired to St Albans late in January, avoiding attendance in the House of Lords.[233] On 27 January, when Clarendon talked with the Prince and Princess of Denmark, Prince George told him that reports that the princess had agreed that William should be king for life were false 'and that neither he nor his wife would consent to alter the succession'.[234] Within the next ten days, however, the princess was forced into an accommodation with the Prince of Orange, and Lord Churchill and Gilbert Burnet, William's advisor, were announcing to all the world that the princess had agreed that William should be king for his lifetime. When Clarendon taxed the prince and princess with their double game on 5 February, they flatly denied any such agreement, although the princess asked Clarendon to burn her letters to him on the subject, which Clarendon refused to do,

> since I found she had said to Lord Churchill, that she had written to me not to say any thing in the House from her. I thought, it would be most necessary for me to keep the note, if there should be any occasion

to show it; since both she and the Prince had not only told me that they would not consent to any thing to the prejudice of their right, but she had said the same to the Duke of Ormonde, Lord Digby, the Bishops of Ely, Peterborough, Bristol, Bath & Wells, and others. They both seemed concerned that I pressed the matter so close; and that I reflected upon Lord Churchill.[235]

Despite the princess's denials to her uncle of any agreement, the following day, 6 February, during a conference between the two houses of Parliament, Churchill and Dorset carried a message from the princess to the Convention that she would give up her rights to William.[236]

Having once agreed to the settlement, the princess was anxious to make it work and to regain favour with William by using her influence with those who refused to recognize the new monarchs – particularly clergymen – even at the expense of making her uncle look ridiculous. A month later Danby visited the dissident William Sancroft, Archbishop of Canterbury, commissioned by the princess to tell him 'that she desired he should know she was extremely pleased' with the regulation of the succession. When Sancroft quoted Clarendon's statements to the contrary, Danby swore that the princess had disowned her uncle's words. 'This is an admirable part of the Princess', Clarendon noted sarcastically, 'and shows great favour to me, enough, I think, to make me look to myself.'[237] The princess also cut herself off from all non-jurors (those who refused to swear the oaths of allegiance to the new monarchs), including her uncle. She instructed Sir Benjamin Bathurst: 'I would have you tell him [Clarendon], if there weare no other reason for my not seeing him, I can't do it since he does not see the King.'[238]

On 12 February 1689 the Princess of Orange arrived in London, to be met at Whitehall 'by the Prince [of Orange] and divers of the Nobility, and was led to the new Apartment facing the Privy Garden by her Sister, the Princess of Denmark'.[239] On the following day, William and Mary accepted the crowns of England and Ireland (that of Scotland was to follow a month later) in a ceremony in the Banqueting Hall, where they were presented with the Declaration of Rights which the Convention had drawn up to remedy the abuses of James II's reign. Following this ceremony, which the Prince and Princess of Denmark attended, the royal family repaired to a service in the Chapel Royal, where they heard the Bishop of London preach a sermon on the text, 'Neither circumcision availeth any thing nor uncircumcision, but a new creature'.[240] At the great drawing-room held in celebration that evening,

the Princess Anne displayed her knowledge of the minute laws of royal etiquette. The attendants had placed her tabouret too near the royal

71

chairs, so that it was partly overshadowed by the canopy of state. The Princess Anne would not seat herself under it, until it was removed to a correct distance from the state-chair of the Queen her sister.[241]

A day would soon come when the princess would prove much less compliant to her sister's authority.

There were royal rewards to recompense the Prince and Princess of Denmark for their role in the Revolution and their agreement to the Convention settlement, although the new king and queen were well aware that the princess's consent was, at best, grudging. On 21 February the princess was granted the magnificent apartments in White-hall which had formerly belonged to Charles II's mistress, the Duchess of Portsmouth;[242] on 20 March, Prince George was created Duke of Cumberland which gave him a seat in the House of Lords, and on 3 April the king signed a bill passed by Parliament naturalizing the prince.[243] Churchill was made a privy councillor and a gentleman of the king's bedchamber and, in the coronation honours, was raised in the peerage to the earldom of Marlborough. Because of the princess's pregnancy, she and her husband attended the coronation on 11 April incognito, although they had places of honour at the banquet following the ceremony.

Her seventh pregnancy dominated the princess's thoughts and ruled her actions in the months following the Convention. True to her determination to avoid London, she retired to Hampton Court to await the birth of her child. As spring became summer and no child appeared, some observers began to cast doubts; John Evelyn noted in his diary that the princess was 'so monstroustly s[w]ollen, that its doubted, her being thought with child, may proove a Tympane* onely'.[244] However, on 24 July 1689 the official *London Gazette* announced:

> This morning, about four o'clock, Her Royal Highness the Princess
> Anne of Denmark was safely delivered of a son, at Hampton Court.
> Queen Mary was present the whole time, about three hours, and the
> King, with most of the persons of quality about the Court, came into
> Her Royal Highness's bedchamber before she was delivered.[245]

Not only did her son survive the immediate rigours of childbirth, but he seemed likely to live beyond infancy. To the princess, the birth of her son was the culmination – and, indeed, the justification – of her role in the Revolution. On 27 July the child was christened by Bishop Compton and given the names William Henry, in honour of the king, who stood as godfather along with the Earl of Dorset. The birth of a Protestant heir – to whom the king immediately gave the title of Duke of

*Tympanites – a distention of the abdomen caused by accumulation of air or gas.

Gloucester – immeasurably increased the political stature of the princess. 'Upon the birth of a Son', commented one of her early biographers, 'the interest of the Princess of Denmark seem'd to be very much advanc'd, and all the world began to make their Court that way, how much soever they had slighted her before.'[246]

3

'Never any body was so used'
William and Mary,
1689–94

Prior to the reign of James II, Stuart monarchs co-operated closely with their heirs apparent; from the Revolution, however, the heir to the throne was usually the nominal head of the opposition. The success of the Revolution had legitimized opposition to the personal wishes of the monarch, but not to the crown; as the distinction between monarch and crown remained uncertain, politicians who were not in royal favour sought the aid of the heir apparent to cloak their activities with some degree of respectability. Given this new structure of politics, it was not surprising that personal and political hostility quickly developed between the new king and queen on the one hand, and the Princess of Denmark on the other; what are remarkable are the princess's hesitation to go into opposition and, when she had taken that step, the moderation of her conduct. Apart from the fact that Princess Anne was steeped in the seventeenth-century tradition that opposition to the crown was factious, if not treasonable, the continued Jacobite threat to the whole structure of post-revolutionary England accounted in large part for the princess's moderation.

Courts in the seventeenth century did not lack grounds for grievances and feuds: lodgings, pensions, employments, and the rapacity of royal favourites were only the most obvious causes of dissension. In the new court of William and Mary, the supreme favourites were the former childhood playmates of the princess, the son and daughters of Sir Edward and Lady Frances Villiers. This prominence was due to the fact that one of the daughters, Elizabeth Villiers, who had accompanied the Princess of Orange to the Dutch republic on her marriage in 1677, had become the *maîtresse en titre* to William III, though exercising more social than sexual influence over the new king. When Willem Bentinck, William III's closest friend from childhood, came to England in 1685 to congratulate James II on his accession, the Princess of Denmark had upbraided Bentinck, telling him 'to check the insolence of Elizabeth

74

Villiers to the Princess of Orange'.[1] Princess Anne's choice of a messenger was singularly undiplomatic, as Bentinck was at the time married to Elizabeth Villiers' sister, Anne (who died in November 1688). The eldest sister was Princess Anne's close friend and the Duke of Gloucester's governess, Barbara, the wife of Colonel John Berkeley, who succeeded to the barony of Fitzharding in 1690; Lady Fitzharding's intimate ties with the new regime were to lead eventually to the deterioration of her friendship with the princess. Finally, Sir Edward Villiers, the only brother of these ladies, was ennobled in 1690, raised to the earldom of Jersey in 1697, and showered with honours throughout William's reign, honours which his very ordinary talents did not warrant; during the early days of the reign, he served as Queen Mary's master of the horse.

Inevitably, there was competition and hostility between the favourites of the princess, the Earl and Countess of Marlborough, and the Villierses, to whom Marlborough was distantly related; the rivalry was particularly intense between Marlborough and Bentinck, who was created Earl of Portland in 1689. While this hostility was undoubtedly a contributing factor to the breach within the royal family, there were more important causes. The king remained acutely conscious that Princess Anne possessed a better hereditary claim to the throne than he, and that his position was merely that of an elective monarch, scarcely better than the position of Kings of Poland. His jealousy of the princess's superior hereditary right was paralleled by the queen's inevitable jealousy of her sister's happy marriage and of her ability to produce children. Furthermore, there were profound personal differences between the two sisters, who had not seen each other for ten years; the queen was voluble and self-assured, while the princess was shy and taciturn. Sarah commented on

> the different characters and humours of the two sisters. It was indeed
> impossible that they should be very agreeable companions to each
> other because Queen Mary grew weary of anybody who would not
> talk a great deal; and the Princess was so silent that she rarely spoke
> more than was necessary to answer a question.[2]

This incompatibility of tempers soon led to conflicts exacerbated by the people surrounding the royal sisters.

In any court, the question of lodgings was by far the most likely to produce grievances, for not only did adequate lodgings mean physical and material comfort but their size and convenience also illustrated the owners' political and social standing. In the old Palace of Whitehall (which was almost entirely destroyed by fire later in William's reign), the most elegant apartments after those of the king and queen had belonged to the Duchess of Portsmouth. Immediately after the accession of William and Mary, the princess requested – and was given – the Portsmouth apartments.[3] Not content with this, however, the princess requested the adjoining apartments for her servants, in return for which she was willing to give up the Cockpit, which had been settled absolutely upon her and her heirs by Charles II. But the adjoining apartments in Whitehall which the princess desired had already been promised to the Earl of Devonshire, who – according to Sarah – tenaciously held on to them in the hope that the princess, disgusted by her failure to secure them, would give up Portsmouth's apartments as well, which Devonshire could then claim. In discussing this question with her sister, the queen told the princess that no decision could be reached until Devonshire had decided whether he would retain his Whitehall apartments or exchange them for a part of the Cockpit, 'to which [Princess Anne] reply'd then she would stay where she was, for she would not have my Lord Devonshire's leavings'. To prevent Devonshire from accomplishing his purpose, the princess retained Portsmouth's apartments 'for her children'.[4] At about the same time, the princess requested possession of the palace at Richmond, where she had spent so much of her childhood and where she wished to raise her children outside the polluted air of London. However, another Villiers sister, Catherine, Marquise de Puissiers, held her mother's reversionary rights to occupancy at Richmond, and refused to give them up; accordingly, the princess's request was refused.[5] This denial of Richmond was particularly distressing to the princess, because of the precarious health of the Duke of Gloucester. Described at his birth as a 'brave livly-like boy',[6] only a month later, in September 1689, Gloucester 'was seized with convulsion fits, every day they expect his death, no one of the doctors thinks he can live'.[7] Following Gloucester's surprising recovery from this illness, the princess rented 'my Lord Craven's house, at Kensington gravel-pits', well outside central London and near the newly purchased Kensington Palace, which William and Mary were extensively remodelling as their principal residence in the capital (William's chronic lung afflictions would not allow him to reside in the polluted air of Westminster). This rental of Craven House and, in 1690, that of Campden House west of Kensington Palace, which was to remain Gloucester's London home throughout his life, imposed a heavy financial burden on the princess who, as we have seen, was neither well endowed with money nor, in her youth, exceptionally careful in managing it. This added expense led to the princess's attempt to augment her income and into a direct confrontation with the king and queen.

The princess might well have expected to be awarded half of the estate which her father, as Duke of York, had owned as a private individual and which had not been merged with crown lands during his reign. Although the extent of this estate in the three kingdoms has not been ascertained, the income from it was huge; Burnet (who had now been appointed Bishop of Salisbury) estimated that James's private income was £120,000 per year, derived in part from 87,330 acres which James owned in Ireland alone.[8] By William's reign, James's Irish estate was producing an annual income of £26,000, with £3,000 per annum charged during the lives of two former mistresses, one of whom was Arabella Churchill (who had married Colonel Charles Godfrey).[9] During the first years of his reign, William simply assumed the management of James's estates, although he later gave the Irish property to Elizabeth Villiers; Princess Anne received nothing whatsoever from her father's private fortune, a source of continuing grievance against the king.

Prince George also had a financial grievance against William III. In July 1689, when the Maritime Powers (as Great Britain and the Dutch republic were now commonly called) were mediating the peace of Altona between Denmark and Sweden, William asked Prince George to surrender to the Duke of Holstein, as part of the peace, mortgages which he held on the Isle of Femern and the villages of Tremsbuttel and Steinhorst, 'his Majesty having engaged to procure payment of the moneys due or to pay it himself, and meantime to pay his Highness interest for it'.[10] The amount due was 428,000 Rix dollars.[11] By 1691, the prince had still received neither principal nor interest, because the Dutch States-General refused to pay above 120,000 Rix dollars to satisfy their half of the debt. The prince complained to Daniel Finch, the Earl of Nottingham and secretary of state with whom he had negotiated the arrangement, adding 'I will not tell you of your own honour being concerned in this business'. In the hope of payment, Prince George agreed to drop his demands to 340,000 Rix dollars.[12] The king, however, did not choose to recommend payment of the debt to Parliament until 1699; consequently, the prince and princess found themselves cut off from the Danish income which had been an essential element in their marriage settlement.

Confronted with increased expenditure and a diminished income, the princess and her friends concluded that her allowance should not only be increased but also guaranteed by a parliamentary grant. Such a grant to the heir to the throne, independent of the monarch's control, was unprecedented, but the princess's abdication of her hereditary right was also unprecedented and she felt that a parliamentary grant was only just compensation. The motion for the grant was first introduced in the

House of Commons in March 1689,[13] but was not debated until December. During the interim, the queen noticed that the princess 'avoided carefully . . . all occasions of being alone with me'.[14] The queen 'with a great deal of displeasure' taxed her sister with the question, 'What was the meaning of those proceedings?' The princess answered that 'She had heard her friends had a mind to make her some settlement'. According to Sarah, 'The Queen hastily replied with a very imperious air, "Pray, what friends have you but the King and Me?"' The princess was outraged: Sarah, who was not present, recorded that when the princess returned to the Cockpit that night, 'I never saw her express so much resentment as she did at this usage'.[15] Well might the princess be angry, for her sister had made it clear that she was to be completely dependent financially upon William and Mary. During the autumn of 1689, the king and queen on the one hand and the princess and the Marlboroughs on the other campaigned furiously to secure political support in the Commons for their respective positions and the hostility between the two courts became public knowledge.[16] From the king's point of view, a parliamentary grant would make the princess dangerously independent of royal control; as one of the leading Whigs, Thomas, Lord Wharton, warned William,

> The design was plain to give the Princess a great revenue, and make her independent upon Your Majesty, that she might be the head of a great party against you. This was laboured by the Tories and high church men, and carried for you by the honest old Whig interest.[17]

When the matter came before the House of Commons on 16 December, there were three parties concerned with the question: the princess's adherents proposed that she should be granted £70,000 annually ('Is it not seasonable that the Prince and Princess and the Duke of Gloucester should have meat, drink, and cloths?' asked one); a second party proposed that the sum should be only £50,000, while the king's adherents argued that the princess should rely exclusively upon the king's generosity. One member warned of the danger of giving a pension to a 'Princess who had a claim to the Crown independent of the King'.[18]

On 17 December the king sent two of his Whig ministers, Shrewsbury and Wharton, to the princess to attempt to dissuade her from pursuing her course; according to Queen Mary, Shrewsbury first spoke with his long-standing friend, Marlborough, 'who begg'd he would not own he found him, his wife would by no means hear of it, but was like a mad woman and said the Princess would retire if her friends would not assist her'.[19] When the princess met with Shrewsbury and Wharton, she refused to desist from her attempts, arguing that the matter was already under the scrutiny of the House of Commons. The next day, the House voted to give the princess £50,000 annually, a humiliating public defeat for the king and queen. Even this triumph did not satisfy the Cockpit circle. As Sarah recalled a few years later,

> *after* I had an account of what the Parliament had don in voting the fifty thousand pound a year, I sent to speak with my Lord Rochester (before I knew hee had soe much mind to make his court to the Queen) & I ask'd his opinion whether hee thought the Princesse should be satisfy'd with that settlement, or if it was reasonable for her to try to get more, upon which I remember hee answered me, that hee did not only think she should be satisfy'd with that but that she should have taken it any way the King & Queen pleased.[20]

Small wonder, then, that there were resentments on both sides, or that the princess's signal victory reinforced William and Mary's apprehensions about the potential strength of her position in the country. Queen Mary, in a private memorandum of 3 March 1690, recorded that the Revolution government was threatened by a republican party, a Jacobite party, 'and I have reason to fear that my sister is forming a third'.[21]

For the moment, these divisions within the royal family were overshadowed by the approaching victory of James II in Ireland, where he had arrived in March 1689; Parliament was hysterical at the thought that a Catholic-Jacobite victory there might allow Ireland to be used as a staging-point for a two-pronged invasion of England from Ireland and France, and pressed William III to go to Ireland in person rather than direct the allied armies in the Spanish Netherlands as he wished to do.* Accordingly, William left London in early June 1690 to retrieve Ireland from James II. He was accompanied by Prince George, who took part in the campaign at his own expense. Professor Baxter has suggested that William agreed to take Prince George in order to ensure Princess Anne's loyalty,[22] but there can be little doubt that the prince wished to join the campaign; Lord Cornbury, his master of the horse, and Lord Falkland, his groom of the stole, were dismissed for refusing to accompany the prince to Ireland and were replace by Lord Lexington and Lord Berkeley.[23] William's treatment of the prince during the campaign was offensive. He offered no thanks for Prince George's participation in the great Protestant victory at the battle of the Boyne on 1 July 1690,[24] nor did he make the least pretence of consulting the prince on military matters. In Sarah's words, 'the King never took more notice of him than if he had been a page of the back stairs' and even refused to allow the

---

* William III's successful invasion of England in 1688 proved to be the first of his campaigns during the Nine Years War (1688–97).

prince to ride in the royal coach.[25] During his absence, relations between the princess, who was again pregnant, and the queen continued to deteriorate. Queen Mary, noting 'the continuance of the coldness between my sister and I', recorded that

> This made us live very uneasily together, and was a reall trouble to me on all accounts, and [might] have proved dangerous to the publick affairs of the nation in making a party; and that all the High Church-men seemed to endeavour and she herself affected to find fault with every thing was done, especially to laugh at afternoon Sermons, and doing in little things contrary to what I did.[26]

The king and the prince returned to London on 10 September[27] and on 14 October, 'two months before her time', the princess gave birth to a daughter, named Mary after the queen. The child lived for two hours.[28]

As the prince had been subjected to such offensive treatment from the king in Ireland, it was quite impossible for him to serve again directly under William, but both he and his wife still wished to find a theatre in which he could acquire military *gloire*; accordingly, it was decided that the prince should follow in the footsteps of the Duke of York by serving as a volunteer in the Navy. When the prince told the king of his plans before William's departure to the Continent in January 1691, the king said nothing and merely embraced the prince, who took William's silence for consent. Accordingly, the prince made plans to sail on the *St Andrew*, commanded by Lord Berkeley. But the king had left Queen Mary instructions that the prince was not to be allowed to serve in any position; after fruitlessly soliciting Lady Marlborough to intervene with the princess, the queen was forced to send Nottingham to the prince in May 1691 with orders forbidding him to serve and to recall his baggage, which had already been dispatched to the ship.[29] This mortification was too profound for the princess to bear quietly; it was reported that 'the two sisters quarreled terribly'.[30] The queen, alarmed by the growing influence of Jacobites and republicans, took a dim view of her sister's political activities and believed that the entire scheme for Prince George to go to sea had been concocted to embarrass the government. 'This was very grievous to me to thinck my sister should be concerned in such things', the queen recorded privately,

> yet twas plain there was a design of growing popular by the Prince's resolution of going to sea without asking leave, only telling the King he intended it, which I had order to hinder, and when perswasions would not do, was obliged to send word by Lord Nottingham he should not, which was desired by them as much as avoided by me, that they might have a pretence to raile, and so in discontent go to Tunbridge.[31]

In a long, undated letter to Lady Marlborough, written during 1691, the princess took great pains to justify her conduct towards the queen and, in the process, proved Sarah's claim that she had urged the princess 'to take all the care in the world to live well with the Queen her sister which I thought was for the interest of both, & for the generall good':

> you must give me leave to endeavour to cleare my self of my behaviour to ye Queen, wch I see you think me to blame in & I find other people take a greate deale of pains to make you beleeve I am more so then I really am; first then ye Queen & I are of very diferent humours and if it were to save my soul I can not make any court to any body I have not a very great inclination for, as she is my sister, if ever it weare posible to lye in my power to serve her I should be ready to do it then any body, as for respect I have always behaved my self towards her with as much as tis posible, for my humour I know I am moros & Grave, therfore may not be so pleasing to her as other Company, but I have bin with her as often & as long at a time as I could.[32]

By the summer of 1691, the relationship between the queen and the princess was only *pro forma*, devoid of all ties of sisterly affection; furthermore, the princess's own emotional make-up was increasingly influenced by her repeated pregnancies and their inevitable tragic results. Alienated from her sister, 'moros & Grave', the princess felt growing devotion and gratitude to Lady Marlborough, whose wise advice and counsel had made her financially secure and whose company was always diverting and amusing. The genesis of the famous cant names of 'Morley' and 'Freeman', under which their correspondence was to be conducted after 1691, lay in the princess's desire to establish in private a relationship of equality between herself and the countess. Eight years earlier, in 1683, the princess had written Sarah to

> lett me beg you not to call me your highness at every word but be as free with me as one freind ought to be with another & you can never give me any greater proofe of your freindship then in telling me your mind freely in all things.[33]

Again, in 1685, the princess had written that

> if I could ever chide you it should be now for calling me at every three words your highnes, espesialy in your last letter I beleeve you repeat it above a hundred times, ceremony is a thing you know I hate with any body & espesialy with you that I have so much kindnes for.[34]

Although previous authorities have followed the intimation in Sarah's *Conduct* that the princess proposed, and she agreed, to use the respective cant names of Morley and Freeman sometime before the death of

Charles II, an examination of the princess's extant letters makes it clear that the names were not used until late in 1691, some months after June of that year when the princess proposed that 'my deare Lady Marlborough' should accept from her a pension of £1,000 per annum:

> I beg you would only look upon it as an ernest of my good will but never mention any thing of it to me for I shall be ashamed to have any notice taken of such a thing from one that deserves more then I shall be ever able to return.[35]

After consulting with Godolphin about the propriety of accepting the offer, Sarah agreed to take the £1,000, which even more closely bound her to the princess's interest.

During 1691 the political and personal intimacy between the Marlboroughs and Godolphin was rapidly increasing and Godolphin was an accepted member of the Cockpit circle, known as 'Mr Montgomery' in the correspondence between the princess and Lady Marlborough. Indeed, so pronounced was Godolphin's attendance at the princess's apartments that it was commented upon by a French agent: 'Mylord Godolphin pays his court much more assiduously to the Princess than to the Queen, whom he almost never visits except when he attends council; by contrast, he regularly visits and gambles with the Princess.'[36] Godolphin and Shrewsbury joined the prince and princess at Tunbridge, where the royal couple spent July and August of 1691.[37] While at Tunbridge, both the prince and the princess wrote letters to the king, pressing him, in Princess Anne's words, 'to remember your promise of a garter for my Lord Marleborough. You cannot sertinly bestowe it upon any one that has bin more servisable to you in the late revolution.'[38] There is no record that the king returned any answer to the requests of the prince and princess. Indeed, by this time, the king may well have suspected their own loyalty to him as well as Marlborough's.

By the autumn of 1691, the Jacobites posed a severe and immediate menace to the stability of the Williamite regime. Although James II had returned to France after his defeat at the battle of the Boyne and the Irish rebellion had been suppressed, approximately 50,000 inhabitants of the British isles had fled to the Continent and there formed a network of agents and supporters working in the interests of the exiled Jacobite court at St Germain-en-Laye. Historical hindsight allows us to see that the political influence of these exiles, most of whom were Roman Catholics, was minimal in Britain and that the Jacobite apparatus was thoroughly infiltrated by William's spies. Yet the possibility of a Jacobite restoration supported by French arms did not appear at all remote to contemporaries; indeed, Cromwell's republican regime had seemed more thoroughly entrenched in 1651 than did William's government in 1691. If James II's unpopularity was too massive to permit a second Stuart restoration, it seemed highly possible that the infant Prince of Wales might one day be restored to his father's throne, particularly if William and Mary accepted the proposals of some of their Catholic allies, notably the Holy Roman emperor, Leopold I, and adopted the prince to rear him as a Protestant. In fact, William toyed with this idea at various times, but the implacable opposition of James II and Mary of Modena to this suggestion rendered it impossible. However, the Cockpit circle viewed the proposal as an implicit threat, and one which had to be circumvented; consequently, in late 1691, the Princess of Denmark and her chief advisors, Marlborough and Godolphin embarked on the double policy *vis-à-vis* St Germain which they were to continue throughout their careers. While actually undertaking every possible measure to prevent a Jacobite restoration, they continually held out false hopes to St Germain that the princess (and later the queen) secretly sympathized with the exiled Prince of Wales and would essay his restoration 'at the right time' (a time carefully left unspecified). By so doing, not only did they insure themselves against the possibility that the Jacobites might succeed in carrying out a second Stuart restoration by the force of French arms, but they also exerted an indirect influence over the political decisions of St Germain by inculcating there the belief that it would prove more profitable to deal with Princess Anne than with William III.

Marlborough and Godolphin, separately, made their first Jacobite contact in January 1691, with Henry Bulkeley (a courtier during James II's reign),[39] but Jacobites in England suspected that Marlborough's growing opposition to William's policies, and particularly to William's reliance upon foreign generals, was designed to benefit the princess, not James II.[40] In order to lend credibility to Marlborough's protestations of Jacobite sympathies, it was necessary to bring the princess into the negotiations. Consequently, the princess wrote her father a letter dated '1 December 1691':

I have been very desirous of some safe opportunity to make you a
sincere and humble offer of my duty and submission to you, and to
beg that you will be assured that I am both truly concerned for the
misfortune of your condition and sensible, as I ought to be, of my own
unhappiness. As to what you may think I have contributed to it, if
wishes could recall what is past, I had long since redeemed my fault.
I am sensible it would have been a great relief to me if I could have
found means to acquaint you earlier with my repentant thoughts, but

> I hope they may find the advantage of coming late, or being less
> suspected of insincerity than perhaps they would have been at any
> time before.

The letter concluded by asking her father's pardon and by making a compliment to Mary of Modena.[41]

The letter, which established the princess's 'Jacobite sympathies', raises more questions than it answers and we are entitled to doubt, as did the court of St Germain, the genuineness of her feelings of repentance. Although the letter was dated '1 December 1691', it was only delivered to James II by Captain David Lloyd on 3 July 1692 NS, after the great English naval victory at Cape La Hogue had prevented an imminent Franco-Jacobite invasion of England. Certainly, the Jacobite network was sufficiently efficient to ensure the delivery of such an important letter in less than eight months. Both the terms of the princess's letter (her repentance 'coming late') and the tone of James II's response ('I am confident that She is truly penitent since She tells me so')[42] suggest that her letter had been antedated in order that her apology might be considered genuine, rather than one extracted by seeming necessity. Indeed, James warned his supporters in Great Britain that, 'being solicited to pardon his son and daughter, the Prince and Princess of Denmark, he could never have a good opinion of them or put any confidence in them'.[43] With his normal rigidity of temper rapidly being reinforced by senility, James II found it impossible to forgive either his children or his protégés, the Marlboroughs.

By the time William and Marlborough returned from the campaign in the Spanish Netherlands in October 1691, it was apparent that a cleavage had developed between the king and his principal English general. The grounds of complaint, William confided to Bishop Burnet, were three-fold: the king 'had very good reason to believe that he [Marlborough] had made his peace with King James and was engaged in a correspondence with France'; it was certain that Marlborough was turning the Army against the Dutch generals, and that he and Lady Marlborough were alienating the princess from the king and queen.[44] On 20 January 1692, after Marlborough had attended the king's levée as part of his routine duties as a gentleman of the bedchamber, the king dispatched Nottingham to inform Marlborough that he was immediately to sell all his offices and to consider himself banned from court. For Marlborough, the blow was severe: his employments were said to be worth from £7,000 to £11,000 per annum.[45]

Consternation and fury greeted this news in the Cockpit, where the princess was pregnant for the ninth time. The ban from court undoubtedly was meant to include Marlborough's wife and inevitably invoked unhappy memories of the Scarsdale affair of December 1687, when James II had forced the prince and princess to dismiss their master of the horse. Hurried conferences between the princess and Marlborough's friends were held and – if an anonymous letter sent to the princess was to be believed – the king and queen were well apprised of their discourse through Lady Fitzharding. Certainly, the princess was disposed to believe the letter, as well as to lend credence to the suggestion that her own person was in some danger:

> Madam, You may billive if I had not all the respect Imagenable for your Heyness I would not give you this trouble. I begg of you for your own sarke that you will have a care of what you say before Lady Fitzharding, rember shee's lord Portland & Betty Villarsis sister. You may depend upon't that these two are not ignorant of what is said and done in your lodgings. Then I leave you to judge whether they make not their court att your expense that's by exposing you & preserving the King as they call it. You know you are but an Honourable Person being in the hands of the Dutch Gards and should there by anny vilence offerd what cann we doe for you? or indeed for our selfs. The King & Queen has been tould that there has not passed a day since lord Marleborrow's being out that you have not shed tears. . . . If it ended in his turning out he meight leave it with patience, but if resolutions hold he will be confinded as soone as the Parlement is up, and if you doe not parte with his Lady of your selfe, you will be obliged to it. . . .
> P.S. It has been taken great notice of Lord Godolphen & Cherrey Russele's [Lord Edward Russell] being at lord Marleborrow's Lodging soe late ye neight he was turn'd out.[46]

Although the princess was unwilling to accept an anonymous letter as absolute proof against Lady Fitzharding, she continually warned Lady Marlborough against trusting her, writing three months later:

> i cant end this without beging deare Mrs. Freeman to have a care of Mrs. Hill [Sarah's note: That was a nick name for Lady Fitzharding] for I doubt She is a Jade & tho one cant be sure she has don any thinge against you, there is to much reason to beleeve She has not bin so sincer as She ought, I am sure She hates your faithful Mrs. Morely, & remember none of her famely weare ever good for any thing.[47]

Two weeks after Marlborough's dismissal, on the evening of 4 February, the princess attended a formal drawing-room at Kensington Palace, presided over by the king and the queen; accompanying the princess, in violation of all etiquette and established precedent, was Lady Marlborough. The princess had obviously decided not to replay the rather ignominious role she had played in the Scarsdale affair, but instead to bring matters to a head in the most public manner possible. She could not have imagined that William and Mary would ignore such a flagrant breach of convention as the presence at court of the wife of a disgraced man, nor did they; the following day, the queen (who subsequently described her letter to the princess as telling her 'in all the gentle and kind wais that could be thought on' that she must part with Lady Marlborough)[48] reprimanded her sister in the harshest possible terms:

> Having something to say to you which I know will not be very pleasing, I choose rather to write it first, being unwilling to surprise you, though I think what I am going to tell you should not, if you give yourself time to think, that never any body was suffered to live at court in Lord Marlborough's circumstances. I need not repeat the cause he has given the King to do what he has done, nor his unwillingness at all times to come to extremities, though people do deserve it.
>
> I hope you do me the justice to believe it is very much against my will that I now tell you that, after this, it is very unfit that Lady Marlborough should stay with you, since that gives her husband so just a pretence of being where he should not. I think I might have expected you should have spoke to me of it; and the King and I, both believing it, made us stay thus long. But seeing you was so far from it that you brought Lady Marlborough hither last night, makes us resolve to put it off no longer, but tell you she must not stay, and that I have all the reason imaginable to look upon your bringing her as the strangest thing that ever was done. Nor could all my kindness for you (which is always ready to turn all you do the best way) at any other time, have hindered me from showing you so that moment, but I considered your condition [i.e. Anne's pregnancy], and that made me master of myself so far as not to take notice of it then.
>
> But now I must tell you, it was very unkind in a sister, would have been very uncivil in an equal; and I need not say I have more to claim. . . . I must tell you I know what is due to me, and expect to have it from you. Tis upon that account I tell you plainly, Lady Marlborough must not continue with you, in the circumstances her lord is. . . .[49]

The princess – particularly stung by the queen's reminder of her own superior rank ('I know what is due to me, and expect to have it from you') – immediately reported to Sarah:

> I have just received such an arbitrary letter from ye Q: as I am sure she nor ye King durst not have writt to any other of theire subjects & wch if I had any inclination to part with deare Mrs. Freeman would make me keep her in spite of theire teeth & wch by ye Grace of God I will

& go to ye utmost verge of ye earth rather than live with such Calibans.[50]

The queen's repeated references to her own kindness did not hide the provocative nature of her letter. Not only did the queen know of the princess's devotion to, and emotional dependence upon, Lady Marlborough; she also directly challenged the princess's right to choose her own servants. There was no doubt in Princess Anne's mind that this time she must stand and fight, and her letter to Sarah shows that the decision was her own. Her reply to the queen on the following day, 6 February, was tantamount to a flat refusal to obey the royal commands:

> Your Majesty was in the right to think that your letter would be very surprising to me; for you must needs be sensible enough of the kindness I have for my Lady Marlborough, to know that a command from you to part from her must be the greatest mortification in the world to me and, indeed, of such a nature, as I might well have hoped your kindness to me would have always prevented. I am satisfied she cannot have been guilty of any fault to you, and it would be extremely to her advantage if I could here repeat every word that ever she had said to me of you in her whole life. . . .
>
> Your care of my present condition is extremely obliging and if you could be pleased to add to it so far as, upon my account, to recall your severe command (as I must beg leave to call it in a matter so tender and so little reasonable, as I think, to be imposed on me, that you would scarce require it from the meanest of your subjects), I should ever acknowledge it as a very agreeable mark of your kindness to me. *And as I must freely own, that as I think this proceeding can be for no other intent than to give me a very sensible mortification,* so there is no misery that I cannot readily resolve to suffer rather than the thoughts of parting with her [Lady Marlborough].[51]

The princess summoned Rochester to the Cockpit and asked him to deliver the letter. After reading it, he refused to be the porter of such a bombshell and instead advised the queen to order the Marlboroughs to vacate the Cockpit, which the queen did by a verbal order to the lord chamberlain on 8 February. This order was even more insulting than the command to dismiss Sarah, for the Cockpit, while within the precincts of the Palace of Whitehall, belonged to the princess. Undoubtedly, the princess had already considered the alternatives and taken her decision, for her answer to the queen was returned on the same day, announcing that she would retire from court until the queen revoked her order.[52] The princess immediately appealed to the Duke of Somerset for the loan of Syon House, situated on the banks of the Thames west of London, as a temporary residence. He agreed to loan the house to the princess and, despite subsequent pressure from the king and queen, refused to go back on his promise, earning Princess Anne's lasting gratitude.[53]

Before leaving the Cockpit permanently on 19 February the princess had a final interview with the queen in which – to quote Sarah – 'the Queen was as Insensible as a Statue' to the princess's arguments.[54] The royal household, particularly Lord Villiers (later created Earl of Jersey), reflected the queen's attitude. Sarah later recalled,

> As the Princesse went away she mett in the next room my Lord Jersey who at that time had not soe much manners as to offer the Princesse his hand to open a door for her, or call her servants who by accident were out of the way, thinking the vissit would have been longe, & the Princesse told me with detestation of my Lord Jerseys behaviour that she was forced to go thru a room, or two alone, tell she mett one of the Queens Gentlman ushers, who lead her to her coach, & sent for her servants.[55]

The immediate royal response to the withdrawal of the Prince and Princess of Denmark to Syon House was to remove their guards: 'ye guards in St. James Park did not stand to theire arms nether when the Prince went nor came', the Princess informed Lady Marlborough on 22 February.

> I cant beleeve it was theire dutch breeding alone with out dutch orders that made them do it becaus they never omitted it before . . . these things are so far from vexing ether ye P: or me that they really please us exstreamly[56]

The royal pressure continued unabated; at the end of February, before his departure for the Continent, the king sent the Duke of Ormonde to the princess 'with a peremptory message that she remove the Countess of Marlborough from her house', and on 2 March the Archbishop of Canterbury and Bishop Compton visited the princess.[57] These journeys to Syon proved to no avail, except to alarm Sarah. The princess's undated letters which are ascribable to March and April 1692 make it clear that Sarah attempted to resign her position; how genuine Lady Marlborough's desire to retire actually was is open to question. The Dutch resident in London, L'Hermitage, reported that Sarah's friends urged her to resign, but 'she responded that she knew the Princess perfectly; if she [Sarah] was separated from her for only two weeks, she would be gone forever; and she hopes to maintain herself in the Princess's favour as long as possible'.[58] The princess adamantly refused to permit Sarah to resign her office, assuring her repeatedly that 'I am more yours than can be exprest & had rather live in a Cottage with you then Reigne Empresse of ye world with out you'.[59]

The princess was quite prepared to incur the full wrath of the king and queen, even if it meant losing her parliamentary grant; on 15 March she assured Sarah that

> if they should take off twenty or thirty thousand pound, have I not lived upon as little before, when I was first marryed we had but twenty . . . & if it should com to that againe, what retrenchments is there in my famely I would not willingly make & be glad of that pretence to do it.[60]

Despite these assurances, Sarah asked the princess to consult Prince George, who continued to attend council meetings, thereby maintaining a tenuous connection between Syon House and Kensington, and might be subject to royal pressure or blandishments. In response, on 19 March, Princess Anne wrote Lady Marlborough a letter which deserves to be quoted in its entirety, for it displays not only the princess's intense hatred of her brother-in-law, the king, but also her aspirations for a 'SunShine day' when she herself would mount the throne:

> In obedience to deare Mrs. Freeman, I have told the Prince all She desired me & he is so far from being of another opinion if there had bin occasion he would have strengthened me in my resolutions, & we both beg you would never mention so cruell a thing any more, can you think ether of us so wretched that for ye sake of twenty thousand pound & to be tormented from morning to night with flattering knaves & fools, we would forsake those we have such obligations to & that we are sertin we are ye occassion of all theire misfortunes, besides can you beleeve we will ever truckle to that Monster who from ye first moment of his coming has used us at that rate as we are sinsible he had don & that all ye world can wittnes, that will not lett there interest weigh more with them then theire reason, but Suppose I did submitt & that the King could change his nature so much as to use me with humanety, how would all reasonable people despise me, how would that Dutch abortive laugh at me & please himself with haveing got ye better & wch is more how could my Conscience reproch me, for haveing sacrificed it, my honor, reputation & all ye Substantiall comforts of this life for transitory interest, which even to those who make it their idol can never aford any reale Satisfaction, much less to a vertuous mind. No my deare Mrs. Freeman never beleeve your faithfull Mrs. Morely will ever submitt, she can waite with patience for a SunShine day & if She does not live to see it yet She hopes England will flourish againe, once more give me leave to beg you would be so kind never to Speake of parting more for lett what will happen that is ye only thing can make me miserable.[61]

In early April, Rochester, upon whom the queen placed increased reliance after William's departure for the Continent, called upon the princess – now in the last stages of her pregnancy – and, in her words, 'talked a great deale of Senseless Stuff'.[62] Rochester's blustering demands that Sarah should immediately be dismissed, far from frightening the prince and princess, merely stiffened their resolve:

> we are both so far from repenting of what we have don that the more
> we think of it ye better we are satisfyed & for Mrs. Morly she is so
> mightely at her ease heare that should the Monsters grow good natured
> & endulge her in everything she could desire, I beleeve she would be
> hardly perswaided to leave her retirement, but of these great changes I
> think there is no great danger.[63]

On 17 April 1692 the princess gave birth to her seventh child, a son who was immediately christened George. The child died one hour after his baptism. Before his birth, the princess had sent Sir Benjamin Bathurst to tell the queen that she was in labour 'and much worse than She us'd to be, as she really was', but, according to Sarah's narrative, the queen refused to see him or to make any answer. After the child's death, the princess sent Lady Charlotte Boeverwart, a Dutch woman who was one of her ladies in waiting and a cousin of both William III and Ormonde, to the queen with the news; after consulting with Rochester, Queen Mary decided to visit her sister that very afternoon. Sarah, naturally, was not present at what proved to be the last interview between the two sisters, but related the story as the princess had described it.

> I could not have believ'd it, that the Queen upon such a Misfortune
> would come to an only Sister, and never ask her how she did, or
> express the least Concern for her Condition, nor so much as take her
> by the hand. The first word she said was, that she had made the first
> step in Coming to her, and that she now expected she would make the
> next, in removing me.

The princess, pale, and suffering from the after effects of a prolonged labour, refused to dismiss Lady Marlborough, but the queen repeated the same order to Prince George as he escorted her to her coach.[64]

To demonstrate her defiance, the princess immediately decided to lease Berkeley House in Piccadilly as a permanent residence, in exchange for which John, Lord Berkeley, the prince's groom of the stole, would take the Cockpit.[65] In retaliation, the queen issued formal orders on 26 April through Nottingham, the secretary of state, that no one should appear at court who had visited the princess.[66] The following day, Rochester wrote to the princess to offer his services towards a reconciliation based on Lady Marlborough's removal.[67] The princess sent Rochester's letter to Sarah with the reassurance that "'tis not in ye power of man to make me ever consent to part with you',[68] and on 29 April replied to her uncle with a spirited letter which was tantamount to an accusation that Rochester himself had induced the queen to forbid courtiers to visit the princess's court:

> I give you many thanks for ye complements & expressions of service wch you make me in your letter, wch I should be much better pleased wth then I am, if I had any reason to think them sincere it is a great mortification to me to find that I still continue under the misfortune of the Queens displeasure. I had hoped that in time, ye occasion of it would have apeared as little reasonable to ye Queen, as it has always don to me, & if you would have me perswaided of ye Sincerety of your intention as you seem to desire, You must give me leave to say I can not think it very hard for you to convince me of it by ye effects, & till then I must beg leave to be excused if I am apt to think this last mortification wch has bin given me can not have proceded from the Queens own temper. . . .[69]

The court's boycott against the princess was immediately effective: 'Her Highness has but a melancholy court at Sion', one observer reported during the following week,[70] and Sarah recorded, 'By this Industry it was so settled that no Body but two or three Jacobite ladies came to the Princess, and it was easy to observe that all of that Interest rejoic'd much in that Difference.'[71]

By the beginning of May, it was obvious that the French intended an invasion of England and that the attempt was imminent; William III was still fighting on the Continent, unable to cross the Channel to mount the defence of the realm, while James II had already made his way to the French coast. James's queen was again pregnant, and the court of St Germain had issued offers of safe conduct within France to William and Mary, to the Princess of Denmark, and to many noble ladies in England, including Lady Fitzharding and Lady Frescheville (but not Lady Marlborough) of the princess's household.[72] These invitations to witness Mary of Modena's lying-in were, of course, ignored; the princess was in no condition to travel, as she was still convalescing after her pregnancy. In this weakened condition, the princess was visited in early May by Elizabeth, Countess of Ailesbury, the wife of one of James II's staunchest adherents in England. Lady Ailesbury warned the princess that a Jacobite invasion force would be in England within twenty-four hours, wind allowing, and that 5,000 troops would be ready to 'escort' her if she returned to her father. Ailesbury recorded in his *Memoirs* that the princess, weighing the threat implicit in this information, 'was very attentive & seemed melancholy and pensive, and fetching a sigh, "Well,

Madam, tell your Lord that I am ready to do what he can advise me to".'
A few days later, however, news arrived in London that Admiral Lord
Edward Russell had destroyed the French fleet at La Hogue, rendering
an invasion impossible. When Ailesbury himself visited the princess
later, he found that her attitude had changed. She refused to write to
James II, saying, 'It is not a proper time for you and I to talk of that
matter any farther.'[73]

Before Russell's great victory at La Hogue, which effectively ended
the French naval challenge to the Maritime Powers in the Channel and
the North Sea for the next quarter of a century, London was in uproar
at the prospect of a Jacobite invasion. On 5 May, acting on the testimony
of a disciple of Titus Oates named Robert Young (whose evidence was
later exposed as false and contrived), the queen ordered the arrest of
Marlborough and a number of Jacobite nobles, all of whom were sent to
the Tower. The princess was convinced that her own arrest was
imminent, as was rumoured,[74] and she wrote immediately to Sarah:

> I hear Lord Marlborough is sent to the Tower; and though I am certain
> they have nothing against him . . . yet I was struck when I was told it;
> for methinks it is a dismal thing to have one's friends sent to that
> place. I have a thousand melancholy thoughts and cannot help fearing
> they should hinder you from coming to me; though how they can do
> that, without making you a prisoner, I cannot imagine.
>
> I am just told by pretty good hands, that as soon as the wind turns
> westerly, there will be a guard set upon the Prince and me. If you hear
> there is any such thing designed, and that 'tis easy to you, pray let me
> see you before the wind changes; for afterwards one does not know
> whether they will let one have opportunities of speaking to one
> another. But let them do what they please, nothing shall ever vex me,
> if I can have the satisfaction of seeing dear Mrs. Freeman; and I swear I
> would live on bread and water; between four walls, with her, without
> repining; for as long as you continue kind, nothing can ever be a real
> mortification to your faithful Mrs. Morley, who wishes she may never
> enjoy a moment's happiness, in this world or the next, if ever she
> proves false to you.[75]

In a second letter of the same day, the princess requested Lady
Marlborough 'to be so just both to Mr. Morly & me to beleeve what ever
lyes in our poor power to serve you we shall be ready on all occasions'.[76]
Unfortunately from the princess's point of view, her powers of action
were nil. She could only write daily reassurances to Lady Marlborough,
who was obliged to bribe clerks in Nottingham's office for permission to
visit her husband in the Tower. On 12 May the princess commented:

> I hope when the Parliament sitts care will be taken that people may not

be clapt up for nothinge or els there will be no liveing in quiet for any
body but insolent dutch & sneaking mercenary english men.[77]

While Sarah spent most of her time in London, preoccupied with the
care of her husband in the Tower and of her youngest son, Charles, who
was seriously ill, the princess decided to call upon the aid of Dr Edward
Stillingfleet, Bishop of Worcester, ostensibly to mediate a reconciliation
with the queen. The princess summoned Stillingfleet to Syon House on
18 May and received 'a very siville answer' from him; on 20 May she
reported to Sarah that

> The Bishop of Worcester was with me this morning before I was drest,
> I gave him my letter to the Queen, & he has promised to second it, &
> seem'd to undertake it very willingly, tho by all the discourse I had
> with him . . . I find him very partial to her, the last time he was here,
> I told him you had several times desired you might go from me & that
> I had as often conjur'd you not to do it, & I have repeated the same
> thing over & over to him today.[78]

The princess's letter, which the bishop delivered to the queen, was
superficially respectful but one which, because of the concluding phrase
and her failure to mention the dismissal of Lady Marlborough, was
intended to be construed as yet another defiance of the queen:

> I have now, God be thanked recovered my strength well enough to go
> abroad. And though my duty and inclination would both lead me to
> wait upon your Majesty as soon as I am able to do it, yet I have of late
> had the misfortune of being so much under your Majesty's displeasure,
> as to apprehend there may be hard constructions made upon anything
> I either do, or not do, with the most respectful intentions.
>   And I am in doubt whether the same arguments that have prevailed
> with your Majesty to forbid people from shewing their usual respects
> to me, may not be carried so much farther as not to permit me to pay
> my duty to you. That, I acknowledge, would be a great increase of
> affliction to me, and nothing but your Majesty's own command shall
> ever willingly make me submit to it; for whatever reason I may think in
> my own mind I have to complain of being hardly used, *yet I will strive
> to hide it as much as possible.*[79]

The last sentence was a glaring falsehood, for the princess's withdrawal
from the Cockpit had been as public as possible and nothing she had
done subsequently had been designed to diminish the talk of the town
concerning the two royal sisters. The princess's letter elicited the desired
response from the queen:

> I have received yours by the bishop of Worcester, and have little to say
> to it, since you cannot but know that as I never use compliments, so

93

now they cannot serve. Tis none of my fault that we live at this
distance, and I have endeavoured to show my willingness to do otherwise; and I will do no more.

Don't give yourself any unnecessary trouble [i.e. by coming to court],
for be assured, 'tis not words can make us live together as we ought.
You know what I required of you; and now I tell you, if you doubted it
before, that I cannot change my mind but expect to be complied
with. . . .[80]

The princess, in reporting the queen's letter to Sarah on 21 May ('I do
not send you the original for fear any accident may happen to ye bearer,
for I love to keep such letters by me for my own Justification'), was
almost flippant in reporting that Bishop Stillingfleet 'was not so well
satisfied' with the queen as he had been before;

> he has promised me to bear witness that I have made all ye advances
> that was reasonable, & I confess I think ye more 'tis told about that I
> would have waited on the Queen but that she refused seeing me 'tis
> the better, & therefore I will not scruple saying it to anybody when it
> comes my way.

So much for trying to hide her differences with her sister, if possible.
News of Russell's victory had reached Syon House before the queen's
letter, and both Lady Fitzharding and Thomas Maul, the prince's groom
of the bedchamber, had urged the prince and princess to send compliments to the queen on the victory,

> but we neither of us thought there was any necessity of it then, &
> much less since I received this arbitrary letter. . . . sure never any body
> was so used by a sister, but I thank God I have nothing to reproach my
> self with in all this business, but the more I think of all that is past the
> better I am satisfied.[81]

The entire negotiation through the Bishop of Worcester was the
princess's idea and was designed to ensure that she would, in the public
eye, appear as the victim beset by the tyranny of the court. Lady
Marlborough was definitely not the princess's counsellor on this
occasion, for on the morning of 21 May, her younger son, Charles, died.
The princess, 'knowing very well what it is to loose a child', sent Sarah a
warm note of sympathy, reminding her that 'time [is] the only cure for
all misfortunes'.[82]

The last attempt at a reconciliation between the queen and princess
was made on 25 May, when the lord president of the council, the
Marquess of Carmarthen (formerly the Earl of Danby), visited the
princess at Syon House for 'a long discours' which failed to heal the
breach.[83] Following this visit, the two rival courts entered a protracted

state of siege warfare, in which the queen held every advantage and the princess none. Marlborough was released from the Tower on an appeal of habeas corpus on 15 June; the queen personally struck his name, along with those of the nobles who stood his £6,000 bail, from the register of privy councillors.[84]

Throughout the early summer of 1692 the princess was subject to an unidentified fever[85] and embroiled in petty disputes with Lady Berkeley over the arrangements between them for the exchange of the Cockpit for Berkeley House. In early August, shortly after the prince and princess had gone to dine with the Marlboroughs at St Albans, 'which is taken notice of',[86] the princess lamented to Sarah,

I will not press her [Lady Berkeley] any more about going out of her house for She must leave it in a month by ye Articles & I wish I was in it that there might be an end of all these disagreeable disputes.[87]

But a week later, she despaired of ever reaching any accommodation with Lady Berkeley:

I was yesterday at Berkly house wch I like very well but my Lady looked so mightely out of humoure that I did not go into all ye Garretts nor the wings as I intended & till She is out of ye house it will be impossible to order anything or see it at ones ease & when She will be pleased to remove God knows.[88]

By the beginning of August the princess knew that she was pregnant again; one of the recurring features of her correspondence with Lady Marlborough was the appearance and departure of 'Lady Charlotte', which was their cant name for menstruation. On 28 July the princess reported to Sarah,

I have not yet seen Lady Charlott, which I wonder very much at for I used to be very regular & I cannot fancy she has taken her leave for nine months becaus since my first three children I have never bred so soon.[89]

Despite the growing certainty of her pregnancy, the prince and princess decided to adhere to their plans to spend August and September in Bath, while Berkeley House was being refitted for their reception. One of the questions which agitated the princess was whether or not to take the three-year-old Duke of Gloucester with her; Lady Fitzharding strongly urged the princess to do so, but the princess bitterly concluded that

there is so much reason to beleeve people considers there own Satisfaction more than mine or then they do the childs good, I think I had better be from him five or six weeks then run ye hazard of his meeting with any accident that one may have cause to repent of ones whole life.[90]

The prince and princess and their entourage left Syon House on 18 August for Bath, where they were received by the mayor and the city corporation with the full honours befitting their rank; news of this reception quickly made its way to Whitehall and provoked the queen's wrath. On 30 August, Nottingham issued formal orders to the mayor (a tallow-chandler, according to Sarah) and the corporation forbidding them from paying the princess 'the same respect and ceremony as has been usually paid to the royal family'.[91] Nottingham privately recorded that Queen Mary, when she approved his letter to the Mayor of Bath, 'could not refrain her tears and said, "Thus it becomes a Queen to act, but I cannot forget she is my sister"'.[92] The princess treated this order with the scorn it deserved: 'I did fancy yesterday', she wrote to Sarah on 6 September,

> as soon as I miste ye Mayour that he was commanded not to go to church with me but I think tis a thing to be laughed at & if they emagin ether to vex me or gaine upon me by such sort of usage they will be mightely disapointed.[93]

During the princess's sojourn in Bath, she was visited by Dr Richard Kingston, formerly a royal chaplain to Charles II, now pretending to be a Jacobite but actually serving as Portland's agent to report upon Marlborough's activities to Nottingham while Portland was on the Continent with the king.[94] Of equal importance, Kingston was to secure the confidence of the princess, and before she had left the Thames valley Kingston had informed Nottingham that 'I grow more and more into the intrigues of Syon House'.[95] On 9 and 10 September, Kingston visited the princess at Bath and promptly reported his conversations with her to Nottingham. While Kingston's account must be treated with the same reserve as the reports of Jacobite agents to St Germain, it contains an interesting portrait of a woman capable of extracting information concerning Jacobite plans from Kingston, while assuring him in vague and impersonal terms of her 'kind sentiments' towards her father. Most importantly, however, Kingston's report depicts the princess as obsessed by the treatment which she had received from William and Mary: 'the Pr[incess] discoursing her sufferings often made a parallel betweene her self and Qu[een] El[izabeth]'. It was no accident that when Anne became queen she adopted the great Elizabeth's motto, *Semper Eadem*. 'Her Highness was pleased to aske severall questions concerning her father', Kingston reported to Nottingham,

> as where he was and what he intended, and seem'd well pleased at the discourse of a winter's descent. A further relation pass'd about the possibility and impossibility of the attempt, which being reconciled to

what was desired it gave her H[ighness] great satisfaction. . . .
Several other discourses were made, as the misfortunes of her
Highness' father and the indignities offered by their Majesties to her
Highness' which she hoped would be all redressed at the sitting of the
next Parliament, to which a brisque and bitter lady [Lady Marlborough?] replyed, I hope, madam, your good father will doe it
himselfe before that time. This lady, whom I yet know not, often inter-
posed with great reflections on theire Majesties, after which her
Highness reassumed the former discourse and in a set and methodized
speech recounted the great services her Highness had done her sister
and the continued ill practises their Majesties had used even from the
beginning against her. More had been said but the Prince his game at
billiards was ended and put a period to our discourse.[96]

Such reports did nothing to contribute to good feelings between the
queen and the princess.

On 14 October the prince and princess returned from Bath to
Campden House and shortly thereafter moved into Berkeley House,
where they were to reside for the next three years. There was one
important new recruit to their diminished circle at Berkeley House: 'The
Duke of Shrewsbury, then out of the Court [i.e. out of office], went
thither constantly.'[97] When William III returned from the Continent the
following week, Prince George wrote to him to ask whether or not he
should appear at court; the king's answer was favourable, and the
prince waited upon him and in November attended the celebrations of
of the king's birthday.[98] Pressure to be reconciled with the king and
queen was apparently placed on the prince by his brother, King
Christian V of Denmark, for the princess reported to Lady Marlborough
that

Mr. Freeman will give deare Mrs. Freeman an account of a letter Mr.
Morly had out of his own Country, by wch tis very plaine Mr. Caliban
has some inclinations towards a reconcilment but if I ever make ye lest
[sic: least] Step, may I be as great a Slave as he would make me if it
weare in his power. Mr. M. is of ye same mind.[99]

Obstinately irreconcilable, the princess continued to endure the petty
malice of the court; the minister at the parish church of St James, where
the princess constantly worshipped 'with little attendance',[100] was
forbidden to place the text of the sermon before her chair, which was the
normal custom. In January 1693 'a scandalous pamphlet' about the
princess was answered by 'a vindication . . . in which are severall
reflections bordering on treason' (neither pamphlet is extant today).[101]
Whatever hope the princess had for a redress of her grievances when
Parliament met came to nothing, for from the parliamentary diary of

Narcissus Luttrell it appears that only veiled allusions were made to the breach within the royal family.[102]

The princess was still subject to spies within her own household, Lady Fitzharding being only the most prominent. Lady Marlborough was convinced that Thomas Maul, a groom of the bedchamber to the prince, was acting as Rochester's agent at Berkeley House. According to Jenkin Lewis, one of the Duke of Gloucester's servants, Mrs Pack, who had been his wet-nurse, bore tales to the queen, for which her husband was rewarded with a position in the custom house before she was forced out of the princess's household.[103] Lord Ailesbury recorded in his *Memoirs* that even the princess's 'foster sister' Margery Fielding, 'a waspish ill natured creature', acted as a spy upon her mistress.[104] Royal pressure was placed on members of the princess's staff to desert her service for more lucrative employments; in February 1693, Lord Lexington, who had urged that Sarah be dismissed, resigned as the prince's master of the horse to become a gentleman of the king's bedchamber.[105] He was succeeded by the Earl of Denbigh, who himself resigned in January 1694 'and kist his majesties hand'.[106] In the same month, Godolphin (who was still first lord of the Treasury) secretly warned Sarah that the king was going to appoint Lord Fitzharding as a teller of the Exchequer, a lifetime sinecure.[107] The princess also suspected that her letters were opened; in the middle of one letter to Lady Marlborough, she broke out of context to add, 'who's ever hands this lights in, I wish they may be so good natured after they have reade it, to lett it go by this nights post'.[108] Nevertheless, despite all the turmoil in her own household and the social ostracism which she faced, the princess had no regrets in February 1693 when she reviewed the events of the year which had passed since her departure from the Cockpit. She assured Lady Marlborough,

> You can not expect any news from Berkly house, but as dull & dispisable as some people may think it, I am so far from being weary of my way of liveing or repenting in ye least of my actions since this time twelvemonth, that weare ye yeare to run over againe I would tread ye same steps.[109]

The princess was reluctant to send the Duke of Gloucester to visit the queen frequently, particularly when these visits, as well as the value of the gifts which the queen gave to her nephew, were regularly announced in the *London Gazette*.[110] Both William and Mary were genuinely fond of their nephew, and the princess's advisors deemed it necessary to maintain Gloucester in the royal esteem. Thus they could prevent any possible accommodation with the exiled Jacobites through the adoption of the 'Pretender' (a name becoming the common description of the Prince of Wales). Reluctantly, the princess bowed to the will of her advisors, telling Sarah on 19 March 1693,

> as to what deare Mrs. Freeman says about my boys going to ye Queen, I must confess I should think it often enough if he went on ye two birthdays & when she asks for him, & as I have often told you it goes extreamly against ye graine, yet since so much better judgments then mine think it necessary, he shall go.[111]

Part of the princess's ill temper was ascribable to the fact that she was nearing the termination of her tenth pregnancy and was feeling the effects ('I have bin on ye rack againe this morning'); four days later she was delivered of a stillborn daughter.[112]

The princess's continued failure to produce live, healthy children undoubtedly contributed to her deepening moroseness. In addition to the social isolation which her quarrel with the king and queen had imposed upon her, throughout the spring and summer of 1693 the princess was deprived of Lady Marlborough's company, for Sarah was at St Albans nursing her mother, Mrs Jennings, who was paralysed from a stroke and dying. A stream of letters flowed from Berkeley House to St Albans, in which the princess implored 'my deare Mrs. Freeman' to have a care for herself and suggested various remedies for Mrs Jennings; she also dispatched doctors and medicines from London. After Mrs Jennings's death on 28 June, Sarah appears to have remained for some time in St Albans, apparently her first prolonged absence from the princess since the beginning of their intimate friendship. Sarah had several reasons for remaining outside London; she had to supervise the education of her five surviving children, Henrietta (born in 1681), Anne (born in 1683 and the god-daughter of the princess), John, Lord Blandford (born in 1685), Elizabeth (born in 1687), and Mary (born in 1689). Attendance at the princess's court was boring, and furthermore Sarah found herself increasingly interested in self-education and in the study of classical authors, an intellectual avocation completely foreign to the princess. Lady Marlborough's absences from the princess's company would continue, although they did not become prolonged until after the princess's accession to the throne.

By August 1693 the princess suspected that she was again pregnant, but she feigned a certain indifference to the outcome and a disinclination to follow precautionary measures to ensure her health and that of her unborn child. 'Lady Charlott I doubt has played ye Jade with me', she notified Lady Marlborough on 4 August, 'for I have mist her now a week, but whatever condition I am in, I do not intend to mind myself any more, then when I am sure I am not with child.'[113] The fatalism which the princess adopted proved to be justified; on 21 January 1694, in the seventh month of her pregnancy, she miscarried a stillborn son.[114]

Of her eleven pregnancies in ten and a half years of marriage, only five had resulted in the birth of living children, and of these two had died immediately after birth. Only Gloucester had survived beyond infancy, and his health was precarious. This latest failure to produce a healthy child resulted in a psychological change in the princess. We are indebted to the Welsh servant of the young duke, Jenkin Lewis, for a charming memoir of his young master's short life and the conditions under which he was reared. It was apparent to the princess, who habitually referred to Gloucester as 'my poor boy', that her son was not normal; he did not learn to talk until he was three or to walk properly until he was five. The post-mortem following his death revealed that he was suffering from water on the brain. During the spring of 1693 and again in the spring of 1694, Gloucester suffered severely from what the doctors diagnosed as an 'ague', a fever of malarial character attended by paroxysms which occurred at regular intervals. In April 1693, for instance, the princess reported to Lady Marlborough that

> my poor boy had his ague againe yesterday & tho Dr. Ratliffe [Dr John Radcliffe, one of the foremost physicians of the period] said it was nothinge I thought it a very long fitt for it lasted seven hours & made him very sick, but an houre after it was gon he was mighty onerry & seemed to be as well as ever he was in his life.[115]

Gloucester's health was a constant source of worry to his mother, who was becoming increasingly morbid; furthermore, the princess's future was tied up with the life of her only son. Should Gloucester die and the princess have no surviving children, it was always possible that the war might be ended with an agreement that William and Mary would adopt the Prince of Wales and rear him as their heir and successor. During the summer of 1694, Marlborough's friends, including the Earl of Sunderland (who had not only been allowed to return to England, from which he had fled at the Revolution, but was now secretly acting as one of William III's most influential advisors) and the Duke of Shrewsbury, who had succeeded Nottingham as secretary of state, tried to settle the quarrel between the monarchs and Berkeley House by bringing Marlborough back into his military posts; but William III refused 'to entrust him with the command of my troops'.[116] There was, in short, no immediate prospect of a reconciliation between the king and the queen on the one hand and the princess on the other.

In the autumn of 1694 the princess believed that she was once again pregnant. Although this 'pregnancy', which was not 'terminated' until the end of June 1695, was false or hysterical, all the normal symptoms of pregnancy, including swelling of the breasts and abdomen, appeared, and her doctors and friends were ready to accept the fact that the pregnancy was genuine. This time Princess Anne resolved to take special care of herself in order to ensure a happy conclusion; in a phrase in Sarah's *Conduct*, which has been overlooked by historians, 'the Princess, *thinking herself with child*, stayed constantly on one floor, by her physicians advice lying very much upon a couch to prevent the misfortune of miscarrying'.[117] It is hardly surprising that Princess Anne underwent a hysterical pregnancy; any woman with her extensive record of ill fortune in childbearing would develop a neurotic obsession; that there were political reasons for providing Gloucester with brothers or sisters only contributed to its development.

In the calculations of courtiers and politicians concerning the future, it was generally assumed that Queen Mary would outlive both her tubercular, asthmatic husband and her younger sister, who was beginning to display signs of the physical deterioration which would leave her an invalid by the end of the decade. The accidental factor in history, however, determined otherwise. During the Christmas celebrations of 1694, the queen, who was thirty-two, fell victim to smallpox. The princess, whose immunity derived from her own smallpox attack at the time of William and Mary's marriage in 1677, sent one of her ladies to Kensington with a message of sympathy and concern, adding 'that if her Majesty would allow her the happiness of waiting on her, she would, notwithstanding the condition she was in, run any hazard for that satisfaction'. The queen's groom of the stole, the Countess of Derby, replied in a letter to Sarah that the queen could not be disturbed and that the princess should defer her projected visit. 'Pray, madam, present my humble duty to the Princess', Lady Derby added as a postscript. 'This civil answer, and my Lady Derby's postscript', Sarah later recorded, 'made me conclude, more than if the college of physicians had told it me, the disease was mortal.'[118]

It was an age when royal deathbed scenes were recorded in minute detail, yet only one reporter, the Prussian resident, Friedrich Bonet, suggested that Queen Mary died on 28 December 1694, 'having declared that she had nothing in her heart against her sister and that she loved the Duke of Gloucester very much'.[119] King William was distraught: so pronounced was his agony that his attendants feared for his health and sanity. His advisors immediately recognized that the king could no longer afford to be estranged from the heiress apparent to the throne, particularly in this unique situation where Princess Anne possessed a

101

better hereditary claim to the crown than did William. On the basis of a statement in favour of the Whig party which Bishop Burnet's wife made to Lady Marlborough ten years later, some historians have concluded that John, Lord Somers, the effective head of the Whig party and lord chancellor in 1694, was the man who convinced the king that it was necessary to reach an accommodation with the princess.[120] While this may be true, Sarah and other members of the princess's entourage attributed the reconciliation to the influence of Sunderland and to the diplomacy of Thomas Tenison, the new Archbishop of Canterbury.[121] On 29 December, the day following the queen's death, the princess wrote a letter of sympathy to the king, which was delivered by the archbishop:[122]

> I beg your Majesties favourable acceptance of my sincere and hearty
> sorrow for the great affliction in the loss of the Queen and doe assure
> your Majestie I am as sensibly touched with this sad misfortune, as if
> I had never been soe unhappy as to have fall'n into her displeasure.
> It is my earnest desire that your Majestie would give me leave to wait
> upon you, as soon as it can be with noe inconveniency to you, or with-
> out danger of increasing your affliction, that I may have an opportunity
> myselfe – not only of repeating this, but of assuring your Majestie of
> my reall intention to omitt noe occasion of giving you constant proofs
> of my sincere respects and concern for your person and interests, as
> becomes your Majesties affectionett sister and Servant, Anne.[123]

There was apparently some hesitation on the king's part as to whether or not he should accept the princess's overture to a reconciliation, although her grief at the death of her only sister was genuine and bitter.[124] The Archbishop of Canterbury, arguing that the quarrel should be settled, reminded the king that 'those Members of either House of Parliament, who had Places under their Highnesses, had always appeared forward in promoting His Majesties Interest'.[125] With the king's permission, Tenison visited the princess on 5 January to arrange for her to call upon William at Kensington two days later 'in some room of your Majesties lower Apartment by reason of her present Condition [i.e. her pregnancy]'.[126] The princess was forced to defer her meeting with the king because of illness, but sent an explanatory note to William by Lord Fitzharding.[127] On 10 January the princess's guards were restored to her,[128] and on Sunday, 13 January, the princess paid her visit to the king at Kensington. The interview, for which the princess had to be carried upstairs in her chair to the presence chamber, was recorded by an eyewitness, Jenkin Lewis.

> The King came and saluted her. She told his Majesty, in faultering
> accents, that she was truly sorry for his loss: who replied, he was much

concerned for hers; both were equally affected, and could scarcely refrain from tears, or speak distinctly. The King then handed the Princess in [to his private closet], who staid with him three quarters of an hour. His Majesty presented the Princess soon after, with most of her sister's jewels.[129]

The goal which the king and the princess shared was to secure the Duke of Gloucester's rights to the throne against the pretensions of the Jacobites, who had great hopes that the death of Queen Mary would remove any semblance of legality to William's regime and would aid a Stuart restoration. The bitter comments of James II's *Memoirs* underline the pivotal importance of the princess's reconciliation with, and public support of, William III:

> the Princess of Denmark (notwithstanding her late pretence of repentence) was better contented, or at least apear'd to be so, to let the Prince of Orange, though he had used her ill, usurp upon her right, than that her father who had always cherished her beyond expression should be restored to the possession of his.[130]

The king made it known that St James's Palace would be given to the princess as her London residence where she would keep court 'as if she were a crowned head'.[131] Predictably, 'as soon as it was known that the quarrel was made up, there was nothing but crouds at Berkeley house of all sorts of people, to show their respect to the Prince and Princess'.[132] The princess was sufficiently cynical to take this in her stride, noting only to Lady Marlborough after her first drawing-room on 15 January: 'I say nothing to you of the great appearance at Mrs. Moreleys because I reckon you will have a much better account of that matter from other hands.'[133] She could not help but be amused, however, by one opportunistic courtier who loudly announced at this reception, 'I hope your Highness will remember that I came to wait upon you, when none of this company did.'[134]

The reconciliation between the king and the princess was, at best, superficial. It did not obliterate William's jealousy of the princess, nor did the king give her or Prince George any significant role in government throughout the remainder of his reign. On the other side, the princess's intense hatred of William continued, although she usually managed to camouflage it when she acted in the largely ceremonial role of his hostess to which her rank and position entitled her. Nor were the Marlboroughs included in the general dispensation following the reconciliation. Although Marlborough himself claimed publicly that he had done everything possible to end the quarrel after the queen's death,[135] Lady Marlborough remained implacably hostile to the king and tended to scorn the reconciliation. Referring to the princess's letter of sympathy to the king, Sarah commented that it was

> full of expressions that the polliticians make nothing of, but it was a great trouble to me to have her write what could not bee true after such usage, & nobody upon earth could have made me have don it, but I was never the councellor upon such great occasions.[136]

It was already clear that Marlborough possessed more political influence than Sarah with the princess, despite the latter's continued devotion to 'my deare Mrs. Freeman'.

Apart from his concern for the general good of the Revolution settlement, Marlborough undoubtedly hoped that the reconciliation would lead to his own return to office. But in this he was required to exercise his patience. At the end of January 1695, Shrewsbury notified Admiral Russell that,

> since the death of the Queen and the reconciliation between the King and Princess, her court is as much crowded as it was before deserted. She has omitted no opportunity to show her zeal for His Majesty and his government; and our friend [Marlborough], who has no small credit with her, seems very resolved to contribute to the continuance of this union. . . . I do not see he is likely, at present, to get much by it, not yet having kissed the King's hand, but his reversion is very fair and great.[137]

It was only on 29 March 1695 that Marlborough kissed hands,[138] but Sarah herself did not meet the king in person for a year after the reconciliation: 'Having taken great Pains till then to avoid all Places where the King was, & I believe I should have continued it, but that my Lord Sunderland disswaded me from it.'[139]

For the princess, passing through this crucible was an experience which she was never to forget and which was to colour the rest of her life. She had learned, to her cost, the disadvantages attendant upon not possessing political power, the wisdom of caution, the practicality of guile rather than overt public display. Perhaps most importantly for the future, she had learned to rely upon the wisdom and patience of Marlborough while, at the same time, gaining a degree of independence from the impetuosity of Sarah.

4

'Mr Caliban'

William Alone,
1695–1702

The seven years between the death of Mary II and the death of William III were, in many ways, the most placid of Princess Anne's adult life. Despite this tranquillity, events were taking place both in her personal life and in the public affairs of Europe which were to determine the course of her reign as queen.

The princess's reconciliation with King William was largely superficial and ceremonial; they made formal calls upon each other frequently after January 1695, the princess served as the king's hostess on court occasions and at the great entertainments to mark his birthday on 5 November, while the king invariably sponsored a birthday ball for the princess on 6 February. In spite of these social courtesies, however, there was little personal warmth of feeling between the two cousins; the causes for their conflict continued and to a degree were intensified by Queen Mary's death.

The king was even more jealous of the princess's superior hereditary claim to the throne after the death of his wife had stressed the parliamentary, elective nature of his tenure in the monarchy; according to the Earl of Dartmouth,

> The Earl of Jersey told me, the King, besides hating her [the princess] most heartily (for he often said, if he had married her, he should have been the miserablest man upon earth), after the Queen died, was extremely jealous of her.[1]

For her part, the princess was angered when, after Queen Mary's death, the king confirmed his grant of James II's Irish estates to Elizabeth Villiers, without taking the princess's claims as an heir to James II into consideration;[2] furthermore the debt due to Prince George for the surrender of his mortgages in Holstein remained unpaid. Most importantly, however, even though the prince continued to attend council meetings regularly, both he and the princess were excluded from all intimate contact with the formulation of governmental policy. When the king left England in the spring of 1695, as he was to do every remaining year of his life, he established a council of regency to exercise the royal powers in his absence, a council composed of leading ministers rather than the heiress apparent, as all precedent dictated. Even the prince was excluded from the council of regency, on the grounds that his dignity would have been impaired had he served on a basis of equality with his social inferiors.[3] Compliments from the princess to the king on matters of state were also unwelcome; in September 1695, when William scored his single great victory during the Nine Years War in the Spanish Netherlands by capturing the citadel of Namur, the princess wrote him a letter of congratulation. When no reply arrived, Marlborough wrote to Portland to inquire about the king's silence but, according to Sarah, the king showed 'his brutal disregard' of the princess by never returning any answer.[4] Despite the unanimous concurrence of his ecclesiastical advisors, the king proved unwilling to appoint Gloucester's tutor, Samuel Pratt, a prebend of Windsor on the recommendation of the princess.[5]

The King's disregard was all the more galling to the princess, for in 1695 she also suffered from the embarrassment of her hysterical pregnancy; the condition which began in the autumn of 1694 continued well into 1695, even though it was secretly doubted at court as early as February 'whether the Princess be with child'.[6] By the princess's reckoning, the child should have been due in April or May 1695, but by April her doctor, Dr John Radcliffe, was publicly stating that the pregnancy was false. Radcliffe swore 'That Her Highness's Distemper was nothing but the Vapours, & that she was in as good a state of Health as any woman breathing, could she but give into the Belief of it'.[7] Although Radcliffe was the foremost physician of his time, the princess was furious with his diagnosis and thereafter harboured an aversion to him.[8] By late June, however, it was obvious that Radcliffe's pronouncement had been correct, that the princess had suffered from pseudocyesis for ten or twelve months, '& now after greate expectations, not with child &c'.[9]

This hysterical pregnancy accelerated the rapid physical decline of the princess. She had suffered severely from rheumatism during the summer of 1692,[10] and during the summer of 1693 had reported to Lady Marlborough that 'I have bin led about my chamber to day & was caryed into ye Garden for a little aire & ye uneasynes that stiring gives me now is very inconsiderable'.[11] By the beginning of 1695 the princess could not climb stairs;[12] a weakness in her legs had made her lame and unable to stand straight, symptoms which had appeared during the previous year.[13] The princess accepted her physical decline and increased disability with stoicism: 'I hope in ye next world I shall be at ease', she told Lady Marlborough, 'but in this I find I must not expect it long togather.'[14] By the end of the decade, when she was only thirty-five, the princess was an invalid, unable to walk without aid for any distance.

Of even greater concern to the princess than her own weakness was the continued ill health of the Duke of Gloucester; the young boy was repeatedly ill of a fever between March and May 1695. Although she should have been confined to Berkeley House because of her supposed pregnancy, she could not leave Gloucester alone at Campden House. Jenkin Lewis recorded that 'The Princess, who loved him to a great degree, came in her sedan chair, and was carried upstairs with short polls'.[15] The ill health of both Gloucester and the princess contributed to the new routine which her household adopted and which was to remain essentially the same throughout the remainder of her life. Shortly after the reconciliation with William, the king had given her St James's Palace as her London town house although, due to the necessity of removing many of its occupants to the Cockpit and undertaking repairs and redecoration, the prince and princess did not occupy it until the end of 1695. In the summers, the prince and princess habitually resided at Windsor, where they had purchased a small house in Windsor Great Park during their quarrel with William and Mary.[16] From 1695 on, however, the prince and princess resided in the main castle. William III sometimes hunted in the park, but he had little interest in the castle and rarely resided there, preferring instead Cardinal Wolsey's great palace at Hampton Court, which Sir Christopher Wren was extensively remodelling to suit seventeenth-century taste. Perhaps because Hampton Court was very much William III's personal project, Princess Anne was never demonstrably interested in it; although the work on Hampton Court continued into her reign and she and Prince George were idealized in the interior frescoes, only once when she was queen – in 1710 – did the court officially reside there. She did, however, use it occasionally as a half-way point between Windsor and London where she could meet her ministers. Windsor was to remain Princess Anne's great love throughout her life.

By the end of 1695 the princess had discovered that she was once again pregnant, but on 17 February 1696 she miscarried a daughter, her twelfth child.[17] The miscarriage came at the very moment when the government, menaced by a new Jacobite invasion headed by James II, who had reached the French coast, had discovered the existence of an 'Assassination Plot' directed against King William. The original Jacobite plan was to ambush the king at Turnham Green as he waited for a barge

107

to carry his hunting party across the Thames to Hampton Court. Politically, the Assassination Plot was a godsend for William III, immensely bolstering his popularity throughout the country, and for the Revolution settlement. Parliament immediately passed an association (modelled on the Elizabethan statute directed against Mary, Queen of Scots) in which William was recognized as the 'rightful and lawful' king, and all office holders under the crown were obliged to swear to avenge his death, should he be killed by treasonable means; even Lady Marlborough and the other ladies of the princess's household took the oath.[18] By providing that Parliament should immediately be assembled upon the death of the king and should remain in existence for six months thereafter, the association guaranteed that Anne would become queen instantly should William be killed. Furthermore, the Assassination Plot, which had been managed by James II's son the Duke of Berwick, ensured that William would be unlikely to listen to proposals to adopt the Prince of Wales. Nevertheless, according to James II's *Memoirs*, in 1696 Princess Anne asked her father to allow her to accept the crown after William's death and 'accompanyd this request with a seeming sence of her duty, and a rediness to make restitution when opertunitys should Serve'. James, who refused this request,[19] might well have wondered what 'restitution' the princess proposed, while her son Gloucester was still living. For the benefit of their French paymasters, the Jacobites at St Germain repeated their allegations that the princess favoured their cause,[20] but while Gloucester lived they could not have seriously believed this.

Gloucester's importance in the public mind as the Protestant heir was growing, largely because it was becoming increasingly doubtful that either the king or the princess would produce additional heirs. On Gloucester's seventh birthday, 24 July 1696, he was inducted into the Order of the Garter at Windsor in a ceremony which was attended by the whole court and followed by a dinner and a ball, all at the expense of the king, who was campaigning in the Spanish Netherlands.[21] Two months later, the princess miscarried a son in the sixth month of her thirteenth pregnancy, a failure which was attributed to a fall she had suffered a month previously.[22] On 25 March 1697, six months later, the princess suffered yet another miscarriage, her third in thirteen months.[23]

The princess, in common with many of William III's ministers, was a mere spectator of the negotiations which the king was conducting with Louis XIV and which were to bring the Nine Years War to a conclusion in the Treaty of Ryswick in September 1697. The most substantial provision of the Ryswick agreement was Louis XIV's recognition of

William III and his heirs as *de facto* monarchs of Great Britain and his promise not to 'give or afford any assistance, directly or indirectly, to any enemy' (i.e. James II and his son) of William III;[24] in effect, Louis acknowledged the loss of French influence over British affairs, which altered the balance of power in Europe. Nevertheless, France still remained the single greatest military power on the Continent and the triumphs of Louis's early years, if dimmed by the inconclusive outcome of the Nine Years War, were yet potent in the minds of the allied powers. What had enabled the Maritime Powers and their allies to withstand the power of the Grand Monarch was the new financial base being laid in England by William III's government, now largely dominated by the Whigs. In 1694 the Bank of England had been established and the concept of the 'national debt' introduced; in 1696 the coinage of the kingdom had been completely revised to place it on a sound basis. The financial expansion to which these two events contributed enabled William III to consolidate his position.

The recoinage affected the princess directly, for it led to her estrangement from her long-time comptroller and personal friend, Sir Benjamin Bathurst, and indirectly contributed to the increased authority of Lady Marlborough within the princess's household. Prior to the recoinage, guineas had usually been reckoned at thirty shillings, but by law their value was now reduced to twenty-one shillings. According to Sarah, writing several years later, Sir Benjamin 'had made up his accounts with the Prince and Princess, as if they had still been 30 shillings which the Duchess [of Marlborough] detected & rectified, with her usual spirit & zeal against everything dishonest & deceitful'.[25] However well-intentioned Sarah's zeal, its effects could hardly be anything but offensive to Sir Benjamin and his wife; the princess, while grateful to Sarah for preserving one third of her fortune, cautioned her to hold her tongue and promised to be more careful herself in supervising her own business (warnings which Sarah later forgot after the princess became queen):

> I think it will be better not to say any thing to ye Lady Bathurst about her husbands faults, for it will do no good, & since there is no body perfect but deare Mrs. Freeman, I must have patience with ye rest of ye world, & look as much into all my afairs as I can, if I weare not satisfyed with you, I should by ye greatest Monster that ever breathed, for as I have often said, I do realy beleive there never was, nor will be, such a freind as deare Mrs. Freeman.[26]

Even more distressing to the princess was her discovery in April 1697 that Sir Benjamin was selling offices in her household '& in a most shameful manner, which has given me a much greater abhorrance of him then ever'.[27] The details were particularly sordid: 'ye Yeoman of ye Wine sellar', the Dutch cook, a new undercook, and Gloucester's cook, among others, had been pressed by Sir Benjamin to give him a 'gratuity' in return for their offices, even though Sir Benjamin had not influenced their appointment.[28] When the princess confronted Sir Benjamin with the confessions of these servants, he claimed that they had given him the money (totalling several hundred pounds) voluntarily, but the princess responded that 'it was soe unlikely a thing that people that had theire places given them by a Master & Mistris should think of offering him money' that 'it was very plaine by his way of speakeing to see that what he said was false'.[29] Bathurst, although he was to continue in the princess's service until his death in 1704, lost any remaining credit with his mistress through this incident, and it strengthened the princess's conviction that she should have 'a Mrs. Freeman in every post in my family':

> I think it is very hard that I who love to live well, should pay more & be worse served then any body upon earth, & therefore I will try if I can put things in a better method, tho it will be impossible for me to have every thing don to my mind unless I could meet with a Mrs · Freeman in every post in my family, but her fellow I doe really beleive is not to be found the world over, & I am sure I never can have any freind that will bee so deare to me as she is.[30]

Sarah seized upon this domestic contretemps in the princess's household to request a place for one of her impecunious relatives when the princess's lifelong nurse, Ellen Bust, should die. Nepotism such as this was not regarded by the age of Anne as being nearly as venal as the sale of offices, which were usually obtained by the highest bidder regardless of merit; indeed, nepotism was time-honoured and commonplace in seventeenth-century courts. The indigent relatives who were recommended were expected to be reasonably competent in performing their assigned duties, whether menial or ceremonial, and the system had the twin advantages of relieving the patron of a financial burden while placing a protégé in a position of potential influence or utility. In this case, however, the appointment was eventually to have explosive consequences.

The position in question was that of a bedchamber woman, which was inferior to that of a lady of the bedchamber (the position which Sarah and, later, her daughters held). Ladies of the bedchamber were women of noble birth or marriage who served as social companions to the princess and attended her at court functions. Bedchamber women, on the other hand, performed the menial tasks of personal maids. In 1728, Sarah's cousin, Abigail Hill, the object of Lady Marlborough's generosity in 1697, wrote a detailed description of the post which eventually made her famous:

> The bedchamber-*woman* came in to waiting before the Queen's prayers, which was before Her Majesty was dressed. The Queen often shifted in a morning: if Her Majesty shifted at noon, the bedchamber-*lady* being by, the bedchamber-*woman* gave the shift to the *lady* without any ceremony, and the *lady* put it on. Sometimes, likewise, the bedchamber-*woman* gave the fan to the *lady* in the same manner; and this was all that the bechamber-*lady* did about the Queen at her dressing.
> When the Queen washed her hands, the page of the back-stairs brought and set down upon a side-table the basin and ewer; then the bedchamber-*woman* set it before the Queen, and knelt on the other side of the table over against the Queen, the bedchamber-*lady* only looking on. The bedchamber-*woman* poured the water out of the ewer upon the Queen's hands.
> The bedchamber-*woman* pulled on the Queen's gloves, when she could not do it herself.
> The page of the back-stairs was called in to put on the Queen's shoes.
> When the Queen dined in public, the page reached the glass to the bedchamber-*woman*, and she to the *lady* in waiting.
> The bedchamber-*woman* brought the chocolate, and gave it without kneeling.
> In general, the bedchamber-*woman* had no dependence on the *lady* of the bedchamber.[31]

In later years Sarah never tired of writing about her cousins the Hills, and her account of them in her *Conduct* is a classic of polished malice. In an earlier, hitherto unpublished account, she provided much more detail about the Hills (who, despite their temporary prominence at the end of Queen Anne's reign, still remain obscure figures to posterity):

> I can't bee possitive whether it was before, or Just after the revolution that Mrs. Chudleigh, a cousen of the Duke of Marlboroughs, came to me & told me that I had a relation, Mrs. Hill, with a husband and four children that she beleived I did not know which were reduced to want of bread by projects [i.e. speculations] & losses at sea, & that Mr. Hill had kept his misfortunes as long as hee could from his wife, but now hee could strugle no longer & they were all in so miserable a condition that she was sure I would doe what I could to releive them, upon which I presently gave her what I had about me for there present ease which was ten Guinneas & after that I did what I could to support them till opertunitys happened that I could provide better for them.

111

Sarah was not acquainted with Mrs Hill, her aunt, as her grandfather had had twenty-two children; nevertheless, she immediately assumed responsibility for the Hills' four children, persuading Godolphin to give the oldest son a post in 'the Publick revenue' which he held until his untimely death from smallpox; the younger son (later 'the Great General'), Jack Hill, she put to school at St Albans, securing him a position as page of honour to the Prince of Denmark in 1694[32] '& I took care of his allowance which was not enough with out some helps just as if I had been his mother'. He was later given a regiment through Sarah's influence with her husband, 'although my lord always said that Jack Hill was good for nothing'.[33]

The two daughters, Abigail and Alice, posed a greater problem, 'it being more difficult to dispose of women'; they were both taken into Sarah's home at St Albans, where Sarah nursed the elder sister, Abigail, through smallpox, 'using her with all the kindnesse imagineable'. When Ellen Bust's health made it obvious in April 1697 that a vacancy for a bedchamber woman to the princess would soon occur, Sarah had some hesitation about asking the princess to appoint Abigail,

> because her misfortunes had obliged her to serve [i.e. as a menial in a private home], & upon that I ask'd advise, to which my friends said, I need not make any difficulty in that for if she had not been a Gentlewoman, there was non in the Princess's family at that time that were Gentlewomen, except Mrs. Danvers [the eldest daughter of the seventh Baron Chandos], who had in some measure lost the advantage of her birth, by having marryd a trads man.[34]

Consequently, in April 1697, apparently bolstered by this reasoning, Sarah put her request to the princess, who replied on 21 April,

> As to what you say about Mrs. Hill you may asure you self she shall have ye place you desire for her when ever Bust dyes, I . . . never will engage myself in nothinge without knowing first whether any thing that lyes in my power can be ye least servisable to deare Mrs. Freeman who need never use any arguments for any thinge she has a mind to.[35]

We know virtually nothing about Abigail Hill, considering that she eventually became a figure of European importance: there are a few surviving letters (written in a strong, well-educated hand), yet she remains today a shadowy figure; even the portrait once thought to be hers has been called into question by the National Portrait Gallery. During the ten crucial years between her appointment as a bedchamber woman in 1697 and her marriage in 1707, we know of her activities only what Lady Marlborough was later to discover in her attempts to elucidate how Abigail had gained such a powerful influence over their mistress. Neither Mrs Morley nor Mrs Freeman had the slightest suspicion in 1697 that the appointment of Abigail Hill as a mere bed-chamber woman would ultimately destroy their friendship.

Of more immediate importance, the princess was becoming in-creasingly concerned in a financial dispute with the king relating to James II's Irish estates which, as Duke of York, he had settled upon his children after his death. As we have already seen, William III had ignored this settlement. These properties had been included in a blind trust early in 1692, immediately after the princess had left the Cockpit, but after Queen Mary's death they had been openly granted to Elizabeth Villiers[36] who subsequently married Lord Orkney. In 1697, despite the fact that 'a great many of the bishops . . . were possessed with a notion that the Princess was mightily against this Bill',[37] Lady Orkney obtained from the Irish Parliament a confirmation of the king's grant in a bill of Outlawries, which had to be confirmed by the Privy Council of England. The princess instructed Bathurst to

> get me a Copy of an Irish bill that is now before ye Councill here . . .
> & ye best way to do it will be to employ some body, without nameing
> me, to give a giney or two to one of ye Clerks of ye Councill for it,
> which is a thing I'me told they will refuse no body.[38]

This surreptitious method apparently did not work, however, and a week later the princess instructed Sir Benjamin 'to go to ye Attorney generall [Sir Thomas Trevor] from me, & tell him I desire a coppy of ye Bill of Outlawrys not knowing but that I may be conserned in it'.[39] Armed with this information, the princess made a direct appeal to the king not to allow the grant to Lady Orkney to be confirmed by an Act of Parliament:

> The occation of my giveing your Majesty the trouble of this letter, pro-ceeds from my having been informed that a Grant which your Majesty made some years sence of the Irish estates which was the late King my fathers when Duke of York, & then settled upon his children after his death, is now designed to be Confirmed by Act of Parliament. I am apt to beleive your Majesty has not been informed of this estates being thus settled & have therefore taken the liberty to speak to my Lord Chamberlain [the Earl of Sunderland] to put a stop to any further steps upon this bill till I had acquainted your Majesty with it.
> I beg leave to asure your Majesty that I doe it with the greatest respect & duty imaginable & with the greatest sence of your kindnesse to me, who shall allways bee very far from enterposeing to hinder the Effects of your Majestys bounty & favor in any case, & I am confident your Majesty is soe well perswaded of this, that being now made

acquainted in what manner this estate has been long since settled, your Majesty will have the goodnesse to lett the grant rest upon its own strength, & not give it your countenance for a conformation by Act of Parliament.[40]

'This letter', Sarah noted upon her copy, 'had no effect upon King William.' The princess never succeeded in gaining control of any of her father's private property.

Another cause for acrimony between the king and the princess was Parliament's grant in 1697 of an additional £100,000 to the civil list for two specific purposes. Some £50,000 was granted for the annual payment of Mary of Modena's marital jointure as provided by the Treaty of Ryswick; William had promised this payment on the mistaken impression that Louis XIV had agreed to 'invite' the Jacobite court to retire to Rome or, at the very least, to Avignon which was still a papal enclave, where the Stuarts' dependence upon the papacy would be constantly visible to the British public. Actually, Louis XIV had no intention of staining his *gloire* by revoking his hospitality to his cousin. James II remained at St Germain-en-Laye and the jointure remained unpaid. William simply pocketed the money.[41] The second £50,000 was granted by Parliament for the establishment of a separate household for the Duke of Gloucester, now eight years old and at the age when boys were usually taken out of women's hands and placed under male governors. Despite Parliament's intention, the king allotted only £15,000 for the maintenance of Gloucester's household, again pocketing the difference and – according to Sarah – forcing the princess to pay out of her own pocket some of the necessary expenses.[42]

Relations between the king and the princess were further embittered by William's determination that the princess would have a minimal influence in the new household. The position of governor was first offered to Shrewsbury, who declined the appointment on grounds of ill health.[43] Whether this first offer was known to the princess remains uncertain, but in December 1697 the king offered the position to Marlborough, who was certainly the princess's first choice.[44] Marlborough's appointment was not due to any change of heart on William's part regarding his sister-in-law, but was influenced by the rapidly growing power of the king's new, young, Dutch favourite, Arnold Joost van Keppel, whom the king had just created Earl of Albemarle. The twenty-seven-year-old earl had largely replaced Portland (who had been dispatched to Paris as ambassador to Louis XIV) as the king's confidant and – some whispered – lover. Portland was insanely jealous of Albemarle's influence and, naturally, Marlborough supported Albemarle against his longstanding enemy, Portland. As a consequence both of Albemarle's influence and the end of the war (when Marl-borough's role as a military commander was no longer a potential danger to William's position), Marlborough found himself once again in favour with the king, a favour which he used over the next four years to pave the way for the princess's accession to the throne.[45] In June 1698, Marlborough entered the cabinet, was restored to the Privy Council and – on William's departure for the Dutch republic – was named one of the lords justices,[46] a position which he was to hold each summer through-out the remainder of William's reign.

At the same time that Marlborough's appointment as Gloucester's governor was decided upon in December 1697 (the formal appointment was not made until 19 June 1698),[47] the king appointed Bishop Burnet as Gloucester's chief preceptor. The princess, who had requested that Dr George Hooper, Dean of Canterbury, be appointed,[48] was furious; according to the Earl of Dartmouth, she always thought Burnet's appointment 'one of the greatest hardships put upon her by the King, who knew how disagreeable he was to her, and [she] believed it was done for that reason'.[49] Burnet himself had some hesitation about becoming Gloucester's preceptor: 'I had some intimations that I was not acceptable to the Princess and though she by my Lord Godolphin sent me assurances to the contrary, yet I had reason to believe there was some ground for it', he recalled. Burnet tried to excuse himself on the grounds that he was mourning the recent death of his wife, but the king insisted that he accept the appointment. 'I saw all that Court except Lord Marlborough and his Lady were against me, I lived well with them and I thought that was enough', Burnet concluded in referring to his tenure in Gloucester's household.[50]

Under pressure from Sunderland and Marlborough to placate the princess, the king sent word that she could choose the lower servants in Gloucester's household. Happy with this prospect, the princess selected Godolphin's nephew, Hugh Boscawen, and the son of the secretary of state, James Vernon jr, as grooms, the sons of the Earls of Bridgewater and Berkeley as pages, and made promises of positions to other people. Shortly before William left England in the summer of 1698 for his annual sojourn in the Dutch republic, Marlborough presented him with the list of the princess's choices. The king flew into a rage, declaring that 'she shall not be Queen before her time', and proclaiming that he alone would nominate all of Gloucester's servants. Even though Marlborough counselled patience, the princess was furious that she would have to go back on promises already made:

> My hart is soe full of this last mortification that has happened to me,
> that I can nether think nor writt on any other Subject, & therefore I

must tell my deare Mrs. Freeman, tho I submitt to this Brutal ussage because my freinds think it fitt (whos Judgment I shall ever prefer before my own) my hart is touched to that degree as is not to be exprest, for to have people imposed upon one (tho all perfection) is soe disagreeable a thing that I can never have no Satisfaction, besides ye melencoly prospect one has of perpetuall uneasyness on one account or another.[51]

In the course of the summer, through Marlborough's influence, Albemarle was able to bring the king to reason, and when the royal nominations were returned to England in September 1698 the king had approved almost all of the princess's choices. Sarah, who had been anxious to provide for Jack Hill, who had 'grown too big' for his position as page to Prince George, had suggested him as a third groom of the bedchamber to the Duke of Gloucester, 'it being reasonable to have more than two Grooms of the Bedchamber, who were to run after a Child from morning till night'; but, 'forseeing that the King would strike out any body who had nothing to support them but their Service to the Prince or Princess', Sarah had kept Jack Hill's name off the list submitted to the king.

I thought the Princess might add him after all the others were fix'd, & that it was impossible at the King's Return for Him to turn him out. This Stratagem succeeded so well, that I am not sure whether the King ever knew Mr. Hill was Groom of the Bedchamber.[52]

While the question of Gloucester's household was being argued, the princess suffered two further miscarriages, the first in December 1697, of twins, 'too early to determine their sex'.[53] During the summer of 1698, her activities were again curtailed by her sixteenth pregnancy. In July, physicians met in consultation to decide whether or not, for fear of miscarriage, she should travel to Windsor;[54] although the princess decided to undertake the journey, it was reported in August that she 'does not stir out, being above twenty weeks gone with child, and she hopes, by care, to avoid those misfortunes she is too subject to'.[55] Such precautions, however, were to no avail. On 4 September she fell seriously ill and on 15 September, in the sixth month of her pregnancy, miscarried a male infant which her surgeon guessed 'might have been dead eight or ten days'.[56] To a limited extent, the princess's grief over the failure of these pregnancies was mitigated by the successful conclusion of negotiations for the marriage of the eldest Marlborough daughter, Lady Henrietta Churchill, to Francis Godolphin, the only son and heir of the princess's close advisor. 'Lady Harriet' had always been the princess's particular favourite among the Marlborough children and she used the

116

occasion of the negotiations to offer to give 'my poor mite . . . being offer'd from a hart, that is with out any reserve, with more passion & sincerely, my deare deare Mrs. Freemans, then any other can be capable off'.[57] The following day, the princess explained that 'my poor mite' was £10,000, a colossal sum by the standards of the day:

> I am ashamed to say how little I can contribute towards it [the marriage], but since Millions could not expresse ye Sincere kindness I have for you, I hope deare Mrs. Freeman will accsept of £10,000, a poor offering from such a faithful hart as mine.[58]

The Marlboroughs, who were already well established financially, decided to accept only half the amount the princess offered, and Sarah's response to the princess bore every mark of gratitude. The princess reassured her that

> My Dear Mrs. Freeman has no reason to be uneasy with the thoughts that She can never do enough to Deserve my Kindness, . . . for she has done more then ever any mortall did to merit anothers friendship & it is very kind in seting so great a vallue upon so poor an expression as I have made of my truth, which upon my word I am not satisfied with, it comeing far short of what my heart is inclined to do, but as long as I live I must be Endeavouring to shew that never any body had a Sincerer passion for another then I have for my Dear Dear Mrs. Freeman.[59]

Francis Godolphin and Lady Harriet Churchill were married in April 1698, thereby cementing the personal friendship which had progressed into a political alliance between Godolphin and the Marlboroughs. The princess was less pleased, however, when the Marlboroughs concluded another alliance with an old friend in the following year by marrying their second daughter (and the princess's namesake and god-daughter), Lady Anne Churchill, to Lord Charles Spencer, the son and heir of Robert, Earl of Sunderland. Despite Sunderland's intervention on her behalf with William III during the reconciliation, the princess had not completely lost her distrust of him, which had been formed during the reign of James II; in this, she mirrored the attitude of almost every politician, Whig or Tory, in England. Also Lord Charles Spencer was an obnoxious young man, hot-headed, intemperate, fiercely partisan; at the time of his second marriage in 1699 (his first wife, a sister of the Duke of Hamilton, had died in childbirth), Spencer was a full-blown republican who publicly wished for the day when the aristocracy would be abolished and he would be plain *Mr* Charles Spencer.

Marlborough himself was not keen on the proposed marriage of his favourite daughter to such a husband,[60] but Sarah, using Godolphin

117

and his sister Mrs Jael Boscawen as her intermediaries with Lord and Lady Sunderland, pressed the marriage; she was enchanted both by Spencer's Whig ideology and by the intellectual prowess of the young man, who was already assembling one of the most important private libraries in England. In terms of temperament, Sarah and Spencer had much in common.

There are fewer extant letters from the princess to Lady Marlborough during the years 1699 and 1700 than during any other period of their friendship. There are two possible explanations of this void: either Lady Marlborough was at St James's more often and there was no need for the princess to write (which seems improbable), or, for reasons of her own, Lady Marlborough chose to destroy the princess's letters during this period. It seems possible, albeit speculative, that the princess and Lady Marlborough may have had some disagreement over the personal merits of Lord Charles Spencer in 1699, a precursor of their quarrel over his political merits in 1705 and 1706. Nevertheless, the princess contributed another £5,000 to the bride's portion and made both Lady Harriet and Lady Anne ladies of her bedchamber.

The marriage of the Marlboroughs' daughters and the princess's generosity, the necessity of spending some of her own income on Gloucester's household, and the increase in her own 'family' all induced the princess to look for further sources of income. One obvious hope was for the repayment of Prince George's Holstein mortgages, which he had surrendered in 1689 and for which he had as yet received not one penny. There appears to be no record of how the king was finally influenced to take steps to honour his debt, but the assumption must be that the growing power of the Tories in the country, and of their leaders who were by 1699 ardently paying their court to the heiress presumptive at St James's Palace, must have been influential.

From the end of the Nine Years War, anti-monarchical feeling in the country had been growing, associated as the monarchy was with a standing army, with favouritism of foreigners (the Dutch in particular), and with heavy wartime taxation. The discretionary powers of the monarch had suffered a severe limitation in 1694, when political exigency had forced William to assent to the Triennial Act, which limited the duration of Parliament's life to a maximum of three years, after which a general election was mandatory. Although William had commenced his reign with a predominantly Tory ministry, regarding the Tories as the natural allies of the monarchy, wartime necessity had led the king to rely increasingly upon the Whigs, who supported British involvement on the Continent while the Tories opted for a 'Little England' naval and colonial strategy against France. Consequently, by

1697 the Tories were ready to oppose the court at every juncture, even going so far as to mandate the return of William's personal Dutch Guards to their native land. While Rochester and Nottingham led the traditional Tories, who were pledged to the defence of the monarchy and the Church of England, an increasingly important but anomalous group in the House of Commons, sometimes referred to as 'country Whigs' (to distinguish them from the 'court Whigs' on whom William had relied), was led by Robert Harley, the scion of a West Country royalist family with a Noncomformist background who had made himself the foremost parliamentary strategist of the day. It is impossible to know exactly when Harley came into close contact with the princess; a private memorandum in which he summarized his career suggests ('Mr. H: often attending on the Princess Anne by her Command') that it began in 1700, but Harley's chronology in the same memoir is deficient in other points, and their contact may well have begun in the autumn of 1699.[61]

Certainly, by this time Harley (who was now speaker of the House) was working closely with Rochester, Marlborough, and Godolphin. The princess was a natural Tory. Not only were the Whigs suspected of being secretly republican at heart (and had they not opposed her parliamentary grant in 1689?), but their influence had also been paramount in the passage of the Toleration Act of 1689, which removed the laws enforcing Anglican conformity and granted freedom of worship to all Protestants (but not to Roman Catholics). The Tories were the natural defenders of the Church of England and as such attracted the princess, to whom the Church increasingly provided consolation for the children which she had lost.

In November 1699, King William recommended to Parliament that Prince George's mortgage debt should be paid in its entirety. In the Commons debates which followed, the Tories seized the opportunity to attack Bishop Burnet's appointment as tutor to the Duke of Gloucester.[62] When a vote was taken on a motion to petition the king to remove Burnet from his position, it was defeated by 173 to 133, partly because Marlborough actively campaigned on the bishop's behalf.[63] When, in February 1700, the House finally agreed to pay William's debt to the prince, the princess attributed the victory entirely to the influence of the Marlboroughs:

> I was once going to endeavour to thank your Lord my Self for what was don last night conserning ye Princes business, it being wholly oweing to your & his kindness, or els I am sure it would never have bin brought to any efect, but I durst not do it, for feare of not being able to express ye true Sense of my poor hart, & therefore I must

119

desire my deare Mrs. Freeman to say a great deale both for Mr. Morly
& my self & tho we are poor in words, be soe Just as to beleeve we are
truly sensible & most faithfull yours, & as for your faithfull Morley be
assur'd She is more if it be possible then ever, my deare deare Mrs.
Freemans.[64]

The Marlboroughs' detractors, both among their contemporaries and
among historians, have found little to justify the honours which the
princess was to shower upon their family immediately after her accession to the throne, but Princess Anne obviously regarded it as a deferred
repayment for great services which the earl and countess had rendered
in the past.

By the time the prince's debt was honoured by Parliament, the
princess had suffered another miscarriage – on 24 January 1700 – of a
male, 'within six weeks of her time', but the baby was judged to have
been 'dead in her a month'.[65] It was the princess's seventeenth
pregnancy, and the seventeenth child she had lost (including twins); of
her progeny, only Gloucester remained. Although her hopes for children
did not die with this loss, she was never again to conceive.

Even more tragic, however, was the death of the only surviving child
of the prince and princess six months later. On 24 July the family
celebrated the Duke of Gloucester's eleventh birthday at Windsor, while
the boy complained of chills and a sore throat; on 26 July he developed a
fever, and the next day the doctors let blood, after which he felt better.
That evening the fever returned, and 'he went into delierium with short
broken sleep and Incoherent Talke'.[66] The princess spent night and day
next to her son's bed but, overcome by fatigue and despair at his
condition, which was now clearly smallpox, she fainted on the evening
of 28 July, reportedly when one of her doctors refused to spend the
night with her son.[67] The Marlboroughs, who were at Althorp visiting
Lord and Lady Sunderland, were hurriedly summoned and they arrived
at Windsor on the afternoon of 29 July.[68] Late that evening, with his
parents at his beside, the young duke developed pronounced breathing
difficulties and early on the morning of 30 July he died. An autopsy was
made the following day, during which 'the head was opened, and out of
the first and second Ventricles of the Cerebrum were taken about four
ounces and halfe of a lympid Humour'.[69]

Gloucester's body was taken by barge from Windsor to Westminster
on 1 August, where it lay in state in the Painted Chamber of the Palace
of Westminster until 9 August, when it was interred in the Stuart Tomb
in Westminster Abbey.[70] The prince and princess remained in seclusion
at Windsor, the princess refusing to see any of her household except
Lady Marlborough.[71] She was 'daily carried in her chair to the garden,

120

to divert her melancholly thoughts'.[72] Although she believed at that time that she might again be pregnant (a hope which proved to be false),[73] the loss of the last surviving child of the eighteen children she had borne was grievous. Princess Anne never entirely recovered from the death of Gloucester and thereafter, in her letters to Sarah, constantly alluded to herself as 'your poor unfortunate faithfull Morley', a deliberate play on the Churchill family motto, 'Faithful but Unfortunate'.

The news of Gloucester's death was also tragic from the king's point of view. When it reached The Hague five days later, William III immediately wrote a note of sympathy to his sister-in-law which, in its simplicity, underlined the fact that Gloucester's death affected him deeply:

> I do not believe it necessary to use many words to tell you of the surprise and sorrow with which I learned of the death of the Duke of Gloucester. It is so great a loss for me and for all England that my heart is pierced with affliction. I assure you that on this occasion and on any other I shall be glad to give you any marks of my friendship.[74]

For the king and the nation, the death of the Duke of Gloucester posed an obvious problem: how should the succession to the crown be delineated after his death and that of the princess? One obvious candidate was the Prince of Wales, now twelve, who might either be reared in, or later converted to, the Church of England. He, of course, would possess a better hereditary claim to the crown than either William or Anne. Such thoughts were equally obvious to the princess and her advisors. After Anne's death in 1714, an unidentified correspondent at The Hague reported to Hanover that, immediately after Gloucester's death, the princess had sent an express to St Germain, asking permission to succeed William and promising to restore the Prince of Wales thereafter. The report further claimed that the British ambassador in Paris, the Earl of Manchester, had learned of the princess's request and had dispatched John Chetwynd to Het Loo, William's country home, with the news.[75]

This account, published by Lamberty in 1730, was contradicted in 1735 by Christian Cole, who had been Manchester's secretary in Paris. Cole published Manchester's letters, which proved that Chetwynd went to Het Loo on quite different business and that he left Paris before news of Gloucester's sudden death arrived in France.[76]

The details of this particular story are therefore not credible, but it seems likely that some such promise was made at this time. In June 1701, Marlborough was holding conferences with the chief Jacobite agent in London (James St Amand, whose code name was 'Berry') on the basis of 'securing Godal's [King James's] Estate to him after Knitely's [King William's] death'. Immediately after James II died in September 1701, Mary of Modena wrote to the princess, describing Anne's dying father's wish 'to confirm you in the resolution of repaireing to his Son the wrong done to himself'. In later years, the Pretender was also convinced that Anne had made this promise to their father.[77] The question is not whether the promise was made, but why. The inescapable conclusion is that the princess was attempting to secure her own peaceful accession to the throne after William III's death by suggesting to the exiled court that, if the Jacobites had patience, they would find their reward in the next reign, now fast approaching because of the visible decline of William's health.

By September 1700, William III and his predominantly Tory ministry had decided that, after the king and the princess and their respective heirs, the succession should be vested in the next Protestant heir to the throne, Sophia, dowager Electress of Brunswick Luneburg (more commonly known in England after its capital city, Hanover) and a granddaughter of James I. This idea had been broached in 1689, immediately after the Revolution, when the king had informed the Privy Council that the Prince and Princess of Denmark agreed that Sophia should be named heiress after their issue, but the birth of the Duke of Gloucester had removed the necessity of further delineating the Protestant succession by statute law.[78] Despite her promises to the Jacobite court, which were only a continuation of the policy which the princess, Marlborough, and Godolphin had initiated in 1691 and which was to continue long into the future to remove the fangs from any Jacobite threat, every piece of evidence suggests that the princess warmly supported the Hanoverian succession. The Act of Settlement passed by Parliament in June 1701 vested the succession in the Electress Sophia and her Protestant heirs, should the king and the Princess of Denmark die without children. Just as the Tories had contributed the crucial balance to the coalition against James II in the Revolution, they were now largely responsible for enacting the Hanoverian succession; among the princess's advisors, Godolphin and Rochester were among the first to support Sophia's pretensions,[79] while Robert Harley guided the Act of Settlement through the House of Commons. Foreign diplomats in London unanimously concluded that the princess supported the Hanoverian succession, particularly the Dutch resident, L'Hermitage,[80] who had close ties with William III's court. The Prussian resident in London, Friedrich Bonet, reached the same conclusion during the parliamentary debates on the Act of Settlement: 'I do not see that Madame the Princess of Denmark takes offense at this succession; very far from that, she looks upon it as a support for her.'[81]

The Act of Settlement, as originally passed, placed severe limitations on the powers of future monarchs. On William's death, future monarchs were to be communicants of the Church of England and were to obtain parliamentary consent for leaving Great Britain (a slap at William's annual trips to the Dutch republic). On the death of the Princess of Denmark, the nation was not to be obliged to fight for Hanoverian interests, all matters were to be considered and approved by the Privy Council (rather than smaller, secret cabinets), and only native-born Englishmen were to be able to hold office under the crown.[82] So onerous were the restrictions placed on the future Hanoverian heirs that the elector, Georg Ludwig, suspected that the Tories wished to make the succession so unpalatable that Hanover would reject it, thereby opening the way to the Prince of Wales.[83]

The Princess of Denmark, as a counter-point to her policy with the Jacobites, was also determined to keep a Hanoverian heir out of the kingdom. In part, this was a feminine foible, but she was mainly intent on preserving her own *gloire*. Like Elizabeth or, to a lesser extent, Victoria, she could bear no thought of an heir, of eyes and thoughts diverted from the setting to the rising sun. Furthermore, her own experience in opposition to William and Mary between 1692 and 1694 had shown her clearly what use the two political parties could make of a rival court in England, headed either by the heiress presumptive the Electress Sophia, or by her grandson the Electoral Prince Georg August (later George II). Therefore, when the king planned to bring the electoral prince to England in the autumn of 1701 for a visit, the princess prevented Georg August's trip by falsely informing the king that she was again pregnant.[84] The princess was chiefly motivated by the Tories assiduously trying to convince her that William planned to establish the electoral prince as heir and to supplant her. According to the second Lord Dartmouth who was a staunch Tory, two Whigs, the Dukes of Bolton and Newcastle, proposed such a plan to him,

> and used the strongest argument to induce me to come into it, which was, that it would be making Lord Marlborough King, at least for her time, if the Princess succeeded; and that I had reason to expect nothing but ill usage during such a reign. Lord Marlborough asked me afterwards in the House of Lords, if I had ever heard of such a design; I told him yes, but did not think it very likely. He said it was very true; but by God, if ever they attempted it, we would walk over their bellies.[85]

Even before William's death, therefore, there was a degree of jealousy and competition between the princess and the house of Hanover which would carry over into her reign and reach its climax during the last years of her life.

While the princess spent most of 1700 and 1701 in seclusion, mourning the death of the Duke of Gloucester, events were taking place which were to affect the future of Europe and determine the future course of her life. From the moment of Carlos II's accession to the Spanish throne at the age of four in 1665, European diplomats had anxiously been awaiting the death of the last of the Spanish Habsburgs. The product of generations of in-breeding between the Vienna and Madrid branches of the Habsburgs, the Spanish king was a classic example of genetic degeneration, feeble in both mind and body. From the division of Charles V's great empire in the sixteenth century, Habsburg policy had been to keep all their possessions in the family, but with the impending end of the Spanish line, no one in Europe except the emperor, Leopold I, believed that Spain and its possessions would be inherited intact by an Austrian Habsburg; indeed, the French had a very good claim to part of the Spanish inheritance, as both Louis XIII and Louis XIV had married the eldest daughters of Spanish kings and their renunciations of their Spanish heritage were at least debatable at law. Although Spain had, throughout the seventeenth century, been declining in wealth and power, its possessions were still formidable: Naples and Sicily, the Milanese, the Spanish Netherlands, the Philippines, and Spanish America. Both Great Britain and the Dutch republic had vested interests in the future disposition of the Spanish Netherlands, so crucial to their safety, and commercial interests in Italy and Spanish America. Foreseeing the imminent death of Carlos II, both Louis XIV and William III worked to avoid a new European war by partitioning the Spanish empire, albeit without prior reference to either Vienna or Madrid. The first Partition Treaty, signed in October 1698, awarded the largest share of the empire to a grandson of the Habsburg Emperor, the Electoral Prince of Bavaria, with Naples and Sicily being given to the dauphin as compensation for France, and the Milanese being assigned to the Archduke Charles, the younger son of the emperor, as the Habsburg compensation. The emperor stubbornly refused to accept the partition agreed upon by Louis and William; Carlos II, dominated by Castilian nobles whose sole thought was to maintain the integrity of the Spanish empire, signed a will leaving the entire inheritance to the Electoral Prince of Bavaria; then, in February 1699, the seven-year-old prince died, negating the efforts of all the powers involved. Undeterred by this stroke of ill fortune, William and Louis returned to new negotiations,

124

agreeing that neither an immediate heir to the French crown nor to the Austrian Habsburg possessions could be allowed to wear the crown of Spain in addition; consequently, the two candidates became the second son of the dauphin, Philippe, duc d'Anjou, and the younger son of the emperor, the Archduke Charles. Under the second Partition Treaty, signed by France, Great Britain, and the Dutch republic in March 1700, the French were to acquire signal advantages; as well as the gains awarded to France under the first treaty, the dauphin was to receive the duchy of Milan, on the condition that it should be exchanged for the duchies of Lorraine and Bar, thereby not only vastly improving France's eastern border, but also cutting the land connection between the Habsburgs in Austria and Spain by giving the Milanese to the Duke of Lorraine. The Archduke Charles was to be given Spain, the Spanish Netherlands, and the Spanish empire overseas.

Again, the emperor refused to agree to anything less than all Spanish possessions, and the Castilian nobility felt equally strongly that all Carlos II's lands should be preserved intact; their only question was which of the two candidates – the French or the Habsburg – would be in a better position to defend the empire's integrity. Shortly after he was induced to sign a new will, the decrepit Carlos II died on 1 November 1700. When the news of his death, and a copy of his will, reached Versailles on 14 November, Louis XIV was confronted with the gravest dilemma of his career. The will provided that the entire Spanish empire should be offered first to the duc d'Anjou; if he (or Louis XIV) refused to accept, the same offer was then to be made to the Archduke Charles. Louis XIV knew full well that, given the opportunity, the Emperor Leopold would immediately accept the Spanish empire for his son; consequently, if Louis was to abide by the second Partition Treaty, war was inevitable if France was to secure its promised share of the Spanish inheritance. But would Great Britain and the Dutch republic support him militarily against their recent ally, the emperor? Louis knew the anti-monarchical, anti-militarist spirit in England and doubted whether William III would be able to rally the Maritime Powers to fight on France's side. On the other hand, if Louis accepted the will, his grandson would be in possession of the entire Spanish empire and the two centuries of Habsburg encirclement of France would be at an end. On 16 November, Louis XIV announced to the French court his acceptance of the will and proclaimed his grandson Philip V of Spain.

Initially, Louis's acceptance of the will was popular in England, where the Tories in particular assumed that the sixteen-year-old Philip would eventually become a good Spaniard; furthermore, the terms of the second Partition Treaty, particularly the grant to France of the com-

125

mercially and agriculturally important Naples and Sicily, were attacked as deliberate sacrifices of English commercial interests. Indeed, four of William's Whig ministers (John, Lord Somers, the head of the Whig party; Lord Edward Russell, Earl of Orford; Charles Montagu, Baron Halifax and the Whig's financial expert; and Lord Portland) were impeached for their alleged roles in negotiating the second Partition Treaty during the parliamentary session in the spring of 1701. The impeachments, carried by a Tory majority in the House of Commons, failed, thanks to a small Whig majority in the House of Lords, but the incident was crucial in exacerbating party animosities in England and was to have profound repercussions during the reign of Queen Anne.

Louis's mistakes, more than William's activities, turned British and Dutch public opinion against the will. In December 1700, Louis registered a decree in the Parlement de Paris that Philip V remained eligible for the succession to the French throne, despite the fact that he had become King of Spain, thereby giving rise to the spectre of the two kingdoms united under one monarch. In February 1701 the English government intercepted and the king furnished to Parliament a letter written by John Drummond, Earl of Melfort, one of the most widely hated members of the Catholic faction during James II's reign and one of the exiled king's leading advisors. In the letter (which was sent from Paris to the English court at St Germain but was accidentally placed in the London mailbag instead), Melfort described the intentions of the French court to procure the restoration of the Prince of Wales, by force of arms if necessary, and quoted extensively as his authority Madame de Maintenon, the morganatic wife of Louis XIV. In March 1701, Louis procured from Philip V an order that French troops rather than Dutch should garrison the fortresses of the Spanish Netherlands; in one stroke, the entire Spanish Netherlands came under French domination and William III saw his life's work swept away without a shot being fired. But this move alarmed both the Dutch and the English publics, and Parliament passed resolutions urging the king to form a new international alliance to counterbalance the expansionary power of France.

William III was sufficiently clear-sighted to realize that his declining health meant he was unlikely to survive another long war, that Great Britain would soon be ruled by his sister-in-law, and that Marlborough would be her chief advisor; patriotic, and determined to achieve his objectives even beyond his grave, the king now placed his chief trust and confidence in the man whom his government had once imprisoned. On 28 June 1701, Marlborough was appointed ambassador extraordinary to the United Provinces and given the powers of a plenipotentiary to negotiate a European alliance against France and Spain.

Although Marlborough's appointment and the confidence which William reposed in him was the king's method of preparing for the future, there is no evidence that the king personally confided in the princess or tried to explain to her the realities of the European situation and his grand design. He merely assumed that she would always be dominated by the superior intelligence of Marlborough. The king's underestimation of the princess's independence and obstinacy was eventually to prove fatal to the Grand Alliance.

On 7 September 1701 the emperor, the Dutch republic, and Great Britain signed a treaty of Grand Alliance, based on a partition of the Spanish empire whereby the house of Habsburg would receive 'satisfactory compensation', the Maritime Powers would receive 'satisfactory' commercial rights in the West Indies, and the contracting powers pledged to negotiate jointly with France rather than separately. Marlborough, upon whom the principal responsibility of negotiating for England had fallen, was careful to send copies of the draft of the treaty to both Whig and Tory leaders in England in order to secure their written approbation before he signed, an obvious hedge against a future impeachment; there is no evidence that he sent a copy to the prince and the princess, but his letters to Lady Marlborough during 1701, which are not extant, undoubtedly contained copies.

The ink was hardly dry on the new treaty when Louis XIV managed to outrage English public opinion and swing the nation solidly behind William III. For several years, the health of James II had been declining; on 4 March 1701, Good Friday, while hearing mass, James had suffered a stroke in the chapel at St Germain while the choir chanted the first two verses from the last chapter of Lamentations: 'Remember, O Lord, what is come upon us: consider and behold our reproach. Our inheritance is turned to Strangers, our houses to Aliens.' A journey to the waters of Bourbon did little to improve his condition and, at the beginning of September, he suffered another serious stroke. It became apparent that he had only a few days to live. On his deathbed, James asked God to forgive his three greatest enemies; the emperor, the Prince of Orange, and his own daughter, the Princess of Denmark.[86] Louis XIV, moved by the entreaties of Mary of Modena and by the powerful influence of his own wife, Madame de Maintenon, decided, against the advice of his ministers, to recognize the Prince of Wales as James III of England, Scotland and Ireland. The recognition, which was against the terms of the Treaty of Ryswick wherein Louis had recognized William, provoked indignation in England. William ordered his envoy in Paris, the Earl of Manchester, to withdraw without notifying the French court. Marlborough, at The Hague with King William, warned Godolphin:

> If the Princesses mourning be not already putt on, I hope you will
> think it reasonable to endeavour to prevaile with her not to doe itt, till
> she heard from the King, which may prevent the malice of a party
> [i.e. the Whigs] that may be but to[o] much inclined to doe her ill
> offices in England.[87]

William decided to mourn his father-in-law only as a private relative
and not as a monarch, the treatment which Versailles and St Germain
had adopted on the death of Queen Mary in 1694. Unfortunately,
without awaiting the royal decision, the princess had already undertaken to put St James's Palace in full mourning. Marlborough warned
Godolphin that, after Louis's recognition of the Pretender, 'if after this
she should putt her house in mourning, for God sake think what an out-
crye itt would make in England'.[88] Although the princess agreed to
conform to William's decision, she was furious. She wrote to Godolphin:

> it is a very great satisfaction to me to find you agree with Mrs. Morley
> concerning the ill-natured, cruel proceedings of Mr. Caliban, which
> vexes me more than you can imagine, and I am out of all patience
> when I think I must do so monstrous a thing as not to put my
> lodgings in mourning for my father.[89]

She cancelled her orders for deep mourning.[90]

Seizing upon the public indignation against Louis XIV for his recognition of the Pretender, William dissolved Parliament in November 1701
and issued writs for a new general election, divesting himself at the
same time of his Tory ministers and beginning the formation of a new,
Whig ministry. The Tories were angry: they had passed the Act of
Settlement, they had laid the groundwork for the war, and now they
were paying the price for humiliations which the king had suffered
years before. The Parliament which met in January 1702 was almost
equally balanced between Tories and Whigs. The king recommended
the passage of an oath of abjuration against the Pretender, which was
enacted after stiff Tory resistance, and consideration of a union between
England and Scotland, which was to become one of the great glories of
his successor's reign.

While the king was hunting in Richmond Park on 21 February 1702,
his horse stumbled on a molehill and fell, throwing the king whose
collar-bone was broken. (For years afterwards, Jacobites toasted the
mole as 'the little gentleman in black velvet'.) William was returned to
Kensington, where the Prince and Princess of Denmark visited him on 24
February and again on 26 February, on their departure for and return
from a weekend at Windsor. At first, the king's condition did not appear
to be serious, and until 6 March he appeared to improve, but the shock

to a system already weakened by long-term tuberculosis caught up with him. On 7 March his condition deteriorated rapidly, and he refused to see the prince and princess.[91] According to Sarah's *Conduct*, Lord and Lady Jersey wrote continually from the king's bedside to inform the princess of his condition;[92] shortly after eight o'clock on the morning of Sunday, 8 March, William III died at Kensington Palace. The Earl of Dartmouth later recorded,

> As soon as the breath was out of King William (by which all expecta-
> tions from him were at an end), the bishop of Salisbury [Burnet] drove
> hard to bring the first tidings to St. James's where he prostrated himself
> at the new Queen's feet, full of joy and duty; but obtained no
> advantage over the Earl of Essex, lord of the bedchamber in waiting,
> whose proper office it was, besides being universally laughed at for his
> officiousness.[93]

For the princess – now the queen – this was the hour for which she had waited all her adult life. She had deserted and betrayed her father to save her religion; she had broken irrevocably with her only sister; she had stoically suffered the slights and humiliations imposed upon her by her brother-in-law. She had become an invalid at the age of thirty-seven through her futile attempts to produce healthy children. Her life, extra-ordinarily replete with physical pain and mental anguish, had fully prepared her for this moment of supreme joy; it was, in the prophecy she had made to Lady Marlborough in 1692, 'a SunShine day . . . England will flourishe againe'.

5

'Thy nursing Mother'

The Role of the Monarch, 1702–14

'Kings shall be thy nursing Fathers, and Queens thy nursing Mothers' (Isaiah 49:23) was the text chosen by the new queen for her coronation sermon. A brief survey of her dominions and of the structure of government at the beginning of the eighteenth century reveals the appropriateness of this choice. Division and strife were the hallmarks of the new queen's inheritance. The three kingdoms of England, Scotland, and Ireland were culturally distinct and mutually hostile. Although Ireland posed the greatest potential threat to the Protestant constitution in Church and State, it was ironically to be the most tranquil of the three kingdoms during Queen Anne's reign. The Irish populace was overwhelmingly Roman Catholic except for the Scottish Presbyterian communities of Ulster. The established Church of Ireland, enjoying the ecclesiastical wealth and revenues of the island, was little more than an Anglican chapel for the English conquerors. Ireland technically was independent with its own Parliament, but in fact the nation was wholly subservient to direct rule from London. As a consequence of the unsuccessful Jacobite rebellion 1689–91, the English suppressed Ireland ruthlessly, establishing absolute Protestant economic, social, and political supremacy. Tories and Whigs were united in their determination to maintain England's domination over the Irish; the queen shared this resolution, telling one of her ministers: 'She understood they had a Mind to be independent, if they could; but they should not.'[1] Throughout her reign, Ireland was to remain largely quiescent and was to be regarded by Whitehall more as a source of preferment for English politicians and ecclesiastics than as an independent kingdom.

Relations between 'North Britain' and 'South Britain' were to present more immediate problems. The personal union between the crowns of Scotland and England, which began when the new queen's great-grandfather James VI of Scotland inherited the English throne in 1603, would seemingly end on the death of Queen Anne. The Hanoverian succession, established in both England and Ireland by the Act of Settlement of 1701, did not apply to Scotland, where there seemed to be little desire to perpetuate the union. Scotland still enjoyed its separate Parliament, church, legal system, and universities. Only during the Cromwellian period had Scottish independence been eliminated and the entire kingdom governed directly from London. The differences between England and Scotland were marked. Scotland had less than one fifth of the population of England and perhaps less than one tenth of England's wealth. While the Church of England was firmly episcopal in structure, the Church of Scotland was Presbyterian. A strong minority, however, adhered to a disestablished episcopal Church of Scotland, and these episcopalians supported the Jacobite cause to regain their national and religious liberties, as did the Highland clans, where Roman Catholicism retained a foothold. True, Scotland was overwhelmingly Protestant, and even the episcopalians had been profoundly influenced by the reforms of John Knox and his successors. The religious and educational equality of self-governing congregations and kirk schools had introduced into Scottish life an element of democracy as yet unknown in England. At the same time, the Scottish aristocracy still maintained its feudal sway, enjoying much greater power than its English counterpart.

In part because of traditional loyalty to the house of Stuart and in part because of a desire for Scottish national independence, Jacobitism enjoyed greater support in Scotland than in England. This support, essentially anti-English, was increased by two events during William III's reign: the massacre of a Highland clan at Glencoe by government soldiers in 1692, and the disastrous collapse of the Scottish colonization attempt at Darien in the isthmus of Panama in 1699, for which the Scots blamed the covert hostility of the English government. As long as the Scottish Parliament refused to endorse the Hanoverian succession, a Stuart restoration in the northern kingdom remained a real possibility. Sensing a dangerous growth of anti-English feeling and realizing that Scotland might prove to be the Achilles' heel of England in the great world conflict into which it was now entering, William III recommended a union between the two kingdoms in his last speech to the English Parliament.

England, the largest and most powerful of the new queen's possessions, boasted a population of perhaps 6.5 million souls, largely concentrated in the southern and eastern areas of the nation. In the age of Anne, English society was characterized by class distinctions. In 1695, Gregory King had noted the existence of 16,500 families 'of rank' with perhaps 150,000 members. Wealth was still predominantly based on the ownership of land, but commercial and financial endeavours were

131

making significant additions to the national economy. For the able and fortunate, social mobility could be rapid, but over 40 per cent of the population were ranked among 'the Poor', those with £10 or less in annual income.[2] Like her sister kingdoms, England was also religiously divided. The majority of the population still supported the Church of England, although a significant minority were Protestant Nonconformists or Dissenters. One out of ten individuals remained true to Rome and the Old Faith.

Queen Anne's England enjoyed a growing sense of wealth and power; its colonial system was flourishing and expanding, and the nation was on the verge of becoming one of the great powers of Europe. This sense of wealth and power was accompanied by growing literary and artistic freedom. The lapsing of the Licensing Act in 1695 brought an end to censorship of the press. Grub Street flourished, and in the ensuing years Swift, Defoe, Pope, Addison and Steele were to be the greatest of the notable authors of Queen Anne's reign. In the arts, Sir Christopher Wren, Grinling Gibbons, Sir John Vanbrugh, and Sir Godfrey Kneller were to make their distinctive contributions to a recognizably English style, while George Frederick Handel was to precede the queen's Hanoverian heirs into the kingdom. In the sciences, Isaac Newton was the father of modern physics, and was knighted by the queen. The vast palaces of Blenheim, Castle Howard, Chatsworth, and Petworth were being created. A whole style in decorative arts, including furniture and silver, which combined beauty, comfort, and practicality, was to be named after Queen Anne.

The growing wealth and the splendid artistic façade which it produced should not obscure from posterity the deep divisions in English society. These divisions, which had first exploded in the violence and bloodshed of the Civil War of the 1640s and had been exacerbated by the Cromwellian military dictatorship of the 1650s, had merely been papered over by the Restoration of 1660. During the reign of Charles II, the first system of organized political parties in Europe had emerged in England. During the post-Revolution period, the Tories and the Whigs managed to divide every level and segment of society. The bitterness of this factional struggle was compounded by the fact that the electorate expanded in every election between 1689 and 1715; the newly liberated press became the handmaiden of the parties, and contributed its share to heightening party tension. Neither party, as events were to demonstrate, stood above resorting to violence to achieve its ends. Neither party was homogeneous; each was composed of factions based on regional, personal, or ideological loyalties. Neither party possessed leaders who could unite their ranks. Yet, each party had a characteristic world-view and each party was playing for the highest possible stakes. The political game was played for keeps: for any politician who managed to reach the top, the prospect of the scaffold remained a real threat, should his enemies regain the initiative.

In terms of electoral appeal, the Tories were the stronger of the two parties. Based on twin pillars of loyalty to the house of Stuart and to the Church of England, the Tories had been shaken by the policies of James II and by the Revolution; nevertheless, one segment of the Tory party was avowedly Jacobite, while others were widely suspected of being willing to procure the restoration of the Prince of Wales, should he be converted to Protestantism. Despite this, the queen correctly argued that 'the revolution had never bin, nor the Succession setel'd as it is now, if the Church party had not Joyned' with the Whigs.[3]

The Tories in general opposed the military strategies of William III and Marlborough in which British troops were concentrated in the Southern Netherlands for the defence of the Dutch republic; they claimed that this strategy merely attacked Louis XIV where he was strongest. In part, this Tory opposition was inspired by hatred of the Dutch as republicans and Calvinists. Instead, the leaders of the party argued that Louis XIV and Philip V of Spain should be attacked where they were weakest, in their colonial empires and on the high seas. In general, the Tory party represented the 'landed interest', the squirearchy and the lower clergy. The numerical strength of the party was blunted by its divisions on the question of the succession and by the lack of a univerally recognized leader. The queen's uncle, Lawrence Hyde, Earl of Rochester, and Daniel Finch, Earl of Nottingham, were widely regarded as the most distinguished Tories in terms of past service, although they did not command universal loyalty within the party's ranks.

In contrast to the Tories, the Whigs were open to accusations of republicanism (the Tories regularly portrayed them as the lineal and spiritual successors of the Roundheads) and lack of religion. Whig policy had led to the Toleration Act of 1689, which effectively emancipated all Trinitarian Protestants from the Penal Acts against religious non-conformity. The new queen was never able to divest herself of the fear that Whig supremacy in the state would undermine her beloved Church: in November 1704 she told Lady Marlborough:

> as to my saying the Church was in some danger in the late Reigne, I
> can not alter my opinion; for tho there was no violent thing don,
> every body that will Speak impartially must own that every thing was
> leaning towards the Whigs, & when ever that is, I shall think the
> Church is beginning to be in danger.[4]

Compared with the Tories, the Whigs drew support from more diverse elements of society. Their ranks included great territorial magnates (the Dukes of Somerset, Newcastle, and Devonshire), commercial interests (particularly in the City of London), military men with a vested interest in the war, and Protestant Dissenters. On the whole, the Whigs enthusiastically supported the strategies of William III and Marlborough. They viewed Louis XIV's France, his domination of the Spanish empire through his grandson, and the Catholicizing policies which characterized the last half of his long reign, as the greatest threats to the liberties of Europe and England. In contrast to the Tories, the Whigs were totally united in supporting the Hanoverian succession.

Finally, the Whigs enjoyed the advantage of a closely knit group of leaders, commonly called the Junto. The acknowledged leader of the Junto was John, Lord Somers, who had served as lord keeper and lord chancellor under William III from 1693 to 1700. The financial expert of the Junto was Charles Montagu, created Baron Halifax in 1700. Thomas, Lord Wharton, was the Junto's principal speaker in the House of Lords and also served as the electoral manager for Junto interests. Edward Russell, Earl of Orford, was one of the 'immortal seven' who had invited the Prince of Orange to invade England in 1688 and who had subsequently won the great naval victory at Cape La Hogue in 1692. Finally, the Junto enjoyed the avid support and services of Lord Charles Spencer (the Marlboroughs' son-in-law), who succeeded his father in September 1702 as the third Earl of Sunderland. Quite apart from the fact that the queen was biased towards the Tories, she hated and feared the cohesion, power, and influence of the Junto, referring to them as 'the five tyranising lords': in her view, the Junto were constantly 'designing . . . to tear that little prerogative the Crown has to peaces' by attempting to impose a party government upon the monarch.[5]

The whole idea of parties was anathema to the queen. She still entertained the Elizabethan concept of national unity, in which parties were equated with factionalism and diversity with national disunity and weakness. Above all, her goal was 'to keep me out of ye power of ye Mercyless men of both partys',[6] and she referred to the parties as her 'bug-bears'. Initially, she leaned to the Tories as 'the Church party', willing to support both the throne and the Church of England: as we shall see, however, the Tories proved unwilling to prosecute the war and enforce the union with Scotland in the way the queen was convinced was necessary. Consequently, she was increasingly obliged to rely on Whigs, although she consistently opposed admittance of Junto members to government, on the grounds that she would thereby become the cat's-paw of one party. Like William III, Queen Anne embraced the concept of a 'mixed ministry', one composed of equal numbers of Tories and Whigs, which would act in the interests of the nation rather than in those of faction. 'All I wish is to be kept out of the power of both [parties]', she told Godolphin in 1705.[7]

To accomplish this goal, the queen relied on 'undertakers', ministers who could keep both parties in check. In 1702, although Marlborough and Godolphin were regarded as nominal Tories, they had never played leading roles in the inner councils of the party; Robert Harley, speaker of the House of Commons, was completing his metamorphosis from country Whig to moderate Tory, thereby rendering himself suspect to the extremists of both parties. To the queen, Marlborough, Godolphin, and Harley represented bridges between the two parties, men who could reconcile the moderates of both factions and thereby carry through the crown's policies. In her choice of servants, the queen was forced again and again to bow to parliamentary necessity, but a 'mixed ministry' still seemed possible. The evolving constitution under which Queen Anne ruled contained elements both modern and medieval. In a real sense, the queen's ministers were still regarded as her personal servants.

War against France was the predominant fact of life for the generation after 1688, and the necessities of war produced a great expansion in the functions and personnel of the English government. Professor Plumb has outlined the causes and effects of this tremendous growth which meant, among other things, that the queen could not, even if she had wished, exercise the close supervisory role undertaken by Elizabeth.[8] The queen enjoyed ultimate authority over the governmental machine because she was the ultimate source of office. She was naturally jealous of her prerogative of appointment: as she told Lady Marlborough in 1709, 'there is no office whatsoever that has ye intire disposal of any thing under them, but I may putt in any one I please when I have a mind to it'.[9] Indeed, without soliciting the advice of responsible ministers, the queen personally initiated a large number of appointments, and those obnoxious to her had difficulty in obtaining important positions, even when political expediency demanded it.[10] Merit and service were chief recommendations to the queen's favour. She was in advance of her time in opposing the customary 'sale of offices', telling Lady Marlborough in July 1703 that 'both the Prince & I are resolved never to let that custom be introduced into his bedchamber'.[11]

Unlike the great expansion in departments of state after the Revolution, the court and the royal household had declined in size. There were four principal court officers: the lord chamberlain was responsible for the court 'above stairs', the lord steward for management 'below stairs', the master of the horse for the stables, and the groom of the stole for the queen's bedchamber and personal attendants. Whether they enjoyed political influence depended largely upon the individuals involved. As lord chamberlain, both the Earl of Jersey (1702–4) and the Duke of Shrewsbury (1710–14) sat in the cabinet, although no one suggested that the Earl of Kent (nicknamed 'the Bug' during his tenure from 1704–10) should be given ministerial rank. The Duke of Somerset, as master of the horse, sat in the cabinet from 1702 to 1710, more by virtue of his influence with the sovereign and with the constituencies than of his office. The groom of the stole, the officer closest to the monarch, had traditionally been the principal favourite; Portland held this post under William III. One of the new queen's first actions was to install Lady Marlborough in this position, which she combined with that of keeper of the privy purse, the queen's personal financial fund.

The queen followed her predecessor in utilizing Kensington Palace as the main residence of the court. Although she occasionally spent the night at St James's, and more frequently dined there when Parliament was in session, the queen preferred Kensington, still regarded as a 'country' residence. The reason, as the queen told Lady Marlborough in June 1702, was that 'tho St. James's is ye best part of London, it must be very Stinking & close at this time of yeare, and can not be wholesome'.[12] The queen was also attracted to Kensington by the large garden which surrounded the palace, although when she came to the throne she was determined to improve it: 'I went to Kensington to walk in ye garden', she informed Sarah two months after her accession,

> which would be a very prety place if it weare well kept but nothing can be worse, it is a great deal of pity & indeed a great Shame that there should be no better use made of soe great an alowance, for I have bin told the King allowed four hundred pound a year for that one garden.[13]

Work on Kensington Palace gardens, including the eventual construction of the orangery, was put in hand under the capable supervision of Henry Wise, the most famous gardener of the day. With the exceptions of 1710 and 1714, the queen habitually spent most of the summer at Windsor. This necessitated some inconvenience for her ministers, who needed to be in almost daily consultation with the monarch. Kensington was an easy drive from Westminster, but the journey to Windsor entailed considerable trouble and expense. The secretaries of state attended at Windsor in weekly turns,[14] while as a group, 'The Ministers go usually down to Windsor on Saturday, and return on Monday or Tuesday following'.[15]

Queen Anne has traditionally been depicted as a weak monarch, subject to the persuasions of favourites, a view underlined by Sarah Marlborough in her *Conduct* (published in 1742) and largely accepted by subsequent historians. The grounds for her weakness are generally alleged to be her poor health, her sex, and her medicore intelligence. No one would attempt to deny that the queen's health was bad; indeed, at the time of her accession, she was virtually an invalid, a fact which naturally contributed to a curtailment of the normal social activities associated with the court. Nevertheless, no student of her reign can help but be struck by the enormous amount of time and hard work involved in carrying out her duties: conferences – often prolonged – with indivi- dual ministers were a daily occurrence; she presided at cabinet meetings at least once, and often twice, each week; every day she was expected to read a number of petitions as well as the précis of foreign news prepared by her secretaries of state. Warrants, orders, and instructions demanded the monarch's signature. The queen also gave formal audiences to foreign envoys and frequently attended debates in the House of Lords. During her periods of relatively good health, she apparently allowed easy access to her closet for anyone who was admitted to court: in 1711 the Duke of Shrewsbury complained to Harley that 'I have lived in four Courts, and this is the first where I have ever seen anybody go up the back stairs unless such as the Prince would have come to him un- observed'.[16] The queen also attended daily religious services. Sheer exhaustion must have been a concomitant of her life. It was hardly surprising that she lamented 'that she was realy so taken up with business, that she had not time to say her prayers'.[17]

The queen's sex was an obvious disadvantage in a reign dominated by a great war. She enjoyed both factual and titular command of the Army, traditionally the ultimate instrument of royal power,[18] and of the Navy. Until his death in 1708, Prince George served as generalissimo of all forces, both land and sea; as lord high admiral, he was also the working head of the Admiralty. Unlike William III, the queen was incapable (both in terms of her health and of convention) of actually leading her troops in battle, and for the greatest part of her reign her husband was also physically incapable of such exertion. In England, however, the age of the warrior king was almost over; with the exception of George II at Dettingen in 1743, British sovereigns of the eighteenth century were content to direct strategy from afar. Apart from military matters, there was no activity of state in which the queen's sex was a positive disadvantage. Indeed, she was determined that it should not be one. In 1707, when the Junto was pressing her to retract promises which she had made to Tory candidates for ecclesiastical appointments, the queen told Godolphin: 'Whoever of ye Whigs thinks I am to be Heckter'd or frighted into a Complyance tho I am a woman, are mightey mistaken in me. I thank God I have a Soul above that & am to[o] much conserned for my reputation to do any thing to forfeit it.'[19]

The queen's intelligence, or lack of it, is perhaps the most highly debatable factor in assessing her influence. Undoubtedly she was neither 'clever' nor erudite, nor did she pretend to be. As she had been excluded from all business during the reigns of her father and her brother-in-law, she did not have the advantage possessed by William III of having served as administrative head of a great nation and a European coalition before her accession to the throne; there was great truth in Sarah's comment that

> Lord Godolphin conducted the Queen, with the care and tenderness of a father, or a guardian, through a state of helpless ignorance, and had faithfully served her in all her difficulties before she was Queen, as well as greatly contributed to the glories she had to boast of after she was so.[20]

The queen, however, was no mere puppet in the hands of others. She was determined to judge questions for herself, in part because she was convinced that her motives were beyond reproach. 'I have no thought but what is for ye good of England,' she assured Marlborough;

> I ame sure I have no other nor never can but will always to ye best of my understanding promote its true interest, & serve my country faithfully, which I look upon to be as much ye Duty of a Sovereing, as of ye meanest Subject.[21]

All observers were struck that 'she has a very good Memory',[22] an invaluable tool for any executive. Furthermore, her entire previous career had schooled the queen in the wisdom of discretion: in Swift's words, 'there was not, perhaps in all England, a person who understood more artificially how to disguise her passions'.[23] As we shall see, the queen was to prove to be a political infighter of no mean ability. Naturally prone to 'backstairs intrigue', she utilized her personal servants to obtain views and information which might be withheld from her by her government ministers. In addition the queen possessed what so many of her Stuart predecessors had lacked: common sense. None of her ministers was ever to underrate her ability to enforce her strongly held convictions.

During the medieval period, the monarch's chief minister had been the lord chancellor (or the lord keeper, should the Great Seal be in commission). Known as the 'keeper of the Queen's conscience', the lord chancellor served as the chief legal officer of the crown, presided over the House of Lords, and was responsible for the ecclesiastical patronage of the crown. The queen's maternal grandfather, the first Earl of Clarendon, had been the last lord chancellor to serve in fact as principal minister. After the Restoration, the Treasury had increasingly become more important. This pre-eminence naturally grew after 1688, when the financial requirements imposed by the Nine Years War became ever more burdensome. Throughout William III's reign, and during the first two months of Queen Anne's, the Treasury had remained in commission. The monarch was ordinarily expected to attend meetings of the Treasury commission, and William had averaged nineteen meetings a year, despite the fact that he habitually spent six months in the Dutch republic. The close connection between the Treasury and the monarch disappeared under Queen Anne, who attended only twenty-two meetings during the eleven months of her reign when the Treasury was in commission.[24] Yet she did meet frequently with her lord treasurers and chancellors of the exchequer to transact departmental business, and her presence at these meetings was felt. On 19 May 1703, for example, having read a petition from 'Sir God: Kneller praying payment of £570 due to him for drawing several pictures of Her Majesty and the late King', the queen decreed that 'Her Majesty does not care for the picture of £350; the others are to be paid for'.[25] In general, however, the queen relied upon her lord treasurer, whether Godolphin or Harley, to conduct financial business and to be responsible for the vast patronage which the Treasury dispensed.

Next in authority to the chancellor and the treasurer were the secretaries of state. The office had evolved from that of the personal secretary to the king into a great office of state during the reign of Henry VIII, but the secretaries were still regarded as peculiarly the queen's personal servants. The queen, for instance, asked Sir Charles Hedges to 'send me some good pens, for those I have are soe bad I can hardly make them writt'.[26] The secretaries were expected to wait upon the queen daily or, if she was absent from London, to be in attendance upon her in rotation. They also prepared a daily précis of foreign news, which they included in their correspondence to her.[27] The office had evolved into two departments, northern and southern. The secretary of state for the north was responsible for diplomatic relations with the Low Countries, Scandinavia, Russia and the empire, as well as for domestic administration in northern England; his southern counterpart had similar diplomatic responsibilities in those areas bordering the Mediterranean, as well as in southern England, Ireland, and the colonies. For domestic administration, the secretaries of state issued their orders through the lords lieutenant of the various counties; generally, these men were

139

great landowners who exercised both economic and social power in their neighbourhoods, and who were appointed by the monarch to serve during the monarch's pleasure. The secretaries also controlled the diplomatic corps. Queen Anne was necessarily more removed from her foreign envoys than was William III, who had often used both Dutch and English representatives in a capital to carry out his policies, but she often appointed diplomats after only courtesy consultation with the responsible secretary. In 1705, at the solicitation of Godolphin, she appointed Sunderland as envoy extraordinary to Vienna, undoubtedly against the wishes of the responsible secretary, Robert Harley. In 1710 she appointed James Cressett to go to Hanover without consulting either her lord treasurer or the northern secretary, Henry Boyle. In 1711, Harley, now the queen's chief minister, suggested that his close friend, Matthew Prior, should be sent to Paris, to which the queen replied: 'You propose my giveing Mr. Prior some inferiour Caracter, what that can be I don't know, for I doubt his Birth will not entitle him to that of Envoy.'[28] Apparently Harley objected to the royal observation, for three days later the queen assured him that 'I have no objection to Mr. Prior then what I mentioned in my last for I always thought it was very rong to send people abroad of meane extraction'.[29] Prior had to wait a year for his appointment and then he had to settle for the lesser position of minister plenipotentiary.

Among other duties, the queen was also expected to meet periodically with foreign envoys. These meetings were generally formal, with a secretary in attendance, and both the diplomat's speech and the queen's response were carefully arranged in advance: 'I must desire you', the queen wrote to Oxford in 1713, 'to send me a few words that you think may be proper for me to say to the Duc d'Aumont when he coms to me.'[30] The queen was also expected to write personally to reigning sovereigns and their families; these letters were drafted by the secretaries but copied (and sometimes changed) by the queen, although gout in her hands often delayed this task. She also took care to inspect gifts given in her name. In August 1710 she inspected a gift – a be-jewelled miniature of herself – for her namesake, the infant Princess Anne of Hanover, and declared 'I think ye pictures is very neatly set, & beleeve ye diamonds are very good.'[31]

The heads of the Army and the Navy sat in the cabinet, as did the lord lieutenant of Ireland, who was responsible for the military and civil administration of the island kingdom. Although he did not exercise departmental duties, the lord privy seal was also generally a member of the cabinet, as was the lord president of the Privy Council. By the time of the queen's accession, the Privy Council was still theoretically the chief administrative body of the realm, but it had become too large and unwieldy to function efficiently in day-to-day administration; in 1708, for instance, fifty-five persons were listed in its rosters.[32] Instead, it had been replaced by a 'cabinet committee', a cabinet council, or – in modern parlance – the cabinet. As Professor Plumb has demonstrated, the cabinet was centred round the person of the queen: indeed, no meeting could be held in her absence. The queen continued William III's habit of holding regular cabinet meetings after dinner on Sundays, although pressure of business frequently necessitated two or more meetings during a week. In 1705 at least sixty-four meetings were held, and between June 1710 and June 1711 the queen presided over sixty-two cabinet meetings. She easily averaged attendance at one meeting for each week of her reign,[33] attending more often than any preceding or subsequent monarch. The composition of the cabinet depended solely upon whom the queen summoned to attend. Usually, the Archbishop of Canterbury was a member, and during the first years of the new reign Thomas Tenison continued to attend. He stopped this practice after September 1710. Whether he ceased to be summoned or whether he voluntarily chose to withdraw to mark his displeasure at the queen's change of ministry remains unknown. As we have already seen, household officers were summoned depending upon the quality and influence of the men who held office. When the first Duke of Devonshire (one of the 'immortal seven' of 1688) died in August 1707, he was succeeded by his son as lord steward. The queen decided that the younger Devonshire would not be summoned to the cabinet until winter, that 'the Queen may let it be seen that must not be taken as inherent to the office'.[34] On the other hand, loss of ministerial office did not necessarily mean the loss of a cabinet seat; in 1713, when John Robinson was translated from the see of Bristol to that of London and lost his position as lord privy seal, he nevertheless remained in the cabinet.[35] Although most issues of importance were first debated by 'the lords of the committee' (a more informal group whose membership did not include the queen or the prince), the drafts of all important dispatches were first read in the cabinet by the secretaries of state and 'the final decision on all matters had to be taken by the Queen, sitting in Cabinet'. This decision, once made, was final, unless subsequently revoked by the queen in cabinet.[36]

Significantly, one of the matters least frequently discussed by this new, emerging institution was the conduct of parliamentary business. Above all, the Revolution had changed the relationship between the crown and Parliament. No longer could a monarch attempt a personal rule, as both Charles II and James II had done. The Bill of Rights assured the supremacy of the King-in-Parliament and statute law

141

over the crown and the prerogative. In particular, the wars following 1688 vastly increased the power and prestige of the House of Commons, the ultimate source of monetary supply which was so important to England, now the financial engine behind the Grand Alliance. The independence of members of the Commons from crown control was highly prized, and one of the perennial features of parliamentary sessions was the introduction of 'place bills', prohibiting members from accepting offices of profit under the crown. The Triennial Act of 1694 had ensured that the maximum life of any Parliament would be three years, at the expiration of which a general election was mandatory. The result was that between 1689 and 1715 there were twelve general elections, more than in any other comparable period of British history.[37] Neither Queen Anne nor her ministers were ever allowed to forget that their policies must be tailored not only to please the members who would be re-assembling each autumn, but also the growing electorate, which would soon pass judgment upon those policies.

Despite the increasing prominence of the House of Commons, it was still overshadowed by the House of Lords in terms of prestige. Indeed, the last half of the seventeenth century had marked a revival in the influence of the aristocracy. Most of the crucial debates and party conflicts took place in the upper rather than in the lower house. Most party leaders, ranging from Godolphin and Marlborough to Harley and St John, took the first opportunity to procure their elevation to the hereditary aristocracy. From 1704 the queen became an avid attender of the most important debates in the House of Lords, reviving the practice of her uncle Charles II. Bishop Burnet approved of this 'as it was of good use for her better information, so it was very serviceable in bringing the House into better order';[38] but it is clear that the queen had other intentions as well. By ignoring some speakers and favouring others with her attention, the queen could demonstrate her own personal views. Lord Cowper noted in 1705, when he presided over the debates concerning the Regency bill in which he was representing the government's position, that 'The Queen and Prince were pleas'd to talk with me very often & kindly during the Debate'.[39]

As the fount of honour, the queen was exceedingly reluctant to dilute the peerage by additional creations. A month after her accession, it was reported that 'the Queene is positively determined not to create or promote any one single person, there are soe very many that aske, and whoever is refused wil be angry'.[40] In this context, Queen Anne is generally remembered for her famous creation of a dozen peers simultaneously in 1712 in order to ensure the success of the Oxford–Bolingbroke peace policy, but this constitutional landmark stands in contrast to the queen's general reluctance to expand the aristocracy. The peerage was largely a Stuart creation: the House of Lords expanded from fifty-nine members in 1603 to one hundred and sixty-eight in 1714. Queen Anne created fewer peers than most of her predecessors or her successors: during her reign, the net total membership of the House of Lords expanded only by six.*

In terms of creation and promotion in the peerage, the queen's personal prejudices were crucial. The best known example is her refusal in 1712 to revive the extinct earldom of Bolingbroke in favour of Henry St John as a reward for his role in peace negotiations with France. Disliking St John's dissolute personal life and unwilling to catapult him into the third highest rank of the aristocracy, the queen awarded him a viscountcy. Bolingbroke's anger against the queen and Oxford (on whom he blamed this decision) contributed to the split between the two ministers which eventually wrecked the Tory party.[41]

The queen's direct role in parliamentary proceedings began with the Queen's Speech at the opening and closing of each session. These orations were of the utmost importance, according to Defoe, because the country was 'particularly attentive' to what she said.[42] In fact, the speeches were usually drafted by her principal minister and subsequently corrected and amended by his cabinet colleagues, although the queen's final approval was necessary before the speech was delivered. Informally, the queen often lobbied for votes by 'closeting' members of both houses. This was particularly true in the case of her favourite clergyman, John Sharp, Archbishop of York, who in December 1706 recorded in his diary that the queen was particularly concerned to protect the rights and privileges of the crown:

> She pressed me earnestly to be on her side in all matters that came before the Parliament relating to the prerogative. . . . She desired I would never promise my vote, till I had acquainted her with my objections; she said, 'I should be her confessor, and she would be mine'; and if she could not satisfy me, then I should vote as I pleased.[43]

The one remaining power the queen held *vis-à-vis* Parliament was the

---

*James I created 62 peers (while 17 titles became extinct) for a net total of 45.
Charles I created 59 peers.
Charles II created 64 peers (53 extinctions) for a net total of 11.
James II created 8 peers (8 extinctions) for no net gain.
William III created 30 peers (21 extinctions) for a net gain of 9.
Queen Anne created 30 peers (24 extinctions), for a net gain of 6.
George I created 28 peers (13 extinctions), for a net gain of 15.
George II created 38 peers (22 extinctions), for a net gain of 16.
For the complete list of Queen Anne's peerage creations, see A. S. Turberville, *The House of Lords in the Eighteenth Century* (Oxford, 1927), 501–3.

right of veto. This right, however, was rarely exercised, and when in March 1708 Queen Anne became the last monarch to use the veto (against the Militia of Scotland bill), the event passed almost unnoticed by contemporaries.[44] The infrequent use of the royal veto indicated the growing success of the queen's ministers in controlling Parliament, at least to the extent of preventing the passage of legislation repugnant to the government of the day.

Apart from her executive and legislative function, the queen also stood at the head of the judiciary. The Bill of Rights prescribed that judges were to be appointed for good behaviour, and were to be removed only on the petition of Parliament (a right which was never exercised). In her judicial role the queen acted as the final court of appeal, particularly in granting executive clemency. The queen was obliged to hold regular consultations with her judges about individual cases; in 1706, for example, the lord chief justice, Sir John Holt, reported to Harley, as secretary of state:

> Last night I waited on the Queen to give Her Majesty an account of my circuit, and particularly of the several prisoners whose cases were referred to me by the Queen's order signified under your hand. As for the first, Thomas Lyford, condemned in Surrey, the Queen in consideration of his youth and hoping that if he be put into some laborious employment he may be reformed, hath been pleased to extend her mercy to him: the like to William Hayes, condemned in Kent. . . .
> But upon my representation of the case of Evan Evans and his brother William Evans, the Queen hath been pleased to leave them to execution, for they are very notorious highwaymen and so have been for many years, and are a common danger to the Queen's people. . . .[45]

The queen, in dealing with such cases, was genuinely moved by feminine compassion: one convict, she notified Secretary Hedges,

> having a wife and six children, makes me think it a case of compassion; however I desire you would inform youself about it as soon as you can possible, and if you find it soe, take care his life may be spared.[46]

In another case, the queen opined that 'it would be a barbarous thing to hang a woman when she is with child'.[47] It was no accident that the reign of Queen Anne had the singular distinction in the history of England before 1760 that there were no political executions, despite the fact that several prominent Jacobites were captured during the abortive invasion attempt in 1708.

Such compassion became a Christian princess, and particularly one whose role made her head and supreme governor of the Church of England. The queen took her role as Defender of the Faith seriously, both in domestic terms and in relation to international Protestantism. As an institution, the Church of England was beset with problems. Many good Anglicans, including five of the seven bishops tried by James II in 1688, had refused to accept the results of the Revolution, and these non-jurors (who refused to swear oaths of loyalty to William and Mary) had created a schism within the Church. Queen Anne attempted to heal this breach by offering to restore Thomas Ken to his former bishopric of Bath and Wells, and Robert Frampton (formerly Bishop of Gloucester) to Hereford, but these royal overtures were rejected.[48] The Toleration Act of 1689, which in effect granted freedom of religious worship to all Trinitarian Protestants, had also undermined the monopoly position of the established Church: not only did Toleration prove that there were many more Dissenters in the country than anyone had previously suspected, but the Act was also widely misinterpreted as repealing the laws of compulsory attendance at organized religious services. As a result, communicants and contributions in the established Church dropped drastically during the 1690s. Although the Tory party employed the slogan for unscrupulous partisan ends, there was a foundation of fact in the Tory battle cry, 'The Church in Danger'.[49]

Internally, the Church was also divided into High and Low parties; although it would be simplistic to equate these divisions with the Tories and Whigs, there were marked similarities. The High Church emphasized ceremony, loyalty to the house of Stuart, and the sanctity of the priesthood. The Low Church party, by contrast, was more markedly Protestant. Thanks to the expulsion of the non-juring bishops, William III had enjoyed an unprecedented opportunity to remodel the episcopal bench, and the Upper House of Convocation was dominated by Low Church bishops. The Lower House, composed of the representatives of the lesser clergy, was fiercely High Church in conviction; consequently Convocation, as a general council of the Church of England, was constantly plagued by struggles between its two component bodies.

As a private individual, the queen was more in sympathy with High Church views and practice; but as monarch she had 'an acid dislike for factious clergymen, or of any discord in religion'.[50] The queen quickly discovered that not only were the High Church clergy factious, but they also wished for a degree of freedom from episcopal (and consequently from royal) control. The queen, bent upon preserving both the Toleration and the royal prerogative, naturally opposed this; the hopes which the High Church clergy had conceived for their triumph under the first genuinely Anglican monarch since Charles I were quickly dashed.

The most important aspect of the royal prerogative in Church affairs was the queen's right to appoint the twenty-six bishops and two arch-

145

bishops who sat in the Upper House of Convocation and in the House of Lords. Despite partisan disputes over these appointments, the calibre of the competing candidates was strikingly high during the queen's reign. Her first criterion for appointment was that the bishop could perform his diocesan work: in 1709, for example, the queen rejected the suggestion that Dean William Hayley should be promoted to the bishopric of Chichester because he could not do diocesan work, 'being a cripple and without hopes of remedy'.[51] Another consideration in the queen's mind was that her ecclesiastical appointees should be men of 'quality': when Lady Marlborough asked her to reward the grandson of her ally in 1692, the Bishop of Worcester, the queen replied:

> as to what dear Mrs. Freeman desires conserning Dr. Stillingfleets Grandson, I shall be glad to do any thing for him when I can . . . I should be glad to know what his name is, & whether he is a gentle-man (for Clergy men do not often consider what aliances they make).[52]

The queen, as a faithful daughter of the Church, was determined to exercise the royal prerogative personally. William III had appointed a commission composed of the two archbishops and four bishops to advise him on ecclesiastical appointments, but on the advice of Bishop Compton the queen dissolved this commission and acted on her own.[53]

For ecclesiastical advice, the queen relied heavily upon John Sharp, appointed Archbishop of York in 1691: in the matter of appointments, 'she would rarely give her promise without his advice and, generally speaking, consent first obtained'.[54] She regarded Sharp as her 'confessor' and regularly consulted him in preparation before taking the sacrament.[55] But, according to Sarah (who made it clear that Sharp was the queen's own choice as her principal ecclesiastical advisor), Sharp was subservient to the queen's wishes after her accession: 'He had now free access at all times to the Queen: & by that means came quickly to know Her Sentiments, & her Resolutions; to which He seem'd immediately to conform his own.'[56] In 1702, Sharp was appointed the queen's lord almoner, which among other prerequisites gave him the opportunity to appoint the clergymen who preached before the queen, a right of which Sharp proved jealous.[57] Sharp's prerequisite, as Lady Marlborough realized, was important. In 1704, Sarah lamented to a friend that she had little influence in clerical appointments:

> I must own to you that I have less opinion of my solicitations of that sort than any other, because whoever speaks to the Queen upon that subject she does always consult with the Bishops before she disposes of the thing; and besides Her Majesty has so many Chaplains who are always importuning her for preferment, that I think they had the advantage of everybody else.[58]

146

In defending her reliance upon Sharp to Lady Marlborough, the queen made it clear that she intended to limit the influence of the clergy to ecclesiastical affairs. Early in her reign she assured Sarah:

> I am intirly of my dear Mrs. Freemans mind that ye heat & ambition of Church men has don a great deale of hurt to this poor Nation, but it will never do it any harm in my time, for I will never give way to theire governing in any thing, only sometimes it is necessary to ask theire advice in church matters, there is but one of all our Bishops that I have any opinion of, & he I take to be a very reasonable as well as a good man, & I'me sure if my dear Mrs. Freeman knew him she would be of that opinion to[o].[59]

From the beginning of the reign, the queen proved reluctant to rely exclusively on lay advice concerning ecclesiastical appointments. Although Godolphin, as her lord treasurer, was her closest advisor in the early years of the reign, he realized the limits of his influence in ecclesiastical affairs. Reporting to Lady Marlborough in 1703 on the prospects of two candidates for the vacant diocese of St Asaph, he wrote: 'I think whoever had spoken to the Queen for either of these worthy persons would but have lost their labour, for though she did not positively say who should, she seemed very well resolved who should not have it.'[60] Just as Godolphin relied upon Robert Harley's extensive contacts with every shade of Church and Dissenting opinion,[61] so the queen consulted Harley concerning episcopal appointments. Harley's influence, however, was never as powerful as Archbishop Sharp's. In 1714 the queen translated Sharp's protégé, William Dawes, from Chester to York as her final tribute to Sharp, without consulting Harley, then her chief minister.[62]

The two archbishops and the twenty-six bishops had seats in the House of Lords, which they attended more regularly than many lay members and where they consequently exercised a disproportionate influence. During her reign the queen largely succeeded in reversing the Whiggish trend of William III's episcopate. In December 1703, for example, thirteen of the late king's episcopal nominees voted against the second bill against Occasional Conformity, while only two were in favour. In contrast, in December 1718, when the House of Lords voted on a proposal to repeal the Occasional Conformity and Schism Acts, ten of the bishops appointed by the queen opposed repeal, while only three favoured it.[63]

Perhaps the most curious affirmation of the queen's quasi-religious role as sovereign was her decision to resurrect the practice of 'touching' for the king's evil (the disease of scrofula, a tuberculous condition with enlargement of the lymphatic glands). This medieval practice, originated in 1058 by Edward the Confessor and used by subsequent monarchs to demonstrate the divine origins of the kingly office,[64] had been discontinued by William III. In April 1703 the queen informed Lady Marlborough:

> I intend (an it please God) when I com from Windsor to touch as many poor people as I can before hott wheather coms, I do that business now in ye Banqueting house which I like very well, that being a very cool room, & ye doing of it there keeps my own house sweet & free from crouds.[65]

The frequency of the touching ceremonies depended largely upon the queen's health ('it may be at a day's warning'),[66] which was undermined by the strain involved: 'the Queen disorders herself by preparing herself to touch', one observer reported in 1714, '. . . no one about her cares she should doe it, for she fasts the day before and abstains severall days, which they think does her hurt'.[67] At the beginning of the reign the queen received groups of only forty sufferers, but hoped 'as she has strength (for she has lately had the gout in both her hands) to increase her number, and from forty will I hope come to touch two hundred or three hundred at a time'.[68] The queen was apparently successful in expanding these numbers. Each person who was touched was given a small medal, a piece of 'healing gold'. In the year from 16 May 1706 to 31 May 1707, some 1,877 pieces of healing gold were ordered and 1,793 pieces were sent to the queen for distribution.[69] Despite these large numbers, admission to the ceremony was difficult to obtain and the queen's chief ministers received requests for tickets of admission.[70] The practice of touching was permanently discontinued after the accession of George I.

Opponents of the queen's Hanoverian successors later claimed that she had revived the practice of touching for the king's evil as a demonstration of her belief in the principle of hereditary right and – implicitly – of her support for a Jacobite restoration in the person of her half-brother, the Pretender. Non-jurors and Jacobites cherished this thought: three months after the queen's accession, William Lloyd, the deprived Bishop of Norwich, opined in a confidential letter to one of his close friends that

> The Queen is truly zealous for the Church of England, though there may be some about her that are not so, yet it's hoped there are many great ministers in her interest that may in due time assist her in giving ease to those that suffer from conscience sake, and for the true interest of the Royal family and hereditary monarchy.[71]

It was in the queen's interest to encourage the continuation of such false hopes, because of the potential seriousness of the Jacobite menace.

During the reign of William III, Jacobites in England had enjoyed no opportunity to display the strength of their numbers, but almost half of Scotland and three-quarters of Ireland were suspected of being loyal to the titular James III. Furthermore, at the moment of the queen's accession, the Pretender was receiving monetary aid from Pope Clement XI, while Louis XIV was prepared to aid him actively after William's death.[72] While Jacobites at home continued to flatter themselves that the queen would eventually help to restore her half-brother, the French were more realistic, noting that the queen alone could not change the laws in favour of Hanover and that it would be impossible for her to bring foreign troops into England to support a Jacobite restoration.[73]

In reality, there is every reason to believe that the queen was pro-Hanoverian and strongly anti-Jacobite. She realized full well, as the Earl of Marchmont put it to her in a memorandum in the summer of 1702, that 'if the Queen have a good title, the pretended prince has none; and if the pretended prince have a good title, the Queen and her progeny have none. There is no medium.'[74] While the queen realistically tended to discount the size of the Jacobite movement in England, she was nevertheless well aware of the danger which it posed to her own security. In August 1702 she assured Lady Marlborough:

> I must own I am not apt to beleeve all ye reports one heares, soe can not give into ye opinion that there are many Jacobites in England, but I'me as well satisfyed as you can be, that those that are soe, are as much my enemies as ye papists, & I am very sensible these people will allways have designes against me, for as long as ye young man in France lives (which by ye laws of nature will be longer then me) no body can doubt but theire will be plots both against my crown & life, you may be sure I'le take as much care of both as I can . . .[75]

At the end of the year, when Bishop Burnet warned the queen that her life would be in danger when the Jacobites attempted to bring in the Prince of Wales, 'the Queen responded that she understood that well, and that she was grateful for what he told her'.[76] By that time, the Hanoverian envoy to London, Ludwig von Schütz, was convinced that the queen was well-intentioned towards Hanover 'dans les fonds'.[77] In small but significant ways the queen demonstrated her adherence to the Protestant constitution from the opening of the reign. She forbade entry to court to non-jurors, including her uncle, the Earl of Clarendon (although she privately gave him an annual pension of £1,500), while at the same time she received (and continued to do so throughout her reign) the congratulations of Dissenters through delegations of their pastors.[78] There is no proof worthy of the name that the queen contemplated the restoration of the Pretender, even if he should become converted to Protestantism.

Throughout the queen's reign, her ministers constantly received reports, both at home and abroad, that plans were afoot to murder the sovereign; the Assassination Plot of 1696 was still a fresh memory and these warnings were assiduously investigated. The 1711 attempt by the marquis de Guiscard to assassinate Harley lent a dreadful reality to such rumours. Despite constant threats to her life, the queen apparently took few precautions and stoically faced such dangers, telling Harley in 1712:

> these accounts that are com of a designe against my person dos not
> give me any uneasynes, knowing God Almightys protection is above
> all things, & as he has hitherto bin infinitely gracious to me, I hope he
> will continue being soe.[79]

Such stoicism was reinforced, no doubt, by the enormous popularity accorded the queen until the last months of her life. She worked hard to maintain the most fervent and continuous public support enjoyed by any monarch since Elizabeth. A history of her reign published in 1721 described this popularity in recording the queen's visit to Newmarket in October 1706:

> Crouds of people from all parts of the Country came to see Her
> Majesty and wish her a long Life and Happy Reign; and, indeed, thus
> it was in whatever part of England she was pleased to appear amongst
> them. Nor was their sincerity, I believe, ever doubted . . . they ever
> looked upon her as their common Parent. She found no necessity of
> following the Turkish Maxim of immuring her self for fear of being
> assassinated, the affections of the people were her surest Guard, and
> she was never safer than when she was surrounded by them.[80]

Most of her subjects, of course, saw her not in the flesh, but as the triumphant figure portrayed by the propagandists of her reign. No depiction could stand in greater contrast to the pathetic invalid which the queen was in reality. Surrounded by political rancour and personal sorrow, burdened by her deteriorating physical condition, subject to the unrelenting demands of daily business, the queen's spirits were sustained by her personal popularity and by her sense of mission: 'as long as I live', she told Godolphin in 1705, 'it shall be my endeavour to make my Country and my friends easy'.[81] Her determination to succeed in this mission was to be among the greater glories of her reign.

6

'Unreasonableness, Impertinence, and Brutality'

The Opening Years, March 1702 – April 1704

From the moment Bishop Burnet informed her early on Sunday morning, 8 March 1702, that the king was dead, the new queen was plunged into a bewildering whirlwind of activity. The customs of the Sabbath gave way to the needs of the state. An accession council was immediately held at St James's Palace, at which the queen swore the oath prescribed by law to uphold and defend the Protestant religion; she then, according to Burnet, made a 'well considered speech . . . with great weight and authority', in which she promised to follow the policies of William III.[1] Then both houses of Parliament assembled to recognize the Princess of Denmark as the new sovereign, while the queen remained at St James's to swear and sign the Coronation Oath of Scotland, administered by the Earl of Seafield, secretary of state in Scotland. Shortly after, most of the Lords and Commons repaired to St James's to kiss her hand; only at four o'clock in the afternoon did the formal proclamation of Queen Anne by the royal heralds begin throughout London.[2] L'Hermitage, the Dutch resident in London, reported that on the evening after her accession, the queen felt so exhausted by this activity that she refused to see anyone. 'So great is this princess's sadness since the death of the Duke of Gloucester that she takes pleasure only in solitude; and her elevation to the throne has renewed her sense of loss.'[3]

The smoothness of the transition from William III to Queen Anne was not fortuitous; in the days immediately preceding the king's death, Marlborough, Godolphin, and Robert Harley had been quietly meeting to lay contingency plans for Anne's accession.[4] In consultation with the princess, they decided that continuity of policy between the old and new regimes should be stressed, both at home and abroad. On the day of her accession the queen announced that all major office holders would remain in place for at least a month, and she forbade solicitation for office, while Marlborough assured Count Wratislaw, the Imperial ambassador, that the queen would make use of men from both parties.[5] In addition, the queen assured her Privy Council that she would maintain the Protestant succession and reduce the power of France.[6] On the day following her accession it was announced that Marlborough, in his role as ambassador extraordinary to the States-General, would immediately be dispatched to The Hague to reassure the Dutch republic that Great Britain would remain faithful to the Treaty of Grand Alliance.

The most pressing concern of the new queen and her advisors was her first formal speech to Parliament, scheduled for Wednesday, 11 March. The Queen's Speech presented both ideological and practical problems. While stressing continuity of policy, the new government naturally wished to secure for the queen a degree of popularity which William III had never been able to attain. William's favouritism towards the Whigs during the last weeks of his life had made his name anathema among the Tories. The text of the speech was the subject of acrimonious debate in the cabinet: Rochester, the queen's uncle, insisted that the new monarch distinguish herself from her predecessor by stressing her English birth. Although Rochester's proposal was opposed by Marlborough, Somerset, Devonshire, and the Earl of Carlisle, the first lord of the Treasury, the queen chose to follow her uncle's advice to appeal to Tory and nationalist sentiment.[7]

The queen, in preparing for her speech, also had to overcome the practical problem of her physical invalidism. On the evening of her accession, Godolphin asked Harley, speaker of the Commons: 'She is very unwieldy and lame; must she come in person to the House of Lords, or may she send for the two houses to come to her?'[8] Harley advised Godolphin that the queen should make the journey to the Palace of Westminster. The queen's decision to speak personally in the House of Lords was a recognition of Parliament's central role in the constitution and of her own role as a parliamentary sovereign. When she appeared before Parliament on 11 March, accompanied only by the Marlboroughs,[9] it was obvious that the new queen had taken great care in choosing what to wear. She was dressed in a robe of red velvet lined with ermine and edged in gold galloon, she wore the crown and heavy gold chains with the badge of St George, and bore the ribbon of the Garter on her left arm. Her costume was modelled on a portrait of Queen Elizabeth,[10] whose motto, *Semper Eadem*, she was to adopt before the end of the year.[11]

The Queen's Speech, as finally approved, pledged loyalty to the late sovereign's foreign policy and also stressed the immediate need for a union with Scotland. What was memorable, however, was Rochester's insertion: 'I know my own heart to be entirely English', a declaration which was popularly interpreted to be a reflection on the memory of William III, but one which was also a slap at Mary of Modena and the French-educated Prince of Wales. The queen's statement was widely quoted and approved. Her performance in those first few days established the immense popularity which she was to enjoy throughout her reign. 'Her Majesty charm'd both Houses on Wednesday last [11 March]', one observer reported,

> for never any woman spoke more audibly or with better grace. And her pressing to support our allyances abroad will commute for what the Dutch may take amiss in that emphasis which Her Majesty layd on her English heart. But it did very well at home and rais'd a hum from all that heard her.[12]

Others, however, noted what appeared to be the queen's lack of personal satisfaction in her new role and her innate shyness: 'The Queen happening to blush very much when she spoke her speech from the throne, some compared her to the sign of the Rose and Crown.'[13]

For both personal and political reasons, however, the queen took satisfaction in being able to reward the Marlboroughs for their long support. In 1691, William III had ignored her request that Marlborough be given the Garter; within five days of her accession the new queen had given him the crown's highest honour. On 14 March, Marlborough left London for The Hague ('he sails with a full Gale of Favour')[14] to reassure the Dutch and particularly Anthonie Heinsius, the pensionary of Holland and the *de facto* executive head of the Dutch state, of England's adherence to her alliances. Marlborough was also successful in securing the agreement of all contracting parties to the Grand Alliance to an additional article to demand the expulsion of the pretended Prince of Wales from France.[15] On the day of his departure, the queen created Marlborough captain-general of the Army, master-general of the ordnance, and ambassador extraordinary to the Dutch republic. In addition, Sarah became groom of the stole (the officer in charge of the queen's bedchamber and personal household), mistress of the robes, and keeper of the privy purse; the Marlboroughs' two married daughters were appointed ladies of the bedchamber. Furthermore, during his short stay at The Hague before his return to London and the queen's coronation, Marlborough was elected deputy captain-general of the Dutch land forces, thereby consolidating the military position enjoyed by William III. At the height of their power and influence with the queen, the Marlboroughs enjoyed a joint income of £60,000 per annum, which exceeded that of the Princess of Denmark during the previous reign.

The events of the new queen's life had established the tenacity and

153

independence of her character. She had intrigued against her father and had later defied William and Mary. The world, however, believed that the new queen was the puppet of the Marlboroughs; because of her personal shyness and reticence, and also her retired life and isolation from society, her strength of character was as yet widely unappreciated. Within three weeks of her accession, however, after Parliament had unanimously granted her the same income which William III had enjoyed on the civil list, the queen on her own initiative surrendered £100,000 to supplement governmental revenues for the duration of the war.[16] The £100,000 had been added to William III's civil list in 1697 to provide £50,000 per annum for the support of the Duke of Gloucester, and the same amount for the payment of Mary of Modena's marital jointure. Not only did the queen's surrender of this income increase her general popularity, but it also gave her a reasonable excuse for declining to provide an English household for the heiress apparent, the dowager Electress Sophia of Hanover, for the duration of the war. There is no evidence that Marlborough (who was still at The Hague) or his wife or Godolphin advised the queen to take this step: in all probability the idea was hers alone.[17]

The preparations of the queen's coronation were elaborate but rushed: the date chosen, 23 April, was St George's Day and the seventeenth anniversary of her father's coronation. On the great day, the queen was carried to Westminster Abbey in 'a low open chair', but at the main entrance she left the chair and proceeded by foot to the choir: 'her robe . . . was of gold tissue, very rich embroydery of jewells about it' and she wore the George with a blue ribbon; 'her head was well dress'd with diamonds mixed in the haire which at the least motion brill'd and flamed'.[18] At the queen's request,[19] John Sharp, Archbishop of York, preached the sermon,[20] and at about four o'clock in the afternoon the queen was crowned by Thomas Tenison, Archbishop of Canterbury. At the end of the ceremony 'the Queen walked to the doors of the Abby with obligeing lookes and bows to all that saluted her'.[21] She proceeded to Westminster Hall, where the traditional coronation banquet was held. A mounted knight in armour entered the hall to challenge to combat anyone who would deny the queen's title to the crown. It was only at half past eight that evening that the queen, exhausted, was able to return to St James's[22] and to the task of reconstructing the government which she had inherited from her predecessor.

From the moment of her accession, the queen was the focus of a struggle for power and influence. The advent of her reign was hailed by the Tories with enthusiasm: after the covertly Catholic Charles II, the openly papist James II, and the Calvinist William III, the queen was an undoubted (and undoubting) daughter of the Church of England; consequently, she was expected to support those whose tradition it was to defend the Church and the house of Stuart. Sensing the strength of Tory support in the country and anxious to maintain her popularity, the queen was ready to turn to the Tories. Fear of Whig domination played a part in this decision, as it was to do throughout her reign, but Sarah Marlborough grossly exaggerated this fear when, at the height of her bitterness, she wrote of the queen:

> She had been always bred with an utter aversion to all that went under the name of Whigs. She had been told strange frightfull things of Them: & her Impressions to their disadvantage were as Strong, as they were unjust. She believed them sworn Enemies to the Rights of Princes: & had been taught to look upon them all as Rank Republicans, & as always in readiness to rebell. This aversion was heighten'd by the usage she had met with from King William & her Sister which (tho no more owing to one party than the other, & perhaps more to my Lord Rochester than to any one man living) was now all to be charg'd to the account of the Whigs, against whom she had from her tender years imbibed the most unconquerable prejudices.[23]

In truth, as Sarah's statement suggests, the queen was more influenced by issues than personalities, but the issues involved were not those which Lady Marlborough later chose to present. Like most politicians, the queen did not forget personal slights, and in a few instances took revenge on those she considered her enemies. One man who fell into this category was William III's former favourite, the Earl of Portland. In May 1702 the queen reported to Sarah:

> Lord and Lady Portland took there leave of me this morning. She, I thought, looked a little grave, but he was in one of his gracious ways, and I fancy is fool enough to think his unreasonable demands [i.e. for £10,000 which Portland claimed to have loaned William III] will some time or other be complyed with. But if they were never soe just, and that one had mony to throw away, I think he should be one of the last to be considered.[24]

In contrast to the queen's treatment of Portland, she agreed that after William III's personal debts had been paid, the remainder of his privy purse should be given to the Earl of Albermarle.[25] Personal preferences aside, the queen was determined to appoint men who would support the war effort. Indeed, the queen, Marlborough, and Godolphin stood alone in considering the war abroad as the government's first priority; other politicians of both parties considered domestic issues to be more important. The queen turned to the Tories on the strength of their promises 'to carry on the war and to maintain the alliances'.[26] Marlborough reassured Heinsius: 'I hope the alterations the Queen has [made] & will make will give you noe uneassyness, for I can and doe assure you that the Queen will never indure anybody about her, that dose not shoe a zeall for the common cause.'[27]

In the last months of William's life, Godolphin had warned him that the Whigs were 'an angry party, who breath nothing but violence and confusion when the whole power of the government is not entirely in the hands of their own creatures'.[28] The queen was soon to find that the same strictures applied equally well to the Tories. Led by her uncle, the Earl of Rochester, and by Daniel Finch, Earl of Nottingham, the High Tories were determined to oust the Whigs from every office under the crown. In constructing a new ministry, the queen was not a free agent. Despite the best efforts of the Whigs ('You can't imagine how assiduous the Whigs are to curry favour with her', one disgruntled Tory commented two weeks after the queen's accession)[29] and the support of Marlborough and Godolphin in favour of moderation, the queen found herself forced to concede many of the demands of the Tory leaders.[30] Marlborough told Wratislaw, the Imperial envoy, that 'it is not in my power to intervene in everything'.[31] In so far as they could, the queen, Marlborough, and Godolphin attempted to propitiate the more moderate Whigs. Nottingham, for instance, refused to become secretary of state unless he was assured that a Tory loyalist, Sir Charles Hedges, would replace James Vernon as his fellow secretary:[32] as compensation to Vernon ('I was too obnoxious to the [Tory] party to be continued in'), the queen gave him an annual pension of £1,000, the arrears of his salary were paid in full, and his son was appointed a groom of the bedchamber to Prince George.[33] By contrast, the leaders of the Junto were treated more harshly: Somers, Halifax, Wharton, and Orford were struck from the rolls of the Privy Council. The queen, who personally disapproved of Wharton's licentious and ungodly modes of life and speech, handed his staff as comptroller of the household to the longstanding Tory leader, Sir Edward Seymour, in Wharton's presence.[34]

The household posts were divided between High Tories and moderate Whigs. Edward Villiers, Earl of Jersey, became lord chamberlain and Sir Edward Seymour was appointed comptroller of the household, as just mentioned, while the Duke of Devonshire continued in office as lord steward. After a period of indecision during which the queen, Marlborough, and Godolphin hoped that the Duke of Shrewsbury would return from Rome (where he had retired for health reasons in 1700),[35] the Duke of Somerset was named master of the horse. On 2 May, Vernon was replaced by Sir Charles Hedges as secretary of state for the northern department, while the Earl of Manchester was replaced by Nottingham as secretary for the southern department. John Sheffield, now Marquess of Normanby, became lord privy seal, while Sir Nathan Wright, a Tory appointee, retained his position as lord keeper. There were surprisingly few alterations in subordinate offices, even in the lords lieutenancies, and none in the diplomatic corps. 'You will have noticed that the changes did not go as far as had been imagined', Vernon's son reported to Hanover.[36] Nevertheless, the Whigs were disgruntled by what they regarded as the queen's Tory partisanship. The wife of John Hervey, a West Country Whig, lamented the social predominance of her husband's hereditary rivals: 'We mett last night at Court, which was full of nothing but Sey[mours], it was the saddest drawing room that ever was seen.'[37]

The High Tories, for their part, were dissatisfied with anything less than a thoroughgoing purge at every level. Rochester protested most loudly against the queen's moderation,[38] particularly against her support of Marlborough in resisting a purge of the Army,[39] and it was reported: 'My Lord Rochester threatens to lay down, and I have ground to believe that he is in earnest.'[40] Rochester's irritation was increased by the most important change in government: the queen decided to take the Treasury out of commission and to appoint Godolphin as lord treasurer. Rochester's heart was set on this office, which had last been his during the opening years of James II's reign. He was convinced that he deserved it both by virtue of his near relationship to the queen and his leadership of the Tory party. The queen, however, had other thoughts. Rochester had done little to serve her during her dispute with William and Mary; from that time forward, Lady Marlborough had been his sworn enemy.[41] The queen was already irritated by Rochester's cool reception of her call for a union with Scotland. Finally, Marlborough also distrusted the hot-tempered Rochester's lust for power, warning his wife, 'You will never live to see [Rochester] like anything which he is not the author off.'[42]

From her accession, Godolphin had acted as one of the queen's chief advisors, despite the fact that he did not yet hold governmental office; he spoke to foreign envoys in her name and co-ordinated the queen's activities.[43] The services which 'Mr Montgomery' had rendered to the queen in past reigns were a sure recommendation to her favour. As far as the queen was concerned, the case for Godolphin was clinched when Marlborough refused to command British forces on the Continent unless his ally was appointed lord treasurer and was in a position to provide regular financial support for Marlborough's operations.[44] On 4 May the queen declared Godolphin's appointment publicly.[45] For the next eight years, Godolphin was to be the queen's closest advisor, rarely spending more than a few days each year away from her side. Although Marlborough directed his confidential, cyphered correspondence to his political ally, the lord treasurer, his letters were invariably read by Godolphin to the queen during the early years of the reign.*

Rochester was retained in his position as lord lieutenant of Ireland, but it was intimated to him that he would do well to proceed to Dublin to take up his duties there.[46] From a combination of pique and conviction, Rochester vehemently opposed the proclamation of war against France and Spain on 4/15 May, although Marlborough had already agreed on a joint declaration with the allies at The Hague.[47] In the cabinet, Rochester argued that England should not act as a principal, the role envisioned in the Treaty of Grand Alliance, but rather as an auxiliary, exploiting its naval and colonial role in the struggle against the Bourbon powers.[48] Rochester's protests, supported by Normanby and Jersey,[49] proved to be of no avail, although it renewed suspicions that the three lords shared Jacobite sympathies (a charge which was certainly untrue in Rochester's case); these suspicions were sharpened when Normanby opposed the queen's orders that the dowager Electress Sophia should be specifically named in the prayers for the royal family in *The Book of Common Prayer*.[50]

This Tory opposition to Marlborough's war plans irritated both Lord and Lady Marlborough, who shortly after the declaration of war left London for Margate, where Marlborough awaited favourable winds to embark for the Continent. Godolphin reported to the Marlboroughs Rochester's demands for additional Tory appointments. Characteristically, husband and wife differed in their reactions, Marlborough merely remarking that 'I am sorry gentlemen persist in pressing unreasonable things'.[51] Sarah, the fiery Whig, reacted more vehemently, regarding the loss of positions for Whigs as intolerable. Significantly, in her protest to Godolphin (and through him, to the queen), Sarah added, 'I know my opinion is very insignificant upon most occasions.'[52] Godolphin reassured Sarah that the Whig dismissals 'are much fewer than I thought would have been pressed';[53] on the same day, the queen hastened to mollify the countess by offering her Portland's position as ranger of the Great Park at Windsor. The position would be for Sarah's life and included the office's major prerequisite, a lodge, which became Sarah's main residence for the next few years. The queen, in offering this gift,

---

*The queen, the Marlboroughs, and Godolphin, well aware that the mails were liable to interception and tampering, employed a series of numerical cyphers to represent proper names. Names in italics which appear in quotations cited hereafter appeared only as numerals in the original letters.

158

expressed the wish that Sarah might have the lodge 'for all her days which I pray God may be many and as truly happy as this world can make you'.[54] Sarah's happiness, however, depended upon supporting the projects of her lord against the Tories, whom she chose to regard as hell-bent upon the restoration of the Prince of Wales. During the summer and autumn of 1702, Sarah embarked upon a campaign to convince the queen that the Tories were her secret enemies, while her only hope of retaining the crown rested with the Whigs. The queen, displaying her sense of moderation, refused to be influenced by such extremely partisan propaganda. A year later, in replying to Sarah's interminable arguments, the queen remarked,

> you don't say that among ye Whigs there is not knaves, & you hope no body will disown there is that misfortune with Torys. I wish they had not that misfortune with all my hart, but I do not at all doubt, there are knaves among them as well as among ye Whigs, & I beleeve there are some good reasonable people that are Whigs, I wish there weare more of that number in both partys.[55]

In May 1702 the queen's natural inclinations lay with the Tories, who in her view had consistently supported and defended the Church of England. In the structure of early eighteenth-century politics, the queen's personal views were crucial; as George I's lord chancellor was to inform him in 1714,

> the parties are so near an equality, and the generality of the world so much in love with the advantages a King of Great Britain has to bestow without the least exceeding the bounds of law, that it is wholly in Your Majesty's power, by showing your favour in due time (before the elections) to one or the other of them, to give which of them you please a clear majority in all succeeding Parliaments.[56]

The queen had carried out her changes in government before dissolving William III's last Parliament; governmental patronage, so important to the forthcoming elections, would be securely in Tory hands. In her speech dissolving Parliament on 25 May the queen delivered the new government's election manifesto. While stressing her personal devotion to the principles of national unity and moderation, she nevertheless invited her subjects to join her in supporting the Tory party. 'I shall be very careful to preserve and maintain the Act of Toleration, and to set the minds of all my people at quiet', the queen stated. 'My own principles must always keep me entirely firm to the interests and religion of the Church of England and will incline me to countenance those who have the truest zeal to support it.'[57] Rochester and Notting-ham had been successful in persuading the queen to insert this clause in her speech, over the objections of Godolphin.[58] Although the results of the elections held in June and July were not to become entirely clear until the new Parliament assembled in October, the Tories managed to secure a comfortable majority of 113 members in the House of Commons.[59]

Aside from the elections, the eyes of England were upon the opening campaign of the war being mounted by Marlborough. Between July and October 1702, although faced by an imposing French army under Maréchal Boufflers, Marlborough managed to force the French out of the territories of Cleves and Cologne, between the Rhine and the lower Maas, and then to capture the major fortresses of Venloo, Ruremond, Stevensweert, and Liège. This ensured that Louis XIV would not be able to invade the Dutch republic by the route of 1672.[60] The success of Marlborough's 1702 campaign – startling by comparison with those which William III had recently undertaken with so little success – proved irritating to the Tories. Opposing Continental involvement as they did, the Tory ministers favoured the dispatch of the English and Dutch fleets to seize either Cadiz or Gibraltar and thereby establish an allied foothold in the Iberian peninsula. The naval units were under the command of a Tory officer, Sir George Rooke, and the infantry, 10,000 strong, was headed by Rochester's former son-in-law James Butler, Duke of Ormonde, whom the Tories were attempting to bring forward as a Tory military hero to rival Marlborough. Intra-service rivalries, as well as disputes between the English and the Dutch, prevented any direct attempt upon Cadiz, although the expedition did succeed before returning to England in destroying the main Franco-Spanish treasure fleet from the Caribbean, after the ships had been largely emptied of their treasure while at anchor at Vigo Bay.[61]

By August 1702, Rochester's inveterate opposition to Marlborough's plans led the captain-general to suggest again that he should be dispatched to Dublin to carry out his duties as lord lieutenant of Ireland.[62] Marlborough was particularly worried that Rochester might be able to gain an advantage with the queen because of Marlborough's failure to secure one of her most coveted goals: the election of Prince George as captain-general of the Dutch republic. On 17 April, Prince George had been named generalissimo of all English land and sea forces, although he was given no administrative duties;[63] on 20 May the prince had been appointed lord high admiral with a council of four to six naval advisors.[64] Although the prince was the nominal head of the Admiralty, Marlborough's younger brother, George Churchill, was the leading spirit on the prince's council and the effective head of the Navy. Two days after her accession to the throne, the queen had made it clear to the

Dutch envoys in London that she wished to see the prince placed at the head of the Dutch forces as well.[65] This was not merely a personal whim; William III's death had severed the administrative unity of the Maritime Powers, the continuance of which was made necessary by war. Acting on the queen's instructions, Marlborough had raised the issue with Heinsius during his first visit to The Hague immediately following the queen's accession,[66] and then had subsequently pursued the matter in his correspondence with Heinsius, as well as soliciting Imperial pressure on the Dutch.[67] The queen herself wrote a personal letter to the States-General, asking them to elect her husband, to which the Dutch legislature deemed it most diplomatic to make no reply.[68] In June 1702 she personally spoke to the Dutch envoys in London concerning the possibility of the prince's appointment, and Marlborough had urged Godolphin to press them on the issue in order to establish a unified allied command and to avoid nationalist disputes within the armies.[69] Republican and anti-Orangist elements, however, were now in the ascendant in the republic. They refused to elect any stadhouder or captain-general, especially the consort of the English monarch who would enjoy a political base independent of the control of the States.[70] Faced by Dutch intransigence on this issue Marlborough, by August, was seriously alarmed that his old protagonist (and Prince George's closest Danish friend) Christian Siegfried von Plessen, who was passing through The Hague en route to London to serve as the new Danish envoy, would convince the queen and the prince that Marlborough had prevented an offer of the Dutch command to the prince in order that Marlborough might enjoy it himself.[71] Marlborough appealed to Heinsius, assuring him that Plessen 'is imposed upon by My Lord Rochesters means, who would be glade to have him come into England with this opinion'.[72] By the end of the month, however, both the queen and the prince had reassured Marlborough of their continued confidence in him.[73]

By then, it was clearly impossible for the prince to undertake any active military service. In August 1702 he suffered a serious and prolonged asthmatic attack while at Windsor, the first manifestation of pulmonary disorders which were to end his life within six years. The queen was distraught by her husband's illness, telling Lady Marlborough, 'I am very much in the Spleen to see these Complaints return soe often upon him & with more violence this time then ever they did before.'[74] The royal doctors recommended that the prince should take the cure at Bath, and the queen was determined to accompany her husband. The queen and the prince began their journey from Windsor on 26 August; they were accompanied by Godolphin, Lady Marlborough, Sir Charles Hedges as secretary in attendance, and 'a great court'.[75] The first day involved a reception by the university of Oxford, the night of 27 August was spent at Cirencester, and Bath was reached on 28 August. The royal party was met 'within half a mile of the city by two hundred maids richly dress'd, and carrying Bows and Arrows like Amazons', and escorted into the city in great state, where it was greeted by the lord mayor and the corporation, in striking contrast to the official boycott in 1692.[76] The queen and the prince remained at Bath for six weeks, and the queen took the opportunity to visit Bristol between 3 and 6 September. The royal couple finally returned to Windsor on 10 October and to Kensington on 12 October.[77] Their journey to Bath, however, had little permanent effect on the prince's health; by the end of October, he had to be bled three times in as many days, and for over a week his life seemed to be in danger.[78] 'The Queen would not be persuaded to lie from him during all his illness', reported one observer, 'though in many nights she had very little rest.'[79] The prince's serious illness and his subsequent lack of physical stamina apparently ended plans which some Tories had suggested should be proposed in Parliament that he should be made king, with the right to reign alone should he survive the queen.[80]

By the time the newly elected Parliament opened its first session on 20 October, both the queen and Godolphin were shying away from the High Tories. According to the Hanoverian envoy, Ludwig von Schütz, Godolphin had let the Whigs know that they must work closely with moderate Tories, led by Harley, in order to frustrate the designs of Rochester and Nottingham.[81] Despite Tory bitterness against the Whigs, a French agent in London noticed a seeming contradiction in the personal attitude of the Queen:

> While the Cabinet and the English Parliament use such harsh means to suppress the Whigs, the Queen wishes only to use *douceurs* to gain the support of Whig leaders. She accorded Lord Orford a very favourable reception when he was presented to her.[82]

The queen was exercising caution, refusing to burn her bridges to the Whigs in case Rochester should continue to prove obstreperous.

On most major issues, however, the queen was pleased by the Tory majority in the House of Commons. Keeping to their promise to support the war, the Commons voted all necessary financial supplies with great dispatch.[83] Futhermore, the queen agreed with her High Tory ministers on the most controversial issue considered during the first session of her first Parliament: their bill against Occasional Conformity. The passage of the Toleration Act of 1689, which effectively granted freedom of religion to all non-Anglican Protestants, had led to a serious decline both in attendance and tithing in the Church of England, a decline which the Tories lamented in their slogan 'The Church in Danger'. Also many Nonconformists had evaded the clear intention of the Corporation Act of 1661 and the Test Act of 1673 (both of which limited office-holders to those who accepted the Anglican sacrament) by visiting their parish church to accept the sacrament according to the rites of the Church of England, thereby qualifying for office, and thereafter reverting to their Dissenting chapels. This obvious undermining of the Church of England's monopoly position within the state infuriated the High Tories. Nottingham was probably the author of the first bill against Occasional Conformity,[84] which provided crippling financial penalties for those men who, after qualifying for office, attended non-Anglican services. The bill easily passed the Tory dominated House of Commons, and was enthusiastically supported by the queen, who as a loyal daughter of the Church of England was convinced that the bill was necessary for its preservation. None the less, even she had her doubts, largely occasioned by the position of Prince George who attended both Anglican services and those of his private Lutheran chapel at St James's.[85]

Marlborough and Godolphin, on the other hand, were lukewarm about the proposed bill. As always, their primary consideration was the prosecution of the war, and they viewed the Occasional Conformity bill as a Tory measure to sow discord between the parties and within the country. On 10 December, Godolphin asked Robert Harley,

Does anybody think England will be persuaded that this Queen won't take care to preserve the Church of England? And do they forget that not only the fate of England but of all Europe depends upon the appearance of our concord in the dispatch of our supplies?[86]

In the event Marlborough and Godolphin voted for the bill in the House of Lords, but did nothing else to support it. The queen dispatched Prince George, in his capacity as Duke of Cumberland, to the House of Lords to vote for the bill, but the prince sadly told Wharton, one of the opposition tellers, 'My heart is vid you.'[87] The Whigs, unwilling to rely exclusively upon their slim majority in the upper house, loaded the bill with so many amendments which were unacceptable to the Tory House of Commons that an impasse developed. The Occasional Conformity bill was dead for the 1702-3 parliamentary session.[88]

Apart from disputes on domestic matters, Parliament proved to be delighted with the progress of the war. One of the first actions of the House of Lords was to pass an address to the queen commending her for her choice of Marlborough. In consultation with Godolphin, the queen decided that the occasion was appropriate to elevate Marlborough in the peerage to the rank of duke, despite the queen's apprehension that Sarah might object that it was done upon her account.[89] On 22 October the queen informed Sarah of her decision, adding, 'I know my dear Mrs. Freeman does not care for any thing of that kind.'[90]

Sarah's major objection to the proposed promotion (which was to be kept secret until Marlborough's return to England) was that their family did not have the financial resources necessary to support the new rank. Godolphin conveyed Sarah's apprehensions to the queen,[91] which formed the genesis of the queen's ill-fated proposal to Parliament that Marlborough and his heirs should be given an annual pension of £5,000 in perpetuity.

Significantly, within seven months of the queen's accession, personal contacts between 'Mrs Freeman' and 'Mrs Morley' were so infrequent and uncertain that the lord treasurer felt it necessary to act as an intermediary. This tension was largely due to Sarah's unsuccessful efforts to convince the queen that most Tories were secret Jacobites at heart. Sarah seized upon this new offer of money to continue her partisan controversy with the queen, a dispute which was eventually to wreck their friendship. The Occasional Conformity bill, as well as Rochester's continued opposition to the war schemes of Marlborough and Godolphin, had infuriated Sarah. The queen, at Sarah's request, regularly burned Sarah's letters; the first surviving letter from the queen to Sarah which indicated a fundamental division of opinion between the two women on the question of politics was written on 24 October:

> I can not help being exstreamly conserned, you are so partiall to ye
> Whigs, becaus I would never have you & your poor unfortunat faith-
> full Morly differ in opinion in ye least thing; what I said when I writt
> last on this Subject, dos not proceed from any Insinuations of ye other
> other party, but I know ye Principles of the Church of England, & I
> know those of ye Whigs, & it is that, & no other reason which makes
> me think as I do of ye last.

The queen then bluntly (and for the first time) told Sarah that she was wrong:

> My dear Mrs. Freeman, you are mightely mistaken in your notion of a
> true Whig, for ye Character you give them, dos not in ye least belong
> to them, but to ye Church, but I will say no more on this Subject, only
> beg, for my poor Sake, that you would not shew more countenance to
> those you seem to have soe much inclination for, then to the Church
> party.[92]

Despite the queen's hint that the topic should not be raised again ('I will say no more on this subject'), Sarah was not content to drop the argument. Early in November the Tory majority in the Commons combined their thanks to the queen for Marlborough's services (which, in an affront to William III's memory, they declared to 'have singularly retrieved the ancient honour and glory of the English nation') with an equal commendation of the expedition to Vigo Bay. Lady Marlborough obviously protested that this demeaned her husband's services. On 10 November the queen assured her:

> I am very sory you think I can be offended at you for any thing, espessialy for finding fault with ye address of ye house of Commons, you know I never looked upon ye Sea fight as a victory, & I think what has bin said upon it, as rediculous as any body can do. I wish that every body that dos not do theire Duty, may be found out, & punished as they deserve. I am sure I shall be as willing to do it, as to reward those that do well.[93]

To demonstrate publicly her support for Marlborough's campaign, the queen resurrected the Elizabethan practice of victory services at the new St Paul's Cathedral, which Sir Christopher Wren was now rapidly bringing to completion. She took special care to examine the prayers to be used in the service before they were printed.[94] On 12 November she rode in state to the City, passing the Ludgate monument on which this verse was tacked:

> As threatening Spain did to Eliza bow,
> So France and Spain shall do to Anna now,
> France that protects false Claims t'another's Throne,
> Shall find enough to do to keep her own.

At St Paul's, a *Te Deum* was sung, and Jonathan Trelawney, Bishop of Exeter, preached on the text of Joshua, 22: 8–9: 'Return with much riches unto your tents, and with very much cattle, with silver, and with gold, and with brass, and with iron, and with very much raiment: divide the spoil of your enemies with your brethren.'[95]

The first division of the spoils, to the queen's mind, should go to the Marlboroughs. On 29 November she privately announced to her cabinet her decision to give Marlborough the title of duke and to grant him, for her lifetime, a pension of £5,000 per annum by which the dignity might be supported.[96] Marlborough, who had returned to London on the previous day, was not content with this example of royal bounty. He wished to have the pension granted by Act of Parliament in perpetuity to his heirs.[97] On 2 December the queen publicly proclaimed Marlborough a duke, and on 10 December the proposal for Marlborough's cherished pension for himself and his descendants was introduced in the House of Commons with the support of the speaker, Robert Harley. The High Tories, however, were appalled by the blatant favouritism displayed by the queen at the very moment when they were attacking the memory of William III for similar largesse given to his Dutch confidants. Tory opposition to Marlborough's pension was prompted by Rochester[98] and led by Sir Edward Seymour and Sir Christopher Musgrave – 'those of whom I thought we had deserved better', Godolphin lamented to Harley.[99] Faced by implacable Tory opposition, the queen was forced to withdraw her request on 15 December, the first major setback which her government had received.[100]

'The Queen and her Two Favourites were nettled to the Quick at their Disappointment', reported one contemporary.[101] The failure of the proposed pension not only confirmed Sarah in her inveterate opposition to the Tories, but also helped to alienate Marlborough and Godolphin from their erstwhile allies, particularly from Rochester. The queen was furious at 'what has been so maliciously hindred in the parliament' and, on 16 December, offered the Marlboroughs £2,000 per annum from the privy purse in addition to the £5,000 from the Post Office. 'This can draw no envy', she explained to the new duchess,

> for no body need know it, not that I wou'd disown what I give to people that deserve, especialy where it is imposible ever to return the deserts, but you may keep it a secret or not as you please.[102]

In 1702, thinking she 'had enough', Sarah declined the queen's offer:[103] eight years later, at the height of her bitterness, Sarah demanded – and received – this gift with arrears from the queen.

While the House of Commons had frustrated the queen's attempts to reward Marlborough, it had speedily granted her request that Prince George be given £100,000 per annum, should he survive his wife: this was double the jointure previously awarded to any royal consort. In the House of Lords the Whigs took issue with a clause which specifically exempted the Prince of Denmark from a provision in the Act of Settlement which barred naturalized subjects from sitting in Parliament or on the Privy Council. The ban was to take effect on the accession of a Hanoverian monarch, but the Whigs feared that the clause exempting the prince might later be construed to ban any subject naturalized in the reigns of William III or Queen Anne.[104] The Marlboroughs' son-in-law, the Earl of Sunderland, was the most vociferous leader in the Lords against the clause, embarrassing the Marlboroughs and infuriating the queen.[105] After the judges had ruled that William III's Dutch peers

166

would not be affected by the clause, the prince's bill passed the Lords by a small majority of four votes on 19 January 1703. The queen attributed this success to the efforts of the Marlboroughs, profusely and affectionately thanking Sarah for 'ye pains you & Mr. Freeman has taken . . . but neither words nor actions can ever express ye true servise Mr. Morly and I have of your sincer kindness in this & on all other occasions.'[106]

Sunderland's opposition to the prince's bill was doubly mortifying to the Marlboroughs because it came at the very moment when they were concluding negotiations for the marriage of their third daughter, Elizabeth, to Scroop Egerton, fourth Earl of Bridgewater. Yet on this occasion the queen once again demonstrated her unparalled generosity. On 5 February, four days before the wedding, the queen voluntarily offered a dowry of £10,000.

> My Lord Bridgwater being in hast[e] to be Marryed, I can't any longer deffer telling my dear Mrs. Freeman what I have intended a great while, that I hope she will now give me leave to do what I had a mind to, when dear Lady Harriett was marryed, & lett me speak to Lord Treasurer about it when I see him, that your poor unfortunat faithful Morly may not be any ocassion of delay to other peoples happyness.[107]

After his marriage to Lady Elizabeth Churchill, Bridgewater was made a gentleman of the horse to Prince George, but the Marlboroughs aimed at the post of master of the horse to the prince, held by the deranged Earl of Sandwich to whose appointment Sarah had objected violently in May 1702. Their pretensions were based not on Bridgewater's abilities, but on the fact that all other Churchill connections held some official position. As Marlborough put it to Sarah in 1704, Bridgewater 'is not fit for everything; but I think for our own sakes as well as his, something should be done for him or he would have just reason to take itt unkindly'.[108] The queen agreed with Marlborough's estimate of his son-in-law's limited abilities. Three months after his marriage, the queen notified Sarah:

> I have heard nothing more of Lord Sandwich, so I conclude he has not bin soe ill as it was reported, but if that, or any other vacancy happens that you think proper for Lord Bridgewater, I shall be glad to lett him have it; for though he is no Solomon, he is a man of great quality and young enough to improve. But I must confess that which weights most with me, is the neare relation he has to my dear, dear Mrs. Freeman.[109]

Bridgewater finally obtained the post when Sandwich's mental condition made his removal from office essential in 1705.

At the same time that the queen was re-inforcing her financial support for the Marlboroughs, she was also extending her political support of

167

the Duumvirs (as Marlborough and Godolphin were now generally called). She was heartily weary of Rochester's presumption and insolence. Through Nottingham, she ordered her uncle to take up his office as lord lieutenant of Ireland by going to Dublin, and she specifically forbade his future attendance at the cabinet, saying it was not reasonable that he 'should come to the council only when he pleased'. When Rochester angrily refused to leave England she calmly dismissed him from office, and on 5 February appointed his former son-in-law the Duke of Ormonde in his place.[110] The dismissal of Rochester marked the queen's final break with her mother's family. Rochester went into open opposition, for which the queen never forgave him, particularly for his misuse (in her eyes) of his edition of her maternal grandfather's *History of the Great Rebellion* which Rochester had begun to publish in 1702. In the autumn of 1703, the second volume of Clarendon's *History* appeared with a dedication by Rochester to the queen which, in effect, was a warning to adhere to the Tory party unless she wished to share the fate of her paternal grandfather Charles I. The queen reported to Sarah:

> Sir B. Bathurst sent me Ld Clarendons history last week, but haveing not quite made an end of ye first part, I did not unpack it, but I shall have that Curiosety now, to See this extraordinary dedication, which I should never have looked for in ye Second part of a book, & me thinks it is very wonderfull that people that dont want sense in some things, should be soe rediculous as to shew theire vanity.[111]

Two years later, in the summer of 1705, it was noted that 'My Lord R———r was att Court & saw ye Queen att dinner; but no notice was taken of him'.[112] Although political necessity forced the queen to recall Rochester to office as lord president in 1710, there is no evidence to suggest that he exercised any influence over her during the remaining eight months of his life.

Hard upon these events – the dismissal of Rochester and the marriage of Elizabeth Churchill to one of the wealthiest noblemen in England – occurred a tragedy which was to alter fundamentally the Marlboroughs' lives: the death of their only son John, Lord Blandford. A student at Cambridge, Blandford was stricken with smallpox. The duchess rushed to his bedside. Her departure from London was followed by a series of anxious letters from the queen, asking Mrs Freeman to 'give me leave once more to beg you for Christ Jesus sake to have a care of your dear precious self'.[113] The queen dispatched her own doctors to Cambridge to attend Blandford.[114] By 19 February, however, word had reached London that his condition was hopeless and the queen sent a heartfelt letter to the distraught mother, praying that 'Christ Jesus comfort & support you under this terrible affliction, & it is his mercy alone that can do it'.[115] With his parents by his bedside, Blandford died on Saturday morning, 20 February. The Marlboroughs retired from Cambridge to their country home at St Albans to mourn the passing of their son and heir.

For this remarkable couple, the death of Blandford deprived them of their favourite child and shattered their dreams of establishing a dynasty. Marlborough was able to find some degree of consolation by returning to the Dutch republic and his military duties on 6 March. He also nourished the hope – which proved false – that the duchess was again pregnant and might yet produce another male heir. For Sarah, the death of her only son was much more disastrous, for it coincided with her climacteric, the menopausal period in which, as in so many women, her personality was subtly but profoundly affected. Her wit, which had been sharp, became piercing; her humour, which had been biting, became mordant; her convictions, which had been firm, became absolute; her manner, which had been bold and assured, became precipitous and arrogant. Indeed, so changed was she by Blandford's death that one observer commented: 'We hear the Duchess of Marlborough bears not her affliction like her mistress, if report be true that it hath near touched her head.'[116]

In 1714, Jonathan Swift was to claim that he had it 'from unquestionable Authority, that the Duchess of Marlborough's Favour began to decline very soon after the Queen's Accession to the Throne'.[117] Like all such generalizations, there is an element of truth in Swift's assertion. From the beginning and throughout their careers, Marlborough and Godolphin treated the queen as she expected, with the deference and submission normal to a servant–mistress relationship. Sarah, however, had long since ceased to treat Mrs Morley as her mistress. The death of Blandford, which should have linked the queen and Sarah in mutual tragedy, served instead to increase the duchess's presumption. It also contributed to her prolonged absences from court.

From the queen's extant letters to Sarah attributable to 1702, it is clear that Sarah spent long periods away from London; she did not even come to court during Prince George's illness in November 1702.[118] Her absence from court seemed to be a luxury for one whose offices involved close attendance upon the queen. The queen still relied upon her judgment, informing her that 'I am now at liberty to take another maid of Honour' and, mentioning a potential candidate, adding 'but if She dos not live civilly enough with you . . . do not Constrain your self, but lett me know who you think will be proper to order to acquaint her with it'.[119] The alienation between the two friends began in the summer of 1702, thanks to Sarah's campaign against the Tories, but it was vastly accelerated by Blandford's death in 1703, after which the duchess became a virtual recluse at St Albans or at Windsor Lodge. She compensated for her prolonged absences from the queen with long epistles packed with her own political views.

Immediately after Blandford's death, the queen – remembering her own losses – offered in a moving letter to join her friend at St Albans, 'for I must have one look of my dear Mrs. Freeman & I would com ye way that will be least uneasy to you'.[120] Sarah, however, was so distraught that she would not even see her own daughters and rejected the queen's suggestion that 'ye unfortunat ought to come to ye unfortunat'.[121] Godolphin returned to London on 26 February and found the queen hurt and surprised by Sarah's attitude.[122] Part of Sarah's cold reaction to the queen's offer may be attributed to natural feminine jealousy: at this time it was rumoured that the queen was once again pregnant.[123] Although she was now an invalid, the queen still hoped, as she later told the duchess, 'for the inexpressible blessing of another child, for though I do not flatter myself with the thought of it, I would leave no reasonable thing undon that might be a means towards it'.[124] Sarah's sorrow and jealousy led her to retire to Windsor Lodge for virtually the remainder of the year.

The spring of 1703 was the lowest point, from a political and a personal point of view, which the Marlboroughs and Godolphin were to experience in the early years of the queen's reign. Marlborough was to be hampered throughout the 1703 campaign by the obstreperous delaying tactics of the Dutch field deputies. Godolphin was increasingly beset by difficulties with Scotland. Both men had to work continuously against some of their High Tory colleagues who were less than enthusiastic about the war. This lack of enthusiasm was definitely not shared by the queen. When news reached London at the end of April that Marlborough had captured Bonn, one disgruntled Whig, suspecting that some Tory ministers wished to make peace with France, wrote,

> But the Queen her self with out advise of Council (& against ye inclination as is thought of some there), sent to ye Tower to have ye Gunns fir'd, & to ye City to have ye Bells rung on this Gloriouse News; & express'd reall Joy when more than half her Court were said to have sad Looks.[125]

It was against this background that Marlborough, for the first time, threatened to resign, promising Sarah, 'I shall meadle with nether partys . . . I know by this methode which ever party is uppermost will be angry with mee, soe that at last the Queen will be obliged by them to let me retir[e].'[126] Confronted by this possibility, the queen demonstrated her obstinacy and her determination to proceed along the course which had already been charted. On 22 May she wrote one of her most famous letters to Sarah:

> The thoughts that both my dear Mrs. Freeman & Mr. Freeman seems to have of retyering gives me no small uneasyness & therfore I must say something on that Subject, it is no wonder at all people in your posts should be weary of ye world who are soe continually troubld with all ye hurry & impertinencys of it, but give me leave to say, you should a litle consider your faithfull freinds & poor Country, which must be ruined if ever you should putt your melencoly thoughts in execution, as for your poor unfortunat faithfull Morly she could not beare it, for if ever you should forsake me, I would have nothing more to do with the world, but make another abdycation, for what is a Crown, when ye support of it is gon, I never will forsake your dear self, Mr. Freeman nor Mr. Montgomery, but allways be your constant faithfull servant, & we four must never part, till death mows us down with his impartiall hand.[127]

No more ringing endorsement could be expected from a monarch to her servants, but one startling omission suggests that, consciously or unconsciously, the queen was beginning to view the Marlboroughs and Godolphin in a political rather than in a personal context. For twenty years her happiest and bitterest moments had been shared with her husband, Prince George; by every account (except Sarah's, written at the moment of her greatest bitterness) the queen was a loyal and devoted wife, deeply in love with her husband. If, as Sir Winston Churchill says of this letter, 'It was the Cockpit against the world!', would the queen deliberately have omitted her husband? This subtle shift in the queen's reactions to the Marlboroughs and Godolphin was largely inspired by Sarah's own tactic, the ostentatious use of titles rather than the old and comfortable names of Freeman and Morley. Five days before this letter was written, the queen had complained to the duchess:

> I must disobey my dear Mrs. Freeman & answer her letter in writting, becaus I can't help being uneasy that you call me twice Majesty, & not once mention your poor unfortunat faithfull Morly & therfore I beg if it is not very troublesom that you would writt two words before you goe to bed, to lett me know if your are ether angry with me or take any thing ill, that I may Justify my self if you have any hard thought of me.[128]

The disappointments of the summer of 1703 were to test the queen's enthusiasm for the war; in contrast to the preceding campaign, Marlborough's achievements were limited by the hesitancy of his Dutch field deputies. Although he was able to capture Bonn, Huy, Limburg and Guelders, thereby liberating the whole of Spanish Guelderland and the bishopric of Liège from French control, the Dutch prevented him from bringing Louis XIV's Army of Flanders into a decisive battle which might have changed the course of the war. From the outset of the campaign, the allies had to contend with the desertion to Louis XIV of Maximilian Emmanuel, Elector of Bavaria, whose hereditary possessions were now at the disposal of the French for an invasion of Austria and an attack upon Vienna in 1704. In the east, the French were secretly subsidizing a revolt by Hungarian Protestants against the Catholic Habsburgs.[129] In the west, the allied cause was strengthened and its goals changed by the successful conclusion of the Methuen Treaty in May 1703, an Anglo-Portuguese alliance negotiated by John Methuen under the supervision of Nottingham. Not only did this alliance give the allies a base in the Iberian peninsula, but England and the Dutch republic also agreed to Portugal's demands to support the claims of the Habsburg heir, the Archduke Charles, as 'Carlos III of Spain'. The original Treaty of Grand Alliance had envisioned a partition of the Spanish possessions between the Habsburg and Bourbon candidates; by the Methuen Treaty the allies demanded the entire Spanish empire for the Habsburgs, with no compensation whatsoever for the duc d'Anjou. It was Nottingham who coined the slogan 'No Peace without Spain',[130] and the recovery of Spain from the house of Bourbon quickly proved to be the only major goal shared by the Whigs and the Tories. The queen also embraced this new policy, 'I haveing no ambition after the King of Spaine is seteld on his throne, but to see an honnorable peace', as she told Godolphin in 1706.[131]

Despite the great events which were taking place on the Continent, the queen's mind during the summer of 1703 was largely occupied with attempts to propitiate her dearest friend and closest servant, the Duchess of Marlborough. After her first Parliament was prorogued on 27 February 1703, the queen had overcome her reluctance to create new peers in order to give the Tories a working majority in the House of Lords. The Marquess of Normanby was elevated to the dukedom of Buckinghamshire and four new Tory peers (Finch, Gower, Granville, and Seymour-Conway) were created. At Sarah's personal request, the queen had also ennobled a Whig, John Hervey, as Baron Hervey. This royal compliance merely encouraged Sarah to become even bolder. At the end of May 1703 the queen complained to the Duchess of Marlborough about the Duke of Somerset and the new Duke of Buckingham, and their extravagant demands of courtiers' prerogatives as master of the horse and lord privy seal respectively, concluding:

> it is very troublesom to have any thing to do with these great men, but one must have patience which is ye only remedy for every thing; the unreasonableness, impertinence, & Brutalety that one sees in all sorts of people every day, makes me more & more sensible of ye great Blessing God Almighty has given me in three such friends as your dear self, Mr. Freeman, & Mr. Montgomery, a happyness I beleeve no body in my Sphere ever enjoy'd before, & which I will allways value as I ought.[132]

The queen concerned herself intensely with the duchess's ill health (lameness and a shortness of breath); on 5 June she asked Godolphin to 'perswaid her to ask some advice, for this complaint may prove of ill Consequence if She dos not take some thing'.[133] At the same time, the queen recognized the emotional roots of Sarah's illness, telling her at the end of June, 'I am very sory my dear Mrs. Freeman will not hearken to any advice conserning her Self, I know no Doctor can do your mind any good, but Sertainly they may mend your health.'[134] Partly to please the duchess, the queen at first encouraged her intervention on politics. On 7 June the queen told Sarah:

> I beg my dear Mrs. Freeman would banish that hard thought out of her head that I can ever be displeased at anything that comes from you, for sure I must be void of all reason if I weare not sensible that there can not be a greater mark of kindness then telling one every thing freely, it is what has allways bin my request to you to do, & I do againe beg you would Continue that goodness to your poor unfortunat faithfull Morly.[135]

Sarah, encouraged by this, again took up her favourite theme: the Tories were simply Jacobites in disguise. On 11 June the queen replied to this assertion with an analysis of recent history which has largely been endorsed by twentieth-century historians:

> I own I can not have that good opinion of some sort of people that you have, nor that ill one of others, & lett the Whigs brag never soe much of theire great Services to their Country & of theire numbers, I beleeve the revolution had never bin, nor the Succession setel'd as it is now, if the Church party had not Joyned with them, & why those people that agreed with them in these two things should all now be branded with ye name of Jacobit I can't imagin, have they not great Stakes as well as them, & that if they had nether consience nor honnour would prevaile with them not to give into what would be for theire destruction, sure ye same argument will hold for both Whig & Tory. I do not deny but

there are some for ye P. of Wales, but that number, I believe is very small, & I dare say there are millions that are call'd Jacobitts, that abhor theire principles as much as you do.[136]

To demonstrate that she did not stand alone in her hostility to the High Tories, the duchess sent the queen a letter which Marlborough had written to her on 3 June saying,

Wee are bound not to wish for anybody's death, but if *Sir Edward Seymour* should dye, I am convinced it would be noe great lose [*sic*] to *the queen*, nor the nation, and you may be sure the visset intended by *Rochester* and his friend [Sir Christopher Musgrave] could be for noe other end but to flatter *Seymour* to doe such mischiefs as they dare not openly owne.[137]

The Queen returned Marlborough's letter to Sarah on 14 June, endorsing the views of the husband but not those of the wife: 'I do not at all doubt but the person [Seymour] that Mr. Freeman thinks would be better out of the world than in it, and the other [Rochester] that is gon a progress, are of that violent temper that they will do all the mischiefe they can', she assured Sarah, 'and I can see as well as anybody all the faults and follys of others exsept that great one [Jacobitism] you think them guilty of, & that I must own againe I want faith to beleeve.'[138] The queen's lack of faith soon led to exasperation, and on 16 June the queen attempted to break off her political correspondence with Sarah:

I can not help thanking my dear Mrs. Freeman for ye letter she sent me last night, becaus I'me sure she means it out of kindness to me, but I will not go about answering any one part of it, finding you are soe fixed in ye good opinion you have of some, & ye ill opinion you have of other people, that it is to no manner of purpose to argue any thing with you, therfore shall leave it to providence & time to convince you of ye mistakes you are in in severall things.

In a remarkably accurate prophecy, the queen demonstrated her caution and judgment when she warned Sarah: 'When you have had a few yeares more experience of that sort of people you are now so partiall to, you will find they are not what they would be thought to be.' This was as close to an open rebuke as the queen had ever come with Sarah, and she softened her tone adding,

I must Confess it is no small mortification to me that differences of opinion should make you cold to your poor unfortunat faithful Morly, & hinder you from Coming to me, for whatever you say I can never take it ill, knowing as I have said already, that you mean it kindly.[139]

Sarah was slow to appreciate how serious the queen was, and two days later another rebuke was administered: 'I am very sory to find that every body who are not Whigs must be reckoned Jacobites, I meane all that are in any employment.'[140]

Confronted by the queen's 'want of faith', Sarah switched her tactics: instead of indicating the entire Tory party, she proceeded to undermine the faith of her husband, of Godolphin, and of the queen in individual Tory ministers. She did not have difficulty in convincing the Duumvirs. In June 1703, Marlborough warned Godolphin that Nottingham was working against the treasurer,[141] and a month later, when Nottingham refused to give John Methuen the title of ambassador extraordinary to Portugal and Methuen complained to the duchess, Marlborough commented to Godolphin: 'If you should oblige him [Nottingham] in this, and in almost everything he askes . . . *the Queen* must expect that he will underhand endeavour to obstruct everything.'[142] Sarah retailed Methuen's complaints to the queen, but the latter replied with some exasperation: 'I allways took it for granted that Mr. Methuen was to have ye title of Ambassadour extraordinary . . . soe you may lett him know it shall be don.'[143] The queen's alienation from her High Tory ministers had not proceeded as far as that of Marlborough, who agreed with Sarah that at least Jersey and Buckingham should be dismissed from office for their support of Rochester's attacks upon the management of the war.[144] Marlborough even at times appeared to accept his wife's equation of the Tories with Jacobitism: 'There are a thousand reasons for preserving our friendship with the Dutch', he told Sarah in September, 'for as we save them, so they preserve us from the arbitrary power of *Rochester* and *the Tories*, which must be entirely governed by *the Pretender.*'[145]

In undermining the reputations of the Tory ministers, Sarah concentrated much of her fire on Buckingham, reporting to the queen the rumour that Buckingham was going to apply for a grant from the privy purse. The queen disingenuously replied that

> the only reason that I never answered what you said about the Duke of Buckingham was forgetfullnes, he has never yet mentioned anything of a grant, but if he dos as it is very likely he will, you may be assured I will never Consent to it, for no body can have a worse opinnion of him then I have.[146]

Earlier, the queen had given Buckingham permission to build a town house in St James's Park (the genesis of the present Buckingham Palace). The Duchess of Marlborough now reported that Buckingham had exceeded his boundaries and was actually constructing a wall on the Queen's property. The queen asked Sarah to consult with Godolphin 'what is proper for me to do to putt a Stop to this impertinence of Ld. Nor[manby]' and promised on her next visit to London to 'see this addition of his insolence my self, & then I confess if one can't make him pull ye wall down that goes further then ye ground I gave him, I should make no Scruple to order it to be done'.[147] There is no evidence, however, that the queen found that Sarah's story was true. Despite the queen's statement that 'no body can have a worse opinnion of him then I have', on 20 August 1703 Buckingham was given £1,000 as a 'free gift' from the secret service accounts.[148] This was the first occasion when the queen was less than candid with her best friend.

The growing divergence between the two women was underlined by the fact that when, on 22 July, the queen notified the duchess that she and the prince had decided to visit Bath during the following month, she did not suggest that Sarah should accompany them.[149] On 18 August the royal couple departed from Windsor, once again accompanied by Godolphin, for a sojourn in Bath which was to last for seven weeks. The duchess did not join the queen until 9 September.[150] When the queen returned to Windsor on 9 October, she learned that Nottingham had managed to conclude an alliance with Victor Amadeus, Duke of Savoy. Victor Amadeus had deserted William III in 1696 and had subsequently married his two elder daughters to the two elder grandsons of Louis XIV. Now Savoy's desertion to the Grand Alliance threatened to put an end to Franco-Spanish domination of the Italian peninsula. The queen, though aware of the Duke of Savoy's lack of sincerity, objected strongly to Sarah's charge that the Tories regretted the Savoyard alliance: 'I will not say who is glad or sory for it', she wrote sharply to Sarah on 20 October, 'nor whether my eyes are shutt or open, but this I am very sure off, that *the queen* will venture & do more for ye true interest of this poor Country than all those [Sarah's note: 'by them she means the Whigs'] who boast soe much of theire good intentions towards it.'[151]

The political situation which the queen faced on her return from Bath in the weeks leading up to the opening of Parliament was grim. Party disputes were increasing, as were difficulties with Scotland; despite the Portuguese and Savoyard alliances, the 1703 military campaign had produced disappointing results. Her personal dispute with the Duchess of Marlborough did not contribute to the queen's peace of mind: 'your poor unfortunat faithfull Morly . . . expects nothing but uneasyness this winter', she told Sarah on 16 October, '& your Coldness added to it will make it unsupportable'.[152] The queen officially opened Parliament on 9 November, asking in her speech for 'perfect Peace and Union' between all her subjects, but the two parties had other ideas. On 23 November a

notice appeared in the official *London Gazette* of the impending introduction of a second Occasional Conformity bill, and on 25 November it
was introduced by a High Tory, William Bromley, representative for the
university of Oxford, supposedly with cabinet approval.[153] Marlborough (who had returned to London on 10 November) and
Godolphin, increasingly dependent upon the support of moderate
Tories and Whigs for financial supplies with which to prosecute the war,
again voted for the bill in the House of Lords, but covertly did everything possible to defeat it. More importantly, the queen's attitude
towards the bill had changed during the summer. She now believed that
its reintroduction was a 'pretence . . . for quarelling' and firmly
supported her Lutheran husband's refusal to vote again for it ('I think
him very much in ye right'). However, she still believed that the bill
would serve to strengthen the Church of England and rejected the
standard Whig arguments against it ('I see nothing like persecution in
this Bill'). In presenting the Whig arguments, the duchess had insinuated
that the queen's failure to agree with her was due to 'secret influences'.
This the queen hotly resented. In response to the duchess's 'long letter'
against the bill, the queen wrote on 10 December:

> I must own to you that I never cared to mention any thing on this
> Subject to you becaus I knew you would not be of my mind, but since
> you have given me this occassion, I can't forbeare saying that I see
> nothing like persecution in this Bill, you may think this is a notion Ld.
> Nott: has putt into my head, but upon my word it is my own thought.

In the same letter, for the first time the queen made a significant plea:
she 'begs She [Sarah] would never lett difference of opinnion hinder us
from liveing togather as we used to do'.[154] On 13 December, the day
before the second Occasional Conformity bill came to a vote in the
Lords, the queen once again assured the duchess that the prince would
not vote for it.[155] The absence of Prince George from the House of Lords
was probably crucial in encouraging five peers, previously considered to
be securely within Tory ranks, to absent themselves, too, from the
debate. In a frontal assault on the issue, the Whigs defeated the bill by
twelve votes.[156]

The failure of the second Occasional Conformity bill infuriated the
Tories, who had viewed it as a means to undermine Toleration,
suppress Dissenters, and generally outwit the Whigs. They were
particularly distressed by the position which the queen – hitherto regarded as a Tory heroine – had taken. 'The clergy over England',
recorded Bishop Burnet, 'who were generally inflamed with this matter,
could hardly forgive the Queen and the Prince the coldness that they

expressed on this occasion.'[157] In their propaganda attacks, the Tories went so far as to equate her with William III.[158] Both the queen and her chief ministers suspected that these attacks were directly inspired by a few Tory leaders, and that the bulk of the party remained loyal to the Protestant constitution. Marlborough, in writing to his wife in December 1703, obviously described the queen's position when he stated: 'I can't by noe means allow that all the Tory party is for King James, and consequently against the Queen. I think it is in her power to make use of allmost *all but some of the heads*, to the true interest of England, which I take to be the Protestant Succession.'[159] Marlborough himself had advised the queen to dismiss Sir Edward Seymour from office before the parliamentary session began. She had demurred, but by January 1704 Marlborough confided to Schütz, the Hanoverian envoy, that the queen had agreed to dismiss Seymour as soon as Parliament rose.[160] The position of the Tories, and particularly of Nottingham, had been undermined by their handling of the 'Scotch Plot'. Simon Fraser, Lord Lovat, whose career in treachery was to end on the scaffold in 1747, had reported his contacts with the exiled court of St Germain-en-Laye to the queen's principal minister in Scotland, the Duke of Queensberry. In his report, Lovat had unfairly implicated his personal enemy and Queensberry's political rival, the Duke of Atholl. Queensberry had dispatched Lovat back to France to contact the Jacobite court again and had first brought the 'Plot' to the attention of the English government in the summer of 1703. When Queensberry visited London in October 1703, he told Nottingham that he was sending an unnamed double agent back to France for more information. When Atholl discovered Lovat's intrigue, he protested to Queen Anne;[161] and the Whigs in the House of Lords had unscrupulously seized upon the whole affair to discredit Nottingham.

During the storms raised by the Scotch Plot and by the Tory attitude to Church matters, the queen played hostess to the new allied candidate for the Spanish throne in what was to prove the most elaborate state visit of her reign. The Archduke Charles of Austria (now recognized by the allies as Carlos III of Spain) landed at Spithead on 26 December 1703 and arrived at Windsor on 29 December, accompanied by Prince George and the Duke of Somerset. After two nights of lavish entertainment and banqueting, the King of Spain left Windsor on 31 December to sail for Portugal six days later.[162]

The Queen, during and after the state visit, was increasingly disturbed by the Tory cry of 'The Church in Danger', which she interpreted as a personal insult. Fortunately, the resourceful Robert Harley had a plan in hand to counteract Tory propaganda following the failure of the second Occasional Conformity bill, a plan for the financial relief of the poorer clergy which had originally been suggested by Bishop Burnet to William III. On the queen's thirty-ninth birthday, 6 February 1704, the government introduced in the House of Commons plans for what became known as Queen Anne's Bounty: the crown would surrender its traditional income from first fruits and tenths (amounting from £16,000 to £17,000 per annum) to the Church to supplement the pitifully in-adequate clerical stipends in the poorest parishes.[163] The Bounty was immediately popular and did much to counteract High Tory propa-ganda. As the queen pointed out in her message to Parliament, she sought 'the advantage of the Church of England as by law established, for which nobody can have a more true and real concern than myself'.[164]

In her message proroguing Parliament on 3 April, the queen admonished the members of both houses to 'go down into your several countries so disposed to moderation and unity, as becomes all those who are joined together in the same religion and interest',[165] but it was obvious that moderation and unity could not be attained without changes in her government. The following day the process began. Henry St John, a young follower of Robert Harley and a particular favourite of the Duke of Marlborough, kissed hands on his appointment as secretary at war,[166] replacing William Blaythwayt, a civil servant from the reign of Charles II who was 'grown somewhat stiff and rusty'.[167] St John's appointment represented a real strengthening of Marlborough's control over the disposal of military forces, and was a challenge which Nottingham could not ignore. On 8 April, Marlborough warned Godolphin from Harwich (where the captain-general was to embark for the Continent) that Nottingham was assuring the Tories that 'the Queen is desirous to doe everything that would give them satisfaction, but that she is hindered by you and mee'; furthermore, Marlborough predicted that Nottingham would soon press for major changes in the cabinet.[168]

Within ten days, Marlborough's prophecy came true. On 18 April, in a long conference with the queen, Nottingham demanded that the re-maining Whigs be dismissed from government; specifically, he de-manded that the Duke of Somerset and the Archbishop of Canterbury be removed from the cabinet, Somerset because he had been the chairman of the House of Lords investigation into the Scotch Plot, in which an attempt had been made to smear Nottingham, and Tenison because he had opposed the Occasional Conformity bill. 'He was very positive', Godolphin reported to the Duchess, 'that the Queen could not govern but by one party or the other.' The queen was angered by Nottingham's presumption and refused to be intimidated. She wished to take stronger measures against the High Tories than she had previ-ously agreed upon with Marlborough and Godolphin: 'she seemed to

179

think it was not equall to displace some that had misbehaved and keep in others', Godolphin told Sarah, 'but after a little talk she resolved to send her messages Thursday morning', 20 April, to Sir Edward Seymour and to the Earl of Jersey.[169] Although Seymour's dismissal had been long predicted, the dismissal of Jersey at the same time came as a complete surprise to the High Tories, including Jersey himself.[170] Godolphin predicted that despite provocation Nottingham would cling to his office;[171] but the queen, in a letter to Sarah announcing the dismissals on 20 April, implied that she believed that Nottingham would resign:

> I am told by a very good hand that *the Queen* has sent a message to *Jersey* & *Seymour* that they will not like, sur[e] this will convince *the duchess* that *the queen* never had any partiality to one of these persons, for if that had bin soe, this would sertinly never have bin don; Something more of this nature its beleeved will soon happen that will not be disagreeable to *the duchess*.[172]

In fact, the queen was already certain of Nottingham's resignation; he had visited her earlier that day and had offered her the seals of his office. She thrice refused to accept them, largely because no successor had been agreed upon. On the afternoon of 22 April, however, she did accept the seals from Nottingham.[173] Within the next month, the ministry was reconstructed. Seymour's reaction to his dismissal is not known, but Jersey, in his own words, 'argued my case a little with her majesty, not for my Staff, but for my own justification'. The only explanation which the queen chose to give to Jersey was 'that some of her servants had taken measures she did not approve'.[174] Sir Edward Seymour (whose political influence was already on the decline when he died in February 1708) was replaced by Harley's political ally and neighbour, Sir Thomas Mansell; Jersey was replaced as lord chamberlain on 23 April by a Whig nonentity, the Earl of Kent (who the High Tories claimed had received his post as a reward for losing £10,000 to Sarah at the gambling tables).[175] Kent's appointment did nothing to satisfy the Junto. It was a month, however, before Harley agreed, on 18 May, to accept the seals as secretary of state in succession to Nottingham, and to exercise his executive functions while he continued to serve as speaker. Harley delayed both because of his desire to remain independent of party pressures and from his fear of accepting ministerial responsibility. He later recorded that he took the office 'forced by the Queen's express command' as well as by pressure from Marlborough and Godolphin.[176]

For the queen, the ministerial changes in the spring of 1704 marked a political and personal watershed. Events on the Continent and in

Scotland were moving towards a crisis. At home, the queen, Marlborough, and Godolphin had broken the unity of the Tory party by
dividing its leaders and by bringing Harley and his associates into the
ministry, without satisfying the ambitions of the Whig Junto. 'We are far
from being in a Whig interest', St John truthfully remarked in May
1704.[177] Upon the military skills of Marlborough, the financial and diplomatic expertise of Godolphin, and the political management of Harley
hung the future of the Protestant establishment in Great Britain. For the
queen personally, the course of her reign had been determined. 'Moderation' became her watchword and, increasingly, Harley became its
representative in her eyes. She had known Harley for several years.
Although he had advised her before and after her accession, as secretary
of state he now enjoyed daily access to her both as minister and a
personal servant. This was to prove crucial for the future. The queen
continued to rely chiefly upon Marlborough and Godolphin for advice,
but by the spring of 1704 her friendship with Sarah was on shaky
ground. On 24 April, Godolphin warned the Duchess that she was
absent from court too frequently: 'your quiett . . . is much in your own
power; you see you may take it when you will, but you should not abuse
that great indulgence of Mrs. Morley'.[178] Upset by this warning, Sarah
began to doubt her hold on the queen's affections. Two days later,
Godolphin reassured her that 'I know so much of [the queen's goodness
and indulgence], particularly of my own knowledg, that I am very sure a
little time will undeceive you in that matter'.[179] Sarah later concluded
that the queen at this time 'took pains to make Lord Godolphin beleive
she loved me, and she could desimble as well as any Lady that I ever saw
in my life'. In truth, it was Sarah who had changed, not the queen.
During the next three years, while the queen's 'mixed ministry' presided
over the liberation of Germany, Italy, and the Netherlands from French
influence, as well as over the union between Scotland and England,
Sarah's ceaseless verbal bombardment of her friend and sovereign was
to destroy the queen's friendship for her and was to undermine the
political position of Marlborough and Godolphin.

7

'Soe Glorious a Victory'

The Year of Blenheim,
April 1704 – April 1705

During the opening years of her reign, oppressed by constant political problems, Queen Anne also suffered a marked deterioration of her physical condition, particularly the use of her arms and legs. Her malady, labelled 'gout' by early eighteenth-century medical practitioners, was to become more and more confining. In June 1703 she notified Sarah that 'I am I thank God very well in my health, & can walk a little with ye help of two Sticks, but I feare it will be a great while before I shall walk alone'.[1] Her fear proved justified: in November 1704 Lady Russell reported of the queen, 'She cannot set her foot to the ground; has a chair made so well that it is lifted with her in it into the coach, and then she moves herself to the seat, and the chair [is] taken away.'[2] While her increasing disability did not prevent the queen from regularly attending cabinet meetings and holding interviews with her ministers, it could sometimes impede the routine of government. In the winter of 1704 one of her secretaries explained that the queen was unable to write with her own hand, 'her eyes being a little sore', while a year later Godolphin noted: 'The Queen's right hand is bound up so that she can't write.'[3]

The queen's visibly declining health made the question of the succession more crucial as her reign progressed. During the years of victory between 1704 and 1706, the security of the Hanoverian succession, without personal or political embarrassment to the queen, was to be one of the major concerns of her government. Accordingly, the wishes and desires of the heiress apparent to the English throne, the dowager Electress Sophia of Hanover, now aged seventy-four, played a more important role in the calculations of the British government. From the beginning of the queen's reign, Sophia had been angered by the failure of the English government to offer what she considered to be the prerogatives of the heir: a household, a pension, and even the title of 'Princess of Wales' (although there was no legal precedent for a female heir being given this rank). Having enjoyed her closest contacts with Englishmen through the exiled court of Charles II during the Inter-regnum, Sophia's natural inclinations were to the Tories, and to Rochester as the son of the great Clarendon. Rochester, in his fierce desire to revenge himself upon his niece once the queen had dismissed him from office in February 1703, had established contact with the electress through his own agent Dr John Hutton. By the end of 1703 it was known that Rochester was contemplating moving a parliamentary invitation to the electress to take up residence in England.[4] Such a motion would have a triple advantage to the Tories: it would establish Sophia in England as the titular head of the opposition; it would humili-ate the queen; and should the Whigs oppose the invitation they could easily be labelled as republicans.

The queen had been acutely aware of such a possibility before the opening of her reign, when rumours had swept London that William III intended to bring in the electoral prince (the future George II) and perhaps displace the Princess of Denmark. In early 1702, Lady Marl-borough had assured Mrs Gilbert Burnet that the queen herself would propose to Parliament that she would send for the electoral prince.[5] Apparently, Sarah proposed such a scheme to Marlborough in the summer of 1703, for on 1 July he replied to her:

> What you mention . . . concerning *the Elector of Hanover's* son . . . it is not practicable, for the father will less consent to itt now, then he would some time agoe, and att that time I know he was possitively re-solved not to suffer it.[6]

By Christmas 1703, when rumours of Rochester's plans had reached the ears of Schütz, the Hanoverian envoy in London, Marlborough in-formed Portland, and the duchess told Bishop Burnet, that rather than be forced into giving the invitation, the queen herself would invite the electoral prince to reside in England and would treat him as her own son.[7] There is no direct evidence that the queen was consulted on this question or, if so, if she regarded such 'promises' as anything more than ploys to prevent Hanover from falling in with the schemes of opposition leaders, whether Whig or Tory. The dismissal of the High Tories from office in April 1704, however, changed the situation: the animus and wrath of the Tory party was now directed against the queen personally, and the widely mooted invitation scheme was accordingly supplemen-ted by a plan (if the invitation to Sophia should be approved by Parlia-ment) to introduce a motion that the electoral prince should be made generalissimo – thereby humiliating the queen, the Prince of Denmark, and Marlborough. 'Nothing better demonstrates the rage of this party against the Queen', Schütz reported to the elector. 'They were never more animated against the late King than they are now against the Queen.'[8] Before the spring of 1704 the queen had relied upon the elector's well-known aversion to sending his unpredictable son to England and upon the personal regard which the elector had expressed for her.[9] Now, a strong party seemed intent on forcing the queen to accept the presence of a potential successor in England which, as Godolphin informed Harley, 'tis not imaginable how uneasy this will be to the Queen'.[10]

One pretence for the invitation was the continued refusal of the Scottish Parliament to establish the Hanoverian succession in the northern kingdom: should the queen die, there were no legal guarantees that the personal union of the two kingdoms would be continued. In her first speech to Parliament, the queen had recommended the union of the two kingdoms, and had been irritated when the English Tories had proved less than enthusiastic.[11] She was soon to discover that Scottish politics were exceptionally complex, and that the Scottish nobility had no hesitation in appealing over the head of her commissioner, the Duke of Queensbury, to the monarch herself. 'The Queen is pestered out of her life with these Scotch lords', Godolphin reported to Sarah in October 1702. 'She says five of them came to see her together this morning and in the afternoon she was to have the Duke of Queensberry.'[12] Much to the distress of the queen and her English government, in the spring of 1703 the Scottish Parliament passed a bill of Security, which provided that the next sovereign of Scotland should be a Protestant but not the person who inherited the English crown. Scottish Jacobites (who interpreted the bill as an invitation to the Pretender to be converted) supported this measure, as did those Scottish politicans who wished to apply pressure on England to provide Scotland with extensive commercial concessions. The queen, on the advice of her English ministers, vetoed the bill, remaining staunchly committed to the policy of the union as the best means for securing the succession. On 7 June 1703 the queen informed the Duchess of Marlborough:

> I have read & heard read all ye accounts that are com from Scotland, & am very sory to see things go soe ill there, the disaffected people heare [i.e. the English Jacobites] have no doubt a good understanding with those there & will allways help to make distractions in both kingdoms. I must beg my dear Mrs. Freemans pardon for differing with her in that matter as to ye Succession, for sertinly if ye Union can ever be compassed, there would be no occassion of nameing a Successer, for then we should be one people & ye endeavouring to make any Settle-

ment now would in my poor opinnion putt an end to ye Union, which every body that wishes well to theire Country must own would be a great happyness to both Nations.[13]

Such an answer did not please Sarah, who accused the queen of being influenced by the High Tories to delay a settlement of the Hanoverian succession in the northern kingdom. Four days later, the queen again defended her position, assuming as axiomatic the necessity of securing Hanover's rights:

you are pleased to say, what I say about ye Succession is what I have bin told from some people heare, I do asure you what I ground my poor opinion upon, is what I have heard from all ye Scotch ministers long before they went into theire own Country, for as to this particular Scotch business, according to ye best of my remembrance, I have spoke very little to those people you suspect, & that some months agoe. I do agree interily it would be very good to have ye Succession setel'd, but since ye Unnion will do that, I must confess I can't see why one should be in greater hast[e] now then we have bin all this time, if that should not Succeed, then indeed it will be absolutely necessary.[14]

In order to stress her interest in Scotland (and to reward those who supported her position), in the winter of 1703–4 the queen revived the ancient Order of the Thistle as the highest honour which the crown could bestow on a Scottish subject.[15]

By this time, in conjunction with Godolphin and Harley, the queen was determined to force the Hanoverian succession on the Scottish Parliament. In March 1704 George Baillie of Jerviswood described an interview with the queen which she handled adroitly without the presence of an English minister, and in which she stated 'that she designed to settle the succession next session, which she thought would tend very much to the security of the Protestant religion, and safety of both kingdoms, and asked our opinions about it'.[16] Unfortunately for the queen, however, the Scots were determined to use the succession as a weapon to force the English into extensive commercial concessions to their kingdom. In the summer of 1704 the Scottish Parliament again passed the bill of Security, which not only separated the Scottish succession from that of England, but also specified that Scotland was not to be drawn into England's wars. Her Scottish ministers unanimously advised her to sign it;[17] because of the grim international situation which she faced and the implicit threat that Scotland would not only withdraw from the present war but also become a base for France, on 6 August much against her will the queen assented to the Act of Security. Four days later, she received news of the greatest of Marl-

185

borough's victories, which transformed both the queen's domestic and international positions.

The 1704 campaign on the Continent had begun with the threat of the dissolution of the Grand Alliance. The Holy Roman emperor, Leopold I, was threatened in the east by a rebellion in Hungary which had already contributed to Austria's failure to live up to its treaty obligations; in the west the French and Bavarian armies were preparing to unite in a march through the Danube valley for an attack upon Vienna itself. The only possible salvation for the empire could come from the Maritime Powers, and during the winter of 1703–4 Marlborough had formulated a plan for such aid, which involved marching British troops into the heart of Europe. It was vital, of course, that the queen should be minutely informed of Marlborough's secret plans, for in the event of failure her help and support would be indispensable in preventing an impeachment of the captain-general. Godolphin was also brought into the secret, for it would fall upon him to provide the finance for a march to the Danube. When Marlborough left England in April 1704 he had the vague permission of the cabinet to 'go to the aid of the Emperor', although how this was to be accomplished was not specified. This is not the place to detail how Marlborough, working in collusion with Heinsius, misled both the States-General and Versailles into believing that he intended to attack France on the Moselle, or to recount his long march down the Rhine on the most perilous Continental expedition which British troops had ever attempted.

No letters from the queen to Sarah survive which reflect the terrible anxiety which must have afflicted her during the summer of 1704. The Tory party still commanded a majority in the House of Commons; her new 'mixed ministry' was as yet untried in that forum. The march to the Danube went against the whole Tory theory of how the war should be waged. Should Marlborough's expedition prove to be unsuccessful, there would be little doubt that the queen's government would face almost insuperable hurdles in the autumn. Marlborough, despite his acknowledged skill at manoeuvre and sieges, had yet to win a major battle; should he fail, the empire would be overrun, the Grand Alliance would collapse, and the Dutch republic and England itself would be exposed to the danger of French attack. On 30 May/10 June, Marlborough's forces joined the imperial armies under the command of Prince Eugene of Savoy and Prince Louis of Baden; on 21 June/2 July, they attacked the Schellenberg, the principal Bavarian fortress. The capture of the Schellenberg – at the cost of many lives – enabled Marlborough to devastate Bavaria, but the allied armies were unable to prevent the conjunction of the principal French army, under Maréchal

Tallard, and the Elector of Bavaria's forces. The High Tories could – and did – deprecate Marlborough's victory at the Schellenberg as costly and useless.

It was, however, the necessary preparation for the greatest of Marlborough's victories, fought on 2/13 August along the banks of the Danube between the small villages of Höchstadt and Blenheim. In the day-long battle, Louis XIV's armies – for the first time in the Grand Monarch's reign – suffered a total defeat, twenty-eight regiments surrendering and Maréchal Tallard and many other high French officers being captured. Marlborough had saved the empire, and in the aftermath of the battle the remaining Franco-Bavarian forces evacuated Germany. France could not seriously threaten the integrity of the empire for the remainder of the war. The battle of Blenheim was nearing its end when Marlborough, using a pencil and a bill of tavern expenses, penned his famous message to the duchess:

> I have not time to say more, but to beg you will give my duty to the queen, and let her know her army has had a glorious victory. Monsieur Tallard and two other generals are in my coach, and I am following the rest. The bearer, my aide de camp Collonel Parkes, will give her an account of what has passed. I shal doe it in a day or two by another more at large.[18]

It took Colonel Daniel Parke eight days to cross Europe and the Channel; he arrived in London in the late afternoon of 10 August and presented Marlborough's letter to the duchess at St James's. Sarah in turn immediately dispatched Parke with his letter to Windsor, where legend has it that the queen and the prince were seated on the terrace of the castle, playing checkers. It was reported that the queen told Parke 'he had given her more joy than ever she had received in her life'.[19] She was so ecstatic that she granted his request for her picture by presenting him with a miniature set in diamonds and doubled the normal reward for a bearer of good tidings by giving him 1,000 guineas. (In the following year, Parke was appointed governor of the Leeward Islands.)[20] The queen immediately wrote to Sarah:

> I have had the happiness of receiving my dear Mrs. Freemans by Coll. Parke with the good news of this glorious victory, which next to God Almighty is wholly owing to dear Mr. Freeman, whos safety I congratulate with you with all my Soul, may the same providence that has hitherto preserved, still watch over & send him well home to you, we can never thank God Almighty enough for these great blessings, but must make it our endeavour to deserve them & then I hope he will continue his goodness to us, in delivering us from the attempts of all our other enemys.[21]

After overnight consideration of this news, the queen easily foresaw that the victory would have domestic as well as international consequences, a point which she stressed in her letter of congratulation to Marlborough:

> You will very easily beleeve ye good news Coll: Parks brought me yesterday was very wellcom, but not more I do assure you then hearing you weare well after soe Glorious a Victory, which will not only humble our enemyes abroad but Contribute very much to ye putting a Stop to ye ill designes of those at home. I will not give you any account of what passes hear, knowing you have it from other hands, but end this with my sincer wishes, that God Almighty would continue his protection over you, & send you safe home to ye Joy of your friends, none I'me sure is more truly, & without any Compliment soe, then your faithful servant, ANNE R. The Prince congratulats your great Success & safety.[22]

The queen's letter to Marlborough was considerably warmer in tone than her letter to Sarah, who had throughout the spring and summer of 1704 sustained a campaign which, in ardour and audacity, was comparable to that of her husband: Sarah's goal was nothing less than the elimination of all remaining Tories from the government. On 27 April, five days after Nottingham's resignation, Sir Benjamin Bathurst died and the queen immediately granted Sarah's request of his place as cofferer of the household for her son-in-law, Francis Godolphin.[23] In her response to the queen's letter, the duchess stressed her favourite theme – that the queen had changed towards her simply because she was a faithful servant who dared to tell the truth:

> Tho one can scarce help being pleased at the first reading of a letter from Your Majesty which in words is kind, yet that pleasure is very short when I consider the kindnesse of your heart is quite gon from me . . . *for noe fault of my own, but only that I have not been deceived as well as your self in the opinion you had of others* . . . all my thoughts of your affairs seem to agree so much with those you appear to trust most [i.e. Marlborough and Godolphin], that I durst appeal to them upon any occation of defference.[24]

The queen vehemently denied that she had changed towards Sarah, but, significantly, in her postscript she requested that Sarah's answer should be in writing.[25] A few days later, there was an angry confrontation between the queen and her groom of the stole, when Sarah asked the queen to appoint a rising young Whig divine Benjamin Hoadley (successively Bishop of Bangor, Hereford, Salisbury, and Winchester under George I and George II) to the vacant office of Prebend of Canterbury. The queen had replied that 'you may easily emagin I will do any thing you desire, but intending to be always very carefull in disposing of any thing of this nature', she would ask the Tory Archbishop Sharp 'to inform himself if he be proper for it, & if he finds him to be soe, he shall be sure to have it'.[26] Not surprisingly, Sharp told the queen that Hoadley 'was young & might stay for preferment better then others', recommending instead a Tory candidate as 'ye fittest man for this liveing . . . & upon his saying soe I told him he should have it'.[27] On 25 May the queen and the duchess had a violent argument over the appointment, in which Sarah accused the queen of secretly being influenced by both Jersey and Sir Charles Hedges. The following morning the queen wrote a letter to Sarah in which, after her routine apology, she could hardly contain her anger or her sarcasm:

> Tho I am in ye greatest hast[e] emaginable, I must beg my dear Mrs. Freemans pardon if I weare to[o] warm in my discours last night, & that She would not give it ye name of being angry, which I can never be with you, knowing that every thing you say is meant kindly, but it was impossible to help being very much conserned, to find after all ye assurances I had formerly given you that I had no manner of value for Ld. Jersey, you still thought him one of my Oracles, & that you seem'd to think I would putt any body into a church preferment with out being rightly informed of ye person, & by ye way I can't help saying, I beleeve Mr. Secretary Hedges to be too honest a man to say any man was a good man if he did not know him to be soe. I know ye people you beleeve have not this opininion of him soe that I feare my Character of him will not be credited; . . .
>
> I wish with all my soul God Almighty may inspire you with just and right thoughts of your poor unfortunat faithfull Morly, who is not changed, nor never will, for I beleeve it will not be in ye power of any Mortall to convince you of that truth, as long as you have soe very good and opininion of some sort of people as you have now.[28]

'Some sort of people' referred, of course, to the Junto and – as the queen now suspected – Sarah had become their captive and their tool. The Whigs were outraged that they had been passed over after the dismissal of the High Tories and, as Godolphin informed the duchess, 'till they have the power in their hands, thay will be always against everything that may bee an assistance to the Queen and the government'.[29] Sarah switched her tactics with the queen, launching an attack on the remaining High Tories in the cabinet, Sir Nathan Wright, the lord keeper,[30] and Buckingham, the lord privy seal. By July both Godolphin and Harley had agreed that Wright should be dismissed,[31] but the difficulty was to find a suitable replacement for him. Godolphin was also willing to replace Buckingham with the moderate Whig Duke of Newcastle although, as he informed Sarah, 'I don't see how it can be reasonable for [the queen] to doe it now till *Buckingham's* own humours give a proper occasion.'[32] The queen apparently agreed with Godolphin, and for her part did what she could to drive Buckingham into open opposition. When he complained to her in June that his pension had not been paid for a year, the queen 'told me gravely, though she must laugh att me in her heart, that I had less need of £100 than herself'.[33] At the same time, the queen granted a £2,500 annual pension to the Earl of Pembroke, even if he could not carry out the duties of lord president; 'I beleeve no reasonable body will think it too much for him whatever they might do for another', she told Godolphin.[34]

The queen had immediately perceived that Blenheim represented a turning-point ('a Victory which will not only humble our enemyes abroad but Contribute very much to ye putting a Stop to ye ill designes of those at home'), but the Tories were thunderstruck at the victory. They attempted to place it on an equal footing with the capture of Gibraltar by an English naval expedition under the command of the Tory admiral, Sir George Rooke, and Rooke's subsequent defeat of the French and Spanish in the naval battle of Malaga; but the main thrust of their propaganda was to belittle Marlborough's victory as one which would scarcely diminish the resources of France. As Sarah put it in her *Conduct*, 'by the visible dissatisfaction of some people on the news of it, one would have imagined, that instead of beating the French, he had beat the Church'.[35] The queen, however, rejected Sarah's complaints as ill-founded and staunchly defended the loyalty of her Tory subjects:

as to what you say Conserning *the Tories*, it is impossible to see into
any bodys hart, or to know what there Conversation is with other
people, but I must do them that Justice as to say, they made me
Compliments upon ye coming of the first good news, as well as for ye
last, & looked with as much Satisfaction in theire face as any body. I
feare what I have now sayd will rather increase then lessen ye ill
opinnion you have of me, which I never did nor never will deserve.[36]

A long and tedious correspondence ensued throughout the summer of 1704, in which the queen adamantly maintained, 'I am not Changed.'[37] So bitter was the duchess at the queen's obstinate refusal to accept her political advice that Godolphin attempted to mediate in the quarrel, telling Sarah on 1 September:

I am very sorry to find Mrs. Morley & Mrs. Freeman cannot yett bring
things quite right. I am sure they will doe it at last, and when the case
happens betwixt people that love one another soe well, it is not
impossible that both may be a little in the wrong.[38]

Such was the state of their relationship when, on 7 September, the duchess accompanied the queen and the prince to St Paul's for the great thanksgiving service for Marlborough's victory at Blenheim.

Godolphin's hint that the duchess should take stock of her own conduct was completely lost upon Sarah who proceeded to concentrate her fire upon Marlborough and Godolphin, knowing that in the long run her influence over both men was greater than her influence with the queen, and that their support was indispensable in advancing the Whig cause. Marlborough, in the first instance, reacted adversely, expressing moderate sentiments which the queen could have endorsed: 'I will endeavour to leave a good name behind mee, in countrys that have hardly any blessing but that of not knowing the detested nam[e]s of Wigg and Torry.'[39] In a subsequent letter Marlborough attempted to avoid Sarah's importunities for the Whigs: 'he hopes he shal never be desired [by Sarah] to recomend anybody into a place of trust, it being what I have possativly resolved never to do'.[40] The duchess used the same tactics on Marlborough as she did on the queen and on Godolphin; on 19 October, Sarah informed the lord treasurer:

> I find I have won a good wager when I said *Nottingham* would keep his winter quarters in the Queen's hous [in the Privy Garden, St James's] to caball with all her enemys. Indeed it is a very sertain case that those gentlemen who have been soe much favoured will never serve the Queen thorowly, though they will be very unwilling to part with their employments. And why the Queen should accept of such servises, from people that have no reputation, Lord Marlborough and you will find it a pritty hard thing to give a good reason when the whole world knows, that there has not been ever upon the thrown, a person with more vertue, and good qualitys for the publick nor more truely in their interest.[41]

As he always eventually did, Marlborough submitted to the logic and reasoning of his wife, warning Godolphin on 23 October that Buckingham was working in league with Nottingham and Rochester 'to give all the obstruction that is in their power to the carrying on the publick business with vigor this sessions' and recommending that Buckingham should be replaced by the Duke of Newcastle, to whom Marlborough had earlier objected as too strong a Whig but was now assured that Newcastle 'would be everything that the Queen would have him'.[42]

By the time Marlborough's advice arrived in London, the opening of Parliament on 24 October was upon the queen, and it was deemed inappropriate to inflame the Tories further by dismissing Buckingham. The queen in her speech once more pleaded for national unity, pointing out: 'It is plain, our enemies have no encouragement left, but what

191

arises from their hopes of our divisions.' It was already known, however, that the Tories intended to attack the government on two fronts: in
the House of Lords, John Thompson, first Lord Haversham (formerly a
discontented Whig who had become a discontented Tory), planned to
attack Godolphin for advising the queen to sign the Act of Security,
while in the Commons the Tories planned to 'tack' the Occasional Conformity bill to the land tax. 'The Tack' was a particularly invidious
constitutional innovation: it was already accepted that the House of
Commons had exclusive responsibility for financial measures, but if
extraneous amendments could successfully be added to financial
measures in the Commons and thereby be forced through the upper
house, the legislative power of the House of Lords would be ruined.
Godolphin, slowly moving closer to the Whigs, had already decided
that he would oppose, for the first time, the Occasional Conformity bill,
apparently with the queen's approval. When Archbishop Sharp visited
the queen in November 1704, he proposed to her that Godolphin should
summon the leading Tories and promise them that, if they dropped the
Tack, when the bill against Occasional Conformity came to the Lords in
the normal manner, he would support it; 'but', Sharp recorded in his
diary, 'I found she liked not this proposal'. Instead, the queen asked
Sharp, and he agreed, to use his influence with the Yorkshire members
against the Tack.[43]

At the height of the battle against the Tack, when Godolphin was
urging the queen to speak with the prince to ensure that those
dependent upon the Admiralty voted right, Sarah re-entered the fray
with a letter to the queen in which she once again indicted all Tories as
Jacobites. On 17 November the queen, while again urging national unity
('sertinly union is very necessary to be preached at all timess, espessialy
now that we are soe devided amongst our selves'), responded hotly to
Sarah's accusations:

> I . . . must own I have ye same opinnion of Whig & tory, that ever I
> had, I know both theire principles very well, *& when I know my self to be
> in ye right, nothing can make me alter mine*, it is very sertin that there are
> good & ill people of both sorts, I can see ye faults of ye one as well as
> ye other, & am not deluded by any bodys calling themselves of the
> Church, for God knows there are too many that talks of religion that
> have no true Sense of it, but becaus there are som hott headed men
> among these that are call'd Torys, I can't for my life think it reasonable
> to brand them all with ye name of Jacobit, when with out doubt there
> are as many of them, that will be as much for ye liberty of theire
> religion & Country, as any of those [i.e. the Whigs] who would have
> none thought soe but themselves.[44]

Sarah's impertinent reply to the queen was to lead to an open breach between them. Growing hotter and more acerbic as she wielded her pen, she concluded her long letter by telling her monarch and her mistress:

> It will be very hard to impose such a blind passion upon me if you don't say something more, then that you will allways think as you do of Whigg & Tory.[45]

The queen's bitter response to Sarah's diatribe was that

> every thing I say is imputed ether to partialety, or being imposed upon by knaves or fools. I am very sory any body should have ether of those Characters given them, for any fault in my understanding, since all I say proceeds purely from my own poor Judgment, which tho it may not be soe good as other people, I'me sure is a very honest one.[46]

Not only did the queen refuse to engage in further argument with the duchess, but in private she had given Sarah up. On 24 November the queen confided to Godolphin:

> I agree that all Lady Marl: unkindness proceeds from ye real Consern She has for my good, but I can't hope as you do, that She will ever be easy with me again. I quite despaire of it now, which is no small mortification to me, however I will ever be ye Same, & be ready on all occassions to do her all ye Service that lyes in my poor power.[47]

Godolphin (who was supervising the battle against the Tack from his home, where he was confined with a cold) notified Sarah of the queen's opinion, and on 25 November the duchess retaliated by threatening to exile herself from the queen's side.[48] The day had long since passed when Mrs Morley could not bear the thought of parting with Mrs Freeman. The queen was now exhausted with the duchess's importunities on behalf of the Whigs, and in her reply she conspicuously failed to ask Sarah to reconsider her decision.[49] Unknown to the general public, the first long estrangement between the queen and the Duchess of Marlborough began with the Tack. Throughout 1705, Mrs Morley was rarely to see or write to Mrs Freeman, but Sarah's loss of the queen's favour was obscured for some time to come by the queen's continued ardent support of both Marlborough and Godolphin.

The Tack was defeated in the House of Commons on 28 November by a vote of 251 to 134, the majority being a combination of moderate Tories led by Harley and his followers, court supporters, and the Whigs.[50] Having defeated one of the High Tories' two major attacks, Godolphin assured Harley that the government was safe from 'the small shitt of the party, Wee have nothing now to fear but Lord Haversham's bomb'.[51] It

193

was in defence of Godolphin that the queen began a practice which she was to continue for the remainder of her reign. Bishop Burnet recorded:

> The Queen began this winter to come to the House of Peers upon great occasions to hear their debates which, as it was of good use for her better information, so it was very serviceable in bringing the House into better order. The first time she came, was, when the debate was taken up concerning the Scots act; she knew the Lord Treasurer was aimed at by it, and she diverted the storm by her endeavours, as well as she restrained it by her presence.[52]

Ostensibly, the queen was present incognito, 'at first on the Throne and after (it being cold) on a bench at the fire'.[53] Between 29 November and 16 December the queen attended five debates in the Lords, hearing among other things Nottingham castigating William III for negotiating the Partition Treaties and Somers replying

> That it was unbecoming a member of that House to sully the memory of so great a prince; and he doubted not, but a man who could reflect upon King William before his successor, would do the same by her present Majesty, when she was gone.[54]

The major theme of the debates which the queen attended was the Scottish Act of Security: Somers and the Whigs, supported by the government, introduced and secured the passage of the Aliens Act, which authorized the queen to appoint English commissioners to negotiate a union with Scotland, while suspending commerce with Scotland until the northern kingdom also authorized the appointment of commissioners for the union. On 15 December, while attending the Scottish debates, the queen was present for the Lords' overwhelming rejection (by a vote of 71 against, 50 for) of the third Occasional Conformity bill.[55] The queen's presence at this debate, combined with the fact that both Godolphin and Marlborough voted openly against the bill, effectively implied that she too had abandoned it.

The queen's resolute support of Godolphin, and the Whig dedication to the concept of union, saved the lord treasurer; the queen also demonstrated her continued support of Marlborough, who returned to London on 14 December to receive the laurels for his great victory. On 15 December both houses of Parliament offered their thanks to the duke, and on 16 December the queen informed the House of Commons of her decision to grant Marlborough the royal estates at Woodstock. She asked the House for an equivalent grant to build a great palace to commemorate the victory of Blenheim, to which the Commons speedily agreed. Sir John Vanbrugh was appointed as architect, and soon a scale model of his projected house was presented to the queen at Kensington.

Although Marlborough was anxious to spend his remaining years at Blenheim, the duchess 'saw the maddnesse of the whole Design [and] I opposed it all that was possible for me to doe'.[56] The duchess became obsessed by a running battle with Vanbrugh over the costs of Blenheim, and she frequently journeyed to Woodstock to oversee the progress of the works. The queen never visited the site of the most famous building of her reign.

Despite the queen's coolness towards Sarah, she none the less re-united the Cockpit circle on 23 January 1705, the day of the great victory parade through London. From Lord Fitzharding's lodgings in St James's, surrounded by the prince, the Marlboroughs, Godolphin, and the Fitzhardings, the queen watched the procession bearing the twenty-eight French standards which Marlborough had captured at Blenheim, 'forty Guns in the Park being fired at the same time'.[57] She also patronized Marlborough in a private matter close to his heart, the marriage of his youngest daughter, Lady Mary Churchill.

In a corrupt age, Ralph, Earl of Montagu, had acquired a singular reputation of profitable dishonour; his construction of Montagu House in Bloomsbury (the site of the present British Museum) showed that he was one of the wealthiest peers of the realm. When, in May 1703, Montagu had first proposed the marriage of his son and heir Viscount Monthermer to Lady Mary, Marlborough had objected that the pro-posed partners were only fourteen. 'I am confident', he told the duchess, 'whenever you shal see the young man and Mis Mary to-gether, you will think she is to much a woman for him.'[58] When Lord Bradford's grandson was mentioned as a possible husband a month later, the queen seconded Marlborough's advice to Sarah that they should wait.

> By what the Duke of M[arlborough] say of Lord B[radford's] grandson,
> I fancy the other proposall [i.e. Montagu's] dos not go on. I wish
> whenever you do dispose of that charming person, you may have the
> best match that it to be had. I know nothing of this young man, but I
> am of the Duke of Marlborough's opinion she is young enough to stay
> some time longer, and you need never feare haveing all the best
> offers.[59]

None the less, Sarah persevered in striking a bargain with Montagu which would redound to the benefit of their children, an agreement which Marlborough endorsed and to which the queen acquiesced. The marriage took place on 20 March 1705 in the Marlboroughs' private apartments in St James's, in the presence of the queen and the prince. The queen gave a dowry of £10,000 and on the day of the marriage she created Montagu a duke and ordered the reversion of the post of master of the great wardrobe, which Montagu had purchased for life, to his son.[60] Finally, the queen agreed enthusiastically to the offer of Leopold I, the Holy Roman emperor, to create Marlborough a prince of the empire which, in Marlborough's words, 'as none ever of his nation have had the like, he thinkes it may remain in after times as an honour to *the queen* and *Marlborough*'.[61] With the queen's permission, Marlborough was given the small principality of Mindelheim in Bavaria. In terms of royal favour, the Marlboroughs had reached the apotheosis.

On 14 March the queen made her final speech to Parliament, after which it was prorogued until its dissolution on 5 April and the issuance of writs for new elections on 23 April. During this period, the queen intervened openly in the electoral process. The careful preparations for the forthcoming campaign were characterized by a marked swing to the Whigs by both the queen and the Duumvirs. The government had already decided to purge those members who had voted for the Tack: as Godolphin had told Sarah the previous November, 'when the session is over, I shall never think any man fitt to continue in his employment, who gives his vote to this Tack'.[62] In the purge of 1705 the Tories lost as much, if not more, than they had gained after the queen's accession in 1702.[63] On 23 March, to stress the seriousness of the government's intentions, Marlborough personally called upon the Duke of Buckingham to demand the return of the privy seal, which was given to John Holles, Duke of Newcastle, one week later. This was the government's first turn to the moderate Whigs and one for which Harley was responsible, having been in negotiation with Newcastle since April 1703.[64] In addition, the Whig Earl of Peterborough was appointed commander of the Allied troops in Spain, and other changes, including six lords lieutenancies, were made in favour of the Whigs.[65]

The queen took a hand in proscribing the Tackers: Bishop Burnet recorded that he did not meddle in parliamentary elections during the previous reign, but after the Tack, the queen

> her selfe spoke to me with relation to the elections. She said we [i.e. the Whigs] saw she trusted to us, and in particular she spoke severely of Mr. [Charles] Fox the Citisen for Salisbury. This made me set my whole strength to keep him out

(an effort which was unsuccessful and provoked increased Tory wrath against the Whig bishop).[66] Furthermore, the queen dispatched one of her chaplains to Oxford to vote against a Tacker.[67] On 10 April the queen and the prince embarked on a journey to Newmarket which, while ostensibly a pleasure trip, was in effect a campaign expedition on behalf of the Whigs. The queen dined with one of the Junto members, the Earl of Orford, in his nearby country home, and she also visited the university at Cambridge where she hoped to aid the election of Francis Godolphin as one of the university's two members (in the event, two Tackers were elected).[68] While at Cambridge, she knighted Isaac Newton and James Montagu, the brother of Junto leader Charles, Lord Halifax.[69] By the time of the queen's return to London on 23 April and the issuance of writs for a new election, she had personally demonstrated that the Whigs were no longer to be excluded from the royal favour. The queen was now irrevocably committed to 'moderation' between the extremes of the two parties, a position which she was to maintain throughout the remainder of her life.

Her attitude was reinforced by the violence of the High Tory campaign, in which the queen was personally attacked in the pamphlet warfare.[70] Although she was angry at the constant repetition of the Tory slogan 'The Church in Danger', the queen still feared the Junto. On 1 May, after discussing possible dismissals in the offices of the Cinque Ports with Godolphin, the queen assured him:

> as I shall at all times very willingly discourage all violent torys, soe I
> would not have any punished that do not deserve it, nor encourage
> violent Whigs, & I flatter my self you are of ye same mind, lett me beg
> you once more to inform your self thoroughly of this matter that I may
> know ye truth, & in this & in every thing els for Gods sake tell me
> your mind freely for I would not err in any thing, when ever I do, it
> will be my misfortune but shall never be my fault, & as long as I live
> it shall be my endeavour to make my Country & my freinds easy, &
> tho those that Com after me may be more Capable of soe great a trust
> as it has pleased God to putt into my poor hands, I am sure they can
> never discharge it more faithfully than her that is Sincerly your
> Humble Servant.[71]

The results of the general election of 1705 were something of a personal triumph for the queen, for neither the Whigs nor the Tories were able to secure an absolute majority. The government's campaign to proscribe the Tackers was obviously a failure, 90 out of the 134 being returned. Yet the Whigs managed to increase their overall representation from 184 to 246, while the number of Tories fell from 329 to 267.[72] The balance of power in the new House of Commons would be held by the 'moderate' Tories (or the 'sneakers', as the Tackers called them), led by Harley. Marlborough and Godolphin calculated (as events proved, correctly) that the Tory party would regain its cohesion and they consequently began to think of further concessions to the Whigs. Harley, by contrast, continued to assure the queen throughout the summer of 1705

197

that most of the Tories would disassociate themselves from the Tackers and continue to support the ministry.[73] The queen, heavily influenced by Harley's optimistic assessment, was willing to 'discourage all violent torys', but refused to punish those 'that do not deserve it'.

The queen, standing above faction, might reject the 'violent' men of both parties and support political moderation by maintaining a 'mixed ministry', but for her ministers the balance of power within such a government might prove crucial. Harley had irretrievably alienated the Whigs; Marlborough and Godolphin had now burned their bridges to the Tories. In the electoral victory of 1705 which the Blenheim campaign had produced lay the seeds of political disagreement which were eventually to destroy their working relationship and would force the queen to choose between her lifelong friends and the political principles which she had so ardently embraced.

8

'Ye Mercyless Men of both Partys'

The Attempt at Moderation,
April 1705 – December 1706

The first challenge to the queen's determination to support political moderation came from the Whigs. The Junto, encouraged by their electoral success and demanding rewards for their previous support of the Duumvirs' war policies, selected their candidate to breach the walls of the cabinet: the son-in-law of the Duke and Duchess of Marlborough, Charles, Earl of Sunderland. They had already advanced Sunderland's claims to succeed Nottingham in April 1704, but Marlborough had then rejected him.[1] In the spring of 1705, Godolphin, particularly irritated by the loss of his son's election at Cambridge ('no small mortification to mee, and I have now the same occasion to complain myself of the behaviour of the clergy, as some of my friends had before'), knew that the queen would be reluctant to appoint Sunderland to any office. Indeed, the Junto had seriously overestimated the strength of the queen's friendship with the Marlboroughs, for Sunderland was the last Whig whom she would willingly have accepted for office. As means of placating the Junto, on 23 May the treasurer asked the queen to appoint Sunderland as envoy extraordinary to the court of Vienna, to present condolences on the death of Leopold I and congratulations on the election of his eldest son, Joseph I, as well as to assist the permanent envoy, George Stepney, in mediating in the Hungarian rebellion against the Habsburgs. The queen initially objected to Sunderland's appointment on the basis of his political extremism. Godolphin threatened to resign if he could not secure Sunderland's appointment to conciliate the Junto. Confronted by the possible loss of her lord treasurer, the queen later in the day had second thoughts: 'I am very sory to find', she wrote to Godolphin,

> that what I said this morning has given you soe much uneasynes as
> you express, there being nothing I desire more than to have you easy
> in everything, and to convince you of that, I desire you would speake to

ye Person [i.e. Sunderland] you proposed should go to Viena, to try whether he will care for that employment. I am truly sensinbel of every thing you say proceeds from ye sincerity of your hart, and from no other motive, and I beg you would be soe just to me as to believe I am intirely satisfyed with you in every thing, and that I have no thought or desire to have you joyne your self to any one party. All I wish is to be kept out of the power of both. I beg you would not be so unkind as to think I am uneasy at what you say, for indeed I am not, but take all things that com from you as they are meant. I depend intirly on your friendship, which I hope you will continu to me as long as I live, and never think of leaving me, for that would be a blow I could never support.[2]

Significantly, Godolphin did not confide the burden of this transaction to Robert Harley, his closest ministerial collaborator, merely informing Harley a week later of his belief that 'the Queen will resolve to send Lord Sunderland' to Vienna.[3] When Sunderland kissed hands on 18 June, Godolphin reported to Sarah: 'The Queen seem'd to bee very well satisfyed with Lord Sunderland's behaviour to her, and I think he had reason to bee soe with hers.'[4]

Godolphin was forced to resort to the same tactics – repeated threats to resign – in order to secure ecclesiastical appointments for Whig divines. Between 1702 and 1705 the queen appointed five Tory bishops, largely on the advice of Archbishop Sharp. On 1 March 1705, James Gardiner, Bishop of Lincoln, died and Thomas Tenison, Archbishop of Canterbury, was determined to secure the diocese for one of his protégés, Dr William Wake, Dean of Exeter. Godolphin supported Tenison's efforts as part of his rapprochement with the Whigs, while Sharp supported his own candidate, Sir William Dawes. The queen assured Sharp that 'she would always desire that the bishops she put in should vote on the side of they who call themselves the Church party do vote on'. Nevertheless, Godolphin proved to be 'exceedingly firm' in his representations to the queen, who finally conceded the point and signed Wake's *congé d'élire* on 16 July. Sharp interpreted this defeat as meaning that the queen 'refused persons . . . for being Tories'.[5]

Despite these successes, both Godolphin and Sarah were dissatisfied with the queen's unwillingness to displace moderate Tories, and they suspected that she was influenced through George Clarke, the prince's secretary at the Admiralty, who had in May furnished the prince with reasons why three members from the Cinque Ports should not be replaced by the Whig deputy warden, Lord Westmorland.[6] The Tory admiral, Sir George Rooke, had incurred the queen's wrath for refusing to promise the prince his vote against the Tack.[7] It had therefore been decided to reconstitute the prince's council to eliminate Rooke, to transfer James Brydges to the lucrative post of paymaster-general, and to appoint a promising young Whig, Robert Walpole. Clarke, however, slipped past the prince a new commission which included Rooke's name: on 6 June the queen – angry at Clarke – promised Godolphin that 'I will use my utmost endeavours to get him [the prince] to part with' Clarke.[8] Apparently she had earlier promised the same thing to both Marlborough and Godolphin, for four days later, Marlborough wrote to the duchess: 'If *George Clarke* comites so many unreasonable things, why is not *the queen* acquainted with them, for she told *Godolphin* and myself that she would take the first occasion of putting him out.'[9] Either because of the queen's unwillingness, or because of the prince's refusal to dismiss him, Clarke retained his office throughout the summer of 1705.

In England the queen had been forced to turn to the Whigs; similarly in Scotland she was forced to turn to the Whigs' allies. So far as Scottish policy was concerned, the Junto demanded that the English government concentrate on securing a treaty of union rather than on the succession alone. The young John Campbell, second Duke of Argyll, was appointed lord commissioner, the Earl of Seafield remained lord chancellor, the Earl of Annandale was appointed secretary of state and – to the queen's great anger – the Whigs insisted that the Duke of Queensberry be returned to office as lord privy seal. On 6 June she told Godolphin that

> it would be very uneasy to me to have any thing said to him [Queens-berry] that might look like a command to go down into Scotland, being sure if upon that, he and his friends behaves themselves well in ye Parliament, he will expect to be taken into my Service, which is a thing I can never consent to, his last tricking behaviour haveing made him more odious to me than ever.[10]

Argyll, however, insisted that Queensberry's presence in the Scottish ministry was indispensable to carry the union negotiations through the northern Parliament; furthermore, the queen's personal candidates could not be given office. On 14 June, in a mood of despair, the queen informed Godolphin that she could 'not help venting my thoughts upon the Scotch affairs':

> & in ye first place I think those people use me very hardly in opposeing Lord Forfars being of ye Treasury & I should be very glad to know your oppinion whether upon this refusal, I might not writt to ye Commissioner [Argyll] to lett him know . . . that I do expect he should comply with this one desire of mine, in return of all ye complyances I have made to him. This may displease his grace's touche temper, but I

> can't see it can do any prejudice to my service, & in my poor oppinion such usage should be resented.

Not only was she furious at Argyll's high-handed behaviour, but she was outraged at the thought of taking Queensberry back into office:

> as to the Duke of Queensburry, tho it is none of my choise, I own it goes mightely against me, it grates my soul to take a man into my Service, that has not only betrayed me, but tricked me several times, one that has bin obnoxious to his own country men these many yeares, & one that I can never be convinced can be of any use but after all this, since my freinds may be censured, & it may be said if I had not bin obstinat every thing would have gon well, I will do my self ye violence these unreasonable Scots men desire, & indeed it is an unexpressible one.

Argyll had recommended that the government in the forthcoming Parliament should attempt to secure the union, something which could more easily be established than the succession alone, but Tory accusations that the English government (principally Godolphin, but by implication the queen as well) did not truly have the succession at heart led the ministry to decide to press the succession alone. The queen assured Godolphin that 'ye draught of ye letter & instructions as you propose, will sertinly be much better than those that are com out of Scotland, but I am intirely of your oppinnion that no method will succeed'.[11] Argyll, much to the queen's surprise and delight, managed not only to secure the agreement of the Scottish Parliament to the appointment of commissioners to negotiate a union, but also that the queen should have the right to appoint them: on 25 September 1705 she was able to sign this legislation.

Distracted as she was by Scottish affairs throughout the summer of 1705, the queen's chief concern continued to be English domestic affairs. For the first time, she was having serious difficulty with both Marlborough and Godolphin because of their anxiety to make further concessions to the Whigs. After the dismissal of the High Tories in 1704, it had been agreed by all concerned that the lord keeper, Sir Nathan Wright, should be dismissed. In Sarah's words, Wright was

> a man of no use to the Crown, one despised by all Parties, whose weak & wretched Conduct in the Court of Chancery had almost brought his very office into Contempt; & whose sordid & undisguised Covetousness had render'd his personal Character vile & scandalous all over the nation.[12]

The Whigs complained bitterly that Wright had turned out several hundred justices of the peace between 1700 and 1704[13] and in March

1705, apparently with the queen's approval, Harley offered Wright's position to the lord chief justice, Thomas Trevor, a moderate Tory. However, Trevor declined the office.[14] Marlborough and Godolphin were determined that the position should go to a moderate Whig, but they found it difficult to convince the queen. Indeed, they had to resort to surreptitious means to do so. In early June 1705, Marlborough cautioned Godolphin: 'one point gives me a good deal of trouble, which is, that you find difficulty in perswaiding Mrs. Morley to do what is good for herself'. Marlborough suggested that Godolphin should 'loos no time in writing such a letter to me as may be proper for Mrs. Morley to read. You must mingle some other things in the letter so as it may not look as a designed thing.'[15]

On 12 June the queen gave Marlborough an opportunity to offer advice when she wrote him, 'I wish you may find the restless spirits of both parties quiet when you come back, but I mightily fear it; every-thing, in my opinion, having a melancholy prospect.'[16] In his reply, based upon Godolphin's draft,[17] Marlborough once again wrote of his desire to retire after the current campaign and, in the light of the Tackers' electoral successes, he urged the queen to 'advise with Lord Treasurer what encouragement may be proper to give the Whigs, that they may look upon it as their own concern early to beat down and oppose' any proposals which might frighten the allies into a precipitate peace. Marlborough concluded his letter by striking a maudlin note which was to be repeated later in his correspondence and which the queen was to find increasingly grating:

> By the vexation and trouble I undergo, I find a daily decay, which may deprive me of the honour of seeing Your Majesty any more, which thought makes me take the liberty to beg of your Majesty, that for your own sake and the happiness of your kingdoms, you will never suffer any body to do Lord Treasurer an ill office. For besides his integrity for your service, his temper and abilities are such, that he is the only man in England capable of giving such advice as may keep you out of the hands of both parties, which may at last make you happy, if quietness can be had in a country where there is so much faction.[18]

The queen, in her reply to Marlborough of 3 July, postponed any discussion of Marlborough's desire to retire until his return to England, and quickly came to the main point, repeating her desire to rely exclusively upon Godolphin's advice:

> What you desire Concerning Lord Treasurer was not at all necessary, for I have soe true a sense of his freindship to me, & soe real a value & Esteem for him, that if ever any body should endeavour to do him any

203

ill office, it would have no effect upon me, you know every one that I converse with all, & I dare say none of them have a thought against him. Great care must be taken that no cause be given to our friends abroad to think there is any feare of buisness going ill in England, & you may be assured I will advice in every thing with those you desire, the partys are such bug beares that I dare not venture to writt my mind freely of ether of them with out a Cypher, for feare of any accident. I pray God keep me out of ye hands of both of them.[19]

In truth, the queen was listening to advice which ran counter to Godolphin's: Robert Harley, who waited upon her every day as secretary of state, was opposed to the appointment of a Whig[20] as lord keeper and particularly feared that the Junto would put forward Somers, who had served in the post with distinction from 1693 to 1700. In the short run, the lord chancellor controlled a great deal of ecclesiastical patronage, which hitherto had been at the disposal of Harley and Archbishop Sharp; in the long run, Harley could no more turn to the Whigs than Godolphin and Marlborough could return to the Tories. Harley's advice was more agreeable to the queen, who wished to maintain a strict balance between the two parties, than was Godolphin's. On 11 July the queen appealed to the lord treasurer not to be influenced by Sarah to recommend the appointment of Somers:

I can not help saying I wish very much that there may be a moderate tory found for this employment, for I must own to you I dread ye falling into ye hands of ether party, & ye Whigs have had soe many fayvours shewed them of late, that I feare a very few more will pull me insensibly into theire power which is what I'me sure you would not have happen no more than I.

I know my dear unkind friend [i.e. Sarah] has soe good an oppinion of all that party, that to be sure she will use all her endeavour to get you to prevaile with me to putt one of them into this great post, & I can not help being aprehensive that not only she but others may be desiorous to have one of ye heads of them [i.e. Somers] in possession of ye Seale, but I hope in God you will never think that reasonable, for that would be an unexpressible uneasyness & mortification to me. There is no body I can rely upon but your self to bring me out of all my difficultys, & I do putt an intire confidence in you, not doubting but you will do all you can to keep me out of ye power of ye Mercyless men of both partys, & to that end make choice of one for Lord Keeper that will be ye likelyest to prevent that danger.[21]

Marlborough, accepting at face value the queen's assurances that she consulted only Godolphin, took Harley's opposition to a Whig chancellor lightly, telling Godolphin that the lord treasurer could, 'with some pains, do whatever he thinkes is right with *the queen'*.[22] Godolphin, however, discovered differently when the Whigs put forward as their preferred candidate not Somers, but Sir William Cowper, a noted barrister and a political moderate. Throughout July and August the queen continued to procrastinate and to reject Godolphin's entreaties to appoint Cowper. Reacting to the treasurer's complaints, Marlborough again wrote to the queen on 18/29 September, pointing out that if she refused to accept Godolphin's advice,

> I see no remedy under heaven, but that of sending for Lord Rochester and Lord Nottingham, and let them take your business into their hands, the consequences of which are very much to be feared; for I think they have neither courage nor temper enough to serve your Majesty and the nation in this difficult time, nor have they any support in England, but what they have from being thought violently at the head of a party, which will have the consequence of the other party's opposing them with all their strength.[23]

The queen certainly had no intention of returning to the High Tories. Her reply to Marlborough on 27 September was an eloquent analysis of her duty, but it evaded the main issue of how the chancery should be disposed:

> I give you a thousand thanks for ye kind conserne you expresse for me in your last letter, & indeed I think my Condition is very much to be lamented, but as for those two persons [Rochester and Nottingham] you mention, they have made it wholly impossible to employ them, if I had never soe much inclination to doe it, & I am soe intirely satisfyed of ye Sincerity & ye capacity of him I trust [i.e. Godolphin], that I shall never repent of that Choice whatever my fortune may be, I wish all ye assurances & professions that are made to him, & to me, may be made good; if they are, I beleive one may depend upon Success, but I must own I can't help fearing I shall meet with some disagreable things this next session of Parliament. . . .
>
> You are very Just to me in beleeveing I have no thought but what is for ye good of England, I ame sure I have no other, nor never can, but will always to ye best of my understanding promote its true interest, & serve my country faithfully, which I look upon to be as much ye Duty of a Sovereing, as of ye meanest Subject.[24]

The 'disagreeable things' which the queen anticipated in the rapidly approaching session of Parliament centred principally upon the invitation to the Electress Sophia, which the Tories were openly boasting they would introduce. Godolphin undoubtedly pointed out to the queen that Whig support would be indispensable if such a proposal was to be averted, and by the end of September the queen agreed to appoint

Cowper, although she ordered Secretary Hedges to delay visiting Wright to demand the seals of office,[25] and the Whigs complained bitterly of 'this tedious way of proceeding'.[26] The delay was used to establish certain conditions which the queen wished to impose on Cowper: all ecclesiastical livings with an annual value above £40 which were at the disposal of the lord chancellor were actually to be given by the queen. This arrangement was inspired by Harley,[27] and in establishing it the queen ignored the Archbishop of Canterbury who 'fear'd it would be under a worse Management than when under the late Keeper's Servants by the Importunity of the Women & Hangers-on at Court'.[28] The queen plainly intended to continue to rely upon Harley and Archbishop Sharp for advice. In the following year, the queen answered complaints from the Duchess of Marlborough concerning

> my Lord Keeper & his liveings. I have a very good opinnion of him, & would depend upon his recommendation on any occasion sooner then on most peoples, but as to this particular, I think ye Crown can never have too many liveings at its disposal, & therfore tho there may be some trouble in it, it is a power I can never think reasonable to part with, & I hope those that Com after me will be of ye same mind.[29]

The seals were taken from Wright on 6 October, the queen returned from Windsor to Kensington on 10 October, and the following day the seals were given to Cowper. At the age of forty-one, Cowper was the youngest lord keeper in living memory. His daughter later recalled: 'He looked very young, & wearing his own hair made him appear yet more so; which the Queen observing, obliged him to cut it off, telling him the world would say she had given the Seals to a boy.'[30]

Sarah later claimed in her memoirs that she had induced the queen to dismiss Wright and appoint Cowper,[31] although the queen subsequently told her Whig doctor (and Cowper's close friend) Sir David Hamilton 'that the putting out of Wright, and putting in of Cowper, made no difference between the Duchess and her, for the Duchess had never spoke but once to her of it'.[32] Sarah, indeed, had maintained her self-imposed exile from the queen throughout the first half of 1705; her absence from court became so noticeable that Godolphin advised the duchess to use it as an excuse to avoid importunities, saying 'that while you indulge yourself by staying in the country, you can't think it reasonable to give the Queen the same trouble as if you saw her every day'.[33] The scarcity of letters from the queen to Sarah which are attributable to 1705 suggests a degree of alienation on both sides. In July, for instance, after many excuses for delaying an answer to a letter from Mrs Freeman, Mrs Morley concluded, 'it is now to[o] late for me to say much, &

therfore I must defer answering all your letters till another time'.[34] In August, however, the duchess, conscious of her decline in the queen's favour, managed a reconciliation between the two women, in which both Marlborough and Godolphin rejoiced. Marlborough advised his wife:

> It is a pleasure to me when I find by any of yours that you are easier with *the queen*. I think for the good of everything you should make itt your business to have it so, for I am very confident by *Godolphin's* letters it would be of great use to him.[35]

Sarah accompanied the queen, the prince, and the court on an expedition to Winchester, where they spent ten days in late August and early September examining the grandiose palace which Sir Christopher Wren had begun for Charles II but which had been abandoned after that monarch's death. While at Winchester, Sarah entered into a violent altercation with one of the queen's attendants, Lady Charlotte Frescheville 'upon an occation that was very extraordinary, her Lady-ship having been madder than ordinary'.[36] When the court returned to London on 8 September, Sarah retired to Woodstock to inspect the Blenheim works, and from there complained to the queen of Lady Frescheville's malicious remarks. After a long delay, the queen replied on 17 September 'to endeavour to clear my self as to this business of Lady Fretschevilles impertinence':

> I hope too you will [be] soe just to me as to beleeve I do resent her Brutal useage of you & that I am ready to do any thing you can think reasonable. . . . She has exprest a great deale of sorrow that you & I should be angry with her, & denys all, which is an additional lye to all she has told before, if she should go on in her impertinences to you, you may be assured I will not keep her in my family for such behaviour is not to be sufferd by any body, much less by your poor unfortunat faithfull Morly, who has soe tender a passion for her dear Mrs. Freeman & ever will have till her last moment.
>   I have bin soe unfortunat as to be unjustly thought of by you soe long that I feare what I say now will be no more credited then all ye former assurances I have given you of my truth.[37]

This uneasy feeling of mutual mistrust was to continue between the queen and the duchess throughout the parliamentary session of 1705–6.

The forthcoming Parliament dominated the thoughts of the queen and her principal advisors during the autumn of 1705. By September, Harley was becoming alarmed that the court was making too many concessions to the Whigs, concessions which – if carried to their logical conclusion – might result in his own exclusion from government. He believed, as he informed Godolphin in September, 'that no party in the House can carry it for themselves without the Queen's servants join with them. That the foundation is, persons or parties are to com in to the Queen, and not the Queen to them.' In the subtle language of a courtier with the dark overtones of a prophet, he stressed the necessity of separating the moderate Tories from the Tackers: 'If the gentlemen of England are made sensible that the Queen is the Head, and not a Party, everything will be easy, and the Queen will be courted and not a Party; but if otherwise —'[38]

The first action of the new House of Commons, scheduled to meet on 27 October, would be the election of a speaker. The High Tories put forward as their candidate William Bromley, the member for Oxford University. Harley had originally backed his ally, Simon Harcourt, to be selected as the court candidate, but in the summer Godolphin had decided that a moderate Whig should be nominated: his choice, enthusiastically backed by the queen, was John Smith, widely identified as a 'lord treasurer's Whig', who kissed the queen's hand in August.[39] In order to procure Smith's election, the queen personally intervened wherever she could. On 23 October she appealed to her lifelong friend, Lady Frances Bathurst, to influence the vote of her son, Allen (whom the queen had privately opined was possessed of 'ye Cuning of his famely'):[40]

> I doubt what I am now going to say will come too late to obtain my wishes, the meeting of Parliament being soe very neare that one may reasonable beleeve every body has taken theire resolution who they will give theire votes for to be speaker: however I cannot help asking you whether your son is engaged or no. If he be not, I hope you will give me your interest with him to be for Mr. Smith. . . . I do not at all doubt of his good inclinations to serve me, and therfore hope, tho' it should be too late to recall his resolutions as to ye speaker, *he will be carefull never to engage himself soe far into any party as not to be at liberty to leave them when he sees them running into things that are unreasonable.* . . .[41]

The court actively canvassed every possible supporter in favour of Smith, but the vote on 27 October came as a shock: Smith received 248 votes, Bromley garnered 205. To Godolphin's mind, based on three decades of experience, the vote put paid to any hope that the bulk of the Tory party would accept moderate counsels and shun the High Tories: a close working alliance with the Whigs was indispensable to the government. Indeed, he had already shown the Whig leaders the queen's letter to Marlborough of 27 September, in which she had promised that she would never take Rochester and Nottingham back into office.[42] To

Harley's mind, by contrast, the vote was proof of his contention that the court had already gone too far to conciliate the Whigs and had thereby alienated the moderate Tories. There can be little doubt that the election of John Smith as speaker inspired Harley, who had hitherto acted as a faithful subordinate of Godolphin, to begin exerting his influence with the queen to bolster her natural antipathy towards the Whigs. The reluctance of the moderate Tories, led by Harley, to co-operate with the Whigs on questions of disputed elections was soon made plain.[43] Despite this growing tension, the anger of the court was visited upon those who had voted for Bromley: George Clarke was immediately dismissed by the prince as secretary of the Admiralty.[44]

The major difficulty faced by the queen and the government in Parliament was the long projected Tory invitation to the Electress Sophia. In October 1702, James Cressett had reported from Hanover that the queen's discontented subjects, both Whig and Tory, were intriguing with the electress and suggesting that she might soon be invited to London:

> their batteries are planted at present against the weake part of the
> House of Hannover, an aged Princesse cannot be so wel fortify'd
> against their attacks or surprizes, but there is one comfort, that a
> breach made there would signify nothing.[45]

Sophia, who was keen to reside in England,[46] and her chief advisor, the famous philosopher Gottfried von Leibniz, began a series of intrigues with both parties, hoping to obtain a pension, a household, and most importantly an invitation from the queen or Parliament. Their intermediary with the Whigs was Sophia's 'personal', unofficial representative in London, Pierre de Falaiseau, formerly a Prussian diplomat.[47] The advice which the Whigs conveyed to Sophia through Falaiseau after the dismissal of the High Flyers in 1704 was unpalatable to the electress: they promised Sophia that the Duchess of Marlborough would eventually induce the queen to consent to the invitation.[48] Falaiseau made the serious mistake of assuring Sophia and Leibniz that the queen was a cypher, entirely dominated by favourites.[49] After the invitation crisis of 1705–6, Falaiseau revised his opinion: 'the Queen . . . is very opinionated and quite ferocious', he reported to Leibniz.[50]

The Tories maintained their contacts with Sophia and Leibniz through Sophia's niece, the Raugravine Louise, and Henry Davenant, the English resident at Frankfurt.[51] The electress had always leaned towards the Tories, numbering Rochester and Nottingham among her friends. As the queen cooled towards the Tories, Sophia's attitude towards them became warmer, even towards suspected Jacobites: she was quick to express her regret when Buckingham was forced to resign from the government in March 1705.[52]

One of the major proponents of the invitation was Sir Rowland Gwynne, a Whig MP who had lost his seat in the 1702 elections. Gwynne arrived in Hanover in November 1703,[53] where he quickly became a close confidant of the dowager electress. Gwynne, realizing that the only way to further Sophia's wishes (and hence his own preferment) was to join the discontented Tories, was quite prepared to work with Rochester, Nottingham, Buckingham, and Jersey. Rochester's agent at the electoral court was Dr John Hutton, formerly William III's chief physician. Dr Hutton first visited Hanover in February 1703, after Rochester's dismissal from office.[54] He returned again on Rochester's behalf in September 1705 and resided there for one year.[55] Hutton and Gwynne co-operated in assuring leading figures in England, including the Archbishops of Canterbury and York, that Sophia was willing to reside in England 'whenever the Queen and Parliament call her'. Hutton mistakenly assured Rochester that the elector, 'though exceeding modest on this point', agreed with his mother in supporting the invitation.[56]

In reality, the elector was totally opposed to the concept of the invitation which the Tories wished to force upon the queen. He had no wish to let his mother, much less his son, reside in England where they might be manoeuvred into open opposition to the queen. He agreed with his own London envoy, Ludwig von Schütz, and with Emmanuel Scrope Howe, the British envoy to Hanover from 1705 until his death in 1709, that the Tory goal was to disrupt relations between the two courts.[57] Indeed, Georg Ludwig believed that the High Flyers aimed at nothing less than sabotaging the Grand Alliance. He told Howe that the Tory goal in pressing the invitation 'was to create all ye Jealousies & missunderstanding between and breake this great allayance which is ye Safety & Support of all Europe against ye Common Enemy'.[58] Yet the elector could not publicly announce that Hanover would refuse an invitation as this would lend fresh ammunition to Tory charges that he cared nothing about England or the succession.

The Junto were most anxious to co-operate with the government in opposing the invitation in the hope of obtaining royal favour, and the Duumvirs were able to concert measures with the Whigs in advance.[59] Nevertheless, the queen remained anxious that the Tories might be able to carry their proposal in the absence of a firm declaration against the invitation by the elector. She relied upon Marlborough, who after the conclusion of the 1705 campaign was planning to visit Berlin and Hanover. On 13 November she wrote to her captain-general:

The disagreeable proposall of Bringing some of the house of Hanover into England (which I have bin afraid of soe long) is now very neare being brought into both houses of Parliament which gives me a great deal of uneasynes, for I am of a temper always to feare ye worst. There has bin assurances given that M. Schutes should have instructions to discourage the propositions, but as yet he has said nothinge of them, which makes me feare there may be some alterations in theire resolution at ye court of Hanover. I shall depend upon your freindship & kindness to sett them right in notions of things heare, & if they will be quiet I may be soe to[o], or els I must expect to meet with a great many mortifications.[60]

Marlborough was confident that the elector would take care to prevent his mother from accepting any invitation. On 20 November he wrote to Godolphin (and through the treasurer, to the queen):

I am very much of your mind that if *the elector* be reasonable, as they say he is, it will be very easy to convince him that the jorny of *Electress Sophia* is very unseasonable, and may be prejudicial to his interest. I shall make use of your arguments, but I beleive there will be a necessity of making use of *the queen's* name.[61]

The queen was certainly not reluctant to have her name used: indeed, it was common knowledge that the Tories planned to introduce the invitation to irritate the queen personally. She had already summoned Archbishop Sharp to Kensington to warn him that the Tories would introduce the invitation and to persuade him 'to use my interest with my friends not to come into that motion', which Sharp agreed to do, believing that the invitation was 'nothing but a pique to her Majesty'.[62]

On 15 November the queen attended the first of a long series of debates in the House of Lords concerning the succession. Lord Haversham led off for the Tories in his annual 'state of the nation' speech, in which he objected to the queen's presence at the debates as inhibiting nobles from free expression.[63] After Haversham had moved an address to the queen that she invite the electress to reside in England, the motion was warmly supported by the High Tories, particularly the Duke of Buckingham who – according to Sarah – said 'that the Queen might live till she did not know what she did, and be like a child in the hands of others'. The queen was incensed by Nottingham's support of the invitation, for which she never forgave him.[64] She later told the Earl of Dartmouth:

Sure he [Nottingham] had forgot that he told her, whoever proposed bringing over her successor in her lifetime, did it with a design to depose her, or he must think she had forgot that he was the first man that made the proposal, to imagine any body could do him worse offices than he had done himself.[65]

The government, firmly supported by the Whigs, successfully opposed Haversham's motion, which attracted only fifteen votes. Though relieved at the result, the queen was furious with the Tories, believing that they had aimed at nothing less than limiting her authority as sovereign. That night, in her anger, she came close to endorsing Sarah's political opinions when she wrote to the duchess:

I believe dear Mrs. Freeman and I shall not disagree as we have
formerly done, for I am sensible of the services those people have done
me that you have a good opinion of, and will countenance them, and
am thoroughly convinced of the malice and insolence of them, that you
have always been speaking against.[66]

The Whigs, in a counter-attack against the Tories, moved a bill to establish a regency council on the death of the queen to exercise the sovereign power until the successor arrived in England. Seven great officers of state (the Archbishop of Canterbury, the lord chancellor, the lord treasurer, the lord president, the lord high admiral, the lord privy seal, and the lord chief justice at the time) were to serve automatically, as well as the successor's nominees contained in a sealed list which was to be opened on the queen's death. With the support of the queen and the government, the Regency Act passed through both houses and became law in February 1706. In addition, an Act of Naturalization was passed to accord all Protestant members of the Hanoverian family the status of English subjects. The regency legislation meant that the Protestant succession was now established by law and there was effective machinery to protect it in case of need. In justifying the Whig opposition to the invitation and their support of the Regency Act, Falaiseau informed Leibniz and Sophia:

In their judgement, these were the most convenient means to succeed
in this affair without shocking the Queen, and I can tell you frankly
that those who believe that the goal could have been reached by any
other means or high-handedly, know neither the Queen, who is very
opinionated and quite ferocious, nor England.[67]

The queen found herself in a difficult position: she wished to stress her support for the Protestant succession without having one of the Hanoverian family reside in England. Shortly before the invitation debates, she instructed Bishop Burnet, as chancellor of the Order of the Garter, to check the precedents to discover whether a father and son (other than a reigning king and a Prince of Wales) had ever held the

Garter simultaneously, as she wished to give it to the electoral prince.[68] On 5 April 1706 the queen awarded the Garter to her young kinsman. As a gesture of thanks to the Whigs for their support on the invitation question, the queen agreed to appoint Lord Halifax, a Junto member, as her special envoy to Hanover to convey the Act of Regency and the electoral prince's Garter to that court. While at Hanover in the summer of 1706, Halifax discovered that the electoral prince had 'a mind to be an English duke'.[69] On his return to The Hague, Halifax consulted Marlborough and both men agreed to support the proposal.[70] The queen, however, realized that to give the electoral prince a seat in the House of Lords might one day be used as an excuse to advocate his residence in England: she 'was not very easy at the first proposall of it in your letter', Godolphin reported to Marlborough,

> apprehending it might bee a farther handle for the invitation. But I have endeavored to lett her see, that it must rather have a quite contrary effect, and furnish her servants with a strong argument against it. So she has promised to give directions in it immediately.[71]

Although Halifax boasted to Hanover that the prince's ennoblement 'was done in the best manner here, upon the first Representation I made',[72] the patent of nobility as Duke of Cambridge, issued in November 1706, expressly stated that the war prevented the electoral prince from visiting England or sitting in Parliament, but despite these impediments the queen wished to honour him and his family.[73] The royal hint could not have been broader.

The queen's suspicion that the invitation attempt would be renewed was not simply because 'I am of a temper always to feare ye worst'. In February 1706 a pamphlet appeared in London containing two letters: the first was one which the Electress Sophia had written to the Archbishop of Canterbury in November 1705, couched in cautious terms but clearly demonstrating her eagerness to come to England; the second was a letter from Sir Rowland Gwynne to a Whig peer, which intimated that those who had opposed the invitation were motivated by Jacobite principles.[74] Gwynne's letter, which had in fact been composed by Leibniz and only translated and signed by Gwynne,[75] created a storm in London and was condemned by the Lords. Sophia, who had strongly desired the publication of her own letter,[76] proved staunchly unrepentant.[77] Her son, however, was furious with Gwynne.[78] Marlborough and Godolphin warned the elector through Schütz that Gwynne must be forbidden from attending the electoral court;[79] Gwynne was accordingly forced to retire to Hamburg, where he remained until the queen's death.

Although the queen was disturbed by the invitation crisis, the parliamentary session of 1705–6 was one of the smoothest in her reign, thanks to the close co-operation between the court and the Junto. On 6 December 1705 the queen had the pleasure of attending the House of Lords debate in which Rochester's motion that 'the Church was in danger' under her administration was rejected by 61 to 30. On 19 December both houses presented the queen with an address which stated that the Church,

> under the happy reign of Her Majesty, is in a most safe and flourishing condition; and that whoever goes about to suggest and insinuate, that the Church is in Danger, under her Majesty's administration, is an enemy to the Queen, the Church, and the Kingdom.[80]

Even more importantly, in December 1705 the English Parliament repealed the Aliens Act over the protests of the High Tories,[81] as a gesture of conciliation to Scotland. In the opinion of the elector, the queen, and her ministers, the greatest support for the Hanoverian succession would be the successful conclusion of a union between England and Scotland. By the votes of the Parliaments of both kingdoms, the queen was empowered to nominate an equal number of commissioners from each nation to draw up a treaty. On 27 February 1706 the queen nominated thirty-one Scottish commissioners and on 10 April an equal number of English commissioners. With the exception of Archbishop Sharp, all the English commissioners were Whigs or court Tories; apart from George Lockhart, a Scottish Jacobite, all the Scottish commissioners (suggested by Argyll and Queensberry) had already proved themselves to be in favour of the union. On 16 April the meetings of the commission began in the Cockpit (which was symbolic as it was the queen's former home), and within nine weeks a treaty was agreed upon. The major provisions were that the Hanoverian succession was to apply in Scotland as well as in England; an imperial Parliament sitting at Westminster would be composed of the English Parliament as it was constituted, with sixteen representative Scottish peers in the House of Lords and forty-five Scottish members in the House of Commons; universal free trade was to be established between the two kingdoms and colonial trade was henceforth to be open to Scottish merchants; and the independence of the Presbyterian Church of Scotland was guaranteed.

The queen visited the commission only upon formal occasions, such as the meeting of 21 May, when she exhorted the members to finish their work quickly, and that of 26 June,[82] but she took a keen interest in their proceedings. On 4 July she assured Godolphin: 'I am very glad all ye difficultys in the union are at an end heare, & wish with all my hart, it may meet with none in Scotland.'[83] On 23 July a great ceremony was held at St James's in which the treaty was formally presented to the queen by her commissioners. After speeches by Cowper and Seafield, the two chancellors, 'Her Majesty made a very handsome return, with a very graceful pronunciation and tone of voice.'[84] Godolphin and Robert Harley were the chief English ministers on the commission, which was almost their last harmonious joint undertaking.

The negotiations for the union took place against the background of Marlborough's single most successful campaign in the Southern Nether-lands. Marlborough left England on 12 April with the warmest good wishes of the queen. On 14 May, knowing that Marlborough was preparing for a major action, the queen wrote Godolphin a short note:

> I have nothing to trouble you with at this time, but only to desire ye fayvour of you to give my Service to the Duke of Marlborough, & tell him I beg whatever great designs he undertakes, that he would in ye first place take care of his own person, & if he be Safe I do not doubt but by the Blessing of God Almighty, he will be the means of quieting ye world, & then I hope he & all his Humble Servants may enjoy quiet together.[85]

In his letter to Marlborough of the same evening, Godolphin forwarded the queen's note 'which shows so much kindness and concern for you, that I thought I could not express it so well as she had don herself'.[86] Although neither the queen nor Godolphin knew it at the time, the allied army had two days previously, on 12/23 May, defeated the French under Maréchal Villeroy at Ramillies. So overwhelming was Marl-borough's victory that the French were forced to evacuate virtually all of the Southern Netherlands and to retire to their own fortified borders. Such great prizes as Antwerp and Ostend fell into allied hands without a shot being fired. The news of the great victory at Ramillies reached London on the evening of 16 May, carried by Colonel Michael Richards, who Marlborough suggested should be given no more than £500 as a reward. Godolphin replied, 'Care shall be taken that his present bee according to your direction, though the Queen was so pleased with his news, that she would willingly have exceeded it.'[87] The following day Marlborough's 'humble Servant' sent him her congratulations in an extraordinary letter from a sovereign to a subject:

> I want words to express the true sense I have of the great Service which by the Blessing of God you have don your Country, & so in this great and Glorious victory, *I hope in God it will be a means to Confirm all good & honest people in theire principalls, & frighten others from being troublesom.* You must give me leave again once more to repeat ye request I have

made before, of your being carefull of your self, for it is a great alay to all ye satisfaction this good news gives me, to consider what hazards you are exposed to. I congratulate your great delivirances from my hart & soul & pray God to preserve you from all accidents.[88]

As the French continued their retreat, city after city in the Southern Netherlands fell into the hands of the allies. On 21 May, the queen congratulated Marlborough for a second time:

it is impossible for me ever to say soe much as I ought in return of your great & faithfull services to me, but I will endeavour by all ye actions of my life to shew you how truly sensible I am of them, the account you send . . . of ye great progres you have made since ye Batle is astonishing, the Blessing of God is sertinly with you, may he continue to protect you, & make you the happy instrument of giveing a lasting peace to Europe.[89]

On 27 June the queen, accompanied by the Duchess of Marlborough, attended a great thanksgiving at St Paul's, and the same service was celebrated throughout the three kingdoms. But this time, the Southern Netherlands had been virtually conquered by Marlborough's armies, and the titular 'Carlos III' offered to Marlborough the governor-generalship of the Netherlands, worth £60,000 per annum, a position and an income which Marlborough dearly wished to make his own. The Habsburg offer, however, instilled in the Dutch a permanent suspicion of England's motives, and of Marlborough's in particular. The republic wished to maintain its economic and political superiority over its southern neighbour, and the prospect of English control of the Southern Netherlands was displeasing to every faction in the United Provinces. In order to preserve allied unity, Marlborough chose to refuse the 'King of Spain's' offer in favour of an Anglo-Dutch condominium. On 9 July the queen assured Marlborough,

you know I left it wholly to you to doe what you thought most proper Conserning the King of Spains commission & therefore I need not say any more on that Subject, but that I should have bin very glad both for your particular, & ye good of ye Common cause, that you had ye Government of Flanders in your hands, being sertin it can be given to none that can be soe capable of that trust.[90]

For the queen, the Ramillies campaign had one overriding significance: 'now', she told Godolphin, 'we have God be thanked soe hopefull a prospect of a peace'.[91] While in the north the French forces were obliged to retreat to their own borders in the summer of 1706, in the south Prince Eugene of Savoy won the battle of Turin in September, which drove Franco-Spanish forces from northern Italy. In Spain, where the Earl of

Peterborough had succeeded in conquering Barcelona and the province of Catalonia in 1705, a joint invasion of Castile from Portugal and Catalonia in 1706 had allowed 'Carlos III' to occupy Madrid for several weeks between June and August 1706. Indeed, the allied victories of the *annus mirabilis* of 1706 induced Louis XIV to make his first serious overtures of peace to the Dutch, and these proposals were conveyed through the Elector of Bavaria and revealed by Heinsius to Marlborough in late July. France proposed that Spain should be divided between Philip V and 'Carlos III', with the Spanish Netherlands and the Indies going to Charles, the Milanese to Philip, and Naples and Sicily to the Elector of Bavaria.[92] The queen, worried that Dutch suspicion of English ambitions in the Netherlands would wreck the alliance, had already summarized the English peace conditions of 'No Peace without Spain' in a letter to Godolphin of 4 July:

> I am very sory to find the french party have still soe much power in
> holland as to fill ye States with such Jealousys, if they knew my temper,
> they would be very easy, I haveing no ambition after the King of
> Spaine is seteled on his throne, but to see an honnorable peace, that
> whenever it pleased God I shall dye, I may have the Satisfaction of
> leaveing my poor Country & all my friends in Peace & quiet.[93]

Marlborough, in his reply to Heinsius, echoed the queen's sentiments: 'as a good Englishman I must be of the opinion of my country, that both my treaty and intirest, we are obliged to preserve the Monarque [*sic*: monarchy] of Spain intier'.[94] In August, Louis XIV expanded his offers: he was willing to see the archduke take all of Spain and the Indies, while the States-General would be allowed to determine the fate of the Spanish Netherlands and Philip V would be compensated by the Spanish possessions in Italy (the kingdoms of Naples and Sicily, the duchy of Milan, and the Spanish ports in Tuscany).[95] Nevertheless, the English government stood firmly on the principle that all Spanish possessions should go to 'Carlos III', and that Philip V should receive nothing. In September, Godolphin reinforced this position in a letter to Willem Buys, the Pensionary of Amsterdam and the reputed leader of the 'peace party' in the republic: 'No good Englishman nor servant to the Queen can advise the dismembering of the Spanish monarchy.'[96]

In a self-justifying memorial written after the queen's death, Robert Harley claimed that

> Mr. Harley being then Secretary of State, the Queen requires him to
> give his Opinion without reserve, he advises to Enter into the Negotia-
> tion of Peace & if sufficient Terms were not offered, that the Duke [of
> Marlborough] shou'd be order'd to march into the Heart of France,

there being no Army then to oppose him. From this time the D: of
Marlborough & My Lord Godolphin projected the ruin of Mr. H: upon
a Jealousy that the Queen had too great a regard for him.[97]

Despite Harley's later claims, there is no hard evidence to indicate that
he seriously opposed the policy of Marlborough and Godolphin in 1706
or, because of the allied rejection of Louis XIV's offers, 'that he began
dragging his feet on the war issue'.[98]

In truth, the Duumvirs and their principal associate in the government had come to a parting of the ways by the autumn of 1706, but their
differences of opinion revolved around domestic issues, not foreign
affairs. The questions over which they differed were the increasing
demands of the Junto for rewards for their support of the government in
the previous session of Parliament. Early in 1706, Marlborough and
Godolphin had drawn up 'a formal pact' with the Junto which was
essentially an agreement that future ecclesiastical preferments would
not be awarded on the nomination of Harley or Archbishop Sharp.[99]
Marlborough and Godolphin had severed their connections with the
High Tories, and they were now prepared to cut their ties with the
moderates in the party. In March, Godolphin explained to Harley his
belief that it would be easier for the government to retain Whig support
rather than regain that of the Tories, whose 'behaviour in this Session
has shown as much inveteracy and as little sense as possible'.[100]
Although the Junto had not yet succeeded in putting one of their
members into governmental office, they held veto power over appointments. The most notable example was that of Charles Talbot, Duke of
Shrewsbury and one of the architects of the Glorious Revolution. In
January 1706, Shrewsbury returned to England after a five-year self-
imposed exile in Rome, where he had acquired an Italian-born wife who
quickly became the object of scorn of the court ladies (and of the Duchess of
Marlborough in particular) for her 'foreign' manners. Marlborough and
Godolphin had hoped to offer their longstanding friend a position in the
cabinet, but the Junto – still resentful that Shrewsbury had deserted the
Whigs and fled to Rome at the end of William III's reign – vetoed his
appointment. For the next two years, Shrewsbury avoided attendance at
court and Parliament while Harley, whom the Junto regarded as their
foremost enemy in the cabinet, maintained increasingly close contact
with Shrewsbury.[101]

By the beginning of 1706 the Junto, flushed with newly acquired
influence and self-righteous because of their continued support of the
government, aimed at nothing less than replacing Harley as secretary of
state with the young Earl of Sunderland. When they discovered that

neither the queen nor Godolphin nor Marlborough would consider such a plan, they switched targets, demanding that Sunderland replace the other Secretary, Sir Charles Hedges.[102] Hedges was a much less formidable target than Harley: in Sarah's words, Hedges 'has noe capasity, noe quality, no interest, nor never could have been in that post but that every body knows my Lord Rochester cares for nothing so much as a man that hee thinks will depend upon him'.[103] The Junto mistakenly reasoned that Sunderland, as the son-in-law of the Marlboroughs and the husband of the queen's god-daughter and namesake, would be the easiest of their members to force into high governmental office. The Whig pressure upon Godolphin and, to a lesser extent, upon Marlborough was relentless because they could not believe that the Duumvirs could not bend the queen to their will.

In truth, Sunderland was perhaps the most difficult member of the Junto to foist upon the queen. She had long hated his parents; his own youthful republicanism made him suspect. As we have seen, there is a real possibility that the Princess of Denmark had opposed his marriage to Lady Anne Churchill; in addition, Sunderland had led the opposition to the prince's bill in 1702, which the queen took to heart. Most importantly, however, Sunderland's membership of the Junto itself disqualified him in the queen's eyes from high office. She had escaped the overbearing extremism of Rochester and Nottingham and had no wish to have another extremist in government office. The battle to obtain office for Sunderland was to prove crucial in the future development of the queen's reign: it finally ruined Sarah in the queen's opinion, it estranged the queen from Godolphin, and it increased her reliance upon Robert Harley.

Sarah, at first, remained in the background. Since her complaints against Lady Frescheville after the royal party's return from Winchester in September 1705, her relations with the queen had been infrequent and formal. She was devoted heart and soul, none the less, to procuring the post of secretary of state for her son-in-law, even against the wishes of Marlborough and Godolphin. On 19 April 1706, Godolphin informed Marlborough that he had paid a special visit to the duchess at Windsor 'chiefly to lett her see the unreasonableness of her friends [the Whigs] in some particulars'.[104] Godolphin found himself caught on the issue between the duchess and the queen. Three days later he complained to Marlborough that the queen was unreasonably biased against the Junto:

> I have had some discourses with Mrs. Morley about the *papers* you
> have redd to her before you went away, and some other thoughts of
> that nature [i.e. rewarding the Junto]. But all that matter goes so much

uphill with her, that she will hate one for endeavoring to perswade her to half what is really necessary for her own good. I doubt this temper must have ill consequences of many kinds.[105]

During May several Tories were dismissed from lords lieutenancies and were replaced by Whigs, including Lord Wharton in Westmorland;[106] during the summer the queen agreed to restore Wharton to his former position as chief justice of the royal forests and parks south of the Trent, which considerably strengthened Wharton's electoral influence.[107]

While she was making these concessions to the Junto, the queen avoided answering Sarah's long, importunate letters. On 23 May, for instance, she replied to Sarah:

> I am very sorry when ever I happen to make any mistakes in what dear Mrs. Freeman says to me as I find I have don in her letter that was writt on Munday, that which I received today is soe long, that I hope you will not think it unreasonable if I deffer ye answering it till tomorrow, more particularly then I can do now being a going to take ye air, & if it weare not for that, I would desire your permission to do soe, to have time to read it over & over againe, before I begin to writt, for feare of makeing any more mistakes.[108]

The fact that the queen avoided replying was a red rag to the duchess, who ostentatiously complained to the queen that she would cease informing her of people's pretensions, as her letters did no good. Despite a conciliatory reply from the queen,[109] the duchess held firm to her resolution not to write, and almost two weeks later, on 3 July, the queen wrote again:

> Not haveing heard from my dear Mrs. Freeman since my two last, I am almost afraid of ventureing to trouble her with a few lines from her poor unfortunat ever faithfull Morly, but not being Consious to my self, of ever haveing don any thing that deserves soe much coldnes from you as you have againe shewed of late, I can't help putting you in mind of her who you thought worthy of your esteem, & will to her last moment be with all truth & tenderness my dear Mrs. Freemans.[110]

The suppliant tone of the queen's letter encouraged the duchess to write again, complaining that two Tories, Henry Graham and Charles Seymour, were retained as grooms of the prince's bedchamber, despite their votes against the government in the House of Commons. Her complaint brought an immediate answer: on 5 July the queen assured Sarah that 'what you said concerning Mr. Graham & Mr. Seymour, seemed so reasonable to me that . . . I can now tell dear Mrs. Freeman, that ye first of these Gentlemen has had his Sentence, & ye other will have it very soon'.[111] Graham was replaced by Marlborough's nephew, Colonel Charles Godfrey, jr, and Seymour was replaced by Colonel Samuel Masham, of whom we shall hear more.

However, in her correspondence with Sarah and her conversations with Godolphin, the queen tried to avoid the main point, the Junto's desire to secure Sunderland's appointment. Both Godolphin and Sarah suspected that someone was secretly encouraging the queen's resistance to the Whigs in general and to Sunderland in particular; their suspicions fell first upon Prince George and his favourite, George Churchill. In June, Godolphin complained to Marlborough that his younger brother 'has contributed to make some things easy. But at the same time, Mr. Morley [Prince George] has shown uneasiness in some things which nobody can tell hcw to impute to any other influence than that of *George Churchill*'.[112] Marlborough did not believe that Admiral Churchill had much influence with the queen and assured both Godolphin and the duchess: 'I am afraid there is somebody else that makes *Prince George* and Mrs. Morley uneasy.'[113] Godolphin, despairing of changing the queen's will by himself, appealed to Marlborough to bring his influence to bear in Sunderland's behalf.[114] On 27 June, Marlborough wrote to the queen to announce the surrender of Ostend, and at the same time advised her to appoint Sunderland as secretary of state. The queen, true to her policy of avoiding the issue as long as possible, replied to Marlborough on 9 July:

> You may easily beleeve I shall be very willing to grant any request you
> make for any body that I can, espesialy for one who is soe neare to you
> & that has shewn soe much Zeale for my Service as my Lord
> Sunderland has lately don, but you know very well it is not in my
> power at this time to Comply with your desire.[115]

The queen did not consult Godolphin on her reply to Marlborough, 'though she has had a very fair occasion to have done so', the treasurer reported to Marlborough two days later.[116] Nor did she speak to the duchess about Marlborough's request. Marlborough wrote to Sarah:

> I agree with you that Mrs. Morley's saying nothing of my letter must
> proceed from not likeing the subject matter . . . as she is very sincere
> and a great many other good quality's in which we aught to think
> ourselves happy, I think *Sunderland* and his friends aught not to take itt
> unkindly; for as she is every day sensible of the undutyfull and unkind
> usidge she meets with from the greatest part of *the Tories*, [it] will bring
> her to what I am afraid she is yet uneasy att. . . . . I can't but think
> you lay a great deal more to *George Churchill's* charge than he deserves,
> for *the queen* has no good opinion nor never speakes to him.[117]

221

Sarah did not share her husband's sanguine belief that the queen's intransigence could gradually be overcome, and on 29 July Marlborough deprecated his wife's search for a 'secret influence' on the queen:

> You know that I have often disputes with you concerning *the queen*, and by what I have always observed that *when she thinkes herself in the right, she needs no advice to help her to be very ferm and possative*. But I do not doubt but a very little time will sett this of *Sunderland* very right, for you may see by the letter [of 9 July] that *the queen* has a good opinion of *Sunderland*.[118]

The queen remained inflexible, refusing to discuss with Godolphin the possibility of appointing Sunderland to any important governmental position. Finally, on 20 August, Godolphin informed the queen, possibly in writing, that he would be forced to resign as lord treasurer if she refused to accede to the Junto's demands.[119] At this point the queen privately turned to Harley for advice. An undated memorandum, in Harley's hand, of his conversation with the queen in which he urged her to stand fast against Sunderland's appointment, can safely be attributed to this moment:

> Nothing wil satisfie them.
> If so much pressed now to take him in, when most think him unfit, wil it be possible to part with him when he appears to be so.
> All power is given them.
> Those that press it must be delivered from the engagements or terrors they are under.
> If you stop it now, it wil make you better served and observed by al sides, it is gon so far it wil be too late hereafter – Everybody wil worship the Idol party that is set up.
> Ballance the good and the evil of taking him or keeping him out.[120]

The queen, however, was more concerned at the possibility that Godolphin might resign (she had written 'for God Almighty sake make me easy, which I can never be if you leave me') than she was to keep Sunderland out of office. On 23 August she proposed 'an expedient' to the lord treasurer: let Sunderland be given a seat in the cabinet and a pension but no office, 'till some post is vacant'.[121] But the queen's expedient was unacceptable, because the Junto refused to consider anything less for Sunderland than Sir Charles Hedges's seals.[122] On 27 August the duchess entered the fray, for the first time openly advocating Sunderland's appointment. 'Tis certain', she told the queen, 'that your government can't be carryd on with a part of the Torrys, & the Whigs disoblidged, who when that happens will joyn with any people to torment you & those that are your true servants.' The blunt threat that

222

the Whigs might oppose the government if they did not get their way enraged the queen, but the bombshell was in Sarah's final sentence:

> Your security & the nations is my cheif wish, & I beg of God Allmighty as earnestly as I shall do for his pardon at my last hour, that Mr. and Mrs. Morley may see their errors as to this *notion* before it is too late, but considering how little impression any thing makes that comes from your faithfull Freeman, I have troubled you too much & I beg your pardon for it. [123]

The queen misread 'notion' as 'nation' and was mortally offended: instead of answering Sarah, she complained bitterly to Godolphin of the duchess. On 30 August, Sarah wrote again to the queen, protesting 'Your Majesty's great indifferency & contempt in taking noe notice of my last letter', summarizing the points which she had made in her original letter, and asking the queen to show the first letter to Godolphin. [124] Instead, the queen wrote to the lord treasurer, again refusing to appoint Sunderland on the grounds that to do so would make her a slave of party and faction; once more she advocated a balanced or 'mixed' ministry composed of representatives of both parties. Although her anger against the High Tories had not abated (she wrote 'I am not inclined nor never will be to employ any of those violent persons that have behaved them selves soe ill towards me'), she had no desire to embrace the Whigs. Instead, she harked back to the Elizbethan concept of national unity and turned her face against the trend of the future:

> All I desire is my liberty in encourageing & employing all those that Concur faithfully in my Service whether they are call'd Whigs or Torys, not to be tyed to one, nor to ye other, for if I should be soe unfortunat as to fall into ye hands of ether, I shall look upon my self tho I have the name of Queen, to be in realety but theire slave, which as it will be my personal ruin, soe it will be ye destroying of all Government, for instead of putting an end to faction, it will lay a lasting foundation for it. . . .

In a *cri de coeur* the queen expressed her concept of the sovereign's role, that of the impartial arbitress:

> Why for God sake, must I who have no interest, no end, no thought but for ye good of my Country, be made soe miserable as to be brought into ye power of one sett of men, & why may I not be trusted, since I meane nothing but what is equally for ye good of all my subjects?

In an allusion to her disputes with the duchess, the queen concluded:

223

> There is another aprehension I have of Lord Sunderland being
> Secretary, which I think is a matterial one; & proceeds from what you
> told me of his temper. I am afraid, he & I would not agree long
> togather, finding by experience my humour, & those that are of a
> warmer, will often have misunderstandings between one another.[125]

Godolphin replied the following morning, matching the queen's
intransigence with his own ('I cannot struggle against the difficulties of
Your Majestie's business, and yourself at the same time') and again
threatening to resign.[126] On 1 September, in a long conversation with
the queen, Godolphin discovered that she had read 'nation' for 'notion'
in Sarah's letter and attempted to smooth matters over.[127] Despite
Godolphin's entreaties, the queen delayed any reply to Sarah until 6
September, when she pointed out that 'my complaint was not with out
some ground, & a mistake any body might make upon ye first reading,
for you had made an *a*, instead of an *o*, which quite alter'd ye word', and
reassured the duchess that Godolphin's 'leaveing my service is a
thought I can not bear'.[128] Sarah fired back an answer four times the
length of the queen's letter, recapitulating her arguments and then
answering the queen's assertions in her letter to Godolphin of 30
August, castigating the Tories ('the Heros of the Church'), and concluding: 'I beg your Majestys pardon for not waiting upon you, I
persuade myself that, long as my letter is, it will be less troublesome to
your Majesty.'[129] A friendship which could be threatened by a misread
vowel was not very seaworthy; what was to follow was to sink it
irretrievably.

On 7 September, Godolphin visited the queen at Windsor and again
pressed her to accept Sunderland. 'He found however', Godolphin
reported to Sarah,

> it had no sort of effect but to disturb & grieve *the queen*, who after
> having agin repeated the arguments used in Mrs. Morley's letter [of 30
> August], and percieving that they made very little impression upon
> *Godolphin*, burst into a passion of weeping and sayd it was plain *the
> queen* was to bee miserable as long as they lived, whatever they did.

This outburst so upset the normally stolid lord treasurer that he agreed
to the queen's suggestion that they await Marlborough's response to the
'expedient' proposed by the queen.

> After some pause, *Godolphin* says *the queen* complained of a letter she
> had received from Mrs. Freeman, which she said with a great deal of
> stiffness and reservedness in her looks, was *very extraordinary* in her
> opinion, but she said she was not composed enough to mention the
> particulars at that time.[130]

224

The result, as Godolphin reported to Marlborough on 10 September, was deadlock:

> The uneasiness betwixt *the queen* and Mr. Montgomery about the affair
> of *Sunderland* continues as it was . . . one cannot goe about to show
> them [the Whigs] these difficulties without too much exposing of *the
> queen* . . . there is no room to hope for the least assistance from Mrs.
> Freeman in this matter.[131]

On 13 September, Godolphin wrote a long letter to the queen in which he attempted to answer her objections to the proposed change. First, he pointed out, the change could not be a hardship to Sir Charles Hedges, who had expressed a desire to retire; second, Sunderland was zealous for the queen's interest and the warmth of his temper was consequently directed in the right way; third, as for throwing herself into the hands of a party, 'after what they did unasked to serve your Majesty last winter & to keep you even from uneasyness' during the invitation crisis, the Whigs now deserved a reward.[132] Godolphin was distraught by the queen's unwillingness to appoint Sunderland, and also by the Duchess of Marlborough's unrestrained anger at the queen's intransigence. 'You are much better natured in effect than you sometimes appear to bee', he wrote to Sarah on 14 September,

> and though you chide me for being touched with the condition in
> which I saw *the queen*, you would have been so too, if you had seen the
> same sight I did. But what troubles mee most in all this affair is that
> one can't yett find any way of making Mrs. Morley sensible of her
> mistakes, for I am very sure she thinks herself intirely in the right.[133]

Godolphin certainly did not underestimate the queen's emotional revulsion against the appointment of Sunderland. A few days later, she assured Godolphin that she would reply in writing to his letter. He privately complained, 'since this hurly burly I have never had one easy conversation, but all coldness and constraint'.[134]

The queen wanted her response to Godolphin to be in writing, to give her time to consult with Harley, who was already frightened by the growing power of the Junto.[135] He encouraged the queen in her obstinacy, and in her reply to Godolphin on 21 September she predicted that the Junto's demands on behalf of Sunderland were only the first steps in their campaign: 'if this be complyd with, you will then in a little time find they must be gratifyd in some thing else, or they will not goe on heartyly in my businesse'. Flatly refusing to be 'in the hands of a party', the queen again offered to take Sunderland into 'the Cabinet Councell with a pension till some vacancy happens', but she absolutely refused to appoint him secretary of state.[136]

225

Meanwhile, Sarah had retired to Woodstock in high dudgeon at what she considered to be her ill treatment by the queen. Godolphin joined her there and, on 25 September, the treasurer replied to the queen's letter, pointing out that the parliamentary session

> in this next winter . . . is like to bee the most criticall of your whole reign, & when many things of very great consiquence will come to bear all at once. I doubt whether all we can doe will be able to keep off the peace this winter.

Again, Godolphin threatened to resign if the queen did not follow his advice: 'you have an opertunity of making your Government strong, which you will never have again'.[137] The following day Sarah re-entered the lists ('Mrs. Morley may very well wonder that I should trouble her again after the last contempt to Mrs. Freeman, not to mention any other') to support Godolphin:

> I must once more represent that I find that lady is going to ruin all her affairs, the parliament is going to sett very soon, & by all one hears is likly to bee a sessions soe criticall that in all probability your future happynesse & the nations will depend upon it.

Sarah predicted that the queen would force Godolphin out of her service and – for the first time – suggested to the queen that a 'secret influence' was at work:

> the only fear I have is that there is sombody artfull that takes pains to mislead Mrs. Morley for otherwise how is it possible that one who I have formerly heard say, she was not fond of her own Judgment, could persist in such a thing soe very contrary to the advise of two men that has certainly don more services both to the Crown & Country than can be found in any history.[138]

Sarah was correct in fearing 'sombody artfull', although as yet she had not identified the individual. Harley was engaged in the tug of war for both the queen's mind and her affections. On 25 September, according to his own memorandum, he had presented arguments to the queen with which she undoubtedly agreed:

> The foundation of the Church is in the Queen, the foundation of Liberty is in her? Let her therefore be Arbitress between them.
> Should the Whigs be complied with in everything they ask, can you carry on business? Certainly no.
> Releve therefore those [i.e. Marlborough and Godolphin] who are gon too farre – Can you stop the Whigs that they will not possess themselves (as a faction) of your Authority, if you stand not heer?
> Do the Whigs deserve to enjoy all the Queen's successes? & nobody else?[139]

Emboldened by Harley's reasoning, and hopeful that his prediction ('I have the Remedy') that the 'reasonable' men could be drawn away from the 'violent' Tories in support of the ministry, the queen totally ignored Sarah's letter and merely temporized with Godolphin, proposing that the entire matter be postponed until Marlborough's return to England.[140] Even before the queen could appeal to her captain-general, however, Marlborough had dispatched a letter to her, totally supporting Godolphin's position:

> the behaviour of Lord Rochester and all the hot heads of that party is so extravagant, that there is no doubt to be made of their exposing you and the liberties of England to the rage of France, rather than not be revenged.

The lord treasurer, Marlborough warned the queen, 'can't be supported but by the Whigs, for the others seek his destruction, which in effect is yours'.[141]

In letters now lost, the queen appealed to Marlborough on 27 September and again on 1 October to take her side in the dispute. In response to these letters, Marlborough wrote even more strongly on 13/24 October, attacking the concept of a 'moderate' ministry. 'It is true', he told the queen,

> that your reign has been so manifestly blessed by God, that one might reasonably think you might govern without making use of the heads of either party, but as it might be easy for yourself. This might be practicable if both parties sought your favour, as in reason and duty they ought. But, madam, the truth is, that the heads of one party have declared against you and your government, as far as it is possible without going into open rebellion. Now, should your Majesty disoblige the others, how is it possible to obtain near five millions for carrying on the war with vigour, without which all is undone.[142]

The queen herself was a witness to Tory hostility to the government when she and the prince spent ten days at Newmarket at the beginning of October 1706. One Tory noted that 'there was a small appearance at Newmarket, of which 'tis said the Queen took notice that the Gentry did not meet Her Majesty, which makes me think few but Whigs were there'.[143] Still, the queen remained inflexible on the question of making Sunderland a secretary of state. Her obstinacy could not be attributed entirely to personal contact with Harley, for he left London on 10 October to visit his country home and did not return to town until 15 November.[144] Despite his absence, Harley and his friends, particularly Henry St John – alarmed at the Junto's hold on Godolphin – began a steady obstruction of business, opposing minor appointments, cultivating the discontented, and delaying the dispatch of matters connected with the war. Godolphin quickly discovered that 'Harley, St John and one or two more of *Marlborough's* particular friends were underhand endeavouring to bring all the difficultys they could think of, upon the publick business in the next sessions', as he informed Marlborough on 18 October.[145] In spite of the awakening suspicions of the lord treasurer, Marlborough continued to trust Harley. He urged Godolphin to take Harley into his confidence and explain the necessity for changes in the ministry, thereby governing the other moderate Tories through Harley.[146]

On 20 October the Duchess of Marlborough once more entered the battle on behalf of her son-in-law, attempting to deploy tact ('I must in the first place beg leave to revive the name of Mrs. Morley & your faithfull Freeman') in forwarding to the queen Marlborough's letter to his wife of 7/18 October, in which he complained that 'I did flatter myself that my zeal and sincerity for *the queen* was so well known to her, that my representations would have had more waite then I find they have'. Sarah, after elaborating on the risks and sacrifices which her husband was making in the queen's service, proceeded to a general indictment of the house of Stuart:

> I desire you would reflect whether you have never heard that the greatest misfortunes that ever happen'd to any of your family has not been occasion'd by having ill advises & an obstanacy in their tempers that is very unaccountable.[147]

Between private individuals, such an insult would be intolerable; between subject and sovereign, it was unforgivable. The queen waited a week before replying to Sarah's letter on 27 October, and her response was a pointed rebuke:

> It would be more pleasing whenever you are pleased to let me have ye Satisfaction of heareing from you, if you would write in ye Stile you used to do, & why it was alterd I can't emagin for I'me sure I never gave no Cause for it. I had resolvd before I received your letter not to dispose of ye liveing you mention till the D. of Marl: coms home, & what you say you may be assured will not alter my mind, for I am as little inclined as any body to encourage those that do not deserve well. I have nothing more to add at present but that as unkind as you are to your poor unfortunat faithfull Morly, I will ever be with all truth & tenderness my dear Mrs. Freemans.[148]

This merely served to provoke a bitter response from the duchess, who accused the queen of ignoring the points which she had made in her original letter, and particularly of failing to comment on Marlborough's letter which Sarah had forwarded to the queen. On 30 October, the queen reassured Sarah that there was 'no reason to have Suspissions of any ones haveing power with Mrs. Morly besides Mr. Free: & Mr. Mont: & I hope they will beleeve mee', and she concluded with a heartfelt plea that Sarah would not press Marlborough and Godolphin to resign:

> I never did nor never will give them any Just reason to forsake me, & they have too much honnor & too sincer a love for theire Country to leave me with out a Cause, & I beg you would not add to my other misfortunes, of pushing them on to such an unjust & unjustifyable an action. [149]

The queen was not being disingenuous when she assured Sarah that 'she had no reason to have Suspissions of any ones haveing power with Mrs. Morly besides Mr. Free: & Mr. Mont:'. As yet Harley had only reinforced the queen's own opinion; he had not yet attempted to guide her into paths divergent from those being taken by Marlborough and Godolphin. The queen's greatest fear was that Sarah would influence Marlborough and Godolphin to resign if she remained obstinate regarding Sunderland. For this reason, the queen, despite the sharpness of her rebuke to Sarah, attempted to resurrect her personal relationship with the duchess. On 2 November, in a kind letter, she promised Sarah that 'tho we have the misfortune to differ in some things I will ever be the same to my Dear Dear Mrs. Freeman'. [150] Sarah's influence, the queen well realized, might prove paramount in shaping the reactions of Marlborough and Godolphin to a 'moderate scheme' which Harley was projecting in a last effort to prevent Sunderland's appointment. Harley's plan, which was similar in scope and personnel to what he was to attempt in 1708 and to accomplish in 1710, was to join the 'moderate' Tories, such as James Brydges, one of the court's managers in the Commons, with the non-Junto Whig magnates, such as the Duke of Newcastle, lord privy seal, in support of the Duumvirs. Godolphin, however, rejected out of hand the feasibility of such a scheme. Harley pinned his hopes on Marlborough. [151]

On 18 November the captain-general returned to London, and two days later the Duumvirs met with Harley to deliver their final rejection of his plan. Sensing that he might be risking his own dismissal, Harley backed down and dropped his open objections to Sunderland's appointment. [152] The queen, to her chagrin, was forced to face parliamentary facts: no majority would be forthcoming to support the court without the aid of the Junto. Without Harley's scheme in action, Whig support was indispensable to secure the supplies necessary to carry on the war. Nevertheless, the queen drove a hard bargain in agreeing to take

Sunderland into her cabinet: eighteen months later, she reminded Marlborough

> of ye promis you made to me when I first took this person into my
> Service, which was that if ever he did anything I did not like (or some
> thing to that purpose), you would bring him to make his leg & take his
> leave.[153]

In addition, she promised Sir Charles Hedges that he would be given the first vacancy in the prerogative court of Canterbury (for which he had to wait until January 1711).[154]

On the day Parliament reassembled, 3 December, Sir Charles Hedges was dismissed and the seals were given to Sunderland.[155] The queen successfully covered her inner resentment with a gracious veneer: three months later, Godolphin reported to Marlborough: 'The Queen was very easy in giving to my Lord and Lady Sunderland the house where my Lord Nottingham lived, in the privy garden.'[156] Her civility was due, in part, to the fact that she remained bitterly estranged from the High Tories: on 9 December, Archbishop Sharp recorded in his diary that 'She desired I would not be governed by my friends (meaning Lord Nottingham and that party) in my votes in Parliament'.[157] In addition to Sunderland's appointment, the queen made a series of lesser concessions to the Whigs; several Whigs were promoted in the peerage, notably Cowper who became a baron and Wharton who was elevated to an earldom. Godolphin himself was also given the same rank. Sir James Montagu, the brother of Lord Halifax, was appointed solicitor-general and the Commission of Trade was reconstituted with three new Whig members.[158] Rochester, Nottingham, Jersey, and Buckingham were struck from the registers of the Privy Council.[159] The only Tories left in high positions were Harley and his allies, Henry St John, Simon Harcourt, and Sir Thomas Mansell. Despite these royal concessions to the Whigs, the Junto were not satisfied. Irritated at the prolonged delays and suspecting that Marlborough and Godolphin were not dealing honestly with them, the Junto were determined to force their remaining members into office – as the queen had foreseen.

From 1704 to 1706 the 'moderate ministry' had accomplished great things. The union was virtually completed; the Hanoverian succession was made as secure as statute law could allow; Germany and the Spanish Netherlands had been liberated from French influence; Louis XIV's power in Italy had been mortally wounded. The war had now been carried to the borders of France itself, and in Spain the allies had a firm base in Catalonia and a staunch ally in Portugal. In spite of these accomplishments, largely attributable to the skill and sagacity of the

Duumvirs, Marlborough and Godolphin had lost the unquestioning allegiance of the queen by their failure to protect her from the rapacity of the Junto. Furthermore, her lifelong friendship with Sarah was dead. On 23 November she had written to the duchess, apologizing for her silence during their last meeting ('I knew if I had begun to speake I should not have bin fitt to be seen by any body') and asking Sarah to put her complaints in writing.[160] Although couched in the language of affection, the queen's letter was a subtle hint that Sarah's presence was not desired, and Sarah reacted accordingly, rarely coming to court after Sunderland's appointment. When in January 1707 the queen asked Parliament to entail Marlborough's title and Post Office pension of £5,000 per annum to his female posterity,[161] she totally ignored Sarah's future interest in the pension. As the duchess later recorded, 'Her Majesty never took the least care of me in this matter, tho' she had often said in many heaps of letters that I had by me, that no crown was rich enough to repay the services I had done her.'[162] Sarah, to demonstrate 'that I did not omitt takeing any reasonable occation to please her even when I saw she was changed to me', wrote a formal letter of thanks to the queen which she signed 'your poor forsaken Freeman'.[163]

Except for Prince George, whose own health was rapidly deteriorating, the queen was now alone. The best pen-portrait we possess of her physical and mental state during this period was written by Sir John Clerk of Penicuik, one of the Scottish commissioners for the union. During the summer of 1706, when Clerk and the Duke of Queensberry visited the queen at Kensington, Clerk recorded in his journal:

I had occasion to observe the Calamities which attend humane nature even to the greatest dignities of Life. Her Majesty was labouring under a fit of the Gout, and in extream pain and agony, and on this occasion everything about her was much in the same disorder as about the meanest of her subjects. Her face, which was red and spotted, was rendered something frightful by her negligent dress, and the foot affected was tied up with a pultis and some nasty bandages. I was much affected by this sight, and the more when she had occasion to mention her people of Scotland, which she did frequently to the Duke. What are you, poor mean-like Mortal, thought I, who talks in the style of a Sovereign? Nature seems to be inverted when a poor infirm Woman becomes one of the Rulers of the World.[164]

When in the spring of 1707 Sir John took his leave of the queen to return to Scotland as a baron of the exchequer, this most perceptive of observers noticed her essential loneliness and isolation:

She appeared to me the most despicable mortal I had ever seen in any station. The poor Lady, as I saw her twice before, was again under a

231

very severe fit of the Gout, ill dressed, blotted in her countenance, and surrounded with plaisters, cataplasims, and dirty-like rags. The extremity of her pain was not then upon her, and it diverted her a little to see company with whom she was not to use ceremonies, otherways I have not been allowed access to her.

However, I believe she was not displeased to see any body, for no Court Attenders ever came near her. All the Incence and adoration offered at Courts were to her Ministers, particularly the Earl of Godolphin, her chief Minister, and the two Secretarys of State [Harley and Sunderland], her palace at Kensington where she commonly resided, was a perfect solitude. . . . I never saw any body attending there but some of her Guards in the outter Rooms, with one at most of the Gentlemen of her Bedchamber. Her frequent fits of sickness, and the distance of the place from London, did not admit of what we commonly called Drawing-Room nights, so that I had many occasions to think that few Houses in England belonging to persons of Quality were keept in a more privat way than the Queen's Royal Palace of Kensington.[165]

Observers might regard her as 'a poor infirm Woman', but the queen never for a moment forgot that she was 'one of the Rulers of the World'. The forced admission of Sunderland into high office marked a turning-point in her life. For eighteen months, she had fought Sunderland's appointment, standing alone against the Junto, the duchess, Godolphin, and Marlborough. Only in the last five months had she found a new ally in Robert Harley. Their combined efforts, due to lack of time and co-ordination, had proved unsuccessful in winning the battle for political moderation. But the queen was determined to win the war, to strike back at the Junto. She was prepared to do this in alliance with Marlborough and Godolphin or – if needs be – without them.

9

'Hector'd or Frighted'

The Bishoprics Crisis,
January – October 1707

The queen's political acumen had greatly increased during her five years on the throne and she was less susceptible to domination by others. From 'being led by the hand' through unfamiliar territory by Godolphin in 1702, she had grown capable of conducting – largely unaided – an obstinate, highly skilled, year and a half campaign against the treasurer over the appointment of Sunderland. That her campaign had ended in defeat rankled; that subsequent events proved her prediction that Sunderland's appointment was merely the first step in the Junto's effort to force themselves upon her only reinforced the queen's confidence in her own perception.

The principal casualties of the battle over Sunderland were the queen's friendships of a lifetime. For all practical purposes, her friendship with Sarah was not only dead but rapidly decaying into aversion. Although Mrs Morley in the future would again appeal to Mrs Freeman in attempts to restore personal harmony between them, the queen now regarded Sarah as an object of fear, not only for her harangues and importunities, but also for the adverse publicity which she might create and which the queen dreaded. Most importantly, the queen feared Sarah's immense influence over Marlborough and Godolphin. The queen also felt estranged from Godolphin, albeit to a lesser degree. He had proved unable (and, in the queen's opinion, unwilling) to maintain moderation and had finally succeeded in forcing Sunderland upon her. She was not yet willing to part with the lord treasurer: she hoped that could be avoided, but she no longer regarded him as indispensable. Marlborough, on the other hand, was indispensable as long as the war continued; the queen realized full well that no government could be maintained in wartime without the presence of her great captain-general. Marlborough had also been less directly involved in the struggle over Sunderland than the duchess or the treasurer; further-more, his involvement could be attributed to their influence. Marlborough, in the queen's eyes, appeared to have remained closer to Toryism than had Godolphin and to fear the High Tories less than did the treasurer. Marlborough maintained close personal friendships with a number of Tories, including Henry St John and Sir Simon Harcourt. In her future struggles against the Junto, almost all of the queen's impassioned appeals against further Whig encroachments were to be directed to the captain-general.

As Sir John Clerk had realized, the queen stood alone at the summit of the political world, but she remained isolated socially as well as politically. Despite the fact that Great Britain's power and prestige had reached hitherto undreamed of heights, the sovereign felt fettered. As she gradually turned away from Godolphin, she relied increasingly upon her husband, but Prince George's health was declining as he fought violent asthmatic attacks. As an invalid herself, the queen was also growing more dependent upon her personal and household servants. One of her private confidants among her medical consultants was a Scot named Dr John Arbuthnot; he attended the queen from 1703 and in October 1705 was appointed her physician extraordinary. Arbuthnot's brother, Robert, was an active Franco-Jacobite agent in Rouen.[1] A few years later, one courtier noted that Dr Arbuthnot, a High Tory, was 'a very cunning man, and not much talk't of, but I believe what he says is as much heard [by the queen] as any that give advise now'.[2] Another, and more important, confidante was Sarah's first cousin, Mistress Abigail Hill.

Contemporary opinion concerning Abigail was mixed. Jonathan Swift, a leading Tory propagandist, subsequently described Abigail as

> a Person of a plain sound Understanding, of great Truth and Sincerity, without the least Mixture of Falshood or Disguise; of an honest Boldness and Courage superiour to her Sex; firm and disinterested in her friendship, and full of Love, Duty, and Veneration for the Queen Her Mistress.[3]

Lord Dartmouth, also a Tory, took a radically different view of Abigail, saying, 'She was exceeding mean and vulgar in her manner, of a very unequal temper, childishly exceptious and passionate.'[4] Almost all our information concerning her growing importance in the queen's personal life, after her appointment as a bedchamber woman in 1697, is based on the later discoveries of her cousin, the Duchess of Marlborough. Sarah's evidence must be treated with the greatest caution: but there are some suggestions that, during the duchess's increasing absences from court even before the queen's accession, Abigail acted as Sarah's palace lieutenant. A contemporary historian described Abigail as 'a Dependent and Relation, in whom she [Sarah] entirely confided'.[5] Sarah dated the first manifestation of the queen's favour to Abigail from the royal visit to Bath in August 1703. On a letter dated 20 August, from the queen to the duchess ('oh my dear Mrs. Freeman you can never emagin how Sincerly & tenderly I love you, & be assured nothing can ever change me'), Sarah later noted:

> Mrs. Danvers told me some yeares after this leter was writt, when she
> was angry with Mrs. Masham, that the Queen was very fond of her at
> the bath, & that upon Mrs. Hills dislikeing the lodging that was
> marked for her, she told the Queen that she would sett up, upon
> which there was the most rediculous sceen as Mrs. Danvers acted it
> that ever I saw, of Mrs. Hills sorley ill bred manner, & the Queen
> goeing about the room after her & beging her to goe to bed, calling her
> Dear Hill twenty times over.[6]

By 1705, 'Mrs.' Hill could afford on an annual salary of £500 to give twenty guineas as a christening gift,[7] and she was regarded as second in influence only to the duchess within the bedchamber.[8] Indeed, from the privy purse records it appears that Abigail was informally acting as the duchess's deputy, receiving the payments for the queen's own pocket money.[9] The first concrete example of the queen's favour to Abigail appeared in May 1705, when she asked Godolphin to obtain Marlborough's permission for James Stanhope to sell his army regiment to Abigail's younger brother, John Hill:

> I can not Seale up this with out telling you that [Abigail] Hill has bin
> speaking to me this morning about her Brothers business. . . . I must
> own to you I should be glad the thing weare don (tho I am against
> Sellings) becaus I find Mr. Hill has perswaided his sister this would be
> of soe much advantage to him, that She seems to be desirous of it, &
> she is soe good a Creature that I shall be glad at any time to do any-
> thing for her that is not unreasonable.[10]

Perhaps encouraged by the fact that the queen regarded her cousin Abigail as 'soe good a Creature', in August 1705 the Duchess of Marlborough suggested that she should take Abigail's younger sister Alice, who had served as laundress to the Duke of Gloucester, as an additional bedchamber woman. The queen, however, postponed any decision with a graceful tribute to Abigail: 'if at any time there should happen a vacancy, I shall like to take Mrs. Hill better then any body, beleeving She is very good, if She is like her Sister, I am sure she must be soe'. The queen proposed that, until a vacancy in the bedchamber occurred, Alice Hill should be given a pension of £200 per annum.[11] Sarah, always the efficient business woman, proposed instead that the queen purchase an annuity of £150 which Alice Hill could enjoy for the remainder of her own lifetime, while the total cost to the queen would be only £2,400 ('12 yeares pension at once').[12]

One may only speculate, but the fact that Sarah's intervention reduced Alice Hill's annual pension by £50 may have influenced Abigail to turn for aid at court to another relative. Robert Harley was Abigail's second cousin on her father's side of the family.* We know nothing of the early relationship between Harley and Abigail, but it is certain that Sarah's absence from court and her growing estrangement from the queen made her useless as an intermediary, particularly in the advancement of Abigail's suitor, Samuel Masham, who had first entered the royal service in 1692 at the age of thirteen as a page to the Prince of Denmark. In 1697, Masham became an ensign of the Coldstream Guards and was named captain and lieutenant-colonel in January 1704 and brevet colonel in October of the same year.[14] In July 1706 he was made a groom of the bedchamber to the prince. Sarah later recorded that Masham

> allways attended his wife & the basset table & lived in the Court
> twenty years at least without ever being taken notice of, being only a
> good natural soft insignifycant man, making low bows to every body &
> being ready to run to open a door.

Presumably Masham's return to court in the summer of 1706 led to the flowering of his courtship of Abigail Hill, with the queen enjoying the role of a beneficent fairy godmother, aided and abetted by Abigail's cousin, Robert Harley. In the spring of 1707 the queen decided to give Lord Windsor's regiment to Masham, wishing, however, to keep it stationed in Ireland, while Masham remained at court. To do so, the queen made a special appointment with Secretary Harley, 'being impatient to know what you have don about ye Irish regiments, & have other things to speake to you about which I should be glad to do when

---

*The family connection of Abigail Masham with Robert Harley and Sarah, Duchess of Marlborough:[13]

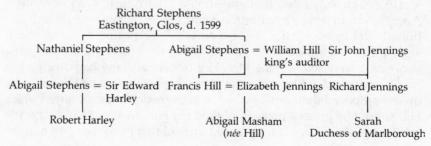

Richard Stephens
Eastington, Glos, d. 1599

Nathaniel Stephens   Abigail Stephens = William Hill   Sir John Jennings
                                    king's auditor

Abigail Stephens = Sir Edward   Francis Hill = Elizabeth Jennings   Richard Jennings
             Harley

Robert Harley   Abigail Masham   Sarah
                              (*née* Hill)   Duchess of Marlborough

no body is by'.[15] The queen was so anxious to keep her patronage of Abigail and Masham secret that she enjoined Harley not to tell his closest political ally, the secretary of war Henry St John, 'that he may not suspect what you say to him about the Regiment coms from me'.[16]

Apparently, the queen and Abigail agreed that the Duchess of Marlborough had become so difficult and unpredictable that news of Abigail's romantic prospects should be kept from her ears. The courtship of Abigail and Samuel Masham culminated in a secret marriage, held in Dr Arbuthnot's lodging in Kensington Palace, probably between 5 April and 12 June 1707, while the queen was resident at the palace.[17] On 11 June the queen called for 2,000 guineas from the privy purse, to be delivered in cash;[18] subsequently, after her 'great discovery' three months later, the duchess suspected that this money was intended as a dowry for Abigail. If this was so, compared to the beneficence which the queen had showered upon the Marlboroughs, their children, and their connections (among whom the Hills were numbered), her favouritism for Abigail was calibrated on a minor scale.

When Sarah later discovered the queen's patronage of Abigail, and put these facts together, her paranoia led her to declare: 'I discovered that my cousin was become an absolute favourite . . . & I likewise then discovered beyond all dispute Mr. Harley's correspondence and interest at Court by means of this woman.'[19] But Sarah's view, which misled both contemporaries and later historians, was wrong: the queen never regarded Abigail as more than an excellent servant and nurse. Certainly, she did not view her as a social equal, as Mrs Morley had once treated Mrs Freeman. It was therefore impossible for Abigail to establish Robert Harley politically, and we have already examined the independent reasons for his rise in the queen's esteem. Abigail, however, was important to Harley: through her influence, he could establish a personal relationship with the queen in a way to rival Mr and Mrs Freeman and Mr Montgomery. After Harley's resignation in February 1708, Abigail proved useful to him as an intermediary, a reporter, and a spy. Abigail's influence with the queen was essentially negative, as Harley bluntly told her in the last months of the queen's life: 'You cannot set any one up: you can pull any one down.'[20]

The queen was fond of Harley; when he was ill with a cold in January 1707, Henry St John reported to Harley that

> when I waited on the queen yesterday she enquired after your health, and expressed her concern for your illness in such terms as I am sure came from the bottom of her heart. She said so much of your having prejudiced your health in her service, and showed so much trouble, that I thought it was proper for me to tell you particularly of it.[21]

Furthermore, both the queen and Harley (in her view) were working together to support the Duumvirs by creating a genuine centrist government, excluding the high priests of both Toryism and Whiggism. Burning with resentment against her defeat over Sunderland, the queen at the beginning of 1707 was determined to exert her authority against both the High Whigs and the High Tories. There can be no doubt that Harley advised her and encouraged her to do so, but the decision was fundamentally hers. In the resulting 'bishoprics crisis', which became the centrepiece of the queen's struggle against the Junto throughout 1707, she always claimed that she had made the final decisions, an assertion which the latest authority agrees has 'the ring of truth'.[22]

The first phase of the 'bishoprics crisis' originated in November 1706, when Peter Mews, Bishop of Winchester, died. Winchester, the richest diocese in England, was a prize which the Junto coveted for one of their followers, and they regarded it as a test case of the 1706 agreement between themselves and the Duumvirs concerning ecclesiastical patronage. Godolphin, unfortunately, had long ago promised to translate Bishop Jonathan Trelawny of Exeter, a Tory divine, to this see in return for Trelawny's help in the 1705 elections. Working in collusion with Harley, Godolphin smuggled the Bishop of Exeter into a secret audience with the Queen to kiss hands and to receive her promise of nomination to Winchester.[23] The Junto were furious, and Somers virtually ordered Archbishop Tenison to remonstrate personally with the queen; when the primate visited Her Majesty, however, he reported a frosty reception: 'My discourse', he reported to Somers, 'was short, it being said to me on my entrance on it, that the thing was already determined, though the person was not declared.'[24]

Godolphin saw an opportunity to make amends to the Junto by giving the see of Exeter to a Whig; furthermore, within a month of the queen's interview with Trelawny, in mid-January 1707, Nicholas Stratford, Bishop of Chester, was dead, and so was William Jane, regius professor of divinity at Oxford. There were consequently three high ecclesiastical positions available to satisfy the Junto. In consultations with Somers, Tenison, and Marlborough, Godolphin agreed to nominate Samuel Freeman, Dean of Peterborough, and Charles Trimnell, Rector of St James's, Westminster, for the two bishoprics, Dr White Kennett for the vacancy in the deanery of Peterborough, and Marlborough's candidate, Dr John Potter, as regius professor.[25] However, when the treasurer presented these names to the queen, she delayed and evaded the issue, determined to exercise her ecclesiastical prerogatives without consulting her chief minister. In fact, she had already promised the regius professorship to George Smallridge, a protégé of Harley, and she was seriously considering the claims of two of Sharp's friends, Dr Offspring Blackall, Rector of St Mary Aldermary, and Sir William Dawes, two Tory divines who had preached impressively at court. Harley's decision to back Smallridge for the Oxford professorship was a clear break with Marlborough, who wished to establish his political influence in the university to support his power in the county at large. Six months earlier, in July 1706, Marlborough had privately warned Harley: 'I have been inform'd that the Dean of Carlile [Dr Francis Atterbury] and Dr Smallridge make compliments to Her Majesty, but at the same time are as violent as if they were govern'd by Lord Rochester.'[26]

The Junto naturally were furious when the candidates they had agreed upon were not routinely approved, although they could make no objections to the fitness of Blackall and Dawes except for their politics.[27] The brunt of the blame fell upon Godolphin rather than upon the queen: as Cowper told the lord treasurer, 'The world cannot believe he could not hinder her.'[28] Apparently, Marlborough, Godolphin, and Harley held one or more meetings in the queen's presence to discuss ecclesiastical patronage, but without reaching any decision. By June 1707, Godolphin was complaining to Marlborough of

> those spirituall affairs which seem to grow rather worse and worse, ever since I saw you last with *the queen* and *Godolphin* and another person [Harley] who I doubt, has not much altered his mind in those matters though he won't own anything like that to Mr Montgomery.[29]

The question of future appointments was held in abeyance until the government had weathered the parliamentary session of 1706–7.

The session of Parliament which began in December 1706 was perhaps the easiest of the queen's reign. Unprecedented votes of money for the forthcoming campaign were immediately granted by the House of Commons, both in tribute to the victories of 1706 and in the hope of final victory in 1707. The principal business of the session was to carry the English ratification of the Act of Union (which was approved by the Scottish Parliament on 16 January): this was bitterly opposed by the High Tories, on the ground that the treaty guaranteed Presbyterianism as the established Church of Scotland, a guarantee the High Flyers claimed could place the Church of England in danger. The union was dear to the queen's heart, and she used all her influence with Archbishop Sharp and others to gain their support, but in vain.[30] The government sponsored the Act for the Security of the Church of England, which blunted the principal High Tory objections to the union. Finally, on 6 March 1707, the ratification completed all parliamentary stages and the queen gave her assent: 'La Reyne le veult.'[31]

The union which took place on 1 May 1707, was marked by a thanks-giving service at St Paul's in London which was attended by the queen, the prince, and all the great officers of state. To symbolize the union, the queen wore the combined Order of the Garter and Order of the Thistle, and 'Prayers of Thanksgiving were very heartily put up for the success of the Union, at least no body on this occasion appeared more sincerely devout and thankful than the Queen her self'.[32] The establishment of the United Kingdom of Great Britain entailed the dissolution of the separate English and Scottish governments and their reconstitution as one united body: at the first Privy Council meeting following the union, the queen named five Scottish members who had supported the union, and at the same time dropped fourteen High Tories from the council's roster.[33]

In comparison with the previous *annus mirabilis*, the military campaign of 1707 ranged from disappointing to disastrous. Marlborough, in the Spanish Netherlands, confronted the great ring of barrier fortresses constructed by Louis XIV's military engineer, Vauban, to defend the northern approaches to the Isle de France and Paris. The captain-general pinned his hopes for the year on an ambitious amphibious campaign, mounted by British ships with Savoyard and imperial forces, which would attack Toulon, the largest French port on the Mediterranean. Due to increasing friction between Turin and Vienna, however, the invasion proved to be a failure. More seriously, in Spain the queen's half-brother James FitzJames, Duke of Berwick, decisively defeated the principal allied army in the battle of Almanza in April 1707, pushing the allies back into Catalonia and Portugal and securing the bulk of the peninsula for Philip V. It became clear that the allies had seriously underrated the difficulty of conquering Spain. In 1714, Henry St John was to claim that he, Harley, and the queen agreed, after the disaster at Almanza, that Spain would never be won and that consequently some partition of the inheritance of Carlos II was inevitable.[34] This seems unlikely, for in the year after Almanza the queen again personally endorsed the policy of securing the entire Spanish empire for the allied candidate, 'Carlos III'. Indeed, by this time Marlborough had formulated a policy, which was enthusiastically supported by the Whigs, that Spain could be won through France: only if Louis XIV was reduced to the utmost extremity would French support be withdrawn from Philip V and the allies allowed to enthrone 'Carlos III'. What is probable is that the queen began to look at the Duumvirs' foreign policy with the same sceptical eye as she now regarded their domestic policies.

The spring and summer of 1707 witnessed a continued struggle between the queen and the lord treasurer over the vacant bishoprics.

240

Even before Professor Jane's death on 23 February, the queen had promised both Harley and Archbishop Sharp that she would appoint Jane's Tory deputy, George Smallridge, in his place; after complaints by Marlborough and Godolphin, however, she hedged on her promise, telling Sharp 'She had been told that [Smallridge] was One of those who flew in ye face of the Government by representing the Church to be in Danger'.[35] Sarah subsequently claimed that the queen had promised the regius professorship to both Smallridge and to Marlborough's candidate, Dr John Potter, 'which was probable enough, many months passing, & many delays & difficulties being pretended, before Her Ministry could obtain the promise she had made to them'.[36] In April 1707, Godolphin reported to Marlborough: '*the queen* has never said the least word to mee of Oxford, or the professorship, but in all other things, she leans that way, as much as she did in that while you were here'.[37] In the middle of April the queen secretly sent for Dr Blackall and offered him his choice of Exeter or Chester; when he opted for the first, she sent for Sir William Dawes and offered him the bishopric of Chester.[38]

Little could be kept secret in Queen Anne's court, and within a month both Sarah and Godolphin had elicited the fundamental facts of the queen's duplicity. The queen, however, proved intransigent in the face of Godolphin's remonstrances. The treasurer's situation and the Junto's anger at the unexplained delays, were compounded when Simon Patrick, Bishop of Ely, died on 31 May and the queen translated John Moor, Bishop of Norwich, to Ely. 'There are three bishopricks vacant [Exeter, Chester, Norwich]', Godolphin reported to Marlborough on 11 June, 'and I find *Godolphin* has soe little hopes of them being well filled that he seems resolved to use all his endeavors to keep them vacant till he can have Mr. Freeman's assistance in these spirituall affairs.'[39] Godolphin, in short, was caught between the obstinacy of the queen and the fury of the Junto: on 14 June, Godolphin asked Harley to introduce Bishop Trelawny to the queen for his formal audience of appointment to Winchester, 'knowing so much of my Lord Sunderland's mind in that matter . . . I find something will happen which may be shocking and uneasy to the Queen'.[40]

Realizing his colleague's predicament, Marlborough (in a letter which the queen later called 'spleenatick')[41] advised Godolphin on 16/27 June to take Harley with him to the queen 'to lett *the Queen* see with all the freedome and plainess imaginable her trew interest'.[42] Godolphin replied that such a confrontation would prove useless:

> *Harley* does so hate and fear *Somers, Sunderland* and *Wharton* that he
> omitts no occasion of filling *the queen's* head with their projects and
> designs; and if Mr. Montgomery should take him with him [i.e. to the

241

queen] upon any occasion of that kind, he would either say nothing or argue against what the other says as he did upon some subjects, some months since when Mr. Freeman himself was present.[43]

The queen, in her arguments with Godolphin, stressed the fact that her royal word had been given, and that her promises to Blackall and Dawes could not now be retracted. On 27 June, Godolphin reported to Marlborough:

> *the queen* has indulged his own inclination in the choyce of some persons to succeed *the bishops* and which give the greatest offence to *the Whigs* that can bee . . . *the queen* has gone so farr in this matter (even against my warning) as really to bee no more able than willing to retract this wrong step.[44]

Marlborough saw clearly that soon the queen would be forced to choose between Godolphin and Harley. This was the burden of his warning to the queen on 7 July:

> it must end in betraying your quiet, whoever goes about to persuaide you that you can be served at this time by the Torrys, considering the mallice of their chiefs, and the behavior of the greatest part of the cleargy, besides the Nation is of opinion that if they had the management of your affaires, thay would not carry this warr on with vigor, on which depends your happyness and the safety of our. religion.
>
> I would beg as a favour, if anybody near your person is of opinion that the Torrys may be trusted, and at this time made use off, that you would be pleased to order them to put their project in writting, and know if thay will charge themselves with the execution, then you will see their sincerity by excusing themselves.[45]

No reply of the queen's to Marlborough's indirect attack upon Harley and his defence of Godolphin has survived; Godolphin noted that the queen 'did not say the least word of her having had a letter from you'. On the question of the ecclesiastical nominations, the queen remained inflexible: in late July she again confirmed her promises to Blackall and Dawes, demonstrating 'the power of the Crown to act without consultation with its ministers'.[46]

The bishoprics crisis was not overshadowed by Sarah's 'great discovery'. In her *Conduct*, published a generation later, Sarah implied that her discovery was made 'in less than a week's time',[47] but a close examination of the facts makes it clear that Sarah fitted together bits and pieces of the puzzle of the queen's changed behaviour throughout the summer of 1707. Bitter, hostile, searching for a 'secret influence' over the queen, Sarah was psychologically prepared to discover what she considered the height of treachery of the part of her cousin, Abigail Hill. By the spring of 1707, the duchess's prolonged absences from court were drawing public attention[48] and on 4 May, Marlborough commiserated with his wife on 'the little satisfaction you have of the inclinations and behaviour of *the queen*'.[49] Between 9 and 13 May, Sarah discovered, in the words of Marlborough's reply to her four letters of that period, 'that *Abigail* does speak of business to *the queen*'. From the tone of Marlborough's reply, it is clear that neither husband nor wife attributed crucial importance to this fact: 'I should think you might speak to her with some caution, which might do good, for she certainly is gratefull, and will mind what you say.'[50] On 11 June the queen called for 2,000 guineas from the privy purse, and two days later Sarah reported to Marlborough her suspicions that the money was intended for Abigail; on 23 June, Marlborough replied: 'What *Sarah* says concerning *the queen* giving *money* depends upon what the gold may be for. Play and charity may take up a great deal.'[51] Apparently, the duchess told the queen of her suspicions (which still did not include Abigail's secret marriage). On 17 June the queen wrote to Sarah:

> By what my dear Mrs. Freeman said a little before She went from me this evening, I can not help feareing She may have heard some new Lye of her poor unfortunat faithfull Morly, & therefore I beg you to open your dear hart, hide nothing, but tell me every ye least thing that gives you any hard thoughts of me, that I may Justefy my self, which I am sure I can do, never haveing don any thing willingly to diserve your displeasure.[52]

Sarah's answer in writing accused the queen of having changed towards her because of the secret influence of others, and she complained that the queen sent to her only on business. Her letter provoked an immediate reply from the queen:

> I am exstreamly Conserned to find my dear Mrs. Freemans unkind & unjust thoughts continue still of my being changed, & that you can think me capable of being catched with flattery, indeed I am nether, for I have ye same sincere tender passion for you as ever, which I will preserve intire to my last moment, & as for my haveing any reserve I have none upon my word, but will open my hart as freely to you at any time as I used to do.
> I must own I have of late bin a litle afraid to speak on any Subjects that we differd upon, becaus you have bin pleased to think I have shutt my eyes, that I am infatuated, that I am fond of some people (who I care no more for then I do for ye pen in my hand) & when I happen not to agree in ye very good opinion you have some, & ye very ill of others, then you think that proceeds from ye wrong informations

& notions that some sort of people give me, & and all I can say to justefy my self is not to be beleeved, these are ye reasons that have made me seem reserved tho I am not soe in my hart. . . .[53]

During the next month, the duchess's intelligence system ferreted out many instances of the queen's favour to Abigail, and of Abigail's commerce with Harley. On 13 July, the queen wrote to Sarah (in the latter's words) 'to assure me that all your notions were your own, & I doe really believe that you think soe, but you must give me leave to say that wee differ in matter of fact, which is not call'd notions'.[54] In order to set the queen right on 'matter of fact', the duchess appealed for an interview with her, a measure of how strained their relationship had become. On 16 July the queen replied

to lett my dear Mrs. Freeman know if she can com to me at five a clock this afternoon I will be redy to receive you in my Gallery at ye Castle, & shall think my self very happy if that meeting sett every thing right between us.[55]

Their explosive exchange on 17 July became known in their future correspondence as 'the Gallery visit'. Sarah began by attacking the Tory candidate for the regius professorship, George Smallridge ('hee has been as violent as any in everything of late'[56]) and then proceeded onto ground which neither Marlborough nor Godolphin had yet essayed, an open attack on Robert Harley. In 1709 the duchess recalled to the queen 'when I gave you Mr. Harleys character long since in the closet in the Gallery at Windsor, how angry you were with me upon that occation'.[57] Almost in passing, Sarah mentioned Abigail Hill as a source of the queen's 'notion'; the queen's response was so abrupt that Sarah felt impelled the following day to elaborate:

You seem'd soe much offended when I named my cousen Hill's speaking to you of businesse, that I have a mind to explain that further, & asure you I should bee as much offended at my self, if I did her any wrong, for I believe you have nobody in your family that has more honour or better intentions to serve you & sence you say she does not speake to you, I doe believe she does not derectly medle in any thing of that nature, but with out knowing it, or intending it, she is one occation of feeding Mrs. Morleys passion for torrys by taking all occations to speake well of some of them, & by giving you a prejudice to those that are truely in your interest, for she converses with nobody but those that have an interest or Inclenation to make wrong representations of all things, & all people that would keep you out of the power of your Enemys. . . .

Sarah then indicted the Tories in general ('they design bringing in the

2 *The Family of James, Duke of York*, by Sir Peter Lely and Benedetto Gennari

Sir Peter Lely portrayed the Duke of York and his first duchess, Anne Hyde, between 1668 and 1670; their two surviving children, Lady Mary (*left*) and Lady Anne, were added by Gennari about 1680. Windsor Castle is seen in the background.

3 *The Lady Anne*, artist unknown

This portrait of the Lady Anne and her King Charles spaniel was painted in France during her stay there from 1668 to 1670 while she was receiving treatment for her 'sore eyes'.

4 *Princess Anne of Denmark about 1683*, by Willem
Wissing
The Dutch artist Wissing depicted the eighteen-year-old
Lady Anne about the time of her marriage to Prince
George of Denmark in 1683. She gave this portrait to her
sister, Princess Mary of Orange, in 1685 and commented of
her likeness, 'It is really true.'

5 *Prince George of Denmark about 1687*, by John Riley

This was Queen Anne's favourite portrait of her husband, and it was hung over the chimney of her bedchamber in the 'garden house' at Windsor.

6 *Mary of Modena about 1685*, by Willem Wissing

The second wife of James II became an object of hatred to her step-daughter, who was only seven years her junior.

7 and 8 *William III and Mary, Prince and Princess of Orange, in 1685,* by Willem Wissing

James II commissioned these companion portraits of his elder daughter and his son-in-law in 1685. Three years later they mounted his throne.

9 *Princess Anne of Denmark about 1690*, by Michael Dahl
Dahl was the Princess's favourite painter. She regarded his
portraits as 'more like flesh and bloud' than those of
Kneller.

10 *The Earl and Countess of Marlborough and their
Children,* by Johann Baptist Closterman

Closterman executed this huge canvas about 1694,
depicting the future Duke and Duchess of Marlborough
and their five children. *From left:* Marlborough; Lady
Elizabeth Churchill (later Countess of Bridgewater); Lady
Mary Churchill (later Duchess of Montagu); Lady
Marlborough; Lady Henrietta Churchill (later Countess of
Godolphin); Lady Anne Churchill (later Countess of
Sunderland); and Lord John Churchill, later Marquess of
Blandford, who died in 1703.

11 *Princess Anne of Denmark and the Duke of Gloucester,* after Sir Godfrey Kneller

The princess, who habitually referred to her son as 'my poore boy', was depicted with the three-year-old Gloucester (shown here in skirts) shortly before Easter 1694, when he was breeched.

12 *James Francis Edward Stuart and Louisa Maria Theresa Stuart,* by Nicholas de Largillière

Queen Anne's half-brother, 'the Pretender', and her half-sister (whom she never saw) were painted in formal French court dress by Largillière in 1695, at the ages of seven and three respectively.

13 *William Henry, Duke of Gloucester*, by Sir Godfrey
Kneller
Painted by Kneller in 1699, the ten-year-old Gloucester
was already being portrayed as a Protestant champion who
would prevent the restoration of his uncle, the Pretender.
One year later Gloucester was dead.

14 *Sarah, Duchess of Marlborough*, after Sir Godfrey Kneller

This portrait of Sarah – one of the great beauties of her age – was probably painted about 1700. The gold key of her office as keeper of the privy purse was probably added after Queen Anne's accession in 1702.

15 *Sidney, Earl Godolphin*, after Sir Godfrey Kneller

This portrait of Godolphin was painted about 1705; he is seen wearing the Garter and holding the white staff of office as lord high treasurer.

16 *Portrait said to be that of Abigail, Lady Masham,* artist unknown

The authenticity of this portrait has been questioned; the nineteenth-century label identifying the sitter dates her life from 1670 to 1734, which is our only evidence regarding the date of her birth.

17 *Robert Harley, Earl of Oxford,* by Sir Godfrey Kneller

Kneller painted Oxford in 1714, showing him in the formal dress of a knight of the Garter and holding the white staff of office as lord high treasurer.

18 *Henry St John, Viscount Bolingbroke*, attributed to
Alexis Simon Belle

This portrait was presumably painted immediately after
Bolingbroke's elevation to the peerage and during his
diplomatic mission to France in August 1712; the map on
the table shows the fortifications of Dunkirk and the letter
is addressed 'A la Reine'.

19 *Charles Talbot, Duke of Shrewsbury*, after Sir Godfrey Kneller

From 1688, when he signed the invitation to the Prince of Orange, until 1714, when he became the last lord treasurer as Queen Anne was dying,

Shrewsbury was one of the most important and influential figures of the period.

20 *George I*, studio of Sir Godfrey Kneller

Georg Ludwig, Elector of Hanover, succeeded his second cousin, Queen Anne, in 1714. He was five years her senior.

P[rince] of W[ales]') and concluded with her favourite self-characterization, that of the injured but ever faithful servant:

> These are truths that have been often told you by one that has served you more then twenty years with fedelity . . . & in saying you wish nobody medled with businesse more then Mrs. Hill, is not that very unkind & very hard usage?[58]

The queen was stung to the soul, and immediately replied in a letter which Churchill termed 'a masterpiece of sarcasm and polished hostility':[59]

> your Cousin Hill, who is very far from being an occassion of feeding Mrs. Morly in her passion (as you are pleased to call it), she never medleing with any thing. I believe others that have bin in her Station in former Reigns have bin tateling & very impertinent, but She is not at all that temper, & as for ye Company she keeps, it is with her as with most other people I fancy, that theire lott in ye world makes them move with some out of common sivility, rather then choice, & I realy beleeve for one that is soe much in ye way of Company, she has less acquaintance then any one upon earth.[60]

The duchess replied on 21 July, apparently oblivious to the hostility in the queen's letter. After defending her own actions by claiming that she represented the opinions of Marlborough and Godolphin, Sarah again attacked Abigail:

> Mrs. Morley seems more desirous to vindicate a person that I have said as much good of as one can doe of any body, & till I see cause, I will allways beleive she deserves it, tho I can't agree to what Mrs. Morley says as to the clearing of her from being infested by the company she keeps . . . tho it is sure that she does not have many vissiters, it is as certain, that all the people she does converse with are Jacobites, open or in disguise, mislead torrys, that are tackers, or opposers of you in whatever lyes in their way.[61]

Despite Sarah's protests, the queen remained unrepentant: the same day, she fired back a response, telling the duchess

> as to what you say of my being afraid of another Gallery vissitt, I do assure you I am not, being soe Consious to my self of never haveing don any thing to deserve your ill oppinion that I can beare any reproches that my dear Mrs. Freeman is pleas'd to make to her poor unfortunat ever faithfull Morly.[62]

The situation was reminiscent of 1692, when the Princess of Denmark had defended her servants from attack; now, however, the persecuted had become the persecutors. As the sovereign, the queen believed –

245

and the constitution was still largely on her side – that it was within her prerogative to select her own ministerial servants: she regarded the appointment of Sunderland as a gross violation of this principle. As a private individual, the queen believed equally that she had the right to select – and consequently to defend – her personal attendants. Quite apart from the fact that Abigail was an excellent servant and nurse and that the queen was physically dependent upon her ministrations, she would have been obliged to defend her bedchamber woman as a matter of pride, particularly against the increasingly bitter onslaughts mounted by the duchess.

It was the queen who initiated the next stage of the disagreement when she notified the duchess, on 9 August, that she was at last willing to take Alice Hill into her service as one of her bedchamber women. Her reasons were that Sarah had requested the appointment and that Abigail was so overworked that 'I think it would be cruel not to give her some ease'.[63] Sarah, whose suspicions of Abigail were now rapidly growing and who labelled this as 'an Equivocating leter', replied to the queen the next day, complaining of 'Mrs. Morleys unkind & unjust usage of Mrs. Freeman' and hinting that the queen's favouritism to Abigail could damage the royal reputation:

> my greatest concern now is to think of the prejudice it must doe Mrs.
> Morley when the true cause of it is known, which will make her
> character soe very different from that which has allways been given by
> her faithfull Freeman.[64]

In combating the influence of Abigail, Sarah resorted to a tactic which had proved a failure when she had attempted to equate the Tories with Jacobitism: she attempted to frighten the queen. Her vague reference to the queen's reputation was, as we shall see, to become a new theme which time and desperation would expand.

The duchess apparently wrote another letter to the queen in which she further expostulated with her on the influence of Abigail. On 1 September the queen foreclosed further discussion by informing Sarah that, as groom of the stole, it was her duty to introduce Alice Hill formally into the queen's bedchamber. The date she chose was 3 September.[65] Sarah later recorded that Abigail, who wished to hide her intimacy with the queen, was present when the duchess arrived at Windsor to present Alice Hill:

> When I came to present her sister to the Queen, she was waiting with
> her in a little room next to the Queen's closset at the garden hous,
> upon which I asked her to tell the Queen that I was come, & she
> started back I remember, & said her Majesty was in her closset,

poynting to it as if she would have me goe, & as if she had not so
much liberty as to scrap at the door but soon after this, it all came out
of her being so often shutt up with her [the queen] & her marriage
which the Queen was at in Doc: Arburth[not's] Chamber, & Her
Majesty was met going to his chamber alone by a boy of the kitchin, at
Kinsington.[66]

It was in mid-September that Sarah learned of Abigail's secret marriage,
which had occurred three to five months earlier. In her *Conduct*, Sarah
recounted that

I went presently to the Queen and asked her, 'why she had not been
so kind as to tell me of my cousin's marriage?' but all the answer I
could obtain from her Majesty was this, 'I have a hundred times bid
Masham tell it to you, and she would not'.[67]

Sarah was naturally astounded, not only that the queen had kept
Abigail's marriage a secret from her but also by the extent of Abigail's
power with the queen. On 23 September the duchess wrote to her
cousin, complaining that by her secret marriage Abigail had 'made me
returns very unsuitable to what I might have expected'; the next day
Abigail sent an impertinent reply and in her rejoinder Sarah effectively
broke off relations between them.[68] Abigail reported to Harley that
when 'a great lady' next visited the court,

as she passed by me I had a very low curtsey, which I returned in the
same manner, but not one word passed between us, and as for her
looks, indeed they are not to be described by any mortal but her own
self.[69]

For Sarah, Abigail and Harley merged disastrously in her own mind,
and when she attacked one to the queen, she was in effect attacking the
other. It is impossible to know whether or not the queen realized the
degree of co-operation which existed between Harley and his cousin,
Mrs Masham, although it seems probable that she did. What is certain,
however, is that the queen believed that Sarah was influencing Marlborough and Godolphin against Harley, and against the political
moderation which Harley represented.

Two months prior to Sarah's discovery of Abigail's marriage, during
the 'Gallery visit' of 17 July, she had attacked Harley openly, reading to
the Queen extracts from Marlborough's letter to his wife of 30 June in
which he had said:

I am very sorry that you think you have reason to believe that *Harley*
takes all occasion of doing hurt to *England*. If *Godolphin* can't find a
remidy, and that before the next winter, I should think his wisest and

honestest way should be to tel *the queen* very plainly which way he thinks *the queen's* business may be carryed on, and if that be not agreable, that she would lose no time in knowing of *Harley* what his scheem is, and follow that, so that *Godolphin* might not be answerable for what might happen.[70]

Six weeks later, on 16 August, Godolphin for the first time endorsed Sarah's analysis of the situation, telling Marlborough:

I reckon one great occasion to Mrs. Morley's obstinacy, and of the uneasyness she gives herself and others, especially about the clergy, proceeds from an inclination of talking more freely than usually to *Abigail*. And this is layd hold of, and improved by *Harley* upon all such matters, if not upon others, to insinuate his notions (which in those affairs) you know by your own experience, from the conversation wee had together before you left England, are as wrong as is possible. I am apt also to think, he makes use of the same person to improve all the ill offices to *the Whigs*, which both hee, and that person are as naturally inclined to, as *the queen* is to receive the impression of them.[71]

Marlborough and Godolphin agreed that the political situation, and their difficulties with the Junto, would soon force them to speak plainly to the queen against Harley's influence. If she would not accept their advice, their alternative in Marlborough's words was 'to be quiet, and let *Harley* and *Abigail* do what thay please'.[72] Privately, and without the queen realizing it, the Duumvirs were moving closer to the position which the Junto adopted at the end of August. The five great lords, meeting at Sunderland's country home at Althorp, agreed that their first priority must be to force Harley out of office.[73]

By the end of August, the queen was facing the beginning of a crisis within her government as well as within her personal life. On 25 August the duchess and Godolphin decided to read to the queen Marlborough's letter of 18/29 August (omitting Harley's name) in which he said that if the queen would not accept the Duumvirs' advice,

I think *Godolphin* and *Marlborough* should honestly lett her know, that thay shall not be able to carry on her business with success, so that she might have time to take her measures with such as will be able to serve her.

That night, Godolphin reported to the captain-general that the reading of his letter had only increased the queen's uneasiness with the duchess: Godolphin suggested that henceforward Marlborough should write letters to be seen by the queen, and 'letters apart' meant only for the treasurer's eyes.[74] Within two weeks, Godolphin had formally notified Harley that his fellow ministers considered him to be disturbing the public business, and he consulted Cowper rather than Harley in preparing the Queen's Speech for the forthcoming session of Parliament.[75]

On 25 August, after hearing Marlborough's letter ready by Godolphin, the queen wrote a long letter to the captain-general, defending 'my own choice' of Dawes and Blackall as bishops ('all ye Clamour that is raised against them proceeds only from ye Malice of *the Whigs*') and denying that she was secretly working with Harley to the exclusion of the Duumvirs. She expressed astonishment that Sarah could inform Marlborough that she had 'an intire Confidence' in Harley, 'when she has soe often bin assured by me, that *the Queen* relyed entirely on none but Mr. Freeman & Mr. Montgomery'.[76]

The Duke of Marlborough replied to the queen on 4 September with a vigorous defence of Godolphin and offered to come to England for a short visit if his journey could put things right; at the conclusion of his letter, Marlborough added a justification of his wife:

> It is impossible for me to finish this letter without assuring You of what
> I have been witness off for many Yeares, I mean the Zeal and Constant
> Love with which *Sarah* has serv'd *the queen* and I know their greatest
> Concern at this time, is the apprehensions of your being made uneasy
> – and I must do their Judgement that right, that they have forseen
> many things that I thought cou'd never have hapn'd.[77]

On 10 September, knowing that Marlborough's letter had arrived, Godolphin in a long audience with the queen urged her to compromise on at least one of the bishoprics and, instead of sending Dr Blackall to Exeter, to appoint a Whig candidate. The queen refused, and the next day Godolphin wrote a long letter offering to resign, asking the queen:

> what colour of reason can incline your Majesty to discourage &
> dissatisfy those whose principle, & Interest lead them with so much
> warmth & Zeal to carry you through the difficultys of this warr, and
> have already given you so many unquestionable proofs of their pre-
> ferring your Majesty's interest & the support of your Government, above
> all others, and what appearance will it have, what reflexion will it not
> cause in the world, that all these weighty things together, can not
> stand in the ballance with this single point, whether Dr. Blackall at this
> time bee made a Bishop or a Dean or a prebend.[78]

The queen, in her reply of 12 September, again refused to retract Blackall's nomination ('I could not answer it nether to God Almighty nor my Self, my consience & honnour being to far ingaged in that matter') and, in terms similar to those she had used in her defiance of William and Mary in 1692, warned the lord treasurer:

Whoever of ye Whigs thinks I am to be Hecktor'd or frighted into a Complyance tho I am a woman, are mightely mistaken in me. I thank God I have a Soul above that, & am too much conserned for my reputation to do any thing to forfeit it, as this would.

As for Godolphin's resignation, the queen implored him, 'do not think any more of that Cruel request you mention in your letter for I can never consent to it & if you should put it in practice I realy beleeve it will be my death'. The queen closed her letter: 'I beg you would not lett this be seen by any body, no, not by my unkind friend [Sarah].'[79]

Two days later, the duchess forwarded to the queen Marlborough's letter to his wife of 8 September[80] ('which I can't resist sending, tho I am pretty sure how fruitless it will prove') in which he complained that he had no credit with the queen because his candidate had not yet been appointed regius professor at Oxford. In her covering letter Sarah launched direct attacks upon Harley and Abigail:

It must appear that after the faithfulest Services that were ever done to any Prince, a Man that was never knowne but lately, had by twenty Artifices work't all this mischeife, & that which makes it yet more unaccountable, few people in the World are so ignorant, as not to know, that he has not Reputation enough to carry on your business two months. . . .

Mr. Harleys insinuations from himselfe or some he is known to employ, has made your Majesty Deaf to all the representations that could be made by those you have had so great experience of. . . .[81]

Apparently, in the copy which Sarah kept to show Marlborough and Godolphin, she omitted a more direct attack upon Abigail at which the queen took offence. She replied to the duchess on 16 September, returning Marlborough's letter:

As to your own letter there is very litle in it I think I need give any answer to, you haveing shewn on many occassions you give no Creditt to what I say, & therfore I shall only Just touch upon two things, the first is to what you say, that it shews plainly by what the D: of M: says in ye end of your letter, he thinks he has not much Creditt with me, to that I answer, I am of oppinion, & soe I beleeve all impartiall people must be, that I have all my life given demonstration to the world he has a great deale of Creditt with me; the other is to beg you would not mention that person [Abigail] any more who you are pleased to call ye object of my fayvour, for whatever caracter ye Malittious world may give her, I do assure you it will never have any weight with me, knowing She dos not deserve it, nor I can never change ye good impressions you once gave me of her, unless She should give me Cause, which I am very sure She never will. . . .[82]

Within the next few days, of course, Sarah discovered Abigail's secret marriage and the stage was set for a political crisis which was to last throughout the autumn and winter of 1707–8. On 12 and 16 September the queen repeated, in appeals to Marlborough which are now lost, her determination not to make further concessions to the Junto. On 26 September, Marlborough replied:

> I am not able to express the trouble and concern I have to see every thing that has been hethertoo so prosperous runing so fast to ruin. . . . I am in my Judgment persuaded that if you do not alter the resolution You seem to have taken, by which you will make it impossible for *Godolphin* to serve You with any Success, You will not only disturb the quiet of your own life, but also ruin the prodistant Religion, and all the libertys of Europ.
> . . . For God sake Consider when England shall see after the faithfull Services for so many years perform'd with success by *Godolphin* and *Marlborough* that thay have not Credit enough left to persuade You to do what is good for Your Self, how farr this must discorage others from entering into Your Service, with that Zeal and Love which is necessary for the Carrying on of Your business. I shou'd not write with this earnestness were it not for the Duty I have for You, for I have no ambition left, and shou'd I serve a thousand Years, I have nothing to aske for my self. . . .[83]

The queen's response to this remarkable warning does not survive, but from her subsequent actions it is clear that she discounted Marlborough's talk of resignation and believed that he could be induced to enter a scheme which included neither the Junto nor Godolphin.

Godolphin, surprisingly, was much more sanguine than the duke and duchess about the extent of his influence with the queen and his belief that Harley did not represent a serious threat. He believed that the queen had rashly involved herself in promises to Blackall and Dawes for the bishoprics of Exeter and Chester and that this was the root of her uneasiness. On 7 October he reported to Marlborough:

> In severall of *Marlborough's* letters to Mrs. Morley, I find he often repeats, *that the rashness of some people's schemes may prove fatall*. But there is really no such thing as a scheme or anything like it from any-body else; nor has *the queen* as yett thought of taking a scheme, but from Mr. Freeman and Mr. Montgomery. The misfortune is that *the queen* happens to bee intangled in a promise that is extreamly incon-venient, and upon which so much weight is layd, and such inference made, that to affect this promise would be destruction; at the same time *the queen* is uneasy with everybody that but endeavours to shew the consequences which attend it.[84]

251

By this time the crisis was upon them. The Whigs, in retaliation against the queen and the Duumvirs for their 'betrayal' over the ecclesiastical question, were determined to attack the conduct of Admiralty affairs, of particular consequence to the queen because Prince George was in titular control of the Navy while his close associate, Admiral George Churchill, was the real manager.[85] Earlier in the summer, Marlborough had wished that his younger brother would resign to forestall Whig protests.[86] To Godolphin, the Admiralty issue – not Harley's activities – presaged disaster, not least because the queen was personally concerned. On 25 October he predicted to Harley that, despite any possible naval success,

> all this will not hinder the great clamours which I hear are preparing against the management of our sea affairs, which must needs be very disagreeable to the Queen and particularly uneasy to the Prince; in short, I expect to see the whole government torn to pieces.[87]

Shortly thereafter, the queen and the Duchess of Marlborough had another interview in which Sarah, as she later described it to the queen, expressed herself

> with soe little passion, that the last time I waited upon you, there were very long spaces on both sides when it was a profound silence, I never stir'd once from behind the screen where I first stood, that I remember, I never in the whole conversation once pull'd out my pockitt hankerchese, till after I had taken my leave, when att the door you were pleased to give me a mark of your favour, that brought teares into my eyes.

Nevertheless, the queen made 'heavy complaints to Mr. Montgomery' about two of Sarah's themes. She apparently construed a phrase the duchess used to describe the prince and Admiral Churchill as implying that they were lovers. Sarah, in her letter of 29 October, protested that

> if this were my last hour . . . I did mean what I said of Mr. Morley only as a comparison, & not with any disrespectfull thought or reflection upon him, to shew what a sort of friendship it was, & if I had thought, or ever heard, that hee had any such Inclenation it would have been the last thing that ever I should have touched upon, for in my whole life I never did any thing soe ill breed, or soe foolish, as to say a thing only to offend you, without doing you any servise.

The queen also objected to the duchess 'saying perpetually ill things of Mrs. Hill', particularly that she would accept bribes. Sarah explained, 'I never said Mrs. Hill took mony, but I said she had acquaintance that every body knew would take mony for any thing upon earth.' Sarah concluded her letter by blasting the Tories as 'devided madd men, & for the P: of W:, who neither will nor can support you'.[88] The queen ignored Sarah's letter. A month later, Sarah dispatched a similar epistle and received a curt answer: 'if I thought any thing I could say would make us live easyer togather', the queen wrote at the end of November,

I should be encouraged to writt at large a volum to you, but I am afraid that would not do. I must repeat what I have often don, & must ever do, that if you will be ye Same to your poor unfortunat faithfull Morly as you used to be, She will be soe to you.[89]

Relations between the two women, sovereign and subject, continued to deteriorate as the queen (in Sarah's opinion) perversely clung to Harley and Abigail. On 24 December the duchess visited the queen at Kensington: 'when I came in', Sarah later recounted,

she used me extream coldly, stood all the time to make me go away, which I did at last, telling her I was sorry I had waited upon her so unseasonably, as I made my courtsie she lookt disordered very much, came up to me without making any answer & took me by the hand upon which I offer'd to kiss hers, stooping lower & she took me up with a cold embrace.

Brooding over this incident, three days later Sarah again wrote to the queen, attempting to retrieve their friendship from the ruins:

If Mrs. Morley has any remains of the tenderness she once profess'd for her faithfull Freeman, I wou'd beg she might be treated one of these two ways, either with the openness & confidence of a friend as she was for twenty years, for to pretend kindness without trust & openness of heart is a treatment for children, not friends, or else in that manner that is necessary for the post she is in, which unavoidably forces her to be often troubling Mrs. Morley upon the account of others, & if she pleases to chuse which of these ways or any other she likes to have Mrs. Freeman live in, she promises to follow any rule that is laid down.[90]

By the end of 1707, however, the queen had chosen her path. Sarah received no answer.

10

'Utter Destruction to Me'

The Failure of Moderation, October 1707 – October 1708

The first session of the first parliament of the United Kingdom of Great Britain, which opened on 23 October, was essentially the last session of the English parliament which had been elected in 1705, with the addition of forty-five Scottish commoners and sixteen representative Scottish peers. All parties knew that there would be a general election in the spring of 1708, and their lines were drawn accordingly. Shortly before the session began, Whig members of the House of Commons met with the Dukes of Somerset and Devonshire, both members of the cabinet, who informed them that although the queen could not back down on her promises to Blackall and Dawes, 'yet for the future she was resolved to give them [the Whigs] full content'. This was diametrically opposed to what Harley, St John, and Harcourt were informing their followers, and it was widely labelled 'double-dealing' on the part of the queen.[1] Under attack, the government was in danger of losing its majorities in both houses of Parliament. Against the government's wishes, the High Tories and the Whigs united to abolish the Scottish Privy Council; it was an issue which touched the queen personally, for the abolition weakened the crown's influence in Scottish elections.[2] In both houses, the Whigs launched their attacks upon mismanagement at the Admiralty,[3] to which the queen took personal offence. George Churchill was the immediate Whig target, as he controlled the day-to-day business of the Admiralty. The prince rarely appeared in the administrative offices, but everything was done under his signature and in his name.[4] On 13 November, Archbishop Sharp recorded in his diary that the queen

> spoke to me for my assistance or vote in matters that were likely to come before the Parliament with relation to the Admiralty. She said the design was against Admiral Churchill, who was one of the ablest men for that service that could be found.[5]

254

The queen was so bitter against Peter King, a young Whig lawyer who led the attack in the Commons, that during the remainder of her reign King was never to rise higher than the Recordership of London and a knighthood, although he subsequently served both George I and George II as lord chancellor.[6] It appeared that Godolphin had predicted correctly when he had expected 'to see the whole Government torn to pieces'.

Marlborough returned from the Continent to London and, after a month of consultations with his colleagues, on 5 December he and Godolphin entered into an agreement with Harley to explore a 'moderate scheme' to reconstruct the government, a scheme 'to rescue the ministry and defeat the Junto'.[7] The details of Harley's scheme remain sketchy, but apparently the reconstruction of the government was to be based upon Harley's own followers (St John, Harcourt, Mansell), the territorial magnates (the Dukes of Devonshire, Somerset, and Newcastle), the 'lord treasurer's Whigs' (John Smith, Henry Boyle, Robert Walpole), Tories who were detachable from Rochester and Nottingham (such as the Duke of Buckingham), and – significantly for the future – Charles Talbot, Duke of Shrewsbury. Shrewsbury, who was a lifelong friend of the queen, Marlborough, and Godolphin, had remained absent from the court because it considered his Italian wife vulgar and eccentric; consequently, he realized better than the Duumvirs the burden which the war was placing on England, although he was still reluctantly endorsing the policy of 'No Peace without Spain'. 'A Peace is much wanted & desired in the Country', Shrewsbury had written a year earlier,

> for tho we have plenty of all things, money is so scarce, that nobodys
> rents are payd which makes the land tax felt heavily. I speak not for
> my self, who am less sensible of it than others, mine being an old
> Estate, set much under value & the Tenants pay all the taxes, but I speak
> the general voice, tho at the same time if the Peace be not good, any
> warr is better than a Peace that does not settle King Charles in Spain.[8]

There can be no doubt that the queen encouraged and supported Harley's moderate scheme. On 16 December she gave Archbishop Sharp early notice

> that she meant to change her measures, and give no countenance to
> the Whig Lords, but that all the Tories, if they would, should come in;
> and all the Whigs likewise, that would show themselves to be in her
> interests, should have favour.[9]

It remains unclear how far Harley wished to proceed – whether or not he aimed to replace Godolphin as lord treasurer – and how far the queen was informed of these intentions. She was later to claim that she had no wish to part with Godolphin; judging by her subsequent behaviour, particularly in 1710, this was probably true, although the queen 'was not averse to lying her way out of a tight corner, not to putting on a convincing act when it suited her'.[10] What is clear is that both the queen and Harley believed that Marlborough could be separated politically from Godolphin in the right circumstances.[11]

The 'scheme' was carried out against the background of parliamentary debates on the management of the war in Spain, particularly the conduct of the Earl of Peterborough who, after a series of disputes with his home government and with the ministers of 'Carlos III', had been summoned home in disgrace and replaced by James Stanhope.[12] On 22 December both houses of Parliament passed resolutions which became the official policy of the British government: 'nothing could restore a just ballance of power in Europe, but the reducing the whole Spanish monarchy to the obedience of the House of Austria'.[13] 'No Peace without Spain', initially a Tory policy enthusiastically supported by the Whigs, became the nation's ultimate – and impossible – war aim.

At the time of the agreement between the Duumvirs and Harley, Godolphin gave way to the queen's insistence on Blackall and Dawes for the bishoprics of Exeter and Chester. The queen sent the following message to the Junto:

> They will receive no satisfaction for the two bishops that are making.
> The Queen says . . . she had given her word and honour, and that she
> will through all difficulties abide by it with this addition, she had much
> rather heal the breach and engages preferments for the future shall be
> as they approve. But if the breach is once made . . . that she will never
> more return to consult them any more than Lord Rochester and that
> form of men, but she will ever after trust herself in the hands of such
> as have never been on the stage in either party. This she hopes will
> carry her right intentions along in her administration.[14]

On 18 December, in a speech to the House of Lords in which she gave her assent to the annual financial bills, the queen made it clear that there would be an all-party government. The 'moderate scheme' was riding high, but Harley's personal position was severely weakened on 31 December when it was discovered that William Greg, a clerk in Harley's office, had been retailing state papers to the French. Greg, who was immediately arrested and interrogated, pleaded guilty and was convicted of high treason on 19 January 1708. Although he denied that Harley was in any way involved in his treachery, the Greg affair left Harley open at least to accusations of incompetent management of his office and perhaps, at the hands of unscrupulous opponents, to an impeachment.

The agreement between the Duumvirs and Harley lasted at least until the conviction of Greg; a few days previously, a large meeting of the government's supporters in both houses agreed to bring some Tories into the administration.[15] During the last days of January, however, Marlborough and Godolphin became convinced that Harley was aiming to become the principal minister in any new combination. On 24 January, in an audience with the queen, Harley said something to her, probably concerning mismanagement of the war in Spain, at which Marlborough and Godolphin took umbrage.[16] It seems likely that Harley revealed to the queen what his associate, Henry St John, was to admit in the House of Commons five days later: fewer than half of the English troops authorized by Parliament for the Spanish theatre had been present at the battle of Almanza.[17] Apparently, Harley pinned the responsibility for this on Godolphin and unveiled to the queen the details of his scheme for reconstructing the government, an administration in which the lord treasurer would not be included.[18] The queen must have encouraged Harley to proceed; significantly, during the following days she was to make no effort to keep Godolphin in office.[19]

Within four days, both Marlborough and Godolphin discovered what had transpired during this conference, probably from the queen herself. Godolphin was shocked and Marlborough was incensed. On 28 January the queen told Harley that Marlborough had complained bitterly about his conduct,[20] and on 30 January Harley visited Marlborough to learn the particulars of the captain-general's complaints.[21] Harley's plan had been discovered before he had time to secure adequate Tory support in either house of Parliament, and he was reduced to protesting to both Marlborough and Godolphin that he had no design to overthrow the Duumvirs.[22] Godolphin was understandably bitter at what he considered to be Harley's treachery. 'I have received your letter', he told Harley on 30 January,

> and am very sorry for what has happened to lose the good opinion I had so much inclination to have of you, but I cannot help seeing and hearing, nor believing my senses. I am very far from having deserved it from you. God forgive you![23]

On 1 February, Marlborough wrote to the queen that he and Godolphin would resign rather than continue in the same cabinet 'with so vile a person' as Harley. The queen summoned the Duumvirs to a meeting on 2 February in which she urged a reconciliation between them and Harley and their continued adherence to the moderate reconstruction of the government previously agreed upon. This had no effect, and the agony of disagreement with her lifelong friends affected the queen's health. On 4 February it was reported that 'the Queen is not well, grieves much, has had ye gout in her stomach'.[24] Indeed, the queen's indisposition cast a pall on the celebrations of her forty-third birthday on 6 February: 'there has been a great appearance at Kensington and will be a greater this evening', it was reported. 'Her Majesty did not come to town and has not ordered any ball or comedy'.[25] On her birthday, the queen reached her decision that she must part with Godolphin: she sent Marlborough a letter, which was delivered by Henry St John, telling the captain-general that she was prepared to part with the lord treasurer.[26] While she was ready to sever her ties with Godolphin, neither the queen nor Harley believed that any new administration could survive without the support of Marlborough.[27]

On Sunday evening, 8 February, the Duke and Duchess of Marl-borough and the Earl of Godolphin visited the queen to offer their resignations if she did not agree to the dismissal of Harley.[28] The names of Morley, Freeman, and Montgomery were not used in this dramatic confrontation between the queen and her most powerful subjects. According to Sir John Cropley, who had his information from Godol-phin's close friend, James Stanhope, the queen was prepared to see Godolphin and the duchess resign, but could not allow Marlborough to do so. 'I must tel you some parts of ye Dialogue', Cropley wrote to his friend, the Earl of Shaftesbury:

Lord Treasurer told ye Queen he came to resign ye Staff, that serving her longer with one so perfidious as Mr. H[arley] was impossible, she reply'd in respect of his long Service, she would give him til tomorrow to Consider when he should doe as he pleas'd with all she could find enough glad of that Staff.

Then came Lady Dutchess with great Duty and Submission, that She had serv'd her ever with affec[tion] & tenderness, &c., her utmost had been her Duty and she had been faythefull in it. Ye reply is said to be, 'You shall Consider of this til tomorrow, then if you desire it, you shall have my leave to retire as you desire. I shall then advise you to goe to your Little house at St. Albans and there stay til Blenheim house is ready for your Grace'.

Then enter'd ye Duke, prepar'd with his utmost address. He told her he had ever served her with obedience and fidelity . . . that he must lament he came in Competition with so vile a creature as H[arley]; that his Fidelity and Duty should continue as long as his breath. That it was his Duty to be speedy in resigning his Commands, that she might put the sword into some other hand immediately, and it was also his Duty to tel her he fear'd ye Dutch would immediately on ye news make a peace very injurious for England.

'And then, my Lord,' says She, 'will you resign me your sword'. 'Let me tel you', says he, 'Your Service I have regarded to ye utmost of my power'. 'And if you doe my Lord, resign your sword, let me tel you, you will run it through my head'.

She went to Council beging him to follow, he refusing. . . .[29]

Harley's minutes of the cabinet meeting which followed the queen's interview with Marlborough show that the secretary of state proceeded through several routine items of business before the Duke of Somerset (supported by the Earl of Pembroke, lord president of the council, and most other members) refused to continue the meeting in the absence of the captain-general and the lord treasurer: the cabinet broke up in confusion.

News that the queen had publicly broken with the Marlboroughs and Godolphin in favour of Harley and political moderation spread rapidly throughout London. The adverse reaction to this news in both houses of Parliament the next day made it apparent that Harley could not find adequate political support to sustain a new administration; furthermore, the possibility that Harley might be exposed to parliamentary attack over the Greg affair shook the queen's resolve.[30] While Harley's own followers were prepared to stand beside him, the territorial magnates, including Somerset, Newcastle, and Devonshire, rallied to Marlborough and Godolphin.[31] The most crucial role, however, was played by Prince George of Denmark. Sarah later recorded that Marlborough and Godolphin triumphed 'by the interposition of the Prince',[32] and Peter Wentworth, an equerry to the prince, recorded two years later that Harley's dismissal 'would never have been effected if my Master had not been prevailed upon at last to persuade 'twas for the good of the nation'.[33] On 9 February the queen summoned Marlborough to Kensington and informed him that she would dismiss Harley; the following day, Harley surrendered his seals of office, and St John, Harcourt, and Mansell resigned with their leader. These resignations were important to the development of future cabinet solidarity, and they underlined the degree to which these younger, moderate Tories felt betrayed by Marlborough and Godolphin.

The queen was humiliated by her loss of this power struggle, which was discussed in every coffee house in town. She had risked sundering personal relationships of a quarter of a century's duration for the principle of political moderation. Nevertheless, the balance of evidence suggests that, on a personal level, the queen still preferred Marlborough and Godolphin to Harley. She habitually signed her letters to Harley

'ANNE R'; those to the Duumvirs, by contrast, were signed 'your humble Servant'. After the February 1708 crisis, the queen obviously blamed her humiliation to a large degree on Harley, believing that he had publicly exposed her without adequate preparation or support for his 'scheme'.[34] In the months immediately after Harley's forced resignation, the queen suspended contact with him, relying heavily upon the support of her husband in her continuing struggle against the Junto, despite the prince's rapidly declining health. Although he had influenced the queen on behalf of the Duumvirs during the February crisis, the prince was embittered by Whig assaults on his management of the Admiralty, and throughout 1708 the royal couple presented a united front against further incursions by the Junto. Harley and his adherents were replaced not by Junto men but by 'lord treasurer's Whigs', headed by Henry Boyle, who became secretary of state in place of Harley, and Robert Walpole, who became secretary at war in place of Henry St John. Both Marlborough and Godolphin were well aware of the new, crucial importance of the Prince of Denmark during the last months of his life.[35]

Despite the obvious influence of the prince, the Duchess of Marlborough – now very embittered against her mistress – was convinced that the queen maintained secret contacts with Harley, particularly during the summer of 1708 which the queen spent at the 'little house' at Windsor. When Sarah accused her of this,

> she often said, & wrote, & sometimes very solemnly affirmed that she receiv'd no such advices; & that Mr. Harley never came near Her; nay, she sometimes thought fit to carry it so far, as to declare to the Duke & Dutchess of Marlborough, that She had a very ill opinion of the man; & this in such a manner, as that the Duke believ'd Her, whilst the Dutchess, who had had more experience of how small account words & assurances were come to be with Her, was but little moved by such protestations.[36]

In spite of Sarah's scepticism, Harley's correspondence bears out the truth of the queen's assertion. Harley's first surviving letter to Abigail after the crisis was dated 10 October 1708,[37] although he drew up a cypher of cant names for their correspondence dated 14 May 1708.[38] In a letter of 16 October from Harley to Abigail, undoubtedly meant to be shown to the queen, Harley wrote:

> It is now Eight months since I have had no sort of communication with her [the queen]; & several months that I have been at this great distance so that ye difficultys (I am wel informed) they [Godolphin and the duchess] complain of are not to be imputed to me; & therefore they

should consider that its arises from ye unreasonableness of their own demands & my Aunts true judgment & right understanding.[39]

The queen's disinclination to correspond with Harley indicated the degree of her humiliation at losing in the February power struggle; it was not caused by pressure from the Duumvirs. When Marlborough, during the summer of 1708, reported that Harley's agents in the Dutch republic were libelling the Duumvirs, Godolphin read Marlborough's letter to the queen 'without offering the least observation upon it, having often found upon many other occasions, that it is always best to lett [her] make [her] own reflexions'.[40] Abigail Masham also noted the change, and believed that the queen was afraid to take an independent line: 'Oh, my poor aunt Stephens [the queen] is to be pitied very much,' Abigail told Harley in the summer of 1708, 'they press her harder than ever, since what happened lately she is altered more than is to be imagined, no ready money [courage] at all to supply her with common necessaries.'[41] Abigail's surviving letters to Harley during the summer of 1708 make it clear that the queen discouraged Abigail from travelling to meet her cousin, at least in part because Abigail was undergoing her first pregnancy. Furthermore, Harley was out of London for most of the summer, residing at Brampton Bryan, his Herefordshire estate. From there, at the end of October, he complained to Abigail, 'I have not heard one tittle from you since I came into the country.'[42]

The queen was undoubtedly reluctant to associate openly with Harley because of the Greg affair. After Harley's forced resignation, the Duumvirs and the Whigs attempted to link Harley with Greg's treason; a committee of the House of Lords, of which Sunderland was the leader,[43] was appointed to examine Greg and it was rumoured that Greg would produce 'startling' revelations. Greg, however, went to the scaffold at the end of April proclaiming Harley's innocence.[44] This incident naturally exacerbated the bitterness which the February crisis had engendered, particularly as the Junto attempt to link Harley with the French and the Jacobites coincided with an invasion attempt launched by the Pretender.

Popular dissatisfaction in Scotland with the union and with the loss of Scotland's national independence had made the northern kingdom ripe for a Jacobite attempt; anti-union feeling was more important than traditional loyalty to the house of Stuart in paving the way for James Francis Edward Stuart, now twenty years old. Many Scots suspected that the queen might be secretly sympathetic to the establishment of her half-brother on the Scottish throne, and Jacobites in Scotland had assiduously cultivated this impression, which had no basis in fact. Louis XIV's decision to play his Jacobite card was a measure of his desperation by the spring of 1708. At most, the French hoped that an invasion of Scotland would result in sizeable withdrawals of British troops from Flanders and a quickly negotiated peace settlement. Unfortunately for French hopes, the ill fate which plagued the later Stuarts was in the ascendant. No sooner had the Pretender reached Le Havre, from where his invasion fleet was to be launched, than he came down with measles. His doctors forbade him to travel, the expedition was delayed by one week, and the British and Dutch intelligence services were able to report the Jacobite plans to London and The Hague. By the time the expedition sailed on 6/17 March, a combined Anglo-Dutch fleet under the command of Sir George Byng was in the Channel and it followed the French Admiral Forbin closely in his path towards Scotland. When the French fleet arrived off the eastern coast of Scotland, the signals agreed upon were not given by Jacobite rebels on the shore, Forbin refused to land, and the French fleet made it safely home, eluding Byng's squadrons. The Pretender did not set foot on British soil.

The first warnings of the Pretender's intentions reached London on 4 March, but it was not until 11 March that news arrived that the French fleet had passed Byng in the Channel and was headed north. It was reported that the 'Duke of Marlborough, Lord Treasurer, and Lord Sunderland went to Kensington at 5 o'clock in the morning, and there was a Councel summon'd immediately, which mett between 7 and 8'.[45] Later that day, the queen went to the House of Lords to inform them that Byng was pursuing the French with a superior fleet.[46] That night she did not return to Kensington but slept at St James's in order to dispatch necessary orders.[47]

The next day, 'being much alarmed with the danger of this invasion', the queen responded to the Lords' unanimous address of support with an indirect endorsement of the Whig Party: 'I must always place my chief dependance upon those who have given such repeated proofs of the greatest warmth and concern for the support of the Revolution, the security of my person, and of the Protestant Succession'.[48] There can be little doubt about the queen's fear. In 1715 the Duchess of Marlborough recorded:

> When the Nation was allarm'd with the Pretender's attempt to land in Scotland, the Queen herself had terrible impressions about his coming in a forcible manner, & shew'd the greatest signs of fear & concern about the matter. . . . Such sort of frights would work upon Her Temper, when better arguments had no manner of force.[49]

The queen's fears evaporated – quite simply because the Jacobite attempt proved to be a fiasco. While the main French fleet eluded Sir

George Byng, one ship, the *Salisbury*, was captured and 500 prisoners were taken, among whom were two sons of Charles, Lord Middleton (the Pretender's principal advisor), and the aged Edward, Lord Griffin. Griffin was tried and sentenced to death for high treason in June 1708, but was reprieved on a month-to-month basis by the queen and died in the Tower of natural causes in November 1710.[50] When the Dutch envoy, Vryberg, and the Dutch resident in London, L'Hermitage, had their public audience with the queen to congratulate her on the failure of the Pretender's attempt, L'Hermitage recorded that 'it appeared that Her Majesty was very pleased with Vryberg's congratulations, her expression revealing that she was quite satisfied'.[51]

In the immediate aftermath of the Jacobite invasion attempt the government seized upon the favourable opportunity, and dissolved Parliament on 15 April and held a general election. Predictably, the Whigs scored a major triumph, securing a majority in the House of Commons of sixty-nine seats.[52] This victory encouraged the Junto to increase their demands, insisting that Somers should be appointed lord president in place of the Earl of Pembroke, and – even more disagreeably for the queen – that Wharton should be named lord lieutenant of Ireland (an office which Pembroke had assumed when Ormonde was dismissed in 1707). The queen was adamantly opposed to any ministerial changes, and Godolphin, like Sarah, suspected that a secret influence was at work. On 19 April he complained to Marlborough: 'Mrs. Morley continues so very difficult to doe anything that is good for herself, that it puts us into all the distraction and uneasyness imaginable. I really believe this humour proceeds more from her husband than from herself, and in him is very much kept up by your brother George.'[53]

On the evening of 21 April the Dukes of Newcastle and Devonshire visited the queen to propose that she bring Somers into the cabinet as lord president; when she responded that it would be doing a disservice to Pembroke to dismiss him without cause, they countered by proposing that she add Somers to the cabinet without any office, the 'expedient' which the queen herself had suggested when she had tried to avoid appointing Sunderland as secretary of state (although they did not dare to remind her explicitly of this). This proposal 'being new to her, and unexpected, she was much at a loss what to say', Godolphin reported to Marlborough.

> At last, she sayd she thought it was very unusuall, upon which they offer'd some instances of its being done. And then she said, she thought the Cabinet Counsell was full enough already, so they took leave in much discontent.

263

The next morning the queen summoned Godolphin 'to complain that she saw there was to bee no end of her troubles' and she proved 'very uneasy and very unwilling' when Godolphin advised her to follow the suggestion of Newcastle and Devonshire.[54] It was clear to the queen that she could put no further reliance upon Godolphin to prevent the Junto from taking over the cabinet; her only remaining hope was Marlborough, and her letters to the captain-general during the 1708 campaign reflect her overwhelming fear of Sarah's influence over her husband. On the evening of her conversation with Godolphin, the queen appealed to Marlborough,

> looking upon it to be utter destruction to me to bring Ld. Sommers into my Service, & I hope you will not Joyne in Soliciting me in this thing tho Lord Treasurer tells me you will, for it is what I can never consent to.[55]

Marlborough's reply was far from reassuring. The February 1708 crisis had severely shaken him. He warned the queen that the Dutch were likely to embark on peace negotiations with Louis XIV, not from apprehension of French power 'but from what passed in England last winter, and from the continued intelligences they have of your Majesty's being resolved to change hands and parties'. Embracing the line which Sarah had been preaching for years, that the Tories were secretly Jacobites at heart and as such represented a danger to the queen, Marlborough suggested that 'the greatest part of that party' had known of or supported the Pretender's invasion attempt and that she could find safety only with the Whigs. If she refused to appoint Somers, Marlborough predicted, 'it will be a demonstration . . . to every body, that Lord Treasurer and I have no credit with your Majesty, but that you are guided by the insinuation of Mr. Harley'.[56]

The queen received Marlborough's letter on 4 May and begged off an immediate response ('haveing bin kept a great while at Councill this evening that makes me soe weary & sleepy') but could not resist answering Marlborough's parting shot about Harley:

> whatever I may say will proceed from no insinuations, nor pursuasions but of my own thoughts & ye Sincerety of my hart, which wishes you all Success imaginable in your undertakeings, & I pray God Almighty with all my Soul to direct you in all things & to send you safe home againe.[57]

Two days later, on 6 May, the queen responded to Marlborough at greater length, totally ignoring the issue of Somers but backing Marlborough on the war issue:

264

I have bin soe tyerd to day with importunetys that come from *the Whigs* that I have not spirits left to open my afflicted hart soe freely & soe fully as I intended. . . . I can now only tell you that as to what you mention, & what *Godolphin* told me some time agoe of your being prest in two Conferences for ye makeing steps towards a peace, I am Intirly of your oppinion thinking it nether for my honnor nor Interest, & do assure you (whatever insinuations my enemies may make to ye Contrary) I shall never at any time give my consent to a peace but upon Safe & Honorable terms; excuse my answering nothing more of your letter at this time, & be soe just to me as not to lett any misrepresentations that may be made of *the queen* have any weight with *Marlborough* for that would be a greater trouble to me then can be exprest.[58]

On the same day, Godolphin reported to Marlborough that

though Mr. Montgomery has had two conversations with Mrs. Morley of 2 hours a piece, upon the subject of Mr. Freeman's letter, *the queen* continues hitherto inflexible on that poynt, and resists all the plainest reasons and arguments that ever were used in any case whatsoever. At the [same time], *the queen* renounces and disclaims any talk or the least commerce with Mr. Harley, at first or secondhand, and [is] positive that she never speaks with anybody but *Prince George* upon anything of that kind. From whence *Prince George's* notions come, is not hard to conjecture [i.e. from George Churchill].[59]

The queen also proved obstinate on questions of secondary importance, particularly the proposal to appoint Halifax's younger brother, Sir James Montagu, as attorney-general in the place of Simon Harcourt. Montagu had supported the abolition of the Scottish Privy Council during the previous session of Parliament, and the queen took umbrage against him.[60] On 20 May the queen proposed to Godolphin that Sir Thomas Parker be appointed attorney-general and that Robert Eyres replace Montagu as solicitor-general.[61] Both Parker and Eyres were staunch Whigs, but they were not tied to the Junto. This suggestion, of course, proved totally unacceptable to both Godolphin and the Junto. On 1 June the lord treasurer reported to Marlborough his conversation that morning with the queen,

which ended with the greatest dissatisfaction possible to both. They have had of late many great contests, as I am told, upon the subject of *Halifax's* brother, but with out any ground gained on either side. This day it held longer than ever. The particulars, as they have been repeated to mee, are both too tedious and unnecessary to trouble you with them. In short, the obstinacy was unaccountable, and the battel

265

might have lasted till [evening], if after the clock had struck 3, *Prince George* had not thought fitt to come in and look as if he thought it were dinner time.[62]

The Whigs were now angry and resentful about their treatment by the queen. No longer deluded that Marlborough and Godolphin were secretly conniving to delay and to prevent Whig appointments, the Junto were determined to display their force to the court and to the queen, whom they now recognized as a powerful and tenacious enemy. As soon as the composition of the new House of Commons became clear in the spring of 1708, the Junto rejected the government's proposed candidate for speaker, Sir Richard Onslow, a 'lord treasurer's Whig', in favour of their own candidate, Sir Peter King, who had led the attack on the Admiralty.[63] Furthermore, the Junto were determined to renew their attacks on the Admiralty as the best means of distressing the queen and the prince. Such a strategy had popular support, for Admiralty mis-management had contributed to enormous shipping losses to French pirates. As one observer put it shortly after the ministerial crisis in February 1708:

> I am of opinion people will be willing enough to overlook ye Queen's mistake in the matter of the Ministry, provided the Admiralty be better provided for; but ye generality are soe exceedingly dissatisfyed with ye present management of that, they will never cease clamoureing till that great trust be in other hands. And, indeed, I wonder at the indiscretion of those counsells which influence the continueing of the Prince in such a post, where he is only to bear ye blame of other men's mis-carriages.[64]

'Other men's miscarriages' to be attacked were primarily those of the prince's favourite, Admiral George Churchill. As we have seen, Churchill, a High Tory, was becoming daily more distasteful to both Godolphin and to the Duchess of Marlborough and was increasingly difficult to manage. During the summer of 1708, Churchill became engaged in a violent quarrel with Robert Walpole, who had replaced Henry St John as secretary at war. The dispute arose over the disposal of Lillingston's regiment to his lieutenant-colonel, James Jones, who Marlborough was told had been recommended to the queen by Harley. When Marlborough wrote to his brother to this effect, Churchill told the queen and the prince that Walpole had informed Marlborough that he (Walpole) and Harley had recommended Jones to the prince, and that Walpole had publicly confirmed this fact. The queen, knowing perfectly well that Harley had not recommended Jones to such a post, was furious with Walpole and complained bitterly to Godolphin. Walpole, in turn, informed the lord treasurer that he had never heard of Jones and demanded an apology from George Churchill.[65]

Godolphin, in reporting this imbroglio to Marlborough, informed him that George Churchill was entirely to blame for the quarrel:

> I must need add upon this occasion that *George Churchill* does certainly contribute very much to keep up both in *Prince George* and *the queen* the naturall, but inconvenient averseness they have to *the Whigs* . . . and nothing is more certain than that the general dislike of *George Churchill* in that station is stronger than ever, and much harder to be supported.[66]

Marlborough himself wished that his brother would resign, 'but I am told *Prince George* will not hear of itt'.[67] The final blow, as far as the Marlboroughs and Godolphin were concerned, came in mid-July, when George Churchill journeyed to Oxford to confer there with Harley.[68] Before the end of the summer Marlborough wrote to his brother, virtually ordering him to retire from the Admiralty[69] but, protected by the queen and the prince, Churchill obdurately remained at his post.

During the summer of 1708, Marlborough and the queen clashed more directly on another issue, the conduct of Sunderland. During the 1708 Scottish elections, the Junto – largely at Sunderland's instigation – and their Scottish allies had struck an electoral alliance with a number of nobles recently imprisoned on suspicion of complicity in the Pretender's invasion attempt, including Sunderland's former brother-in-law, the Duke of Hamilton. The result of this alliance was that over one third of the government's nominees for representative peerages were defeated in June 1708 and nominees of the Junto, including Hamilton, were elected instead. The queen, hearing this news from one of her favourite Scottish nobles, John Erskine, Earl of Mar,[70] complained angrily to Godolphin (who, perhaps not surprisingly, did not relay her complaints to Marlborough). On 18 June the queen wrote directly to Marlborough concerning Sunderland's role in the Scottish elections:

> One would not loos ye least assistance at such a Critical time as this that there is such a mighty Strugle, & there is no wonder opposition should encreas when one of my own Servants [i.e. Sunderland] are at ye head of it, as you will see by ye enclosed, which I could not forbear sending you, to give you a view of ye ill treatment I receive from ye person that is mentioned in it, there are larger accounts com today from other hands, all to ye same purpose; it is such a behaviour I beleeve as never was known, & what I realy can not beare, nor what no other I dare say would one minute, but I am willing out of sincere kindnes & Consideration I have for you, to deffer takeing away ye Seals, till I receive againe more confirmation of what ye enclosed

Containes, not that I have doubt of ye truth of it, all Ld. S[underland's] own actions haveing shewn soe much of ye same spirit.

I have told my thoughts very freely to *Godolphin* on this subject, & I do not doubt but he will give you an account off what past between us, & what his oppinion is, & therfore will not say any more on a thing that must be soe disagreeable to you; only that it is impossible to beare such usage, & I am sure you are too reasonable (if you consider this matter impartialy) to Blame me when I send for ye Seals, & be assured I shall ever be ye same sincere & faithfull freind to you as ever.[71]

The queen also challenged Sunderland, who denied any guilt in the matter, but the incident served to bring to a head the frustration which the queen had felt since she had been forced to bring him into office. On 22 June she wrote again to Marlborough, complaining of 'such exstrodinary ways used to get an ill Election' and lamenting that, but for Sunderland's activities, 'ye whole list would have bin such as would have voted as I would have them'. She reminded Marlborough of his promise 'when I first took this person into my Service, which was that if ever he did anything I did not like (or some thing to that purpose), you would bring him to make his leg & take his leave', and again repeated her determination to dismiss Sunderland.[72]

Despite her anger with Sunderland and her disillusionment with Marlborough and Godolphin, the queen had to continue to rely upon them, not least because the question of the invitation to a member of the Hanoverian family was once again alive. It had been raised by the Earl of Peterborough, characteristically acting on his own without the support of any party, who petitioned both the elector and the Electress Sophia to send the electoral prince, in his capacity as Duke of Cambridge, to England after he had served in the 1708 campaign in Marlborough's armies.[73] Jean de Robethon, the elector's secretary, immediately notified Marlborough of this proposal, and Marlborough forwarded Robethon's letter to Godolphin and the queen.[74] Godolphin hoped to use the threat of the electoral prince's arrival in England as a means to induce the queen to accept more Whigs, but this did not succeed. On 17 May he reported that he had read Marlborough's letter to the queen,

who was not surprised at it and seems prepared to expect a great deal of trouble upon that matter in the winter, but can't bee prevailed with upon that or any other account to doe what can only in my opinion prevent it.[75]

Certainly, the queen was worried about the possibility: on 22 May, in the postscript of a long letter to Godolphin, she added:

tho I have said soe much already, I can't conclud this with out telling you what the D. of M. says about the Electoral Prince, gives me a great deale of uneasynes, seeing many disagreable things will happen to me upon it.[76]

In seeming confirmation of the queen's forebodings, the Whigs seized upon the issue, and in mid-June Sarah warned Marlborough that they were planning to introduce the invitation in Parliament.[77] Harley's followers spread rumours that the Duumvirs were secretly supporting the invitation as a way to control the queen.[78]

On 21 July, Lord Haversham, the perpetual political rebel, visited the queen at Windsor to warn her that Marlborough, Godolphin, and the Junto were secretly planning an invitation for the next session of Parliament; the queen's gracious reception of Haversham, who had relentlessly opposed the government in the House of Lords, was unprecedented and, as Godolphin later informed Marlborough, 'I could not help observing to Mrs. Morley upon it, that it was not hard to make a judgment of what was like to happen next winter, when people of his behaviour could meet with encouragement to come to Court.'[79] In reporting the meeting to Marlborough, the queen disingenuously excused her reception of Haversham ('I thought it was not proper to refuse any man of quality that desired to speake with me') and appealed for Marlborough's help to prevent the electoral prince from entering England:

> if this matter should be brought into Parliament, whoever proposed it whether Whig or Tory, *I should look upon nether of them as my friends nor would never make any invitation nether to the young man, nor his father, nor Grandmother. . . .*
>
> I . . . beg you would find whether there is any designe where you are *that ye young man should make a vissit in ye winter & contrive some way to putt any such thoughts out of theire heads, that ye difficulty may not be brought upon me of refusing him leave to com if he should ask it, or of forbiding him to com if he should attempt it with out asking, for one of these two things I must do if ether he or his father should have any desires to have him see this Country, it being a thing I can not beare to have any successour heare tho it weare but for a week.*[80]

Before the queen had written this appeal to her captain-general, Marlborough had won the third of his great victories, the battle of Oudenarde (30 June/11 July), which destroyed the remnants of French power in the Southern Netherlands and exposed the second largest city in France, Lille, to the allied armies. News of Marlborough's victory was carried to Windsor on 5 July by John Dalrymple, Earl of Stair, and the queen immediately wrote a warm letter of congratulations to Marlborough, although she could not resist alluding to the political differences between them:

> I want words to express ye Joy I have that you are well after your Glorious Success, for which next to God Almighty my thanks are due to you & indeed I can never say enough for all the great & faithfull Services you have ever don me, but be soe Just as to beleeve I am as truly Sensible of them as a gratfull hart can be, & shall be ready to shew it upon all occassions; I hope you can not doubt of my esteeme & friendship for you, nor think that becaus I differ with you in some things, it is for want of ether. No, I do assure you, if you weare heare I am sure you would not think me so much in ye wrong in some things as I feare you do now.[81]

No similar letter of congratulation went from the queen to the Duchess of Marlborough. Sarah decided to show to the queen the letter which Marlborough had written to his wife, immediately after the battle, in which he said: 'I do, and you must give thankes to God for his goodness in protecting and making me the instrument of so much happyness to the Queen and nation, if she will please to make use of itt.'[82] The queen immediately seized upon Marlborough's equivocal phrase and, on 13 July, asked him:

> I was shewd a letter ye other day by a friend of yours that you writt Just after ye battel, & I must beg you would explaine to me one expression in it, you say after being thankfull for being ye instrument of soe much good to the Nation & me, *if I would please to make use of it*. I am sure I will never make an ill use of soe great a Blessing, but according to ye best of my understanding make ye best of it I can, & should be glad to know what is ye use you would have me make & then I will tell you my thoughts very freely & sincerly.[83]

The queen's letter crossed one in the post which Marlborough had written on the previous day, in which he attributed his success to 'the hand of God' and reminded the queen;

> As I have formerly told your Majesty that I am desirous to serve you in the Army, but not as a minister, I am every day more and more confirmed in that opinion. . . . But as I have taken this resolution to myself, give me leave to say, that I think you are obliged, in conscience, and as a good Christian, to forgive, and to have no more resentments to any particular person or party, but to make of such as will carry on this just war with vigour, which is the only way to preserve our religion and liberties, and the Crown upon your head.[84]

Marlborough's allusion, of course, was to the queen's complaints concerning Sunderland, to which as yet Marlborough had not responded directly. This, as the queen wrote to Marlborough on 22 July, 'I must own Surprizes me, expecting some notice should have bin taken of them'. She refused to regard him merely as a general and promised to continue to consult him as a minister, although she was obviously irritated by Marlborough's lecture on the requirements of Christianity:

> I thank God, I do forgive all my enemies with all my hart, but it is wholly impossible for human nature to forget peoples behaviour in things soe fresh in ones memory, soe far as to have a good oppinion of them, or any relyance on them, espesialy when one sees for all theire professions they are still pursueing ye same measures, & you may depend upon it they will allways do soe, for theire is no washing a Blackamore whit[e].
>
> I am truly sensible & thankfull for God Almighty['s] great Goodnes shower'd on your head & mine, & hope he will give me grace never to make an ill use of his Signall Blessings, *but I can never be Convinced that Christianity requres me, nor that it can be for my Service to putt my self intirly into ye hands of any one party.*[85]

In reply to the queen's letters, Marlborough responded that Sunderland had justified himself and, alluding to Harley's supposed influence with the queen, he went on,

> I did not flatter myself nobody could have prevailed with you, to carry your resentment so far against him [Sunderland] in my absence, as is mentioned in your letters, and to give me so great a mortification in the face of all Europe, at a time when I was so zealously endeavouring to serve you at the hazard of both my reputation and of my blood.

Marlborough added that his remark to Sarah ('if she will please to make use of itt') meant

> that you can make no good use of this victory, nor of any other blessing but by following the advice of my Lord Treasurer, who has been so long faithfull to you; for any other advisers do but lead you into a labyrinth, to play their own game at your expense. Nothing but your commands should have obliged me to say so much, having taken my resolution to suffer with you, but not to advise, being sensible that if there was not something very extraordinary, your Majesty would follow the advice of those that have served you so long, faithfully, and with success.[86]

The queen, in her reply to Marlborough of 6 August, denied that she was influenced by Harley and Abigail and pointedly asked Marlborough why it was 'something very extraordinary' that she did not automatically adopt his opinions:

And why then should it be wonderful that you and I should differ in some things, as well as other people, especially since my thoughts are the same of the Whigs that ever they were from the time that ever I have been capable of having notions of things and people; and I must own I can see no reason to alter mine.[87]

The queen's intransigence, her flat refusal to alter her 'notions of things and people', resulted in Marlborough yet again threatening to resign. Godolphin also threatened to retire if the queen did not agree to placate the Junto. On 27 August the queen wrote an impassioned appeal to Marlborough that he and the treasurer should 'not do an action that will bring me and your country into confusion'. Nevertheless, as she told Marlborough, she was adamant that she would make no further concessions to 'the five tyrannizing Lords' of the Junto.[88]

By the time the queen had pronounced this final defiance of the Junto, she had been forced to sever all but her formal connections with the Duchess of Marlborough. In 1707 Sarah had formed a firm friendship with Arthur Maynwaring[89] (her self-styled 'secretary'), a playwright and pamphleteer of note who was a close associate of the Junto, particularly of Somers; indeed, some non-Junto Whigs suspected that Somers was using Maynwaring's association with the duchess to serve his own ends.[90] Maynwaring proved to be a fatal influence on Sarah, feeding her passion and, if anything, making her more mercurial than before in her dealings with the queen. Shortly after the February crisis which resulted in Harley's resignation, Sarah returned to court and the queen 'put on a great smile . . . & she seem'd to be pleas'd'.[91] Sarah seized upon the queen's affability to solicit what she later invariably described as the queen's 'solemn promis': Sarah asked that, when she resigned her offices, the queen would distribute them among Sarah's daughters.

The Queen heard all I said but would not comply with my desire, not that she disaproved of it but out of seeming kindness, for she said she & I must never part, but upon my pressing her extreamly . . . att last the Queen promis'd that if I did ever leave her (which she stil continued to say cou'd never be), she wou'd give my employments to my children & she bound that promise with a solemn asservation upon which I kissed her hand.[92]

What also seems probable – although Sarah carefully avoided mentioning it in her subsequent accounts – was that the duchess also secured the renewal of the queen's offer of an annual pension of £2,000.

It will be recalled that, in 1702 when Sarah was at the height of royal favour, the queen had offered her a secret pension from the privy purse in lieu of the £5,000 annual pension to Marlborough which the Tories in the House of Commons had blocked. Sarah at that time had refused the offer but, as she recorded in her *Conduct*, when she was finally dismissed from office in January 1711, she sent the last volume of her privy purse accounts to the queen, with a copy of the queen's letter offering the pension and with £18,000 deducted from the privy purse in payment of that debt. Unfortunately, this last volume of Sarah's accounts, from January 1710 to January 1711, has not survived. We will therefore be forced to follow the duchess's steps in her role as keeper of the privy purse in some detail during the latter years of her tenure. On 18 March 1708, ten days after the sixth anniversary of the queen's accession, the duchess paid herself £12,000, the largest single withdrawal recorded in the extant account books.[93] The coincidence of the date suggests that this was a first payment of the promised pension.

If this payment marked a partial restoration of the friendship between the queen and the duchess, it did not last long. Shortly after, Sarah discovered that Abigail had moved into part of the duchess's lodgings at Kensington (which Sarah rarely used, preferring to stay at St James's 'because I was so ill with the Queen'). When Sarah expostulated with the queen, the response was that a mistake had been made. Sarah again checked her facts, again went to the queen, and a violent argument between the two women ensued. Sarah promptly retired from court, and on 29 March wrote to the queen to announce her intention not to return.[94]

The queen was at the end of her patience, and on 10 April she wrote to the duchess, placing the major blame for the quarrel on Sarah:

> I am very sory all I can say will not prevail with you to live with your
> faithfull Morly as we did Seven yeare agoe, that being ye Manner I am
> & shall allways be desirous to live with you, & whenever you will be
> easy with me I will be soe to[o] . . . it has not bin my fault, that we
> have lived in ye Manner we have don ever since I came to the
> Crown.[95]

Both Maynwaring and Sunderland urged the duchess to return to court, Sunderland advising his mother-in-law that despite her loss of the queen's favour 'sure it would be right to endeavour to deceive the world, at least in this point'.[96] Maynwaring gave the duchess advice in dealing with Abigail which Sarah was to follow with fatal results: 'A good ridicule has often gone a good way in doing a business; and this I am sure is of such a kind, that it needs only to be mentioned to make it ridiculous.'[97] Apparently, Sarah attempted another reconciliation with the queen, for one Whig reported on 20 April: 'Her Grace ye D[uchess] of M[arlborough] is constantly again with ye Queen at Court; & we hope all things will hold as well as they are if not mend.'[98]

It was at this point that Sarah discovered that Abigail, despite the queen's assurances to the contrary, had reoccupied her own apartments at Kensington. Sarah again retired angrily from court, and on 22 May, fearing the consequences of a total disruption of their association, the queen addressed a remarkable plea to her groom of the stole, begging 'for Jesus Sake, that you would not give way to these dismall unkind thoughts of leaveing me'.[99] On the same day, the queen appealed to Godolphin to mediate between her and the duchess, who was 'againe relapsed into her cold unkind ways'. Significantly, the queen's concern was not so much to retrieve Sarah's friendship as to prevent disagreeable gossip when it became known that the duchess no longer visited her privately:

> She may impose upon some poor Simple people, but how can she emagin she can on any that has a grain of sense, can she think the D[uchess] of Somerset & my Lady Fitz[harding] (who are two of ye most observeing, pryeing Ladys in England) wont find out that she never coms neare me, nor looks on me as she used to do, nor that ye tateling Vice [Vice-Chamberlain Peregrine Bertie] will not in a litle time make us ye Jest of the town, some people will blame her, others me, & a great many both, what a disagreable noise will She be ye occassion of makeing in ye world, besides God knows what ill consequences it may be off, therfore for God Almightys sake, for the Duke of Marlboroughs, your own, & my poor sake endeavour all you can to perswaid Mrs. Freeman out of this strange unreasonable resolution.[100]

Nothing could restrain Sarah in the heat of anger against the queen. As we have seen, the duchess sent to the queen Marlborough's letter of 1 July, written immediately after the battle of Oudenarde ('if she will please to make use of itt'); Sarah's accompanying explanation, as she subsequently complained to the queen, 'put your Majesty into soe much passion that you quite mistook the whole meaning of the letter'. Sarah, as she reconstructed her original note,

> added that it made me melancholly when I reflected that after three such battles won for your servisses, hee apprehended that hee had not much credit with you or that the influence of some ill meaning people might disappoint whatever your most faithfull servants could doe; that I knew your Majesty's answer to this would bee, that there were noe such people, but everybody knows that impressions must be given by somebody, that the object of the Prince's favour [George Churchill] had so sad a character in the world that it could not bee supposed to take informations from him; and since you would not indure to have one

think you suffered your own faverit [Abigail] to talk to you upon anything of businesse, what account could bee given of your Majestys doing contrary to the advise of soe many of your most considerable subjects and old experienced friends?[101]

The queen apparently returned no answer to this diatribe, which infuriated the duchess even more. Shortly before the end of July, in one of her rare appearances at court, Sarah showed the queen two current ballads, one attacking Harley ('Verses upon Mr. Harley being Lord Treasurer') and the other ridiculing Abigail ('A New Ballad to the tune of Fair Rosamond'). The latter – probably written by Maynwaring – was particularly libellous:

> When as Queen Anne of great Renown
> Great Britain's Scepter sway'd,
> Besides the Church, she dearly lov'd
> A Dirty Chamber-Maid.
>
> O! Abigail that was her Name,
> She stich'd and starch'd full well,
> But how she pierc'd this Royal Heart,
> No Mortal Man can tell.
>
> However, for sweet Service done
> And Causes of great Weight,
> Her Royal Mistress made her, Oh!
> A Minister of State.
>
> Her Secretary she was not
> Because she could not write
> But had the Conduct and the Care
> Of some dark Deeds at Night.[102]

Not content with merely showing the ballads to the queen, in an explanatory letter on 26 July Sarah directly accused the queen of lesbian tendencies.

and tho your Majesty was pleased to desire me not to speake any more of her [Abigail], which I know to bee her own request & what would bee of great advantage to all her designs if she could obtain it, yet I must humbly beg pardon if I cannot obay that command, the rather because I remember you said att the same time of all things in this world, you valued most your reputation, which I confess surpris'd me very much, that your Majesty should so soon mention that word after having discover'd so great a passion for such a woman, for sure there

275

can bee noe great reputation in a thing so strange & unaccountable, to say noe more of it, nor can I think the having noe inclenation for any but of one's own sex is enough to maintain such a charecter as I wish may still bee yours.

Such a charge, odious between equals, was insupportable from a subject to a sovereign. But Sarah's wrath did not stop there. Claiming that the queen, working in league with Harley and Abigail, had attempted to dismiss Marlborough and Godolphin, Sarah warned the queen: 'I earnestly desire of your Majesty not to make a second tryall of removing them, which will certainly cost you much dearer than the last.'[103]

The queen returned no reply to this remarkable invective, and Marlborough warned his wife: 'You say Mrs. Morley has taken no notice of your letter. I think that is a trew sign she is angry.' He believed that Abigail was depicted as telling the morganatic wife of Louis XIV: trouble ourselves to no purpose'.[104] Neither Sarah nor Maynwaring, however, were willing to drop the theme which suggested that the relationship between the queen and Mrs Masham had a sexual basis. Shortly after this incident, a pamphlet (probably written by Maynwaring) appeared in London entitled *The Rival Dutchess: Or Court-Incendiary: A Dialogue between madam Maintenon, and Madam M*, in which Abigail was depicted as telling the morganatic wife of Louis XIV: 'Especially at Court I was taken for a more modish lady, was rather addicted to another Sort of Passion, of having too great a Regard for my own Sex, insomuch that few People thought I would ever have Married.'

The queen never forgave Sarah for making such accusations, and here personal contact between the two women came to an end until 19 August, the day scheduled for the thanksgiving services at St Paul's for the victory at Oudenarde. The queen had spent most of the summer at Windsor, where she was nursing the prince, whose chronic respiratory problems were becoming much worse. Weary from the long coach ride to St James's, where she was to dress for the ceremony, the queen declined to wear the heavy jewels which Sarah, as groom of the stole, had laid out for her. The duchess interpreted this refusal as a new example of Abigail's power, and as the queen, accompanied by Sarah and the Countess of Burlington, rode in the royal coach through the London streets to St Paul's, an argument broke out between the queen and the duchess. As they arrived at the cathedral, Sarah apparently said to the queen, 'Be quiet!', for fear that their altercation would be overheard. The queen was greatly offended. She sat through the sermon preached by William Fleetwood, Bishop of St Asaph, a personal encomium to Marlborough as 'a most Valient, Wise and Fortunate Commander, crowned with Fresh Laurels every other Year, because it seems they wither faster in our unkindly Climate than elsewhere'.[105] The return of the royal party to St James's was hindered by the popular demonstrations of joy, 'the crowds of people which followed Her Majesty's carriage being so great that it could scarcely move'.[106]

The duchess, because 'our conversations of late are so disagreeable',[107] had previously considered sending to the queen Marlborough's letter of 9/20 August, in which he said that 'I am so tired of what I hear, and what I think must happen in England' that he would seize the earliest opportunity to retire. 'I must be in some maner answerable for the actions of *the queen*', Marlborough wrote to Sarah, 'who is noways governed by anything I can say or do. God knows who it is that influences, but as I love her and my country, I dread the consequences.'[108] Two days after the thanksgiving confrontation, Sarah forwarded this letter to the queen with a sarcastic covering note, complaining that 'your Majesty chose a very wrong day to mortify me, when you were Just going to return thanks for a victory obtained by Lord Marlborough'.[109]

The Queen's response was chilling:

> After the commands you gave me on the thanksgiving day of not answering you, I shou'd not have troubled you with these lines, but to return the D: of Marlboroughs letter safe into your hands, & for the same reason do not say anything to that nor to yours which enclosed it.[110]

Sarah attempted to explain, rather unconvincingly, that she had feared that she and the queen would be overheard at St Paul's, but realizing that she had overstepped the bounds of decorum, attempted to make apologies:

> The word command which you use in the begining of your leter, is very unfitly supposed to come from me, for tho I have allways writt to you as a friend & lived with you as such, so very many yeares, with all the truth & honesty & Zeal for your serviss that was possible, yet I shall never forget that I am your subject, nor ever cease to bee a faithful one.[111]

Although the queen chose not to respond to Sarah's letter, she did take Marlborough's attitude to heart. On 27 August she appealed to the captain-general not to retire:

> I am sorry to find you in such a spleenytick way as to talk of retireing, it being a thing I can never consent to, & what your country nor your truely faithfull friends can never think right, what ever melancholy thoughts they may have all this time, besides in my poor opinion, when after all the Glorious successes God Allmighty has blessed you

277

with, hee is pleased to make you the hapy instrument of giveing a
lasting peace to Europe, you are bound in conscience both to God &
man to lend your helping hand & how can you doe that if you retire
from businesse.[112]

The queen found herself in an alarming dilemma. She did not wish
for, nor could she afford, Marlborough's resignation. Yet her personal
relationship with Sarah – her groom of the stole, first lady of the bedchamber, keeper of the privy purse – had broken down irretrievably. If
Sarah was to be retained in office (and such, the queen believed, was the
price to be paid for Marlborough's retention at the head of the Army),
personal contact between the two women would, of necessity, continue.
Sarah's offices were closely concerned with the queen's private business
and comfort. At the same time, Sarah was being encouraged to continue
her assaults upon the queen by Arthur Maynwaring, who wrote to the
duchess:

since Mrs. Morley disclaims so loudly the influence of Mr. Harley &
since the object of the Prince's affection [George Churchill] is so freshly
discovered in such notorious falshoods that she must be ashamed to
own herself directed by him, who in the Name of God can she pretend
advises her contrary to the opinion of all her Ministers & Council?[113]

On 4 September, Peregrine Bertie, the vice-chamberlain of the household, told Maynwaring that 'the Dutchess of Marlborough has lately had
two terrible Battles with the Queen, & that she came out from her in
great heat, & when the Queen was seen afterwards her Eyes were red, &
it was plain she had been crying very much'.[114] The subject of these
battles is best illustrated by Sarah's 'Heads of the Conversation with
Mrs. Morley', dated 9 September 1708:

No body countenanced, or trusted by her but who is some way or
other influenced by Mr. Harly.
    Mr. Harley never had a good reputation in the world . . . but since
hee was tempted by the favour of Abigaill to sett up for himself & to
betray & ruin those that had brought him into her servise, & her servise
itself allsoe, nobody alive can either bee more odious than hee is, or
more contemptable to all partys. . . . [115]

This conversation, not surprisingly, produced yet another rupture in
the relations between the queen and the duchess; the latter retired to
Windsor Lodge for over six weeks. It was at this time that the duchess
began to make heavy financial inroads on the privy purse, presumably
to help finance the construction of Marlborough House, located cheek-
by-jowl with St James's Palace. In July 1703, Sarah had obtained from
the queen a promise of the reversion of a land grant in St James's Park,

originally given to Catherine of Braganza (who died in December 1705), on which the duchess might build a town house; to secure the land, Sarah had paid £2,000. On 18 August 1708 the privy purse paid the duchess £2,000 'being borrowed'. Her next withdrawal came ten months later, on 20 and 21 June 1709, when Sarah withdrew a total of £7,000; in July of that year, Sarah borrowed another £1,800 and in September and October she borrowed an additional £10,000, to make a total of £20,800.[116] These huge withdrawals (for which no repayments are shown in the extant records) began at the time when the duchess was securing the land and beginning the construction of Marlborough House[117] and, we must note, were in addition to the £12,000 paid to Sarah in March 1708. These payments were presumably made with the queen's knowledge, as she regularly checked and approved Sarah's privy purse account books, but as the quarrel deepened between the two women, the financial stakes correspondingly heightened.

In the autumn of 1708 domestic politics were temporarily suspended as the queen – and Britain with her – closely followed the fortunes of Marlborough's siege of Lille, the strongest fortress in Europe and one which was considered impregnable. Lille was invested on 2/13 August, and on 12/23 October the second largest city in France surrendered to Marlborough. It was the greatest loss of French territory which Louis XIV had so far sustained in his long and glorious reign. Even before this great triumph, however, the queen was distracted by the rapid decline of her husband's health. In the early autumn, 'a dropsical humour . . . seized his Legs, this was attended with a sleepiness, Cough, and an encrease of his Asthma'.[118] On 4 October, Godolphin notified Marlborough: 'The Prince has been very ill of a violent cold, and the Queen much alarmed at it. But he is much better.'[119] Due to the prince's illness, the queen did not attend the christening on 5 October of Abigail Masham's first child, a daughter to whom the queen was to be godmother (Lady Frescheville acted as the queen's proxy).[120] The queen's gift of eighty ounces of gilt plate (worth £40)[121] compared poorly with the 1,000 guineas which she had presented the year before to the Marlborough's youngest daughter, Lady Monthermer, on the birth of her first child.[122] Nevertheless, as Lord Dartmouth later recorded, at night Abigail 'slept on a pallet in the ante room of her Majesty's bedroom within call; the Queen often supported Prince George when he was labouring under the dreadful attacks of asthma, and she required some help beyond what her strength could afford'.[123]

On 23 October the prince became seriously ill,[124] and two days later Godolphin warned Sarah: 'The Prince seems to bee in no good way at all (in my opinion) as to his health, and I think the Queen herself seems now much more apprehensive of his condition, than I have formerly remembered upon the same occasion.'[125] The duchess, alarmed at the adverse publicity which might result if she should be absent from court at such a crucial moment, wrote to the queen on 26 October:

> Tho the last time I had the honour to waite upon your Majesty your usage of me was such as was scarse possible for me to imagin or for any body else to believe, yet I can not hear of so great a misfortune & affliction to you, as the condition which the Prince is in, without coming to pay my duty in inquiring after your health, & to see if in any particular whatsoever my service can either bee agreeable or usefull to you, for which satisfaction I would doe more than I will trouble your majesty to read att this time.

To guard against the possibility of a royal rebuff, the duchess travelled during the night from Windsor Lodge to Kensington, where on the morning of 27 October she gave her letter to Mrs Danvers, 'after I had inquired after the Queen & Prince, & desired her to send to me if Her Majesty had any commands for me, which she did in the evening, & I waited upon her in her closset, but she received me very coldly, & like a stranger'.[126] This reception was not surprising, considering both the tenor of the duchess's letter and the fact that the queen was exhausted, having spent the whole of the previous night at her husband's bedside. On the night of 27 October the queen again personally nursed her husband, in Bishop Burnet's words, 'with such care and concern, that she was looked on very deservedly as a pattern in this respect'.[127] At half past one on the afternoon of 28 October 1708,[128] the prince died in his fifty-sixth year and after a quarter of a century of marriage to the queen. 'His death', it was reported,

> has flung the Queen into an unspeakable grief. She never left him till he was dead, but continued kissing him the very moment his breath went out of his body, and 'twas with a great deal of difficulty my Lady Marlborough prevailed upon her to leave him.[129]

This moment marked the nadir of the queen's life. She had lost eighteen children; her dearest friend and confidante had become estranged from her; her own health was precarious and she was to a great extent living the life of an invalid. Now her husband, her partner in a marriage which scandal had never touched and in which harmony had reigned, was taken from her. Inevitably, this final tragedy temporarily broke the spirit of this 'poor mean-like Mortal'; but it did not break her will to be recognized as 'one of the Rulers of the World'.

11

'A Very Disconsolate Condition'

The Triumph of the Whigs,
November 1708 – November 1709

After the death of Prince George in October 1708, Queen Anne was isolated, both politically and – to a large extent – personally: as Abigail Masham wrote to Harley, 'my poor aunt [the queen] is in a very deplorable condition, for now her ready money [courage] is all gone. . . . She has shut and bolted the door upon herself.' To be sure, her once close friend the Duchess of Marlborough had intruded, uninvited, into the prince's last hours and afterwards had taken care, as Abigail complained, that the queen should not be left alone, 'for since the misfortune the Lady Pye [Sarah] has hardly left her so long as to let her say her private prayers but stays constantly with her'.[1] Immediately after the prince's death, Sarah later recalled that she led the queen from his bedchamber

> into her closet at Kensington . . . then I knelt down to the Queen and said all that I could imagine from a faithful servant, and one that she had professed so much kindness to; but she seemed not to mind me, but clapt her hands together, with other marks of passion; and when I had expressed all I could think of to moderate her grief, I knelt by her without speaking for some time, and then asked her to go to St. James's; upon which she answered she would stay there. I said that was impossible; what could she do in such a dismal place? and I made use of all the arguments that are common upon that head, but all in vain; she persisted that she would stay at Kensington.[2]

Sarah attributed the queen's refusal to remove to St James's (where the duchess resided) to the 'fear she could not have so much of Mrs. Masham's company as she desired'. The queen then ordered Sarah to bring Masham to her, which the duchess later excused doing, as 'I thought it would make a disagreeable noise, when there were bishops and ladies of the bedchamber without, that she did not care to see'. Nevertheless, Abigail managed to be in the long gallery at Kensington as the queen was leaving for St James's and, as Sarah recorded of the queen,

> notwithstanding her great affection for the Prince, at the sight of that charming lady, as her arm was upon mine, which she leaned upon, I found she had strength to bend down towards Mrs. Masham like a sail, and in passing by, went some steps more than was necessary, to be nearer her.

Embittered by this slight, the duchess was led into the worst mistake and the least creditable action in her relationship with the queen: she consistently disparaged the queen's sorrow for the death of the prince. Sarah found it an 'extraordinary thought' that the queen should order Godolphin to check the vaults of Westminster Abbey to determine where the prince should be buried and where the queen could later join him. Sarah repeatedly referred to the fact that, despite her grief, the queen enjoyed a healthy appetite:

> When we came to St. James's, I carried her privately through my lodgings into her green closet, and gave her a cup of broth, and afterwards she ate a very good dinner, and at night I found her at a table again, where she had been eating.

Later, the queen sent the duchess a note, 'at which I could not help smiling':

> I Scratched twice at dear Mrs. Freemans door as soon as Ld Treasurer went from me, in hopes to have spoke one word more to him before he was gon, but no body heareing me, I writt this not careing to send what I had to say by word of mouth, which was to desire him that when he sends his orders to Kensington that I he desired, he would give directions there may be a great many yeomen of ye Guards to cary the Princes dear body that it may not be lett fall, ye Great Stairs being very Steep & Slipery.[3]

What would seem a normal precautionary step for any widow to take, made the duchess smile; when the queen looked into precedents for the prince's funeral (his body was removed from Kensington on 11 November and privately interred in the abbey on 13 November), Sarah thought this 'unusual and not very decent'. Sarah's concluding words on the topic of the queen and the prince were:

> I did see the tears in her eyes two or three times after his death, upon his subject, and, I believe, she fancied she loved him; and she was certainly more concerned for him than she was for the fate of Gloucester; but her nature was very hard and she was not apt to cry.[4]

Sarah's unsympathetic analysis of the queen's grief is contradicted by every contemporary authority.[5] When Archbishop Sharp, for example, arrived in London two weeks after the prince's death, he recorded: 'I waited upon the Queen, who received me very kindly. We both wept at my first coming in. She is in a very disconsolate condition.'[6] Sarah, however, was confident that she alone knew how to deal with grief and mourning. One of the duchess's first actions was to order the removal of the prince's portrait from the queen's bedchamber. The first letter which the queen wrote to the duchess after the prince's funeral concluded: 'I can not end this with out beging you once more for God sake to lett the Dear picture you have of mine, be putt into my Bedchamber for I can not be with out it any longer.' Sarah noted that she only took the portrait away 'because I thought she loved him, & if she had been like other people tis terrible to see a picture while the afliction is just upon one'.[7]

Given the past history of their relationship, and the scornful attitude which the duchess adopted towards the queen's loss of her husband, no reconciliation between the two women could last long. Predictably, by early December the duchess had again retired from court, this time in anger when the queen refused her request to give part of the stables at St James's to the Duke of Marlborough.[8] When Sarah left the court at this point, there was no longer any pretence of a friendship between the two women.

The prince's illness had weakened the queen's intransigence on political matters. Even before his death, on 22 October, she had finally agreed to appoint Halifax's brother, Sir James Montagu, as attorney-general in the place of Simon Harcourt.[9] The queen's resistance to further Whig incursions in her cabinet was broken by her husband's death; the Admiralty went automatically into commission and the queen became the last monarch to administer it personally until a successor was named.[10] On the first occasion when the secretary of the Admiralty brought papers for the queen to sign, as he had brought them to the prince previously, she broke into tears and the business had to be postponed.[11] The prince's death was particularly fortuitous for the Whigs, for it meant that the Earl of Pembroke could be placed at the head of a new Admiralty commission and his offices as lord president of the council and lord lieutenant of Ireland could be given to Somers and Wharton respectively. Nevertheless, the queen delayed two weeks before finally agreeing to the ministerial changes, and on 15 November Somers and Wharton kissed hands.[12] Marlborough, responding to this news, told Sarah: 'I should hope everything might mend, especially since you think that *Godolphin* is as well with *the queen* as ever. If that continues, *Abigail* may vex, but never do much mischief.'[13] The Whigs, aided and abetted by Godolphin, had cold-bloodedly used the prince's death as an opportunity to ride roughshod over the queen's wishes and to limit the prerogative of the crown by establishing a clearly Whig party government. Despite the queen's demonstrated tenacity in the past, the Whigs still believed that the Duumvirs possessed paramount influence with her, and they consistently underrated her constancy and determination. As Sunderland had told Sarah a few months earlier of the Tories: 'I believe they nor any other Party don't much value Mrs. Morley's never forgiving them, because they all know that goes backwards & forwards, just as those that govern her think it for their interest.'[14]

The queen, however, was quickly to prove her determination again. By temporarily assuming the management of the Admiralty herself, she made it clear that she regarded it as her own special prerogative to vindicate the memory of the prince. By contrast, the Junto were determined to secure control of naval affairs for one of their members, the Earl of Orford, one of the prince's leading critics. The queen regarded Pembroke's appointment as first lord on 29 November as a reward for a faithful servant, who was also a moderate, while the Whigs regarded it merely as a stop-gap measure.[15] The struggle raged on throughout 1709, with the Whigs increasing their pressure upon the queen and Godolphin, until Pembroke voluntarily resigned in October; even then, the queen battled on for another month against giving subordinate offices under Orford to two leading critics of the prince's regime, Sir George Byng and Sir John Jennings. Finally, in November, an agreement was reached by which Orford was willing to become first lord.[16] By then, only one Junto member, Halifax, was not in the cabinet.

In her struggles against Whig encroachments, it is impossible to know how much 'backstairs' advice the queen received from Robert Harley. As noted earlier, Harley, on his own testimony, had 'no sort of communication' with the queen from the time of his dismissal until October 1708.[17] Then, as Abigail reported to him, the queen rejected Harley's 'wise and good advice'.[18] The burden of Abigail Masham's surviving letters to Harley throughout 1709 was that the queen was reluctant to negotiate directly with her former secretary of state. On 9 August, for example, Abigail informed her mentor that she had read his letter to the queen,

> who wants such good instructions, and though she has had the same advice last year, yet I think it cannot be too often repeated to one that shows so little courage and resolution as she has hitherto done. . . . As for your writing a letter for me to show my friend, you had better not do it, for I fear she will be afraid of being examined about it, so I dare answer she would much rather know nothing of the matter.[19]

Certainly, except as a conduit for Harley, Abigail exercised little political influence over the queen. 'She keeps me in ignorance', Abigail complained to Harley, 'and is very reserved, does not care to tell me any thing.'[20] In one undated, and undatable, letter, Abigail summarized her own subordinate status and the queen's lack of reliance on her:

> I wou'd fain have enter'd into some discourse which might have led us
> to have talk'd of the main point in hand, but whenever I said anything
> relating to business, She answer'd 'pray goe for if You begin to talk
> you will make it soe late I shall not gett to bed in any time', tho I think
> she is in good humour and has not a disponding countenance as
> sometimes she has.[21]

It would appear that, in her struggles with the Duumvirs and the Junto throughout 1709, the queen had only indirect advice from Harley and that his secret visits to her were rare.

Domestic politics during this period were largely overshadowed by the approaching climax of the war against Louis XIV and the prospect of international peace. In the parliamentary session of 1708–9 which opened on 16 November, the Tories were reduced to an ineffective minority. To forestall any new proposal for an invitation to Hanover, Whig majorities in both houses introduced and passed addresses asking the queen to remarry in order to produce an heir, however unlikely that prospect might be. The queen perfectly understood the parliamentary tactics involved, but the necessity of such an address – and the consequent notoriety – undoubtedly rankled; as Peter Wentworth, one of the late prince's equerries, reported to his brother, 'They cry'd about the street *The hasty Widdow or the Sooner the Better*; there was nothing in the paper but a parcel of proverbs, but the impudence was the title and coming out after the Address to the Queen.'[22] More importantly for the future, a resolution of both houses defined the minimum British terms for a European peace: Louis XIV should recognize the queen's title and the Protestant succession as by law established, remove the Pretender from his dominions, destroy the harbour and fortifications of Dunkirk, and recall Philip V from Spain.

By the time this resolution was passed in March 1709, it seemed that France was on the brink of collapse. The winter of 1708–9 was one of the most severe in modern European history: in London, the Thames froze solid, as did the Seine in Paris. In France, after a February thaw, there was a second severe freeze which effectively destroyed all spring crops. In addition, the financial strain of maintaining armies on four fronts against a European coalition had proved to be too much for the French treasury. To stave off bankruptcy, Louis XIV was reduced to melting down the famous silver furniture which had decorated the Galerie des Glaces in the château of Versailles. In March 1709, questioning whether France and the absolutist system could weather the strain of another campaign, Louis dispatched one of his leading diplomats, Pierre Rouillé, to The Hague to open secret peace negotiations with the Dutch. For the first time in his long reign, Louis appeared in the guise of a suppliant. The allies were convinced that France would be forced to accept peace at any price, and the allied demands escalated accordingly. In London, as spring brought welcome relief from the rigours of the harsh winter, it was universally assumed that peace was at hand, and new questions were emerging concerning the future.

Twenty years of warfare had greatly expanded the role and the power of the central state in English life. If Britain and her allies should secure their demands of France, would Britain then revert, as she had after the peace of Ryswick in 1697, to a peace-time economy and political organization? Or would those men who had profited from the war, particularly the military leaders, retain a leading position in the nation? These were not theoretical questions, but real issues which closely touched the royal prerogative and therefore the queen. They were brought home to her by the actions of her longstanding friend and advisor, Marlborough, probably when he returned home from the Continent on 1 March 1709. Sometime during this visit, Marlborough asked the queen to give him the office of captain-general for his lifetime. The nature and extent of Marlborough's request, although recently explored by Professor Snyder,[23] remain shadowy, because Marlborough later destroyed the pertinent correspondence and on this ocasion, significantly, did not confide in either Godolphin or Sarah. Marlborough believed that the grant of his office for his lifetime would demonstrate that his influence with the queen had not declined and it would fortify his personal position as head of the Grand Alliance. What he did not foresee was that his request would alienate the queen.

To the queen's mind, the equation was simple: Marlborough's request was unprecedented and outside the scope of the constitution. The monarch could not grant offices beyond her own lifetime; to do so would require ratification by Act of Parliament. The support of the Whig majorities in both houses would be necessary to secure the passage of such an Act, and the end result would be the permanent militarization of the state in alliance with the Whigs. To give Marlborough his position for life would put him outside the control of the crown and monarch. For the generation which grew up in the shadow of Cromwell, 'no standing army' was an absolute article of political faith. Later, when the news of Marlborough's request became public knowledge, the Tories referred to him as 'Oliver' or, more sinisterly, 'King John'.[24] It is improbable that the queen accepted their more radical propaganda, that Marlborough aimed at the throne itself; but it is clear that she was deeply disturbed by his request. When Marlborough first made it, the queen appeared ambivalent and suggested that Marlborough should search for legal precedents for such an action. In fact, she was inwardly alarmed and immediately consulted her new lord president, one of the foremost lawyers of his day, and the head of the Whig party, John, Lord Somers. Somers, according to Lord Dartmouth, told the queen of 'the danger she ran' if Marlborough's attempt to pass his grant through Parliament should succeed, 'which put an effectual stop, and gave the Queen a grateful sense of Lord Somer's fidelity and integrity ever after'.[25] During the course of the peace negotiations at The Hague during the spring of 1709, Marlborough consulted both the lord chancellor, Cowper, and his own 'man of business', James Craggs the elder, asking them to seek out legal precedents. They both discouraged Marlborough from pursuing the topic futher; but although Marlborough assured Cowper that 'I have so great a . . . deference to your Judgement, that I intierly submit to it, and shal think no more of that matter',[26] he continued to pursue the issue with the queen. The extent of the queen's anxiety might be measured by the fact that, for the first time in her reign, she began to take a direct, active role in the distribution of Army commands. In May 1709, General George Maccartney, one of Marlborough's favourite commanders, was convicted in London of raping his housekeeper, a parson's widow. On the advice of Henry Compton, Bishop of London, the queen relieved Maccartney of his positions as commander of an expedition to Newfoundland and Governor of Jamaica.[27] Marlborough's closest associates in the administration attempted to induce the queen to reverse her ruling, without success. Although Robert Walpole, secretary at war, spoke to the queen strongly on Maccartney's behalf, 'the Queen is not to be prevail[ed] on to pardon him'.[28] In the summer Godolphin informed Marlborough that 'for all the Duke of Somerset and I could say together t'other day in his [Maccartney's] behalf, wee could not gett the Queen to say she would ever employ him again'.[29] In this small but clear way, the queen was demonstrating to Marlborough that she was still the titular and actual head of the Army.

The struggle between the queen and the captain-general was still below the surface and unknown to the public, when the leaders of the Grand Alliance gathered at The Hague in April 1709 to negotiate with the representatives of Louis XIV. Heinsius for the Dutch and Prince Eugene for the imperialists were joined by Marlborough and an additional British delegate upon whom the ever-suspicious Junto lords had insisted, Charles, Viscount Townshend.[30] In early May, Louis XIV dispatched his secretary for foreign affairs, the Marquis de Torcy, to The Hague. The allied demands were enormous: the Imperialists demanded the restoration of all Habsburg losses since 1648, while the Dutch and the British demanded extensive commercial concessions from both France and Spain. Most importantly, the allies supported the British demand of 'No Peace without Spain': the entire Spanish monarchy was to be handed to 'Carlos III', while Philip V was to receive no compensation whatsoever. The forty preliminary articles agreed upon by the allies demanded that Louis XIV immediately hand over to the allied armies in Flanders four 'cautionary' towns, to be held for two months while Louis recalled his grandson from Spain; should Philip V refuse to sacrifice his empire without compensation, the war would recommence with the allies in a position to invade France and capture Paris. Marlborough was so confident that peace was at hand that he asked Sarah to arrange for the shipment of his plate, chair of state, and canopy as ambassador extraordinary to the Dutch republic in order that he would be prepared for the formal signature of a peace treaty.[31] Marlborough's confidence was reflected throughout London, based both on popular war-weariness and the conviction that Philip V was essentially his grandfather's puppet.

The first blow to public confidence came on 17/28 May, when the allies presented the forty preliminary articles to the French delegates and Torcy refused to sign them, warning the allies that his master might refuse to accept such onerous terms. In truth, Louis XIV knew that Philip V would not give up the Spanish throne voluntarily, and Louis refused to use French troops against his own grandson. On 24 May/4 June, Louis publicly rejected the preliminary articles and, in an unprecedented appeal to his people, issued a manifesto to be read throughout his kingdom, summoning his subjects to give their last exertions in defence of *la patrie*. Even this news could not suppress the conviction in the highest circles in London that France was on the verge of collapse and that 'ye Peace is not far off'.[32] Godolphin, for instance, assured his supporter, Lord Coningsby:

> I can hardly yett bring my self [to think] the French will persist in not signing the preliminarys, nothing but the hopes of peace has kept their people within any bounds for this last month, and if they find themselves like to bee disappointed, I believe we shall hear of no small disorders in that kingdome, & if to that a blow be added from without, their government is in danger of being changed.[33]

288

There is no direct evidence of the queen's attitude to the collapse of The Hague negotiations, but there is little reason to doubt that she agreed with Godolphin's assessment of the situation and hoped, as did most of her subjects, that France would not be able to weather another campaign.

On 24 August/4 September, the French Army of Flanders under the command of the Maréchal-Duc de Villars met the allied armies under the command of Marlborough and Eugene in the battle of Malplaquet, the bloodiest in Europe in the eighteenth century. Both sides claimed a victory, the French because their army retired with its formations intact, the allied because the French losses of 25,000 men exceeded those of the allies, who lost 20,000 soldiers. Whatever the military results, the political consequences of Malplaquet were enormous: this conclusive proof that France's will and ability to fight was not yet extinguished produced a psychological convulsion in Great Britain, and particularly in the Dutch republic which had sustained tremendous casualties. It appeared unlikely that the Dutch would remain in the war merely to support the British policy of 'No Peace without Spain'; because of the Francophile 'peace party' in the republic, both the French and the English had always regarded the States as the weak link in the allied chain. Now, determined to keep the republic in the Grand Alliance at any cost, the Whig cabinet agreed to enormous concessions in the first Anglo-Dutch Barrier Treaty, signed by Townshend for Great Britain on 18/29 October. The Barrier Treaty gave the Dutch effective military and economic control over the Southern (soon to become the Austrian) Netherlands and was construed by the Tories as a serious blow to English commercial interest in the Low Countries. Godolphin, under the influence of Somers, approved of the Barrier Treaty.[34] Marlborough, knowing full well that such a treaty would be a target for serious objections in Parliament, refused to sign, telling the queen (according to Lord Dartmouth) that 'he would have lost his right hand rather than have signed it'.[35] Instead, contrary to the advice of both Cowper and Craggs, Marlborough renewed his request for the captain-generalcy for life. This time the queen flatly refused to grant it.[36] Her reaction to the news of Malplaquet is perhaps apocryphal, but nevertheless it mirrored the emotional state of her kingdoms: 'When will this bloodshed ever cease?'

Just as the war on the Continent seemed endless, so did the running confrontation at home between the queen and the Duchess of Marlborough. Though friendship was dead, the two women remained tied together as long as Marlborough was at the head of the Army. Sarah's conduct was becoming increasingly irresponsible. The queen gave orders that no ladies wearing colours were to be admitted to her presence during the official mourning for Prince George: 'the first night the Queen saw company upon her bed', Peter Wentworth reported to his brother, 'the Dutchess of Marlborough was the only one that had powder in her hair, or a patch upon her face'.[37] In dealing with Sarah in 1709, the queen pioneered the tactics which she was to employ in 1710 to undermine the status of Godolphin and Marlborough: she simply failed to honour the prerogatives, formal or informal, of Sarah's offices. In February 1709 the queen, without consulting Sarah as groom of the stole raised the salary of Mrs Elizabeth Abrahal, the royal laundress, which the duchess regarded as a plot put forward by Abigail.[38]

Sarah, of course, was furious at what she considered to be the queen's gross interference in her office, but for the moment she stayed her protests: the queen had indicated that she was willing to employ another bedchamber woman, a position for which there was general competition,[39] and Sarah saw an opportunity to establish a rival to Abigail's influence. The duchess's candidate was the sister of James Stanhope, Mary Fane, who before her marriage had been a maid of honour to the queen. In April, James Craggs reported to Stanhope:

> And now I will tell you a very great Secrett, The Duke, Duchess &
> Lord Treasurer made an Essay to bring your Sister Fane into the
> Queens Bedchamber, but the Queen avoyded it for this time (as she
> called it), which is no small indication of Mrs. Mashams power, who is
> afraid Her Majesty's inclinations would returne againe if she [Mrs
> Fane] were once about Her Majesty, but I dair say they won't rest till it
> is brought about.[40]

Having Sarah as one's champion was more hindrance than help, for the duchess now rarely visited the queen; often Sarah was absent from court for two or three months at a time.[41] On 24 July the queen coldly notified Sarah that she had decided to appoint Belle Danvers, the daughter of one of Sarah's enemies in the bedchamber:[42] Sarah was naturally vexed at what she considered to be a bold display of Abigail's power. Belle Danvers, 'who did not look like a human creature', in the next year was to marry John Harstonge, Bishop of Ossory, who in 1714 was created Bishop of Derry. According to Sarah's close friend, Lady Cowper,

> She married an Irish Bishop who hoped to have been made an English
> Bishop by marrying one of the Queen's Dressers; but, I don't know
> how it happened, he missed his Aim, and got only one of the fright-
> fullest, disagreeablest Wives in the Kingdom.[43]

On 31 July, Sarah visited Windsor to present Belle Danvers to the queen. In their conversation after the ceremony, the queen and the duchess fell into a violent argument. The queen later dispatched to Sarah an angry letter, the original of which has not survived but which Sarah summarized in her *Conduct*:

> . . . She charges me *with invetercy* (as her word is) *against poor Masham, and with having nothing so much at heart as the ruin of my cousin.* In speaking of the misunderstandings betwixt her Majesty and me, she says *they are for nothing that she knows of, but because she cannot see with my eyes, and hear with my ears.* And adds, *that it is impossible for me to recover her former kindness, but that she shall behave herself to me as the Duke of Marlborough's wife and her Groom of the Stole.*[44]

These were fighting words, and the passionate duchess was not one to ignore them. In her reply to the queen on 6 August, Sarah boldly proclaimed that Marlborough would always stand by her, even in her quarrel with the queen. She also hinted that she still had the queen's earlier letters in her possession and, after pointing out how badly used she had been in the appointments of Alice Hill and Belle Danvers, Sarah attacked the queen for raising Elizabeth Abrahal's salary ('I defy any body to shew that att any time, or in any reign that an inconsiderable under-officer had ever any sort of addition to their place without acquainting the principal').[45]

The queen returned no answer to this diatribe, but Sarah was not content to let the matter rest. On 18 August she, 'with much adoe', spent 'one whole hour at ye little House'.[46] Afterwards, Maynwaring informed Sarah, 'it was commonly reported that *Sarah* made at Windsor an open complaint of having been worse used than *the Duke of Somerset* or even the Bug [the Earl of Kent]', respectively master of the horse and lord chamberlain.[47] By now Sarah suspected that both the Duke and the Duchess of Somerset were secretly working to undermine her influence with the queen, and her suspicions were confirmed by Godolphin.[48]

At Windsor, the queen was depressed both physically and emotionally. On 14 September, Abigail reported to Harley, 'now She's afflicted with very sore eies which makes her mighty Malincholy together with the thoughts of Lady Pyes [Sarah] being to be near her this night and is to stay as long as my Aunt does'.[49] Apparently, the queen and the duchess did not meet again until after the queen's return to London. On 30 September the duchess waited on the queen to ask for some vacant rooms at St James's with which to expand her own apartments. When the queen refused her request, Sarah, 'being resolved that I would vex her a little longer', then asked the queen's permission to repeat their conversation publicly, confident that it would be thought strange 'that after the servise Lord Marlborough had done her, she would not give him a miserable hole to make him a clean way to his lodgings'. It was with great difficulty that the queen controlled her anger:

> Yes, she replyd, but she did not answer that without seeming to think, & looked extreamly disagreeable, then I made my chursey, saying I hoped she would some time or other reflect upon all that had passed, to which she made no reply but . . . dropt a churtsey.[50]

As well as threatening to cause disagreeable publicity, which the queen loathed, Sarah also apparently raised the lesbian question again. In a later letter, she reminded the queen that

> there was somthing so very unusuall in the manner of the last conversation I had the honour to have with your Majesty in your declaring that you would give no answer to whatever I said, & in the disorder that appear'd by your turning away from the candle when you thought I was going to mention a disagreeable subject,

presumably the queen's 'intimacy' with Abigail.

Not satisfied, on 16 October the duchess wrote the queen an extremely long letter, which began by complaining that the queen had not kept her promise to 'write me an answer to a great deal that I had said', attacked Harley for attempting to overthrow Marlborough and Godolphin ('I hope your Majesty will forgive the freedome of my expression, if I say never anybody was so much exposed as you were in all that proceeding'), and condemned Abigail and her supporters. In this letter Sarah repeated an earlier answer from the queen which lay at the heart of their dispute:

> I appeal to your Majesty if I have not often asked you what my fault was, for I was sure I could mend, & if you have not as often answered not, till one day upon such pressing you said it was that I beleived you had such an intimacy with Masham.[51]

To the queen, Sarah's actions had become 'teasing & tormenting'. But what was important was that Sarah had dragged her husband into the fray. On 29 September, Marlborough wrote a bitter letter to the queen, complaining of 'your Majestys Change from Lady Marlborough To Mrs. Masham, & the severall indignitys Mrs. Masham has made her suffer', as well as the queen's refusal to grant him the captain-generalcy for life ('this made me very uneasy but noe ways lessened my Zeal'). Marlborough explained that he had made his request because

> I was asured last winter of what I am convinced is true, that Mrs. Masham has asured Mr. Harley & some of his wretches that let my

servises or success's bee what they would, from thence forward I
should receive noe incouragement from your Majesty, which she was
very confydent must oblige me to retire.

Marlborough concluded his letter with a threat to resign on the
termination of the war,

hoping that in time you will bee sensible of the long & faithfull servises
of Lady Marlborough & that God will bless you with the opening of
your eyes, so that you may avoid the danger these people are running
you into.[52]

The queen had reached the limits of her patience with both the duke
and the duchess. Her answer to Marlborough, written on 25 October
after a long delay, was remarkable for the absence of her beseeching
pleas of the past that Marlborough should not resign; indeed, the tenor
of her response indicates that she was fully prepared to part with the
duchess and, while holding open the hope that she might relent on the
captain-generalcy, if needs be part with Marlborough himself:

I am very Sory for ye resolution you have taken of quiting my Service
when ye War is ended. . . . It is not to be wonderd that you should be
so incensed against poor Masham since the Dutchesse of Marlborough
is soe & has used her soe very hardly as she has done for some yeares
past, which I know she dos not deserve, but it is vaine to go about
vindicateing one against whom there is soe great a prejudice, onely this
I must say, that I dare be answerable, She never said to Mr. Harley or
any body, what you are informed She did. . . .
   I saw very plainly your uneasynes at my refuseing ye Mark of
fayvour you desired, & beleeved by another letter I had from you on
that subject you fancyed that advice came from Masham, but I do
assure you, you wrong her most exstreamly, ffor upon my word she
knows nothing of it & as I told you in another letter, what I said was
my own thoughts, not thinking for your Service nor mine to do a thing
of that Nature, however if when you come home you still continue in
ye same mind, I will Comply with your desires.

The queen had no intention of allowing Marlborough's criticism of her
treatment of Sarah to go unanswered. In terms reminiscent of those
employed by Queen Mary in 1692, the queen reminded Marlborough
that she was the sovereign and should be treated with due respect:

You seem to be disatisfyed with my behaviour to the Dutchesse of
Marlborough. I do not love Complaineing, but it is impossible to help
saying on this occassion, I beleeve no body was ever soe used by a
freind as I have bin by her ever since my coming to ye Crown. I desire
nothinge but that she would leave off teasing & tormenting me &

293

behave herself with the desensy she ought both to her freind & Queen, & this I hope you will make her do, & is what I am sure no reasonable body can wonder I should desire of you, whatever her behaviour is to me, mine to her shall be always as becoms me.

I shall end this letter as you did yours to me, wishing both your eyes & the Dutchesse of Marlboroughs may be opened & that you may ever be happy.[53]

The brutal frankness of the queen's letter must have shocked Marlborough, as it appears likely that he did not know the details of the duchess's vituperative exchanges with the queen. Certainly, when he returned to London early in November he was temporarily successful in forcing Sarah to stop her letter writing campaign. Unfortunately, the queen's letter to Marlborough of 25 October was dispatched to the captain-general only one day before Sarah initiated the next stage of the correspondence battle. The royal seamstress, Mrs Anne Rainsford, was near death; 'that place', the duchess warned the queen, 'is in the disposal of my office as much as a footman in the Duke of Somersets', and she demanded that she be consulted, for fear that Mrs Masham would recommend Elizabeth Abrahal.[54] The queen's immediate reply was sarcastic and determined:

> You need not have bin in such hast for Rainsford is pretty well againe & I hope will live a great while, if she should dye, I will then turn my thoughts to consider who I know that I Could like in that place, that being a post that next to my bedchamber women is ye nearest to my person of any of my Servants, & I beleeve no body, nay even you yourself if you would Judg impartially, could think it unreasonable that I should take one in a place soe neare my person that weare agreeable to me.

The queen, for the first time, rebuked Sarah for her official conduct, pointing out that Somerset's recommendations were always submitted for the queen's final confirmation and sarcastically adding that Abigail 'will not goe about recommending any body'. If Mrs Rainsford should die, the queen concluded, 'I shall then hearken to no bodys recommendation but my own'.[55]

This answer incensed the duchess and was directly responsible for her self-styled 'Narrative' of 29 October. Sarah explained to Maynwaring her reasons for writing the 'Narrative', 'for tho it will never cure her passion, yet it does certainly keep it from being own'd in a disagreable manner, & the truths I tell her, tho it makes her hate me, makes it more easy for the ministers to govern her'.[56] The 'Narrative' was an extremely long and tedious recital in three parts, recounting Sarah's great services to the queen dating from the reign of James II, enjoining the queen to follow the precepts of *The Whole Duty of Man*, particularly those calling for self-examination and confession before receiving the Holy Sacrament, and establishing (to Sarah's own satisfaction) Mrs Masham's entire dominion over the queen ('such things can proceed from nothing but extravagant passion'). After copying some of the queen's earlier letters, Sarah ended the 'Narrative' with a threat which, in the context, intimated that she might publish the queen's letters:

> . . . I find by your last leter that there is an Expedient found for all manner of hardships & breaking the Custome in your great offices, since you are pleased to say that there is noe officer that has the intire disposall of anything under them, but that you may put in any one if you have a mind to it, & so far Mrs. Masham is in the right, for 'tis generally true, there being no law against it, but then it is as true that [if] you use that officer ill & unkindly & without reading any of the Narratives I send you, *I will appeal to the whole earth* (exsept my dear Cousen) whether Lord Marlborough or I have deserved hard usage from Mrs. Morley or from the Queen.[57]

The queen's first response to the 'Narrative' came on 7 November, in a letter in which she requested 500 guineas from the privy purse and 'a hundred gines to be sent to Mr. Gueche for ye Cure of my eyes'. She concluded, 'I have not yet had leasure to read all your paypers but as soon as I have I will writt you some answer.'[58] Four days later, the queen again promised to write an answer ('I hope you do not expect any answer to ye narative tho this goes by a safe hand, for it would take me up more time then I could get to day . . . but you shall have it as soon as it is possible'); the promise appeared in a business letter remarkable only for the conclusion, in which she for the last time revived the names which had been used so long: 'I have nothing more to add, but that I wish my self with my dear Mrs. Freeman, & am with all truth & tenderness your poor unfortunate faithfull Morly.'[59]

The queen could not realistically hope that this gesture would soften the duchess, nor did it. The 'profession at the end' merely emboldened the duchesss to write yet another letter, of the same length as the 'Narrative', attacking Abigail, summarizing Maynwaring's pamphlet, *Dialogue between Madame de Maintenon and Madam Masham* ('there is stuff, not fit to be mentioned, of passions between women'), and transcribing whole portions of *The New Atlantis*, a scurrilous semi-pornographic attack on the Marlboroughs written by one of Harley's agents, Della de la Rivière Manley.[60] On this note, the correspondence between the queen and the duchess ended, largely because Marlborough returned to London on 10 November and persuaded his wife that further communication would prove useless. He further promised the queen that

295

Sarah would never again write to her on political topics or about Mrs Masham.

Marlborough's return to England came at the moment when the Whigs had reached the zenith of their power: they had just forced the queen to include Orford in the cabinet and to accept his nominees as commissioners of the Admiralty. The queen felt that she had been reduced to a cypher. The cabinet approved the Queen's Speech, which she read when Parliament reassembled on 15 November. The speech referred to Malplaquet as 'a most remarkable Victory' and suggested that 'France is thereby become much more exposed and open to the impression of our arms and consequently more in need of a peace, than it was at the beginning of this campaign'. Maynwaring reported to the duchess that 'it was observed that she spoke it in a much fainter voice than she used to have, and her manner was more careless and less moving than it has been on other occasions',[61] perhaps reflecting the queen's personal disbelief in her cabinet's prophecies. On 22 November the queen attended a thanksgiving for Malplaquet at St Paul's, during which the Whig Dean of Peterborough, White Kennett, preached on Luke 17:17, 'in effect comparing the opponents of the ministry to the nine healed lepers who had neglected to give thanks to Christ'.[62] No one present realized that the weapon which the queen would use to break the Duumvirs and the Whigs was already at hand.

12

'Many Unkind Returns'

The Queen's Revenge,
November 1709 – January 1711

On 5 November 1709, the joint anniversary of the Gunpowder Plot of 1605 and the landing of William III at Torbay in 1688, a crypto-Jacobite fanatic, Dr Henry Sacheverell, preached by invitation of the Tory Lord Mayor in St Paul's Cathedral.[1] Sacheverell's sermon, 'The Perils of False Brethren both in Church and State', was a thinly veiled attack upon the government, the Revolution settlement, and – by implication – the Hanoverian succession. Sacheverell's audacity was quickly compounded by that of the lord mayor, who published the sermon: so great was public demand that an astounding 40,000 copies were printed.[2] The government, hoping to silence its clerical enemies, impeached Sacheverell for high crimes, apparently with the queen's approval. After his impeachment was brought before the House of Lords, she told Bishop Burnet that Sacheverell's 'was a bad sermon and that he deserved well to be punished for it'.[3]

The fundamental point of contention in Sacheverell's impeachment was whether the British monarchy was based on hereditary or parliamentary right. The Whigs, united in their interpretation of the Glorious Revolution, argued that James II had broken his fundamental contract with the English people; resistance to his illegal acts, therefore, had been justified, and William and Mary owed their title, as did Queen Anne, to a decision of Parliament. To buttress their case against hereditary right and to demonstrate that the queen reigned lawfully as a parliamentary monarch in contravention of her half-brother's strict hereditary claim, the Whigs announced that the warming-pan story was a convenient lie which had served its purpose in 1688; by doing this, they inadvertently weakened the Hanoverian settlement. The exposure of the warming-pan fraud revealed the Whigs as self-confessed liars, and left them open to Jacobite rebuttals that the son – whom the Whigs now recognized by implication as the hereditary heir – was being penalized for the sins of the father.

297

The several Tory views of the succession which Sacheverell's defenders exposed were not recognized in 1710 as conflicting, but they portended the ultimate Tory divisions and disasters of 1714–15. However, it was not the Pretender but the Church of England round which Harley and the Tories rallied. The Tories supported Sacheverell against a Whig attack on the political liberties of the Anglican clergy.[4] The impeachment of Sacheverell in December 1709 united the entire Tory party in opposition to the government. Harley himself was kept out of London by illness, and did not arrive in town until the first week in January 1710; in the absence of hard evidence, it seems probable that it was at this time that Harley began his surreptitious visits to the queen, initiating a secret consultative process which was to result in the dismissal of the Godolphin administration within the year.

Harley accomplished this feat, aided not only by the extraordinary public passions produced by the Sacheverell trial but also by the war-weariness of the English nation. Public expenditure had risen from £3 million in the last year of peace to £13 million;[5] the national debt was to rise from £10 million to £50 million during the queen's reign;[6] the harsh winter of 1708–9, which the Whig ministers believed had ruined France, had also crippled Britain; the price of grain rose astronomically and, by January 1710, had never been higher in London.[7] Private charity was diverted from native to alien recipients by the influx of 'poor Palatine' Protestant refugees; this in turn exacerbated the latent anti-German prejudice of the English public. The government's financial situation was so desperate, concluded one observer, that England would inevitably be forced to sue for peace after the 1710 campaign.[8] High taxes, declining trade, the growing scarcity of specie, and forced recruiting had rendered the war – and the Whig policies which perpetuated it – increasingly unpopular. Public discontent was inevitably fanned by jealousy of the Marlboroughs and their connections, who were allegedly prolonging the war for private profit: and in truth some of Marlborough's closest associates (including William Cadogan and James Brydges) made war profits through less than honourable means.[9] Universal disappointment at Louis XIV's rejection of The Hague preliminaries was largely vented upon the Duumvirs and, to a lesser extent, upon the Whigs whose policy 'No Peace without Spain' had really been responsible for the continuation of the war.

The opposition party which Harley created after 1708, therefore, was united by two principles: the queen should be liberated from the 'tyranny' of the Marlborough family and England should quickly be given a respite from war. These principles were inextricably linked in Harley's own mind, for as long as the war continued, Marlborough's presence in the Army was the *sine qua non* for the survival of any ministry. Harley's desire for peace was sincere and of long standing, but he also wished to drive Marlborough from public life. The heart of the opposition was composed of Harley's protégés who had left office with him in 1708: Henry St John, Simon Harcourt, and Thomas Mansell. Rochester, Nottingham (with whom Harley had never been on good personal or political terms), and William Bromley, the leaders of the High Church Tories, disliked Harley as the man who had split the Tory party in 1704: necessity, however, forced them to forgive him, for Harley offered them the only possible road back to the queen's favour – and to power.

Harley's most important converts between 1708 and 1710 were three great lords of the 'middle party', the Dukes of Shrewsbury, Somerset, and Argyll. All three men were staunch supporters of the Hanoverian succession; all were nominal Whigs; all possessed the open access to the queen which was still denied to Harley. Capturing these three magnates proved indispensable to Harley's return to power in 1710: his loss of their support was instrumental in his fall in 1714. Of the three, Charles Talbot, Duke of Shrewsbury, was by far the most important and influential. As we saw earlier, Shrewsbury had been vetoed by the Junto in 1706 when the Duumvirs had wished to bring him into government. By December 1707, Shrewsbury was corresponding with Buckingham, one of the promoters of Harley's coalition scheme, and was writing that 'men of moderation should be employed', sentiments which tallied exactly with those of the queen.[10] Throughout the summer of 1708, Shrewsbury privately corresponded with Harley,[11] but it was only after he had learned from the forthright Sarah herself that her credit with the queen was irretrievably lost that he moved into open opposition to the Whig ministry.[12] By the summer of 1709 the queen was frequently consulting Shrewsbury.[13]

Harley's second important convert was Charles Seymour, Duke of Somerset, who had won the queen's lasting gratitude in 1692 when he had loaned her Syon House after William and Mary had driven her from the Cockpit. Somerset, who became master of the horse in 1702, served the queen longer than any other minister; furthermore, the Duchess of Somerset, rather than Abigail Masham, had replaced Sarah as the queen's favourite companion.[14] Unfortunately for the historian it appears 'that a great number of letters from Queen Anne to Lady Elizabeth Percy, first wife of Charles, Duke of Somerset, had been burnt by his Grace's order' after the deaths of the two women.[15] Somerset had taken a leading role in driving Harley from the cabinet in 1708, but later became increasingly dissatisfied with the Duumvirs and the Junto.

Harley and his co-conspirators flattered Somerset's high estimate of his own abilities and reinforced his delusion that he would lead any ministry which replaced that of Marlborough and Godolphin.

The third 'man of the centre' was the head of the Campbells and a hereditary enemy of the Stuarts, John, Duke of Argyll. Immensely influential in Scotland,[16] Argyll was also covetous and grasping for power and honours: no government could entirely satisfy his desires and he was therefore the most irritating of friends but an even more dangerous enemy. Along with other military rivals of Marlborough (including the Earls of Peterborough, Orrery, and Rivers), Argyll was ripe for Harley's schemes. Even the diplomatic corps contained dissidents, for Lord Raby at Berlin was sympathetic to the former secretary of state.[17]

From the beginning of 1710, there were persistent rumours of ministerial changes in the offing and it was common knowledge that Harley was the queen's backstairs advisor.[18] To both the queen and Harley, it was obvious that the crucial power possessed by the Duumvirs was Marlborough's control of the Army. Indeed, without Harley's aid, the queen had made cautious moves towards breaking this during 1709, particularly by her blunt refusal to consider any employment for General Maccartney. She also intervened in more minor affairs. In April 1709, Peter Wentworth, who wished to sell his regiment because the prince's servants had not been paid their pensions, reported to his brother: 'Mr. Walpool told me that when he had ask't the Queen's leave by the Duke of Marlborough's order, she said, "Mr. Wentworth sell, he has not ask't my leave & I'll have nothing done in't till he speak[s] himself".'[19]

The death of the Earl of Essex on 10 January 1710 gave the queen an opportunity to challenge Marlborough directly. Essex held both a regiment and the lieutenancy of the Tower of London. Ordinarily the queen would have consulted with her captain-general in disposing of these positions. Marlborough planned to give the Tower to the Duke of Northumberland and, in an attempt to pacify Somerset, to give the regiment to Somerset's heir, Lord Hertford. One of the first candidates to visit Marlborough was Harley's close associate, the Earl Rivers, who requested Marlborough's support for the Tower governorship; Marlborough disingenuously replied that he would have no personal objections to Rivers's appointment. When the captain-general visited the queen on 13 January to recommend Northumberland, the queen replied that, as Malborough had assured Rivers that he had no objection to him, she had already appointed Rivers. To make it quite clear that her action was not accidental, the queen immediately following this interview, sent Marlborough a written order to appoint Captain John Hill, Abigail Masham's younger brother, as colonel of Essex's regiment. Marlborough rightly interpreted this order as a direct challenge to his authority in the Army, and on Saturday, 14 January, the duke and duchess retired from London to Windsor Lodge.

The queen, according to Dartmouth, was 'incensed beyond measure'[20] when Marlborough deliberately failed to attend the usual Sunday cabinet. He obviously hoped that his absence would disrupt the meeting, as it had in February 1708. It did not. The timidity of Godolphin and the 'lord treasurer's whigs', combined with the suspicion which the Junto members still entertained of Marlborough, led both groups to attempt a compromise. The following day, when Godolphin conferred with the queen, she did not mention Marlborough's absence from the cabinet.[21] The same day, both Somers and Cowper visited the queen. There are two accounts of Somers's visit: the truth concerning his conversation with the queen probably lies somewhere between the two. The first, recounted many years later by Erasmus Lewis, an under-secretary in Harley's office and one of his confidants, suggests that

> Queen Anne sent for Lord Somers, and told him, when they were alone, she having an opinion of his judgment and impartiality, desired him to tell her his opinion of the Duke of Marlborough. He said he would; and told her that he was the worst man that God Almighty every made; that his ambition was boundless and his avarice insatiable; and that he had neither honour nor conscience to restrain him from any wicked attempt, even against her person, as well as against his country, etc. Somers (as the Queen was weary of the Duchess) expected to be made first minister, but was baulked. The Queen had expressed herself advantageously of his honour, integrity, and capacity.[22]

The second account of Somers's meeting with the queen was the one which he himself sent to Marlborough at Windsor Lodge. In this, Somers claimed to have explained to the queen that appointments in the Army without Marlborough's approval would lead to factions and would undermine discipline; furthermore, Somers suggested 'there are some persons who endeavour to do him ill offices with your Majesty'. After a short pause, according to Somers, the queen replied: 'I have a full and lasting sense of his long and great services, and no one dares attempt to do him ill offices with me, because if they did, their malice would recoil on themselves.' Nevertheless, she remained adamant that John Hill should be appointed.[23] The queen took the same line in her interview with Cowper. 'I thought her Majesty very much concerned that anything should make you uneasy', Cowper reported to Marlborough, 'but at the same time she was pleased to insist she hoped you had no reason to be so, since it was [only] the second time she had imposed in anything of that kind and that few princes could say the like'; furthermore, the queen added, the fact that she had known John Hill so long 'might make it reasonably believ'd Her Majesty's own thought to propose him'.[24]

Marlborough's response to Cowper on 18 January, written under the eye and the influence of the duchess, was directed squarely against Abigail:

> If Her Majesty wou'd be pleas'd to reflect for some time past, She
> wou'd find that my uneasiness does not proceed only from Her
> intention for Mr. Hill, that being but one of the many Mortifications I
> have receiv'd, it is the Queen's change to me that has brook my sperit,
> and my silence has been the effect of my great Concern and respect for
> Her Majesty, for I can't but think the Nation wou'd be of opinion that I
> have deserv'd better than to be made a sacrifice to the unreasonable
> passion of a bedchamber woman.[25]

Marlborough wrote in a similar vein to Godolphin but, according to Maynwaring's report to Sarah, both the chancellor and the treasurer suppressed Marlborough's letters rather than show them to the queen. On Thursday, 19 January, Maynwaring conferred with Somers and Sunderland, who concluded that the queen would eventually place the regiment at Marlborough's disposal; however, Maynwaring advised that Abigail's removal be demanded as the price for Marlborough's continuation in office: 'It is Childrens play, for any men to hold the first Posts in a government, & not have it in their power to remove such a Slut as that', he told Sarah.[26] Godolphin was not nearly so confident as his Junto colleagues that the queen could be brought to heel. The same day, he reported to Marlborough:

> I waited on *the queen* again this morning, and endeavoured once more
> to show the ruinous consequences of the indifference and little notice
> she took of *Marlborough's* mortification and concern for her unkind-
> ness. . . . She made mee a bow, but gave me not one word of answer.
> This makes me think she has taken her resolution and is prepared for
> everything.[27]

It was apparently on 19 January, in his meeting with Somers and Sunderland that Maynwaring proposed, and they accepted, the idea of introducing a petition in the House of Commons asking the queen to remove Abigail from her household.[28] They decided to introduce it on Monday, 23 January. This suggestion won scant support among more prudent Whigs, who thought 'it was impossible for any man of sense, honour, or honesty to come into an Address to remove a dresser from the Queen . . . only to gratifie my Lady Marlborough's passions'.[29] The proposal, however, outraged the queen when she heard of it: her anger was such, reported one of Nottingham's correspondents, that 'Lady Fretchvill says in thirty years she has served, she never saw the like'.[30] Direct parliamentary interference in her household was much more insulting than anything William and Mary had attempted, and the only precedent (particularly unhappy in the light of Sarah's insinuations) for removing a personal – as opposed to a ministerial – servant was that of Edward II's lover, Piers Gaveston, in the fourteenth century. Furthermore, such a parliamentary address would deny the queen 'the liberty allow'd to the meanest housekeeper in her dominions, viz. that of choosing her own domestic servants'.[31] The queen immediately 'gave orders to tell all her friends in the House of Commons, that is to say all that had any dependants, that any such address wou'd be very disagreeable to her'.[32] She also began a widely publicized series of interviews with a great many lords and gentry of all political persuasions, imploring them 'with tears in her eyes' to oppose the motion.[33] Among others, she summoned Maynwaring 'to whom she spoke very plain'.[34] Her tactics proved successful and bore out what Harley had told Marlborough in 1704: 'there is no one party, nay not both of them, can stand against the Queen frowns'.[35]

This display of the queen's influence was necessary not only to defend Abigail but also to protect the queen herself: should such a motion have been carried by Whig majorities, the queen would have had every reason to regard herself as 'in bondage'. Furthermore, the queen had good reason to fear that a successful address against Abigail would immediately be followed by a motion to give the captain-generalcy to Marlborough for his lifetime.[36] Nevertheless, as long as the war continued, Marlborough was still necessary and, in dealing with him, the queen attempted to disguise her anger. On 19 January, she had a second long conversation with Somers in which, he reported to Marlborough, the queen appeared 'so entirely full of affection to you'.[37] Marlborough, meanwhile, had drafted a letter to the queen in which he demanded that she dismiss either Abigail or himself,[38] but at the thought of the timidity of his colleagues and the determination of the queen, he softened his request: the letter which was actually delivered to the queen asked only for permission to retire if Hill was given the regiment.[39]

On the evening of Friday, 20 January, the queen told Godolphin that Hill would not be appointed, but when Godolphin urged her to write to Marlborough, she said she would tell the captain-general when he returned to town.[40] The next day, she promised the treasurer she would write to Marlborough, but did not do so.[41] Marlborough saw that it was useless to persevere in his demands that Abigail be dismissed, because of lack of support from his colleagues. Maynwaring complained to Sarah,

> I take it for granted that *Godolphin* and *Henry Boyle* are now the greatest favourites that ever were in England, & well they deserve to be so, for they have sav'd that wicked Jade [Abigail] at the Expence of their best Friend, which is more than Mr. Harley cou'd have done.[42]

After this ten-day crisis, the queen told Sir David Hamilton (one of her Whig doctors whose diary is to become one of our most important sources of information concerning her later life) that she was pleased with Godolphin's conduct throughout the crisis.[43] She had good reason: Godolphin's timidity had allowed the queen to mortify Marlborough without really sacrificing anything in return.

His absence having been ignored by the queen, Marlborough returned to London on Monday, 23 January, and had an audience the next morning.[44] Marlborough disingenuously assured her, concerning the rumours that an address against Abigail had been planned, 'that it never enter'd into his thoughts to Stir up the Parliament to prescrib[e] to her what servants she shou'd keep about her person'.[45] Although she accepted this plea of innocence, the queen's subsequent actions demonstrated that she did not believe it. To assuage any pain which John Hill might have felt for being deprived of Essex's regiment, the queen promised him a pension of £1,000 for her life.[46]

Both the queen and Harley were anxious to remove Marlborough from England as quickly as possible. The Whig majorities in Parliament unwittingly fell in with this by passing addresses to the queen that Marlborough's presence was necessary in the Dutch republic, where a second round of peace negotiations was to open between the French and the Dutch at Geertruydenberg on 26 February/9 March.[47] The response which Godolphin drafted for the queen was an encomium on the victorious general:

> I thank you for your address, and am very well pleased with this declaration of your just sense of the Duke of Marlborough's eminent services, which I am so fully convinced of, that I shall always esteem him as God Almighty's chief instrument of my glory, and my people's happiness, and I will give the necessary orders for sending him immediately into Holland.

When Godolphin presented this draft to the queen, she refused to accept it, proposing instead to state that she had previously given orders for Marlborough's departure, thereby imputing that he had been reluctant to proceed to the Continent. When Godolphin protested and hinted that this formula had been devised by her secret advisors, the queen 'made the most solemn asservations that it was her own thought'. She finally agreed to an answer which was much less laudatory of Marlborough personally:

> I am so sensible of the necessity of the Duke of Marlborough's presence in Holland, at this critical juncture, that I have already given the necessary directions for his immediate departure; and I am very glad to find by this address, that you concur with me in a just sense of the Duke of Marlborough's eminent services.[48]

On 18 February, Marlborough left London for Harwich, accompanied by the duchess. In the year to come, he would receive no more appeals from the queen; instead, she was prepared to inflict unparalleled humiliations upon him. He was warned by his son-in-law, Sunderland, 'none of our heads are safe, if we can't get the better of what I am convinced Mrs. Morley designs'.[49]

Thus was the ground laid, both in court and country, for an astonishing outburst of resentment against the Whig government and for a resurgence of the Jacobite movement produced by the trial of Dr Henry Sacheverell. By early February the queen was already cautiously disassociating herself from her government: she told Dr Hamilton 'that there ought to be a punishment but a mild one, least the mobb appearing on his side should occasion great commotions and that his Impeachment had been better left alone'.[50] The preparations for the trial before the House of Lords were elaborate, and Sir Christopher Wren was ordered to construct special scaffolds in Westminster Hall, including an area in which the queen and her ladies could attend incognito. During the debates concerning these arrangements, Godolphin told the upper house 'that the Queen was possitive she wou'd have no body over her head, which made the House laught coming so pat to what had been so lately the discourse of the town'.[51]

The trial, which began on 27 February and lasted three weeks, immediately became the focus of all public discontent against the Whig government. Riots began in London on 1 March: Dissenting chapels were sacked, and the only troops which the government had at its disposal were those guarding the royal precincts of Whitehall and St James's. When Sunderland called upon the queen late that evening to report the government's fear that, if these troops were sent into the City, the mob might get through to sack St James's, she resolved the dilemma herself. Earlier, on the first news of the riots, she reportedly was 'seized with a paleness and trembling', but she now ordered Sunderland to take both her horse and foot guards, adding that 'God would be her guard'.[52] The threat of civil war hung in the air. Hoffmann, the imperial resident in London since 1685, believed that the kingdom had not experienced such convulsions since Cromwell's time.[53]

The queen, accompanied by her ladies, attended every session of the trial. Although she agreed with her ministers that Sacheverell should be punished for his impudent sermon, she was reticent about expressing a personal judgment. Abigail Masham, for instance, complained to Harley:

> I was with my aunt [the queen] last night on purpose to speak to her about Dr. S[acheverell] and asked her if she did not let people know her mind in the matter. She said, 'No, she did not meddle one way or other, and that it was her friends' advice not to meddle'.[54]

When the lord chamberlain, the Earl of Kent, asked her advice, 'the Queen told him she thought the Commons had reason to be sattisfied that they had made their allegations good, and the mildest punishment inflicted upon the Doctor she thought the best'.[55] Certainly, she had no sympathy with the High Tory defence of divine right, a claim which she thought 'unfit to be given to anybody'.[56] During the trial, she did not flinch when Wharton announced in her presence that her best title to the throne was a parliamentary one: later in the same debate, however, when Lord Guernsey (Nottingham's brother and a High Tory) was busily 'clearing himself of the Revolution', the queen angrily 'riss & left them, which so much confounded him that [he] had much ado to proceed'.[57]

The trial ended as a fiasco for the government. Although Sacheverell was convicted by seventeen votes (69 to 52), his punishment – three years' suspension from the pulpit – was extremely light. The open repudiation of the government's position by Harley's converts (Shrewsbury, Somerset, Argyll) was correctly regarded as a dire omen for the ministry's survival.[58] Godolphin complained bitterly to Marlborough that

> *Somerset* labours hard against us, and makes use of *the queen's* name to South and North Brittains with a good deal of freedom. I doubt he is pretty sure of not being disavowed, and I believe him entirely linked with the opposite party, upon a foot of knowing *the queen's* inclinations and flattering them.[59]

Marlborough for his part was convinced that Shrewsbury would not have opposed the government 'but that he knew the inclinations of *the queen'*.[60]

The real goal of Sacheverell's defenders had been the creation of public division over an issue which could carry the Tories to electoral victory: in this they succeeded handsomely.[61] Gloucestershire, quickly followed by other counties and boroughs, presented fiery addresses to the queen demanding the dissolution of Parliament. From the moment the trial ended, it was confidently predicted that elections would soon follow.[62] Tories – and even Jacobites – who had long since ceased paying court, now flocked to Kensington. 'Your Majesty', the Jacobite Duke of Beaufort informed the sovereign, 'is now Queen indeed.'[63]

By this point, relations between the queen and the Duchess of Marlborough had broken down irretrievably. Indeed, before Marlborough's departure for the Continent, he had received the queen's permission for Sarah to spend most of her time in the country, away from court. Mrs Morley and Mrs Freeman were memories from the past. The duchess, who suspected that her enemies had been filling the queen's ears 'with what we properly call Grub-Street storys',[64] asked the queen for an interview 'to vindicate my self'. The queen, however, did not wish to see Sarah alone and on 3 April commanded her to put her thoughts in writing.[65] Sarah was not one to succumb to such evasive tactics, and on Maundy Thursday, 6 April, she indicated that she would use every means possible to run the queen to earth:

> If this Afternoon be not convenient, I will come every day, and wait till You please to allow me to speak to you. And one thing more I assure Your Majesty which is, *that what I have to say will have no Consequence either in obliging You to answer* or to see me oftner hereafter than will be easy to You.[66]

We possess only Sarah's commentary on the famous last interview between the two women, which took place the same afternoon at Kensington. In one of her many versions, the duchess made use of dialogue form. The queen had just received Sarah's letter when the duchess entered her closet and she obviously seized upon the last phrase of it ('that what I have to say will have no Consequence . . . in obliging You to answer') to avoid conversation. During the first part of the interview, the queen repeatedly responded, 'There is nothing you can have to say but you may write it.' Sarah then went to the heart of the matter:

> *Lady Marlborough:* There is a thousand lyes made of me, which are so rediculous that I should never have thought it necessary to goe about to clear my self of what never entered into my head . . . & I doe assure your Majesty that there is severall things which I have heard has been told to your Majesty, that I have said of you, that I am no more capable of, then I am of killing my children.

In her dialogue, the duchess did not repeat the particular lie, but it undoubtedly referred to lesbianism, for when she repeated the story to the queen 'she turned her face from me, as if she fear'd blushing upon something I might say to her'.

> *Queen:* There is without doubt many lyes told.
> *Lady Marlborough:* Pray, Madam, tell me what you have heard of me, that I may not trouble you to repeat more disagreeable things then is necessary.
> *Queen:* You said you desired no answer, & I shall give you none.

Sarah then told the queen that her informant had urged her to vindicate herself to the queen personally, although Sarah did not know who had told lies of her:

> *Lady Marlborough:* I never pressed her to know, & much less should I ask of your Majesty who had said things to my prejudice, I only beg to know what you have heard that I might be able to clear my self in any thing in which I was wronged.
> *Queen:* You said you desired noe answer & I shall give you none.

Sarah then launched into an attack on the Duke and Duchess of Somerset, to which 'I observed all the time I talked to the Queen upon that matter she had a more then ordinary attention, but answerd not one word'. She begged the queen yet again to tell her what her enemies had said of her:

> *Queen:* I shall make you noe answer to any thing you say.
> *Lady Marlborough:* Will your Majesty make me some answer att some other time, since you won't now.
> *Queen:* I shall make you no answer.
> Then my tears dropt again, which was strange, but I could not help it, & I suppose it must bee at such inhuman usage.
> *Lady Marlborough:* You know, Madam, how much I have dispised interest in comparison of serving you, & of doing what was right, & you are sure I would not disown any thing that were true, & I assure your Majesty I have never don any thing that you have reason to bee displeased att, then I cryd again.
> *Queen:* I shall make you noe answer to any thing you say,
> att which I made my chursey, saying I was confydent she would suffer in this world, or the next for so much inhumanity, & to that she answerd, that would bee to her self.[67]

The queen later explained to her doctor, Sir David Hamilton,

> that when the Duchess left her, she said, that God would punish her either in this world, or in the next for what she had done to her this day. The Queen said that it was a very hard passing a Sentence upon any body, for that was a thing between God and themselves.[68]

Incredibly, this remarkable interview did not end here. Sarah, having left the queen's closet, attempted to collect herself. She realized that not only her own position, but also that of her husband, could be affected by adverse accounts of her meeting with the queen. 'Therefore, after I had come out from the Queen and sat me down in a long Gallary to wipe my eyes, before I came within sight of any body, I went back again to the closet & scratch'd at the door', which the queen opened. Sarah told the queen that when she went to Windsor, Sarah would take care not to be at the lodge. 'To this she readily answer'd that I might come to her to the Castle and that she should not be uneasy at it.'[69] Regardless of what the queen may have said to pacify the duchess, she obviously had no intention of seeing Sarah again, particularly as the duchess had promised before Marlborough's departure never again to mention politics or Mrs Masham. The following day, 7 April, Sarah forwarded a letter from Marlborough to Godolphin, in which the captain-general warned of foreign plots against the queen's life: in her covering letter to the queen, Sarah complained of 'the strange usage I received yesterday' and attacked both Lord Rivers and the Duke of Somerset. The queen's immediate reply was curt: 'I received yours with one enclosed from the D: of M: to Lord Treasurer Just as I was coming down Stairs from St. James's, soe could not return ye enclosed back till I came to this place [Kensington].'[70] Mrs Morley was never again to see Mrs Freeman.

Personally and politically, the queen was now ready to use the divisions and jealousies within her cabinet (which the proposed address against Abigail had exposed) and the widespread public demonstrations in favour of Sacheverell to break the power of the Junto. The timing of the 'great changes' of 1710 was largely the queen's; in the next year, Lord Poulett, one of Harley's closest associates, noted that 'a thorough change' was an undertaking which 'none of her servants could perswade her to at first'.[71] Harley acquiesced in this: 'Act by her own judgment', he noted in the spring of 1710, '& I wil be ready to obey and promote it.'[72] Caution was necesssary, for the Whigs possessed one ultimate weapon: majorities in both houses of a Parliament, the legal life of which did not expire until the spring of 1711. That Parliament, prorogued on 5 April, could never be allowed to meet again. On 14 April, without consulting her ministers, the queen dismissed the Earl of Kent as lord chamberlain (placating him with the title of duke and appointed Shrewsbury in his stead. This move was made at Harley's suggestion, but it is possible that both the queen and Shrewsbury – who were equally cautious – realized that the Whigs could hardly object to the queen's selection of a lord chamberlain who as major-domo of the royal household bore a personal relationship to the sovereign. The day before Shrewsbury's appointment the queen notified Godolphin of her intentions while the lord treasurer was taking a short holiday in Newmarket, adding in a carefully contrived epilogue: 'I have not yet declared my intentions of giveing the Staff & ye key to the Duke of Shrewsbury becaus I would be ye first that should acquaint you with it.'[73]

Although Shrewsbury's appointment was the first manifestation of Harley's power, it was difficult for the ministers to complain effectively: Shrewsbury was a Whig of the first rank whom Marlborough and Godolphin had formerly wished to bring into the cabinet; furthermore, the office of lord chamberlain did not automatically confer a seat in the cabinet, although Shrewsbury immediately was summoned by the queen to attend.[74] Finally, there was a general hope among the Whigs that Shrewsbury would prove to be his own man. Maynwaring assured Sarah that Shrewsbury

> will trim and shuffle between [the two parties] as well and as long as he can, professing and lying to both sides, and making his court all the while to *the queen* by doing so, which *Henry Boyle* says is the only way to gain her favour.[75]

Godolphin, convinced that the queen's letter to him concerning Shrewsbury 'was certainly of her own writing',[76] immediately protested against her decision in terms designed to frighten her: Harley and his associates, Godolphin warned her, would be willing to accept any peace, particularly if it left 'France at liberty to take their time of imposing the Pretender upon this country'.[77] Bishop Burnet also warned the queen of her danger from the Pretender: 'she was for the most part silent', Burnet recalled, 'yet by what she said, she seemed desirous to make me think she agreed to what I laid before her' (to which Dartmouth later commented, 'The Queen, who was the best bred person in her dominions, would give him a patient hearing, when she despised his impertinence').[78] On 17 April, when he returned to London, Godolphin waited on the queen, who told him that he appeared more upset than the Whigs about Shrewsbury's appointment. Godolphin replied

> that I believed my letter would bee found, though perhaps too late, to bee a very true prophesy of what was to happen. Wee parted dryly enough, but I found she had a mind to make me think she did not design any other alterations, though I had told her the noise of the town ran very high upon that subject.[79]

The queen did not repeat this to Godolphin alone: she twice assured Cowper that 'she had no thoughts of dissolving the Parliament, nor would hear any one talk to her upon that Subject'.[80] The queen was quite pleased with herself because she had brought Shrewsbury into office while avoiding a major crisis. On 19 April, Sir David Hamilton recorded, 'Her Majesty told me she had made the Duke of Shrewsburry with less trouble then she expected, and now hop'd she should be easy, and to show her remaining inclinations to, and her good opinion of my Lord Godolphin.'[81]

Although the major rivals for the queen's trust and reliance appeared to be Godolphin and Harley, Shrewsbury was in fact a third competitor: he did not aspire to the role of day-to-day manager of the government, but he was soon to acquire an influence with the queen which he was to enjoy until his death. Godolphin quickly realized this. Before the month was out, he had warned Sarah: 'I incline to think that he [Shrewsbury] may soon come to have as much influence with *the queen* as Godolphin used to have heretofore.'[82]

Before he had received word of Shrewsbury's appointment, Marlborough had taken steps which reawakened all the unpleasantness of the January crisis and made the queen less likely than ever to listen to complaints from the Duumvirs. He ordered Walpole to present to the queen promotion lists which stopped short of John Hill in the list of brigadier-generals and of Samuel Masham in the list of colonels.[83] The queen correctly surmised that Marlborough had done this deliberately, and insisted that both Hill and Masham be included, particularly because Masham's commission had been antedated 'by the Prince's favour'.[84] On 18 April the queen told Walpole that she positively ordered the promotions of Masham and Hill and she refused to sign any other commissions until Walpole procured Marlborough's agreement.[85] The struggle between the queen and the captain-general over the promotions continued throughout May and June, although the queen wished to keep it a private matter. Walpole reported to Marlborough that 'she commanded me strictly not to tell any body, and in particular, not to let you know that she stopt the commissions upon this account, but would have it thought . . . that the delay was accidental'.[86] Walpole noted in his conversations with the queen concerning the promotions that 'there seem'd a great struggle betwixt the desire of doeing the thing, and not putting a mortification upon *Marlborough*'.[87] Finally, at the beginning of June, Marlborough agreed to make both promotions at the end of the campaign.[88]

This altercation between the queen and Marlborough began while there was general uncertainty as to whether Shrewsbury's appointment signalled the beginning of other ministerial changes. For several weeks, the Duumvirs and the Whigs hoped that the queen intended no further

311

changes.[89] Nevertheless, on 5 May Godolphin reported to Marlborough that,

> at the part of Lord Townshend's letter which mentioned the forreign ministers writing from hence, that the Treasury was to bee putt in commission, [the queen] gave a sort of scornfull smile, but did not think fitt to say a word to mee upon it.

Godolphin correctly suspected that the queen had not yet brought herself to part with him, but that this was Harley's goal.[90] Two weeks later, Godolphin advised Marlborough to agree to the promotions of Masham and Hill, as their enemies were making Marlborough's intransigence appear as though the queen had no authority over the Army.

> Notwithstanding all the noyse of alterations and changes which was continued now for three weeks together, Mrs. Morley has never once opened her lips to Mr. Montogomery upon that subject, though upon all other ordinary transactions it is between them two just as it used to bee,

Godolphin told Marlborough.[91]

By this time, it was clear that the next person to be removed from office was the queen's *bête noire*, Sunderland.[92] According to his successor, Lord Dartmouth, 'The Queen said, Lord Sunderland always treated her with great rudeness and neglect, & chose to reflect in a very injurious manner upon all princes before her, as a proper entertainment for her.'[93] The queen was eager to dismiss Sunderland as soon as possible,[94] but the month's delay in his removal was largely due to the number of candidates for his office, including Harley's close associate, Lord Poulett;[95] in fact, the queen offered the position to Poulett, but he declined it because of Godolphin's opposition. When, on 2 June, the treasurer warned the queen that she would undermine Marlborough's position abroad by dismissing his son-in-law, '*the queen* said *Marlborough* was too reasonable to lett a thing of this kind doe so much prejudice to himself, and to the whole world,' by resigning 'and that nobody knew better than *Marlborough* and myself, the repeated provocations that *Sunderland* had given'.[96] Significantly, Sunderland's Whig colleagues – seduced by Harley's proposals for a 'moderate' administration of the centre and hopeful of salvaging their own interests thereby – failed to lift a finger to save him, thus further confirming the queen's opinion that Sunderland was 'obnoxious to all people, exsept a few'.[97] The queen sought and received Somers's approval (but not Godolphin's) before offering Sunderland's position to George Legge, first Earl of Dartmouth.[98]

Before Dartmouth's appointment could be made, however, the Duchess of Marlborough resumed her correspondence with the queen for the last time. On 7 June she sent the queen an extremely long letter in which she emphasized that the dismissal of his son-in-law might drive Marlborough into resignation. Sarah claimed that, if the queen's husband was still alive, 'I am sure the Prince would have prevented your going into a scheeme with a collection of the worst people in the kingdom'. With more than a hint of blackmail, Sarah stressed that she possessed 'a thousand letters' written by the queen: to underscore this, she enclosed a letter which Mrs Freeman had received from Mrs Morley immediately after the news of Blenheim had arrived, as well as a letter which the Duke of Somerset had written to Sarah when their relations were happier.[99] On 12 June the queen wrote the last of her many letters to Sarah: we do not possess the original, which Sarah described in her reply the following day as 'your short, harsh, and I must beg leave to think, very undeserved answer'. The queen had complained that she 'had my Lord Marlborough's promise & mine that I should never say one word of politicks, or of Mrs. Masham', a promise which Sarah claimed she was justified in breaking because the queen had failed to reply to her 'Narrative'.[100] In a postscript, the queen had asked Sarah to return all the letters which she had ever written to her.[101] Sarah's insolent (and, to the queen's mind, threatening) response was, 'Your Majestys refusing to send mee back ye Letres as I humbly desired, obliges mee to take a little better care of the rest.'[102]

As her resentment against Sarah increased, the queen was naturally less willing than ever to listen to Marlborough's advice, particularly when it concerned Sunderland. On 9 June, Marlborough addressed to Godolphin an appeal, which he intended the treasurer should read to the queen, that Sunderland should not be removed from office:

I am sorry Lord Sunderland is not agreable to the Queen, but his being at this time singled out, has no other reason but that of being my son-in-law. When this appears in its treu light, I am very confident every man in England will be sensible that my enemys have prevailled to have this done, in order to make it impossible for me with honour to continue at the head of this glorious army.[103]

On 12 June, the day before Marlborough's letter arrived in London, the queen summoned Somers to tell him that she intended to dismiss Sunderland 'and to assure him at the same time that she was entirely for moderation; that she did not intend to make any other alterations, but

313

this was a resolution she had taken for a long time, and that nothing could divert her from it. The next day, 13 June, Godolphin read Marlborough's letter to the queen. He later reported to Marlborough,

> when I had the reading of it to *the queen*, I could not observe that it had any effect, but to give her an uneasiness from the thought it might make the matter more difficult, and the consequences of it worse. But I saw a dryness at the same time which fully convinced mee that nothing I could add to the letter was capable of changing *the queen's* opinion.[104]

Indeed, shortly before her conference with Godolphin, the queen had ordered Henry Boyle, Sunderland's fellow secretary of state, to demand the seals from Sunderland. Boyle had demurred, on the grounds that he was Sunderland's friend. 'She replyd, therfore best done by a friend.' When Boyle asked if Sunderland could present the seals himself, 'She said that would be a trouble to himselfe as well as her.'[105]

Later that day, having reflected on Marlborough's letter, the queen notified Godolphin that she refused to change her mind:

> & I do not see why the Duke of Marlboroughs letter should make me alter my resolution, unless I could agree with him that I had don him hardships, which I am not Concious to my self I have, & I can't but think all impartial people will be of ye same oppinion, it is true indeed that ye turning a Son-in-law out of his office may be a mortification to the D: of Marl:, *but must the fate of Europe depend on that*, & must he be gratefyed in all his desires, & I not in soe reasonable a thing as parting with a man who I took into my Service with all ye uneasynes emaginable & whos behaviour to me has bin soe ever since, & who I must add is I beleive obnoxious to all people exsept a few. . . .[106]

Godolphin attempted one more protest, writing to the queen that night and warning her that Marlborough would resign if Sunderland was dismissed. The next morning the queen replied to Godolphin, telling him for the first time that she had selected Dartmouth and reassuring him that

> I have no thoughts of takeing the Duke of Marlborough from the heade of ye army, nor I dare say no body els [has], if he & you should doe soe wrong a thing at any time, espesialy at this Critical Juncture, as to desert my Service, what Confusion might happen would lye at your doors & you alone would be answearable & no body els.[107]

In this letter, the queen appeared anxious that neither Godolphin nor Marlborough should resign. Possibly she had some foreknowledge of a letter which was sent on the same day, 14 June, to Marlborough, signed by Godolphin, Cowper, Newcastle, Devonshire, and the five Junto lords, asking Marlborough not to resign his commands in retaliation for the dismissal of his son-in-law. Despite the queen's appeal to Godolphin not to resign, within two months the queen was to dismiss him from office, which led to accusations that she had acted with duplicity. Yet an examination of the contemporary situation suggests that the queen genuinely wished to retain Godolphin's services, but three factors intervened: the peace negotiations in progress at Geertruydenberg, Godolphin's attachment to the Duchess of Marlborough, and his refusal to agree to the dissolution of Parliament.

As we noted earlier, the French had once again opened peace negotiations with the Dutch in February 1710 at Geertruydenberg.[108] The negotiations had so far proved slow and tortuous, largely because the allies remained inflexible in their onerous demands, particularly that Louis XIV should force Philip V to withdraw from Spain. Nevertheless, the queen naturally hesitated to make substantial changes in her ministry as long as the possibility of an immediate peace existed. The dismissal of Sunderland, however, encouraged the French to break off the negotiations on 1/12 July, in the hope that further changes in the British government would produce a more favourable diplomatic situation for France. The end of negotiations made it possible, in the context of the war, for the queen to change her chief minister.

A second factor was Godolphin's refusal to sever his ties with the Duchess of Marlborough. As early as 11 May the queen complained to Sir David Hamilton,

> that the Duchess made my Lord Marlborough and my Lord Godolphin do any thing, and that when my Lord Godolphin was ever so finally resolv'd when with her Majesty, yet when he went to her [Sarah], she impress'd him to the Contrary.

Hamilton quoted the queen as 'often Expressing her self thus, "O, that my Lord Godolphin would be parted from the Duchess of Marlborough, I should be very happy"'.[109] On 15 May the queen asked Hamilton

> to see, if it was possible, to bring my Lord Godolphin off from the Duchess; for that would be one of the happiest things imaginable. That she did believe the City would be in an Uproar, if he was turn'd out, and she was perswaded that he greatly study'd her Ease.

Godolphin's response to Hamilton's inquiries was not encouraging. The following day, Hamilton told the queen that he had visited Godolphin, who said 'it was impossible their Relation being so near, and their Circumstances so united, for him to break off from the Duchess'.[110] The queen accepted this answer as definitive: even though she continued to use Hamilton as her intermediary with the Marlboroughs and Godolphin, she never again expressed the hope that their interests might be divided.

The third, and fundamental, question was the future of the Parliament elected in 1708. On 15 June, the day after Sunderland's dismissal, a deputation from the Bank of England visited the queen. Peter Wentworth reported to his brother as 'a true matter of fact' that these commissioners 'did receive this equivocal assurance from her that she had *at present* no intentions to make any alterations in the Ministry . . . and now 'tis agreed on all hands that neither they nor [the queen] mentioned any thing concerning a parliament'.[111] The next evening, Sir David Hamilton visited Godolphin: 'he told me', Hamilton recorded,

> that he found it was the Queen's inclination, that it should be known
> that she would make no other Changes, but my Lord Sunderlands;
> which I coud Easily believe, because her Majesty her self order'd me to
> say the same, viz. that she would make no other Change, but not to
> disown the dissolution of Parliament.[112]

The Bank of England, to demonstrate the power and vested resources of the Whigs, refused on 16 June a routine request from the government for a loan of £120,000 (although it reversed its decision later the same day). This gave Harley the opportunity to tell the queen: 'you must preserve your character and spirit and speak to Lord Treasurer. Get quit of him.'[113] The queen was becoming alienated personally by Godolphin's sourness: on 26 June, Godolphin assured Sarah that he talked 'so plainly and in such a manner, as I can say has not, nor will not be sayd by anybody else in the world to *the queen*'.[114] Furthermore, the treasurer made it quite clear that he would never consent to an immediate dissolution of Parliament. On 29 June he reported to Marlborough:

> I have told *the queen* very plainly that to think of parting with *Parliament*
> was present ruine and distraction, and therefore it was never possible
> for *Godolphin* to consent to it, but in that case, he must begg his
> dismission before that resolution came to bee declared. All the answer
> he had to it was, that it was a matter which required to be very well
> considered.[115]

Godolphin was becoming more outspoken because he saw the growing indications that the queen was listening to Harley, who was now conferring with her every evening. On 25 June the queen shattered a cherished plan of the treasurer to send his nephew, Sir Philip Meadows, as envoy to Hanover,[116] and instead named a cousin of Harley's, James Cressett, who had served as envoy to the Hanoverian court from 1694 to 1703; 'I would not give my orders to Mr. Secretary

[Boyle] in this matter until I had first acquainted you with my intentions', the queen told Godolphin.[117] This appointment added insult to injury, for Cressett (who suddenly died on 25 July before he could leave London) and Harley instigated rumours that Cressett would offer Marlborough's command to the Elector of Hanover and that some member of the electoral family would be invited to London for a short, complimentary visit.[118]

Conscious of the need to retain control of the queen, uphold public credit, and maintain the Grand Alliance, Harley was – in Godolphin's words – 'exceedingly desirous to be thought moderate'.[119] Harley was well aware that the major obstacle to dissolution and new elections was Godolphin, who as treasurer continued to control vast areas of patronage. Yet six weeks after Sunderland's dismissal, Harley and his associates had not been able to bring the queen to resolve finally to part with Godolphin.[120] In this endeavour, they were inadvertently aided by a Whig strategy which backfired. After Sunderland's dismissal, the queen had dispatched Shrewsbury to the imperial and Dutch envoys in London to assure them that this ministerial change did not portend any fundamental alteration in Britain's war role; in addition the queen had personally assured Count von Gallas, the imperial envoy, that she intended to continue the war until an honourable peace had been procured.[121] Seizing upon these facts, Marlborough and the Whigs secretly and successfully instigated attempts to support the Godolphin ministry by the States-General, the emperor, and the Elector of Hanover.[122] Gallas and Vryberg, the Dutch envoy in London, and Hans Caspar von Bothmer, the Hanoverian envoy at The Hague, were intimately associated with the Whig government. Through these diplomats, and at specific Whig behest, the three allies expressed thanks for the queen's voluntary promises that no ministerial changes would affect the conduct of the war or the Hanoverian succession; each ally, however, went further in making an explicit appeal that the queen should neither dismiss a ministry nor dissolve a Parliament which had contributed so much to the 'common cause'.[123]

Such appeals were open to the Tory rejoinder that foreign powers were interfering in British domestic affairs. The letters from the emperor and the States-General received the widest publicity: that of the Elector of Hanover, news of which might produce unfavourable electoral repercussions for the Tories, was suppressed.[124] Harley, now in his own words 'obliged to almost daily attendance on *the queen* and at such unreasonable hours',[125] used these allied protests to inflame the queen against foreign interference in the conduct of her affairs.[126] At a cabinet meeting on 2 July, the Queen ordered (her self) an answer to be wrotte by Mr. Boyle to Lord Townshend to aquaint the States she was verry much surprissed at so extraordinary a prosseeding but that nothing should lessen her affections to the States, but as it was the first of this kind, she hoped it would be the last and ordered Mr. Boyle to show her the letter before he sent it.[127]

Both the queen and her secret advisors suspected that Marlborough and Godolphin had been responsible for this allied intervention.[128] As a warning to the treasurer, on 7 July the queen suddenly dismissed one of Godolphin's closest allies, Lord Coningsby, from his post as vice-treasurer of Ireland and appointed the Earl of Anglesey in his stead; when Coningsby, in his farewell audience, began remonstrating with the queen on the dangers of dismissing the Whigs, he was stopped in mid-sentence by the queen 'rising from her seat . . . with a very angry air'.[129]

Despite all this, the queen remained extremely reluctant to dismiss Godolphin. Her first candidate as a successor to the lord treasurer was Shrewsbury, who declined her offer.[130] During the last week of July, presumably at the queen's instigation, there were secret consultations held between Godolphin and Harley; no reconciliation resulted, however, and these negotiations broke down by the end of the month.[131] At the cabinet held on 30 July, Godolphin, well aware of his loss of influence with the queen,[132] spoke harshly to her. As he reported to Marlborough,

You may depend that *the queen* being by *Abigail* entirely in the hands of *Harley*, *Somerset* and *Shrewsbury* has not the least reguard for *Godolphin*, any farther than while he is necessary in order to bring their ends to bear.

While Godolphin represented all the domestic and foreign dangers inherent in a dissolution of Parliament, '*the queen* seems to bee deaf to all reasons of that nature, and is perswaded to look upon it only as a personall contest for power and favour, and whether *the Whigs* or *the Tories* shall have the greatest sway'. Godolphin believed that the queen was convinced a new Parliament 'will be entirely at *the queen's* disposall, and have nothing so much at heart as to deliver her from the tyranny of *the Whigs* and their supporters'.[133] Orford also spoke out strongly for the continuation of the present Parliament but, as Maynwaring (who was not there) reported to Coningsby, '*the queen* having the Cue given, interrupted him & broke off the Debate, saying they were not ther upon that busines'.[134]

Although the queen did not abruptly silence Godolphin as she did

318

Orford, she nevertheless was offended by his expostulations. As Harley commented, Godolphin 'every day grows sower and indeed ruder to *the queen*, which is unaccountable, & will hear of no accomodation, so that it is impossible he can continue many days'.[135] By 1 August, after what she was later to call 'perpetual teazing',[136] the queen finally agreed to dismiss Godolphin and to put the Treasury into commission.[137] By 5 August she had agreed with her advisors, Shrewsbury and Harley, that Lord Poulett should serve as first lord of the new Treasury commission and that Harley should re-enter government as chancellor of the exchequer.[138] Nevertheless, the queen still wished to avoid the agony of a personal confrontation with the man who had served her more closely than any other minister for over eight years; in their last meeting, on the afternoon of 7 August, Godolphin asked the queen if he was to remain in office, and she unhesitatingly replied, 'Yes.' It was later reported that their interview lasted over two hours, '& when he came out appear'd with an air of cheerfulness & content that had not been seen for some time in his countenance, & was so thoroughly persuaded himself of his success' that Godolphin assured Vryberg, the Dutch envoy, that he had gained his point and Parliament would not be dissolved.[139] The final agreement on a new Treasury commission was presumably reached on the evening of 7 August, for the Duke of Somerset summoned Harley to attend the queen 'at the usuall hour'.[140] the next morning the queen sent her famous letter of dismissal to Godolphin:

> The uneasiness which you have showed for some time has given me very much trouble, though I have borne it; and had your behaviour continued the same it was for a few years after my coming to the crown, I could have no dispute with myself what to do. But the many unkind returns I have received since, especially what you said to me personally before the Lords, makes it impossible for me to continue you any longer in my service; but I will give you a pension of four thousand a year, and I desire that, instead of bringing the staff to me, you will break it, which I believe will be easier to us both.[141]

The fact that the queen commanded Godolphin to break his staff, rather than return it to her in a private audience, was a measure of her personal reluctance to dismiss him; indeed, she later confided to Sir David Hamilton that she resented the fact that she had been manoeuvred into such a position.[142] The queen's reluctance, however, was not shown in the insulting way her letter was conveyed to Godolphin: it was delivered by 'a common groom' of the staff of Somerset, the master of the horse.[143] Godolphin's reply, written that afternoon, was returned to the queen by John Smith, outgoing chancellor of the exchequer.[144] At the same time that the queen issued orders to Dartmouth to notify British officers abroad that 'Shee will take such effectual care their armys shall want for nothing',[145] she personally informed Marlborough in curt language that she had dismissed his closest colleague:

> My Lord Treasurer haveing for some time shewed a great deale of uneasynes in my Service & his behaviour not being ye same to me it was formerly, made it impossible for me to lett him keep ye white Staff any longer, & therfore I order'd him this morning to break it, which I acquaint you with now that ye may receive this news first from me, & I do assure you I will take care that ye army shall want for nothing.[146]

Thus ended for the queen an eight-year association with Godolphin during which they had conferred daily. Sarah later claimed that the queen's offer of a pension of £4,000 per annum

> shew'd that she knew she did him great injustice, but she had not so much honor as to pay it, or ever to mention it to any body after she had given it under her hand that she would pay it, & any body that knew him will be very sure that hee would never ask it.[147]

There appears to be no question that the promised pension was not paid. Whether this was due to the queen's negligence, or to the fact that a few days after his dismissal Godolphin's elder brother died, leaving him the bulk of the family fortune, remains unknown. Whatever the case, it is certain that the queen continued to maintain some communication with her former treasurer; indeed, Dartmouth harboured 'a suspicion that there was an understanding between him and the Queen to the last'.[148] Godolphin took some pains to conceal this connection from his Whig associates: he complained to Cowper, for example, 'If I were not under the misfortune of having lost all access to the Queen' but he did not blame the queen personally for his dismissal ('How miserably has that poor princess been deluded & exposed, by false & malicious insinuations?').[149] On 5 September, when Boyle read to the queen a private letter from Marlborough to her, discussing a proposed descent upon Calais, the queen ordered Boyle to discuss the plans with Godolphin.[150] After the defeat of the allied armies in Castile at Brihuega on 29 November/9 December, the queen solicited Godolphin's advice, which he gave through Sir David Hamilton on 17 December,[151] and on 27 December the queen ordered Hamilton to visit Godolphin to discuss this advice.[152] Throughout 1711 and 1712, Godolphin continued to attend Parliament and to participate in the inner councils of the Whig opposition, but his health rapidly declined and he died on 15 September 1712. When Dartmouth brought the queen news of Godolphin's death, she seemed to be concerned, and told me, she could not help being so, for she had a long acquaintance with him, and did believe, what she or any body else had to complain of, was owing to the influence the Marlborough family had over him.

The queen asked Dartmouth to 'hinder, as much as I could, any scurrilities coming out upon him'.[153]

The queen used her secret contacts with Godolphin to seek advice and also to preserve 'moderation'. She told Archbishop Sharp more than once 'that she would neither be in the hands of the Whigs nor of the Tories'.[154] Shrewsbury had earlier assured Godolphin that 'the queen has not any inclinations to be entire with the Tories but is persuaded that it is absolutely necessary to humble the Whigs'.[155] During the summer of 1710,

> an old Chaplain, thinking to make his court, preacht in St. James's Chapel before the Queen a very high and foolish Sermon, and had orders sent to him by the present Lord Chamberlain [Shrewsbury] that he need not trouble him self to preach before the Queen, for she had provided one to do it when it came to his turn.

The queen's orders were later extended to 'all the parsons that preach before the Queen not to entertain her with politicks'.[156]

Although he professed to be a 'moderate', Harley had never the same degree of influence with the queen which Marlborough and Godolphin had enjoyed at the height of their power. It was of supreme importance to Harley's own authority as a political manager that it be thought that he was, in St John's words, 'the only true channel through which the Queen's pleasure is conveyed'.[157] The reality was quite different. Harley found that the queen, once liberated from the 'tyranny' of Sarah and the Junto, proved very difficult: in Swift's words, 'after the usuall Mistake of those who think they have been often imposed on' the queen 'became so very suspicious that She overshot the mark and erred in the other Extream'.[158] Harley's immediate problem was that the queen was reluctant to part with Whigs like Boyle and Cowper who had become personal favourites. She even held Somers, head of the Junto, in high personal regard. Dartmouth recorded that the queen 'often told me she thought herself very much obliged to him and that he was a man that had never deceived her'.[159] Harley was well aware that he would never be safe until Parliament was dissolved, while the Whigs demanded its retention in return for their co-operation. While, at the queen's request, he approached some Whig ministers with improbable assurances of his intentions ('A Whig game intended at bottom'),[160] his real goal, as he noted both privately and to his sister four years later, was to forestall the inevitable attacks from the right wing of the Tory party, once it had been restored to power through his agency. It therefore became imperative for him to set himself at the head of 'the French party'.[161] Because there was little basis for mutual co-operation, Harley's appeals to the Whigs (excepting only the Duke of Newcastle, to whose daughter and heiress Harley wished to marry his only son) were half-hearted and correspondingly unsuccessful. The Whigs stood their ground, confident that Harley and the Tories could never surmount the problems which the dismissal of the Whig ministry and the dissolution of Parliament would inevitably entail. The Whigs believed that only they could successfully maintain public credit and support the Grand Alliance. Harley's great skill as a financial administrator soon robbed them of the first issue and his adroitness in pacifying the allies while secretly destroying the Grand Alliance was soon to change the structure of European affairs.

From her dismissal of Sunderland, it is certain that the queen had no intention of allowing the Whig Parliament to meet again. James Brydges, commenting upon 'this Revolution' produced by the dismissal of Godolphin, remarked that 'the Queen has show'd such a resolution in it, that nobody doubts her going thro' with it'.[162] Harley offered a seat on the treasury commission to Richard Hampden, who refused, telling the queen that there must be no new Parliament. Her crushing response was 'that though she offer'd him an employment, yet she did not ask his advise'.[163] Within five weeks of Godolphin's dismissal, the queen and Harley felt confident that Treasury patronage had been sufficiently altered to ensure a favourable general election. Harley notified Newcastle on 14 September that the queen had agreed to the dissolution, 'it being resolved in her own breast'.[164] On the same day, Shrewsbury and Harley notified Halifax (one of those Whigs with whom Harley had been secretly negotiating) that Halifax's brother, Sir James Montagu, would be immediately dismissed as attorney-general: 'his days are number'd and Sir Simon Harcourt is to reassume his place very suddenly'.[165] The appointment of Harcourt was required in order that he might secretly draw up the necessary proclamations and writs for the dissolution of Parliament and the summoning of a new one. On 20 September, at a meeting of the Privy Council,

> the Queen asked if the Proclamation was ready. The Attorney General [Harcourt] . . . Immediately took it out of his pocket, and in a Minute the Clerk had read almost the half of it (which was a Sign he had practic'd it before). When it was read the Queen imdiatly withdrew, and would not hear any person Speak.[166]

The following day most of the Whig ministers resigned. The queen clearly regretted the loss of Somers: she ordered Dartmouth to tell him 'that she had not lessened her esteem for him and designed to continue the pension, and should be glad if he came often to her'.[167] Although Harley had maintained contact with Henry Boyle from the spring of 1709 and had worked hard to keep him from resigning, Boyle followed his colleagues; the queen told Sir David Hamilton 'that Mr. Boyles going out was his own doing'.[168] In the case of Cowper, the lord chancellor noted in his diary that he tried to surrender the Great Seal to the queen:

> She strongly oppos'd my doing it, and giving it me again at least five times after I had laid it down, & at last would not take it, but commanded me to hold it, adding 'I beg it as a Favour of you, if I may use that Expression'; on which I took it again; but after some pause told her, 'I could not carry it out of her Palace, unless she would promise me to accept tomorrow of it, if I brought it'; which I think she did, saying, she hoped I would alter my mind.[169]

The next day, the queen accepted Cowper's resignation 'in great Concern, begging him not to do so, with tears'.[170] Cowper suspected that the queen was anxious because she and Harley had no obvious candidate at hand to replace him.

This may well have been true, because it is clear that Harley feared that both Simon Harcourt (the obvious 'moderate' Tory successor to Cowper) and Henry St John were too closely linked in friendship with the Duke of Marlborough. In the autumn of 1710, Harley suspected that St John in particular was revealing the new ministry's secrets to Marlborough.[171] It is possible that this suspicion was justified, for Marlborough had certainly acquired a new source of secret information[172] and, throughout the spring of 1711, St John met periodically with Marlborough's confidential agent, James Craggs (whose letters to Marlborough during this period are not extant).[173] During the same period, while informing the captain-general through James Brydges of his 'very cordiall Respect',[174] St John aided and abetted Marlborough in sabotaging the effectiveness of the war office committee which Harley had established to remove political control of the Army from Marlborough's hands.[175] Harley, acting on his fears and supported by the queen's personal dislike of both St John and Harcourt, offered only to reinstate them in their former positions as secretary at war and attorney-general, rather than give them the offices which they coveted, secretary of state and lord keeper. Harley was finally forced to relent when both men refused to serve on such terms (Harcourt was only given the seals on 19 October), but insult and injury had been sustained on both sides.[176] The divisions which were to plague and ultimately wreck the queen's last ministry began at its inception.

Apart from St John and Dartmouth as secretaries of state and Harcourt as lord keeper, the new administration was a mixture of High Tories and Harley's adherents. Having spent seven years in the wilderness since his dismissal in 1703, Rochester had learned that strict adherence to a party line could cost him his niece's favour: as lord president until his sudden death in May 1711, Rochester proved to be a leading force of political moderation in government.[177] Other important positions went to Buckingham (who replaced the Duke of Devonshire as lord steward), the Duke of Ormonde (who succeeded Wharton as lord lieutenant of Ireland), and Thomas Wentworth, Lord Raby (soon to succeed Townshend at The Hague and to be created Earl of Strafford). The 'great changes' of 1710 proved to be more extensive than any ministerial reorganization since 1689: with the exceptions of Shrewsbury, Somerset (deceived in his hopes of becoming first minister and actively opposing Harley after the introduction of a Tory ministry and the dissolution of Parliament), and Newcastle (whose double-dealing rendered him universally suspect and politically impotent), no prominent Whig remained in high ministerial office by the end of 1710.[178] On 8 November, when a general thanksgiving was celebrated for Marlborough's success in capturing Douai, Bethune, St Venant, and Air-sur-Luys, Swift noted: 'I was at Court, where the Queen past by us with all Tories about her; not one Whig.'[179]

The 1710 elections were fought by all sides with unprecedented violence. Although the Whigs claimed that the ministerial changes had been made to pave the way for bringing in the Pretender, their stories of his imminent arrival could not outweigh public hopes for a quick peace under the Tories. The queen did not participate directly in the elections, as she had in 1705, but her sentiments could hardly be doubted by the public. The result was a Tory landslide which produced a majority of 151 in the House of Commons, the greatest party majority since her accession.[180] This Tory majority was both larger and more revengeful than either the queen or Harley had anticipated, and its existence was to complicate the future considerably.

For the moment, however, the queen's greatest personal concern throughout the autumn of 1710 was the future position of the Duke and Duchess of Marlborough. The queen was determined to get rid of Sarah, but at the same time Marlborough remained indispensable until peace had been reached. To negotiate a solution would be a delicate task, further complicated by Sarah's vehemence and obstinate determination to salvage as much as possible from her fall from favour.

After their final interview on 6 April, the queen had decided that ''twas to no purpose' for Godolphin to speak with Sarah. Instead, she asked her Whig doctor, Sir David Hamilton, to act as her intermediary with the duchess, a role which Hamilton was to fill until Sarah's dismissal from office.[181] From Hamilton's diary, it appears that he first saw the duchess on 15 June, the day after Sunderland's dismissal from office. At the end of June, Sarah renewed her threat to publish the queen's letters,[182] and Hamilton advised the queen

> that my Lady Marlborough being [put] out be done in a way the least provoking. For a woman of Sense and Passion, provok'd, dos often turn Malicious, and that may force her to Print what has happen'd, for her own Justification.

The queen agreed with this advice, adding 'that when People are fond of one another, they say many things, however indifferent, they would not desire the world to know'. On 10 July, Hamilton reported to the queen that 'the Duchess said that she took more pleasure in justifying herself, than your Majesty did in wearing your Crown, and that she wondered that when your Majesty was so much in her Power, you should treat her so', virtually a blackmail threat.[183] The duchess now began to write letters, ostensibly directed to Hamilton, which she knew the doctor would read to the queen. In tone and substance, these were similar to the correspondence which Sarah had formerly conducted with the queen; indeed the queen told Hamilton (he noted in his diary) 'that the Duchess wrote to me as she us'd to do to her'.[184] In her first letter to Hamilton, Sarah mentioned 'the famous history that is to bee',[185] although both Marlborough and the Duke of Devonshire (to whom she had shown a rough draft of her 'justification') had already advised her 'not to make publick the harsh usidge she has meet with'.[186]

On 24 July, Sarah raised the issue of the 'solemn promis' which the queen had made in February 1708 that, when Sarah left the court, her positions would be distributed among her daughters.[187] Hamilton apparently did not introduce this question to the queen until 16 September, and he met an abrupt refusal to honour the promise. 'Her Majesty answered that persons may Promise, and yet upon Occurrences, change', although Hamilton quoted scriptural authority concerning the sanctity of oaths.[188] That circumstances had changed was to be the queen's undeviating rationale for refusing to honour the 'solemn promis'. The final explosion in the relationship between the queen and her groom of the stole came on 23 November, when Jonathan Swift published his famous essay on 'British Ingratitude' in the government backed *Examiner*. Swift attacked the Marlboroughs for gross avarice and, as Sarah complained to Hamilton on 28 November, 'to be printed & cry'd about the country for a common cheat & pickpocket is too much for human nature to bear'. Sarah then threatened 'to publish other papers of a very different kind' in her own justification, 'since any body that knows what honour or a principle is, wou'd rather loose their life than be murdered in their reputation'.[189]

The next day, Hamilton relayed this letter to the queen. Sarah noted on her copy, 'All the Queen said to this letter was "Nobody thinks cheating is the Dutches of Marlboroughs fault"', a remark which can only be interpreted by knowing where the oral emphasis was placed. The queen made it clear to Hamilton that she desired the return of her letters, and she hoped that Marlborough might co-operate in this project on his return to England. The queen kept the duchess's letter overnight. When she returned it to Hamilton on 30 November, she was obviously less sure of Marlborough's attitude; without mentioning Marlborough's disappointment when she refused him the captain-generalcy for life, the queen told Hamilton 'how good nature'd the Duke us'd to be, that he could not give any Creature a harsh word; whereas lately he appears so ill natur'd, and swearing, that he could not forbear swearing in her Presence'.[190]

The duchess, aware of the queen's increasing truculence from her conversations with Hamilton, began to write to the doctor every day. On 6 December, in a letter on which the queen commented, 'The Duchess wrote free',[191] Sarah again obliquely raised the issue of lesbianism:

> I hear there is some [pamphlets] lately come out which they said were not fit for me to see, by which I guess they are upon a subject that you may remember I complain'd to you, & really it troubl'd me very much upon my own account as well as others, because it was very disagreeable & what I know to be a lye, but something of that disagreeable turn there was in an odious ballad to the tune of fair Rosamond, printed a good while ago, in which the Queen gives an account of Mr. Harleys & Mrs. Mashams base designs against all those that had brought them to court, & rediculed her very Justly, but that which I hated was the disrespect to the Queen & the disagreeable expressions of the dark deeds in the night.[192]

By once again raising the possibility of physical intimacy between the queen and Abigail, the duchess succeeded only in hardening the queen's determination to be rid of her. On 9 December, Hamilton recorded: 'The Queen was then positive she would never see her more, and it would look odd to keep her in [office], and she never come to her'. The queen's chief fear was Sarah's influence over Marlborough: she had already ordered Hamilton to try to prevent Sarah from meeting the duke on the coast and, on 11 December, 'the Queen order'd me to insist that she might not inflame the Duke. She hoped my Lord Marlborough would be calm, and submissive.'[193]

It called upon Marlborough's greatest resources to be 'calm and submissive', for Harley had done everything possible to reduce his control of the Army. In September, Adam de Cardonnel, Marlborough's personal secretary, was replaced as secretary at war by George Granville (created Lord Lansdowne in December 1711), a personal enemy of Marlborough's and a known Jacobite.[194] In December three of Marlborough's protégés (Generals Thomas Meredith, George Maccartney, and Philip Honeywood) were cashiered for allegedly drinking damnation to the duke's ministerial enemies: the dismissals, signed by the queen, were sent sealed to Marlborough, to be delivered unopened by him.[195] The queen obviously intended the cashierings as a warning to Marlborough. She told Hamilton that those who 'went up and down in the Army, making factious Officers' would be dismissed; when Hamilton asked whether she wished Marlborough to continue in the service, 'She answer'd, to be sure, if he would go into Her Measures, and not divide and make partys'.[196] Unknown to the queen, under pressure from both the Whigs and the Elector of Hanover, Marlborough had agreed not to resign his command, and he notified the elector to this effect before his return to London (accompanied by the new Hanoverian envoy to Great Britain, Hans Caspar von Bothmer) on 26 December.[197]

For the queen, the issue of central importance was the necessity to be rid of Sarah. On 27 December, before Marlborough called upon her, she had a long conversation with Hamilton, in which she explained why her friendship with Sarah was dead: 'That the Duchess had said shocking things even to her self, Yea as much to her self, and afterwards in Company, as that she lied.' The queen also made it clear that she did not intend to keep the 'solemn promis'; quite apart from Sarah's subsequent undutiful behaviour, her daughters were unsuitable. Anne Sunderland was too 'cunning and dangerous to be in the Family', Henrietta Godolphin was 'Silly and Imprudent, and [had] lost her reputation', and Mary Montagu (worst of all) 'was just like her Mother'.[198] On 28 December, when Marlborough had his first audience with the queen, she told him bluntly that he must not expect votes of thanks from either house of Parliament; he proved to be, in her own words, 'very humble and submissive'.[199] The next evening, Hamilton visited the duke and on 30 December he reported the captain-general's 'Duty and Submission' to the queen, as well as the fact that 'he long'd to have his wife quiet'; this report, Hamilton noted, 'quite melted' the queen. 'Her Majesty said she was sorry to see him so broken. That there was no thought of puting him out.'[200]

327

Encouraged by this reaction, Hamilton concocted a three-part scheme whereby Marlborough and Harley would first reconcile their differences, which would then lead to a reconciliation between Sarah and the queen and finally (and most improbably) a reconciliation between Sarah and Abigail. The queen, however, was sufficiently realistic to find this plan impractical. On 5 January 1711 in a long conversation with Hamilton, the queen described her final meeting with Sarah:

> The Queen . . . said the Reason why she desir'd the Duchess to write without coming to her was, because one can write ones thoughts as well as say them, especially its better in her, because when she speak them it is always in passion, which is uneasie to me.[201]

That evening, Hamilton conferred with both Godolphin and Marlborough, and Marlborough apparently learned for the first time some of the more sordid details of his wife's correspondence with the queen; the next day, Hamilton told the queen 'how angry my Lord Duke was to hear that the Duchess shou'd have spoke so to her Majesty, with which she was extreamly pleas'd'.[202] To Dartmouth, Marlborough also 'complained of his wife who, he said, acted strangely, but there was no help for that, and a man must bear with a good deal, to be quiet at home'.[203]

Despite the evident fondness which the queen still displayed for Marlborough, she remained inflexible in her determination that Sarah must go and that the 'solemn promis' would be ignored. When Hamilton reported this to the Marlboroughs on 10 January, the duchess, in an angry outburst ('theres nothing like this in Turky, in Neros time, or in any History'), darkly threatened that 'Such Things are in my Power, that if known by a Man, that wou'd apprehend and was a right Politician, might lose a Crown'.[204] On 12 January, Shrewsbury and St John assured the Hanoverian envoy, Bothmer (whom Harley had avoided), that they desired Marlborough to remain in the queen's service; at the same time, they made it clear to both Bothmer and Marlborough that Sarah's resignation was mandatory.[205] Two days later, Bothmer, accompanied by Sunderland as interpreter, visited Sarah to convey the Elector of Hanover's wish that Marlborough retain his command at all costs: Sarah submitted.[206] On 17 January, in a final desperate attempt to save his wife's positions, Marlborough carried a humble letter of apology from Sarah to the queen. The queen refused to relent and gave Marlborough a fortnight in which to procure his wife's resignation.[207] The next morning Marlborough returned Sarah's gold key of office to the Queen.[208]

One question remained unresolved – Sarah's threat to publish the queen's letters in her own justification. The queen had no legal recourse either to compel the return of her letters or to prevent their publication. In her *Conduct*, published thirty years after these events when most of the major participants were long dead, the duchess claimed that in her last privy purse accounts she copied the queen's 1702 letter offering her a private pension of £2,000 per annum and deducted £18,000 from her final reckonings for the nine years which she had served. The queen, according to Sarah, kept these accounts a fortnight before returning them with her approval. Apparently, the queen agreed to this on the understanding that Sarah would not publish. In the absence of the account books, one may only speculate. It seems highly probable that, instead of £18,000 in cash, the duchess wiped out the £20,800 which she had borrowed from the privy purse to finance the construction of Marlborough House. This, in addition to the £12,000 which she withdrew as a free grant in March 1708, would mean that Sarah gained £32,800 above and beyond her normal salary and prerequisites.

Thus drew to an end the sad and poignant last stage of a friendship which had lasted for thirty years. Inevitably, there was one further contretemps. Later in the spring, when Sarah was vacating her apartments at St James's, she sent the queen word through Shrewsbury that she wished to store her furniture in the palace until Marlborough House was completed; the answer which the queen (stung by Sarah's financial exactions) returned was that the duchess could rent storage space for ten shillings a week.[209] Infuriated, Sarah removed all portable fixtures from her apartments, down to the mantelpieces and the door-knobs. In retaliation, the queen ordered a temporary halt to the construction of Blenheim, angrily saying 'that she would not build the Duke a house when the Duchess was pulling hers to pieces'.

The queen had secured her revenge. She had freed herself from the 'tyranny' of the Marlboroughs and the Junto. There are, however, few indications that this brought her peace of mind. During the remaining three years of her life, there is every reason to believe that Mrs Morley privately regretted the disappearance of Mr and Mrs Freeman and Mr Montgomery. She had freed herself from her bondage only to find herself slipping into another sort of captivity.

13

'Ye Peace soe much at Hart'

The Peace of Utrecht,
January 1711 – April 1713

I

Peace and the succession were the principal themes which were to dominate the last years of the queen's life. To the queen, 'peace' meant a search for personal tranquillity as well as the restoration of European harmony; the two goals were exceptionally difficult, if not impossible, to separate for one reared as a child of state and whose watchword was 'duty'. She found emotional repose difficult to achieve, in part because of her declining physical condition. She was a captive of her own innate shyness and her limited eyesight. Jonathan Swift recorded in August 1711 the queen's limitations in standard social intercourse:

> There was a drawing room today at Court; but so few company, that the Queen sent for us into her bedchamber, where we made our bows, and stood about twenty of us round the room, while she looked at us round with her fan in her mouth, and once a minute said about three words to some that were nearest her, and then she was told dinner was ready, and went out.[1]

To an increasing extent, the queen was a captive of her invalidism; from 1710 onwards, she rarely walked without support, and eyewitness accounts of her usually mention either her sedan-chairs or her wheel-chairs. Finally, some of her 'family' had been appointed purely for political reasons and they were to remain in the queen's service for the remainder of her life.

The most important of her personal attendants was Elizabeth Percy, Duchess of Somerset. After the Duchess of Marlborough's dismissal, the Duchess of Somerset received Sarah's principal offices, groom of the stole and first lady of the bedchamber. She was two years younger than the queen, and had had a chequered past; married to Henry Cavendish,

330

Earl of Ogle, at the age of twelve, she was left a widow at thirteen. In 1681, at the age of fourteen, she was married to Thomas Thynne of Longleat, from whom she immediately fled to The Hague; Thynne was murdered in February 1682 by the Count von Königsmark, a jealous suitor, and three months later the twice widowed Lady Thynne married the Duke of Somerset. As the heiress of the eleventh and last Earl of Northumberland, one of the oldest aristocratic families in the country, she was, according to Dartmouth, 'the best bred as well as the best born lady in England'.[2] She was to remain the closest royal companion during the last years of the queen's life: 'she was by much the greatest favourite when the Queen died', Dartmouth recalled.[3] In contrast to both Sarah and Abigail, the Duchess of Somerset 'never press'd the Queen hard, nothing makes the Queen more Uneasie than that', according to Sir David Hamilton.[4] The new ministers apparently tried to hinder her appointment as groom of the stole but, according to Swift, 'the Queen said, if . . . she could not have what Servants she liked, she did not find how her Condition was mended'.[5] The duchess's influence with the queen continued to grow, despite the fact that her husband was the first of the 'middle party' to desert Harley. Disappointed in his ambition to succeed Godolphin as head of government in 1710, Somerset had been enraged by the dissolution of Parliament and had retired to Petworth 'to keep out as many Tories and Jacobites in this new Parliament as I can'.[6] Somerset and his duchess, now regarded as wreckers by both parties, became as virulent against their new colleagues as against their predecessors, but neither Harley not his colleagues were unduly concerned by Somerset's desertion.[7] Somerset's prime importance was his influence with the queen through his wife who, in Swift's opinion, had 'quickly won so far upon the affections of Her Majesty, that she had more Personall Credit than all the Queen's Servants put together'.[8] This was an influence which Somerset did not scruple to use, and it gave him access to the queen.[9] The Duchess of Somerset represented the remaining Whig influence in the queen's household. Sir David Hamilton, regarding the duchess as his political ally, attempted to reinforce her position in his conversations with the queen: 'I took notice of my Lady Massams Passion as unsuitable to the Queen's Temper, and of the Duchess of Somerset's more Suitable, to which she reply'd, "Yes, by farr".'[10]

Abigail Masham, of course, was the Tory rival of the Duchess of Somerset. On the dismissal of her cousin, Abigail was given Sarah's former post as keeper of the privy purse (with her sister, Alice Hill, serving as her deputy). In May 1711, Samuel Masham was appointed comptroller of the household in the place of Francis Godolphin.

Abigail's attendance on the queen and her potential influence, however, were repeatedly interrupted by long absences due to six pregnancies during her first seven years of marriage.* The concern which she displayed for the welfare of her children did not please her Tory partisans who resented every moment she was absent from the queen's side. In 1713, when Abigail was at the bedside of her eldest son who she believed was dying, Swift complained:

> She is so excessively fond it makes me mad; she should never leave the Queen, but leave every thing to stick to what is so much the Interest of the Publick as well as her own. This I tell her, but talk to the Winds.[11]

Undoubtedly, Abigail's repeated pregnancies struck a chord of sympathy with the queen. In October 1712, when Abigail was about to give birth to her second son, it was reported that 'the Queen was very much concerned for her. . . . She was pleased to sitt by her three hours late at night by her bedside.'[12] Despite Sarah's accusations that the queen displayed a 'passion' for Abigail, the last four years of the queen's life make it clear that, while she treated the Duchess of Somerset as a companion, she continued to regard Abigail as a servant.

If political divisions within her own 'family' made it difficult for the queen to find tranquillity, political peace in the country at large was impossible to achieve, at least in part due to the queen's own actions in 1710. In spite of the establishment of a new, and largely Tory, ministry, the queen still maintained her hostility towards organized political parties: she told Cowper in 1713, 'That when one was in a Party, it was the Influence of That, that guided their discourse and Opinion, and till he show'd himself by his Actions not to be in a Party, She could not trust his Opinion.'[13] Never again was she unhesitatingly to trust her ministers. One striking aspect of the queen's last ministry is that she frequently consulted Whig leaders in private: as Swift noted in March 1711, 'Lord Somers has been twice in the Queen's closet, once very lately.'[14] As his diary reveals, the queen often used Sir David Hamilton as her intermediary with the opposition party, particularly with Hamilton's close friend, Lord Cowper. Significantly, she was never

---

*As in everything else concerning the Mashams, the facts of these pregnancies remain unclear. Mrs Masham certainly gave birth to four children during the queen's reign: Anne (September 1708 – March 1727), Elizabeth (1709 – October 1724), George (August 1711 – ??), and Samuel (November 1712 – 1776). George may have died in April 1713, as Swift reported that 'he will not live' (Journal to Stella, 658: 10 April 1713). A fifth child, Francis, was born, possibly in early 1714 (Swift Correspondence, I, 409: John Arbuthnot to Swift [November 1713]), but the dates of his birth and death are not available. Mrs Masham also suffered a miscarriage in March 1713 (Journal to Stella, 632: 5 March 1713).

again to allow herself to be manoeuvred into the position in which she had found herself after the dismissal of Harley in 1708 – cut off from all advice but that of her official ministers.

The queen's hatred of parties naturally attracted her to the Duke of Shrewsbury. The last member of one of the oldest noble houses in England, Shrewsbury was suave and debonair in his personal conduct (his nickname was the 'King of Hearts') and widely experienced in foreign and domestic affairs. Like the queen Shrewsbury stood apart from faction and, also like the queen, he was extremely cautious. According to the Duchess of Marlborough, the queen

> us'd to send her own chair she was carried about the rooms in, when she had the goute, to bring him up when he was lame, or pretended to be so, for upon every thing of consequence, that was to come out, he was frighted I believe, & pretended to be sick, but the Queen sent for him perpetually, & kept him two hours together with her.[15]

The queen herself described to Harley her reliance on Shrewsbury's counsel: 'I speake to him of every thing & advice with him on all occasions & will continue doeing soe.'[16] In 1711, according to Cowper, 'when some Lords told the Queen that they would Vote for the Interest of the Nation, she bid them vote as Lord Chamberlain did'.[17] Always reluctant to accept any governmental post which required continuous application to business, Shrewsbury none the less resented those who did. As Dartmouth later recalled, Shrewsbury 'had not resolution enough to be chief minister, but could not bear that another should be what he so often refused: and could not help shewing his dissatisfaction, even to invidiousness'.[18] Shrewsbury's timidity kept him in the shadows, but his influence could prove decisive. He repeatedly impinged upon Harley's peace policy and was the only new minister of importance who was unabashedly pro-Hanoverian, both publicly and privately, throughout the last four years of the queen's life. Harley was suspicious of Shrewsbury's fondness for St John and the fact that, despite their political differences, Shrewsbury maintained his personal friendship with Marlborough.[19] Furthermore, Shrewsbury acted as mediator in the frequent quarrels between Harley and St John, thereby shoring up the younger man's position.[20] Finally, because of his dedicated Anglicanism, his anti-Junto Whiggism, and his reputation as one of the chief architects of the Revolution, Shrewsbury enjoyed more influence with the queen (on those rare occasions when he chose to exercise it) than any other minister, including Harley.[21] It is not surprising that Harley, while trying to diminish Shrewsbury's influence with the queen,[22] also worked to secure the duke's honourable removal from England, and that St John was equally determined to keep Shrewsbury at home for as long as possible.[23]

All of this posed problems for Harley, the minister responsible for the day-to-day management of the government. Part of the queen's suspicion and independence was Harley's own fault: according to Swift, the new ministers 'have cautioned the Queen so much against being governed, that she observes it too much'.[24] As the queen told Harley in 1712,

> You can not wonder that I who have bin ill used soe many yeares should desire to keep my self from being againe enslaved, & if I must always Comply, & not be complyed with, is I think very hard, & what I can not submit to.[25]

According to Dr Hamilton, Harley and his colleagues attempted to circumscribe the Queen's independence by increasing her isolation: 'She was kept not only from Persons of a Contrary Opinion, but from the Knowledge of things.'[26] Despite this growing isolation, the queen was never again to prove as pliable as in the opening years of her reign.

Harley's foremost problem was that his parliamentary majority was divided between the court party, on which he could depend as long as he enjoyed the queen's active support, and a group of young High Tories who quickly formed themselves into the October Club, so named after the month in which the malt for their favourite beverage was harvested.[27] The members of the October Club were mostly Hanoverian when sober, Jacobite when drunk. The leadership of this group was seized by Harley's younger colleagues, St John and Harcourt. The group desired vengeance against the previous administration and, as a sop to them, the government initiated an investigation (which proved to be abortive) of Godolphin's financial administration. The queen told Sir David Hamilton 'That it was Mr. Harley's Misfortune that St. Johns high and Lord Keeper [Harcourt] who took Fees of little lords was with him'.[28] The foresighted Harley was already undertaking measures to clip the wings of an incipient rebellion within the ministry's ranks and to preserve his own power and the supremacy of the court faction in the uneasy partnership which formed his majority in Parliament.

II

Even before the dismissal of Godolphin, Harley had entered into secret negotiations with the French court through the Earl of Jersey and the obscure Abbé François Gaultier, a Roman Catholic priest in the imperial embassy chapel and the Marquis de Torcy's London agent. Jersey's wife was a Roman Catholic and it was through her that Gaultier approached the former lord chamberlain. Gaultier became the principal medium of Anglo-French communications, a position which he retained until the death of Queen Anne. He was the perfect instrument for the new ministers, for he spoke English, was sufficiently obscure to remain unnoticed by Britain's watchful allies, and could easily be disavowed if necessary.

The three principles which Jersey outlined to Gaultier in the autumn of 1710 were substantially those on which Harley and his colleagues operated until the conclusion of the Treaty of Utrecht in April 1713.[29] First, peace was to be negotiated on the basis of a secret understanding with France at the expense of the allies: only the Duke of Savoy was to be conciliated, for Britain needed to carry one other ally with her in order to destroy the Grand Alliance. The threat of a separate Anglo-French peace was to be the sword of Damocles hanging over allied statesmen, compelling them to accept whatever bargain Britain and France had arranged in advance. To cover this stark betrayal of the allies, Jersey proposed the 'two-tier' negotiations which Harley later successfully conducted: official negotiations in the Dutch republic, secret negotiations in London and Paris; official British support for all allied demands (including the restoration of the entire Spanish monarchy to the Habsburgs), but a previous secret agreement with France which would only be revealed to the allies in stages. The second British principle was that Philip V should retain Spain and the Indies; in return, Great Britain would receive exclusive and extensive commercial advantages in Europe and the Americas. The 1709 Anglo-Dutch Barrier Treaty was to be scrapped and the Dutch were to receive a barrier 'agreeable to the English nation'. Under cover of returning to the partition of the Spanish possessions demanded by the original Treaty of Grand Alliance, Jersey and Harley were ready to take the first step in undoing the life-work of William III: the dissolution of the union of the Maritime Powers.[30] To secure themselves after the queen's death against retribution for such a gross betrayal of the allies (including, of course, the Hanoverian heir), Jersey informed Gaultier in September 1710 that the new ministers' third proposal was to restore the Pretender 'if he thinks like them', principally on religion.[31] Both the French and the allies later regarded a Stuart restoration as the logical conclusion of the new regime's peace proposals.

After the arrival in London of the news of General James Stanhope's defeat at Brihuega on 29 November/9 December 1710 and the loss of all Castile to Philip V, Harley was ready to act. In January 1711, Gaultier was dispatched on a secret mission to Versailles to consult with Torcy and to present Harley's proposals to the French minister. In April, Gaultier made a second trip to the French capital, and returned to London with 'French proposals' in writing. These were the proposals which were first presented to the cabinet, as though the French had initiated the negotiations rather than Harley. It is highly improbable that the queen knew of the existence of Gaultier, or of the secret negotiations before this point. Certainly, Jersey was in close contact with Harley, hoping to find a position in the new administration. The queen, however, would not hear of Jersey, remaining implacably hostile to him because he was a suspected Jacobite. She never knew that the basic principle of the 'Jersey period' of the peace negotiations was the restoration of her half-brother. When Gaultier asked Jersey point-blank whether the queen approved of his first mission to France, Jersey refused to answer.[32]

In a campaign reminiscent of that conducted by Sarah and Godolphin on Sunderland's behalf in 1706, Harley and his 'female solicitrix', Abigail,[33] continually attempted throughout late 1710 and early 1711 to secure an office for Jersey (either as first lord of the Admiralty or lord privy seal), but the queen refused to employ him because of his Jacobite sympathies.[34] It took Harley nearly a year to overcome the queen's aversion to Jersey. In August 1711, Jersey was forced to write a letter, ostensibly to Harley but undoubtedly for the queen's eyes, in which he denied rumours that he was a Jacobite, admitting that 'the consequence of this to me is no less than the entire loss of the Queen's favour'.[35] Jersey's formal disavowal of Jacobite sympathies, combined with Harley's warning to the queen that the peace would languish without Jersey's help ('yr ministry wil crumble al to peices, & what is of the last consequence, I cannot have any one *to help me in your service*'), did the trick. The queen reluctantly agreed that Jersey should be appointed lord privy seal, but on 26 August, the very day the appointment was to be announced, Jersey suddenly died.[36] (The position went to John Robinson, an experienced diplomat whom the queen had recently named Bishop of Bristol.)

Harley's negotiations with the Jacobites through Jersey and Gaultier were necessary because Jacobite strength was greater in the Parliament elected in 1710 than in any House of Commons since the queen's accession.[37] Harley wished to gain Jacobite support for the ministry, in order to strengthen his hand in buttressing 'moderation' against the excessive partisanship of the October Club. The Pretender, hopeful that Harley would work for a Stuart restoration, dispatched orders to his friends in England to support the government and helped contribute to

Harley's success by subduing his radical supporters. With only slight exaggeration, the Pretender later informed Torcy that Harley could never have achieved peace without Jacobite support in Parliament,[38] support which was to last almost to the end of Harley's tenure in office.

On the evening of 7 March 1711, the day before the ninth anniversary of her accession to the throne, the queen granted a private audience to Anthonie de Guiscard, a French refugee previously employed by the government to help plan an invasion of Normandy (a scheme which never reached fruition). After Harley became chancellor of the exchequer, he halved Guiscard's pension; financially pressed, Guiscard entered into treasonable correspondence with Versailles. Dartmouth later recalled that 'the Queen told me, he was very pressing for an augmentation in his pension and complained that he was ill paid'.[39] The next morning, Guiscard was arrested and, while being interrogated by the council, he attempted to assassinate Harley by stabbing a penknife into his breast; Harley was saved because Guiscard's blows were blunted by the heavy gold brocade waistcoat which he had donned for the accession anniversary. Nevertheless, Harley sustained serious wounds, while Guiscard was run through by the Duke of Ormonde and St John, and died in prison a few days later. The queen was so distraught by the news of the attempted assassination that she wept uncontrollably for two hours, and by 10 March had developed such a high fever that four doctors had to be summoned to her bedside at five in the morning.[40]

It took almost two months for Harley to recover from this attempt on his life. During his absence from governmental affairs, St John embittered his quarrel with Harley by claiming (with some appearance of probability) that he, rather than Harley, had been Guiscard's intended victim, but Harley's wounds and his slow recovery lent him a martyr's image and added an extra fillip to his personal popularity. St John also seized upon Harley's absence to begin building his credit with Abigail Masham: he persuaded the queen to agree to a plan which Sunderland had previously formulated for an invasion of French Canada. In the cabinet on 25 March while Harley was still absent, 'The Queen declared the design of the expedition to Canada to the Lords' and ordered St John to give the details.[41] The most important of these was that the expedition (which Harley opposed and which ended in abysmal failure) was to be commanded by Abigail's younger brother, John Hill.

The international situation was transformed on 6/17 April by the sudden and unexpected death of the Holy Roman emperor, Joseph I. His sole male heir was his younger brother, the Archduke Charles (who was elected emperor the following October). Suddenly, 'No Peace without

337

Spain' – the policy supported by both British parties – meant that the empire of Charles V would be reunited in the person of Charles VI; the dreaded spectre of 'universal monarchy' was now personified by the house of Habsburg rather than the house of Bourbon. The death of the emperor coincided with Gaultier's second trip to Versailles; on 26 April, while Harley was still convalescent, the queen ordered the proposals from Torcy, which Gaultier had carried back to London, to be read in the cabinet and then ordered St John to send a copy to Heinsius at The Hague.[42] This was the last information which the allies were to receive from London concerning the secret Anglo-French negotiations until the autumn, when Harley's plans were complete.

On 2 May the Earl of Rochester, the queen's uncle, unexpectedly died. Rochester was the lord president of her council, and his death meant that the queen would be forced to reorganize her cabinet. Following her moderate instincts and wishing to consult those from her former ministry for whom she had conceived a high personal regard, she summoned Somers and Cowper to a secret conference.[43] The Whigs, full of soaring hopes that the queen and Harley would bring them back into office as a balance to the power of the October Club, played into Harley's hands by advising the queen to promote him to the position of lord treasurer.[44] On 4 May, Harley introduced to the House of Commons his South Sea Company scheme for trading in the Spanish Indies: the plan was intended to rival the Whig dominated Bank of England, and it received general Tory applause. On 23 May, Harley was created Earl of Oxford and Mortimer, a promotion to which the queen had agreed a month earlier.[45] His nomination as lord treasurer was delayed until 29 May. The significance of the date – the fifty-first anniversary of the Restoration – did not go unnoticed by contemporaries.[46] The day Oxford (as he will henceforth be known) was given the white staff, Dr Hamilton recorded: 'The Queen told me she believed Mr. Harley (now Earl of Oxford) was an honest Man.'[47] On 12 June, Parliament was prorogued and then the full extent of Oxford's power (which he had tricked the Whigs into aiding and abetting) became clear; among his personal allies, Robert Benson (a genial Tory nonentity) was appointed chancellor of the exchequer, Buckingham was promoted to the lord presidency, replacing Rochester, and Poulett replaced Buckingham as lord steward.[48]

While Oxford was consolidating his domestic power, Marlborough – in what proved to be his last campaign – was moving closer to a full-scale invasion of France. The campaign of 1711 made it virtually certain that the allied armies would march on Paris in 1712. On 5 August 1711, Marlborough's army circumvented Maréchal Villars's much vaunted *ne plus ultra* lines and, on 12 September, captured Bouchain.

Marlborough and Prince Eugene viewed 'this hole of Bouchain', in the sarcastic words of the Earl of Strafford, as the passage 'through which our whole army is to creep into the heart of France & so force Spain from them'.[49] Oxford, however, had no intention of letting the war progress to this stage, for to abase France utterly would prevent Britain from achieving the separate and exclusive advantages on which the secret Anglo-French negotiations were based.

The queen's introduction of the cabinet into the secret negotiations also foiled Oxford's original intention to keep St John out of the business. St John suppressed whatever chagrin and displeasure he may have felt at being excluded previously and he entered enthusiastically into the plans which Oxford had formed. The lord treasurer, however, soon expressed indignation that his junior colleague was assuming a leading role in the negotiations, and by July Torcy was well aware of Oxford's resentment.[50] The queen also showed a marked coolness towards St John, who later complained that she had treated him as a lackey during the peace negotiations.[51] In the autumn of 1711, explaining this to Swift,

> The secretary [St John] told me last night, that he had found the reason why the Queen was cold to him for some months past . . . it was, that they suspected he was at bottom with the Duke of Marlborough.[52]

St John's position and vigour, his knowledge of French and his grasp of the European political situation, as well as his connection with Shrewsbury, soon made him indispensable in negotiating the details of the larger scheme which Oxford had conceived. Yet the lord treasurer was determined to control the negotiations and, in Oxford's own words, 'the Treasurer's Hands were full of negotiating the Peace in all Courts Abroad' during the summer of 1711.[53] Later Harleyite propaganda alleging that St John was the principal Jacobite sympathizer in the queen's last government (and as such was opposed by that 'Sincere Hanoverian', Oxford) seemingly received *ex post facto* confirmation by St John's precipitate flight to Paris and the Pretender in 1715. Yet we may note that, until October 1713, Oxford remained the sole ministerial negotiator with the exiled court of St Germain, while St John displayed little or no interest in furthering Jacobite fortunes. Although he knew or suspected the lord treasurer's connections with St Germain through Gaultier, St John did not know the details: he remained unaware, for instance, that Oxford had successfully solicited St Germain's orders for Jacobite support in Parliament.[54]

In July 1711, to hasten the pace of the secret Anglo-French talks, Matthew, Prior, poet and diplomat, was dispatched to France with

Gaultier. The queen, at Oxford's urging, agreed to shield Prior against charges of high treason for visiting France during wartime (and Oxford against any charges of responsibility for Prior's mission) by signing the famous 'three line power' without the customary counter-signature of a minister:[55]

> ANNE R.
> Le sieur Prior est pleinement instruit et
> authorise de communiquer a la France nos demandes
> Preliminaires, et de nous en rapporter la response.
> A.R.*

The French reception of Prior constituted a *de facto* recognition of Anne as queen of Great Britain. On 10 August, Gaultier and Prior left Paris for London, accompanied by Torcy's leading commercial expert, Nicholas Mesnager. Mesnager spent almost two months in London, secretly engaging in detailed negotiations with Oxford and St John. The queen, in residence at Windsor, was kept closely informed of the progress of these talks. On 19 September she assured Oxford:

> I am very willing to receive ye Compliment you mention [i.e. from Mesnager] if you can Contrive a very privat way to do it. Since I saw you, Lord Chamberlain [Shrewsbury] has talked a good deale to me about ye Peace, & I hope he will act very hartely in it tho he seems a little fearfull.[56]

The next day, while urging that Strafford should be dispatched immediately to his post as envoy at The Hague, the queen told Oxford: 'I give you many thanks for ye account you send me of ye Conversation you had last night, & am very glad the great affair is in soe good a way, I pray God send a happy Conclusion of it.'[57]

With agreement in sight, it came as a rude shock to Mesnager when the British – under pressure from Shrewsbury and St John – raised the question of the Pretender. Shrewsbury was zealous to secure a peace agreement, but he had already protested to St John against what appeared to be the ministry's gross betrayal of the allies.[58] Now he was determined to secure ample guarantees for the Hanoverian succession. On 20 September, Mesnager met a full cabinet delegation for the first time, which included Oxford, St John, Dartmouth, Shrewsbury, and Prior. A long silence was broken by St John whose voice, according to the French diplomat, betrayed his embarrassment; the House of Lords' resolution of March 1709 prevented Britain entering into a treaty with

* 'Mr. Prior is fully instructed and authorized to communicate our preliminary demands to France, and to bring us the response.'

any prince harbouring the Pretender. St John, therefore, informed Mesnager that James had to leave France. Aware that his hosts had been involved in a heated controversy before the meeting and having studied the faces of the group, Mesnager believed that Shrewsbury was the only member who had insisted upon this condition. Mesnager pointed out that they were only negotiating a preliminary agreement, and that when full-scale formal negotiations opened, the Pretender might choose to leave France voluntarily. This expedient was met with smiles, particularly from the enigmatic lord treasurer: even Shrewsbury lost 'son serieuse'.[59]

The queen was determined that nothing should prevent her king-doms from enjoying the benefits of peace. On 24 September she told Oxford:

> I have this buisnes of ye Peace soe much at hart, that I can not help giveing you this trouble to ask if it may not be proper to order Mr. Secretary [St John], in case he finds Mr. Menager very averse to ye new proposition [i.e. the Pretender's expulsion], not to insist upon it, & if you think it right I hope you will take care Mr. Secretary has such an order in my name, *for I think there is nothing soe much to be fear'd as ye letting ye Treaty goe out of our hands.*[60]

On 27 September three documents which constituted the preliminary articles were signed. The first, signed by Mesnager alone, was to be shown to the allies: these 'public' preliminaries contained Louix XIV's promise to recognize the queen 'and the Succession as presently established' after the treaty's conclusion, to prevent any union of the crowns of France and Spain, to satisfy all nations at the forthcoming peace congress, to restore international commerce, to allow undefined 'barriers' for the Dutch and the empire, and to destroy the port of Dunkirk if Britain provided an equivalent. The second document (a secret addition to the first and again signed only by Mesnager) promised that France would co-operate in securing those parts of Italy for the Duke of Savoy which the British government judged necessary. The third document contained specific French concessions to the British and was to be kept secret from the allies until both contracting parties agreed to reveal its contents: it was signed by Mesnager for France and by Dartmouth and St John for Great Britain. These 'secret' preliminaries again provided for Louis's eventual recognition of the queen and the established succession, negotiations for an Anglo-French commercial treaty, the conditional destruction of Dunkirk, British retention of Gibraltar and Port Mahon, British acquisition of the Spanish American slave trade (the *Asiento*) for thirty years, and the same commercial privileges in Spain as France enjoyed.[61]

Oxford's intention in negotiating both 'public' and 'secret' preliminary articles was to reveal the true extent and nature of the Anglo-French agreement by stages, in order to avoid concerted foreign and domestic opposition to the peace. One week after the signature of the preliminary articles, Oxford was still pretending to the imperial resident, Hoffmann, that the war in Spain would be continued with vigour, and reacted with false incredulity to Hoffmann's suggestion that Spain and the Indies had already been consigned to the house of Bourbon.[62] On 11 October the British government presented copies of the public preliminaries to allied diplomats: on 13 October the Imperial ambassador, Count von Gallas, printed them in the Whig *Daily Courant*, for which the government immediately denied him access to court and demanded his recall.[63] Despite the ministry's contention that the preliminaries did not constitute a treaty, but were merely an outline for discussion at the forthcoming general peace conference, the published documents left both Whigs and Tories aghast at so great a departure from the allied position of 1709.[64]

III

Motives, personal and political, noble and base, quickly led Somerset, Nottingham, and Marlborough to reinforce the emerging Whig opposition to the 'Jacobite peace'. Somerset, as we have seen, was the first of the 'middle party' to desert Oxford and was now in violent opposition to the ministry. The second important dissenter on the issue of war or peace was 'party sense in person', the Earl of Nottingham. He had entertained great hopes of re-entering office in 1710 but the queen, enraged by his support of the invitation in 1705, would not hear of him; Oxford, who disliked 'Dismal' and feared his influence, warmly supported her in this. The cabinet reshuffle after Rochester's death in May 1711 made it clear beyond all doubt that there was no place in Oxford's ministry for Nottingham.[65] When Oxford tried to win Nottingham's support for the preliminaries in October, Nottingham (who had made 'No Peace without Spain' a part of Tory dogma) remained sarcastically unimpressed. 'I am very glad to hear from your Lordship so good a character of this treaty as your Lordship gives it', Nottingham replied, 'for I may conclude that the accounts of it in the prints must be very imperfect.'[66] When Nottingham came up to London in November, his exclusion from the Tory government still rankled. 'I find Nottingham as sour and fiercely wild as you can imagine anything to be that has lived long in the desert', Oxford's ally Poulett reported.[67] The Whigs, willing to sacrifice the interests of their Dissenting adherents in order to thwart the Tory peace proposals, easily secured Nottingham's support by promising to endorse his Occasional Conformity bill.

The third and most important of the anti-ministerial recruits was Marlborough. During the siege of Bouchain in August, Marlborough dispatched the Earl of Stair to London with plans for wintering his forces on the French frontier, thereby ensuring an early opening for the 1712 campaign: at the same time, he secretly communicated these plans to the Elector of Hanover, who heartily endorsed them 'as the surest means of reducing France to the necessity of concurring in a reasonable peace'.[68] Oxford indicated his willingness to accept Marlborough's plan, but the Dutch – already suspicious of negotiations between France and the Tories – refused to agree.[69] This left Oxford in the most advantageous situation possible: allied armies remained in the best position ever for an invasion of France,[70] and the queen was now convinced, as she told Oxford, that 'ye Duke of Marlborough shews plainer than ever by this new project his unwillingness for a peace, but I hope our negotiations will Succeed & then it will not be in his power to prevent it'.[71] To keep Marlborough in line, the government was sponsoring a parliamentary investigation of the captain-general's accounts, particularly charges that Marlborough had misappropriated the 2½ per cent of the payments from foreign princes which traditionally went to the commander for secret service purposes.

The queen's anxiety to procure peace had a harmful effect on her health. During the summer at Windsor, she had enjoyed hunting in the Great Park: 'she hunts in a chaise with one horse', Swift noted, 'which she drives herself, and drives furiously like Jehu, and is a mighty hunter like Nimrod'. A week later, he commented that 'she drove in her chaise above forty miles'.[72] At the beginning of September the queen suffered a debilitating attack of 'gout' (as her affliction was then labelled), and throughout the autumn she repeatedly complained of her lameness. Nevertheless, she closely followed the diplomatic negotiations of her ministers, in particular their conferences with Willem Buys, the special envoy of the Dutch republic with whom they were attempting to arrange the details of the forthcoming peace conference. The queen personally received Buys, and on 26 October she told Oxford:

I hope every thing is now soe well seteld with Mr. Buys that he will be ready to go in a few days tho the Parliament should not meet soe soon as we now intend, & I fancy it can not for something must be said in my Speech of ye Peace & I question whether in Holland they will make any hast[e] to make any answer to what Mr. Buys is to say to them.[73]

343

The oligarchs who controlled Dutch political life were under intense public pressure to procure peace, but were highly suspicious of the separate and secret negotiations with France which the British government had initiated. Throughout 1711 and 1712, the Dutch consistently proved to be the weak link in the chain of allied and Whig resistance to the terms which Oxford and France sought to impose upon them. Frightened by Strafford's threats not to concert the forthcoming campaign with them (which implied a Tory willingness to make a separate peace with France) and hoping that the opposition in London was now so strong that the ministry would fall and the projected peace congress would never open, the States-General on 21 November/2 December named Utrecht as the place for negotiations.[74]

The queen dreaded the opening of Parliament, as much on personal as on political grounds. 'As to the Parliament', she notified Oxford on 3 November, 'I can not tell yet when I shall be able to open it for tho I thank God I am much better then I was, I am not out of paine & ye weaknes always Continues a good while after.'[75] She was also worried about whether or not the government would be able to command a majority in the upper house in support of its peace policy. 'At this Juncture', she warned Oxford a month before Parliament was to meet, 'we cannot part with one vote out of the house of Lords.'[76] To shore up the ministry's defences, the queen personally interviewed a large number of nobles, including the Dukes of Grafton and St Albans, the Earls of Dorset and Scarborough, and Lords Somers and Cowper. She told Bishop Burnet 'she hoped bishops would not be against peace',[77] and the day before Parliament opened she spoke to the Duke of Kent, who later voted with the Tories.[78] Although she later made light of it, she was visibly disturbed by Burnet's warning that her ministers intended to introduce the Pretender, that her life was not safe, and that the fires of Smithfield would soon burn again.[79] Nothing showed the depth of her determination to procure peace for her country better than her handling of Marlborough.

Oxford had used the caution of Shrewsbury and the military plans of Marlborough to undermine the reputation of them both with the queen. This was particularly necessary in the case of Marlborough, for the queen still retained great affection for him: in September 1711 it was reported that 'at Court no one was so inquisitive of my Lord Duke's health as the Queen her self'.[80] Oxford's campaign against Marlborough and Shrewsbury was reflected in the queen's letter to the lord treasurer of 15 November:

the news you sent me . . . conserning the Duke of Marlborough is something prodigious, & . . . his proceedings since, I think is very extraordinary. I am sorry the Duke of Shrewsbury should make complaints of me, I am sure I do not deserve them for I speake to him of every thing & advice with him on all occasions & will continue doing soe, thinking it very right to keep him in good humour, but I can not see how I can say anything to soften him, for I suppose I am not to know he Complains of me.[81]

She had already determined, in her own mind,

> When the Duke of Marlborough coms, I should think it will be best for me just to begin to open the matter of the Peace to him and refer him to you and Mr. Secretary [St John] for a fuller account of all that is passed.[82]

Marlborough returned to London on 17 November, and the next day he had his first audience with the queen. 'The Duke of Marlborough came to me yesterday,' she told Oxford, 'made a great many of his usiall professions of duty and affection to me. He seemed dejected and very uneasy about this matter of the publick accounts, stayed neare an hour and saw nobody heare but my self.'[83] This interview in fact lasted only about fifteen minutes. On 23 November, Marlborough returned to Hampton Court to meet the queen privately.[84] According to Sarah,

> when He waited upon Her again, to lay before Her what was doing against Him by ye Commissioners of Accounts, She put on ye guise of great kindness, & said 'She was sure, Her Servants would not encourage such proceedings', or to that effect. Yet it appear'd afterwards that not only Her Servants, but She herself encouraged this very proceeding against Him, & particularly took care that it should not be deferr'd, but that their Representation against Him should be laid before ye House of Commons before ye End of that Session.[85]

According to Marlborough's version, which he reported to Bothmer, the queen entreated Marlborough to resume his place in the cabinet and to support the peace proposals. This Marlborough refused to do, warning her that Oxford's ultimate goal was the restoration of the Pretender and, alluding to the 'mysterious' circumstances of Charles II's sudden death, he declared that her life would then be in danger from the Catholics.[86] The queen was well aware of the party purposes behind such warnings, and it was undoubtedly after this second interview, when Marlborough offended her by refusing to attend the cabinet, that she finally resolved to dismiss the captain-general. On the same day Oxford assured Gaultier (who was now the lord treasurer's confidant) and through him, Torcy, that Marlborough would not be allowed to command in the 1712 campaign, an assurance which he would hardly have made without knowing that the queen would agree.[87] Whatever her outward resolution, the queen was inwardly troubled by these warnings, delivered by men like Marlborough and Burnet with whom she had been intimately associated many years before Robert Harley had entered her life. Even more shocking to the queen was the public expression of opposition to her policies made by Baron von Bothmer, the London representative of her heir presumptive, the Elector of Hanover.

The government had not neglected the arts of propaganda: on 27 November, Jonathan Swift published *The Conduct of the Allies*, a highly partisan and deliberately misleading history of the Grand Alliance written under the direct supervision of Oxford and St John. The following day Bothmer presented the elector's formal protest against the preliminary articles to St John, who read it and promised an answer.[88] No answer was immediately forthcoming and, following the elector's orders, Bothmer circulated handwritten copies among opponents of the peace. To counter the tremendous popular success of Swift's appeal to British xenophobia, the *Daily Courant* published an English translation of Bothmer's memorial on 6 December, the day before Parliament opened. This sensational document placed the elector squarely and publicly on the side of the Whigs. The memorial[89] condemned the preliminaries as vague, general, and meaningless, accused the British government of violating the Treaty of Grand Alliance by secretly negotiating with the French, and suggested that as soon as Philip V was secure on the throne of Spain, the house of Bourbon would actively support the Pretender. Bothmer's memorial created a sensation: he claimed that 1,000 copies had been sold on the first day and the *Flying Post* immediately reprinted it.[90]

The memorial had a profound effect upon Oxford, who declared that it was 'not to be borne by a free nation; and whoever advised that memorial have given the succession a terrible wound, and we must do our best to calm the spirits of the people upon that head'.[91] In reality the treasurer, knowing full well that the memorial was the elector's, was determined to stand his ground. Some Whig leaders, convinced that they were on the verge of destroying the ministry, made one final attempt to induce Oxford to head a new coalition of 'moderate' Whig and Tory elements.[92] Oxford, following his established pattern, listened to these Whig suggestions, but once again rebuffed the proffered alliance. The day before Parliament opened he was convinced that he had a majority of ten peers at his disposal.[93] The great swell of public opinion in favour of peace, expressed in letters he was daily receiving from 'the gentlemen of England', assured Oxford of success despite the fact that sentiment in the House of Commons was virtually unanimous that Spain should go to an anti-Bourbon candidate.[94] Oxford calculated that the Tory majority could be managed until the government could afford to admit publicly that Philip V would retain his throne. At the root of Oxford's subsequent policy lay his alienation from Hanover: 'If the Elector prefers Bothmer to Brittain . . .', he noted darkly to himself.[95] Gaultier, now Oxford's confidant, reported to Torcy: 'The impertinent memorial of Bothmer advances the prospects of Montgoulin [James] and does not hurt our own.'[96]

The queen's ministers had kept her in ignorance of Bothmer's memorial: although it had been presented to St John on 28 November, the queen knew nothing of it until the Duchess of Somerset called her attention to the printed version in the *Daily Courant*. The opposition of the elector to her measures and the suppression of that fact by her ministers came as a great shock to her.[97] Nevertheless, she remained resolute for peace. Bothmer compared her entry into the House of Lords for the crucial opening debates on 7 December, passing through lines of nobles, to a general reviewing his troops.[98] The last minute designation of Utrecht by the States-General as the site for the peace congress allowed Oxford, after a dig at Marlborough, to insert words into the Queen's Speech which the emperor's publicly announced opposition to a conference, Bothmer's memorial, and the previous Dutch position rendered false and were publicly known to be false:

> Notwithstanding the arts of those who delight in war, both time and
> place are appointed for the opening of the Treaty of a general peace.
> Our Allies, especially the States-General, whose interest I look upon as
> inseparable from my own, have, by their ready concurrence, expressed
> their intire confidence in me.[99]

As soon as the queen had finished her speech and she had returned incognito to the House, Nottingham proposed his famous motion that 'No Peace could be safe or honourable to Great Britain or Europe, if Spain and the West Indies were allotted to any branch of the House of Bourbon'. So sure of success were the Whigs that Sunderland reminded Oxford 'that in the late reign, four Lords were impeached for having made a Partition Treaty'.[100] Nottingham's motion was carried by a majority of eight votes (62 to 54). The queen was undoubtedly shaken by the government's defeat on this crucial issue. It was widely noted that when Shrewsbury, the lord chamberlain, asked the queen whether he or the Earl of Lindsey, the hereditary great chamberlain, should escort her from the house, 'she answered short, "Neither of you", and gave her hand to the Duke of Somerset, who was louder than any in the house for the clause against Peace'.[101]

Well might minor Tory functionaries worry, and St John and Mrs

Masham give Swift 'some lights to suspect the Queen is changed'.[102] The preliminary articles, flimsy in themselves, had thoroughly shaken cabinet unity. Shrewsbury and Buckingham had been notably silent during the debate on Nottingham's motion.[103] The following day, Dartmouth deserted the ministry during its next defeat by five votes on an issue involving the queen's right to create British peerages: the majority decision not to seat the Duke of Hamilton under his new British title, Duke of Brandon, was a further exacerbation of Anglo-Scottish relations.[104] The queen, who thought ''twas pitty the Prerogative should be so Lessen'd',[105] none the less adamantly refused Hamilton's demand that Dartmouth should be turned out of office for voting against Hamilton's patent: 'she believed', according to Dartmouth, 'it would give great offence to the English lords, and do the Scotch more harm than good'.[106] It was clear, however, that for the first time in the queen's reign her government had lost control of one of the two houses of Parliament.

IV

The events of December 1711 shook the queen's confidence in Oxford. Had she not warned him earlier that the government's majority in the House of Lords was questionable? Politically, the easiest task which Oxford's hand, of the queen's last letter to her most longstanding and had agreed to this on 23 November. On 10 December, when Sir David Hamilton taxed the queen with her slur on Marlborough ('the arts of those who delight in war') 'as not suitable to her Calm Temper', she defended herself by saying 'they were the words of the Common Prayer'.[107] On the same day Oxford secretly divided Marlborough's offices for future distribution.[108] But the dismissal was delayed until the commissioners of accounts could lay before the House of Commons a prima facie case of peculation against Marlborough, after which the Commons were immediately adjourned on 22 December before the report could be debated. On 29 December the queen's letter of dismissal was delivered to the captain-general, who was so angry that he threw it into the fire. Oxford's memoranda contain an imperfect draft copy, in Oxford's hand, of the queen's last letter to her most longstanding and famous servant:

> You desir'd to hear from me & not any other way, my resolution concerning Your self; I appeal to your own conscience how little I have deserved the Treatment I have met with; Since I thought never to have had occasion of writing to you what I now do, I leave it to your

reflection rather than mention the occasions. I am sorry for your own
Sake the reasons are becom so *Public* which makes it necessary for me
to let you know you have render'd it impracticable for you to continue
yet longer in my service.

But I wil be. . . .[109]

We do not know how the queen concluded her letter, nor does
Marlborough's reply shed any light on the queen's last words. In his
reply, written the same day, Marlborough complained that the queen
had dismissed him 'in the manner that is most injurious to me' and, in
defending himself against the queen's implied complaint that he had not
fulfilled the responsibilities of a royal servant, Marlborough advanced
the relatively new constitutional doctrine of collective responsibility:

> But I am much more concerned at an expression in Your Majesty's
> letter, which seems to complain of the Treatment you had met with. I
> know not how to understand that word, nor what construction to make
> of it. I know I have always endeavoured to serve Your Majesty faith-
> fully, and zealously, through a great many undeserved mortifications.
>
> But if Your Majesty does intend by that expression to find fault with
> my not coming to the Cabinet Council, I am very free to acknowledge
> that my duty to Your Majesty and country would not give me leave to
> join in the counsel of a man who, in my opinion, puts Your Majesty
> upon all manner of extremities. And it is not my opinion only, but the
> opinion of all mankind, that the friendship of France must needs to be
> destructive to Your Majesty, there being in that court a root of enmity,
> irreconcileable to Your Majestys government, and the religion of these
> kingdoms.[110]

Oxford never succeeded in completely destroying the queen's affection for Marlborough. Despite his attempts to play upon her fears of
'King John' and his insistence that Marlborough must be dismissed if the
queen was to remain on the throne,[111] her break with Marlborough was
not personal and irrevocable, as had been the case with Sarah, but
political, as it had been with Godolphin. As the queen told Dr Hamilton,
'the Duke of Marlborough was out; for he had not carry'd himself Well
to her Majesty since he came home. That she did not mean to her
Personally, but in her business.'[112] No one realized more fully than
Oxford the incompleteness of his victory on this battlefield, and he
continued to regard Marlborough as his most dangerous enemy.

A much more difficult task for Oxford was to persuade the queen to
create enough new peers to provide a working majority for the government in the House of Lords. She had always been reluctant to dilute the
peerage through excessive creations, and earlier in December she had
told Cowper 'That the House of Lords was already full enough. "I'll

warrant you, I shall take Care not to make them more in hast[e]".'[113]
Oxford, however, warned the queen that new creations were necessary
to preserve her throne against the encroachments of 'King John', the
Whigs, and Hanover.[114] The advice to create twelve new peers came
from Oxford alone and there was no consultation in the cabinet.[115] In
any event, the queen was unwilling to allow her cabinet to advise her in
the exercise of her prerogative; a year later, when she informed Oxford
that she had signed Robert Benson's patents as Baron Bingley, she

> did not think it proper to acquaint the Lords [of the cabinet] with it,
> because in my oppinion it would have given them a handle to
> prentend [sic] for the future to give me there advice what peers to
> make, everybody being too apt to encroach upon my right.[116]

Dartmouth, the senior secretary, was amazed 'when the Queen drew a
list of twelve lords out of her pocket, and ordered me to bring warrants
for them'. When he registered surprise, the queen asked if he had any
doubts of the legality of such a large creation.

> She said, she had made fewer lords than any of her predecessors, and
> I saw the Duke of Marlborough and the Whigs were resolved to distress
> her as much as they could, and she must do what she could to help
> herself.[117]

On 31 December the official *London Gazette* announced the dismissal of
Marlborough from all his offices and the simultaneous creation of twelve
peers, including three suspected Jacobites (Lords Bruce and Bathurst
and George Granville, created Lord Lansdowne), two relatives of
Oxford (Dupplin, his son-in-law, and Foley, his cousin), and two
Oxford allies (Mansell and Trevor).

Against her better judgment, the queen also allowed Oxford to
persuade her to give a peerage to Samuel Masham. In his private
memoranda, Oxford noted:

> Mr. Masham wil, I beleive, have a Peerage now. I mentioned him to
> the Queen but she desired me not to put it into his head, for she was
> sure Mrs. Mas: did not desire it. She took me up very Short last night
> only for mentioning it.[118]

Nevertheless, Oxford managed to overcome the queen's reluctance. The
queen, who was displeased 'that anybody should apply by' Abigail, was
reluctant to lose a good body servant by elevating Abigail's husband to
the peerage; as Dartmouth recorded,

> I was desired to propose her husband's being made a lord, which I
> found was not very acceptable. The Queen told me, she never had any

design to make a great lady of her, and should lose a useful servant about her person: for it would give offence to have a peeress lie upon the floor, and do several other inferior offices; but at last consented, upon condition she remained a dresser and did as she used to do.[119]

Two weeks after Masham's elevation,

The Queen took all her cloaths, and devided them herself in six several heaps, and stood by whilst the bechamber Women choose as they were eldest [i.e. in terms of service], and that Lady Masham took in her turn, and 'tis given out as if she will continue Bedchamber Woman.[120]

It was also reported that the queen had ordered Abigail not to pay or receive formal visits, 'to live very privately that she may not get the envy of the People, like the Duchess of Marlborough'.[121] Certainly, she did not wish Abigail to receive any honours above her humble station. When, later in the peace negotiations, Louis XIV dispatched special wheelchairs to England as a courtesy gift to the queen, she ordered Oxford:

My Lady Masham told me she heard one of the chaises that are com out of France was intended to be given to her, do not take any notice of it to her but find out if it bee soe and endeavour to prevent it, for I think it would not be right.[122]

According to Dartmouth, in the last years of her life the queen developed a suspicion that Lady Masham and her sister, Alice Hill, were spying on her and she thought of gently easing them out of office.[123]

The queen found it impossible to prevent the further politicization of her 'family'. Among other things, the ministers were determined to get rid of Somerset and his seditious duchess. Yet this was treading on dangerous ground: any attempt to interfere with her personal servants smacked too much of the 'tyranny' from which the queen had so lately escaped. Somerset's opposition to the peace and his behaviour during the Duke of Hamilton case contributed to his eventual dismissal. When the queen interviewed Somerset, who was widely known to be against admitting Hamilton as Duke of Brandon, he equivocated, saying that he would leave London and would give his proxy to someone who would vote for Hamilton, knowing full well that Hamilton was scheduled to have legal counsel and in such cases proxies were not allowed. The queen was so angry with this trick 'that a letter was writ to dismiss him, and given the Dutchess to send him'. Somerset's reply was that if he went, the duchess would leave the queen's service too. This effectively delayed Somerset's dismissal, because the queen was loath to lose the companionship of his duchess.[124]

On 23 December, Jonathan Swift wrote *The Windsor Prophecy*, an attack on the Duchess of Somerset which saw print the next day. On 26 December he visited Mrs Masham who 'desired me not to let the *Prophecy* be published, for fear of angering the Queen about the Duchess of Somerset';[125] unfortunately for Swift, enough copies had already circulated to give it wide publicity. The lines which related to the Duchess of Somerset (called 'Carrots' because of her red hair) mentioned the murder of her second husband, Thomas Thynne, by a rival suitor, Count von Königsmark:

> Their Conyngs mark thou, for I have been told,
> They Assassine when young, and Poison when Old.
> Root out these Carrots, O Thou whose Name
> Is backwards and forwards always the same: [Anna]
> And keep close to Thee always that Name,
> Which backwards and forwards is allmost the same.
>
> [Masham][126]

Dr Hamilton urged the queen 'to keep the Duchess of Somerset for her Own quiet' and the queen was obviously willing to do so.[127] Nevertheless, she dismissed Somerset after a personal interview on 19 January 1712[128] and placed the office of master of the horse in commission. On 23 January, in a conversation with Dr Hamilton, the queen 'express'd Her desire that the Duchess of Somerset Shou'd be kept in' and the next day she ordered Hamilton to solicit Cowper's help and influence with Somerset.[129] 'The Duke', Hamilton reported, 'took Ill the harshness of some Expressions in the Letter and in the way of putting him out', although Cowper advised him that 'it was done [i.e. by the ministers] on purpose to irritate him and provoke him to take the Duchess away'.[130] After a week of delicate negotiations with the proud duke, Cowper and Dr Hamilton persuaded Somerset to allow his wife to continue in the queen's service. When the affair was concluded Dr Hamilton recorded, 'I never saw the Queen Look with a more pleasant and Healthfull Countenance, saying that "Now, it was done".'[131] The Duchess of Somerset was not the only lady the queen retained in her household despite her husband's opposition to the ministry. Lady Strafford, wife of the envoy to the Dutch republic, lamented to her husband: 'I wish the Queen would make me a Lady of the Bedchamber. I wonder Lady Scarborough keeps her place, for Lord Scarborough opposes the Queen in every thing that's in his power with all the violence in the world.'[132]

The Windsor Prophecy had disastrous consequences for Swift's ecclesiastical career.[133] When Dr Hamilton mentioned the poem to the queen, 'She said, "that wou'd have no Influence on her, to turn Her respect from the Duchess"'.[134] In discussing 'Dr. Swift's Character' the queen said, 'He was good for some things. . . . But had not dispos'd of that Benefice [deanery of Wells] to him, nor would not'.[135] Despite pressure from her ministers, the queen steadfastly refused to bestow any living within her gift on the author of the *Prophecy* and the equally objectionable *Tale of a Tub*, generally regarded as an attack on all religion. In the autumn of 1712, when Dr Hamilton said 'it was talk'd that Dr. Swift was to be Dean of Wells, she said it was false, and desir'd that nothing they said might Impress me'.[136] The Whig physician encouraged her obstinacy in refusing to heed Oxford's solicitations for Swift's preferment, telling her

> she was teaz'd to preffer Dr. Swift, and said that in conversation, I did not contradict it, because such a report look's well on her Side, and it made it look the better that their Teazing did not make her yeild.[137]

When Swift received his promotion, it was not in the English but in the Irish Church: he was nominated Dean of St Patrick's in Dublin by the lord lieutenant of Ireland, the Duke of Ormonde. In April 1713 the queen made it clear to Dr Hamilton that Swift's preferment was none of her doing:

> She discours'd of Dr. Swifts being a Dean in Ireland, saying that all the Deanerys in Ireland were of the Lord Lieutenants gift, but the Bishopricks of Hers. I told Her most know that she was press'd to prefer him, and it was Honourable to Her as a Pious Queen, to refuse it.

She was obviously pleased when, a few days later, Hamilton 'told Her how few knew that Swift was prefer'd by the Duke of Ormond, and not by Her, but that I had remov'd the Mistake where I went, by what she told me Her self'.[138]

V

The most important matter confronting the queen remained the completion of a general peace treaty. Bothmer, Marlborough, and the Whigs hoped that the arrival of the famous imperial general, Prince Eugene of Savoy, in England to protest personally against the Tory peace policy would yet save the Grand Alliance. Despite the efforts of the ministers in London and of Strafford in The Hague to prevent the visit of the great popular hero, Eugene arrived in London on 5 January. Oxford and St John immediately reassured Torcy through Abbé Gaultier that Eugene's presence in London would not hinder the Utrecht conference or change

353

the resolutions of the British government.[139] Prince Eugene soon discovered that the Tories had no desire to improve relations with Vienna, sorely strained by the Gallas incident, or to drop the preliminary articles in return for the emperor's promise to double his army in the field and to accept the burden for three-quarters of the allied forces in Spain. During his stay in London between January and March 1712, the queen received Eugene several times, the most notable occasion being 6 February, the forty-seventh anniversary of her birth. 'On her Birth Day', Peter Wentworth reported to his brother, Strafford,

> she gave Prince Eugene a sword sett with diamonds, the Queen being to be carried in her chair from her dressing room to the great Drawing Room, everybody but the ladies in waiting and my Lord Chamberlain [Shrewsbury] was kept out of that apartment.[140]

It was apparent that the ministry was determined to destroy the Grand Alliance. The House of Commons, after indicting Marlborough, Walpole, and Adam de Cardonnel for peculation on flimsy evidence, proceeded to a project dear to Tory hearts: the repeal of the Anglo-Dutch Barrier Treaty of 1709. Shortly after the Commons had passed a motion condemning the allies for alleged shortcomings in the prosecution of the war, particularly in Spain, they censured Townshend 'and all those who advised the ratifying' of the Barrier Treaty as 'enemies to the Queen and Kingdom'.[141] The claim that the Whigs were planning riots to overthrow the government became standard ministerial fare during the winter of 1712. The appearance of 'Mohawks', a group of young bloods who nightly molested pedestrians in the streets of London, added credence to the government's continuing anti-allied, anti-Whig campaign that a conspiracy was afoot to kidnap the queen and to assassinate her ministers. The royal guard was reinforced and Oxford and Shrewsbury were given apartments at St James's, allegedly to render murder attempts less likely.[142]

The fundamental factor in Oxford's peace policy following the signature of the preliminary articles was his determination that Great Britain would fight no campaign in the Netherlands during 1712. Gaultier's letters between November 1711 and May 1712 clearly reveal that Oxford was the real author of the notorious 'restraining orders'. In late November 1711, Oxford informed Gaultier: 'We are absolutely resolved not to bear the expense of another campaign.'[143] As he subsequently explained to Torcy through Gaultier, Oxford was convinced that a quick, separate Anglo-French peace could be concluded by April 1712, thereby eliminating the need for a campaign.[144] For this reason, the queen and Oxford felt safe in dismissing Marlborough.

Immediately after the opening of the Utrecht conference (where Great Britain was represented by Bishop Robinson and the Earl of Strafford) on 18/29 January, a series of deaths in the house of Bourbon imperilled the basis of Oxford's negotiations. Louis XIV's only legitimate heir, the grand dauphin, had died in April 1711, leaving three sons (the duc de Bourgogne, Philip V, and the duc de Berri). On 7/18 February 1712, Bourgogne succumbed to a measles epidemic, only to be followed to the grave by his elder son three weeks later. The senior male line of France was virtually extinct. Only a sickly infant of two years (later Louis XV), whose early death was universally predicted, stood between Philip V and the throne of France. For ten years, Europe had struggled against the union of France and Spain in one family; it now appeared probable that the two crowns would be united in one person.

The first response of the British government to this new problem was to propose that Philip V should renounce for ever his rights, and those of his heirs, to the French throne in favour of his youngest brother, the duc de Berri, and of Louis XIV's nephew, the duc d'Orléans. Louis and his advisors rejected this renunciation scheme out of hand, claiming that primogeniture was the manifestation of God's divine will.[145] After this blunt rejection, Oxford proposed a second plan to settle the French succession: Philip V should immediately hand over Spain and Spanish America to Victor Amadeus of Savoy, in return for Savoy, Piedmont, Sicily, and a royal title. If and when Philip came to the French throne, Sicily would be given to the emperor and the remainder of Philip's Italian possessions would be united to the French crown. This plan was exclusively Oxford's. As St John informed Strafford, 'I am not in this part of his secret.'[146] The 'Savoy plan' had three advantages in the lord treasurer's eyes: first, it would remove the Bourbons from Spain, thereby fulfilling the cry of 'No Peace without Spain'; second, it would in some measure conciliate the emperor by preventing his hated rival, Philip V, from retaining the Spanish throne; third, Victor Amadeus would definitely adhere to the British peace plans and thereby ensure the dissolution of the alliance.[147]

In the event and to the surprise of all concerned in the secret negotiations, Philip chose to remain in Spain and to renounce his French rights. It was an age of slow and unsure communications, and the secret negotiations between Whitehall and Versailles concerning the future of Philip V, initiated on 4/15 March, took well over two months. Meanwhile, the onset of spring meant that a new campaign would soon be under way and the French military situation was precarious: the allied army in Flanders possessed 25,000 more troops than that commanded by Villars and was much better equipped. Louis XIV himself recognized the acute danger involved if the allies should take Le Quesnoy – the last remaining northern frontier fortress – or force Villars into open battle. The seventy-five-year-old Louis informed Villars that if ultimate disaster threatened he would 'collect all my troops and with you risk a last effort, determined to perish or save the state'.[148] For his part, Oxford was determined to prevent a final allied victory which would lead to a march into the heart of France and a general peace which would rob Britain of the separate advantages granted in the preliminary articles. There is no evidence that the queen seriously disagreed with Oxford's policy or that he had great difficulty in inducing her to undertake the most discreditable action of her reign. Together, the queen and the lord treasurer, aided and abetted by St John, saved France as surely, though scarcely as nobly, as Jeanne d'Arc.

On 9 April, Marlborough's successor, the Duke of Ormonde, left London for The Hague, 'well satisfied', in Burnet's words, 'both with his instructions and his appointments; for he had the same allowances that had been lately voted criminal in the Duke of Marlborough'.[149] Ormonde's formal orders were to meet with Heinsius, Prince Eugene, and other allied generals 'to concert the proper Measures for entering an Action'.[150] However, Oxford had no intention of letting Ormonde undertake any action if a separate Anglo-French peace could be rapidly concluded. In late April, Abbé Gaultier returned to London from the Continent, bearing a plan which the British and French plenipotentiaries at Utrecht had agreed to use as a basis for terms. All that remained to be settled between Whitehall and Versailles was the fate of Philip V.

On 9 May, Torcy's letter of 2/13 May arrived in London, announcing that Louis XIV had dispatched an ultimatum to Philip to choose between the renunciation and the Savoy plans.[151] On the strength of the dispatch of a French messenger to Madrid, Oxford and St John, confident that Philip would accept the Savoy plan, called upon the queen on 10 May and obtained her sanction for what became infamous as the 'restraining orders'. In a letter to Ormonde which subsequently became the principal reason for St John's impeachment in 1715, he informed the general of 'the Queen's positive command to your Grace, that you avoid engaging in any siege, or hazarding a battle' until further notice. After instructing Ormonde to keep the order secret from the allies, St John added in a carefully contrived postscript:

> I had almost forgot to tell your Grace that communication is given of this order to the Court of France; so that if the Mareschal de Villars takes, in any private way, notice of it to you, your Grace will answer accordingly.[152]

St John, who immediately informed Gaultier of these orders, was asked by the abbé what Villars should do if Eugene threatened a battle. 'He told me', Gaultier informed Torcy, 'that there would be nothing to do but to fall upon him and tear him to pieces, him and his army.'[153]

The 'restraining orders' were, of course, tantamount to a British desertion of the allies in the field. The allied generals were not deceived by Ormonde's flimsy pretexts for delaying action and they immediately informed their masters. The British position was quickly made clear. On 22 May/2 June, acting on St John's orders conveyed through Oxford's cousin, Thomas Harley, Bishop Robinson informed the allied delegates at Utrecht that the queen now considered herself absolved of all obligations to them and at liberty to proceed to a separate peace with France.[154] The one remaining Whig hope, that the queen personally would refuse to conclude a separate peace if the Dutch and the emperor held firm,[155] was shattered by the restraining orders.

On 28 May, Marlborough and the Whigs confidently expected a victory in the House of Lords[156] when Halifax raised the question of the restraining orders and moved that the queen be asked to order Ormonde 'to prosecute the War with the utmost vigour'. Nottingham, insinuating that the ultimate ministerial goal was a Stuart restoration, declared

> that he could not comprehend why orders had been given to our
> General not to fight, unless certain persons were apprehensive of
> weakening the French, so far as to disable them to assist them in
> bringing about designs which they durst not yet own.

Oxford admitted that 'if the Duke of Ormonde declined to act offensively, he did not doubt but he had followed his instructions'. Oxford lied, however, in stating that Ormonde had orders to engage in a siege. Such was the trend of opinion in the house that Oxford survived only by offering hostages to the future. He promised that the basic Anglo-French peace agreement would be laid before Parliament within a few days and, in a further lie, 'He also affirmed, that the Allies knew of it and were satisfied with it'. Finally, he offered an eloquent denunciation of his own previous policy and thereby effectively foreclosed his option to make a separate peace:

> Nothing of that nature was ever intended; and that such a Peace would
> be so base, so knavish, and so villainous a thing, that every one who
> served the Queen knew they must answer it with their heads to the
> nation.[157]

The margin of Oxford's majority (68 to 40) in this crucial debate was decisive, but not as great as those which were to follow. On 6 June the

queen revealed to Parliament the true contents of the 'secret' preliminary articles with the important and exclusive commercial concessions to Britain, and Philip V's acceptance of the renunciation scheme.
The allure of commercial advantage outweighed Whig complaints that
the allies were being deserted and the succession endangered. In the
Lords' debate the following day, twenty-four Whig lords protested
against the renunciation plan as 'so fallacious that no reasonable man,
much less whole nations, can ever look upon it as any security' and as a
violation of the Treaty of Grand Alliance 'which recited the usurpation
of the Spanish monarchy by the French King for the Duke of Anjou, as
the principal cause of this war'. This protest was expunged from the
records by a vote of 90 to 54. [158] By the time Parliament was adjourned on
21 June, the strength of the queen's government and the overwhelming
public desire for peace was readily apparent. Oxford exaggerated only
slightly when he reported to Thomas Harley, 'The bent of the Nation is
so strong for the Queens Measures, that there is scarce one in a Thousand
against them.' [159] The popular basis of Whig opposition to the peace had
been destroyed, because the public had been misled into believing that
the allies supported the peace proposals and that no separate peace had
ever been intended.

The military result of 'perfidious Albion's' desertion of her allies was
immediate and decisive. On 8 July the British received their promised
reward from France: John Hill, Lady Masham's brother, had the honour
of taking over Dunkirk with a small British force. [160] On 12/23 July,
Villars defeated the allied army at the battle of Denain (the only French
victory in the Netherlands during the war), and by the autumn Villars
had swept the allies out of Douai, Quesnoy and Bouchain, nullifying
Marlborough's achievements of 1711. [161] The crushing French victory at
Denain broke the back of Dutch resistance to the Tory peace proposals.
Although the long and complex formal negotiations at Utrecht continued into the spring of 1713, there could be no doubt that the signing
of a formal peace treaty by the Maritime Powers would be shortly
forthcoming.

While they were working jointly to destroy the Grand Alliance, the
quarrel between Oxford and St John took on greater dimensions. As we
have seen, Oxford had kept St John in the dark concerning his
negotiations with France before the Guiscard attack; during Oxford's
convalescence, St John succeeded in launching an ill-fated expedition
against Quebec against Oxford's wishes and winning the lasting
gratitude of Lady Masham, whose brother was the commander.
Oxford's unconcealed glee that the expedition came to a disastrous end
did little to endear him to either St John or Abigail. [162] The breaking-

point came in June 1712, when St John was elevated to the House of Lords. He expected to succeed to the earldom of Bolingbroke, which had lately become extinct in a senior branch of the St John family. The queen, however, disapproved of St John's dissolute personal life and his wide reputation for debauchery. Oxford did little or nothing to soften the queen's hostility towards him. She refused to give St John anything more than a viscountcy, a slight which embittered the new Lord Bolingbroke against his mistress and for which he and his family never forgave Oxford.[163] In August 1712, Bolingbroke visited Paris to complete the detailed negotiations for the peace with Torcy. During his stay there, he appeared at the Opera, sitting directly across from a box occupied by the Pretender. When Dr Hamilton told the queen of this incident she was angry, and 'said he ought to have gone out imediately'.[164]

Throughout the spring and summer of 1712, the queen enjoyed remarkably good health.[165] Peter Wentworth commented during the summer that the queen 'has the use of her limbs more than I have known her for this five or six years past'.[166] Soon after Bolingbroke's return to London in September, however, the queen suffered a short but severe illness. On 18 September, Swift recorded:

> Yesterday we were allarmed with the Queen's being ill. She had an Augish & Feaverish Fitt and you never saw such Countenances as we all had. . . . Her Physicians from Town were sent for; but towards night she grew better, today she misst her Fit and was up; We are not now in any Fear.[167]

In part, her illness may have been induced by the growing crisis in her cabinet. Bolingbroke, on his return to London, discovered that Oxford had attempted to place the Anglo-French negotiations in Dartmouth's hands. The cabinet meeting held on 28 September was stormy; Arthur Maynwaring reported to the Duchess of Marlborough that 'there are differences among the great men, & . . . the Duke of Shrewsbury, the Keeper [Harcourt] & St. John are fallen out with the Treasurer'.[168] The Hanoverian resident in London, C. F. von Kreyenberg, reported to the elector that Oxford and Bolingbroke had been at each other's throats, and that the queen wept the entire evening following the meeting.[169] Oxford's attempt collapsed because Dartmouth possessed neither Bolingbroke's ability nor his knowledge of the previous negotiations,[170] although the queen's sympathies were entirely on Dartmouth's side. Dartmouth was so irritated by the presumption of his fellow secretary that he threatened to resign. On 21 October the queen urgently appealed to Oxford to prevent this denouement:

359

Last night Lord Dartmouth was here with me to desire I would give
him leave to go into ye country for a little while, he made no Complaints but seem'd very uneasy, I said all I could to perswaid him from
going & desired him to Consider of it againe, & to com to no resolution
till he Came to London. I fear he is determined not only in this but to
quit, which I should be very sorry for, for I beleeve him an honest
man, & I think it would be prejudicial to my service, therfore I hope
you & his other freinds will endeavour to perswaid him out of these
thoughts.[171]

Dartmouth did not resign, but the queen again showed her low opinion
of Bolingbroke by ignoring him when, at the end of October, she created
six knights of the Garter (including Oxford, Poulett, Strafford, and the
Duke of Hamilton). Despite his valuable contributions to the peace
negotiations, the queen passed over Bolingbroke's claims in silence;[172]
even during the last months of her life, Bolingbroke could not restrain
his resentment of this slight by the queen.[173]

November 1712 brought the general peace nearer to completion with
the solemn renunciation of his rights to the French throne by Philip V
before the Spanish Cortes. 'I am very glad the form of the renunciation
is over in Spain', the queen told Oxford. 'I think one may reasonable
hope now the great work of the Peace is in a faire way of Coming to a
happy Conclusion.'[174] Domestic peace, however, remained as elusive as
ever. In November, after killing Lord Mohun in a private duel, the Duke
of Hamilton in turn was killed by Mohun's second, General Maccartney
(who immediately fled from the country). Hamilton had already been
promised that he would be named as the queen's first ambassador to the
court of Versailles. Oxford, afraid of the Duke of Shrewsbury's influence
and wishing to remove him from the English political scene and from
the queen's side,[175] nominated Shrewsbury to replace Hamilton, over
the objections of Bolingbroke and Harcourt, Shrewsbury's cabinet
allies.[176] Shrewsbury was in France as ambassador from January until
September 1713; he was then allowed to spend only one month in
England before he was packed off to Ireland as lord lieutenant, a post
which Oxford had urged him to accept since the spring of 1712.[177]
Shrewsbury was not the only major figure to be temporarily exiled from
English political life. In November 1712, the Duke of Marlborough left
England for a self-imposed exile on the Continent, where he was joined
by the duchess in February 1713. The queen was relieved to see Marlborough remove himself from the opposition to her government's peace
programme. Commenting to Dr Hamilton on Marlborough's trip, the
queen 'said it was prudent in him'.[178] The queen and her ministers did
not know that the Marlboroughs voluntarily left England in order to

encourage the emperor, the Dutch, and the Elector of Hanover to invade Great Britain, overthrow the Tory ministry, and prevent the completion of a European peace. The allied responses to Marlborough's proposals were entirely negative and, throughout their exile, most of which was spent in Antwerp, the Marlboroughs remained in the closest communication with the Hanoverian court, Baron von Bothmer (who had been transferred from London to The Hague), and the Whigs in England.[179]

The closing months of 1712 and the first part of 1713 marked the last tranquil period in the queen's personal and political life, and her health was tolerable. In December 1712 it was noticed that 'in the coldest winter ever felt . . . in all the snow the Queen goes out every day to take the aire'.[180] In early February 1713 she was very ill for ten days with 'Gout in the Stomach', but by 28 February Swift 'saw the Queen carryed out in her Chair to take the Air in the Garden'.[181] She was not distracted, as in the previous winters of her reign, by a session of Parliament, for it was repeatedly prorogued until the plenipotentiaries at Utrecht could complete the final details of the formal settlement.

The Treaty of Utrecht was finally signed on 31 March/11 April 1713 by the representatives of France, Great Britain, and the Dutch republic; the emperor and his German allies (including the Elector of Hanover) vowed to continue the war in the vain hope of forcing the French to more advantageous terms. (They finally accepted the general settlement in the Treaties of Rastadt and Baden in 1714.) The Utrecht settlement decisively marked Great Britain's emergence as a world power. Louis XIV recognized Queen Anne's title and the Protestant succession, and the Pretender was expelled from France to Bar-le-Duc in the duchy of Lorraine. In the Mediterranean, Great Britain became the dominant naval power; she was allowed to retain Gibraltar and Port Mahon, while her ally, Victor Amadeus of Savoy, was given the kingdom of Sicily and the remainder of the Spanish possessions in Italy were transferred to the emperor. The Spanish Netherlands now became the Austrian Netherlands, representing a real security for both the British and the Dutch; furthermore, Louis XIV formally promised to destroy the naval fortifications at Dunkirk, previously a haven for French privateers. The treaty also greatly expanded Britain's American empire: British possession of St Kitts Island and Acadia, Newfoundland and Hudson's Bay was recognized by France. Finally, both France and Spain promised to negotiate commercial treaties giving Britain exclusive trade rights, and the English were given the *Asiento* monopoly of the slave trade within Spanish America for a thirty-year period.[182] The European settlement embodied in the Treaty of Utrecht was so successful that the map of

Europe remained substantially the same until the revolutionary passions of 1792 swept away the *ancien régime*.

Oxford and Bolingbroke were the principal architects of the Utrecht accord, but they could not have accomplished their goals without the steadfast support of the queen. Her actions during the peace negotiations were to have profound repercussions in the future. The constitutional precedent represented by her creation of a dozen peers in 1711 to impose the will of the crown and the House of Commons on the House of Lords was to be used again: the First Reform Act of 1832 and the Parliament Act of 1911 would be imposed upon recalcitrant majorities in the House of Lords by threats of massive creations in order to support the government of the day. Even more importantly, the restraining orders of 1712 and the queen's desertion of her allies in the field gave rise to the legend of 'perfidious Albion', a Britain which would desert her friends as soon as her own ends had been achieved. The restraining orders and the Utrecht settlement marked a renewal of Britain's isolation from Continental affairs, of which the island kingdom was to reap the full harvest during the reign of George III and the loss of the first British empire.

There is no evidence to suggest that the queen regretted her actions, or had second thoughts. For her, the end – peace at last – more than justified the means. What she did not anticipate was that the means employed would lead a growing number of her subjects to suspect that she intended to subvert the Protestant constitution by bringing in her half-brother, and that as a consequence the last year of her life would prove tumultuous beyond belief.

14

'For ye good of her Kingdome'

The Protestant Succession,
April 1713 – August 1714

I

By the spring of 1713, the queen and her Tory ministers were widely suspected of wishing to bring in the Pretender. After the queen's death, both the Whigs and the Jacobites had a vested interest in portraying her as a committed Jacobite. The Jacobites, who used this myth as an additional proof of the Pretender's legitimacy, hoped to benefit from the residue of the queen's great personal popularity. The Whigs found it useful in attempting to prove that her Tory ministers had been determined upon a Jacobite restoration. Even her Tory ministers found the story useful: just as they falsely claimed that the restraining orders of 1712 had been the queen's own idea, so they also suggested that she favoured a Jacobite restoration in order to cover themselves against Whig charges. In all three cases, as the author of the 1715 pamphlet, *Queen Anne Vindicated*, remarked, 'They knew that dead Lyons could not bite.'[1]

In the case of the queen's ministers, these suspicions were not without cause. The ministry's warm and public reception of an attainted (and unpardoned) Jacobite rebel, Sir Patrick Lawless, as Spanish resident in London[2] was complemented by the blind eye which it turned upon the flood of Jacobites who returned to Britain, either with or without the queen's permission. Indeed, the willingness of the government, and particularly Oxford, to pardon returned rebels encouraged St Germain to believe that the Tories would pardon many more.[3] Kreyenberg, reporting to Hanover that the numbers of returning rebels (particulary Irish officers) continued to grow, added: 'This is not a rumour spread to frighten women and children here, but a fact of which I have certain knowledge.'[4] Futhermore, Oxford did not neglect the art of which he was a master and one which was so important for the ultimate success of his goal, the use of propaganda to influence public opinion. In February 1713 his son-in-law, Viscount Dupplin, presented an address from the city of Perth to the queen which was deliberately equivocal on the subject of the succession and ended with the wish that 'the Royal Crown of Your Majesty will fall peacfully on the heads of those, who by the Laws of God and of the Nation have the right to inherit it'.[5] In October 1713 a 300-page book entitled *The Hereditary Right to the Crown of these Kingdoms Asserted . . . and the True ENGLISH Constitution vindicated* appeared, which dealt at length both with the justification of divine hereditary right and with the admirable solution which Henry VIII had found when he privately willed his crown to his three children in order of precedence. The contemporary parallel was obvious. It was a notorious fact that William Lowndes, Oxford's chief civil servant in the Treasury, had conducted a search of the public archives for a copy of Henry VIII's will[6] and that other supporting documents came from Oxford's own celebrated collection of manuscripts. The book, when first published, was advertised in the official *London Gazette*.[7] A non-juring divine, the Reverend Hilkiah Bedford, was arrested and convicted as the author of *Hereditary Right* which indirectly attacked the Hanoverian settlement;[8] but at the height of Oxford's resurgent power with the queen in May 1714, Bedford received a royal pardon.[9] The reason was that the real author was George Harbin, a close friend of Oxford's son.[10]

Oxford sponsored Jacobite propaganda because he knew full well that the Elector of Hanover – a staunch supporter of Habsburg interests – was alienated from the Tory ministers who had concluded the Treaty of Utrecht. In his contacts with the court of St Germain through the Abbé Gaultier and the Marquis de Torcy, Oxford followed the same policy as Marlborough and Godolphin, with one major difference: unlike the Duumvirs, Oxford repeatedly stressed that the Pretender's conversion to Protestantism was essential if a Stuart restoration was to be secured.[11] The elector's secretary, Jean de Robethon, concluded in early 1713 that 'Oxford is too far engaged with France and the Pretender ever to retreat from them, and even if he wished to do so, it would not be possible for him to lead the Queen away from them'.[12] Foreign diplomats in London believed, in L'Hermitage's words, 'The Queen above all disposed to favour the Prince of Wales'.[13] Significantly, the Whigs who knew her best did not believe that the queen ever intended to give up her throne: Halifax, for instance, informed Hanover of his conviction that the queen was not for bringing in the Pretender, much less for giving him the crown during her own lifetime.[14]

In truth, there is no valid reason to believe that the queen favoured her half-brother, or that she intended in any way to contravene the

Hanoverian settlement. She repeatedly denied in conversations with those closest to her that she had any Jacobite sympathies. In April 1712 the Pretender's sister, Princess Louisa-Maria, died of smallpox at the age of twenty. Louis XIV wrote a standard letter of condolence to Queen Anne on the death of her 'sister', but the queen's reply carefully avoided any mention of the late princess, merely saying that life and death were questions beyond the sphere of mere mortals.[15] On 12 July, Sir David Hamilton had a long conversation with the queen in which he reported public fears that 'there was a design to bring in the Pretender'. When he told her 'they said that Tho' his coming in might not be directly with Her consent, Yet they [the ministry] might bring Her to do Such Things, as would Necessarily force Her to yield to it', the queen brusquely replied, 'Can any think me so blind as not to see through these Things.' Again in September 1712 the queen reassured Hamilton 'there was nothing in it, as to the Pretender, and desir'd that none might impose upon me such Impressions'.[16] When in October 1712 Hamilton reported Cowper's belief that 'Things look'd as tho' the Pretender was design'd, and all in Places, who are for him', the queen angrily retorted, 'O fye . . . do they think I'm a Child, and to be imposed upon, and that I have only Integrity?'[17] In November, Hamilton had a long conversation with the queen to prove 'that the Pretender was not the real son of King James', reviving the 'warming-pan' myth which the Princess of Denmark had embraced so many years ago. 'Her Majesty received this with Chearfulness', Hamilton noted, 'and by asking me several questions about the Thing.'[18]

The queen perhaps underrated the effects of constant Whig propaganda. In January 1713, when Dr Hamilton mentioned Bishop Burnet, the queen replied with sarcasm, 'He knows all Things, and says more than any body, and that last Summer he said the Pretender would be Here before six weeks.'[19] In February 1713, Pope Clement XI made Torcy's cousin, the Abbé de Polignac, a cardinal on the nomination of 'James III'. Hanover used this news in England to demonstrate James's continued adherence to Roman Catholicism. When Dr Hamilton mentioned the news to the queen, her scornful comment was, 'Poor Creature, he has Influence to do Nothing.'[20] In March 1713, Dr Hamilton informed the queen that the Duke of Kent and Lord Dorset said that when the queen denied to them that she favoured the Pretender, 'She spoke so low about the Pretender that they could not tell what to make of it'. Her crushing response was, 'did they expect I should speak in a Passion?'[21] It was not only to Hamilton that the queen denied any interest in the Pretender. It was reported to Hanover that 'to others who expressed their apprehensions of the Pretender, she expressed herself as astonished that anyone could have such thoughts'.[22] Her half-brother wrote a series of letters to the queen, but he was never sure that they were delivered and he certainly – on his own testimony – never received any response, either directly or indirectly. It was the Queen's most inveterate critic (once her most intimate friend) who recognized that her instinct for self-preservation precluded any support for a Jacobite restoration. At the height of the succession crisis in July 1714, the Duchess of Marlborough, referring to the queen by two numbers, wrote: '7's great love of 40 may save us at last.'[23]

Compared with her denials of Jacobite sympathies, the queen's private comments concerning the Elector of Hanover, her heir presumptive, were surprisingly mild, despite the fact that the elector had publicly opposed the policies of her ministry and had remained outside the Utrecht settlement to fight alongside the emperor. In the summer of 1712 the queen told Dr Hamilton that 'His Treatment to me had not been Civil, if I had done or Treated King William my Predecessour so, it would have been thought so [i.e. uncivil]'.[24] In January 1713 she commented,' 'There were many things said of the Elector that were not true.'[25] Whatever the suspicions or the fears of the queen's ministers, she had none of the elector. By the time of her death, the queen was unfairly suspected of being party to a plot to subvert the established order in the state. In fact, the queen was loyal to the existing constitution. During the crises which marked the last year of her life, the queen pursued her personal policy regarding the succession: wholehearted support for the Hanoverian settlement and continued opposition to any member of the electoral family establishing permanent residence in England during her lifetime.

The opening of the last session of the Parliament elected in 1710 coincided with the signing of the Peace of Utrecht. On 3 April, Bolingbroke's younger brother arrived in London with the news and the queen announced it in her speech to Parliament on 7 April. 'The Queen delivered her Speech very well, but a little weaker in her Voice', Swift noted.[26] With his eyes on the forthcoming general election, Oxford had cleverly constructed the Queen's Speech. To the shock of the Whigs and the Hanoverian court, the queen proclaimed that there was a 'perfect friendship' between her and the house of Hanover. The elector's friends, Kreyenberg reported to Robethon, were unanimous that 'the Treasurer [Oxford] could not have given a more fatal blow to their influence in the nation and to the security of the Protestant Succession'.[27] Oxford knew the value of placing a blatant lie in the queen's mouth. If the Whigs sought to publicize Hanover's grievances, they ran the risk of seeming to challenge the veracity of the queen's word. The implication of the speech that the peace was 'general' was scarcely less remarkable. As if to challenge the accuracy of both statements, the elector did not appoint a new envoy to England until the autumn of 1713 and made preparations to continue the war against France with the emperor.

During the 1713 session of Parliament, the most serious opposition to the government came not from the extreme Tories (as in 1711), for Oxford had now secured Jacobite support, but from the Whigs and – increasingly – from the Scots. The first set-piece battle took place between 18 and 22 May, when the Tories in the Commons voted to apply the malt tax to Scotland, a technical violation of the Act of Union. This united all Scots irrespective of party.[28] Oxford's personal role in this incident remains unclear, but many observers suspected that Oxford covertly supported the malt tax as the opening step towards the dissolution of the union and a revision of the succession.[29] In a counter-attack, the Whigs and the Scots in the House of Lords proposed on 1 June a motion for the dissolution of the union, albeit with adequate safeguards for the Hanoverian succession. The government opposed the motion, both on tactical grounds and because the queen remained a determined supporter of the union. Dr Hamilton noticed the queen's 'Uneasiness about the Scots proposing the Dissolution of the Union'[30] and Baron von Forstner, the envoy from Lorraine, reported that

> The Queen was thunderstruck by this move by the Scots. She is terribly upset by it, and I know from a good source that she fears a civil war. She has surrendered herself to a minister [Oxford] who causes her terrible embarassments.[31]

The contest over the union was universally regarded as a test of political strength rather than a reflection of the true beliefs of either party. But Oxford was beginning to lose his grip on Parliament. The Scots' motion was defeated by a mere four votes.[32] The queen told Dr Hamilton

> that what was done, was done to hinder Business, and from personal Disrespect to Her, to which I said, I hop'd it was rather to my Lord Oxford, but begg'd she would not be disquieted Since the Event Happen'd on Her Side.[33]

On 10 June the government was defeated in the House of Commons, which rejected the Anglo-French commercial treaty by nine votes (194 to 185).[34] This defeat was a serious portent for the future: first, the Whigs were joined by Sir Thomas Hanmer and a group of 'Whimsicals' or Hanoverian Tories who opposed closer connections with France; second, it was widely believed that Oxford had been content to witness the defeat of Bolingbroke's pet project.[35] On 29 June in the House of

Lords the ministers were astonished when Wharton introduced a motion calling for the Pretender's expulsion from Lorraine. Kreyenberg concluded that Oxford only supported this motion, which was passed unanimously, because the Whigs appeared certain to carry their point. The queen naturally turned to Oxford for advice on how to respond to this motion and a similar one passed by the House of Commons, and her reply repeated Oxford's insinuation during the debate that formal complaints had already been made to the Duke of Lorraine, a statement which was not strictly true.[36] Certainly, neither Oxford nor the French wished to force James from Lorraine when his only alternative residence would be Rome. To prevent the Whigs from cross-examining the Lorraine envoy, Baron von Forstner, on the ministry's failure to press the Pretender's expulsion from Lorraine wholeheartedly, the government carefully awaited Forstner's departure from London in November before instructing Matthew Prior in Paris to make the formal demand which resulted from the House of Lords' resolution in July.[37] Futhermore, Oxford and Bolingbroke privately requested the Duke of Lorraine, through Gaultier and Torcy, to refuse the formal British demand, which Leopold accordingly did.[38] Nevertheless, Oxford and his associates repeatedly assured the queen[39] and the public that the Pretender's departure from Lorraine to Venice, or Cologne, or Switzerland was imminent,[40] and at Oxford's behest[41] James co-operated to the extent that his courtiers publicly announced his desire for a warmer climate and wrote to London of his 'forthcoming' departure from Lorraine.[42]

The queen was unable to attend the last great ceremonial event of her reign, the thanksgiving held at St Paul's on 5 July 1713 to celebrate the completion of the Treaty of Utrecht. Although she was generally in a good state of health, foreign diplomats were notified that she was so indisposed by gout that she could not stand during formal audiences.[43] On Dr Hamilton's advice,[44] she decided not to attend the thanksgiving. 'I find myself soe much tyerd with the little fatigue of yesterday', she told Oxford after meeting the French ambassador,

> that it will be impossible for one to undertake that of going to St.
> Paul's; but however I think both Houses should go thither and I will
> perform my devotions at St. James's and be contented without a
> sermon. It is really very uneasy for me that I cannot go, which I hope
> all my friends beleeve.[45]

On 16 July, Parliament was dissolved and writs were issued for new elections. The peace issue – still fresh in the public mind – produced an increased Tory majority of approximately 150 votes.[46] In strict Tory–Whig terms, this was the largest party majority of the queen's reign, but it was endangered by the division within the Tory party on the great issue of the succession. About eighty Tories, characterized by youth and zeal, were committed Jacobites, while a larger number were probably ready to support a Protestant Stuart if the queen gave the lead.[47] On the other hand, there was an 'absolute maximum of seventy-five Hanoverian Tories',[48] who would not accept the Pretender on any condition, even if he should be converted to the Church of England. Either of these factions could imperil the government's majority if they should join with the Whigs. In Scotland, Oxford's nominees for the sixteen representative peerages in the new Parliament (who naturally won) were regarded by Hanover and its supporters as disastrous for the succession, twelve of the sixteen being classified as Jacobites;[49] even Daniel Defoe, later writing as Oxford's apologist, was forced to admit that most of the lord treasurer's Scottish nominees were 'avowedly and professedly in the Jacobite Interest'.[50] In the elections for the forty-five Scottish seats in the Commons, however, the Whigs enjoyed the aid of the Duke of Argyll, who, disenchanted by the inadequacy of his rewards for his part in the 'great changes' of 1710, had by now broken completely with Oxford; with this support, the Whigs captured more than two thirds of the Scottish seats.[51] During the autumn of 1713 there was general uncertainty, both in governmental and Hanoverian circles, about the complexion of the new Parliament, for more than 200 members were newly elected and no one could predict with certainty where they would stand on the matter of the succession.[52]

The queen and her household were drawn into the growing struggle between Oxford and Bolingbroke. Abigail Masham's alienation from Oxford began when he opposed the Quebec expedition of 1711, commanded by her brother. In March 1712, Lady Strafford reported to her husband: 'I am told that Lord Treasurer and Lady Masham begins to be jealous of one another.'[53] Whatever Abigail's attitude was towards her cousin, it apparently had little effect on the queen, who repeatedly inquired about the treasurer's health throughout 1712. By the end of the year, however, she was becoming disturbed by Oxford's propensity for vague generalities. The Duchess of Marlborough echoed the opinion of Oxford's friends and foes when she wrote that Oxford

> had long accustomed himself so much to dissemble his real intentions
> & to use the ambiguous & obscure way of speaking that he could hardly
> ever be understood when he really designed it or be believed when he
> never so much desired it.[54]

This growing propensity put the queen in mind of something Dr Hamilton had told her in 1710 – that Oxford 'would learn Her to

Equivocate'.[55] In November 1712 she alluded to Oxford's vagueness when she told him: 'I . . . am very sory anything I said on Teusday morning should make you think I was displeased with you. I told you my thoughts freely as I have always and ever will continue to do on all occasions.'[56]

By early 1713 the queen was more frequently listening to the advice of her younger ministers, particularly Simon Harcourt, whom she elevated to the position of lord chancellor in April 1713. Harcourt's growing influence with the queen was demonstrated when she agreed in June 1713 to his suggestion to appoint Francis Atterbury as Bishop of Rochester.[57] Dartmouth's later recollections testify both to the queen's reluctance and to her fundamental good sense concerning Atterbury's appointment: 'I never knew the Queen to do anything with so much reluctancy', Dartmouth wrote,

> as the signing of his *congé d'élire*. She told me, she knew he would be
> as meddling and troublesome as the Bishop of Salisbury [Burnet], had
> more ambition and was less tractable. I told her, I thought she had a
> right notion of the man, therefore wondered she would do it. She said,
> Lord Harcourt had answered for his behaviour, and she had lately dis-
> obliged him, by refusing the like request for Dr. Sacheverell, and found
> if she did not grant this, she must breake with him quite.[58]

This growth in Harcourt's influence was not yet at the expense of Oxford. When in July 1713 Dr Hamilton expressed the hope that 'now Peace was made, My Lord Oxford would keep Her in Constant Ease, She said He was Crazy* and that if any thing happen'd to him, She would have a great loss of him'.[59] Oxford's health, weakened by the Guiscard attack and his fondness for late hours and the bottle, declined visibly in the second half of 1713.[60]

By the end of the 1713 parliamentary session there was ample cause for bad blood between Oxford and Bolingbroke. As Oxford – to his credit – realized, Bolingbroke's reluctance to break politically with the treasurer was partly genuine, but he was continually pressed by many others to do so: for that reason, Oxford's distrust extended to Boling-broke's allies in the Tory party, Harcourt and Thomas, Lord Trevor, chief justice of the Court of Common Pleas.[61] In late July, Bolingbroke proposed a government reformation along strictly Tory party lines, in a direct challenge to Oxford's non-party 'moderation'. This Oxford saw as an attack on himself, concluding that 'he was to have terms put upon him, and a junto'.[62] Oxford's counter-attack was swift and Bolingbroke sustained a severe defeat. Dartmouth replaced Bishop Robinson as lord

---

*'Crazy' in the sense of 'cracked' or being frail or indisposed.

privy seal, while Robinson was translated to the bishopric of London; Oxford's friend, Francis Gwyn, was made secretary at war. Bolingbroke himself was moved to the secretaryship for the southern province, thereby losing the important business of The Hague and Hanover. He was replaced by William Bromley who quickly became, in Oxford's parlance, 'the honest Secretary'.[63] As a further insult to both Bolingbroke and Harcourt, the Earl of Mar was appointed secretary of state for Scotland and the Earl of Findlater became lord chancellor for Scotland: both men were reputed Jacobites. Bolingbroke's only consolation was that his friend, Sir William Wyndham, became chancellor of the exchequer. Immediately after his dismissal in July 1714, to avoid responsibility for the events which had preceded it, Oxford claimed that 'I have had no power since July 25: 1713',[64] a statement which the July–August 1713 ministerial upheaval clearly belies. Bolingbroke recognized the extent of his defeat and was furious, but through the mediation of their mutual friend, Arthur Moore (a commissioner of trade), the quarrel between Oxford and Bolingbroke was yet again patched up.[65]

It was small consolation to Bolingbroke that the Duke of Shrewsbury returned from Paris in September 1713 after the completion of his service as ambassador. The duc d'Aumont, the French ambassador in London, reported to Louis XIV:

> Lord Bolingbroke takes great pleasure in the return of the Duke of Shrewsbury. During a long conversation at Windsor, to which I was a witness, it appeared to me that their alliance will be very strong, the opportunities which they have to approach the Queen – who has great trust in the latter and a growing confidence in the former – give me reason to believe that they will balance the power of the Earl of Oxford or at least make him respect the general views of the Court party.[66]

Shrewsbury, although he was still lord chamberlain, remained in England for only one month before leaving for Dublin to assume his duties as lord lieutenant of Ireland; he was sufficiently concerned by the state of the queen's health to arrange privately with Sir John Shadwell, one of her doctors, to send him reports of her medical progress.

The great change in the queen's attitude towards Oxford took place in August and September 1713, while Bolingbroke and Shrewsbury were consolidating their alliance. One reason for the queen's increasing disillusionment with her lord treasurer was the fact that her household was turning against him, primarily because many of the royal servants had received no salaries since September 1710. In October 1711 the queen told Oxford: 'I wish there could be Money enough found to pay the Princes Servants two quarters of ye five they are in arrears, some of them being in very bad Circumstances.'[67] Nothing was done. In the spring of 1712 it was reported that 'the maids of honour and all the household Servants complain very highly of not having received a farthing this two years, and that they are by it almost reduced to Beggary'.[68] In July 1713, when Dr Hamilton complained to the queen that Oxford had not paid his salary, she attempted to defend her treasurer, saying,

> there had been such Vast occasions for money lately that he could not, but . . . there was no Debt since He came. To which I said it was mostly since he came, and it was pitty Lord Godolphins Memory should Suffer, and his Reputation to Stand on others Disreputation; for when he was put out there was but one half year owing me, but now theres near three Years owing.[69]

The queen also heard complaints from Prince George's Danish confidant, Christian Siegfried von Plessen, whom she had formally engaged in her private service in July 1709 to manage the late prince's estate;[70] although the queen did not know it, von Plessen regularly reported his conversations with her to Hanoverian agents.[71] The queen confided to von Plessen that one party was suspected of wishing to bring in the Pretender during her lifetime while the other party favoured establishing a member of the electoral family in England, but 'she would oppose both the one and other with all her force'. When von Plessen reassured her that the elector would only agree to send someone if invited by both the queen and Parliament, the queen replied that,

> notwithstanding all the reiterated assurances which she had given the Elector, that she was for his succession, it seemed he was not persuaded of it, nor believed that she was in his interests.[72]

Von Plessen's private conversations with the queen aroused the suspicions of her ministers. 'Monsieur Pless[en] has been in with the Queen three or four times', Peter Wentworth noted in August 1713, 'and staid longer then some people cou'd wish.'[73] When in the autumn of 1713 the queen ordered Oxford to pay von Plessen's pension and those due to the servants of the late prince, Oxford only mocked von Plessen to his face, and the Dane complained bitterly to the queen.[74]

Even more importantly, through a combination of neglect and presumption Oxford managed to give the queen the impression that he took her for granted. Nothing made her angrier than Oxford's slipshod business methods and her latent suspicion that the lord treasurer was trying to slip his own candidate as treasurer of the chamber past her by presenting a blank warrant for her signature; on 21 August she delivered a stinging rebuke to Oxford:

I was very much surprised to find by your letter that, though I had told you the last time you weare hear I entended to give the Treasurer of the Chamber to Lord DeLaware, you will bring me a blank warrant. I desire you would not have so ill an oppinion of me as to think when I have determined anything in my mind I will alter it. I have told Lord DeLaware I will give him this office and he has kissed my hand upon it. Therfore when you com hither bring the warrant with his name.[75]

Shortly after this rebuke, Oxford made his 'never enough to be lamented folly in mentioning to her Majesty the titles'. For years, Oxford had hoped to marry his son and heir, Lord Edward Harley, to the only daughter of the Duke of Newcastle, Lady Henrietta Holles, the richest heiress in England. After Newcastle's death in July 1711, Oxford had been forced to negotiate with the dowager duchess, who included among her demands the proviso that the duchy of Newcastle should be resurrected in favour of Lord Edward. As Oxford explained the case to his brother, he obviously believed that the queen had agreed to this condition in 1712. 'Now as to the Title of Newcastle', he wrote in August 1713,

the Case is this. A year since (when the Dutchess made it one of her demands) I ask'd it of the Queen, who said She would make him first Earle, & then Duke as soon as the marriage was over. It is most certain, the gradation of Titles is the best & truly honorable way . . . & to speake plaine, for the Queen to do it before the marriage is neither Honorable to ye Lady, nor fit for the Queen.[76]

It is impossible to know whether Oxford's account of the queen's previous agreement was truthful. What is certain is that Oxford asked the queen for the titles on 16 September, immediately after the marriage of Lord Harley and Lady Henrietta, and the queen coldly refused 'with Seeming Resentment at it'. The breach thus caused between the queen and her chief minister was never completely healed; Lady Masham later confided to Dr Hamilton that Oxford 'had never Acted Right in the Queens Affairs since his being refus'd the Title of Duke of Newcastle'.[77]

The queen also had personal reasons for dissatisfaction with the French policy which Oxford personified. Pierre La Roche, a favourite Huguenot servant of hers for forty-two years, was denied permission by Versailles in September 1713 to visit Montpellier to restore his health. The queen was outraged and made her ministers feel her displeasure.[78] In November 1713 the dowager Countess of Jersey fled to France with her ten-year-old son, Henry Villiers, with the avowed purpose of rearing him in the True Faith; young Villiers was the queen's ward and a student at Westminster School, and Lady Jersey's action reinforced the queen's anti-Catholic prejudices.[79] During the autumn of 1713, Oxford only infrequently attended the queen at Windsor, while Bolingbroke was resident there as the secretary in attendance.[80] The queen was later to complain that Oxford rarely came to her and, when he did, that she could not understand him. Certainly by early December 1713 she no longer completely trusted him. 'Now that I have a pen in my hand', she wrote to the lord treasurer on 8 December,

> I can not help desireing you againe when you com next, to speake plainly, lay everything open and hide nothing from me, or els how is it possible I can judg of anything. I spoke very freely and sincerely to you yesterday, and I expect you should do the same to her that is sincerly your very affectionate friend.[81]

II

During the summer and autumn of 1713 the queen enjoyed remarkably good health.[82] On 13 September the Hanoverian resident, Kreyenberg, visited the court at Windsor. The queen, he reported, was carried to the Royal Chapel, but on her return, she walked for the first time since February, aided only by a cane in her right hand and the support of the Duke of Shrewsbury on her left.[83] The new Hanoverian envoy to London, Georg von Schütz (son of Ludwig von Schütz, envoy from 1693 until his death in 1710), formally presented his credentials to the queen on 29 November; he noticed a great decline in her general physical condition since he had last seen her four years previously.[84] Yet when Schütz again saw her two weeks later, he remarked that her complexion appeared to be healthier than before.[85]

On Christmas Eve 1713 the queen fell suddenly and violently ill. According to the reports of her doctors, she 'complained of a pain in her thigh, and was seized with a violent shivering, which lasted above two hours. Extreme heat followed, with intense thirst, great anxiety, restlessness, and inquietude.' Her doctors were summoned to Windsor from London on Christmas morning, but her illness continued until 28 December.[86] Her medical attendants concluded that she had come close to death. Only on 31 December was she well enough to receive a few members of her household.[87] As the unpublished account of one of her doctors, Sir Hans Sloane, makes clear, the queen continued to be seriously ill throughout January 1714.[88] London was swept by a series of conflicting rumours and the Whigs could scarcely conceal their joy. The ministers later boasted that the Electress Sophia would have

374

been proclaimed immediately queen had Queen Anne died[89] but, at the time of her illness, their pro-Jacobite, anti-Hanoverian bias was effectively exposed. By government order all ports were closed, but Gaultier and Charles D'Iberville, the new French envoy, were allowed to dispatch messengers to Paris, while Hanoverian couriers were forced to hire fishing vessels to transport them clandestinely to the Dutch coast.[90] Despite repeated summons from other ministers who rushed to Windsor upon the news of the queen's illness, Oxford chose to appear in the streets of London in order to maintain public confidence,[91] a decision later represented to the queen as 'neglect' on the treasurer's part.

Death did not take the queen this time, but it was universally recognized that her days were numbered, limited to months if not to weeks. The final crisis of the queen's life and reign was at hand. On 5 January, Oxford's cousin Thomas Harley was chosen to go to Hanover to reassure the electoral court of the queen's continued adherence to the Act of Settlement.[92] The movements of Tom Harley were in counterpoint to the more important negotiations which Oxford was simultaneously conducting with the Pretender. It was announced that Harley would leave London immediately, yet he remained there for almost six weeks after his appointment, carefully avoiding any contact with Hanoverian diplomats. Finally, Bolingbroke forced Harley's departure by composing instructions, in conjunction with the queen, with the aim of procuring from the elector a positive statement of confidence in the Tory ministry. Bolingbroke introduced these instructions in cabinet without consulting Oxford, and once they were approved by the queen, no further excuse remained for Harley to stay in London.[93] Harley left on 14 February, but he spent a further six weeks in Amsterdam and The Hague before proceeding to Hanover. He was awaiting the outcome of Oxford's negotiations with the Pretender.

On 15 January, through the Abbé Gaultier, Oxford asked James to change, or at least to dissimulate, his religion. Gaultier's letters to Torcy and to James were accompanied by a draft declaration which James was to issue upon a signal from Oxford. This declaration, after dwelling upon the profound impression which the misfortunes of his parents had wrought upon James's mind, announced his conversion to the Church of England 'without any earthly view'; it also contained an endorsement of Oxford's 'moderation' ('I do not believe that it can be usefull to a sovereign of Great Britain to sustain himself or fortify himself through a party'), an explicit promise that James would never attempt to regain his throne through force of arms, and a concluding assurance that 'I would rather roam the world than disturb the quiet of my Country'.[94] Oxford dictated this manifesto to Gaultier and corrected part of it in his own hand.[95]

Three weeks after Oxford appealed for James's conversion, Bolingbroke made a similar appeal, separately and secretly, through d'Iberville on 6 February. Bolingbroke later admitted to d'Iberville that he had never considered the prospects for a Stuart restoration before the queen's death to be good and instead relied upon the revolution which would 'infallibly' break out after one year of Hanoverian rule.[96] The only points on which Oxford and Bolingbroke agreed in their separate negotiations with the Pretender were that James should be converted and that he should not depend upon the Scots. Otherwise, Bolingbroke's advice was directly contrary to Oxford's. While Oxford used the spectre of a renewed Grand Alliance and war against France under a Hanoverian successor to frighten Versailles into pressurizing James to be converted, Bolingbroke realized that Louis XIV neither could nor would support such a move. Instead, Bolingbroke used the same spectre to advance his proposed anti-imperial alliance between France, Spain, Savoy-Sicily, and Great Britain.[97] While Oxford was urging the Pretender's immediate conversion, Bolingbroke was opining that the best policy was to do nothing, for an immediate declaration of James's conversion 'would be useless'.[98] Both the French and the Jacobites realized that Bolingbroke was considerably less bold than Oxford. 'There is, it is true, gross naïveté on the part of Sably [Bolinbroke]', the Pretender wrote to Torcy, 'but not the firmness and the resolution which I expected from his character.'[99]

Because Torcy had deliberately kept him in the dark in order to make the Jacobite court more pliable, James never realized that a change of religion had been the original and fundamental basis of Oxford's negotiations since 1710,[100] nor, in assessing Oxford's proposed manifesto, did James appreciate what a master propagandist like Oxford could achieve with such a document. Instead, James reacted to the manifesto like an honest, albeit simple, man. Who of sense or honour, he demanded of Torcy, would believe that temporal consideration had not entered into his supposed renunciation of Roman Catholicism at that moment, or that he would renounce the use of force in attempting to regain his throne in favour of becoming a mendicant roaming the world?[101] Convinced that the Tories had so alienated Hanover that they would be forced to support him, even as a Roman Catholic,[102] James sent the Abbé Gaultier a letter on 2 March in which he stated for the first time his refusal ever to consider conversion.[103] This letter was kept secret in England from all but a few, and the Jacobites continued to encourage the public belief that James might become a Protestant.[104]

James's private refusal to dissimulate his religion was the fatal decision which determined the course of his future career. In this, he displayed his full share of Stuart arrogance and lack of remorse: 'I have chosen my own course, therefore it is for others to change their sentiments', he told Torcy.[105] On 11 March, James's letter of 2 March, rejecting the possibility of changing his religion, was in Gaultier's hands, and Oxford's hopes of restoring the Pretender were smashed. From this point forward, neither Oxford nor Bolingbroke seriously considered the Jacobite alternative; both men tried once more to climb the slippery hill to the good graces of the Elector of Hanover, although their major efforts were to be devoted to undermining each other's achievements.

During the early winter of 1714, Oxford and Bolingbroke kept their Jacobite negotiations secret from each other and also from the queen. The ministers tried to assure the public that the queen had recovered completely, but her serious relapse on 23 January could not be kept secret.[106] During the following week there was a run on the Bank of England, which was halted only by the queen's open letter to the Lord Mayor of London on 1 February, announcing her recovery and her determination to open Parliament personally on 16 February.[107] Whatever optimism the queen showed for the benefit of the public, she was privately extremely worried about her physical condition. In one of her last communications with Oxford, Lady Masham told the treasurer,

> What I write concerning her health She knows nothing off, neither wou'd I for the world have her know it, for our business must be to hearten her, for She is too apprehensive allready of her ill state of health.[108]

The queen and her domestics assured everyone that she was fully recovered,[109] but von Plessen privately informed Schütz, the Hanoverian envoy, that the queen could only live a few days judging from her shocking appearance.[110] Although she was not able to open Parliament as promised on 16 February, she did leave Windsor that day for Hampton Court 'in the most terrible storms of Snow, wind & Haile', and on 17 February completed her journey to London.[111]

During the intervals of surprisingly good health which she was to enjoy during the next five months, the queen proved to be remarkably active politically. Well aware that the Whigs were planning the introduction of an invitation address in Parliament,[112] she immediately summoned wavering peers to her presence to inform them of her implacable opposition to any such scheme.[113] The success of these interviews was immediate: because the Hanoverian Tories (the 'Whimsicals') were reluctant to offend the queen personally and thereby foreclose

377

any chance of future preferment, the Whigs soon realized that the invitation could not be carried in Parliament and the project was quietly dropped.[114] On 22 February the queen appeared publicly at a drawing-room; the French envoy, d'Iberville, reported to Torcy that even the Whigs were surprised by the queen's vivacity, adding that she had not looked so well for three years.[115] The queen's renewed strength and determination were felt not only by court observers and the Whigs, but by her ministers as well. Despite the obvious joy of the Whigs at the prospect of her death during her Christmas illness, the queen vetoed proposed purges by the Tories. As Bolingbroke complained to d'Iberville, 'She continually opposes the most necessary changes, only because she suffers when she hurts anyone.'[116] At the height of Oxford's Jacobite negotiations, the queen honoured the last request of Archbishop Sharp (who died on 2 February) by nominating Sir William Dawes, an outspoken Hanoverian Tory and an open opponent of the ministry, as Sharp's successor to the archdiocese of York without consulting any of her ministers.[117]

Although Parliament opened as scheduled on 16 February, no business of substance was conducted for two weeks until the queen could appear to read her speech, which she did 'very distinctly' on 2 March.[118] The speech had been cleverly constructed: without giving any positive assurances of support for the Hanoverian succession, the queen attacked those

> who are arrived to that height of malice, as to insinuate, that the Protestant Succession in the House of Hanover is in danger under my Government. . . . Attempts to weaken my authority or to render the possession of the Crown uneasy to me, can never be the proper means to strengthen the Protestant Succession.[119]

The two parties in Parliament spent most of March shadow-boxing over disputed elections and debating the temerity of pamphleteers. On 10 March the queen again became very ill, once more displaying the symptoms of extreme fever alternating with chills which had characterized her illness at Windsor; she remained seriously indisposed until 13 March.[120]

On 11 March, as we have seen, the Pretender's definitive refusal to consider religious conversion arrived in London, and it quickly became apparent to Hanoverian observers that the lord treasurer's plans for the parliamentary session were ruined. Indeed, Oxford appeared to be losing his grip. On 23 March, the day before Parliament recessed for the Easter break, Kreyenberg reported to the elector, 'It seems, that there are no longer thoughts of changing the Regency Act, although it is certain that was the design.'[121] The queen, unable to receive the sacrament at Easter because she could not fall to her knees,[122] was forced to confront a crisis within her cabinet. The trouble stemmed from Bolingbroke's insistence that Tory policies should be followed in order to reunite the party or, as Oxford interpreted this demand, that the treasurer 'should have measures put upon him and a junto'.[123] Harcourt, Trevor, and Lady Masham supported Bolingbroke while the other ministers (except for Oxford's allies, Dartmouth and Poulett) remained neutral. The queen appointed the Duke of Ormonde to mediate between the two men[124] and Arthur Moore was again called to perform the same service.[125] At one point, according to Schütz, Oxford tried to resign but his allies convinced the queen – still bent upon 'moderation' – that Oxford's departure would throw her into the arms of either the Whigs or the Tories.[126] Oxford's principal loss in this fracas was Lady Masham, who had actually deserted him for Bolingbroke before the queen's Christmas illness.[127] During the crisis, Lady Masham told Oxford, according to Dr Arbuthnot, 'that she would carry no more Messages nor medle nor make.'[128] Oxford desperately tried to repair this breach in his system, first by threatening to lead a parliamentary investigation into her brother's alleged misconduct as governor of Dunkirk[129] and then by unsuccessfully attempting a reconciliation with Abigail through the queen.[130]

At the time of the March cabinet crisis, however uneasy she felt with Oxford, the queen remained loyal to him when he was challenged by Bolingbroke, Harcourt, and Trevor.[131] Contrary to his later claims that he had lost power, Oxford believed at the time that he had emerged relatively unscathed.[132] One issue on which Oxford had chosen to oppose Bolingbroke was the continued purge of Whig officers from the Army. For Bolingbroke, this was a means of establishing permanent Tory supremacy in the state. Oxford, casting about for new sources of support after the Pretender's refusal to be converted, secretly assured the Whigs that he did not support further purges.[133] He nevertheless supplied Thomas Harley with reasons for defending these measures to the electoral court, adding that 'no one is put in but who is undoubtedly zealous for the House of Hanover'.[134]

The cabinet crisis was the signal for every sort of discontent to be fastened upon Oxford: as the Abbé Gaultier reported, 'there is almost no one who does not say that this man is a double-dealer'.[135] In the face of massive public unpopularity, he was sustained only by the queen's loyalty and, ironically, by Bolingbroke's public defence. In early April, d'Iberville described Oxford's situation.

> For the past ten days, the storm against My Lord Oxford has been terrible. . . . He has been attacked by everyone without exception, the campaign against him in both Houses has gone so far as to treat him as a scoundral, a knave, and a villain without, however, naming him directly, and the universal hatred of him is demonstrated by the fact that no one, not even his relatives, has spoken to justify him except My Lord Bolingbroke, although he is no happier with him than the others.[136]

Oxford's confident prediction in January that he would always have a majority of eighteen in the House of Lords[137] soon proved to be grossly mistaken. On 5 April the government introduced a motion in the upper house insisting that 'The Protestant Succession in the House of Hanover is not in Danger'; Harcourt, as presiding officer, shrewdly added the rider 'under Her Majesty's Administration',[138] thus converting the motion into a vote of confidence in the queen personally. After a prolonged debate, the ministry survived what was tantamount to an accusation of high treason by only fourteen votes, made possible by the Scottish peers and by Oxford's 'dozen'.[139] Immediately after the vote, the Duke of Bolton introduced a motion offering a reward for the apprehension of the Pretender 'dead or alive' if he entered the three kingdoms, and Halifax and Wharton succeeded in passing motions against the Pretender's continued residence in Lorraine and beseeching the queen 'in Conjunction with the States General, to desire the Emperor to enter into the Guaranty of the Protestant Succession in the House of Hanover, and also all such other Princes as Her Majesty shall think proper'.[140] Content to win the main point, that the Protestant succession was not in danger, the court party silently accepted these resolutions.

'Affairs', d'Iberville reported the following day in a judgment echoed by Schütz, 'are moving in such a manner that civil war is becoming inevitable in England.'[141] On 8 April the court party struck back in the House of Lords, moving that the 'dead or alive' provision be deleted from Bolton's motion and that the queen should issue a proclamation for the Pretender's apprehension only when she saw fit. The result was mixed: even though most of the opposition bishops were absent and most of the Tories who had supported the Whig motions on 5 April now returned to the court party, the government's majority declined remorselessly to eleven votes.[142] On the advice of Bolingbroke and Harcourt,[143] the queen declined to endorse the hysteria against the Pretender which the Whigs were attempting to create and replied, 'I do not, at this time, see any occasion for such a proclamation.' Furious at this rebuff, Schütz and the Whigs discounted the queen's promise to issue the proclamation 'whenever I judge it necessary'.[144] The queen's answer was delivered to the House of Lords on the afternoon of 12 April; that evening Schütz visited Harcourt to demand the legal writ summoning the electoral prince to Parliament as Duke of Cambridge.

Schütz, who had been importuning Hanover for months for orders to demand the writ, had received a highly equivocal letter from the Electress Sophia, which she later claimed merely instruced Schütz to ask Harcourt why the writ had not been issued; Schütz, however, interpreted her letter as an order to demand the writ itself. In his conversation with the lord chancellor, Schütz left the impression that the electoral prince's arrival in England was imminent. Harcourt declined to issue the writ before consulting the queen, for no peer resident outside Great Britain had ever received one; Schütz responded by claiming that he was the electoral prince's authorized representative (which he was not) and would receive the writ on his behalf.[145] It was later claimed that Bolingbroke played upon the queen's emotions during the emergency cabinet meeting called the same evening by speaking against issuance of the writ (on the pretext that the prince should claim it in person), while Oxford alienated her by supporting the majority opinion that issuance could not be legally refused.[146] In an indirect attack on both Hanover and Harcourt, Oxford pandered to the queen's anger that Schütz had not first consulted her personally but had gone directly to the lord chancellor, telling Schütz 'that he never saw the Queen in a greater passion'.[147] This affront became the official excuse for denying Schütz access to the court immediately after the writ was granted and for demanding his recall. Acting upon Oxford's personal advice,[148] Schütz left London on 20 April. The court was mortified by widespread popular rejoicing when the news became public that Schütz had demanded the writ,[149] but his precipitate departure left both the government and opposition in the dark as to whether or not Georg August would actually come to London. It was a question which was to hang over the remainder of the parliamentary session.[150]

III

The ministerial divisions revealed by the writ demand had nothing to do with the question of the succession. The queen remained faithful to her personal succession policy – support for Hanover while attempting to prevent the permanent residence of any member of the electoral family in England. After the writ demand, the queen reassured Archbishop Dawes of York, other bishops, and many nobles in a series of interviews that she remained loyal to the Protestant succession and to the Hanoverian settlement.[151] Oxford and Bolingbroke realized after the Pretender's refusal to be converted that a Hanoverian succession was inevitable, and both men were intent upon securing, by different means, their own interests and safety under a Hanoverian monarch. Oxford sought Whig support while Bolingbroke attempted to reunite the Tory party and to ensure its predominance in the state after the queen's death. The traditional story, propagated by the Harley family immediately after the queen's death, was that Oxford, 'a sincere Hanoverian', had clung to the reins of power and thus had prevented Bolingbroke and Harcourt, who were allegedly hellbent upon the Pretender's restoration, from achieving their goal. A close examination of primary, contemporary sources destroys this Harleyite legend. Between the writ demand on 12 April and Oxford's dismissal on 27 July, three distinct periods emerge: from 12 April to 19 May, Oxford was dominant; between 19 May and 1 July, Bolingbroke was resurgent; between 1 and 27 July, Bolingbroke emerged triumphant.

During the period of Oxford's predominance, which lasted until 19 May, Bolingbroke appeared both emotionally despondent and physically ill.[152] He was embittered against the queen (who in April again refused to raise him in the peerage to an earldom),[153] and in early May he confided to d'Iberville that he expected to leave office shortly.[154] As Bolingbroke told Kreyenberg, whom he began to court assiduously, he realized that Oxford was trying to portray him as a remorseless Jacobite.[155] To rally the Tories to his banner, Bolingbroke claimed through such pamphlets as *Hannibal Not at the Gates* that Oxford had surreptitiously inspired the writ demand through Thomas Harley or, alternatively, that Tom Harley had not offered one argument at Hanover to prevent the prince's proposed trip to England. Such was the general distrust of Oxford that Bolingbroke's line 'A certain Gentleman is gone to Hanover to bamboozel'[156] struck a responsive chord in every political camp.

Oxford's double game (or triple, if his continued Jacobite protestations are taken into account) was difficult if not impossible to sustain. His first priority was to retain his hold on the queen by claiming that he and Thomas Harley enjoyed extraordinary influence at Hanover and that he alone could prevent the electoral prince's trip to England. As Bothmer reported to Robethon, 'My Lord Oxford only sustains himself with the Queen through the opinion which she has of the credit of which he boasts having with Monseigneur the Elector, through which he pretends to be very useful to Her Majesty.'[157] Oxford urged the queen to rid her administration of 'suspected' Jacobites: 'Who has brought upon [you] all the renew'd . . . attempts of Hannover?' he inquired.[158] Yet at the same time Oxford attempted to alienate the queen from her successors by assuring her that Robethon's letters to Kreyenberg had been betrayed by the latter to Oxford. These contained (so Oxford claimed) news of Hanoverian plans to land thirteen Russian regiments in Ireland and thirteen in Scotland, where Argyll was to act as generalissimo.[159]

To gain Whig support against Bolingbroke, Oxford secretly assured Whig leaders that he favoured the prince's residence in England. Through his brother, Auditor Edward Harley, Oxford assured the Whigs that 'at bottom' he 'would not be sorry that the Electoral Prince were here, although he is obliged to declare and to publish the contrary, for fear of losing entirely the Queen'.[160] While he was making these assurances, Oxford instructed Thomas Harley, who arrived in Hanover on 13/24 April, to oppose the electoral prince's projected visit.[161] More importantly, Oxford established contact through the Palatine envoy in London, Baron Daniel von Steingens, a notorious but competent tool of Oxford's,[162] with General Johann Mathias von der Schulenburg, a brother of the elector's morganatic wife. Schulenburg forwarded Steingens's letters to the elector.[163] Oxford used this connection through Steingens to urge the appointment of Schulenburg as Hanover's replacement for Schütz and to boast to the queen that he would soon secure the dismissal of Jean de Robethon, the elector's confidential secretary.[164]

The elector, however, was determined to use the writ demand to obtain further securities for the Hanoverian settlement. On 27 April/ 7 May, the elector and the electress presented a formal memorial to Thomas Harley which explictly requested the queen's invitation to 'some one of the Electoral family' to reside in Great Britain 'for the security of her royal person, and for that of her kingdoms, and of the Protestant religion'. The memorial, which also requested a civil list for Sophia and the Pretender's expulsion from Lorraine, asked that all princes of the house of Hanover be given British titles, the elector's hint that he would consider his younger brother, Ernst August, a more suitable candidate than the electoral prince for residence in England.[165] For Georg Ludwig, the memorial represented a compromise of his previous succession policy. After the writ demand, he had been un-decided whether or not to send his son immediately without the queen's invitation[166] and had withstood tremendous pressure from his family and his ministers to do so.[167] In case Oxford and Thomas Harley should suppress the memorial, the elector took care to send copies to Kreyenberg in London and to Bothmer at The Hague, with orders to publicize its demands among Hanover's friends in Great Britain.

Oxford saw that the entire basis of his scheme for continued power was shaken by the memorial. He first learned of it from Kreyenberg on 5 May.[168] He delayed, apparently with Kreyenberg's collusion, in receiving it officially in the hope that Thomas Harley would induce the elector to rescind it. This Harley attempted to do, but the elector adamantly refused to change one word.[169] Harley deliberately delayed his return to England[170] and did not forward the memorial to London or mention it in his letters to his nominal superior, Bromley.[171] After further delays and increased pressure from Kreyenberg, Oxford formally received a copy of the memorial from the Hanoverian resident on 18 May.[172]

The memorial destroyed the premise on which the queen had based her succession policy, the conviction that the elector would never agree to send his son to England. On 19 May, before Tom Harley's return and before Kreyenberg had presented the memorial to any other members of the British government,[173] Oxford dispatched letters from the queen and himself to the electress, the elector and the electoral prince, bluntly informing them that no member of the electoral family would be allowed to enter Great Britain during the queen's lifetime.[174] The language of the queen's letters was so harsh that Hanover suspected that Bolingbroke had composed them, but in fact they were drafted by Oxford.[175] These letters from the queen and Oxford arrived on 25 May/5 June at Hanover. The eighty-four-year-old Electress Sophia was grief-stricken at the collapse of her hopes to establish her grandson in England. Three days later, while walking in the gardens of Herrenhausen, the electress suddenly collapsed and died.

During the second week in May, the queen suffered another occurrence of her illness,[176] possibly a reflection of her anxiety about whether or not the electoral prince would come to London. She was profoundly shaken by news of the elector's memorial and by the change in his attitude. This was why, when Dr Hamilton

> ask'd her if Princess Sophia's Death added any thing to Her quiet or disquiet, . . . she said, that Princess Sophia was Chipping-Porridge [i.e. a thing or matter of little importance], it would neither give more Ease, nor more uneasiness.[177]

The formal response of the British government to Sophia's death was immediate and correct: the queen issued a proclamation to replace 'The Princess Sophia' with 'the Elector of Brunswick' in *The Book of Common Prayer* and forbade any deviation from the new usage.[178] To the queen's distress, the elector – now heir apparent after his mother's death – specifically repeated his request for permission for a member of the electoral family to reside in England.[179] To stress the continuity of Hanoverian policy, he also announced that Oxford's *bête noire*, Baron von Bothmer, would replace Schütz in London. The panic which had produced the queen's letters of 19 May and their utter failure to change the elector's policy, as well as the calculated insult to the leading ministers which Bothmer's return from The Hague implied,[180] destroyed the queen's belief in Oxford's claims that he could manage Hanover. If the letters were ever made public, Oxford's last remaining hope for Whig support would be shattered, too.

IV

From 19 May, therefore, Oxford's period of predominance in his struggle with Bolingbroke was at an end.[181] Bolingbroke was resurgent. The change in the queen's attitude was abrupt and quickly became public knowledge. For months, Bolingbroke had been trying to secure the appointment of his half-brother, George St John, as envoy extraordinary to the King of Sicily, against Oxford's nominee,[182] Theophilus Oglethorpe (who later became the Pretender's agent at Turin). On 21 May the queen determined the issue in Bolingbroke's favour.[183] A second battle was fought over whether General Charles Ross (who had been appointed envoy extraordinary to Versailles in October 1713, despite Oxford's reluctance to remove Matthew Prior)[184] should now be dispatched to France in place of Oxford's confidential agent; again, Bolingbroke was triumphant in securing these orders.[185] In the event, Oxford's powerful hold over the Treasury prevented either George St John or General Ross from obtaining the necessary money with which to embark on their missions before the queen's death.[186]

The most important battle centred upon the appointment of an envoy to Hanover. Oxford's candidate was Lord Paget,[187] who in fact hesitated to serve Oxford at the risk of alienating Hanover.[188] Paget therefore declined to go unless the queen granted him an earldom, an honour which she refused to bestow.[189] On 26 May the queen peremptorily took the matter out of Oxford's hands, appointing Bolingbroke's nominee, her own first cousin the Earl of Clarendon, an outspoken personal enemy of the lord treasurer.[190] Clarendon's appointment was universally regarded as a signal defeat for Oxford and a triumph for Bolingbroke.[191] The queen would brook no delay in Clarendon's departure and she circumvented the treasurer by furnishing Clarendon with money from the privy purse.[192] The queen's formal answer to the elector's memorial explicitly refused either to permit a member of the Hanoverian family to reside in Britain or to grant further titles. It deliberately failed to mention either a household or the civil list requested for the heir apparent.[193] These were the *douceurs* at which Bromley hinted in his instructions to Clarendon:

> if the Resolution is taken, That [the electoral prince] shall not come without the Queen's Consent & Invitation, your Lordship will let the Elector know, that this Deference & Respect to her Majesty will be such an Obligation on her as will entitle him to all the good Effects he can expect from it.[194]

While Clarendon was *en route* to Hanover, Bolingbroke proceeded with his plans to reunite the Tory party and to destroy the lord treasurer. His first step was to introduce a measure which all Tories could support, a Schism bill which required all Dissenting educators to obtain a licence to teach from the Anglican bishop of their diocese. Defoe, writing later on Oxford's behalf, justly characterized the Schism bill as 'a Mine dug to blow up the White Staff'.[195] While there is no direct evidence, it seems apparent that the Queen supported the Schism bill as a means to build an educational monopoly for the Church of England. If Oxford opposed the bill, he would lose the Tories and the queen. If he supported it, he would alienate the Whigs and their Dissenting supporters. Oxford supported the bill during its slow passage through Parliament, albeit with a marked show of reluctance, while all his dependants voted against it.[196]

Privately Bolingbroke was working to convince the queen that he was no Jacobite fanatic. On 21 June, in response to the resolution passed in the House of Lords two months earlier, the queen issued a proclamation against the Pretender and offered a £5,000 reward for his apprehension within the three kingdoms, the same reward which her father had offered against Monmouth in 1685. In the welter of lies and half-truths which surrounded this incident, it seems most probable that Bolingbroke advised the queen to acquiesce to the House of Lords resolution in order to convince her that he was indeed anti-Jacobite.[197] Oxford, who had always played down the Jacobite danger to the queen, advised her against issuing the proclamation. According to his own memorandum, part of which appears to have been deliberately obliterated, of a conversation with the queen on 16 June, Oxford told her: 'You are going now to allarme the Nation againe with a Proclamation [illegible] give the Elector [illegible] to come in & provoke the Pretender.'[198] It was reported that the Duke of Shrewsbury (who returned to London from Ireland in early June) had strongly urged the queen to issue the proclamation.[199] In the event, the queen effectively shielded the author of this advice when, using a favourite technique originally learned from Oxford, she appeared in cabinet and immediately announced her decision, soliciting neither advice nor comment.[200] Both Oxford[201] and Bolingbroke[202] knew two days in advance that the proclamation would be issued and each man naturally claimed to Kreyenberg and to the Whigs that he was responsible.[203] To their French and Jacobite friends, however, both Oxford and Bolingbroke came closer to the truth: Oxford informed Gaultier that Harcourt and Bolingbroke were responsible,[204] while Bolingbroke admitted both to Gaultier and to the Earl of Mar[205] that he had advised the queen to issue the proclamation in order to kill rumours of his pro-Jacobite tendencies.

On 1 July, during a long interview with the queen, Oxford spoke strongly to her, warning her that Bolingbroke would endanger not only the Church of England and the Protestant succession but also her own throne,[206] but the final and fatal attack had already been made against the treasurer. On the same day, printed copies of the 19 May letters from the queen and Oxford to the Electress Sophia and the electoral prince appeared in the London streets. The public could now see that Oxford possessed no influence at Hanover, and the falsity of his assurances to the Whigs was exposed. The Marlboroughs, in constant correspondence with Bothmer and through him having access to Schütz's dispatches, had repeatedly warned the Whigs, through James Craggs, that Oxford was lying when he insinuated that he had inspired the writ demand. On the day before her death, the electress had given Samuel Molyneux, Sarah's agent at Hanover, copies of the letters and had ordered him to send them to the duchess and through her to Hanover's friends in Great Britain. This the Marlboroughs did and they were undoubtedly responsible for the publication of the letters, possibly – as Oxford suspected – with the connivance of Bolingbroke.[207]

In retaliation, Oxford launched his final parliamentary offensive against his colleague, promising to aid the Whigs in attacking Bolingbroke on a case of malversation. On 8 July, in the queen's presence, Nottingham and the Whigs in the House of Lords accused Arthur Moore of corruption in the negotiation of the Anglo-Spanish commercial treaty and hinted that the queen's private share of the *Asiento* had been secretly divided between Moore, Bolingbroke, and Lady Masham. This incident further embittered the Whigs against Oxford, for he failed to give them the public support which he had secretly promised.[208] The following day the queen prorogued Parliament.

V

During the last month of the queen's life, the nation – divided between Whig and Tory, Hanoverian and Jacobite – seemed to be heading towards civil war. Everyone knew that either Oxford or Bolingbroke would soon be dismissed from office, but no one knew which minister would fall. It appears certain that a major domestic political upheaval was on the cards in July 1714 and that it was aborted only by the queen's untimely death. Bolingbroke's triumph was partially due to the growth of his own influence with the queen, but more importantly his success derived from his ability to weld together an unstable coalition of all anti-Oxford elements. It is traditional, but inaccurate, to accord to Bolingbroke the sole credit for securing Oxford's dismissal. In fact, all batteries were firing at the embattled lord treasurer. At court, Bolingbroke had secured the aid of Lady Masham (now said to be conducting her cousin, Lord Trevor, to nocturnal audiences with the queen)[209] and, more significantly, that of the queen's favourite companion, the Duchess of Somerset, through her son-in-law Sir William Wyndham.[210] In the cabinet, however, Bolingbroke remained among the minority. He could only count upon Harcourt and Trevor, while Oxford still held the pro-Jacobite ministers (Buckingham,[211] Ormonde,[212] Mar,[213] and Poulett[214]), as well as his personal allies Mansell and Dartmouth.[215] Others, like Bromley, remained genuinely neutral or marginally pro-Oxford.[216] The Whigs were content to watch Bolingbroke destroy Oxford, confident that Oxford would then have no recourse but to join them in destroying Bolingbroke. The two greatest pillars of Bolingbroke's unwieldy coalition, however, were the surviving architects of the Glorious Revolution, Shrewsbury and Marlborough.

Shrewsbury, as the last of the 'middle party' which had brought Oxford to power in 1710 and one who still retained great influence with the queen, was of immense importance. In February he had received the queen's permission to return to England from Ireland,[217] but timidity had kept him from entering the eye of the hurricane. At Bolingbroke's insistence,[218] however, he had returned to London in mid-June and thereafter had pursued a 'trimming' course. He unsuccessfully opposed the imposition of the Schism bill in Ireland,[219] but on the other hand he was one of the few to defend Bolingbroke and Arthur Moore against charges of corruption in the Anglo-Spanish commercial treaty.[220] By late June, Shrewsbury began to declare for Bolingbroke,[221] although as late as mid-July the secretary was still professing to be unsure of where he stood with Shrewsbury.[222] On 5 July, Shrewsbury held a dinner party, attended by both Oxford and Bolingbroke, with the avowed purpose of reconciling them.[223] When this effort predictably failed, Shrewsbury – always averse to the notion of a 'prime minister' – repeated his conduct of 1710: while assuring Oxford of his continued support, it was confidently reported that Shrewsbury privately advised the queen to dismiss the lord treasurer and that he was instrumental in inviting Marlborough to return to England.[224] On the day following Oxford's dismissal, Shrewsbury visited Bothmer (who had returned to London on 25 June). He politely regretted the fact that Oxford had fallen and showed some anxiety at the prospect of Bolingbroke at the helm, but the real purpose of his visit was to assure Bothmer that he, Shrewsbury, had always enjoyed the best of personal relationships with Bolingbroke's new ally, Marlborough.[225]

Even while he was in self-imposed exile for almost two years, the former captain-general remained a powerful figure on the political scene, not least because of the personal attachment which the queen still retained for him. There is no evidence to support the contemporary belief that Bolingbroke had gained a personal ascendency over the queen or that she had lost her aversion to his notoriously licentious private life. It was even reported, on good authority, that the queen was as tired of Bolingbroke as she was of Oxford.[226] On the day she dismissed Oxford, she confided to Dr Hamilton that, of her ministers, 'most of them sought for themselves, they had neither regarded her Health, her Life, nor her Peace'.[227] What the queen sought was a 'manager', one who stood above party and could undertake a rapprochement with her Hanoverian heir. Of the men who had acted that role during the Revolution settlement, the elder Sunderland and Godolphin were dead and Oxford was thoroughly discredited. The queen now turned to Marlborough, her oldest and greatest servant with whom she had never completely lost contact. After the death of his daughter, Lady Bridgewater, in March 1714, Marlborough had written to the queen. She had personally accepted his letter (the contents of which are unknown) from her namesake and god-daughter, Lady Sunderland.[228] It seems possible that the queen may have indirectly summoned Marlborough home through his closest friend, General William Cadogan. As early as 22 June, Kreyenberg reported: 'Cadogan croit scavoir de la part de la Reyne mesme, que Mylord Duc seroit le bien venu.'[229]* Although no direct evidence has survived, it seems certain that Bolingbroke and the elder Craggs entered into negotiations a fortnight before the queen's death. Marlborough's demands, through

---

*'*Cadogan* believes he knows *from the Queen herself*, that *My Lord Duke* would be *welcome*'. Italicized words in cypher.

Craggs, were that Bolingbroke should effectively secure the succession and discard the proposed Anglo-French commercial treaty. The agreement between Bolingbroke and Craggs was rapidly concluded; Marlborough was to resume all his offices (the Duke of Ormonde being compensated with the viceroyalty of Ireland) and the secretary agreed to a reconciliation with Hanover.[230] The fact that adverse winds delayed the Marlboroughs' return to London, where they were expected on 21 July, undoubtedly contributed to the peculiar delay in the queen's dismissal of Oxford from office.

The queen turned to Marlborough and Bolingbroke in the hope that they would be able to re-establish cordial relations between herself and the elector. On 7 July, two days before Parliament was prorogued, Sir David Hamilton informed the queen that he had received a letter from the Palatine envoy, Steingens (who was visiting Bath), reporting that Oxford had not replied to any of General Schulenburg's letters. The queen responded that she did not understand Oxford's negligence, 'but I'll convey an answer to [Schulenburg] by some other hand'. Dr Hamilton concluded that Oxford was 'declining in the Queens Favour and Trust, Else he would have been the Person she would have spoke to'.[231] By 19 July, Bolingbroke was assured of victory over Oxford, and urgently summoned Harcourt to abandon his short visit to the country and return immediately to London.[232] By the beginning of the last week of the queen's life, it was known that Oxford's dismissal was at hand. On Saturday, 24 July, Dr Arbuthnot informed Swift that 'the fall of the Dragon [Oxford] does not proceed altogether from his old friend [Lady Masham], but from the great person [the queen], whom I perceive to be highly offended, by little hints that I have received'.[233] By Monday Oxford knew that he would be out, probably the next day.[234]

Early on the Tuesday morning, Dr Hamilton visited the queen at Kensington Palace. He recorded that the queen

> told me Lord Oxford would be out that night, and upon Telling Her that Bolingbroke was said to get the Staff, she said 'no', as also my telling Her that Persons said the Reason why my Lord Oxford was to be out, was because he had hinder'd Her Majesty from giving Grants to Lady Massam, to which she answer'd that if he said so, he was very ungrateful to Lady Massam.[235]

Of even greater importance was the fact that Hamilton told the queen that he had spoken with Steingens, who had shown him copies of the elector's letters to General Schulenburg. The queen immediately ordered Hamilton to return to Steingens and to ask the Palatine to write over, so that it might come to the Electour by the hand of [Schulenburg], that the Changes she was about to make, should not injure him nor lessen Her friendship to him . . . and that if he would write to Her upon this Her Profession of friendship, she would Immediately answer it with Her own hand, without the knowledge of any of Her Ministry, and desir'd that his writing might be without the knowledge of any of his.

To consolidate this personal rapprochement between Queen Anne and her heir apparent, the queen proposed that Dr Hamilton transfer his son from Oxford to the university at Leyden or that at Utrecht; Hamilton would then have an excuse to request the queen's permission to see his son and visit the court of Hanover at the same time.

And Then asking Her of my Errand thither, she told me it was to Settle a Sincere Friendship with the Elector, and that all occasions of Jealousie might be remov'd, and in Such a way, as would give Her Self least disquiet. . . . He was to ask leave to come Over to pay a Visit to Her for three or four weeks, by which Means he would have entire Satisfaction, and She Quiet, *she resolving to put it upon him to make Changes* [i.e. in the government].

Dr Hamilton carried out the first step in the queen's remarkable initiative by visiting Steingens later in the day, but fate was not to allow the queen's plans to come to fruition.[236]

Later that same day, 27 July, the queen held a cabinet, which apparently was not attended by Oxford, who was still the lord treasurer. Erasmus Lewis, one of Oxford's closest friends, complained to Swift that

The Queen has told all the Lords the reasons of her parting with him, viz. that he neglected all business, that he was seldom to be understood, that when he did explain himself she could not depend upon the truth of what he said; that he never came to her at the time she appointed, that he often came drunk, that lastly to crown all he behav'd himself towards her with ill manner, indecency, & disrespect.[237]

That evening, between eight and nine o'clock, Oxford visited the queen to surrender the white staff, the symbol of his high office. He was forced to resign in 'rather mortifying, than agreeable Circumstances'. Immediately after this meeting, Oxford confided to Gaultier the substance of his valedictory audience with the queen. His last warning to her was never to trust Marlborough, who was returning to England only to betray her and cause civil unrest. Reserved when she chose to be so, the queen did not deign to reply to this unsolicited advice: Oxford admitted to Gaultier that 'the Queen said very little to this'.[238] After her meeting with

Oxford, the queen attended another cabinet, which dragged on until midnight without producing any results. She left the Council Chamber in a distraught state and spent the night weeping in her bedchamber.[239]

Oxford himself attributed the delay in his dismissal to the fact that no successor had yet been settled upon; in law, Oxford remained lord treasurer until a successor was appointed and duly confirmed, and as such he could participate in government after the queen's death under the terms of the Act of Regency. On Wednesday, 28 July, there was yet a third cabinet meeting, although apparently no final determination on a Treasury commission could be reached in Marlborough's continued absence. The queen was already showing symptoms of profound emotional strain: Daniel Malthus, her apothecary, recorded, 'Her appetite was quite lost and Her Spirits sunk.' It is today generally accepted that her illness was caused by suppressed gout, which culminated in erysipelas (an acute febrile disease associated with intense local inflammation of the skin and subcutaneous tissue, caused by a hemolytic streptococcus). On Thursday the queen felt even more poorly, 'very much dispirited, flushed and Her head full'; the cabinet meeting which had been scheduled was postponed until the queen felt capable of presiding.

She was unable to go to sleep that night and vomited at three o'clock in the morning; but she finally slept until seven o'clock on the morning of Friday, 30 July; 'finding herself pretty well, [she] rose from Bed and got her Head comb'd'. However, she had two violent convulsions, one after the other, which lasted from nine until eleven o'clock. Her doctors were immediately summoned, and for about an hour 'she was speechless, motionless, and unsensible'. The Duchess of Ormonde, in attendance as a lady of the bedchamber, dispatched an urgent message to her husband summoning him to Kensington from Whitehall where the lords of the committee (the cabinet without the queen) were scheduled to meet. The other members immediately followed Ormonde to Kensington,

> Lord Chancelor as soon as he came there going into the Gallery, and finding it empty and the Queen's closet open, ask'd where her Majesty was. And being told in her Closet, he went in, & to his thinking saw her dead in her chair, with her Ladies and Physitians about her. Upon that he went close up to her, look'd in her face & touch'd her hand without her showing the least knowledge of him.

When the queen recovered consciousness, she could not speak beyond answering 'yes' or 'no'.[240]

Even to laymen, it was apparent that the queen could not recover. For

Harcourt, Bolingbroke, and their allies, the immediate task was to ensure that Oxford could not return to office under the Regency Act. When he left the queen's bedchamber, Harcourt proposed to the other ministers that a new lord treasurer should be appointed immediately.

> And Therefore I desire you will command me instantly to recommend one to her Majesty, & I think the Duke of Shrewsbury's abilities, his service to her Majesty, & Zeal for the succession are so well known, that none is fitter for so great a trust.

The ministers unanimously agreed to Shrewsbury's nomination and, shortly after the queen had regained consciousness, Harcourt re-entered her bedchamber, accompanied by Bolingbroke, Buckingham, Poulett, and Dartmouth,

> and told her Majesty he desired in ye name of & by the direction of her whole Council, that she wou'd for ye good of her Kingdome immediately make ye D[uke] Shrewsbury, Lord High Treasurer of Great Britain, & command him to prepare his Patent. She answer'd if they desired it, she wou'd, & taking the White Staff of ye Lord Chamberlain out of Lord Chancelor's hand, she return'd it to ye D[uke] Shrewsbury as Lord Treasurer.

Shrewsbury, now endowed with triple authority as lord treasurer, lord lieutenant of Ireland, and lord chamberlain, assumed the presiding role over the committee, which transformed itself into a Privy Council for the defence of the realm. Shortly after the queen had given the white staff to Shrewsbury, the Dukes of Argyll and Somerset, alerted by a message from the Duchess of Somerset, arrived at Kensington. The membership of the Privy Council had not been altered by the 'great changes' of 1710, the two dukes claimed their rights of membership, and Shrewsbury warmly welcomed them to the council board. All vital decisions were taken unanimously: orders were issued to all lords lieutenant authorizing them to seize the arms and horses of Roman Catholics and to watch suspected persons; several regiments were moved towards London and arrangements were made to transport British troops in the Southern Netherlands to England in case of need; the ports were closed and James Craggs the younger was dispatched to Hanover to warn the elector that the queen could not possibly live; Strafford was ordered to demand Dutch assistance in protecting the Hanoverian settlement and a British squadron was ordered to the Dutch coast to escort the elector to England.[241] During the rush and confusion of these hours at Kensington, Peter Wentworth noted that

> The chaplains desir'd the Queen's servants that were in waiting to come and pray for the Queen, so I and three or four more was the whole congregation, the rest of the company, and there was a great deal of all sorts Whigs and Torys, staid in curiosity to hear what they cou'd pick up.[242]

At four in the afternoon, the queen's physicians appeared before the Privy Council to assure the members that the queen could not live twelve hours longer.[243]

During the afternoon and evening of 30 July the queen gradually weakened, slipping into a deep lethargy and becoming insensible to what was happening about her. The next morning, Saturday, a greatly expanded Privy Council met, composed of all leading Tories and Whigs who happened to be in London, and at eleven o'clock forty members signed an appeal to the elector, asking him to embark for England as quickly as possibly.[244] Bothmer and Kreyenberg were invited to join the council as consultants. In the hour of her extremity, the queen's subjects were unified as never before during her reign. All possible preparations had been made for the smooth transfer of power from the house of Stuart to the house of Hanover. All that now remained was to await the queen's death. Sir John Evelyn recorded that, on visiting Kensington, the first person he met was Dr Richard Mead, one of the queen's doctors, who told him that

> the Queen might perhaps live some hours, but t'was morally impossible she shou'd gett over it, adding that any body wou'd have been in her condition, if they had had the gout in their head six & thirty hours, without anything done to them.

That afternoon, Mead was still freely broadcasting his opinion: 'all the Doctors agreed she would in all probability hold out till tomorrow', Charles Ford reported to Swift, 'except Mead who pronounc'd several hours before she could not live two minutes, and seems uneasie it did not happen so'. The vigil stretched throughout the night.

The High and Mighty Sovereign Princess, Anne, by the Grace of God Queen of Great Britain, France and Ireland, Defender of the Faith, died at Kensington Palace at forty-five minutes past seven o'clock on the morning of Sunday, 1 August 1714. She was forty-nine. To those who knew her best, her release from emotional and physical suffering came as a blessing. 'I believe sleep was never more welcome to a weary traveller than death was to her', Dr Arbuthnot informed Swift.[245] To those who remained loyal to the hereditary principle and to the house of Stuart, her death was a tragedy. To those who unfairly suspected that the queen had been party to a plot to subvert the Protestant succession, her death was an example of divine providence. Dissenting chapels rang with psalms of praise on that Sunday morning, for the queen's death almost certainly guaranteed that the Schism Act, scheduled to take effect that very day, would never be enforced. At St John's, Oxford, the Whig head of college ordered prayers for 'King George' to be said in morning worship; when it was objected that the queen might not yet be dead, '"Dead", says he, "she is as dead as Julius Caesar"'.[246]

Epilogue

Immediately after the queen's death, the Privy Council assembled at Kensington where the regency nominations of the new king were opened, the regency council established and the lords justices sworn in. The proclamation of George I began at Queen Anne's birthplace, St James's Palace, at four in the afternoon. This proclamation of the first Hanoverian monarch was peacefully repeated throughout the three kingdoms. The following day, the Duke and Duchess of Marlborough, who had landed at Dover on the afternoon on 1 August, returned to London and were greeted with tumultuous acclaim by the populace. Marlborough, however, was very offended that he had not been nominated a regent by the new monarch, and he and Sarah quickly retired to the country.

On 3 August two unsigned drafts of the queen's will, 'found in her Majesties Closet', were read before the lords justices.[1] The second draft, dating from 1710–11, specified payments for her funeral expenses, her outstanding debts, and the wages due to her servants. The only specific bequest was that £2,000 should be distributed to the poor in her memory. No executors were named. In private conversation, the queen had once told Dartmouth that she wished her personal jewels to be divided between her only surviving cousin, the Queen of Sicily (Anne-Marie d'Orléans, remembered from the Lady Anne's long-ago days in Paris), and the Duchess of Somerset 'as the fittest person to wear them after her'.[2] The queen's horror of death, however, had been so strong that she had been unable to bring herself to make such bequests in writing or to sign her will: she died intestate.[3] Her estate was assumed by the crown, although George I agreed to pay her bequest of £2,000 to the poor[4] even though he was informed that it was not valid in law.[5]

The new king issued orders that the queen's funeral should take place before his arrival in London. The queen's body remained at Kensington Palace for more than three weeks while preparations were made. Both

397

the time and the cost involved suggest that the proper pomp and circumstance due to the last Stuart monarch were rendered: the funeral cost £10,579 8s. 9d., some £5,000 less than the expenses of the new king's coronation.[6] Orders were issued that guns from the Tower of London should be fired every minute from the time the procession set out from Kensington until the queen's body was finally interred.[7] On the evening of 23 August the queen's body was brought to the Prince's Chamber of the Palace of Westminster 'in a Herse cover'd with Purple Cloth drawn by 8 Horses'. The chamber was magnificently decorated with '45 large silver sconces with double Branches in two Rows in each of which were placed two wax Candles . . . some of the Ladies attended upon the Body all Night'. The next day a 'private' funeral was held in Westminster Abbey under the supervision of Shrewsbury as lord chamberlain and with the Duchess of Somerset as chief mourner. The queen's coffin was lowered into the vault beneath the tomb of her great-great-grandmother, Mary, Queen of Scots, where it was placed alongside the remains of Charles II, William and Mary, and her beloved Prince George of Denmark. The officers of her household then broke their staffs of office and threw them into the tomb. Among those present at this final ceremony were those who had shared happier days with the queen, including two daughters of 'Mrs Freeman', Henrietta, Countess of Godolphin, and Mary, Duchess of Montagu. Also present were the ladies of the bedchamber 'in veils' and the bedchamber women 'in Hoods', including Abigail, Lady Masham.[8]

In all the extensive reports of the queen's final illness and death, there is no mention of Abigail, although Swift was assured on 3 August that 'Poor Lady Masham is almost dead with Grief'.[9] On the same day Peter Wentworth reported to his brother:

> The town tells a world of stories of Lady Masham now; as that a Friday she left the Queen for three hours to go and ransack for things at St. James's. I can't say if this is true or false, a Saturday I remember perticularly I see her go away, but as I thought with too much grief, to have any thoughts of herself. I hope people wrong her, for she would be a monster in nature to be ungratefull and to forget a Queen so soon that raised her from nothing.[10]

Four days before the queen's funeral, however, Wentworth was less charitable: 'Lady Masham, Mrs. Hill and Danvers are cry[d] out upon their behaviour; tho they roar'd and cry'd enough while there was life, as soon as there was none they took care of themselves.'[11] The Mashams faded into obscurity, residing at their estates at Langley Marish near Windsor (which Lord Masham had purchased two weeks before the queen's death) and at Oates in Essex. In 1716, Lord Masham secured the reversion of the remembrancer of the exchequer which had been granted to him by the queen and had enough cash to purchase an additional 122 acres in Buckinghamshire,[12] but by 1718 the Mashams were forced to sell some jewellery to George I at a considerable loss. 'The Ring cost the late Queen a Thousand Pound,' the secretary of state noted, 'she gave it to My Lady Masham, who sold it to Us for £620.'[13] Abigail Masham died in December 1734, being quickly followed to the grave by her brother John Hill in June 1735. Samuel Masham, however, survived to the age of seventy-nine, dying in 1758, and Alice Hill enjoyed the annuity which the queen had provided for her until her death at the age of seventy-seven in 1762.[14]

The chief figures of the queen's last ministry did not enjoy such a peaceful retirement. The new monarch arrived in London on 18 September. He had already ordered Bolingbroke's dismissal and the seizure of his papers, and he received Oxford – as Bolingbroke gleefully noted – 'with a most distinguishing contempt'. The following day the queen's ministers, with the exception of Shrewsbury, were dismissed: 'moderation' was as dead as Queen Anne. The Whigs were to rule Great Britain for forty years. The election of a new, Whig dominated Parliament led to the establishment in March 1715 of the Committee of Secrecy, charged with investigating the Utrecht negotiations and the possible Jacobite plots of Tory ministers. Bolingbroke, fearing for his head, rashly fled to France in April 1715 to join the Pretender, as did the Duke of Ormonde three months later. Acts of attainder were passed against both men. Ormonde survived the abortive Jacobite rebellion of 1715 to die in exile in 1745. While Bolingbroke later managed to secure his conditional pardon from George I, he was specifically denied re-entry into the House of Lords and spent the remainder of his life (he died in 1751) in frustrated opposition to the crown, never again holding high office. Oxford, more phlegmatic than his younger rival and knowing that the only evidence against him was safely in the hands of the French, did not flee the country. After his impeachment in 1715, he was arrested and lodged in the Tower, and he did not emerge until two years later when the case against him was dropped because of procedural disputes between the two houses of Parliament. He was, however, denied access to the court and spent the remainder of his life until 1724 in fruitless correspondence with the Pretender.

The older statesmen rapidly faded from the scene after the death of the queen. Shrewsbury, the last man to hold the office of lord treasurer, was retained by George I as lord chamberlain until his death in 1718, but he no longer sat in the cabinet. Marlborough was restored to all his offices, but the captain-general suffered a series of strokes in 1716 which effectively removed him from political life, although he did not die until 1722. The impartial hand of death soon took the Junto which the queen had so hated: Halifax and Wharton both died in 1715, as did Bishop Burnet, while Somers died in 1716; the youngest member, Sunderland, died in 1722, while the last survivor, Orford, lived in retirement until his death in 1727. The most important casualty of the queen's death was the Tory party: Whig revenge pushed many Tories into the arms of the Pretender in 1715. The union survived the strain of the Jacobite rebellion in Scotland, but the Tory party did not. By the 1720s most Tories had either made their peace with the Hanoverian government and returned to office, as Harcourt did before his death in 1727, or lived in retirement, as did Dartmouth until his death in 1750. The queen's half-brother, the Pretender, found his hopes dashed and his opportunities few: in 1717 he was forced to establish residence in Rome and for the next half century, until his death in 1766, he presided over a movement increasingly enmeshed in the quarrels of the past and without hope for the future.

But what of Mrs Freeman? The passage of the years only accentuated in Sarah those qualities which made her at once delightful to some and repellent to others. Jealously guarding her husband, bitterly quarrelling with her daughters, maliciously playing off her grandchildren against their parents and each other, engaging to her heart's content in extensive litigation, and amassing the largest private fortune in Europe, the Duchess of Marlborough lived into triumphant old age. For thirty years she polished various versions of her memoirs until, two years before her own death, *The Conduct of the dowager Duchess of Marlborough* was published in 1742. Through her *Conduct*, her preservation of the queen's letters, and her own extensive annotations of them, Sarah spent a large portion of her declining years in providing the historian with the raw material to assess the life and reign of Queen Anne.

The twelve years during which Queen Anne reigned over Great Britain proved to be the great watershed between the violence of the seventeenth century and the stability and prosperity of the eighteenth century. The queen and her generation were dominated by fear of the renewal of the horrors of the civil wars of the 1640s. The political views which she imbibed in her childhood (her support of the 'Church party', her suspicions of the Whigs) were natural to a granddaughter of Charles I and Clarendon, and she never completely shed them. As she matured politically, however, her actions both reflected and significantly contributed to the growing stability of British society.

Her personal and public lives were dominated by a conflict between illusion and reality, a conflict which began in her nursery. As a child of state she was reared in an atmosphere of exaltation of royalty; in fact, she was dependent upon the vagaries of her nursery servants, a dependence underlined by the deaths of her grandmother, her aunt, and her mother. These unusual vicissitudes of fortune impressed the introspective child and taught her how to bridge the gap between the shadow of power and the reality of impotence. As a royal personage she was trained to protect her 'family'; all accounts conclude that she was the best of mistresses and the remarkable longevity of servants in her personal employ is best illustrated by Mrs Beata Danvers, who served the royal family from the time Anne Hyde was Duchess of York until the death of her younger daughter forty-nine years later. Yet in dealing with her 'family' (in both senses of the word), Queen Anne learned at an early age the advantages of reserve, even the uses of guile and outright duplicity. Throughout her life when she found herself in tight corners she was to prove less than candid, even deceptive, with those closest to her in blood and politics.

The standard picture of Queen Anne, that of a weak, irresolute woman beset by bedchamber quarrels and deciding high policy on the basis of personalities, was largely propagated by the Duchess of Marlborough. The usage of 'Mrs Morley' and 'Mrs Freeman' to bridge the social gap between the two women, a seeming confirmation of Sarah's thesis, was deceptive – and no one was more deceived than Sarah herself. Never during her life did Queen Anne for one moment forget her position and the deference due to it, although she often found it to her advantage to ignore it temporarily. In her first close friendship, that with Frances Apsley, it is clear that the future queen assumed the dominant role, and she was to do so in every subsequent relationship. Her childhood training had taught her how to choose advisors, and she was never to be blindly led by bedchamber favourites. By the time of her marriage in 1683, she was already her own woman. Even her frequent references to 'my poor opinion' barely conceal the fact that she had a very elevated conception of her own opinions. Her formal education had provided her with one great emotional bulwark: implicit trust in the doctrines of the Church of England and a determination to defend the Protestant cause. She saw herself as a Protestant heroine, but the reality of her situation – a fervent Protestant in a largely pro-Catholic court – taught her the advantages of caution. The illusion of power, and the possibility of her eventual succession to the throne, fuelled in her an ambition which was to characterize the remainder of her life.

Religion and her own dynastic ambition led her into covert opposition to her father, the perpetuation of the 'warming-pan' myth, and active participation in the Revolution. Family ties were easily broken. Like England after 1688, Queen Anne never looked back. She easily jettisoned any belief in divine hereditary right, so cherished by her Stuart predecessors, in favour of a monarchy based on parliamentary statute. Religion and ambition also led her to support the Hanoverian succession: it was Protestant and it was protective, for it excluded from the succession the Catholic half-brother who, under the old dispensation, would have preceded Anne and her children. Never was her capacity for deception better illustrated than by the hopes which she consistently held out to the Jacobites after 1691 that 'at the proper time' she would support the Pretender.

The 1690s proved to be a crucial decade in her personal and political development. It was her own decision to go into opposition to William and Mary and she stoically weathered the social ostracism which that decision entailed; she discovered, however, that the illusory importance of her potential position as heiress apparent did not outweigh the realities of power politics. Her limited triumph over William III in 1695 was produced not by her own exertions but by the unexpected death of Mary II, and by the need to maintain Protestant unity in the face of the Jacobite menace. Her hysterical as well as her real pregnancies during this period show that she knew that her trump card was the possibility that she might produce heirs to the throne. Her ambition, which led to seventeen pregnancies during her first seventeen years of marriage, broke her health, and by the time the Duke of Gloucester died in 1700 it was apparent to everyone – even to Anne despite the hopes which she continued to nourish – that she would never succeed in producing a healthy child. By this time, however, her maternal instincts were so strong, her stoic loyalty to her religion such a comfort, that her ambition took a new form: when the 'SunShine day' came she would be the mother of her people. For this reason, the new queen chose as her coronation text the passage from Isaiah – on the face of it so incongruously inappropriate, considering her series of disastrous pregnancies – 'Kings shall be thy nursing Fathers, and Queens thy nursing Mothers'. Sir John Clerk noted the contrast between the 'Ruler of the World' of illusion and the pathetic invalid of reality, but he did not appreciate the queen's ambition, which bridged the gap between the two: 'as long as I live', she told Godolphin in 1705, 'it shall be my endeavour to make my Country and my freinds easy'. This was to prove the theme of her reign.

Queen Anne ascended the throne as an anomaly, a woman ruler in an age of war, and as a constitutional monarch when the limits on the powers of the monarchy were still new and untried. She found herself at the centre of the political system: no politician could afford to ignore her personal and political opinions, likes and dislikes. The attitudes adopted by Whig and Tory politicians, in and out of office, to the question of importing a Hanoverian heir, for example, were largely determined by whether they wished to cultivate or irritate the queen. Her daily consultations with ministers, her presiding role in the cabinet, her assiduous attendance in the House of Lords, and the contacts which she developed and maintained with all shades of political opinion enabled the queen to influence, if not to dominate, the political developments of her reign.

As befitted the rule of a Christian and pious queen, there was a minimum of official violence. There were no political executions; the single impeachment – that of Sacheverell in 1710 – ended with a ludicrously mild punishment, largely because of the queen's known sympathies; victorious politicians were denied the right to hound their defeated rivals to the scaffold. The queen, although a devotee of the Church of England, refused to support the resurrection of a persecuting Anglican Church and deprived the High Tories of the opportunity to repeal the Act of Toleration.

Caution produced the queen's political moderation. She realized that she was a constitutional monarch, and she never attempted to challenge the supremacy of Parliament or of statute law. At the same time, she jealously guarded the prerogatives of the crown and interpreted the constitution as she chose. She regarded her ministers as *her* servants in a personal sense and refused to concede that majorities in both houses of Parliament gave either party an inherent right to dominate the executive councils of government. Despite her momentary fits of pique, as in 1705 when she told Sarah that she would never again countenance the Tories, her innate caution never allowed her to sever completely her contacts with any major politician or party: yesterday's villains might prove to be tomorrow's heroes.

Above all, the queen was determined that she would not be that cat's-paw of any party or politician: as Marlborough commented in 1706, 'I have always observed that when she thinks herself in the right, she needs no advice to help her to be very ferm and possative.' In 1702 at the beginning of her reign she refused to follow Marlborough and Godolphin blindly, while at the same time she stood firm against High Tory demands for purges of Whig office-holders below cabinet rank. After 1705 the queen opposed the removal of Tories at every step; again and again Marlborough and Godolphin succeeded in imposing Whig ministers on her after long, gruelling, and self-destructive struggles, but only at the last possible moment to save the government's parliamentary majority. Her temporary demoralization following Prince George's death allowed the triumph of 'one sett of men'. In 1710, Harley was forced to follow the same step-by-step process as Marlborough and Godolphin earlier, in inducing the queen to carry through the 'great changes' in the teeth of Whig majorities in both houses of Parliament. Even then, her goals were moderate, the timing was largely the queen's, and only the unexpected refusal of the 'lord treasurer's Whigs' to continue in office under Harley produced a cabinet more dominated by Tories than the queen had originally desired. In the event, the cabinet alone was changed, even the membership of the Privy Council remaining intact; furthermore, the queen maintained surreptitious contacts with Godolphin and the Whigs, and cultivated Whig sources of information such as Dr Hamilton in order to ensure that her bridges to the opposition were open. One effect of the queen's insistence on political moderation and a 'mixed ministry' was to perpetuate political instability in British public life, but to a large extent the queen personally determined the political dynamics of her reign and prevented the triumph of either party. The final victory was only achieved by the Whigs after her death, when George I delivered the domestic machinery of the country into their hands.

In resisting the domination of either party, the queen harked back to the constitutional principles of the seventeenth century and firmly turned her face against the trend of the future. She represented the Elizabethan principle of national unity, the indivisibility of the body politic into factions, and regarded herself as the sole disinterested party in the midst of a struggle between self-seeking opportunists. 'Why for God sake', she had demanded of Godolphin in 1706,

> must I who have no interest, no end, and no thought but for ye good
> of my Country, be made soe miserable as to be brought into ye power
> of one sett of men, & why must I not be trusted, since I meane nothing
> but what is equally for ye good of all my subjects?

For a woman and an invalid, a principal minister was a necessity, but the queen grew more truculent as her own sense of confidence in her powers and perceptions increased throughout her reign. As she warned Oxford in 1712,

> You can not wonder that I who have bin ill used soe many yeares
> should desire to keep my self from being againe enslaved, & if I must
> always Comply, & not be complyed with, is I think very hard, & what
> I can not submit to.

Compliance, as the queen defined it, was support for those policies which she had embraced. Throughout her reign, the queen never hesitated to publicize her support for certain policies, and to make it clear that the road to royal favour could only be traversed by supporting them. Without detracting from the accomplishments of her chief ministers – whether Marlborough, Godolphin, or Oxford – it is fair to record that the triumphs of the reign owed a great deal to Queen Anne personally. There can be no doubt that her warm and fervent support for the union of Scotland and England contributed significantly to its acceptance by both kingdoms. During the early years of the reign, her staunch support of Marlborough and his policies against the ardent opposition of Tory naval–colonial strategists proved crucial in providing ample scope for the captain-general to exercise his diplomatic and military skills and to re-establish the balance of power in Europe. In the same manner, the queen's overriding determination to end the war proved decisive to the success of Oxford's peace policy after 1710. The fact that Oxford used duplicity and deceit, that he deserted Britain's allies in the field in order to reap separate and exclusive advantages for the island kingdom in the general peace, did not disturb the queen. As so often in her career, the ends justified the means. The Christian princess was familiar with the precepts of *The Prince*.

Finally, and most importantly for the future, the queen consistently followed a policy combining both personal ambition and Protestant principle in relation to the future succession to the crown. Self-preservation demanded that she support the parliamentary statutes in favour of the house of Hanover: if her Roman Catholic half-brother had any hereditary rights whatsoever, they superseded hers to the crown. At the same time, self-preservation equally demanded that the queen's Hanoverian heirs be kept safely in their German dominions throughout her reign, lest their presence in England form a magnet for discontented politicians of both parties. In her personal succession policy, keeping out both Hanoverian and Jacobite while maintaining her own authority, the queen proved to be triumphantly successful.

In the end, as her body was lowered into the tomb of her ancestors, illusion and reality were one: the only power which she could exert beyond the grave was that of her example. For twelve hectic years, with an indomitable spirit and 'a good hart', the last of the Stuarts had succeeded in overcoming the limitations of her sex and her ill health to impose her views on the great men of the day, to preserve the Protestant constitution, to provide real ease for her country and friends, and to preside over the turbulent age which paid her the ultimate compliment by adopting her name as its own.

Abbreviations

AAE: Archives des Affaires Étrangères, Quai d'Orsay, Paris
BIHR: Bulletin of the Institute of Historical Research
BM: British Museum, London
CSPD: Calendar of State Papers Domestic
DNB: Dictionary of National Biography
EHR: English Historical Review
GEC: G. E. Cockayne, *The Complete Peerage*
HLQ: Huntington Library Quarterly
HMC: Historical Manuscripts Commission
M&M: Archives de Meurthe-et-Moselle, Nancy
NSA: Niedersächsisches Staatsarchiv, Hanover
PRO: Public Record Office, London
SP: State Papers (Foreign), Public Record Office
SRO: Scottish Record Office
TRHS: Transactions of the Royal Historical Society
TVKA: Royal Danish Archives, Copenhagen
ZHVN: Zeitschrift des Historischen Vereins für Niedersachsen

Notes

Chapter 1:   Child of State

1 J. S. Clarke, ed., *The Life of James the Second . . . collected out of Memoirs writ of his own hand* (London, 1816), I, 378: hereafter cited as James II, *Memoirs*; BM, Add. MSS 18,740, f. 3: Anne Hyde's deposition to Privy Council, 18 February 1661.

2 BM, Add. MSS 18,738, ff. 124–5: Elizabeth, Abbess of Hervorden, to Elizabeth, Queen of Bohemia, 23 February 1661, London; cf. David Jones, *The Life of James II, Late King of England* (London, 3rd edn, 1705), 7; Abel Boyer, *The Life and Reign of Queen Anne* (London, 1735), I, 4; Edward Hyde, Earl of Clarendon, *Life* (Oxford, 1857), I, 324–5.

3 James II, *Memoirs*, I, 387.

4 BM, Add. MSS 18,740, ff. 1, 3, 5: depositions of James, Anne Hyde, Joseph Crowther, 18 February 1661.

5 G. E. C[ockayne], *The Complete Peerage*, II, 264: hereafter cited as GEC.

6 GEC, II, 496.

7 Robert Latham and William Matthews, eds, *The Diary of Samuel Pepys* (Berkeley, 1970), II, 95: 6 May 1661.

8 For Sophia, see Eduard Bodemann, ed., *Briefwechsel der Herzogin Sophie von Hannover mit ihrem Bruder, dem Kurfürsten Karl Ludwig von der Pfalz, und des Letzteren mit seiner Schwägerin, der Pfalzgräfin Anna* (Publicationen aus den K. Preussischen Staatsarchiven, Band 26, Leipzig, 1885), 362, 391: Sophia to Karl Ludwig, 20 June, 30 November 1679 NS; for William III, see Stephen Baxter, *William III* (London, 1966), 129.

9 GEC, VI, Appendix F: 'Bastards of Charles II', 706–8.

10 Roger Coke, *Detection of the Court and State of England* (London, 1719), III, 116; cf. Mrs Dawson's diary in John Buchanan-Brown, ed., *The Remains of Thomas Hearne* (London, 1966), 123.

11 PRO 31/3/114, ff. 105–8: Comenge to Louis XIV, 16 February 1665 NS, London.

12 Sir Arthur Bryant, ed., *The Letters, Speeches, and Declarations of King Charles II* (London, 1968), 178: Charles II to Madame, 9 February, 1665, Whitehall.

13 Edward Chamberlayne, *Angliae Notitia* (19th ed., 1700), 107–9.

14 F. J. Routledge, ed., *Calendar of the Clarendon State Papers*, vol. V, *1660–1726* (Oxford, 1970), 511: Clarendon to Sir Edward Nicholas, 11 October 1665, Oxford.

15 Blenheim G I 10: Sarah's 'A True Account', f. 2.

16 Thurstan Peter, 'Queen Anne's Nurse', *Notes and Queries*, 11th series, V, 508.

17 James J. Cartwright, ed., *The Wentworth Papers, 1705–1739* (London, 1883), 282: Peter Wentworth to Lord Strafford, 28 March 1712, London; cf. PRO, T. 48/23, n.f.: Sarah, Duchess of Marlborough, to Wm Lowndes, 2 August 1721, Windsor Lodge.

18 Dr Edward Chamberlayne, *Angliae Notitia, or the Present State of England*, 1st and 6th edns, 1669 and 1672.

19 Violet Bonham Carter, *Winston Churchill as I Knew Him* (London, Pan edn, 1965), 25.

20 Bevil Higgons, *A Short View of the English History* (London, 1731), 367.

21 Boyer, *Queen Anne*, I, 10.

22 Pepys, *Diary*, V, 268: 12 September 1664.

23 HMC *Stuart*, I, 114–17: 'Rules for the Family of our dearest son, the Prince of Wales', 19 July 1696.

24 Blenheim E 17: Anne to Sarah, Fryday night [25 August 1693].

25 Charles, Comte de Baillon, *Henriette-Anne d'Angleterre* (Paris, 1886), 401.

26 *CSPD, Charles II, Nov. 1667–Sept. 1668*, 476: Sir Jer. Smith to Sir Joseph Williamson, 7 July 1668, PRO, SP 101/15, f. 222: newsletter, 25 July 1668 NS, Paris.

27 Hove Central Library, M 1/112/5, 14 November 1709: 'Paid Mr. Gekie for cureing the Queen's Eyes, £107-10-0'; cf. HMC *Belvoir Castle*, II, 40: Lady Chaworth to Lord Roos, 27 [February 1677]: 'Lady Anne, the Duke's second daughter, is ill of her eies againe'.

28 Blenheim G I 9: 'The Character of Princes', p. 109.

29 AAE, CP Angleterre 250, f. 26: Gaultier to Torcy, 18 October 1713 NS, London.

30 SP 78/126, f. 70: Ralph Montagu to Arlington, 30 March 1669 NS, Paris; ff. 97–8: Sidney Godolphin to Arlington, 31 March–10 April 1669, Paris; SP 101/17, f. 140: Newsletter, 11 September 1669 NS, Paris.

31 Baillon, *Henriette-Anne d'Angleterre*, 402; cf. J. M. Cartwright, *A Life of Henriette, daughter of Charles I and duchess of Orleans* (London, 1903), 298; cf. *CSP Venice*, XXXVI, 244: Piero Morenigo to Doge and Senate, 15 August 1670, London.

32 Gilbert Burnet, *History of His Own Time* (Oxford, 1833 edn), VI, 35, Dartmouth's note; cf. W. Blackley, ed., *The Diplomatic Correspondence of the Rt. Hon. Richard Hill*, I (London, 1845), 58: the queen's instructions to Hill, 9 November 1703: 'and particularly you shall give the Duchess [of Savoy] the real assurance of our kindness as to one so nearly related to us in blood'.

33 SP 78/129, f. 282: William Perwich to [Sir Joseph Williamson], 1 July 1670 NS, Paris; cf. C.F.S. de Grovestins, *Histoire des luttes et rivalités politiques entre les puissances maritimes et la France dans la dernière moitié du XVIIe siècle* (Paris, 1868), II, 176.

34 James II, *Memoirs*, I, 451.

35 Pierpont Morgan Library, Rulers of England, Box 10, #8: James, Duke of York, to Louis XIV, 28 June 1670, St James's.

36 Cartwright, *Life of Henriette*, 373.

37 SP 78/130, f. 27v: Wm Perwich to Arlington, 30 July 1670 NS, Paris; *ibid.*, ff. 16, 24v: Francis Vernon to [Sir Jos. Williamson], 23, 26 July 1670 NS, Paris; cf. *CSPD, Charles II, 1670*, 343: James Welsh to Williamson, 23 July 1670, Rye; 301: [H. Muddiman] to Gilbert Stapleton, 27 June 1670, Whitehall; HMC *Buccleuch*, I, 481: R. Montagu to Arlington, 30 July 1670, Paris.

38 F. C. Turner, *James II* (London, 1948), 91–2.

39 James II, *Memoirs*, I, 440–1; Martin Haile, *Mary of Modena* (London, 1905), 59.

40 Huntington Library, MSS 996: 'A Copy of a Paper Written by the late Duchess of York, 20 August 1670, St. James's'.

41 James II, *Memoirs*, I, 452.

42 *Two Letters Written by the Right Honourable Edward, Earl of Clarendon* (London, 1671).

43 Bodleian, Rawl. C. 983, f. 54: George Morley, Bishop of Winchester, to Henry Compton, 16 June 1682, Farnham Castle.

44 Blenheim G I 9: 'The Character of Princes', f. 174.

45 E. M. Thompson, ed., *Correspondence of the Family Hatton* (Camden Society, 1878) (hereafter cited as *Hatton Correspondence*), I, 57: Sir Charles Lyttleton to Lord Christopher Hatton, 10 October 1670.

46 Émile Bourgeois, ed., *Ezechial Spanheim, Relation de la Cour d'Angleterre en 1704* (Annales de l'Université de Lyon, N.S. II, fasc. 5, Paris and Lyon, 1900), 587.

47 PRO 31/3/201, ff. 2–5: d'Aumont to Louis XIV, 19 January 1713 NS, London.

48 HMC *Bath*, I, 210: Queen Anne to Oxford, 13 September 1711.

49 E. S. de Beer, ed., *The Diary of John Evelyn* (Oxford, 1955) (hereafter cited as *Evelyn Diary*), IV, 49–50: 15 December 1674.

50 Edgar Sheppard, *Memorials of St. James's Palace* (London, 1894), I, 280–1; cf. John Ashton, *Social Life in the Reign of Queen Anne* (London, 1897), 255.

51 Hove Public Library, M 1/112/5: privy purse accounts, 9 January 1710; M 1/112/3: privy purse accounts, 28 June 1707.

52 Burnet, *History of His Own Time*, V, 2, notes by Dartmouth and Onslow; my italics.

53 Blenheim G I 9: Sarah's 'Letter to Mr. Hutchenson', f. 27.

54 R. J. Minney, *Hampton Court Palace* (London, 1970), 198–9; Ernest Law, *Kensington Palace* (London, 1899), 20–1.

55 J. P. Hore, *The History of Newmarket and The Annals of the Turf*, III (London, 1886), 62: Duke of York to Countess of Lichfield, 21 March 1683, Newmarket.

56 *Ibid.*, 148n.; cf. Ashton, *Social Life in the Reign of Queen Anne*, 229, 229–30.

57 *An Abridgment of the Life of James II . . . Extracted from an English Manuscript of the Reverend Father Francis Sanders, of the Society of Jesus and Confessor to his Late Majesty. . . . Done out of the French from the Paris Edition*, 1703 (London, 1704), 68–9.

58 PRO 31/3/125, f. 78v: Croissy to Louis XIV, 23 October 1670 NS, London.

59 Haile, *Mary of Modena*, 5; cf. Turner, *James II*, 112.

60 [Lord John Russell, ed.] *The Letters of Rachel, Lady Russell* (London, 1853) (hereafter cited as *Russell Letters*), I, 12–13: Lady Vaughn to William Russell, 23 September 1673, London; cf. Agnes Strickland, *Lives of the Queens of England* (London, 1852), VI, 52.

61 *CSP Venice*, XXXVIII, pp. 212, 232: Girdamo Alberti to Doge and Senate, 9 February, 9 March 1674, London.

62 James II, *Memoirs*, I 503; cf. Strickland, *Lives of the Queens of England*, VI, 69.

63 Haile, *Mary of Modena*, 21.

64 Haile, *Mary of Modena*, 44: Maria Beatrice to the Superior of Visitation Convent, 8 January 1674 NS, London.

65 *Ibid.*, 52: Countess Lucrezia Vezzani to Rinaldo d'Este, n.d. [*c.* March 1675].

66 Haile, *Mary of Modena*, 51–2: Cattaneo to Duke of Modena, 20 January 1675 NS, London.

67 Turner, *James II*, 113.

68 Edward Carpenter, *The Protestant Bishop, being the Life of Henry Compton, 1632–1713, Bishop of London* (London, 1956), 1–16.

69 Burnet, quoted by Haile, *Mary of Modena*, 57.

70 Turner, *James II*, 97.

71 Philip Roberts, ed., *The Diary of Sir David Hamilton, 1709–1714* (Oxford, 1975), 66: 27 July 1714; hereafter cited as *Hamilton Diary*.

72 Beatrice Curtis Brown, ed., *The Letters and Diplomatic Instructions of Queen Anne* (London, 1968), 16: Anne to Mary, 29 April [1686], Cockpit.

73 Carpenter, *Protestant Bishop*, 34.

74 Haile, *Mary of Modena*, 59.

75 HMC *Belvoir Castle*, II, 42: Lady Chaworth to Lord Roos, 22 [November 1677].

76 George Percy Elliotte, ed., *Diary of Dr. Edward Lake* (Camden Society, 1846), 6–14.

77 *Ibid.*, 29.

78 *CSPD, Charles II, March–December 1678*, 421–2: James, Duke of York, to Prince of Orange, 27 September 1678, London; cf. HMC 3rd Report, 423: Anne, Duchess of Monmouth, to Countess of Weymss, 29 September 1678; Haile, *Mary of Modena*, 72: Mary of Modena to Duke of Modena, 6 October 1678 NS.

79 For Oates, see John Kenyon, *The Popish Plot* (London, 1972), *passim*.

80 James II, *Memoirs*, I, 542.

81 HMC *Ormonde NS*, IV 497–8: Sir Robert Southwell to Ormonde, 8 March 1679 [London]; cf. Strickland, *Lives of the Queens of England*, VI, 83.

82 HMC *Dartmouth*, I, 37: Duke of York to Col. George Legge, 11 August [1679], Brussels.

83 H. C. Foxcroft, *The Life and Letters of Sir George Savile, First Marquis of Halifax* (London, 1898), I, 183: Halifax to Henry Savile, 11/21 August 1679, Windsor.

84 Coke, *Detection of the Court and State of England*, III, 118; cf. HMC *Le Fleming*, 161: newsletter, 19 August 1679 [London]; HMC *Foljambe*, 136: York to Orange, 30 August 1679 NS, Brussels.

85 Bathurst, *Letters of Two Queens*, 106–8: Anne to Lady Apsley, 20 September [1679], Brussels.

86 *Ibid.*; cf. Haile, *Mary of Modena*, 81.

87 Boyer, *Queen Anne*, I, 12; Turner, *James II*, 165.

88 Bathurst, *Letters of Two Queens*, 108–9: Anne to Frances Apsley, 22 September (1679), Brussels.

89 Turner, *James II*, 168.

90 HMC *Foljambe*, 138–9: Duke of York to Prince of Orange, 7 October 1679 NS, Brussels; cf. *CSPD, Charles II, Jan. 1679–Aug. 1680*, 251: [Robt Yard] to Lady [O'Brien?], 25 September 1679, Whitehall.

91 Narcissus Luttrell, *A Brief Historical*

411

Relation of State Affairs from September 1678 to April 1714 (Oxford, 1857), I, 22; Roger Coke, *Detection of the Court and State of England* (London, 1719), III, 118, places the arrival on 12 October.

92 Coke, *Detection of the Court and State of England*, III, 118.

93 Turner, *James II*, 171–2.

94 PRO 31/3/150, f. 145: Barillon to Louis XIV, 29 December 1681 NS, London.

95 Coke, *Detection of the Court and State of England*, III, 118.

96 Bourgeois, *Spanheim*, 594–5.

97 Onno Klopp, *Der Fall des Hauses Stuart und die Succession des Houses Hannover*, II, 247, 286; *Hatton Correspondence*, I, 223: Sir Charles Lyttleton to Lord Hatton, 16 March [1680]; *Russell Letters*, I, 69: Lady Russell to Lord Russell, 17 September 1680, London; HMC *7th Report*, 533: Earl of Yarmouth to [Edward L'Estrange], 12 May 1680.

98 PRO 31/3/147, ff. 19v, 25: Barillon to Louis XIV, 18, 21 November 1680 NS.

99 Edward Gregg, 'Was Queen Anne a Jacobite?', *History*, LVII (October 1972), 367.

100 HMC *9th Report*, pt II, 457: Prince Rupert to Princess Sophia, 18 September 1682.

101 HMC *Dartmouth*, I, 63–4: Duke of York to Col. George Legge, 24 May [1681]; cf. *James II, Memoirs*, I, 682–3.

102 HMC *Dartmouth*, I, 63–4: Duke of York to Col. George Legge, 11, 28 June [1681].

103 Coke, *Detection of the Court and State of England*, III, 119; White Kennet, *Complete History of England*, III (London, 1706), 401; cf. HMC *Ormonde NS*, VI, 98: John Ellis to [?], 12 July 1681, London.

104 *CSPD, Charles II, Sept. 1680–Dec. 1681*, 460: newsletter to Roger Garstell, 20 September 1681, London.

105 Turner, *James II*, 190.

106 Bathurst, *Letters of Two Queens*, 139: Anne to Lady Apsley, 16 September [1681], Edinburgh.

107 Winston S. Churchill, *Marlborough, His Life and Times* (London, 1948), I, 149, quoting Sarah's letter of October 1744, in the Spencer MSS.

108 PRO 31/3/152, f. 34: Barillon to Louis XIV, 8 June 1682 NS; cf. *James II, Memoirs*, I, 731–2.

109 HMC *Kenyon*, 134: William Patten to Roger Kenyon, 9 June [?] 1682, Gray's Inn.

110 HMC *7th Report*, 498: Wm Denton to Sir Ralph Verney, 13 November 1682, London.

111 Lady Newdigate-Newdegate, *Cavalier and Puritan in the Days of the Stuarts* (London, 1901), 256–7: Newsletter, 7, 9 November 1682; cf. HMC *7th Report*, 480: John Verney to Sir R. Verney, 9 November 1682, London; HMC *Egmont*, pt 3, 121: N. Barnette to Sir John Perceval, 31 October 1682, London.

112 HMC *7th Report*, 480: John Verney to Sir R. Verney, 9 November 1682.

113 James Macpherson, ed., *Original Papers* (London, 1775), II, 327–31: Buckingham to Middleton, 1/12 July 1712; cf. Blenheim A I 11: Buckingham to Marlborough, 27 June 1704, St James's Park.

114 Bathurst, *Letters of Two Queens*, 154–6: Princess Mary to Lady Bathurst, 27 November [1682], The Hague.

115 Sarah Churchill, Duchess of Marlborough, *Conduct of the dowager Duchess of Marlborough* (1742), 14.

116 Blenheim G I 9: 'The Character of Princes', f. 173.

117 Herts. R. O., Panshanger MSS, D/EP/F 63, ff. 158–9: Sarah to Lady Cowper, 14 May [1710], Windsor.

118 Sheppard, *St. James's Palace*, I, 279–80.

119 Churchill, *Marlborough*, I, 105–28.

120 Turner, *James II*, 85; *Notes and Queries*, 12th series, VIII, 96: articles by Sir Lee Knowles, Dilloughby Maycock and G.F.R.B.

121 David Green, *Sarah, Duchess of Marlborough* (London, 1967), 236.

122 *Hatton Correspondence*, I, 233: Sir Christopher Lyttleton to Lord Hatton, 3 August 1680.

123 *Hatton Correspondence*, I, 66: Sir Charles Lyttleton to Christopher Hatton, 21 August 1671, Landguard.

124 Burnet, *History of His Own Time*, III, 280–1: Dartmouth's note.

125 *Letters of Sarah, Duchess of Marlborough . . . at Madresfield Court* (London, 1875), 70: Sarah to Robt Jennens, 9 July OS [1713]; hereafter cited as *Madresfield Court*.

126 Hon. Spencer Cowper, ed., *Diary of*

Mary, Countess Cowper (hereafter cited as Lady Cowper's Diary) (London, 2nd edn, 1865), 122.

127 Sarah Churchill, Conduct, 10–11.
128 Green, Sarah, 47.
129 Sarah Churchill, Conduct, 11–12.

Chapter 2:   The Revolution

1 PRO 31/3/154, ff. 46, 54: Barillon to Louis XIV, 29 March, 8 April 1683 NS: cf. Bourgeois, Spanheim, 594; Chr. H. Brasch, Prins Georg af Danmark i hans Aegtestab med Dronning Anna of Storbrittanien (Copenhagen, 1890), 7; J. J. Jusserand, ed., Récueil des instructions donneés aux ambassadeurs . . . de France, Angleterre, 1666–1690 (Paris, 1929), 285–6: Louis XIV to Talladet [24 July 1683 NS].

2 PRO 31/3/154, ff. 39v–40: Barillon to Louis XIV, 18 March 1683 NS, New-market, quoting James.

3 J. P. Kenyon, Robert Spencer Earl of Sunderland, 1641–1702 (London, 1958), 87; cf. Klopp, Der Fall des Hauses Stuart, II, 416.

4 PRO 31/31/154, f. 154: Barillon to Louis XIV, 8 April 1683 NS; PRO 31/31/155, ff. 11, 16, 94–5: same to same, 10, 17 May, 5 August 1683 NS.

5 PRO 31/3/155, ff. 107v–108: Barillon to Louis XIV, 16 August 1683 NS, Windsor.

6 PRO 31/3/155, f. 11: Barillon to Louis XIV, 10 May 1683 NS.

7 PRO 31/3/155, ff. 13–14, 16: Barillon to Louis XIV, 13, 17 May 1683 NS, Windsor; cf. Luttrell, A Brief Historical Relation, I, 257.

8 PRO 31/3/155, ff. 28v–29: Barillon to Louis XIV, 7 June 1683 NS, London, quoting the Duke of York.

9 HMC Buccleuch & Queensberry, I, 189: James, Duke of York, to William, Marquess of Queensberry, 9 May 1683, London.

10 Bathurst, Letters of Two Queens, 165–6: Lady Anne to Lady Bathurst, 4 June [1683], Windsor.

11 Strickland, Lives of the Queens of England, VII, 346; G. J., Viscount Wolseley, John Churchill, Duke of Marlborough (London, 1894), 8, 251; S. J. Reid, John and Sarah, Duke and Duchess of Marlborough (London, 1914), 71.

12 Blenheim E 19: Anne to Sarah, n.d.

13 Blenheim E 19: Anne to Sarah, n.d.

14 William Coxe, Memoirs of John, Duke of Marlborough (London, 2nd edn, 1820), I, 27; Blenheim E 18: Anne to Sarah, n.d.

15 Thomas Lediard, The Life of John, Duke of Marlborough (London, 1736), I, 14.

16 CSPD, Charles II, January–June 1683, 311: Blathwayt to Earl of Conway, 12 June 1683; cf. PRO 31/3/155, ff. 35, 43: Barillon to Louis XIV, 14, 24 June 1683 NS, London.

17 PRO 31/3/155, ff. 94v–95, 98–9: Barillon to Louis XIV, 5, 9 August 1683 NS.

18 Sheppard, St. James's Palace, II, 67.

19 HMC Laing, I, 434: Sir Thomas Clarges to [?], 30 July 1683; cf. BM, Add. MSS 17,677 FF, f. 517v: Van Citters to States, 6 August 1683 NS, London.

20 HMC Laing, I, 434: Sir Thomas Clarges to [?], 30 July 1683.

21 Evelyn Diary, IV, 332: 25 July 1683.

22 SP 101/15, f. 326: newsletter, 18 September 1668, Paris; SP 101/16, f. 52: newsletter, 9/19 April 1669, Paris; CSP Venice, XXXVI, 90: Piero Mocenigo to Doge and Senate, 16 August 1669, London; cf. HMC Le Fleming, 65: newsletter 20 July 1669 [London].

23 HMC 7th Report, 365: O. Wynne to Lord Preston, 19 July 1683, Whitehall.

24 Burnet, History of His Own Time, III, 49: Dartmouth's note.

25 Brasch, Prins Georg, 16–18.

26 G. Steinman, ed., Althorp Memoirs (London, 1869), 50: Griffith had been married to Sarah's sister, Barbara Jennings, who died in 1679.

27 London County Council, Survey of London, XIV: The Parish of St. Margaret, Westminster, eds Montagu H. Cox and Philip Norman (London, 1931), 52.

28 In 1683, the princess served as godmother to their only son, while the Duchess of Grafton was chosen as god-mother to the princess's first child: GEC, VI, 43–5.

29 Burnet, History of His Own Time, III, 212.

30 PRO 31/3/156, f. 39: Barillon to Louis XIV, 1 November 1683 NS, London;

Evelyn Diary, IV, 358: 26 December 1683.

31 BM, Add. MSS 17,677 GG, f. 75: Van Citters to States, 23 May 1684 NS.

32 *Ibid.*, ff. 93v, 116: Van Citters to States, 30 June, 18 August 1684 NS; cf. Haile, *Mary of Modena*, 114.

33 BM, Add. MSS 17,677 GG, ff. 172–172v, 185: Van Citters to States, 19 December 1684, 30 January 1685 NS; cf. Turner, *James II*, 223; Strickland, *Lives of the Queen of England*, VI, 154.

34 [John Sheffield, Duke of Buckingham,] *The Character of Charles II, King of England, with a Short Account of his being Poyson'd. Written by a Person of Honour* (London, 1696), 13–14; cf. Lediard, *John, Duke of Marlborough*, I, 46–8; Higgons, *A Short View of the English History*, 401.

35 Klopp, *Der Fall des Hauses Stuart*, XIV, 672–7: Robethon to Bernstorff, 21 March 1711 NS.

36 Blenheim E 19: Anne to Sarah, Sunday, four a clock [? 6 September 1685].

37 Luttrell, *A Brief Historical Relation*, I, 328; PRO 31/3/174; Bonrepaux's 'Rapport sur l'état d'Angleterre' [December 1687]; cf. Godfrey Davies, 'Cabinet and Council, 1679–1688', *EHR*, XXXVII (1922), 48.

38 PRO 31/3/160, ff. 98v–99: Barillon to Louis XIV, 29 March 1685 NS; cf. N. Japikse, ed., *Correspondentie van Willem III en van Hans Willem Bentinck, Eersten Graaf van Portland* (The Hague, 1927), I, 211: William III's instructions for Bentinck, 4 July 1685 NS: when William offered to help James II in the Monmouth rebellion, he asked 'comment regle les ceremonies entre le Prince de Dennemarck et moy'.

39 Baxter, *William III*, 188, 204.

40 The princess was four months pregnant in December 1684: HMC *Buccleuch & Queensberry*, I, 213: James, Duke of York, to William, Marquess of Queensberry, 22 December 1684.

41 Luttrell, *A Brief Historical Relation*, I, 345.

42 Blenheim E 19: Anne to Lady Churchill, Tuesday [4 August 1685].

43 Blenheim E 17: Anne to Sarah, Fryday night [? 11 September 1685].

44 Blenheim E 17: Anne to Lady Churchill, Saturday t[w]o aclock [?1684].

45 Blenheim E 18: Anne to Lady Churchill, Wensday t[w]o aclock [30 September 1685].

46 Blenheim E 17: Anne to Sarah, Fryday [21 August 1685].

47 Blenheim E 17: Anne to Sarah, Tunbridg, fryday afternoon [24 July 1685].

48 Blenheim E 19: Anne to Sarah, Munday [3 August 1685, Tunbridge].

49 Blenheim E 18: Anne to Lady Churchill, Windsor, Sunday night, 10 a clock [13 September 1685].

50 Blenheim E 18: Anne to Lady Churchill, Thursday [12 August 1686], printed without date, HMC *8th Report*, 52a.

51 Brasch, *Prins Georg*, 8.

52 H. C. Foxcroft, ed., *A Supplement to Burnet's History of My Own Time* (Oxford, 1902), 206–7.

53 Burnet, *History of His Own Time*, III, 125–6, Dartmouth's note; Coke, *Detection of the Court and State of England*, III, 120; HMC *3rd Report*, 267: order signed by Rochester and Ennle, for payment to the prince and princess of £3,000 'in part of £16,000 His Majesty's free gift'.

54 S. W. Singer, ed., *The Correspondence of Henry Hyde, Earl of Clarendon, and of his brother, Laurence Hyde, Earl of Rochester* (London, 1828) (hereafter cited as *Clarendon Correspondence*), II, 197: 23 October 1688; Brown, *Letters and Diplomatic Instructions*, 35: Anne to Mary of Orange, 20 March 1688, Cockpit.

55 Brown, *Letters and Diplomatic Instructions*, 22: Anne to Mary, 10 January 1687.

56 Burnet, *History of His Own Time*, VI, 114: Dartmouth's note, quoting Queen Anne.

57 Strickland, *Lives of the Queens of England*, VI, 177.

58 Andrew Browning, ed., *Memoirs of Sir John Reresby* (Glasgow, 1936), 356: 2 March 1685; cf. Andrew Clark, ed., *The Life and Times of Anthony Wood* (Oxford, 1894), III, 132.

59 *Memoirs of Sir John Reresby*, 405: 4 January 1686.

60 Bodleian, Rawl. C. 983, f. 104: William Stanley to Compton, 15/25 March 1686, Darien.

61 PRO 31/3/161, f. 163v: Barillon to Louis XIV, 28 October 1685 NS.

62 Blenheim E 19: Anne to Sarah, Thursday morning, ten aclock [*c.* 1 October 1685].

63 PRO 31/3/161, f. 163v: Barillon to Louis XIV, 28 October 1685 NS.

64 Brown, *Letters and Diplomatic Instructions*, 18: Anne to Mary of Orange, 10 August [1686], Whitehall.

65 Burnet, *History of His Own Time*, III, 195.

66 PRO 31/3/66: Barillon to Louis XIV, 27 June 1686 NS, Windsor; PRO 31/3/168: Barillon to Louis, 3 April 1687; cf. 165: Bonrepaux to Seignelay, 28 March 1686 NS.

67 E. and M. S. Grew, *The Court of William III* (London, 1910), 194.

68 Godfrey Davies, ed., *Papers of Devotion of James II* (Oxford, The Roxburghe Club, 1925), 24n.; cf. *Copies of Two Papers Written by the Late King Charles II, together with a Copy of a Paper written by the late Duchess of York*: Published by His Majesties command, London: Printed by H. Hills, Printer to the King's Most Excellent Majesty for his Household and Chappel, 1686.

69 Brown, *Letters and Diplomatic Instructions*, 16: Anne to Mary of Orange, 29 April [1686], Cockpit.

70 Klopp, *Der Fall des Hauses Stuart*, III, 19, 205–6, 281.

71 For these efforts, see Mechtild, Comtesse Bentinck, *Lettres et mémoires de Marie, Reine d'Angleterre* (The Hague, 1880), 4–9: James II to Mary of Orange, 4 November 1687, Whitehall; cf. J. R. Jones, *The Revolution of 1688 in England* (New York, 1972), 85; Elizabeth Hamilton, *William's Mary* (London, 1972), 179.

72 PRO 31/3/165, n.f.: Bonrepaux to Seignelay, 28 March 1686 NS, London; cf. Leopold von Ranke, *A History of England, Principally in the Seventeenth Century* (Oxford, 1875), IV, 286–7.

73 Lord Braybrooke, ed., *The Autobiography of Sir John Bramston* (London, Camden Society, 1845), 283: June 1686; cf. Haile, *Mary of Modena*, 36; Emilia, Marquise Campana de Cavelli, *Les Derniers Stuarts à Saint-Germain-en-Laye* (Paris, 1871), II, 74; Terriesi to Secretary of State of Tuscany, 7/17 September 1685, London.

74 PRO 31/3/166: Barillon to Louis XIV, 27 June 1686 NS, Windsor.

75 Blenheim G I 10: Sarah's 'A true account' (1704).

76 Blenheim G I 9: Sarah's 'Character of Princes'.

77 Blenheim E 18: Anne to Lady Churchill, Munday four aclock [19 July 1686]; cf. Coxe, *Marlborough*, I, 33.

78 Brown, *Letters and Diplomatic Instructions*, 23: Anne to Mary, 31 January 1687, Cockpit.

79 Foxcroft, *Supplement to Burnet*, 153–4; for previous fears, see Henry Ellis, *Original Letters*, 2nd series, IV (London, 1826), 85: [?] to John Ellis, 6 April 1686, London.

80 *Autobiography of Sir John Bramston*, 229; HMC *Downshire*, I, 167: Dr Owen Wynne to Sir Wm Turnbull, 13 May 1686; PRO 31/3/166: Barillon to Louis XIV, 23 May 1686 NS.

81 Luttrell, *A Brief Historical Relation*, I, 377.

82 *CSPD, James II*, II, 132: James II to Prince of Orange, 14 May 1686, Windsor.

83 HMC *Belvoir Castle*, II, 109: Sir S. Howe to [Countess of Rutland], 2 June [1686].

84 Blenheim E 17: Anne to Sarah, Tunbridg, Sunday [? 18 July 1686].

85 Blenheim E 18: Anne to Sarah, Tunbridg, Thursday [22 July 1686].

86 PRO 31/3/168: Barillon to Louis XIV, 30 January 1687 NS; BM, Add. MSS 17,677 HH, f. 16v: Van Citters to States, 31 January 1687 NS; George Agar Ellis, ed., *The Ellis Correspondence* (London, 1829), I, 231–2: [?] to John Ellis, 22 January 1687 [London]; Ellis, *Original Letters*, 102 and n.: [?] to John Ellis, 5 February 1687.

87 *CSPD, James II*, II, 347: newsletter to Sir John Fenwick, 22 January 1687.

88 Brown, *Letters and Diplomatic Instructions*, 28: Anne to Mary of Orange, 11 April 1687.

89 Luttrell, *A Brief Historical Relation*, I, 393–4; PRO 31/3/168: Barillon to Louis XIV, 13, 17 February 1687 NS; cf. *CSPD, James II*, II, 361–2: newsletter to Fenwick, 8 February 1687, London.

90 *Russell Letters*, I, 204: Lady Russell to Dr Fitzwilliam, 9 February 1687.

91 *Russell Letters*, I, 212: Lady Russell to Dr Fitzwilliam, 18 February 1687.

92 *Ellis Correspondence*, I, 269: J. F. to John Ellis, 5 April 1687, London; PRO 31/3/169: Barillon to Louis XIV, 11 May 1687 NS.

93 Brown, *Letters and Diplomatic Instructions*, 19: Anne to Mary of Orange, 26 November 1686, Cockpit.

94 Brown, *Letters and Diplomatic Instructions*, 25: Anne to Mary, 13 March 1687.

95 PRO 31/3/168: Barillon to Louis XIV, 13, 17, 24 March 1687 NS.

96 Brown, *Letters and Diplomatic Instructions*, 25: Anne to Mary of Orange, 13 March 1687.

97 PRO 31/3/168: Barillon to Louis XIV, 3 April 1687 NS; PRO 31/3/169: Barillon to Louis XIV, 29 May 1687 NS; cf. BM, Add. MSS 17,677 GG, f. 60v: Van Citters to States, 1/11 April 1687; Luttrell, *A Brief Historical Relation*, I, 27 March 1687.

98 Blenheim E 18: Anne to Lady Churchill, Saturday [25 July 1685].

99 PRO 31/3/165: Bonrepaux to Seignelay, 28 March 1686 NS.

100 PRO 31/3/164: Bonrepaux's 'Rapport sur l'état d'Angleterre' [December 1687]; cf. Brown, *Letters and Diplomatic Instructions*, 31: Anne to Mary of Orange, 9 May 1687, Richmond.

101 PRO 31/3/172: Barillon to Louis XIV, 23 September 1687 NS, Bath.

102 Brown, *Letters and Diplomatic Instructions*, 31: Anne to Mary of Orange, 9 May 1687, Richmond.

103 PRO 31/3/168: Barillon to Louis XIV, 3 April 1687 NS; John Lavicount Anderdon, *The Life of Thomas Ken. Bishop of Bath and Wells* (London, 1854), I, 361: Princess Anne to [Dr Francis Turner], Bishop of Ely, n.d. [c. March 1687]; cf. Norman Sykes, *William Wake, Archbishop of Canterbury, 1657–1737* (Cambridge, 1957), I, 32.

104 *Evelyn Diary*, IV, 541; cf, PRO 31/3/168: Barillon to Louis XIV, 24 March 1687 NS.

105 *Evelyn Diary*, IV, 545: 26 March 1687.

106 PRO 31/3/169: Barillon to Louis XIV, 11 May 1687 NS.

107 For his mission, see James Muilenburg, 'The Embassy of Everaard van Weede, Lord of Dykevelt, to England in 1687', *University of Nebraska Studies*, XX (July–October 1920), 85–155.

108 Brown, *Letters and Diplomatic Instructions*, 26–7: Anne to Mary, 13 March 1687, Cockpit.

109 Sir John Dalrymple, *Memoirs of Great Britain and Ireland* (London, 1790), II, app. to book V, 62–3: Lord Churchill to William III, 17 May 1687.

110 Brown, *Letters and Diplomatic Instructions*, 31: Anne to Mary of Orange, 9 May 1687, Richmond.

111 Brown, *Letters and Diplomatic Instructions*, 33: Anne to Mary of Orange, 22 June 1687, Windsor.

112 Blenheim E 48: Princess of Orange to Lady Churchill, The Hague, 28 May [1686], also letter of 14 June [1686].

113 Brown, *Letters and Diplomatic Instructions*, 20–1: Anne to Mary of Orange, 29 December 1686, Cockpit.

114 PRO 31/3/170: Bonrepaux to Seignelay, 4 June 1687 NS, Windsor; PRO 31/3/168: Barillon to Louis XIV, 24 March 1687 NS; cf. Churchill, *Marlborough*, I, 210.

115 PRO 31/3/169: Barillon to Louis XIV, 11 May 1687 NS.

116 PRO 31/3/171: Bonrepaux to Seignelay, 21 July 1687 NS, Windsor.

117 PRO 31/3/175: Barillon to Louis XIV, 26 January 1688 NS.

118 For the Danish request, see SP 104/2, ff. 98, 98v: Christian V to James II, 26 April 1687, Copenhagen; James II to Christian V, 11 June 1687, Windsor; for the pregnancy, PRO 31/3/168: Barillon to Louis XIV, 28 April 1687 NS; PRO 31/3/169: Barillon to Louis XIV, 29 May 1687 NS.

119 *Evelyn Diary*, IV, 558–9; *CSPD, James II*, III, 13: James Sloane to Sir Joseph Williamson, 18 June 1687.

120 PRO 31/3/170: Bonrepaux to Seignelay, 4 June 1687 NS, Windsor.

121 PRO 31/3/171: Barillon to Louis XIV, 21 July 1687 NS, Windsor; BM, Add. MSS 17,677 HH, f. 140v: Van Citters to States, 22 July 1687 NS.

122 PRO 31/3/170: Bonrepaux to Seignelay, 21 June 1687 NS.

123 PRO 31/3/172: Barillon to Louis XIV, 23 September 1687 NS, Bath; PRO 31/3/174: Bonrepaux's 'Rapport sur l'état d'Angleterre' [December 1687]; cf. Churchill, *Marlborough*, I, 183, n. 1.

124 PRO 31/3/173: Barillon to Louis XIV, 13 October 1687 NS, Windsor; Luttrell, *A Brief Historical Relation*, I, 415; *CSPD, James II*, III, 81: John Rooke to Sir Joseph Williamson, 12 October 1687, London.

125 Bodleian, Rawl. B. 243, f. 3: 'Some few Querys about the Preparatives for the making way for a Prince of Wales in the Year 1687' [1702], printed in HMC *8th Report*, pt II, 87–8; cf. PRO 31/3/173: Barillon to Louis XIV, 3 November 1687 NS.

126 PRO 31/3/153, ff. 20v, 50, 53, 55v: Barillon to Louis XIV, 27 August, 12, 14, 21 October 1682 NS; the daughter.

Charlotte Maria, was born 15 August and died 6 October 1682; John Buchanan-Brown, *The Remains of Thomas Hearne*, 134.

127 PRO 31/3/156, f. 39: Barillon to Louis XIV, 1 November 1683 NS.

128 PRO 31/3/161: Barillon to Louis XIV, 16 April, 15 October 1685 NS; see Barillon's dispatches, *passim*, November 1683–April 1686, for repeated reports of Mary of Modena's poor health; cf. Haile, *Mary of Modena*, 114, 124–5, 130, 137, 149.

129 PRO 31/3/170: Bonrepaux to Seignelay, 4 June 1687 NS, Windsor.

130 PRO 31/3/173: Barillon to Louis XIV, 13 November 1687 NS.

131 Haile, *Mary of Modena*, 168–88.

132 PRO 31/3/173, 174, 175: Barillon to Louis XIV, 17, 27 November 1687, 29 December 1687 NS; 26 February 1688 NS.

133 Haile, *Mary of Modena*, 173: Terriesi to grand duke, 23 December 1687–2 January 1688.

134 BM, Add. MSS 33,286, ff. 5–7: 'An Account of ye Birth of the Pretended Prince of Wales, as it is deliver'd by ye Lord Bishop of Worcester', 15 June 1702; Brown, *Letters and Diplomatic Instructions*, 35; Anne to Mary of Orange, 20 March 1688; Burnet, *History of His Own Time*, III, 247, quoting Prince George.

135 *Clarendon Correspondence*, II, 198.

136 James II, *Memoirs*, II, 200–2.

137 Domenico Carutti, ed., 'Relazione sulla Corte d'Inghilterra de . . . Pietre Mellarede (17 Jan. 1713 NS, London)', *Miscellanea di Storia Italiana*, XXIV (Turin, 1885), 229–30; cf. Matthias Earbery, *The Occasional Historian, No. 1* (London, 1730), 44, citing the eyewitness testimony of Mrs Margaret Dawson, a bedchamber woman to the queen who had seen the princess feel the queen's stomach.

138 James II, *Memoirs*, II, 202.

139 PRO 31/3/174: Barillon to Louis XIV, 11 December 1687 NS.

140 PRO 31/3/174: Barillon to Louis XIV, 15, 22 December 1687 NS; Luttrell, *A Brief Historical Relation*, I, 423, 425; GEC, VI, 659–60; Churchill, *Marlborough*, I, 217–18.

141 Brown, *Letters and Diplomatic Instruc-tions*, 34: Anne to Mary of Orange, 14 March 1688.

142 *Ibid.*, 35: Anne to Mary of Orange, 20 March 1688.

143 *Clarendon Correspondence*, II, 168.

144 *Ellis Correspondence*, I, 345–6: J. F. to John Ellis, 17 April 1686, London; cf. R. J. Kerr and I. C. Duncan, eds, *The Portledge Papers* (London, 1928), 30: Richard Lapthorne to Richard Coffin, 21 April 1688.

145 *Clarendon Correspondence*, II, 169: 16 April 1688; cf. Luttrell, *A Brief Historical Relation*, I, 436: PRO 31/3/176: Barillon to Louis XIV, 22 April 1688 NS.

146 William S. Kroger and S. Charles Freed, *Psychosomatic Gynecology* (Philadelphia, 1951), 216; Irving C. Fischer, 'Hypothalamic Amenorrhea: Pseudocyesis', in *Psychosomatic Obstetrics, Gynecology and Endocrinology*, ed. William S. Kroger (Springfield, Ill., 1962), 291–7; Louis M. Hellman and Jack A. Pritchard, *Williams Obstetrics* (New York, 14th ed., 1971), 287. I am grateful to Michael J. Anders for pro-viding me with copies of these items.

147 *Clarendon Correspondence*, II, 170: 25 April 1688.

148 *Ellis Correspondence*, I, 345–6: J. F. to John Ellis, 17 April 1688, London.

149 BM, Add. MSS 32,096, ff. 43v–44: 'A memorandum of what Mr. St. Amand, Apothecary to King James II related to me [i.e. George Harbin] & Dr. Hicks the Deprived Dean of Worcester', 2 April 1703.

150 Burnet, *History of His Own Time*, III, 249–50.

151 BM, Add. MSS 33,286, ff. 5–7: 'An account of ye birth of the pretended Prince of Wales as it is deliver'd by ye Lord Bishop of Worcester', 5 June 1703.

152 Carutti, 'Relazione sulla Corte d'Inghilterra', 230; James II, *Memoirs*, II, 159–60.

153 Brown, *Letters and Diplomatic Instruc-tions*, 34: Anne to Mary of Orange, 14 March 1688.

154 Luttrell, *A Brief Historical Relation*, I, 411; Burnet, *History of His Own Time*, III, 250; *Clarendon Correspondence*, II, 173.

155 *Lives of Two Illustrious Generals* (1713), 22.

156 For Godolphin's later testimony, see *Depositions taken the 22d of October 1688*

before the Privy-Council and Peers of England Relating to the Birth of the (Then) Prince of Wales. Published by His Majesty's Special Command (October 1688), 23.

157 Haile, *Mary of Modena*, 189: Hoffmann to the emperor, 11/21 June 1688; cf. Klopp, *Der Fall des Hauses Stuart*, IV, 39; Campana de Cavelli, *Les Derniers Stuarts*, II, 223.

158 Luttrell, *A Brief Historical Relation*, I, 444.

159 Brown, *Letters and Diplomatic Instructions*, 35: Anne to Mary of Orange, 20 March 1688, Cockpit.

160 Brown, *Letters and Diplomatic Instructions*, 37: Anne to Mary of Orange, 18 June 1688.

161 Bentinck, *Marie, Reine d'Angleterre*, 45–8: Mary of Orange to Anne, 21 July 1688 NS; Brown, *Letters and Diplomatic Instructions*, 39–43: Anne to Mary of Orange, 24 July 1688, Cockpit.

162 Brown, *Letters and Diplomatic Instructions*, 37–43.

163 Ellis, *Original Letters*, 1st series, III (London, 1824), 349: Mary of Modena to Mary of Orange, 21 September 1688.

164 In 1688, Mulgrave, who was standing at the foot of the bed before drawn curtains, gave inconclusive evidence: *Depositions . . . &c.*, 20; in 1714, during a House of Lords debate on the safety of the Protestant succession, he allegedly testified to the validity of the Pretender's birth: BM, Add. MSS 31,256, ff. 80–2: James Drummond, Earl of Perth, to Cardinal Gualterio, 14 May 1714 NS, St Germain; BM, Add. MSS 46,495, f. 102: James Dempster to Gualterio, 13 May 1714 NS, St Germain. There is no reference to his speech in William Cobbett, *Parliamentary History of England, 1066–1803* (hereafter cited as *Parliamentary History*), VI (London, 1810), 1333–40.

165 BM, Add. MSS 33,286, ff. 3–4: 'A true Account of what Passed in a Conference between Isabella, Lady Wentworth, & Dr. George Hickes, about the Birth of the Prince of Wales, signed by the said Dr. George Hickes and Mrs. Bridget Harrison' [14 April 1702]; cf. Burnet, *History of His Own Time*, III, 324n.

166 Herts. R.O., Panshanger MSS, diary of Dr Hamilton, 22 November 1712.

167 *Clarendon Correspondence*, II, 178: 16 June 1688.

168 Brown, *Letters and Diplomatic Instructions*, 38: Anne to Mary of Orange, 9 July 1688, Cockpit.

169 Brown, *Letters and Diplomatic Instructions*, 31: Anne to Mary of Orange, 9 May 1687, Richmond.

170 Brown, *Letters and Diplomatic Instructions*, 36: Anne to Mary of Orange, 20 March 1688.

171 *Evelyn Diary*, IV, 589–90: 8 July 1688.

172 *Ellis Correspondence*, II, 99: [?] to John Ellis, 2 August 1688, London.

173 Sarah Churchill, *Conduct*, 18.

174 Blenheim G I 9: Sarah's 1704 'Conduct'.

175 Althorp, Marlborough MSS, Box III, 'My Last Will', by Sarah, 18 August 1690, in which she refers to this settlement of 27 July 1688.

176 Churchill, *Marlborough*, I, 240: Churchill to William III, 4 August 1688.

177 Burnet, *History of His Own Time*, III, 282–3.

178 Kenyon, *Sunderland*, 206.

179 *Russell Letters*, I, 248: Dr Tillotson to Lady Russell, 6 September 1688, Canterbury.

180 Strickland, *Lives of the Queens of England*, VI, 233–4.

181 Ellis, *Original Letters*, III, 349: Mary of Modena to Mary of Orange, 21 September 1688; cf. Luttrell, *A Brief Historical Relation*, I, 461; *Clarendon Correspondence*, II, 187.

182 Brasch, *Prins Georg*, 32.

183 *Clarendon Correspondence*, II, 189.

184 *Ellis Correspondence*, II, 228–9 [?] to John Ellis, 29 September 1688, London; Coke, III, 122.

185 Brasch, *Prins Georg*, 33–5.

186 *Clarendon Correspondence*, II, 190–1.

187 *Ibid.*, 194–5; 10, 16 October 1688.

188 *Ibid.*, 194: 12 October 1688.

189 Luttrell, *A Brief Historical Relation*, I, 460, 471; *Ellis Correspondence*, II, 176; [?] to John Ellis, 13 September 1688, London; *Clarendon Correspondence* II, 193: 7 October 1688; for Prince George's explanation, *ibid.*, 216: 5 December 1688.

190 *Clarendon Correspondence*, II, 196: 23 October 1688.

191 *Clarendon Correspondence*, II, 197: 24, 27, 29 October 1688.

192 *Clarendon Correspondence*, II, 198–9: 31 October 1688.

193 *Clarendon Correspondence*, II, 199: 1 November 1688; cf. Campana de Cavelli, *Les Derniers Stuarts*, II, 311: Hoffmann to the emperor, 12 November 1688 NS, London.

194 *Clarendon Correspondence*, II, 200: 3 November 1688.

195 *Ibid.*, 201: 9 November 1688.

196 *Ibid.*, 205–6: 19, 20 November 1688.

197 Dalrymple, *Memoirs*, II, 249: Anne to William III, 18 November 1688; cf. *Calendar of Treasury Books* (hereafter cited as *Cal. Treas. Books*), XVII (1702), ed. William A. Shaw (London, 1947), 525–6.

198 G. W. Keeton, *Lord Chancellor Jeffreys and the Stuart Cause* (London, 1965), 499.

199 Dalrymple, *Memoirs*, II, appendix to book VI, 249–50: Anne to William III, 18 November [1688], Cockpit.

200 Brasch, *Prins Georg*, 33; cf. Haile, *Mary of Modena*, 212: Hoffmann to the emperor, 29 November 1688.

201 James II, *Memoirs*, II, 225.

202 Brasch, *Prins Georg*, 35–6; Lediard, *John, Duke of Marlborough*, I, 81–2.

203 Churchill, *Marlborough*, I, 264: Prince George to James II, 24 November 1688.

204 HMC *7th Report*, 418: Middleton to Preston, 25 November 1688, Harteley Roy at 7.00 p.m.

205 *Clarendon Correspondence*, II, 214, 216: 3, 5 December 1688, quoting the prince and Churchill; cf. Klopp, *Der Fall des Hauses Stuart*, IV, 234–5.

206 Sarah Churchill, *Conduct*, 16.

207 *Hatton Correspondence*, II, 118–19: John Horton to Lord Hatton, 2 December 1688, Nasely.

208 Brown, *Letters and Diplomatic Instructions*, 44–5: Anne to Mary of Modena, 25 November 1688, Cockpit.

209 HMC *Dartmouth*, I, 214: Samuel Pepys to Lord Dartmouth, 26 November 1688, 11 at night.

210 *Reresby*, 550: 2 February 1689, quoting an unnamed 'Court Lady'; cf. Higgons, *A Short View of the English History*, 429.

211 John Sheffield, Duke of Buckingham, *Mémoires du duc de Buckingham sur le règne de Charles II et la Révolution de 1688* (Paris, 1824), 30.

212 *Hatton Correspondence*, II, 118–19: John Horton to Lord Hatton, 2 December 1688, Nasely; for the princess's reasons for choosing Nottingham, see Sir George Duckett, *Penal Laws and Test Act* (London, 1883), 111–13; cf. David H. Hosford, 'The Rising at Nottingham', *Albion*, IV (1972), 158–60.

213 BM, Add. MSS 18,675, f. 48: newsletter to Earl of Abingdon, 8 December 1688 [London]; cf. Churchill, *Marlborough*, I, 267.

214 See the correspondence of Compton and Danby of 4, 5 December 1688, in HMC *11th Report*, pt VII, 27; cf. *Reresby*, 587: Sir John Reresby to Halifax, 9 December 1688, Thirberge.

215 HMC *7th Report*, 502: John Verney to Sir Ralph Verney, 4 December 1688 [London].

216 HMC *Le Fleming*, 227: newsletter, 8 December 1688; cf. Campana de Cavelli, *Les Derniers Stuarts*, II, 472: James II to Dartmouth, 19 January 1689, St Germain.

217 Brown, *Letters and Diplomatic Instructions*, 45: Anne to Sir Benj. Bathurst, 3 December [1688], Nottingham; printed from BM Loan 57/71, f. 19.

218 *Letters of Philip, Second Earl of Chesterfield to Several Celebrated Individuals of the Time of Charles II, James II, William III, and Queen Anne* (London, 1829), 48–51.

219 *Clarendon Correspondence*, II, 250: 17 January 1689, quoting the princess.

220 *Chesterfield*, 51.

221 *Ellis Correspondence*, II, 368: [?] to John Ellis, 19 December 1688, London.

222 HMC *Le Fleming*, 234: newsletter, 19 January 1689, Oxford.

223 Luttrell, *A Brief Historical Relation*, I, 491; *Clarendon Correspondence*, II, 231: 19 December 1688.

224 *Clarendon Correspondence*, II, 249: 17 January 1689.

225 Strickland, *Lives of the Queens of England*, VII, 179.

226 [Anonymous,] *The Life of her late Majesty, Queen Anne* (London, 1721), 29–30.

227 Blenheim G I 10: Sarah's 'A true account'.

228 H. C. Foxcroft, *The Life and Letters of Sir George Savile, First Marquis of Halifax* (London, 1898), II, 202–3: 'Spencer House Journals, conversations of the Prince of Orange and the Marquis of Halifax, 30 Dec. 1688'.

229 *Clarendon Correspondence*, II, 260.

230 *Reresby*, 551: 3 February 1689, quoting Scarsdale.
231 *Clarendon Correspondence*, II, 248: 17 January 1689.
232 Blenheim G I 9: 1704 'Conduct'; in 'The Character of Princes' (1715), Sarah claimed that she, rather than Tillotson, convinced the princess.
233 *Clarendon Correspondence*, II, 254–5: 27 January 1689; cf. *Lives of Two Illustrious Generals* (1713), 27.
234 *Clarendon Correspondence*, II, 254–5: 27 January 1689.
235 *Clarendon Correspondence*, II, 260: 5 February 1689.
236 Henry Horwitz, *Revolution Politicks: The Career of Daniel Finch, Second Earl of Nottingham, 1647–1730* (Cambridge, 1968), 80, n. 1; cf. Lediard, *John, Duke of Marlborough*, I, 86–7; H. Horwitz, 'Parliament and the Glorious Revolution', *BIHR*, XLVII (1974), 49 and n. 5.
237 *Clarendon Correspondence*, II, 269–70: 12 March 1689.

238 Bathurst, *Letters of Two Queens*, 222–3: Anne to Sir Benj. Bathurst, n.d. [early 1689].
239 LCC, *Survey of London*, XIII, 105, quoting *The London Mercury, or Moderate Intelligencer*, 11–14 February 1688/9.
240 Luttrell, *A Brief Historical Relation*, I, 503; HMC *Kenyon*, 217: Wm Assheton to Roger Kenyon, 14 February 1689.
241 Strickland, *Lives of the Queen of England*, VII, 198.
242 LCC, *Survey of London*, XIII, 86 and n.
243 *CSPD, William & Mary, Feb. 1689–April 1690*, 32: warrant of 20 March 1689; Luttrell, *A Brief Historical Relation*, I, 517.
244 *Evelyn Diary*, IV, 645–6; cf. *Russell Letters*, II, 8: Lady Russell to Dr Fitzwilliam, 21 July 1689.
245 Strickland, *Lives of the Queens of England*, VII, 231.
246 Boyer, *Queen Anne*, I, 29–30.

Chapter 3:   William and Mary

1 Strickland, *Lives of the Queens of England*, VII, 159.
2 Sarah Churchill, *Conduct*, 25.
3 LCC, *Survey of London*, XIV, 86 and note.
4 Blenheim G I 10: Sarah's 'A true account', ff. 2–3.
5 Strickland, *Lives of the Queens of England*, VII, 220; 27–8; Blenheim G I 10: Sarah's 'A true account', f. 3.
6 HMC *Hamilton*, 190: Melville to Hamilton, 25 July [1689].
7 HMC *Portland*, III, 440: Abigail Harley to Sir Edward Harley, 7 September 1689; cf. Richard Doebner, ed., *Memoirs of Mary, Queen of England (1689–1694) together with her Letters and those of James II and William III to the Electress Sophia of Hanover* (London, 1886), 14–15.
8 Foxcroft, *Supplement to Burnet*, 206–7; Turner, *James II*, 69, n. 2; J. G. Simms, *The Williamite Confiscation in Ireland, 1690–1703* (London, 1956), 179–80.
9 Simms, *Williamite Confiscation*, 92.
10 HMC *Finch*, II, 223: Nottingham to Ludolfe, 9 July 1689; p. 224: Nottingham to William III, 9 July 1689.
11 SP 75/22, ff. 68–9: Duke of Holstein to

William III, 30 July 1689 NS; ff. 141, 151: statement by C. S. von Plessen, 28 November 1689, Copenhagen; full details are found in SP 75/22, ff. 357–9.
12 HMC *Finch*, III, 5–6: Prince George to Nottingham, 3 February 1691; pp. 181, 206–7: Nottingham to Sidney, 28 July, 14 August 1691.
13 Cobbett, *Parliamentary History*, IV, 207–8.
14 Doebner, *Memoirs of Mary*, 17–18.
15 Sarah Churchill, *Conduct*, 29.
16 Andrew Browning, *Thomas Osborne, Earl of Danby and Duke of Leeds*, II (Glasgow, 1949), 220: Carmarthen to [Marchioness of Carmarthen], 3 December 1689.
17 Dalrymple, *Memoirs of Great Britain and Ireland*, III, 107: Wharton to William III, 29 December 1689.
18 Boyer, *Queen Anne*, I, 29–30; White Kennett, *Complete History of England*, III, 547; Cobbett, *Parliamentary History*, V, 492–500; cf. Hon. Architell Grey, ed., *Debates of the House of Commons from the Year 1667 to the Year 1694* (London, 1769), IX, 477–80, 490–500.
19 Doebner, *Memoirs of Mary*, 17–18.

20 Blenheim G I 10: Sarah's 'A true account', ff. 5–6; cf. Sarah Churchill, *Conduct*, 34–5; my italics.

21 Bentinck, *Marie, Reine d'Angleterre*, 95: Queen Mary's meditation of 3/13 March 1690.

22 Baxter, *William III*, 263.

23 Luttrell, *A Brief Historical Relation*, II, 51.

24 Brasch, *Prins Georg*, 45.

25 Sarah Churchill, *Conduct*, 38.

26 Doebner, *Memoirs of Mary*, 24.

27 Strickland, *Lives of the Queens of England*, VII, 313–14.

28 J. L. Chester, ed., *The Marriage, Baptismal and Burial Registers of the Collegiate Church or Abbey of St. Peter, Westminster* (London, vol. 10 of Harleian Society, 1876), 226; Luttrell, *A Brief Historical Relation*, II, 116.

29 Luttrell, *A Brief Historical Relation*, II, 182, 219, 225; cf. BM, Add. MSS 17,677 LL, 76v: Van Citters to States, 5/15 May 1691; HMC *Portland*, III, 464–5: Robert Harley to [Sir Edward Harley], 2, 5, 12 May 1691; Klopp, *Der Fall des Hauses Stuart*, V, 279–80.

30 Brasch, *Prins Georg*, 45; cf. Grovestins, *Histoire des luttes*, V, 313: L'Hermitage to Heinsius, 4 November 1692.

31 Doebner, *Memoirs of Mary*, 38.

32 Blenheim E 18: Anne to Countess of Marlborough, Wensday night [1691].

33 Blenheim E 18: Anne to Sarah, 20 September [1683], Winchester.

34 Blenheim E 17: Anne to Sarah, fryday afternoon [24 July 1685], Tundbridge.

35 Blenheim E 17: Anne to Sarah, ye Cockpitt Munday [c. 9 June 1691]; misprinted, Brown, *Letters and Diplomatic Instructions*, 50–1.

36 HMC *8th Report*, 562b: newsletter, 14/24 July 1691 [London].

37 Luttrell, *A Brief Historical Relation*, II, 263, 282; cf, HMC *8th Report*, 562v: newsletter, 14/24 July 1691.

38 *CSPD, William & Mary, May 1690 – Oct. 1691*, 468: Princess Anne, Prince George to William III, 2 August 1691, Tunbridge.

39 James II, *Memoirs*, II, 444–5.

40 Macpherson, *Original Papers*, I, 440.

41 Brown, *Letters and Diplomatic Instructions*, 52–3: Anne to James II, 1 December 1691.

42 BM, Add. MSS 37,661, f. 125: James II's 'Message to the Princess of Denmark', 18 July 1692 NS, St Germain, conveyed by Lady Sophia Buckley to the Churchills.

43 Macpherson, *Original Papers*, I, 281, Carte MSS quoting Dr William Sheridan, deprived Bishop of Kilmore.

44 Foxcroft, *Supplement to Burnet*, 373–4; cf. Klopp, *Der Fall des Hauses Stuart*, VI, 375: Stratemann's report of 8 February 1692, London.

45 BM, Add. MSS 17,677 MM, f. 65: Hop to States, 1 February 1692 NS; cf. Klopp, *Der Fall des Hauses Stuart*, VI, 27; W. H. Aiken, ed., *The Conduct of the Earl of Nottingham, 1688–1693* (New Haven, Conn., 1941), 111.

46 Green, *Sarah*, 62–3.

47 Blenheim E 19: Anne to Sarah, Wensday three aclock [27 April 1692]. Both Stuart J. Reid, *John and Sarah, Duke and Duchess of Marlborough*, and A. L. Rowse, *The Early Churchills* (London, 1958), 300, have been misled into believing that Mrs Hill referred to Abigail Masham.

48 Doebner, *Memoirs of Mary*, 45.

49 Strickland, *Lives of the Queens of England*, VII, 344–6: Queen Mary to Anne, 5 February 1692, Kensington.

50 Blenheim E 17: Anne to Sarah, n.d. [5 February 1692].

51 Strickland, *Lives of the Queens of England*, VII, 347: Anne to Queen Mary, 6 February 1692, Cockpit. My italics.

52 Strickland, *Lives of the Queens of England*, VII, 348: Anne to Queen Mary, 8 February 1692.

53 Sarah Churchill, *Conduct*, 59–60.

54 Blenheim G I 9: 1704 'Conduct', f. 5.

55 Blenheim G I 10: 'A true account', f. 11.

56 Blenheim E 17: Anne to Sarah, teusday ten aclock [23 February 1692].

57 Luttrell, *A Brief Historical Relation*, II, 372; Grovestins, *Histoire des luttes*, VI, 314–15: L'Hermitage to Heinsius, 14 March 1692 NS, London.

58 Grovestins, *Histoire des luttes*, VI, 314: L'Hermitage to Heinsius, 23 February/4 March 1692.

59 Blenheim E 18: Anne to Sarah, n.d. [March 1692].

60 Althorp, Marlborough MSS, Book B: Anne to Sarah, Fryday morning [15 March 1692], printed without date, Brown, *Letters and Diplomatic Instructions*, 59–60.

61 Althorp, Marlborough MSS, Book B: Anne to Sarah, teusday morning [19 March 1692].

62 Blenheim E 18: Anne to Countess of Marlborough, Fryday [early April 1692].

63 Blenheim E 18: Anne to Sarah, Saturday night [early April 1692].

64 Blenheim G I 9: 1704 'Conduct', f. 6; Spanheim's account of the last interview between the queen and the princess agrees substantially with Sarah's: Bourgeois, *Spanheim*, 599.

65 *CSPD, William & Mary, Nov. 1691 – Dec. 1692*, 245: R. Yard to Sir Joseph Williamson, 19 April 1692, Whitehall; Luttrell, *A Brief Historical Relation*, II, 424, Grovestins, *Histoire des luttes*, VI, 316: L'Hermitage to Heinsius, 28 April 1692 NS.

66 HMC *Finch*, IV, 100: Nottingham to Blathwayt, 26 April 1692, Whitehall.

67 Sarah Churchill, *Conduct*, 89–91: Rochester to Princess Anne, 27 April 1692.

68 Blenheim E 19: Anne to Sarah, Wensday three aclock [27 April 1692].

69 Blenheim E 48: Anne to Rochester, 29 April 1692, printed without date, Brown, *Letters and Diplomatic Instructions*, 55.

70 *Hatton Correspondence*, II, 176–7: Sir Charles Lyttleton to Lord Hatton, 10 May [1692].

71 Blenheim G I 9: 1704 'Conduct', f. 8; cf. Klopp, *Der Fall des Hauses Stuart*, VI, 59, n. 1: L'Hermitage to Heinsius, n.d.

72 HMC *Finch*, IV, 91: newsletter, 15 April 1692, London; James II, *Memoirs*, II, 475.

73 W. E. Buckley, ed., *Memoirs of Thomas, Earl of Ailesbury, written by Himself* (London, Roxburghe Club, 1890), 292–3, 296–7.

74 *Hatton Correspondence*, II, 176: Sir Charles Lyttleton to Lord Hatton, 5 May [1692].

75 Coxe, *Marlborough*, I, 65–6: Anne to Sarah [5 May 1692].

76 Blenheim E 19: Anne to Sarah [5 May 1692].

77 Althorp, Marlborough MSS, Book B: Anne to Countess of Marlborough, Thursday [12 May 1692]; printed without date, Brown, *Letters and Diplomatic Instructions*, 58.

78 Blenheim G I 7: Anne to Sarah, Friday night [20 May 1692].

79 Brown, *Letters and Diplomatic Instructions*, 54–5: Anne to Queen Mary, 20 May 1692, Syon; my italics.

80 Strickland, *Lives of the Queens of England*, VII, 362–3: Queen Mary to Anne, 21 May 1692.

81 Blenheim G I 7: Anne to Sarah, Saturday seven a clock [21 May 1692], misdated in Brown, *Letters and Diplomatic Instructions*, 56.

82 Blenheim E 17: Anne to Sarah, n.d. [21 May 1692].

83 Blenheim E 17: Anne to Countess of Marlborough, Wensday night [25 May 1692]; cf. BM Add. MSS 17,677 MM, f. 207: Thomas Baden to States, 27 May/6 June 1692.

84 HMC *Finch*, IV, 260: Nottingham to Blatywayt, 24 June 1692; *Hatton Correspondence*, II, 180: Sir Charles Lyttleton to Lord Hatton, 16 June [1692].

85 Luttrell, *A Brief Historical Relation*, II, 491, 497, 499.

86 *Ibid.*, II, 525.

87 Blenheim E 19: Anne to Sarah, Teusday [2 August 1692].

88 Blenheim E 19: Anne to Sarah, teusday [9 August 1692], printed without date, HMC *8th Report*, 53a.

89 Blenheim E 19: Anne to Sarah, Thursday [28 July 1692].

90 Blenheim E 19: Anne to Sarah, teusday [9 August 1692], printed without date, HMC *8th Report*, 53a.

91 HMC *Finch*, IV, 433: Nottingham to Mayor and Corporation of Bath, 30 August 1692.

92 Aiken, *Conduct of the Earl of Nottingham*, 112.

93 Blenheim E 17: Anne to Countess of Marlborough, Munday night [6 September 1692], printed without date, Sarah Churchill, *Conduct*, 97–100.

94 HMC *Finch*, IV, 196: [Dr Richard Kingston] to Nottingham [May or June 1692]; p. 342: Nottingham to Portland, 26 July 1692.

95 HMC *Finch*, IV, 438: [Dr Richard Kingston] to Nottingham [August 1692].

96 HMC *Finch*, IV, 452–3: [Dr Richard Kingston] to Nottingham, 11 or 12 September 1692.

97 Buckley, *Ailesbury Memoirs*, 308.

98 Luttrell, *A Brief Historical Relation*, III, 601; Baxter, *William III*, 308.

99 Blenheim E 17: Anne to Sarah, Munday night [*c*. 9 January 1693]; cf. Blenheim E 18: Anne to Countess of Marlborough, Wensday night [*c*. 11 January 1693].

100 Luttrell, *A Brief Historical Relation*, III, 1.

101 *Ibid.*, III, 15–16.

102 Henry Horwitz, ed., *The Parliamentary*

Diary of Narcissus Luttrell, 1691–1693 (London, 1972), 244.

103 Blenheim G I 9: 1704 'Conduct', f. 7; Jenkin Lewis, *Memoirs of Prince William Henry, Duke of Gloucester* (London, 1789), 34; Strickland, *Lives of the Queens of England*, VII, 429.

104 Buckley, *Ailesbury Memoirs*, 296.

105 Luttrell, *A Brief Historical Relation*, III, 37; Sarah Churchill, *Conduct*, 86; John Macky, *Memoirs of the secret services of John Macky* (London, 1733, reprinted Roxburghe Club, 1895), 77; H. Manners-Sutton, ed., *The Lexington Papers* (London, 1851), 6.

106 Luttrell, *A Brief Historical Relation*, III, 251.

107 Blenheim E 17: Godolphin to Sarah, Wednesday at 2 [31 January 1694]; Luttrell, *A Brief Historical Relation*, III, 262.

108 Blenheim E 17: Anne to Sarah, Thursday night [between 1692 and 1694].

109 Blenheim E 19: Anne to Sarah, Thursday night [February 1693].

110 Strickland, *Lives of the Queens of England*, VII, 409.

111 Blenheim E 19: Anne to Sarah, Sunday ten aclock [19 March 1693].

112 Chester, *Marriage, Baptismal and Burial Registers*, 231; Luttrell, *A Brief Historical Relation*, III, 84; BM, Add. MSS 17,677 NN, f. 97v: Baden to States, 28 March 1693 OS.

113 Blenheim E 18: Anne to Sarah, Fryday night [4 August 1693].

114 Luttrell, *A Brief Historical Relation*, III, 258; BM, Add. MSS 17,677 OO, f. 163: L'Hermitage to States, 2 February 1694 NS.

115 Blenheim E 17: Anne to Sarah, Fryday night [*c.* 28 April 1693].

116 *Shrewsbury Correspondence*, 47: Shrewsbury to William III, 22 June/2 July 1694; p. 53: William to Shrewsbury, 15 July 1694 NS.

117 Sarah Churchill, *Conduct*, 104–5; my italics.

118 *Ibid.*, 105–6.

119 Ranke, *History of England*, VI, 264: Bonet's report of 28 December 1694/7 January 1695.

120 *Private and Original Correspondence of Charles Talbot, Duke of Shrewsbury*, ed. William Coxe (London, 1821) (hereafter cited as *Shrewsbury Correspondence*), 80; Coxe, *Marlborough*, I, 74; Strickland, *Lives of the Queens of England*, VIII, 8.

121 Blenheim G I 9: 1704 'Conduct', f. 11; Lewis, *Memoirs of Prince William Henry*, 42.

122 BM, Add. MSS 17,677 PP, f. 111: L'Hermitage to States, 1/11 January 1695.

123 HMC *Bath*, II, 175–6: Princess Anne to William III, 29 December [1694], Berkley House.

124 Strickland, *Lives of the Queens of England*, VIII, 6.

125 White Kennett, *Complete History of England*, III, 674.

126 Lambeth Palace MSS 930, f. 198: Tenison to William III, 6 January 1695.

127 *CSPD, William & Mary, Nov. 1691 – Dec. 1692*, 88: Princess Anne to William III, 7 January [1695], misdated 1692 by editor; Luttrell, *A Brief Historical Relation*, III, 423.

128 *Hatton Correspondence*, II, 211: Charles Hatton to Lord Hatton, 10 January 1695.

129 Lewis, *Memoirs of Prince William Henry*, 42; Boyer confirms the gift of the jewels: *Queen Anne*, I, 34; cf. BM, Add. MSS 17,677 PP, f. 122: L'Hermitage to States, 15/25 January 1695.

130 James II, *Memoirs*, II, 525.

131 Luttrell, *A Brief Historical Relation*, III, 426.

132 Blenheim G I 10: Sarah's 'A true account', f. 13.

133 Blenheim E 17: Anne to Countess of Marlborough, Tuesday night, 15 January [1695].

134 Sarah Churchill, *Conduct*, 110.

135 BM, Add. MSS 17,677 PP, f. 119: L'Hermitage to States, 11/21 January 1695.

136 Blenheim E 48: Sarah's note on princess to William III, 29 December [1694].

137 *Shrewsbury Correspondence*, 220: Shrewsbury to Russell, 29 January 1695.

138 Kenyon, *Sunderland*, 273.

139 Blenheim G I 9: 1704 'Conduct', f. 12.

Chapter 4:   William Alone

1 Burnett, *History of His Own Time*, V, 268, 451: Dartmouth's notes.

2 Simms, *Williamite Confiscation*, 93.

3 BM, Add. MSS 17,677 PP, f. 259: L'Hermitage to States, 7/17 May 1695; Strickland, *Lives of the Queens of England*, VIII, 22–3.

4 N. Japikse, *Correspondentie*, II, 67–8: Marlborough to Portland, 17 September 1695, St Albans; Sarah Churchill, *Conduct*, 114.

5 Edward Carpenter, *Thomas Tenison, Archbishop of Canterbury: His Life and Times* (London, 1948), 170.

6 *Hatton Correspondence*, II, 212: Lady Nottingham to Lord Hatton, 5 February [1695].

7 BM, Add. MSS 17,677 PP, f. 216: L'Hermitage to States, 2/12 April 1695.

8 W. Pittis, *Dr. Radclife's Life & Letters*, (London, 4th edn, 1736), 31–2.

9 *Evelyn Diary*, V, 213; cf. BM, Add. MSS 17,677 PP, ff. 297v–298, 306: L'Hermitage to States, 14, 25 June 1695 OS; HMC *Downshire*, I, 466: Ezra Lyon to Mr Tibalds, 26 April 1695, Whitehall; p. 487: [?] to Thomas Comynge, 27 June 1695.

10 BM, Add. MSS 17,677 MM, f. 230: Thomas Baden to States, 1/11 July 1692.

11 Blenheim E 18: Anne to Sarah, Thursday night [summer 1693].

12 Lewis, *Memoirs of Prince William Henry*, 42, 49.

13 BM, Add. MSS 17,677 PP, f. 119: L'Hermitage to States, 11/21 January 1695.

14 Blenheim E 19: Anne to Sarah, Thursday night [between 1695 and 1701], St James's.

15 Lewis, *Memoirs of Prince William Henry*, 49; cf. BM, Add. MSS 17,677 PP, f. 189: L'Hermitage to States, 12/22 March 1695; *CSPD, William III*, July/December 1695, 335: newsletter to Earl of Derwentwater, 25 [May] 1695.

16 [John Macky,] *A Journey through England* (London, 5th edn, 1732), I, 50.

17 Luttrell, *A Brief Historical Relation*, IV, 20; cf. BM, Add. MSS 17,677 QQ, f. 279v: L'Hermitage to States, 18 February 1696 OS; cf. HMC *Hastings*, II, 258: [Dr Nathaniel Johnston] to Earl of Huntingdon, 18 February 1696.

18 BM, Add, MSS 17,677 QQ, f. 442: L'Hermitage to States, 26 May/5 June 1696.

19 James II, *Memoirs*, II, 560.

20 Macpherson, *Original Papers*, I, 520, 524–5.

21 BM, Add. MSS 30,000 A, f. 200: Bonet to Elector of Prussia, 21/31 July 1696, London.

22 BM, Add. MSS 17,677 QQ, ff. 544, 546: L'Hermitage to States, 18, 22 September 1696 OS; Add. MSS 30,000 A, f. 217: Bonet to Elector of Prussia, 22 September 1696 OS; *Evelyn Diary*, V, 259; Luttrell, *A Brief Historical Relation*, IV, 114.

23 BM, Add. MSS 17,677 RR, f. 278: L'Hermitage to States, 30 March/9 April 1697; 30,000 A, f. 287: Bonet to Elector of Prussia, 30 March/9 April 1697.

24 See abstract of Treaty of Ryswick in Arthur Trevor, *The Life and Times of William III* (London, 1836), II, 508–14.

25 Blenheim G I 9: 'The Character of Princes', ff. 16–17.

26 Blenheim E 19: Anne to Sarah, 20 October [1696], Windsor.

27 Blenheim E 19: Anne to Sarah, St James's, Wednesday night [7 April 1697].

28 Blenheim E 18: Anne to Sarah, St James's, Fryday night [9 April 1697].

29 Blenheim E 18: Anne to Sarah, St James's, tuesday night [13 April 1697].

30 Blenheim G I 7: Anne to Sarah [copy, n.d.].

31 *Letters to and from Henrietta, Countess of Suffolk, and her second husband, The Hon. George Berkeley, from 1712 to 1767* (London, 1824), I, 292–3: Dr John Arbuthnot to Mrs Henrietta Howard, 29 May [1728], London, quoting Abigail, Lady Masham.

32 Chamberlayne, *Angliae Notitia or The Present State of England* (18th edn, 1694).

33 Sarah Churchill, *Conduct*, 180.

34 Blenheim G I 8: Sarah's 'Account of the Hill Family', c. 1711.

35 Blenheim E 17: Anne to Sarah, Wensday night [21 April 1697].

36 Simms, *Williamite Confiscation*, 86.

37 HMC *Buccleuch*, II, 534: Winchester to Shrewsbury, 15 August 1697, Dublin.

38 BM, Loan 57/71, f. 9: Anne to Sir Benjamin Bathurst, Saturday, 16

October [1697], Windsor; cf. Bathurst, *Letters of Two Queens*, 241.

39 BM, Loan 57/71, f. 11: Anne to Sir Benjamin Bathurst, fryday, 22 October [1697], Windsor; cf. Bathurst, *Letters of Two Queens*, 242.

40 Blenheim G I 7: Princess Anne to William III, n.d. [*c.* 1 November 1697].

41 Mark Thomson, 'Louis XIV and William III, 1689–1697', in *William III and Louis XIV*, ed. R. M. Hatton and J. S. Bromley (Liverpool, 1968), 24–48.

42 BM, Add. MSS 33,045, ff. 13–15: Newcastle papers on royal household, establishment of Gloucester's household, 7 February 1698; cf. *CSPD, William III, 1698*, 395–6: John Ellis to Sir Joseph Williamson, 30 September 1698, Whitehall; *Vernon Correspondence*, II, 124: Vernon to Shrewsbury, 13 July 1698.

43 *CSPD, William III, 1697*, 520: Shrewsbury to Vernon, 19 December 1697, Eyford.

44 *Shrewsbury Correspondence*, 444: Vernon to Shrewsbury, 21 December 1697.

45 *Vernon Correspondence*, II, 12: Vernon to Shrewsbury, 14 February 1698; PRO 31/3/182: Tallard to Louis XIV, 22 January 1699 NS.

46 *Vernon Correspondence*, II, 104, 106, 111: Vernon to Shrewsbury, 11, 14, 21 June 1698.

47 White Kennett, *Complete History of England*, III, 755.

48 Strickland, *Lives of the Queens of England*, VIII, 67; Trevor, *William III*, II, 479–80; William M. Marshall, *George Hooper, 1640–1727, Bishop of Bath and Wells* (Sherborne, Dorset, 1976), 57.

49 Burnet, *History of His Own Time*, V, 386, Dartmouth's note.

50 Foxcroft, *Supplement to Burnet*, 493–4.

51 Blenheim E 18: Anne to Sarah, St James's, Wednesday night [15 June 1698].

52 Blenheim G I 9: Sarah's 1704 'Conduct', f. 12; *CSPD, William III, 1698*, 395–6: John Ellis to Sir Joseph Williamson, 30 September 1698; *Vernon Correspondence*, II, 177–8: Vernon to Shrewsbury, 20 September 1698.

53 BM, Add. MSS 17,677 RR, f. 526: L'Hermitage to States, 7/17 December 1697; cf. *CSPD, William III, 1697*, 598: newsletter to Sir Joseph Williamson, 10 December 1697.

54 Luttrell, *A Brief Historical Relation*, IV, 402.

55 *CSPD, William III, 1698*, 379: John Ellis to Sir Joseph Williamson, 19 August 1698, Whitehall.

56 *Vernon Correspondence*, I, 176: Vernon to Shrewsbury, 17 September 1698; Luttrell, *A Brief Historical Relation*, IV, 428; *CSPD, William III, 1698*, 390: newsletter to Williamson, 20 September 1698.

57 Blenheim E 18: Anne to Countess of Marlborough, n.d. [27 October 1697].

58 Blenheim E 19: Anne to Sarah, Thursday morning [28 October 1697], Windsor.

59 Blenheim G I 7: Anne to Sarah (copy), Saturday [30 October 1697].

60 Churchill, *Marlborough*, I, 437–8.

61 Longleat, Portland Papers, X, ff. 131–4: 'Heads of a Memoriall for the E. of Oxford' [*c.* 1715].

62 HMC *Johnstone*, 114: [?] to Earl of Annandale, 14 December 1699 [London].

63 *Vernon Correspondence*, II, 382–3, 385–7, 387–9: Vernon to Shrewsbury, 9, 12, 14 December 1699.

64 Blenheim E 19: Anne to Countess of Marlborough, Thursday morning [14 February 1700].

65 *Vernon Correspondence*, II, 422: Vernon to Shrewsbury, 23 January 1700; Luttrell, *A Brief Historical Relation*, IV, 607; cf. BM, Add. MSS 17,677 UU, f. 138: L'Hermitage to States, 26 January/5 February 1700; Klopp, *Der Fall des Hauses Stuart*, VIII, 551.

66 BM, Add. MSS 57,862, f. 31: newsletter, 30 July 1700, Whitehall; cf. *Vernon Correspondence*, III, 118–20: Vernon to Shrewsbury, 30 July 1700.

67 BM, Add. MSS 17,677 UU, ff. 286, 289: L'Hermitage to States, 30 July 1700.

68 *Vernon Correspondence*, III, 118–20: Vernon to Shrewsbury, 30 July 1700.

69 Blenheim F I 16: Autopsy report of the Duke of Gloucester, 31 July 1700, by Edward Hannes, MD, Charles Bernard, Edward Greene, William Cowper.

70 Boyer, *Queen Anne*, 33.

71 BM, Add. MSS 17,677 UU, f. 268: L'Hermitage to States, 13/24 August 1700.

72 Luttrell, *A Brief Historical Relation*, IV, 675; cf. HMC *10th Report*, pt IV, 335: William Graham to John Graham, 31 August 1700, Windsor.

73 BM, Add. MSS 17,677 UU, ff. 286, 287: L'Hermitage to States, 30 July, 2 August

1700 OS; cf. Onno Klopp, ed., *Correspondance de Leibniz avec l'électrice Sophie de Brunswick-Lunenbourg* (Hanover, 1874), II, 206: Sophia to Leibniz, 18 August 1700 NS.

74 Pierpont Morgan Library, Rulers of England, Box XI (William and Mary, #22): William III to Princess Anne, 4 August 1700 [OS], Loo.

75 NSA, Hannover 93, 12 A, 11–3, ff. 270–3: 'Rélation de ce qu'on a su à la Haie des affaires arriveés en Angleterre depuis le 7 d'Aout [NS], 1714'.

76 G. Lamberty, *Mémoires pour servir a l'histoire du XVIII*^e *siècle*, VIII (Amsterdam, 1730), 657–9; Christian Cole, ed., *Historical and Political Memoirs . . . Beginning with 1697 to the End of 1708* (London, 1735), 188–9.

77 Gregg, 'Was Queen Anne a Jacobite?' 366.

78 White Kennett, *Complete History of England*, III, 525.

79 Richard Doebner, ed., *Briefe der Königin Sophia Charlotte von Preussen und der Kurfürstin Sophie von Hannover an hannoversche Diplomaten* (Leipzig, 1905), 150: Sophia to Schütz, 23 December 1701, Hanover.

80 Baxter, *William III*, 384–5.

81 Gregg, 'Was Queen Anne a Jacobite?', 366.

82 See Dennis Rubini, *Court and Country, 1688–1702* (London, 1967), Appendix C, pp. 282–3.

83 Edward Gregg, 'The Protestant Succession in International Affairs, 1710–1716' (unpublished London PhD thesis), pp. 16–17.

84 Gregg, 'Was Queen Anne a Jacobite?', 368.

85 Burnet, *History of His Own Time*, IV, 553: Dartmouth's note.

86 Ellis, *Original Letters*, III, 354: W. N. to Rev. Francis Roper, 11 September 1701 (London); cf. *An Abridgement of the Life of James II . . . Extracted from an English Manuscript of the Reverend Father Francis Sanders* (London, 1704), 91; Falconer Madan, ed., *Stuart Papers relating chiefly to Queen Mary of Modena* (Roxburghe Club, 1889), II, 274, 343.

87 Henry L. Snyder, ed., *The Marlborough–Godolphin Correspondence* (Oxford, 1975), I, 34: Marlborough to Godolphin, 15/26 September 1701, The Hague.

88 Snyder, *Marlborough–Godolphin Correspondence*, I, 35: Marlborough to Godolphin, 16/27 September 1701, Loo.

89 Brown, *Letters and Diplomatic Instructions*, 67–8: Anne to Godolphin, Tuesday night (23 September 1701).

90 BM, Add. MSS 15,895, f. 111: Vernon to Rochester, 27 September 1701, Whitehall.

91 Strickland, *Lives of the Queens of England*, VII, 120–3; cf. Grovestins, *Histoire des luttes*, VIII, 194.

92 Sarah Churchill, *Conduct*, 120–1.

93 Burnet, *History of His Own Time*, V, 1: Dartmouth's note; Macky, *Secret Services*, 94; HMC *Egmont*, II, 208: Sir John Perceval to Thomas Knatchbull, 21 March 1702.

Chapter 5:   The Role of the Monarch

1 Edward Craven Hawtrey, ed., *The Private Diary of William, First Earl Cowper* (Eton, 1833), 37: entry of 30 January 1706. Hereafter cited as *Lord Cowper's Diary*.

2 Geoffrey Holmes, 'Post-Revolution Britain and the Historian', in *Britain after the Glorious Revolution, 1689–1714*, ed. G. Holmes (London, 1969), 2–4. King's figures should be used with the greatest caution: see Holmes, 'Gregory King and the Social Structure of pre-Industrial England', *TRHS*, 5th series, XXVII (1977), 41–68.

3 Blenheim E 19: queen to Sarah, Fryday, 11 June [1703], Windsor, misdated 1707 by Brown, *Letters and Diplomatic Instructions*, 227–8.

4 Althorp, Marlborough MSS, Book B: queen to Sarah, 21 November [1704], St James's, misdated 1702 in Brown, *Letters and Diplomatic Instructions*, 99–100.

5 Blenheim G I 4: queen to Marlborough [Sarah's copy], 27 August 1708, printed, Brown, *Letters and Diplomatic Instructions*, 256–8.

6 Brown, *Letters and Diplomatic Instructions*, 172: queen to Godolphin, 11 July [1705], Windsor.

7 HMC *9th Report*, pt 2, 472: queen to Godolphin, Wensday [23 May 1705], Kensington.

8 J. H. Plumb, *The Growth of Political Stability in England, 1675–1725* (London, 1967), 98–128, for 'The Role of the Executive'.

9 Blenheim E 18: queen to Sarah, Thursday noon [27 October 1709], Windsor, printed Brown, *Letters and Diplomatic Instructions*, 286, without date.

10 W. T. Morgan, *English Political Parties and Leaders in the Reign of Queen Anne, 1702–1710* (New Haven, Conn., 1920), 136–7.

11 Blenheim E 18: queen to Sarah, 9 July [1703], Windsor.

12 Blenheim E 18: queen to Sarah, Munday 29 June [1702], Windsor.

13 Blenheim E 19: queen to Sarah, teusday 19 May [1702], St James's.

14 Jonathan Swift, *The Journal to Stella*, ed. Herbert Davis, (Oxford, 1948) (hereafter cited as *Journal to Stella*), 327: 5 August 1711.

15 Harold Williams, ed., *The Correspondence of Jonathan Swift* (Oxford, 1963), 245: Swift to Archbishop King, 15 August 1711.

16 HMC *Bath*, I, 201: Shrewsbury to Harley, 25 April 1711.

17 Thomas Sharp, *The Life of John Sharp, D.D., Lord Archbishop of York*, ed. Thomas Newcome (London, 1825), I, 317, quoting the queen.

18 Major R. E. Scouller, *The Armies of Queen Anne* (Oxford, 1966), 6.

19 BM, Add. MSS 52,540 L: queen to Godolphin, Fryday, 12 September 1707, partly printed in Brown, *Letters and Diplomatic Instructions*, 231–2.

20 *Private Correspondence of Sarah, Duchess of Marlborough*, ed. Lord John Russell (London, 1838) (hereafter cited as *Private Correspondence*), II, 117.

21 Pierpont Morgan Library, Rulers of England, Box XI, Queen Anne #7: queen to Marlborough, 27 September [1705], Windsor.

22 BM, Add. MSS 31,143, f. 315: Peter Wentworth to Lord Raby, 25 March 1709, London.

23 Morgan, *English Political Parties*, 193, quoting Swift's *History of the Queen's Last Ministry*.

24 Doris M. Gill, 'The Treasury, 1660–1714', *EHR*, XLVI (1931), 608.

25 *Cal. Treas. Books*, XVIII (1703), 50.

26 *Monthly Magazine*, XVI (1 December 1803), p. 396: queen to Sir Charles Hedges, Friday night.

27 The most complete examples of this secretarial correspondence with the queen are found in Gilbert Parke, ed., *The Letters and Correspondence of Henry St. John, Viscount Bolingbroke* (London, 1798) (hereafter cited as *Bolingbroke Correspondence*), I, II, and IV *passim*; William Salt Library, Dartmouth D 1778, i, ii *passim*; HMC *Dartmouth*, I, 298–316.

28 Brown, *Letters and Diplomatic Instructions*, 357–8: queen to Oxford, 16 November 1711.

29 HMC *Bath*, I, 217: queen to Oxford, 19 November 1711.

30 *Ibid.*, 225: queen to Oxford, Saturday, 3 January 1713.

31 Longleat, Portland MSS III, f. 29: queen to Robert Harley, Wensday [9 August 1710].

32 William Sachse, *Lord Somers, A Political Portrait* (Madison, Wis., 1975), 272.

33 J. H. Plumb, 'The Organization of the Cabinet in the Reign of Queen Anne', *TRHS*, 5th series, VII (1957), 137–57.

34 HMC *Portland*, II, 200: Cowper to Newcastle, 19 September 1707; Harley to Newcastle, 11 September 1707.

35 *Bolingbroke Correspondence*, IV, 260: Bolingbroke to Robinson, 2 September 1713, Windsor.

36 Plumb, 'The Organization of the Cabinet', 153.

37 Plumb, *Political Stability*, 71.

38 Burnet, *History of His Own Time*, V, 125.

39 *Lord Cowper's Diary*, 16: entries for 19 and 20 November 1705.

40 HMC *Rutland*, II, 171: Lady Russell to Rutland, 14 April 1702.

41 Geoffrey Holmes, 'Harley, St. John, and the Death of the Tory Party', *Britain after the Glorious Revolution*, 224.

42 Morgan, *English Political Parties*, 126, n. 2, quoting Defoe's *Challenge of the Peace*.

43 Sharp, *Life of John Sharp*, I, 300–1: Archbishop Sharp's diary, 9 December 1706.

44 *Notes and Queries*, 12th series, V, 155–6: article by Robert Pierpoint.

45 HMC *Portland*, IV, 334: Holt to Robert Harley, 30 September 1706.

46 *Monthly Magazine*, XVI (1 December 1803), 396: queen to Sir Charles Hedges, Tuesday evening.

47 *Ibid.*, 397: queen to Hedges, Wednesday night.
48 J. H. Overton, *The Non-Jurors* (London, 1902), 65, 73.
49 G. V. Bennett, 'Conflict in the Church', in *England after the Glorious Revolution*, ed. G. Holmes, 161–3; cf. Bennett, *The Tory Crisis in Church and State, 1688–1730: The career of Francis Atterbury, Bishop of Rochester* (Oxford, 1975), esp. chap. 1, 'The Anglican Crisis', 3–22.
50 Bennett, 'Conflict in the Church', 167.
51 Norman Sykes, *Church and State in England in the XVIIIth Century* (Cambridge, 1934), 136.
52 Blenheim E 18: queen to [Sarah], Fryday noon [1 October 1708].
53 Carpenter, *Tenison*, 177; cf. Morgan, *English Political Parties*, 160.
54 Norman Sykes, 'Queen Anne and the Episcopate', *EHR* L (1935), 435.
55 Sharp, *Life of John Sharp*, I, 317–18.
56 Blenheim G I 9: Sarah's 'The Character of Princes', 44.
57 A. T. Hart, *John Sharp, Archbishop of York* (London, 1949), 225–6; cf. Sharp, *Life of John Sharp*, I, 315–16.
58 Trevelyan, *England under Queen Anne*, I, 170–1.
59 Blenheim E 17: queen to Duchess of Marlborough (fragment), n.d. [late 1702 or early 1703].
60 Snyder, *Marlborough–Godolphin Correspondence*, I, 185: Godolphin to Duchess of Marlborough, 15 May 1703.
61 Henry L. Snyder, 'Godolphin and Harley: A Study of their Partnership in Politics', *HLQ*, XXX (1967), 243, 255.
62 Sykes, 'Queen Anne and the Episcopate', 457–9: d'Iberville reported that the Tories attributed Dawes's appointment to Oxford's influence, but in fact the queen did not consult any ministers on this question: AAE, CP Angleterre 255, ff. 59–62, 109–12: d'Iberville to Torcy, 14, 22 April 1714 NS, London. For Dawes's record of opposition to the Oxford government, see BM, Stowe 225, ff. 225–6: Schütz to Robethon, 3 November 1713 NS; NSA, Cal. BR. 24, England 113A, ff. 35–6: Kreyenberg to the elector, 3/14 March 1714.
63 For a detailed analysis, see Sykes, *Church and State in England*, 34–5; for William's bishops, see A. S. Turberville, *The House of Lords in the Reign of William III* (Oxford, 1913), 16–30.
64 Sheppard, *St. James's Palace*, I, 204–8; Marc Bloch, *Les rois thaumaturges, étude sur le caractère surnaturel attribué à la puissance royale* (Paris, Strasbourg, 1924), 157, 390–1.
65 Blenheim E 18: queen to Sarah, 29 April [1703], Kensington, misdated as 1706 in Brown, *Letters and Diplomatic Instructions*, 185.
66 S. A. Hervey, ed., *The Letter Books of John Hervey, First Earl of Bristol . . . 1651–1750* (Wells, 1894) (hereafter cited as *Hervey Letter Books*), I, 253: Lady Hervey to John Hervey, 26 April 1706, London.
67 Lady Margaret Verney, ed., *Letters of the Eighteenth Century* (London, 1930) (hereafter cited as *Verney Letters*), I, 356: Mary Lovett to Lord Fermanagh, 15 May 1714.
68 Hart, *John Sharp*, 222, quoting Sharp to William Lloyd, Bishop of Worcester.
69 Blenheim G I 7: 'An Account of Healing Gold Receiv'd', by Rachel Thomas, 31 May 1707.
70 HMC *Bath*, I, 246: William Jackson to [Oxford], 12 February 1714; cf. Hart, *Sharp*, 222.
71 HMC *3rd Report*, 273: William Lloyd, deprived Bishop of Norwich, to Sir Charles Calthorp, 29 June 1702; cf. A. Aufrere, ed., *The Lockart Papers* (London, 1817), 42.
72 Trevelyan, *England under Queen Anne*, I, 149–50.
73 PRO 31/3/190, f. 34: Nathaniel Hooke's 'Memoire sur les Affaires d' Angleterre par rapport à la mort du Roy Guillaume', 25 March 1702 NS, Paris.
74 *A Selection from the Papers of the Earls of Marchmont, 1685–1750*, ed. G. H. Rose (London, 1831) (hereafter cited as *Marchmont Papers*), III, 250: 'Memorial concerning affairs of Scotland', sent by Marchmont to the queen, 11 July 1702, Holyrood.
75 Blenheim E 18: queen to Sarah, Saturday [22 August 1702], partly printed in Brown, *Letters and Diplomatic Instructions*, 228–9, incorrectly dated as 1707–8; cf. Burnet, *History of His Own Time*, V, 125: the queen expressed similar sentiments to Bishop Burnet.
76 NSA, Cal. Br. 24, England 71, ff. 58–65: Schütz to Robethon, 9 January 1703 NS, London, quoting Bishop Burnet.
77 *Ibid.*, ff. 66–7: Schütz to Robethon, 8/19

January 1703, London.

78 BM, Add. MSS 17,677 XX, ff. 252, 262: L'Hermitage to States-General, 17, 24 March 1702 OS, London; cf. HMC *Rutland*, II, 169: J. Wotton to Rutland, 19 March [1702], London; for Clarendon's pension, Althorp, Marlborough MSS, Box III: Sarah's 'Material for the

Historians' (1744); cf. Morgan, *English Political Parties*, 73.

79 HMC *Bath*, I, 223: queen to Oxford, fryday [21 November 1712], Windsor.

80 Boyer, *Queen Anne*, I, 415.

81 Folger Library V.B. 267: queen to Godolphin [1 May 1705], Hampton Court.

Chapter 6:   The Opening Years

1 Burnet, *History of His Own Time*, V, 1–2.

2 PRO 31/3/190, ff. 19–20: Vaudoncourt to [Torcy], 9/20 March 1702, London; TVKA, B 81: Prince George to Frederick IV, 9 March 1702, St James's; Boyer, *Queen Anne*, I, 40; HMC *14th Report*, pt III, 156: Robert Pringle to Marchmont, 8 March 1702, Whitehall.

3 BM, Add. MSS 17,677 XX, f. 250v: L'Hermitage to States, 10/21 March 1702.

4 Snyder, *Marlborough–Godolphin Correspondence*, I, 49, n. 1.

5 BM, Add. MSS 17,677 XX, f. 250v: L'Hermitage to States, 10/21 March 1702; Klopp, *Der Fall des Hauses Stuart*, IX, 483–4: Wratislaw's report of 8/19 March 1702.

6 Trevelyan, *England under Queen Anne*, I, 163.

7 Horwitz, *Revolution Politicks*, 182; Morgan, *English Political Parties*, 63; Robert Walcott, *English Politics in the Early Eighteenth Century* (Oxford, 1956), 101.

8 HMC *Portland*, IV, 34: Godolphin to Harley, 8 March 1702.

9 Walcott, *English Politics*, 96–7.

10 Churchill, *Marlborough*, I, 499; cf. Klopp, *Der Fall des Hauses Stuart*, X, 9.

11 Klopp, *Der Fall des Hauses Stuart*, X, 234.

12 HMC *2nd Report*, 242: Sir Robert Southwell to William King, 14 March 1702, Spring Garden.

13 HMC *7th Report*, 246: John Percival to Thomas Knatchbull, 21 March 1702.

14 BM, Add. MSS 7,074, f. 101v: John Ellis to George Stepney, 13 March 1702, London.

15 Churchill, *Marlborough*, I, 520, 522.

16 Klopp, *Der Fall des Hauses Stuart*, X, 35–6; Burnet, *History of His Own Time*, V, 4; Boyer, *Queen Anne*, 13.

17 Morgan, *English Political Parties*, 74–5.

18 Christopher Morris, ed., *The Journeys of*

Celia Fiennes (London, 1949), 300.

19 Carpenter, *Tenison*, 178.

20 See The Most Reverend Father in God, John [Sharp], Lord Archbishop of York, *A Sermon Preach'd at the Coronation of Queen Anne, in the Abby-Church of Westminster, April XXIII, MCCII, Published by Her Majesty's Especial Command* (London, 1706).

21 *Journeys of Celia Fiennes*, 300.

22 Boyer, *Queen Anne*, I, 51–3.

23 Blenheim G I 9: Sarah's 'The Character of Princes', 33.

24 Snyder, *Marlborough–Godolphin Correspondence*, I, 66–7: queen to Sarah, 19 May 1702, St James's.

25 *Cal. Treas. Books*, XVII (1702), 41: 9 June 1702.

26 Burnet, *History of His Own Time*, V, 10, quoting Marlborough.

27 B. Van t'Hoff, ed., *The Correspondence of John Churchill, Duke of Marlborough and Anthonie Heinsius, 1701–1711* (The Hague, 1951) (hereafter cited as *Marlborough–Heinsius Correspondence*), 13: Marlborough to Heinsius, 17/28 April 1702, London.

28 Snyder, *Marlborough–Godolphin Correspondence*, I, 32: Godolphin to Marlborough, 9 September 1701.

29 HMC *7th Report*, 246: John Percival to Thomas Knatchbull, 21 March 1702; cf. PRO 31/3/190, ff. 47–8: Vaudoncourt to Torcy, 14 April 1702 NS, London.

30 NSA, Cal. Br. 24, England 71, ff. 486–9: Schütz to Robethon, 6 October 1705 NS, London: Schütz believed that Marlborough and Godolphin lacked the influence at the queen's accession to oppose the appointment of High Tories; had they done so, the Tories might have forced the queen to get rid of them.

31 Churchill, *Marlborough*, I, 533;

Wratislaw's report of 3 May 1702.

32 Horwitz, *Revolution Politicks*, 166; Morgan, *English Political Parties*, 71–2.

33 *Vernon Correspondence*, III, 222: Vernon to Shrewsbury, 1 May 1702; cf. BM, Stowe 222, ff. 140–1: J. Vernon Jr to Robethon, 29 July 1702, Copenhagen.

34 Churchill, *Marlborough*, I, 502; Trevelyan, *England under Queen Anne*, I, 200.

35 Churchill, *Marlborough*, I, 537–8; Sir Tresham Lever, *Godolphin, His Life and Times* (London, 1952), 124; Dorothy H. Somerville, *The King of Hearts* (London, 1962), 210–11.

36 BM, Stowe 222, ff. 140–1: James Vernon Jr to Robethon, 29 July 1702, Copenhagen.

37 *Hervey Letter Books*, I, 168: Lady Hervey to John Hervey, 9 May 1702, London.

38 Morgan, *English Political Parties*, 101.

39 Scouller, *The Armies of Queen Anne*, 272.

40 *Correspondence of George Baillie of Jerviswood, 1702–1708*, ed. Gilbert Elliot, Earl of Minto (Bannatyne Club, 1842), 213: Secretary Johnstone to George Baillie, [?] May 1702, London.

41 NSA, Cal. Br. 24, England 71, ff. 14–15: Schütz to Robethon, 25 August 1702 NS, London.

42 Snyder, *Marlborough–Godolphin Correspondence*, I, 87: Marlborough to Sarah, 13/24 June 1702.

43 Lever, *Godolphin*, 120; Churchill, *Marlborough*, I, 503.

44 Burnet, *History of His Own Time*, V, 8; Churchill, *Marlborough*, I, 532; Trevelyan, *England under Queen Anne*, I, 186.

45 *Hervey Letter Books*, I, 161–2: Lady Hervey to John Hervey, 5 May 1702, London; cf. Klopp, *Der Fall des Hauses Stuart*, X, 56.

46 Horwitz, *Revolution Politicks*, 166; Churchill, *Marlborough*, I, 532, quoting Wratislaw's dispatch of 7 April.

47 Churchill, *Marlborough*, I, 527.

48 Trevelyan, *England under Queen Anne*, I, 204; Holmes, *British Politics*, 73.

49 Horwitz, *Revolution Politicks*, 167; Holmes, *British Politics*, 73.

50 Burnet, *History of His Own Time*, V, 14.

51 Snyder, *Marlborough–Godolphin Correspondence*, I, 59: Marlborough to Godolphin, 18 May 1702, Margate.

52 *Ibid.*, 61: Sarah to Godolphin, 19 May 1702, Margate.

53 *Ibid.*, 63: Godolphin to Sarah, 19 May 1702.

54 *Ibid.*, 66–7: queen to Sarah, 19 May 1702, St James's; cf. 58, 63: Godolphin to Sarah, 16, 19 May 1702.

55 Blenheim E 19: queen to Sarah, Munday ye 14th [June 1703], Windsor.

56 Trevelyan, *England under Queen Anne*, I, 213, quoting Lord Cowper's memoir to George I; cf. Burnet, *History of His Own Time*, V, 45.

57 Trevelyan, *England under Queen Anne*, I, 210.

58 Horwitz, *Revolution Politicks*, 183.

59 W. A. Speck, *Tory and Whig: the Struggle in the Constituencies, 1701–1715* (London, 1970), 113.

60 Churchill, *Marlborough*, I, 572–609.

61 Trevelyan, *England under Queen Anne*, I, 260–72; Churchill, *Marlborough*, I, 609–12.

62 Snyder, *Marlborough–Godolphin Correspondence*, I, 99: Marlborough to Godolphin, 10/21 August 1702.

63 TVKA, England B 81: Hugh to Frederick IV, 21 April/2 May 1702, London; Klopp, *Der Fall des Hauses Stuart*, X, 40; Boyer, *Queen Anne*, 14.

64 TVKA, England B 81: Hugh to Frederick IV, 22 May/2 June 1702; Boyer, *Queen Anne*, 21. For the membership of the prince's council between 1702 and 1708, see G. F. James and J. J. Sutherland Shaw, 'Admiralty Administration and Personnel, 1619–1714', *BIHR*, XIV (1936–7), 23–4.

65 Morgan, *English Political Parties*, 68.

66 Snyder, *Marlborough–Godolphin Correspondence*, I, 55: Marlborough to Godolphin, 31 March/11 April 1702, The Hague.

67 *Marlborough–Heinsius Correspondence*, 13, 14: Marlborough to Heinsius, 17, 27 April 1702, London.

68 Churchill, *Marlborough*, I, 504, 533.

69 Snyder, *Marlborough–Godolphin Correspondence*, I, 71, 75–6: Marlborough to Godolphin, 10/21, 19/30 June 1702, The Hague.

70 Churchill, *Marlborough*, I, 524–6.

71 Snyder, *Marlborough–Godolphin Correspondence*, I, 103 and n. 6: Marlborough to Godolphin, 16/27 August 1702.

72 *Marlborough–Heinsius Correspondence*, 25: Marlborough to Heinsius, 21 August

1702 NS; cf. George Murray, ed., *Letters and Dispatches of John, Duke of Marlborough* (London, 1845), I, 44: Marlborough to Plessen, 8 October 1702 NS.

73 Snyder, *Marlborough–Godolphin Correspondence*, I, 108: Marlborough to Godolphin, 27 August/7 September 1702.

74 Althorp, Marlborough MSS, Book B: queen to Sarah, Fryday night [14 August 1702], Windsor.

75 HMC *Portland*, IV, 46: Henry Guy to Robert Harley, 5 September 1702, Bath.

76 Boyer, *Queen Anne*, I, 94.

77 BM, Add. MSS 17,677 XX, ff. 198, 201, 205, 207v, 239: L'Hermitage to States, 28 August, 1, 8 September, 13 October 1702 OS, London.

78 *Ibid.*, ff. 259v, 267v: L'Hermitage to States, 30 October, 6 November 1702 OS, London.

79 *Vernon Correspondence*, III, 228–9: Vernon to Shrewsbury, 6 November 1702.

80 For the fears of Hanoverian agents that the Tories might make such a proposal, see Lediard, *John, Duke of Marlborough*, II, 202, 204; BM, Stowe 222, ff. 162–4: d'Allonne to Robethon, 28 October 1702, The Hague; Eduard Bodemann, ed., *Briefe der Kurfürstin Sophie von Hannover an die Raugräfinnen und Raugrafen zu Pfalz*, Publicationen aus den K. Preussischen Staatsarchiven, XXXVII (Leipzig, 1888), 326: Sophia to Raugrafin Louise, 12 October 1702, Hanover; TVKA, England B 81: Stocken to Frederick IV, 30 June, 11 July 1702, London.

81 NSA, Cal. Br. 24, England 71, ff. 6–7: [Schütz] to Robethon, 9 August 1702 NS, London.

82 PRO 31/3/190, f. 68: Vaudoncourt to [Torcy], 5 December 1702 NS, London.

83 Burnet, *History of His Own Time*, V, 48.

84 Horwitz, *Revolution Politicks*, 185–6.

85 HMC *Portland*, IV, 50–1: Godolphin to Harley, 10 November 1702.

86 *Ibid.*, 53: Godolphin to Harley, 10 December 1702.

87 Churchill, *Marlborough*, I, 627.

88 Burnet, *History of His Own Time*, V, 52–4; Boyer, *Queen Anne*, 38–42; Henry L. Snyder, 'The Defeat of the Occasional Conformity Bill and the Tack: a Study in the Techniques of Parliamentary Management in the Reign of Queen

Anne', *BIHR*, XLI (1968), 172–4.

89 Snyder, *Marlborough–Godolphin Correspondence*, I, 138: Godolphin to Sarah, 22 October 1702.

90 Brown, *Letters and Diplomatic Instructions*, 97: queen to Sarah, 22 October 1702, St James's.

91 Snyder, *Marlborough–Godolphin Correspondence*, I, 140: Godolphin to Sarah, 24 October 1702.

92 Althorp, Marlborough MSS, Book B: queen to Sarah, St James's, Saturday, 24 October [1702], printed Brown, *Letters and Diplomatic Instructions*, 98–9.

93 Blenheim E 18: queen to Sarah, St James's, teusday morning [10 November 1702], partly printed, Snyder, *Marlborough–Godolphin Correspondence*, I, 148, n. 3.

94 HMC *Portland*, IV, 49: Godolphin to Robert Harley, 3 November 1702.

95 Lediard, *John, Duke of Marlborough*, I, 205–6.

96 Snyder, *Marlborough–Godolphin Correspondence*, I, 149.

97 HMC *Portland*, IV, 53: Godolphin to Harley, 9 December 1702.

98 Horwitz, *Revolution Politicks*, 187.

99 HMC *Portland*, IV, 53: Godolphin to Harley, 12 December 1702.

100 Churchill, *Marlborough*, I, 617–18; Boyer, *Queen Anne*, 37; Henry L. Snyder, 'Godolphin and Harley: A Study of their Partnership in Politics', *HLQ*, XXX (1967), 251–2.

101 Boyer, *Queen Anne*, 37.

102 Brown, *Letters and Diplomatic Instructions*, 103: queen to Sarah, Wednesday, 16 December [1702].

103 Blenheim G I 7: Sarah's endorsement on the queen's letter, 16 December [1702].

104 Burnet, *History of His Own Time*, V, 54–6.

105 Lever, *Godolphin*, 133; Morgan, *English Political Parties*, 100; A. S. Turberville, *The House of Lords in the 18th Century* (Oxford, 1927), 42.

106 Blenheim E 17: queen to Sarah, Teusday night [19 January 1703], partly printed, Brown, *Letters and Diplomatic Instructions*, 104, misdated December 1702.

107 Althorp, Marlborough MSS, Book B: queen to Sarah, Fryday morning [5 February 1703], printed without date,

Brown, *Letters and Diplomatic Instructions*, 115.

108 Snyder, *Marlborough–Godolphin Correspondence*, I, 309: Marlborough to Sarah, 22 May/2 June 1704.

109 *Ibid.*, n. 1: queen to Sarah, 29 May 1703.

110 Morgan, *English Political Parties*, 101–2; Churchill, *Marlborough*, I, 627–9; Klopp, *Der Fall des Hauses Stuart*, X, 236: Hoffmann's report of 9/20 February 1703; Burnet, *History of His Own Time*, V, 58–9; *Marlborough–Heinsius Correspondence*, 54: Marlborough to Heinsius, 5/16 February 1703, London.

111 Blenheim E 19: queen to Sarah, Thursday night [21 October 1703]; cf. University of Kansas, Spencer MSS C. 163: Sir William Simpson to John Methuen, 2 November 1703, London.

112 University of Kansas, Spencer MSS C. 163: Sir William Simpson to John Methuen, 3 July 1705, London.

113 Blenheim E 19: queen to Sarah, Thursday morning [18 February 1703].

114 *Ibid.*, queen to Sarah, Thursday night [18 February 1703].

115 Blenheim E 17: queen to Sarah, Fryday night [19 February 1703].

116 HMC *Portland*, IV, 59: Abigail, Lady Pye, to Abigail Harley, 14 April 1703, Derby.

117 Herbert Davis and Irvin Ehrenpreis, eds, *Some Considerations upon the Consequences hoped and feared from the Death of the Queen*, 101, 110; on 10 October 1710, Swift told Archbishop King, 'The Dutchess of Marlborough's Removall has been seven years working'. *Swift Correspondence*, I, 186.

118 Blenheim E 18: queen to Sarah, St James's, teusday morning [10 November 1702].

119 Blenheim E 18: queen to Sarah, Munday, 29 June [1702], Windsor.

120 Blenheim E 19: queen to Duchess of Marlborough, Sunday noon [21 February 1703].

121 Blenheim E 19: queen to Duchess of Marlborough, St James's, teusday night [23 February 1703], partly printed, Brown, *Letters and Diplomatic Instructions*, 116.

122 Snyder, *Marlborough–Godolphin Correspondence*, I, 152: Godolphin to Marlborough, 26 February 1703.

123 PRO 31/3/191, f. 11v: Vaudoncourt [to Torcy], 6 March 1703 NS, London; for earlier rumours, see *Verney Letters*, I, 112: Lady Gardiner to Sir John Verney, 25 August 1702.

124 Snyder, *Marlborough–Godolphin Correspondence*, I, 186, n. 7: queen to Sarah, 14 [June 1703], Windsor.

125 PRO 30/24/20, pt 1, ff. 173–4: Shaftesbury to Benjamin Furley, 30 April 1703 [London]; cf. Althorp, Marlborough MSS, Book B: queen to Sarah, St James's, Munday night past Eleven [10 May 1703], partly printed without date, *Private Correspondence*, I, 25.

126 Snyder, *Marlborough–Godolphin Correspondence*, I, 183: Marlborough to Sarah, 13/24 May 1703.

127 Blenheim E 18: queen to Duchess of Marlborough, Saturday [22 May 1703], Windsor; printed without date, Brown, *Letters and Diplomatic Instructions*, 125, and with wrong date, Churchill, *Marlborough*, I, 699–700.

128 Blenheim E 19: queen to Sarah, Munday [17 May 1703].

129 Churchill, *Marlborough*, I, 635–8.

130 Trevelyan, *England under Queen Anne*, I, 303; Churchill, *Marlborough*, I, 645–9.

131 Blenheim E 18: queen to [Godolphin], 4 July [1706], Windsor, misaddressed to the duchess by Brown, *Letters and Diplomatic Instructions*, 189.

132 Blenheim E 18: queen to Sarah, Munday [31 May 1703], Windsor.

133 New York Public Library, Montagu Collection, No. 11: queen to Godolphin, 5 June [1703], Windsor; cf. Blenheim E 19: queen to Sarah, 5 June [1703], Windsor.

134 Blenheim E 19: queen to Sarah, Teusday, 29 June [1703].

135 Blenheim E 18: queen to Sarah, Munday, 7 June [1703], Windsor.

136 Blenheim E 19: queen to Sarah, Fryday, 11 June [1703], Windsor, misdated 1707 by Brown, *Letters and Diplomatic Instructions*, 227–8.

137 Snyder, *Marlborough–Godolphin Correspondence*, I, 198: Marlborough to Sarah, 3/14 June 1703.

138 Snyder, *Marlborough–Godolphin Correspondence*, I, 198, n. 5: queen to Sarah 14 [June 1703].

139 Blenheim E 18: queen to Sarah, Wednesday [16 June 1703].

140 *Ibid.*: queen to Sarah, Fryday night [18 June 1703].

141 Snyder, *Marlborough–Godolphin Correspondence*, I, 199: Marlborough to Godolphin, 7/18 June 1703.

142 *Ibid.*, 224: Marlborough to Godolphin, 22 June/2 August 1703.

143 Blenheim E 19: queen to Sarah, Wednesday past four aclock [4 August 1703].

144 Snyder, *Marlborough–Godolphin Correspondence*, I, 202–3: Marlborough to Sarah, 10/21 June 1703.

145 *Ibid.*, 251: Marlborough to Sarah, 30 September/11 October 1703.

146 Blenheim E 19: queen to Sarah, Wensday morning [9 June 1703], Windsor.

147 *Ibid.*: queen to Sarah, Teusday, 29 June [1703].

148 *Cal. Treas. Books*, XXVIII (1714), 416.

149 Blenheim E 18: queen to Sarah, Thursday night [22 July 1703], Windsor.

150 Luttrell, *A Brief Historical Relation*, V, 330, 347; Snyder, *Marlborough–Godolphin Correspondence*, I, 232, n. 5; HMC *Portland*, IV, 66: [Henry Guy to Robert Harley] 11 September 1703, Bath.

151 Althorp, Marlborough MSS, Book B: queen to Sarah, [20] October 1703, Windsor, printed in Brown, *Letters and Diplomatic Instructions*, 127–8.

152 Blenheim E 19: queen to Sarah, Saturday night [16 October 1703].

153 Churchill, *Marlborough*, I, 702.

154 Althorp, Marlborough MSS, Book B: queen to Sarah, Fryday morning [10 December 1703], printed Brown, *Letters and Diplomatic Instructions*, 129.

155 Blenheim E 19: queen to Sarah, Munday morning [13 December 1703].

156 Snyder, 'Defeat of the Occasional Conformity Bill', 174–6.

157 Burnet, *History of His Own Time*, V, 109.

158 Churchill, *Marlborough*, I, 704.

159 Snyder, *Marlborough–Godolphin Correspondence*, I, 259: Marlborough to Sarah [10 December 1703].

160 NSA, Cal. Br. 24, England 71, ff. 183–91: Schütz to Robethon, 4/15 January 1704, London.

161 Horwitz, *Revolution Politicks*, 191–3.

162 Boyer, *Queen Anne*, 101–2; HMC *Rutland*, II, 178–9: Lady Russell to Lady Granby, 1 January 1704.

163 Burnet, *History of His Own Time*, V, 118–22; *Swift Correspondence*, I, 184: Swift to Archbishop King, 10 October 1710; Snyder, 'Godolphin and Harley', 256.

164 Cobbett, *Parliamentary History*, VI, 330; for a complete discussion, see G. F. A. Best, *Temporal Pillars: Queen Anne's Bounty, the Ecclesiastical Commissioners and the Church of England* (Cambridge, 1964).

165 Cobbett, *Parliamentary History*, VI, 336.

166 HMC *Cowper*, III, 32: James Brydges to Thomas Coke, 6 April 1704, London.

167 Boyer, *Queen Anne*, 125.

168 Snyder, *Marlborough–Godolphin Correspondence*, I, 274–5: Marlborough to Godolphin, 8 April 1704, Harwich.

169 Snyder, *Marlborough–Godolphin Correspondence*, I, 280–1: Godolphin to Sarah, 18 April 1704; cf. Burnet, *History of His Own Time*, V, 141.

170 Horwitz, *Revolution Politicks*, 198, n. 4.

171 Snyder, *Marlborough–Godolphin Correspondence*, I, 281: Godolphin to Sarah, 18 April 1704.

172 Blenheim E 18: queen to Sarah, Thursday night 9 aclock [20 April 1704], Kensington, misdated 15 May by Brown, *Letters and Diplomatic Instructions*, 144.

173 Horwitz, *Revolution Politicks*, 198; BM, Loan, 29/70/9: Robert Harley to Auditor Harley, 22 April 1704; HMC *Cowper*, III, 35: James Brydges to Thomas Coke, 22 April 1704.

174 Holmes, *British Politics*, 195.

175 HMC *Portland*, II, 184: Robert Harley to Newcastle, 23 April 1704; Burnet, *History of His Own Time*, V, 142, notes by Dartmouth and Hardwicke; Boyer, *Queen Anne*, 125.

176 Snyder, *Marlborough–Godolphin Correspondence*, I, 254, n. 34; Snyder, 'Godolphin and Harley', 253–4; BM, Loan 29/160/misc. 66: Harley's oath as secretary, 18 May 1704; cf. HMC *Portland*, IV, 84: Privy Council minutes, 18 May 1704.

177 Horwitz, *Revolution Politicks*, 201.

178 Snyder, *Marlborough–Godolphin Correspondence*, I, 285: Godolphin to Sarah, 24 April 1704.

179 *Ibid.*, 287–8: Godolphin to Sarah, 26 April 1704.

Chapter 7:   The Year of Blenheim

1 Blenheim E 19: queen to Sarah, Sunday night [20 June 1703], Windsor.

2 *Russell Letters*, II, 169: Lady Russell to Lady Granby, Tuesday, 2 November [1704].

3 HMC 15th Report, pt VII, 118: Sir Charles Hedges to Somerset, 1 February 1704; Snyder, *Marlborough–Godolphin Correspondence*, I, 413: Godolphin to Sarah, 28 February 1705.

4 NSA, Cal. Br. 24, England 71, ff. 183–91: Schütz to Robethon, 7 January 1704 NS, London.

5 Snyder, *Marlborough–Godolphin Correspondence*, I, 251, n. 1.

6 Snyder, *Marlborough–Godolphin Correspondence*, I, 215: Marlborough to Sarah, 1/12 July 1703.

7 NSA, Cal. Br. 24, England 71, ff. 183–91: Schütz to Robethon, 4/15, 7/18 January 1704, London.

8 *Ibid.*, ff. 276–7: Schütz to Robethon, 12/23 December 1704, London.

9 SP 81/160, f.n.: Cressett to [Hedges], 2 June 1702 NS, Hanover.

10 HMC *Portland*, IV, 154: Godolphin to Robert Harley, n.d. [December 1704].

11 BM, Add. MSS 17,677 XX, f. 266: L'Hermitage to States, 27 March/7 April 1702; cf. PRO 31/3/190, f. 67v: Vaudoncourt to [Torcy], 5 December 1702 NS, London.

12 Snyder, *Marlborough–Godolphin Correspondence*, I, 131: Godolphin to Sarah, 17 October 1702.

13 Blenheim E 18: queen to Sarah, Munday 7 June [1703], Windsor.

14 Blenheim E 19: queen to Sarah, Fryday, 11 June [1703], Windsor, partly printed, Brown, *Letters and Diplomatic Instructions*, 227–8, misdated as 1707.

15 Boyer, *Queen Anne*, I, 228.

16 *Marchmont Papers*, III, 263–7: George Baillie to Lady Grisell Baillie, 9 March 1704, London.

17 Burnet, *History of His Own Time*, V, 176.

18 Snyder, *Marlborough–Godolphin Correspondence*, I, 349: Marlborough to Sarah, 2/13 August 1704.

19 Ellis, *Original Letters*, 2nd series, IV (London, 1826), 242: Dr Charles Davenant to Henry Davenant, 15 August 1704.

20 Snyder, *Marlborough–Godolphin Correspondence*, I, 349, n. 2; Trevelyan, *England under Queen Anne*, I, 397.

21 Coxe, *Marlborough*, II, 38; cf. Blenheim G I 7: queen to Sarah, 10 August [1704], Windsor.

22 Blenheim B II 32: queen to Marlborough, 11 August [1704], Windsor, misdated in Brown, *Letters and Diplomatic Instructions*, 149–50. Prince George's congratulations to Marlborough, dated 15 August, are found in Blenheim F II 15.

23 Blenheim E 19: queen to Sarah, thursday night half an hour past ten [27 April 1704], Kensington, partly printed, Snyder, *Marlborough–Godolphin Correspondence*, I, 288, n. 8.

24 Blenheim G I 7: Sarah to queen (copy), n.d. [*c*. 30 April 1704?]. My italics.

25 Blenheim E 17: queen to Sarah, 5 May [1704], Windsor.

26 Blenheim E 19: queen to Sarah, Wednesday night [17 May 1704].

27 Blenheim E 17: queen to Sarah, Kensington, Wednesday [24 May 1704].

28 Blenheim E 18: queen to Sarah, Fryday morning [26 May 1704].

29 Snyder, *Marlborough–Godolphin Correspondence*, I, 323: Godolphin to Sarah, 14 June 1704.

30 *Ibid.*, 308–9: Marlborough to Sarah, 22 May/2 June 1704.

31 *Ibid.*, 334–5: Marlborough to Godolphin, 2/13 July 1704.

32 *Ibid.*, 288: Godolphin to Sarah, 26 April 1704.

33 *Ibid.*, 343, n. 3: Buckingham to Marlborough, 27 June 1704.

34 BM, Add. MSS 52,540 L: queen to Godolphin, Wednesday morning [24 May 1704]; cf. *Cal. Treas. Books*, XIX, 34–5, for details of the grant to Pembroke.

35 Sarah Churchill, *Conduct*, 146.

36 Blenheim E 18: queen to Sarah, 18 August [1704], Kensington.

37 Blenheim E 19: queen to Sarah, Monday night, 21 August [1704], Windsor, partly printed in Brown, *Letters and Diplomatic Instructions*, 226, misdated 21 May 1707.

38 *Ibid.*, 366: Godolphin to Sarah, 1 September 1704.

39 *Ibid.*, 385: Marlborough to Sarah, 9/20 October 1704.

40 *Ibid.*, 388: Marlborough to Sarah, 15/26 October 1704.

41 *Ibid.*, 390–1: Sarah to Godolphin, 19 October 1704.

42 *Ibid.*, 392: Marlborough to Godolphin, 23 October/3 November 1704; this letter was written at Sarah's behest; see p. 393: Marlborough to Sarah, same date.

43 Sharp, *Life of John Sharp*, I, 306, quoting Archbishop Sharp's diary.

44 Blenheim E 18: queen to Sarah, 17 November [1704], St James's, partly printed, Brown, *Letters and Diplomatic Instructions*, 153. My italics.

45 Blenheim G I 7: Sarah to the queen, 20 November 1704, Windsor Park.

46 Althorp, Marlborough MSS, Book B: queen to Sarah, 21 November [1704], St James's, misdated 1702 by Brown, *Letters and Diplomatic Instructions*, 99–100.

47 Blenheim E 19: queen to Godolphin, Fryday [24 November 1704].

48 Blenheim G I 7: Sarah to the queen, Saturday [25 November 1704].

49 Althorp, Marlborough MSS, Book B: queen to Sarah, n.d. [27 November 1704]; misdated as 1706–7 by Brown, *Letters and Diplomatic Instructions*, 225.

50 See Patricia M. Ansell, 'Harley's Parliamentary Management', *BIHR*, XXXIV (1961), 92–7.

51 Longleat, Portland Papers, Misc. Bound, f. 199: Godolphin to Harley, Sunday 19 [November 1704] at 2. Haversham's speech is printed, Boyer, *Queen Anne*, 163–4.

52 Burnet, *History of His Own Time*, V, 125.

53 *Jerviswood Correspondence*, 14: Sec. Johnstone to George Baillie, 2 December 1704; cf. Lever, *Godolphin*, 175.

54 Cobbett, *Parliamentary History*, VI, 371.

55 BM, Add. MSS 17,677 ZZ, f. 538: L'Hermitage to States, 15/26 December 1704; cf. f. 521: same of 1/12 December; *Vernon Correspondence*, III, 277, 279: Vernon to Shrewsbury, 1, 8 December 1704.

56 Green, *Sarah*, 105.

57 Lediard, *John, Duke of Marlborough*, I, 472–3.

58 Snyder, *Marlborough–Godolphin Correspondence*, I, 178: Marlborough to Sarah, 5/16 May 1703.

59 *Ibid.*, 197, n. 5: queen to Sarah, 14 [June 1703].

60 BM, Add. MSS 17,677 AAA, ff. 202–3: L'Hermitage to States, 23 March/3 April 1705; cf. BM, Loan 29/152: Sir Edward Northey to [Robert Harley], Tues[day] [20 March 1705] with Monthermer's patent. The patent for Montagu's dukedom was dated 14 April: GEC, IX, 107.

61 Snyder, *Marlborough–Godolphin Correspondence*, I, 338: Marlborough to Sarah, 5/16 July 1704.

62 *Ibid.*, 405: Godolphin to Sarah, 27 November 1704.

63 Snyder, 'Godolphin and Harley', 246.

64 A. McInnes, *Robert Harley, Puritan Politician* (London, 1970), 93–4.

65 BM, Add. MSS 17,677 AAA, ff. 210–12: L'Hermitage to States, 27 March 1705; NSA, Cal. Br. 24, England 71, ff. 305–6: Schütz to Robethon, 31 March 1705; Snyder, *Marlborough–Godolphin Correspondence*, I, 418, n. 2; HMC *Bath*, I, 67: [Godolphin to Robert Harley], 1 April 1705.

66 Foxcroft, *Supplement to Burnet*, 512–13.

67 Morgan, *English Political Parties*, 117.

68 Snyder, *Marlborough–Godolphin Correspondence*, I, 432, n. 6; HMC *Portland*, IV, 189: Dyer's newsletter, 19 May 1705.

69 BM, Add. MSS 17,677 AAA, ff. 237, 254: L'Hermitage to States 10, 20 April 1705 OS.

70 Walter Fremen Lord, 'The Development of Political Parties during the Reign of Queen Anne', *TRHS*, 2nd series, XIV (1900), 81.

71 Folger Library, V.B. 267: queen to Godolphin, teusday between four & five aclock [1 May 1705], Hampton Court. Incorrectly printed, in part, by Brown, *Letters and Diplomatic Instructions*, 232, misdated as 1707.

72 Speck, *Tory and Whig*, 106.

73 *Ibid.*, 108.

Chapter 8:   The Attempt at Moderation

1 Morgan, *English Political Parties*, 129.

2 HMC *9th Report*, pt 2, 472: queen to Godolphin, Wednesday [23 May 1705], six a clock, Kensington.

3 HMC *Bath*, I, 69: Godolphin to Robert

Harley, 31 May 1705.

4 Snyder, *Marlborough–Godolphin Correspondence*, I, 451: Godolphin to Sarah, 20 June 1705.

5 Sykes, 'Queen Anne and the Episco-

pate', 435, 439; cf. Carpenter, *Tenison*, 178–9.

6 Folger Library, V.B. 267: queen to Godolphin [1 May 1705].

7 BM, Add. MSS 17,677 AAA, ff. 40–1: L'Hermitage to States, 5 January 1705 OS.

8 Brown, *Letters and Diplomatic Instructions*, 159–60: queen to Godolphin, 6 June [1705], Windsor; cf. BM, Add. MSS 28,070, f. 8.

9 Snyder, *Marlborough–Godolphin Correspondence*, I, 447: Marlborough to Sarah, 10/21 June 1705.

10 Brown, *Letters and Diplomatic Instructions*, 159–60: queen to Godolphin, 6 June [1705], Windsor.

11 Brown, *Letters and Diplomatic Instructions*, 160–1: queen to Godolphin, 14 June [1705], Windsor; cf. BM, Add. MSS 28,070, ff. 10–11.

12 Blenheim G I 9: Sarah's 'The Character of Princes', 54–5; cf. Burnet, *History of His Own Time*, V, 224; Morgan, *English Political Parties*, 128; for Wright's career, see John, Lord Campbell, *Lives of the Lord Chancellors and Keepers of the Great Seal of England* (London, 1846), IV, 241–56.

13 HMC *Portland*, IV, 122, 133–5: Richard Duke to Harley, [?], 20 September 1704, Otterton; Trevelyan, *England under Queen Anne*, I, 207–8.

14 Holmes, *British Politics*, 204.

15 Snyder, *Marlborough–Godolphin Correspondence*, I, 439–40: Marlborough to Godolphin, 2/13 June 1705.

16 Coxe, *Marlborough*, II, 130–1: queen to Marlborough, 12 June 1705, Windsor.

17 Snyder, *Marlborough–Godolphin Correspondence*, I, 452, n. 4.

18 Coxe, *Marlborough*, II, 131–2: Marlborough to the queen [25 June/6 July 1705], misdated 16/27 July.

19 Blenheim B II 32: queen to Marlborough, 3 July [1705], Windsor, partly printed in Brown, *Letters and Diplomatic Instructions*, 251–2, misdated 1708.

20 McInnes, *Harley*, 95.

21 Brown, *Letters and Diplomatic Instructions*, 172: queen to Godolphin, 11 July [1705], Windsor, printed from BM, Add. MSS 28,070, f. 12.

22 Snyder, *Marlborough–Godolphin Correspondence*, I, 467: Marlborough to Godolphin, 26 July/6 August 1705.

23 Coxe, *Marlborough*, II, 235–6: Marl-

borough to the queen, 18/29 September 1705, misdated 29 September 1705 OS by Coxe.

24 Pierpont Morgan Library, Rulers of England, Box XI, Queen Anne, #7: queen to Marlborough, 27 September [1705], Windsor.

25 *Monthly Magazine*, XVI (1 December 1803), 398: queen to Secretary Hedges, 3 October [1705], Windsor.

26 Herts. R.O., Panshanger D/EP/F 55, f. 118: Halifax to Cowper, 5 October 1705.

27 Snyder, 'Godolphin and Harley', 256 and n. 38.

28 *Lord Cowper's Diary*, 15, 19.

29 Blenheim E 19: queen to Sarah, 17 July [1706], Windsor; printed in *Private Correspondence*, I, 58–9.

30 *Lord Cowper's Diary*, 1–3; Campbell, *Lives of the Lord Chancellors*, IV, 294 n.

31 Blenheim G I 9: 'The Character of Princes', 54–5.

32 *Hamilton Diary*, 22.

33 Snyder, *Marlborough–Godolphin Correspondence*, I, 442: Godolphin to Sarah, 4 June 1705.

34 Blenheim E 19: queen to Sarah, 10 July [1705], Windsor.

35 Snyder, *Marlborough–Godolphin Correspondence*, I, 483: Marlborough to Sarah, 22 August/2 September 1705.

36 Blenheim E 19: Sarah's covering essay for the queen's letter of 17 September [1705], Windsor.

37 Blenheim E 19: queen to Sarah, 17 September [1705], Windsor.

38 HMC *Bath*, I, 74–5: [Robert Harley to Godolphin] 4 September 1705.

39 W. A. Speck, 'The Choice of a Speaker in 1705', *BIHR*, XXXVII (1964), 29; cf. HMC *Portland*, IV, 223: Harley to Baron Price, 14 August 1705; Holmes, *British Politics*, 41.

40 Blenheim E 19: queen to Sarah, 10 July [1705], Windsor.

41 Bathurst, *Letters of Two Queens*, 262–3: queen to Lady Bathurst, 23 October [1705], Kensington. My italics.

42 *Lord Cowper's Diary*, 1–2.

43 Snyder, 'Party Configurations in the Early Eighteenth Century House of Commons', *BIHR*, XLV (1972), 47–8; cf. Holmes, *British Politics*, 42–3.

44 HMC *Cleyborne-Popham*, 282–3: memoirs of Dr George Clarke; Speck, 'Choice of a Speaker', 30.

45 SP 81/160, n.f.: Cressett to Hedges, 13 October 1702 NS, Hanover.

46 *Ibid.*, n.f.: Cressett to Hedges, 15 August 1702 NS, Hanover.

47 A. W. Ward, *The Electress Sophia and the Hanoverian Succession* (London, 2nd edn, 1909), 351; Waltraut Fricke, *Leibniz und die englische Sukzession des Hauses Hannover* (Hildesheim, 1957), 37, 46, n. 16.

48 Fricke, *Leibniz*, 48–51.

49 *Ibid.*, 47–8: Falaiseau to Leibniz, 27 July 1705.

50 *Ibid.*, 64: Falaiseau to Leibniz, 19/30 March 1706.

51 Klopp, *Der Fall des Hauses Stuart*, XI, 572–3; Bodemann, *Briefe der Kurfürstin Sophia von Hannover an die Raugräfinnen und Raugrafen zu Pfalz*, 249–53, 363.

52 Klopp, *Der Fall des Hauses Stuart*, XI, 573, n. 2.

53 Doebner, *Briefe . . . der Kurfürstin Sophie von Hannover an hannoversche Diplomaten*, 226: Sophia to Bothmer, 14 November 1703 NS; SP 81/160, n.f.: Edmund Poley to Hedges, 17 December 1703, Hanover.

54 Klopp, *Correspondance de Leibniz avec l'électrice Sophie de Brunswick-Lunenbourg*, III, 7; cf. NSA, Cal. Br. 24, England 71, ff. 110, 129–30: Schütz to Robethon, 20 July, 31 August 1703 NS, London.

55 NSA, Cal. Br. 24, England, ff. 352–3, 373–4: Schütz to Robethon, 18 August, 29 September 1705 NS; Carpenter, *Tenison*, 416; SP 81/162, ff. 208–10: Howe to Harley, 19 October 1706 NS, Hanover.

56 *Clarendon Correspondence*, II, 549–60: Hutton to Rochester, 2 October 1705, Hanover. For the correspondence of Hutton and Gwynne with the two archbishops, see Carpenter, *Tenison*, 416–21, and Sharp, *Life of John Sharp*, I, 270–2.

57 NSA, Cal. Br. 24, England 71, ff. 373–4: Schütz to Robethon, 29 September 1705 NS, London; SP 81/162, ff. 25–8: Howe to Harley, 10 November 1705 NS, Hanover.

58 SP 81/162, f. 97: Howe to Harley, 7/18 December 1705, Hanover.

59 Horwitz, *Revolution Politicks*, 205; Walcott, *English Politics*, 117.

60 Blenheim E 19: queen to Marlborough, 13 November [1705], St James's; partly printed, Brown, *Letters and Diplomatic Instructions*, 176, misdated 24 November.

61 Snyder, *Marlborough–Godolphin Correspondence*, I, 510: Marlborough to Godolphin, 20 November/1 December 1705.

62 Sharp, *Life of John Sharp*, I, 308: Archbishop Sharp's diary, 24 October 1705.

63 BM, Add. MSS 17,677 AAA, ff. 531v–532, 538v–539: L'Hermitage to States, 20, 23 November 1705 OS, London; Haversham's speech is printed in Boyer, *Queen Anne*, 211–13.

64 Horwitz, *Revolution Politicks*, 206–7.

65 Burnet, *History of His Own Time*, V, 233, Dartmouth's note.

66 Sarah Churchill, *Conduct*, 159–60: queen to Sarah, n.d. [15 November 1705].

67 Fricke, *Leibniz*, 64: Falaiseau to Leibniz, 19/30 March 1706, London.

68 NSA, Cal. Br. 24, England 71, ff. 398–9: Schütz to Robethon, 2/13 November 1705, London, quoting Bishop Burnet.

69 Snyder, *Marlborough–Godolphin Correspondence*, II, 631: Marlborough to Godolphin, 22 July/2 August 1706, quoting Halifax.

70 BM, Stowe 222, f. 459: Halifax to Robethon, 12 August 1706, The Hague; cf. Snyder, *Marlborough–Godolphin Correspondence*, II, 631: Marlborough to Godolphin, 22 July/2 August 1706.

71 Snyder, *Marlborough–Godolphin Correspondence*, II, 656: Godolphin to Marlborough, 23 August 1706.

72 BM, Stowe 222, f. 478: Halifax to Robethon, 6/17 September 1706, London.

73 Lewis Melville, *The First George in Hanover and England* (London, 1908), I, 144–6, quoting the patent of 9/20 November [1706], misdated 1705.

74 Both letters are printed by Hauptmann von der Knesebeck, 'Einige Belege zur Geschichte Georg Ludwigs, nachherigen Königs George I', *Archiv des historischen Vereins für Niedersachsen* (Hanover, 1846), 369–84.

75 Klopp, *Der Fall des Hauses Stuart*, XII, 25.

76 NSA, Cal. Br. 24, England 71, ff. 441–2: Schütz to Robethon, 23 March 1706 NS, London.

77 Doebner, *Briefe*, 203–4: Sophia to Schütz, 30 March 1706, Hanover.

78 SP 81/162, ff. 112–13: Howe to Harley, 2 April 1706, Hanover.

79 NSA, Cal. Br. 24, England 71, ff. 441–2, 443–4, 445–6; Schütz to Robethon,23, 26 March, 13 April 1706 NS, London.

80 Cobbett, *Parliamentary History*, VI, 507–10; cf. BM, Add. MSS 17,677 AAA, f. 572: L'Hermitage to States, 7 December 1705 OS, London; Burnet, *History of His Own Time*, V, 242–4.

81 Burnet, *History of His Own Time*, V, 246–7.

82 BM, Add. MSS 17,677 BBB, ff. 296, 336: L'Hermitage to States, 21 May, 25 June 1706 OS, London; the queen's speeches are printed in Boyer, *Queen Anne*, 235.

83 HMC *Marlborough*, 5lb: queen to Godolphin [misaddressed to the duchess by Brown, *Letters and Diplomatic Instructions*, 189], 4 July [1706], Windsor; cf. Blenheim E 18.

84 John M. Gray, ed., *Memoirs of the Life of Sir John Clerk of Penicuik, Baronet, Baron of the Exchequer, Extracted by Himself from his own Journals, 1676–1755* (Roxburghe Club, 1895), 62–3; hereafter cited as *Memoirs of Sir John Clerk*. Cf. HMC *Mar & Kellie*, 271: Mar to James Erskine, 25 July 1706, Whitehall; Boyer, *Queen Anne*, 235–6; BM, Add. MSS 17,677 BBB, ff. 364–5: L'Hermitage to States, 23 July/4 August 1706.

85 Blenheim B II 32: queen to Godolphin, Teusday evening [14 May 1706].

86 Snyder, *Marlborough–Godolphin Correspondence*, I, 549: Godolphin to Marlborough, 14 May 1706.

87 *Ibid.*, 545–6: Marlborough to Godolphin, 13/24 May 1706; p. 551: Godolphin to Marlborough, 17 May 1706.

88 Blenheim B II 32: queen to Marlborough, 17 May 1706, Kensington; misprinted without date, Coxe, *Marlborough*, II, 357. My italics.

89 Blenheim B II 32: queen to Marlborough, 21 May [1706], Kensington.

90 Blenheim B II 32: queen to Marlborough, 9 July [1706], Windsor.

91 Brown, *Letters and Diplomatic Instructions*, 188: queen to Godolphin, 4 June [1706]; printed from original, BM, Add. MSS 28,070, f. 6.

92 *Marlborough–Heinsius Correspondence*, 251: Heinsius to Marlborough, 27 July 1706, The Hague.

93 Blenheim E 18: queen to [Godolphin], 4 July [1706], Windsor; partly printed, HMC *Marlborough*, 5lb, misaddressed to the duchess in Brown, *Letters and Diplomatic Instructions*, 189.

94 *Marlborough–Heinsius Correspondence*, 259: Marlborough to Heinsius, 21 August 1706 NS, Helchin.

95 Arsène Legrelle, *La Diplomatie française et la succession d'Espagne* (2nd edn, Braine-le-Comte, 1899), V, 271.

96 Snyder, *Marlborough–Godolphin Correspondence*, II, 663–6: Godolphin to Buys, 3 September 1706 OS.

97 Longleat, Portland MSS, X, ff. 131–4: 'Heads of a Memoriall for the Earl of Oxford' [c. 1715].

98 McInnes, *Harley*, 90.

99 G. V. Bennett, 'Robert Harley, the Godolphin Ministry, and the Bishoprics Crisis of 1707', *EHR*, LXXXII (1967), 731.

100 HMC *Portland*, IV, 291: Godolphin to Harley, 22 March 1706.

101 Somerville, *King of Hearts*, 227, 232, 235–6.

102 Snyder, *Marlborough–Correspondence*, I, 519, n. 3.

103 Blenheim G I 7: Sarah to queen, Friday night [6 September 1706].

104 Snyder, *Marlborough–Godolphin Correspondence*, I, 522: Godolphin to Marlborough, 19 April 1706.

105 *Ibid.*, 525: Godolphin to Marlborough, 22 April 1706.

106 BM, Add. MSS 17,677 BBB, f. 283: L'Hermitage to States, 14/25 May 1706; Herts. R.O., Panshanger D/EP/F 60, f. 3: Harley to Cowper, 20 May 1706.

107 BM, Add. MSS 17,677 BBB, f. 398v: L'Hermitage to States, 16/27 August 1706; cf. Snyder, *Marlborough–Godolphin Correspondence*, II, 641, n. 1.

108 Blenheim E 19: queen to Sarah, Wensday [23 May 1706].

109 Blenheim E 18: queen to Sarah, 22 June [1706], Windsor.

110 Blenheim E 19: queen to Sarah, 3 July [1706], Windsor.

111 HMC *Marlborough*, 53b: queen to Sarah, 5 July [1706], Windsor, printed from original in Blenheim E 19.

112 Snyder, *Marlborough–Godolphin Correspondence*, I, 583: Godolphin to Marlborough, 11 June 1706.

113 *Ibid.*, II, 594, 596: Marlborough to Godolphin, to Sarah, 20 June/1 July 1706.

114 *Ibid.*, II, 603, n. 3.

115 HMC *Marlborough*, 43b: queen to Marlborough, 9 July [1706], Windsor; cf. Blenheim B II 32.

116 Snyder, *Marlborough–Godolphin*

Correspondence, II, 620: Godolphin to Marlborough, 11 July 1706.

117 *Ibid.*, 628: Marlborough to Sarah, 18/29 July 1706.

118 *Ibid.*, 638: Marlborough to Sarah, 29 July/9 August 1706. My italics.

119 *Ibid.*, 565, n. 4: untraced letter, Godolphin to Marlborough, 20 August 1706.

120 Bennett, 'Bishoprics Crisis', 732.

121 BM, Add. MSS 56,105 L: queen to Godolphin, 23 August [1706].

122 Lever, *Godolphin*, 159.

123 Blenheim G I 7: Sarah to the queen, Tuesday at night [27 August 1706].

124 Coxe, *Marlborough*, III, 112-13: Sarah to the queen, 30 August [1706].

125 Brown, *Letters and Diplomatic Instructions*, 196-7: queen to Godolphin, 30 August [1706], printed from original, BM, Add. MSS 41,340, f. 104.

126 Coxe, *Marlborough*, III, 92-3: Godolphin to the queen, Saturday morning at nine [31 August 1706].

127 Snyder, *Marlborough-Godolphin Correspondence*, II, 661: Godolphin to Sarah, 1 September 1706.

128 Blenheim E 18: queen to Sarah, Fryday morning [6 September 1706], printed by Coxe, *Marlborough*, III, 114-15.

129 Blenheim G I 7: Sarah to queen, Friday night [6 September 1706].

130 Snyder, *Marlborough-Godolphin Correspondence*, II, 670-1: Godolphin to Sarah, 7 September 1706.

131 *Ibid.*, 675: Godolphin to Marlborough, 10 September 1706.

132 BM, Add. MSS 56,105 L: draft of Godolphin's letter to the queen, 13 September 1706.

133 Snyder, *Marlborough-Godolphin Correspondence*, II, 679: Godolphin to Sarah, 14 September 1706, Windsor.

134 *Ibid.*, 688: Godolphin to Sarah, 18 September 1706, Windsor.

135 Snyder, 'Godolphin and Harley', 261.

136 Brown, *Letters and Diplomatic Instructions*, 199-201: queen to Godolphin, 21 September [1706].

137 Coxe, *Marlborough*, III, 106-8: Godolphin to the queen, 25 September [1706], Woodstock; cf. original in Blenheim E 19.

138 Blenheim G I 7: Sarah to the queen, Saturday morning ten a clock [26 September 1706].

139 Bennett, 'Bishoprics Crisis', 733.

140 Brown, *Letters and Diplomatic Instructions*, 202: queen to Godolphin, 28 September [1706]; cf. Blenheim E 19.

141 Coxe, *Marlborough*, III, 100-1: Marlborough to the queen, 26 September/7 October 1706.

142 *Ibid.*, 117-19. Marlborough to the queen, 13/24 October 1706.

143 *Verney Letters*, I, 265: Sir Thomas Cave to Lord Fermanagh, 19 October 1706.

144 Snyder, *Marlborough-Godolphin Correspondence*, II, 725, n. 1.

145 *Ibid.*, 715: Godolphin to Marlborough, 18 October 1706.

146 *Ibid.*, 725-6: Marlborough to Godolphin, 29 October/9 November 1706.

147 *Private Correspondence*, I, 71-5: Sarah to the queen, Sunday morning, 20 October [1706]; cf. Blenheim G I 7.

148 Blenheim E 19: queen to Sarah, 27 October [1706], St James's.

149 Blenheim E 18: queen to Sarah, 30 October [1706], Kensington; printed Brown, *Letters and Diplomatic Instructions*, 203-4.

150 Blenheim G I 7: queen to Sarah, Saturday night [2 November 1706]; cf. Brown, *Letters and Diplomatic Instructions*, 212, without date.

151 Snyder, 'Godolphin and Harley', 261.

152 Bennett, 'Bishoprics Crisis', 734-5; cf. Snyder, 'Godolphin and Harley', 261-2.

153 Blenheim B II 32: queen to Marlborough, 22 June 1708, misaddressed by Brown, *Letters and Diplomatic Instructions*, 250, to Godolphin.

154 *DNB*, IX, 362-3: 'Sir Charles Hedges' by W. P. Courtney.

155 BM, Add. MSS 17,677 BBB, f. 548v: L'Hermitage to States, 3/14 December 1706; cf. HMC *Bath*, I, 132: Sunderland to Rivers, 4 December 1706.

156 Snyder, *Marlborough-Godolphin Correspondence*, II, 741: Godolphin to Marlborough, 28 March 1707.

157 Sharp, *Life of John Sharp*, I, 300-1: Archbishop Sharp's diary, 9 December 1706.

158 Coxe, *Marlborough*, III, 132-3; Boyer, *Queen Anne*, 274.

159 Keith G. Feiling, *History of the Tory Party, 1640-1714* (Oxford, 1924), 395.

160 Blenheim E 17: queen to Sarah,

Wednesday night [23 November 1706].
161 Boyer, *Queen Anne*, 275.
162 Blenheim G I 9: Sarah's 'Letter to Mr. Hutchenson' [1713], 6.

163 Blenheim G I 7: Sarah to the queen, n.d. [*c*. 9 January 1707].
164 *Memoirs of Sir John Clerk*, 62.
165 *Ibid.*, 72.

Chapter 9: The Bishoprics Crisis

1 George A. Aitken, *The Life and Works of John Arbuthnot, M.D., Fellow of the Royal College of Physicians* (Oxford, 1892), 26–7; for Robert Arbuthnot, see P. S.-M. Arbuthnot, *Memoires of the Arbuthnots of Kincardineshire and Aberdeenshire* (London, 1920), 154–67; Legrelle, *La Diplomatie française*, V, 115.

2 *Wentworth Papers*, 138–9: Peter Wentworth to Lord Raby, 25 August 1710.

3 Herbert Davis and Irvin Ehrenpreis, eds, *Jonathan Swift: Political Tracts, 1713–1719*, 'An Enquiry into the Behaviour of the Queen's Last Ministry', 153.

4 Burnet, *History of His Own Time*, VI, 37: Dartmouth's note.

5 Boyer, *Queen Anne*, 322.

6 Blenheim E 18: queen to Sarah, 20 August [1703], Bath, 20 August and Sarah's endorsement.

7 BM, Loan 57/72, f. 140: Lady Wentworth to Raby, 13 March [1705].

8 BM, Add. MSS 31,145, ff. 12v, 72–3: Lady Wentworth to Raby, 7 January, 28 August 1705.

9 National Library of Wales, MSS 18,091 D: privy purse accounts for 1705.

10 Folger Library, V.B. 267: queen to Godolphin [1 May 1705].

11 Blenheim E 19: queen to Sarah, 3 August [1705], Windsor.

12 Blenheim G I 8: Sarah's essay on the Hill family.

13 *Notes and Queries*, 10th series, V, 390: article by R. C. Bostock.

14 Charles Dalton, ed., *English Army Lists and Commission Registers, 1661–1714* (London, 1904), IV, 173; V, 46, 166.

15 Longleat, Portland MSS III, f. 25: queen to Harley, Wensday night [30 April 1707], Kensington.

16 HMC *Bath*, I, 86, 97–8: queen to [Harley], 6 August, 2 September [1707], misdated 1706 by editor.

17 HMC *Portland*, IV, 406: Abigail, Lady Pye, to Abigail Harley, 12 May 1707, Derby.

18 BM, Egerton MSS 2,676, ff. 6–8: privy purse accounts, July 1706–June 1707.

19 Sarah Churchill, *Conduct*, 184.

20 Holmes, *British Politics*, 215.

21 HMC *Bath*, I, 157: St John to Harley, 30 January 1707.

22 Bennett, 'Bishoprics Crisis', 737; cf. Sykes, 'Queen Anne and the Episcopate', 445.

23 Bennett, 'Bishoprics Crisis', 735; cf. Burnet, *History of His Own Time*, V, 337.

24 Bennett, 'Bishoprics Crisis', 736, quoting Tenison to Somers, 19, 23 January 1707.

25 *Ibid.*, 736.

26 HMC *Portland*, IV, 320: Marlborough to Harley, 'for your self', 29 July 1706 NS.

27 Sykes, 'Queen Anne and the Episcopate', 444.

28 H. L. Snyder, 'Formulation of Foreign and Domestic Policy', *Historical Journal*, XI (1968), 157.

29 Snyder, *Marlborough–Godolphin Correspondence*, II, 811: Godolphin to Marlborough, 8 June 1707.

30 Hart, *Sharp*, 212.

31 HMC *Mar & Kellie*, 383: Sir David Nairne to Mar, 6 March 1707.

32 *Memoirs of Sir John Clerk*, 68; for the queen's costume, see *Lockhart Papers*, 410.

33 Snyder, *Marlborough–Godolphin Correspondence*, II, 787–8: Godolphin to Marlborough, 22 May 1707.

34 AAE, CP Angleterre, v. 251, f. 103: d'Iberville to Louis XIV, 5 February 1714 NS, London, quoting Bolingbroke.

35 HMC *Portland*, IV, 388: George Smallridge to Harley, 12 February [1707].

36 Blenheim G I 9: Sarah's 'The Character of Princes', 65.

37 Snyder, *Marlborough–Godolphin Correspondence*, II, 750: Godolphin to Marlborough, 11 April 1707.

38 Bennett, 'Bishoprics Crisis', 737; cf.

Sykes, 'Queen Anne and the Episcopate', 444: Gibson to Wake, 29 August
1707.
39 Snyder, *Marlborough–Godolphin Correspondence*, II, 811: Godolphin to Marlborough, 8 June 1707.
40 HMC *Bath*, I, 173–4: [Godolphin] to
Harley, 14 [June 1707].
41 Snyder, *Marlborough–Godolphin Correspondence*, II, 831: Godolphin to Marlborough, 24 June 1707.
42 *Ibid.*, 824: Marlborough to Godolphin,
16/27 June 1707.
43 *Ibid.*, 830–1: Godolphin to Marlborough,
24 June 1707.
44 *Ibid.*, 834: Godolphin to Marlborough, 27
June 1707.
45 *Ibid.*, 843: Marlborough to the queen, 7/
18 July 1707.
46 Bennett, 'Bishoprics Crisis', 739; Sykes,
'Queen Anne and the Episcopate', 445.
47 Sarah Churchill, *Conduct*, 184.
48 PRO 30/24/20, pt 2, ff. 337–8: [endorsed
'Somers', but not his handwriting] to
Shaftesbury, [?] May 1707.
49 Snyder, *Marlborough–Godolphin Correspondence*, II, 770: Marlborough to Sarah,
4/15 May 1707.
50 *Ibid.*, 790: Marlborough to Sarah, 22
May/2 June 1707.
51 *Ibid.*, 829 and n. 3: Marlborough to
Sarah, 23 June/4 July 1707.
52 Blenheim E 18: queen to Sarah, teusday
night [17 June 1707].
53 Blenheim E 18: queen to Sarah,
Wednesday noon [18 June 1707].
54 Blenheim G I 7: Sarah to the queen, 13
July 1707.
55 Blenheim E 18: queen to Sarah,
Wednesday noon [16 July 1707].
56 Blenheim G I 7: Sarah to the queen, 18
July 1707.
57 Blenheim G I 7: Sarah to the queen, 16
October 1709, Windsor Lodge.
58 Blenheim G I 7: Sarah to the queen, 18
July 1707.
59 Churchill, *Marlborough*, II, 284.
60 Brown, *Letters and Diplomatic Instructions*, 227: queen to Duchess of
Marlborough, fryday, five a clock, 18
July 1707 [date in Sarah's hand], printed
from original, Blenheim E 19.
61 Blenheim G I 7: Sarah to the queen,
Munday evening [21 July 1707].
62 Althorp, Marlborough MSS, Book B:
queen to Sarah, Munday [21 July 1707,

Windsor], misdated, Brown, *Letters and
Diplomatic Instructions*, 210, as 1706.
63 Blenheim E 18: queen to Sarah, Saturday
night [9 August 1707].
64 Blenheim G I 7: Sarah to the queen, 10
[August 1707], printed without date,
Private Correspondence, I, 105–6.
65 Blenheim E 19: queen to Sarah, Sunday
between four and five [1 September
1707].
66 Blenheim E 18: queen to Sarah, Saturday
night [9 August 1707], Sarah's endorsement.
67 Sarah Churchill, *Conduct*, 183.
68 Correspondence published in Sarah
Churchill, *Conduct*, 187–90.
69 HMC *Portland*, IV, 545: [Abigail Masham
to Harley] 29 September 1707, London.
70 Snyder, *Marlborough–Godolphin Correspondence*, II, 837: Marlborough to Sarah,
30 June /11 July 1707.
71 *Ibid.*, 884: Godolphin to Marlborough, 16
August 1707, Windsor.
72 *Ibid.*, 886–7: Marlborough to Godolphin,
to Sarah, 18/29 August 1707.
73 Bennett, 'Bishoprics Crisis', 740; Snyder,
'Godolphin and Harley', 262.
74 Snyder, *Marlborough–Godolphin Correspondence*, II, 890–1: Godolphin to Marlborough, 25 August 1707, Windsor.
75 Bennett, 'Bishoprics Crisis', 740–1;
Snyder, 'Formulation of Foreign and
Domestic Policy', 160n, 73.
76 Blenheim B II 32: queen to Marlborough,
25 August 1707, Windsor, misdated as
early September in Brown, *Letters and
Diplomatic Instructions*, 230–1.
77 Blenheim B II 32: Marlborough to the
queen, 4/15 September 1707, printed by
Coxe, *Marlborough*, III, 373–5.
78 Blenheim B II 32: Godolphin to the
queen, Thursday, 11 September 1707,
partly printed, HMC *Marlborough*, 41b.
79 BM, Add. MSS 52,540 L: queen to
Godolphin, Fryday, 12 September 1707,
partly printed, Brown, *Letters and
Diplomatic Instructions*, 231–2.
80 Snyder, *Marlborough–Godolphin Correspondence*, II, 907: Marlborough to Sarah,
8/19 September 1707.
81 Blenheim G I 7: Sarah to the queen, 14
September 1707.
82 Blenheim E 19: queen to Sarah, Teusday
evening [16 September 1707], partly
printed, Brown, *Letters and Diplomatic
Instructions*, 229, as 1708–9.

83 A. W. Thibadeau, ed., *Catalogue of the Collection of Autograph Letters and Historical Documents formed . . . by Alfred Morrison* (London, 1890), IV, 148: Marlborough to the queen, 26 September/7 October 1707, The Hague.

84 Snyder, *Marlborough–Godolphin Correspondence*, II, 932: Godolphin to Marlborough, 7 October 1707.

85 *Ibid.*, 834: Godolphin to Marlborough, 27 June 1707.

86 *Ibid.*, 834: Marlborough to Godolphin, 7/18 July 1707.

87 HMC *Portland*, IV, 74–5: Godolphin to Harley, 25 October [1707], misdated 1703 by editor.

88 Blenheim G I 7: Sarah to the queen, 29 October [1707], cf. *Private Correspondence*, I, 106–12.

89 Blenheim E 19: queen to Sarah, 30 November [1707], Kensington.

90 Blenheim G I 7: Sarah to the queen, 27 December 1707.

Chapter 10:   The Failure of Moderation

1 Burnet, *History of His Own Time*, V, 340.

2 *Ibid.*, 359–60; Walcott, *English Politics*, 129–32.

3 Burnet, *History of His Own Time*, V, 342–7; Walcott, *English Politics*, 132–5.

4 G. F. James, 'Some Further Aspects of Admiralty Administration, 1689–1714', *BIHR*, XVII (1939–40), 15–16.

5 Sharp, *Life of John Sharp*, I, 302: Archbishop Sharp's diary, 13 November 1707.

6 Holmes, *British Politics*, 203.

7 Bennett, 'Bishoprics Crisis', 743; Snyder, 'Godolphin and Harley', 265; cf. Godfrey Davies, 'The Seamy Side of Marlborough's War', *HLQ*, XV (1951), 38: James Brydges to William Cadogan, 24 December 1707.

8 SP 34/8, f. 160: Shrewsbury to Charles de la Faye, 5 October 1706, Heythorp.

9 Sharp, *Life of John Sharp*, I, 323: Archbishop Sharp's diary, 16 December 1707; Geoffrey Holmes and William Speck, 'The Fall of Harley in 1708 Reconsidered', *EHR*, LXXX (1965), 679–80.

10 Holmes and Speck, 'Fall of Harley', 685.

11 *Ibid.*, 687–9; William Montagu, Duke of Manchester, *Court and Society from Elizabeth to Anne* (London, 1864), II, 295: Addison to Lord Manchester, 27 February 1708.

12 See Godfrey Davies, 'The Fall of Harley in 1708', *EHR*, LXVI (1951), 246–54.

13 Cobbett, *Parliamentary History*, VI, 610.

14 Bennett, 'Bishoprics Crisis', 745: Sir John Cropley to Shaftesbury, 15 December 1707.

15 Holmes and Speck, 'Fall of Harley', 683–4.

16 *Ibid.*, 677–8.

17 Davies, 'Fall of Harley', 246–54.

18 Snyder, 'Godolphin and Harley', 269.

19 Holmes and Speck, 'Fall of Harley', 686.

20 BM, Loan 29/12: Harley to Marlborough, 28 January 1708.

21 Holmes and Speck, 'Fall of Harley', 686–7.

22 HMC *Bath*, I, 189–90: Harley to Godolphin, 30 January 1708; BM, Loan 29/22: Harley to Marlborough, 1 February 1708.

23 HMC *Bath*, I, 190: Godolphin to Harley, 30 January 1708.

24 PRO 30/24/21, pt 1, ff. 7–8: Sir John Cropley to Shaftesbury, 4 February 1708.

25 Manchester, *Court and Society*, II, 275: Addison to Manchester, 6 February 1708.

26 Holmes and Speck, 'Fall of Harley', 694.

27 Burnet, *History of His Own Time*, V, 353.

28 PRO 30/24/21. pt 1, f. 12: Sir John Cropley to Shaftesbury, 9 February 1708.

29 Holmes and Speck, 'Fall of Harley', 695–6, quoting Sir John Cropley to Shaftesbury, n.d. [19 February 1708].

30 Holmes and Speck, 'Fall of Harley', 697.

31 PRO 30/24/21, pt 1, f. 11: [Sir John Cropley] to Shaftesbury, 9 at night, Tuesday [9 February 1708], London.

32 Blenheim G I 9: Sarah's 'Letter to Mr. Hutchenson' [1713], 19; cf. Althorp, Marlborough MSS, Box III: Sarah's 'A Paper of Mem: given to Mr. Mallet', 24 September 1744.

33 *Wentworth Papers*, 105–6: Peter Wentworth to Raby, 30 January 1710; cf. HMC *10th Report*, pt 4, 49–50: 'Memoirs of Thomas, Sixth Earl of Westmorland',

a lord of the bedchamber to Prince George; cf. HMC *Portland*, V, 646: Auditor Harley's memoirs.

34 McInnes, *Harley*, 121.

35 Snyder, *Marlborough–Godolphin Correspondence*, II, 1045–6: Godolphin to Marlborough, 21 July 1708.

36 Blenheim G I 9: Sarah's 'The Character of Princes' [1715], 111.

37 Longleat, Portland MSS X, ff. 51–2: Harley to Abigail Masham, 10 October 1708.

38 BM, Loan 29/38: the cypher is printed in Elizabeth Hamilton, *The Backstairs Dragon* (London, 1969), 128.

39 Holmes, *British Politics*, 207; cf. Longleat, Portland MSS X, ff. 55–6: [Robert Harley to Abigail Masham] 16 October 1708.

40 Snyder, *Marlborough–Godolphin Correspondence*, II, 1059: Marlborough to Godolphin, 2/13 August 1708; p. 1066: Godolphin to Marlborough, 8 August 1708.

41 HMC *Portland*, IV, 496, 499: Abigail Masham to Robert Harley, 21, 27 July 1708.

42 Longleat, Portland MSS X, ff. 59–60: [Harley to Abigail Masham] 31 October 1708.

43 Boyer, *Queen Anne*, 332; cf. Angus McInnes, 'The Appointment of Harley in 1704', *Historical Journal*, XI (1968), 264, n. 36.

44 McInnes, *Harley*, 87–8.

45 *Hervey Letter Books*, I, 231–2: Lady Hervey to Lord Hervey, 11 March 1707 [1708], London.

46 Cobbett, *Parliamentary History*, VI, 728.

47 BM, Add. MSS 17,677 CCC, f. 337, 340–4: L'Hermitage to States, 5/16, 12/23 March 1708.

48 Cobbett, *Parliamentary History*, VI, 729.

49 Blenheim G I 9: Sarah's 'The Character of Princes' [1715], 109–10; cf. Burnet, *History of His Own Time*, V, 369.

50 Boyer, *Queen Anne*, 339.

51 BM, Add. MSS 17,677 CCC, f. 406: L'Hermitage to States, 2/13 April 1708.

52 Speck, *Tory and Whig*, 123.

53 Snyder, *Marlborough–Godolphin Correspondence*, II, 957: Godolphin to Marlborough, 19 April 1708.

54 *Ibid.*, 958–9: Godolphin to Marlborough, 22 April 1708.

55 Brown, *Letters and Diplomatic Instructions*, 246: queen to Marlborough, 22 April 1708, Kensington; printed from the original, Blenheim E 18.

56 Coxe, *Marlborough*, IV, 74–6: Marlborough to the queen, 28 April/9 May 1708.

57 Blenheim B 11 32: queen to Marlborough, 4 May [1708], Kensington.

58 Blenheim E 18: queen to Marlborough, 6 May 1708, Kensington; misdated by Brown, *Letters and Diplomatic Instructions*, 248, as 17 May.

59 Snyder, *Marlborough–Godolphin Correspondence*, II, 974–5: Godolphin to Marlborough, 6 May 1708.

60 *Ibid.*, 1029, n. 1.

61 *Ibid.*, 989, n. 3.

62 *Ibid.*, 999: Godolphin to Marlborough, 1 June 1708.

63 McInnes, *Harley*, 115, n. 12.

64 E. M. Thompson, ed., *Letters of Humphrey Prideaux to John Ellis, 1674–1722* (Campden Society, 1875), 198–9: Prideaux to John Ellis, 31 March 1708, Norwich.

65 Snyder, *Marlborough–Godolphin Correspondence*, II, 1022, n. 4; Coxe, *Walpole*, II, 9–11; Murray, *Marlborough Dispatches*, IV, 67; HMC *Portland*, IV, 494.

66 Snyder, *Marlborough–Godolphin Correspondence*, II, 1028: Godolphin to Marlborough, 6 July 1708.

67 *Ibid.*, 1035: Marlborough to Sarah, 12/23 July 1708.

68 *Ibid.*, 1049, n. 1: Marlborough to Sarah, 22 July/2 August 1708.

69 *Ibid.*, 1083–4: Marlborough to George Churchill, *c.* 23 August/3 September 1708.

70 HMC *Mar & Kellie*, 445, 449–50: Mar to the queen, 14, 18 June 1708, Edinburgh.

71 Blenheim B 11 32: queen to Marlborough, 18 June [1708], printed in Brown, *Letters and Diplomatic Instructions*, 249–50.

72 Blenheim B II 32: queen to Marlborough, 22 June 1708, misprinted Brown, *Letters and Diplomatic Instructions*, 250, and misaddressed to Godolphin; cf. HMC *Mar & Kellie*, 453–4: queen to Mar, 24 June 1708, Kensington.

73 Macpherson, *Original Papers*, II, 110: Peterborough to the elector, 3 April 1708.

74 Snyder, *Marlborough–Godolphin Correspondence*, II, 980–1: Marlborough to Godolphin, 13/24 May 1708.

75 *Ibid.*, 985: Godolphin to Marlborough, 17 May 1708.

76 Blenheim B II 32: queen to [Godolphin], Saturday [22 May 1708].

77 Snyder, *Marlborough–Godolphin Correspondence*, II, 1034–5: Marlborough to Sarah, 12/23 July 1708, replying to hers of 16, 18, 22 June.

78 HMC *Portland*, IV, 490, 491: Erasmus Lewis to Robert Harley, 22, 29 May 1708.

79 Snyder, *Marlborough–Godolphin Correspondence*, II, 1056: Godolphin to Marlborough, 30 July 1708.

80 Blenheim B II 32: queen to Marlborough, 22 July 1708, Windsor; partly printed, Brown, *Letters and Diplomatic Instructions*, 253–4; italics represent the queen's emphasis.

81 Blenheim B II 32: queen to Marlborough, 6 July 1708, Windsor; printed Brown, *Letters and Diplomatic Instructions*, 252.

82 Snyder, *Marlborough–Godolphin Correspondence*, II, 1024–5: Marlborough to Sarah, 1/12 July 1708.

83 Blenheim E 19: queen to [Marlborough], 13 July [1708], Windsor; printed Coxe, *Marlborough*, IV, 184.

84 Coxe, *Marlborough*, IV, 182–3: Marlborough to the queen, 12/23 July 1708.

85 Blenheim B II 32: queen to Marlborough, 22 July 1708, Windsor; misprinted by Brown, *Letters and Diplomatic Instructions*, 253–4.

86 Coxe, *Marlborough*, IV, 186–8: Marlborough to the queen, 22 July/2 August 1708.

87 Brown, *Letters and Diplomatic Instructions*, 255–6: queen to Marlborough, [6] August 1708, misdated as 'middle of August' by editor.

88 Blenheim G I 4: queen to Marlborough [Sarah's copy], 27 August 1708, printed Brown, *Letters and Diplomatic Instructions*, 256–8.

89 For this friendship, see H. L. Snyder, 'Daniel Defoe, the Duchess of Marlborough, and the *Advice to the Electors of Great Britain*', *HLQ*, XXIX (1965), 59.

90 Holmes, *British Politics*, 191; cf. Sir Henry Ellis, ed., 'Lord Coningsby's Account of the State of Political Parties during the Reign of Queen Anne', *Archaeologia*, XXXVIII (1860), 11; hereafter cited as Coningsby.

91 Blenheim E 26: Maynwaring to Sarah, Thursday morning [25 February 1708].

92 Blenheim G I 8: Sarah's essay on Harley's dismissal.

93 Hove Central Library, M/1/112/3: privy purse accounts, 14 June 1707 – 30 June 1708.

94 Coxe, *Marlborough*, IV, 45: Sarah to the queen [29 March 1708]; cf. Blenheim G I 7.

95 Blenheim E 19: queen to Sarah, Saturday evening [10 April 1708]; balance printed in Brown, *Letters and Diplomatic Instructions*, 270, as 1709.

96 Blenheim E 15: Sunderland to Sarah, 6 April 1708.

97 *Private Correspondence*, I, 129: Maynwaring to Sarah, [7] April 1708.

98 Chevening MSS, 66 (1): Horatio Walpole to Stanhope, 20 April 1708, Whitehall; cf. Manchester, *Court and Society*, II, 356: Vanbrugh to Manchester, 11 May 1708.

99 Blenheim E 18: queen to Sarah, Saturday morning [22 May 1708].

100 Blenheim B II 32: queen to [Godolphin], Saturday [22 May 1708]; misprinted, Brown, *Letters and Diplomatic Instructions*, 244–5, as February 1708 and misaddressed to Marlborough.

101 Blenheim G I 7: Sarah to the queen, 7 July [1708], partly printed without date, Green, *Sarah*, 313–14.

102 Frank H. Ellis, ed., *Poems on Affairs of State*, VII: *1704–1715* (New Haven, Conn., 1975), 309 ff.

103 Green, *Sarah*, 318–21: Sarah to the queen, 26 July 1708.

104 Snyder, *Marlborough–Godolphin Correspondence*, II, 1073: Marlborough to Sarah, 12/23 August 1708.

105 Lediard, *John, Duke of Marlborough*, II, 273.

106 BM, Add. MSS 17,677 CCC, f. 537: L'Hermitage to States, 20/31 August 1708, London.

107 Blenheim G I 7: Sarah to the queen, n.d. [Monday, 16 August 1708].

108 Snyder, *Marlborough–Godolphin Correspondence*, II, 1069: Marlborough to Sarah, 9/20 August 1708.

109 Sarah Churchill, *Conduct*, 219: Sarah to the queen, n.d. [21 August 1708].

110 Blenheim G I 7: queen to Sarah, Sunday [22 August 1708], printed without date, Brown, *Letters and Diplomatic Instructions*, 258.

111 Sarah Churchill, *Conduct*, 220–2: Sarah to the queen, n.d. [23 August 1708].

112 Blenheim G I 4: queen to Marlborough [Sarah's copy], 27 August 1708, printed, Brown, *Letters and Diplomatic Instructions*, 256–8; Churchill, *Marlborough*, II, 421.

113 Blenheim E 26: Maynwaring to Sarah, Monday eleven a'clock [30 August 1708].

114 Blenheim E 27: Maynwaring to Sarah, Saturday morning [4 September 1708].

115 Blenheim G I 8: Sarah's 'Heads of the Conversation with Mrs. Morley, 9 September 1708', printed Coxe, *Marlborough*, IV, 210–14.

116 Hove Central Library, Wolseley Papers, M/1/112/4, 5: Sarah's privy purse accounts, from 30 June 1708 –11 January 1710.

117 Snyder, *Marlborough–Godolphin Correspondence*, II, 1016, n. 4; cf. BM, Loan 29/195, ff. 113–14: [Erasmus Lewis] to Harley, 30 September 1708.

118 BM, Add. MSS 6,309, f. 26v: extract from *London Gazette*, no. 4484.

119 Snyder, *Marlborough–Godolphin Correspondence*, II, 1124: Godolphin to Marlborough, 4 October 1708.

120 BM, Loan 29/195, f. 115: [Erasmus Lewis] to Harley, 5 October 1708.

121 *Cal. Treas. Books*, XXIII (1709), 183.

122 BM, Egerton 2,678, ff. 6–11: Sarah's privy purse accounts, entry for 2 January 1707.

123 Morgan, *English Political Parties*, 350, n. 1, quoting Lord Dartmouth.

124 BM, Add. MSS 17,677 CCC, f. 614: L'Hermitage to States, 29 October/9 November 1708, London.

125 Snyder, *Marlborough–Godolphin Correspondence*, II, 1139: Godolphin to Sarah, 25 October 1708.

126 Blenheim G I 7: Sarah to the queen, 26 October 1708, Windsor Lodge, and Sarah's endorsement.

127 Burnet, *History of His Own Time*, V, 391.

128 Rae Blanchard, ed., *Correspondence of Richard Steele* (Oxford, 1941), 242–3: Steele to Mrs Steele, 28 October 1708, Kensington.

129 Godfrey Davies, 'The Seamy Side of Marlborough's War', 40–1: Brydges to Cadogan, 29 October 1708.

Chapter 11:   The Triumph of the Whigs

1 HMC *Portland*, IV, 510–11: Abigail Masham to Harley, 6 November 1708.

2 *Private Correspondence*, I, 412–13: Sarah's account of the queen and Mrs Masham.

3 Blenheim E 19: queen to Sarah, n.d. [28 October 1708], printed Brown, *Letters and Diplomatic Instructions*, 263.

4 *Private Correspondence*, I, 415–16: Sarah's account of the queen and Mrs Masham.

5 Morgan, *English Political Parties*, 355.

6 Sharp, *Life of John Sharp*, I, 332: Archbishop Sharp's diary, 14 November 1708.

7 Blenheim E 19: queen to Sarah, Munday [6 December 1708].

8 Blenheim E 19: queen to Sarah, Munday [6 December 1708], printed Snyder, *Marlborough–Godolphin Correspondence*, II, 1163, n. 2.

9 Morgan, *English Political Parties*, 353.

10 *Vernon Correspondence*, III, 367: Vernon to Shrewsbury, 30 October 1708; G. F. James and J. J. Sutherland Shaw, 'Admiralty Administration and Personnel, 1619–1714', *BIHR*, XIV (1936–7), 24.

11 BM, Add. MSS 17,677 CCC, ff. 168v–169: L'Hermitage to States, 2/13 November 1708, London.

12 *Ibid.*, f. 683v: L'Hermitage to States, 16/27 November 1708; for Wharton's role in Ireland, see Lewis A. Dralle, 'Kingdom in Reversion: The Irish Viceroyalty of the Earl of Wharton, 1708–1710', *HLQ*, XV (1951), 393–431.

13 Snyder, *Marlborough–Godolphin Correspondence*, II, 1158: Marlborough to Sarah, 22 November/3 December 1708.

14 Blenheim E 15: Sunderland to Sarah, 9 August 1708, Althorp.

15 *Swift Correspondence*, I, 115: Swift to Archbishop King, 30 November 1708.

16 For the most detailed account, see H. L. Snyder, 'Queen Anne versus the Junto: The Effort to Place Orford at the Head of the Admiralty in 1709', *HLQ*, XXXV (1972), 323–42.

17 Longleat, Portland MSS X, ff. 55–6:

[Harley to Abigail Masham] 16 October 1708.

18 HMC *Portland*, IV, 511: Abigail Masham to Harley, 6 November 1708.

19 *Ibid.*, 524: Abigail Masham to Harley, 9 August 1709.

20 *Ibid.*, 525: Abigail Masham to Harley, 4 September 1709.

21 BM, Loan 29/38: Abigail Masham to Harley, Teusday night, twelve aclock.

22 *Wentworth Papers*, 70: Peter Wentworth to Raby, 11 January 1709, London.

23 For the following paragraphs, see H. L. Snyder, 'The Duke of Marlborough's Request of his Captain-Generalcy for Life, a Re-examination', *Journal of the Society for Army Historical Research*, XLV (1967), 67–83.

24 Burnet, *History of His Own Time*, V, 149, Dartmouth's note.

25 *Ibid.*, 416, Dartmouth's note.

26 Herts. R.O., Panshanger D/EP/F 63, f. 24: Marlborough to Cowper [30 June]/11 July 1709.

27 Snyder, *Marlborough–Godolphin Correspondence*, III, 1252, n. 4.

28 *Wentworth Papers*, 85–6: Peter Wentworth to Raby, 9 May 1709.

29 Snyder, *Marlborough–Godolphin Correspondence*, III, 1346: Godolphin to Marlborough, 18 August 1709, Windsor.

30 For The Hague negotiations, see Werner Reese, *Das Ringen um Frieden und Sicherheit in den Entscheidungsjahren des Spanischen Erbfolgekrieges, 1708 bis 1709* (Munich, 1933).

31 Snyder, *Marlborough–Godolphin Correspondence*, III, 1250–1: Marlborough to Sarah, 8/19 May 1709.

32 Godfrey Davies and Marion Tinling, 'Letters from James Brydges to Henry St. John', *HLB*, IX (1936), 124: Brydges to St John, 11 June 1709.

33 BM, Add. MSS 57,861, ff. 73–4: Godolphin to Coningsby, Thursday night, 2 June [1709].

34 Snyder, 'Godolphin and Harley', 258.

35 Burnet, *History of His Own Time*, VI, 112, Dartmouth's note.

36 Snyder, 'Marlborough's Request', 75.

37 *Wentworth Papers*, 82: Peter Wentworth to Raby, 5 April 1709, London.

38 Blenheim G I 7: Sarah's essay on her dismissal.

39 BM, Add. MSS 31,143, ff. 335–6: Isabella Arundell to Raby, 31 May 1709; ff. 369–70: Lady Isabella Wentworth to Raby, 3 June 1709.

40 Chevening MSS, 34 (5): James Craggs to Stanhope, 5 April 1709, London.

41 *Wentworth Papers*, 92, 98: Peter Wentworth to Raby, 1 July, 22 August 1709.

42 Blenheim E 18: queen to Sarah, Wensday night [24 July 1709].

43 *Lady Cowper's Diary*, 39–40; cf. Sykes, 'Queen Anne and the Episcopate', 454; *Journal to Stella*, 597, entry for 7 January 1713: 'The Bishop of Ossory will not be Bishop of Hereford, to the great grief of himself and his Wife.'

44 Sarah Churchill, *Conduct*, 224: Sarah dates this letter in the *Conduct* as 26 October 1709, but Sarah's manuscript copy of her reply is dated 6 August. I have accepted the earlier date.

45 Blenheim G I 7: Sarah to the queen, 6 August 1709, St James's.

46 BM, Add. MSS 57,861, f. 123: Robert Walpole to Coningsby, 3 September 1709, Whitehall.

47 *Private Correspondence*, I, 251: Maynwaring to Sarah, Monday evening [August 1709].

48 Snyder, *Marlborough–Godolphin Correspondence*, III, 1350: Godolphin to Sarah, 20 August 1709, Windsor.

49 BM, Loan 29/195, f. 178: [Abigail Masham to Harley] 14 September 1709.

50 Blenheim G I 8: Sarah's 'An account of a conversation with the Queen when she refused to give me an inconsiderable Lodging, to make a clean way to mine'.

51 Blenheim G I 7: Sarah to the queen, 16 October 1709, Windsor Lodge.

52 Snyder, 'Marlborough's Request', 73–4: Marlborough to the queen, 29 September/10 October 1709.

53 Blenheim B II 32: queen to Marlborough, 25 October 1709, Windsor; partly printed, Brown, *Letters and Diplomatic Instructions*, 285–6.

54 Blenheim G I 7: Sarah to the queen, 26 October 1709, St Albans.

55 Blenheim E 18: queen to Sarah, Thursday noon [27 October 1709], Windsor; printed Brown, *Letters and Diplomatic Instructions*, 286, without date.

56 Blenheim G I 4: Sarah to Maynwaring, Thursday, 3 November [1709].

57 Blenheim G I 7: 'Second part of Sarah's Narrative', 29 October 1709.

58 Blenheim E 19: queen to Sarah, Munday morning [7 November 1709].

59 Blenheim E 18: queen to Sarah, fryday night [11 November 1709], Kensington.

60 *Private Correspondence*, I, 240–6: Sarah to the queen [12 November] 1709.

61 *Private Correspondence*, I, 270: Maynwaring to Sarah [18 November 1709].

62 G. V. Bennett, *White Kennett, Bishop of Peterborough* (London, 1957), 105.

Chapter 12: The Queen's Revenge

1 For a complete account, see Geoffrey Holmes, *The Trial of Doctor Sacheverell* (London, 1973).

2 Burnet, *History of His Own Time*, V, 435.

3 *Ibid.*, 446, quoting the queen.

4 Trevelyan, *England under Queen Anne*, III, 75.

5 *Ibid.*, 69.

6 Ottocar Weber, *Der Friede von Utrecht* (Gotha, 1891), 8, n. 1.

7 AAE, CP Angleterre 230, f. 48: Gaultier to Torcy, 21 January 1710 NS, London; see Churchill, *Marlborough*, II, 673, n. 1, for wheat prices, 1706–14.

8 AAE, CP Angleterre 230, ff. 26, 72: Gaultier to Torcy, 10 January, 18 February 1710 NS, London.

9 Davies, 'The Seamy Side of Marlborough's War', 21–44.

10 Feiling, *Tory Party*, 513.

11 HMC *Bath*, I, 191: Shrewsbury to Harley, 6 May, 29 July 1708; cf. Longleat, Portland MSS X, ff. 55–6: [Harley to Abigail Masham] 16 October 1708; Somerville, *King of Hearts*, 254–5.

12 *Private Correspondence*, II, 126.

13 Snyder, *Marlborough–Godolphin Correspondence*, III, 1327–8: Godolphin to Marlborough, 29 July 1709.

14 Holmes, *British Politics*, 215–16, 226; for Somerset's career, see A. A. Locke, *The Seymour Family* (London, 1911), 148–92.

15 C. L. Hopper, *Notes and Queries*, 2nd series, IV, 305, quoting the Birch MSS memoranda of 14 June 1754.

16 For this influence, see Eric Cregeen, 'The Changing Role of the House of Argyll in the Scottish Highlands', in *Scotland in the Age of Improvement*, ed. N. T. Phillipson and Rosalind Mitchison (Edinburgh, 1970), 5–23.

17 Coxe, *Marlborough*, IV, 185: Marlborough to Sarah, 2 August 1708; McInnes, *Harley*, 118–19, n. 26.

18 AAE, CP Angleterre 230, ff. 65, 67, 68, 71, 93: Gaultier to Torcy, 28 January, 4, 7,

15 February, 4 March 1710 NS, London; Klopp, *Der Fall des Hauses Stuart*, XIII, 377; *Wentworth Papers*, 102.

19 BM, Add. MSS 31,143, ff. 327–8: Peter Wentworth to Raby, 8 April 1709.

20 Burnet, *History of His Own Time*, V, 354, Dartmouth's note.

21 Snyder, *Marlborough–Godolphin Correspondence*, III, 1408.

22 Macpherson, *Original Papers*, II, 283: Carte Papers, 10 April 1749.

23 Coxe, *Marlborough*, V, 131–2: Somers to Marlborough, 16 January 1710.

24 Herts. R.O., Panshanger D/EP/F 63, f. 29–30: Cowper to Marlborough, 17 January 1710, London; partly quoted, Snyder, *Marlborough–Godolphin Correspondence*, III, 1410.

25 Herts. R.O., Panshanger D/EP/F 63, f. 31: Marlborough to Cowper, 18 January [1710].

26 Blenheim E 25: Maynwaring to Sarah, Thursday four in the afternoon [19 January 1710].

27 Snyder, *Marlborough–Godolphin Correspondence*, III, 1411–12: Godolphin to Marlborough, 19 January 1710.

28 Lediard, *John, Duke of Marlborough*, III, 21; Klopp, *Der Fall des Hauses Stuart*, XIII, 378: Hoffmann's report of 24 January/4 February 1710.

29 Coningsby, 11.

30 Holmes, *British Politics*, 209.

31 *Lockhart Papers*, 316–17.

32 *Wentworth Papers*, 102–4: Peter Wentworth to Raby, 24 January 1710, London.

33 Clara Buck and Godfrey Davies, 'Letters on Godolphin's Dismissal in 1710', *HLQ*, III (1940), 237: James Brydges to John Drummond, 24 August 1710; cf. AAE, CP Angleterre 230, f. 71: Gaultier to Torcy, 14 February 1710 NS, London; *Wentworth Papers*, 103; Holmes, *British Politics*, 209–10.

34 *Hamilton Diary*, 72, n. 16, quoting con-

temporary newsletter of 28 January 1710.

35 Holmes, *British Politics*, 209–10.

36 Snyder, 'Marlborough's Request', 80.

37 Snyder, *Marlborough–Godolphin Correspondence*, III, 1414: Somers to Marlborough, 19 January 1710.

38 *Ibid.*, 1412: Marlborough to the queen [18 January 1710].

39 Sarah Churchill, *Conduct*, 232–4: Marlborough to the queen [18 January 1710].

40 Snyder, *Marlborough–Godolphin Correspondence*, III, 1415–16: Godolphin to Marlborough, 21 January 1710.

41 *Ibid.*, 1417: Godolphin to Marlborough, 21 January 1710.

42 Blenheim E 27: Maynwaring to Sarah, Sunday noon [22 January 1710].

43 *Hamilton Diary*, 63.

44 BM, Add. MSS 17,677 DDD, ff. 391v–392: L'Hermitage to States, 24 January/4 February 1710.

45 *Wentworth Papers*, 104–6: Peter Wentworth to Raby, 27 January 1710, London.

46 Snyder, *Marlborough–Godolphin Correspondence*, III, 1494: Godolphin to Marlborough, 12 May 1710.

47 Legrelle, *La Diplomatie française*, V, 501–65.

48 Coxe, *Marlborough*, V, 149–51.

49 Lever, *Godolphin*, 225: Sunderland to Marlborough, 21 February 1710.

50 *Hamilton Diary*, 6.

51 *Wentworth Papers*, 111: Peter Wentworth to Raby, 17 February 1710, London.

52 Holmes, *Trial of Sacheverell*, 170.

53 Klopp, *Der Fall des Hauses Stuart*, XIII, 429: Hoffmann's dispatch of 5 May 1710 NS; cf. AAE, CP Angleterre 230, f. 114: Gaultier to Torcy, 21 March 1710 NS.

54 HMC *Portland*, IV, 532: Abigail Masham to Harley [February 1710].

55 *Wentworth Papers*, 146–8: Peter Wentworth to Raby [end of September 1710].

56 HMC *Bath*, I, 199: Shrewsbury to Harley, 20 October 1710, quoting the queen.

57 Holmes, *British Politics*, 187.

58 Klopp, *Der Fall des Hauses Stuart*, XIII, 422: Gallas's report of 29 April 1710 NS.

59 Snyder, *Marlborough–Godolphin Correspondence*, III, 1437: Godolphin to Marlborough, 17 March 1710.

60 *Ibid.*, 1445: Marlborough to Sarah, 24 March/4 April 1710.

61 AAE, CP Angleterre 230, ff. 94, 117: Gaultier to Torcy, 7 March, 1 April 1710 NS, London.

62 *Ibid.*, ff. 118, 119, 120, 122, 123: Gaultier to Torcy, 4, 8, 11, 18, 22 April 1710 NS; see *A Collection of Addresses . . . presented . . . since the Impeachment of the Rev. Dr. Henry Sacheverell* (London, 1711).

63 Coxe, *Marlborough*, V, 278; for the Jacobite sympathies of Beaufort and his family, see P. S. D. Thomas, 'Jacobitism in Wales', *Welsh Historical Review* (1963), 282.

64 Blenheim G I 9: Sarah's 'Letter to Mr. Hutchenson' (1713), ff. 26–7.

65 Althorp, Marlborough MSS, Book B: queen to Sarah, Munday night [3 April 1710], printed Brown, *Letters and Diplomatic Instructions*, 301.

66 Althorp, Marlborough MSS, Book B: Sarah to the queen, 6 April 1710.

67 Blenheim G I 8: Sarah's 'The Account of a conversation with the Queen upon Good Friday, 1710'. The 6th of April was actually Maundy Thursday.

68 *Hamilton Diary*, 25.

69 Blenheim G I 9: Sarah's 'Letter to Mr. Hutchenson' (1713), f. 29.

70 Althorp, Marlborough MSS, Book B: queen to Sarah, three a clock [7 April 1710], Kensington.

71 Holmes, *British Politics*, 208, quoting Poulett to Strafford, 20 December 1711.

72 *Ibid.*, 207, quoting Harley's memorandum of 20 May 1710.

73 Blenheim B II 32: queen to Godolphin, 13 April [1710], St James's; printed Brown, *Letters and Diplomatic Instructions*, 302–3.

74 J. H. Plumb, 'The Organization of the Cabinet in the Reign of Queen Anne', *TRHS*, 5th series, VII (1957), 153.

75 *Private Correspondence*, I, 311–12: Maynwaring to Sarah, 21 April 1710.

76 *Ibid.*, 321: Maynwaring to Sarah [19 April 1710], quoting Godolphin.

77 Coxe, *Marlborough*, V, 217: Godolphin to the queen, 15 April 1710.

78 Burnet, *History of His Own Time*, V, 456, and Dartmouth's note.

79 Snyder, *Marlborough–Godolphin Correspondence*, III, 1463: Godolphin to Sarah, 17 April 1710.

80 *Private Correspondence*, I, 320–3: Maynwaring to Sarah, Wensday night [19 April 1710].

81 *Hamilton Diary*, 8.

82 Snyder, *Marlborough–Godolphin Correspondence*, III, 1478: Godolphin to Sarah, 29 April 1710.

83 Blenheim G I 4: Marlborough to the queen [13]/24 April 1710; cf. Coxe, *Walpole*, II, 11: Marlborough to Walpole, 13/24 April 1710.

84 Snyder, *Marlborough–Godolphin Correspondence*, III, 1461, n. 6.

85 *Ibid.*, 1465: Godolphin to Marlborough, 18 April 1710; *Private Correspondence*, I, 339–41: Maynwaring to Sarah, n.d. [*c.* 18 April 1710]; Coxe, *Walpole*, II, 13–14: Walpole to Marlborough, 18 April 1710.

86 Coxe, *Walpole*, II, 17: Walpole to Marlborough, 12 May 1710.

87 *Ibid.*, 23: Walpole to Marlborough, 26 May 1710.

88 *Ibid.*, 21: Marlborough to Walpole, 1/12 June 1710.

89 Klopp, *Der Fall des Hauses Stuart*, XIII, 430: Hoffmann's dispatch of 13 May 1710 NS.

90 Snyder, *Marlborough–Godolphin Correspondence*, III, 1485: Godolphin to Marlborough, 5 May 1710.

91 *Ibid.*, 1500: Godolphin to Marlborough, 19 May 1710.

92 *Ibid.*, 1493: Godolphin to Marlborough, 12 May 1710.

93 Burnet, *History of His Own Time*, VI, 9, Dartmouth's note.

94 Snyder, *Marlborough–Godolphin Correspondence*, III, 1511–13: Godolphin to Sarah, 1 June 1710, quoting both Newcastle and Poulett.

95 HMC *Portland*, IV, 542–3: Poulett to Harley, 7 June 1710.

96 Snyder, *Marlborough–Godolphin Correspondence*, III, 1515–16: Godolphin to Marlborough, 2 June 1710.

97 Coxe, *Marlborough*, V, 263: Queen to Godolphin, 13 June 1710.

98 Burnet, *History of His Own Time*, VI, 9, Dartmouth's note.

99 Blenheim G I 7: Sarah to the queen, 7 June 1710.

100 Blenheim G I 7: Sarah to the queen, n.d. [13 June 1710].

101 Blenheim G I 4: Sarah's essay on Marlborough's letter to Godolphin concerning Sunderland's removal.

102 Blenheim G I 7: Sarah to the queen, n.d. [13 June 1710].

103 Snyder, *Marlborough–Godolphin Correspondence*, III, 1522: Marlborough to Godolphin, 9/20 June 1710.

104 *Ibid.*, 1526–1527: Godolphin to Marlborough, 13 June 1710.

105 HMC *Rutland*, II, 190: Lady Russell to Lady Granby, 15 June 1710.

106 Blenheim B II 32: queen to Godolphin, Teusday, 13 June 1710, printed Brown, *Letters and Diplomatic Instructions*, 303.

107 Blenheim B II 32: queen to Godolphin, Wensday morning nine a'clock [14 June 1710], printed Brown, *Letters and Diplomatic Instructions*, 304.

108 See John C. Rule, 'France and the Preliminaries to the Gertruydenberg Conference', in *Studies in Diplomatic History*, ed. Ragnhild Hatton and M. S. Anderson (London, 1970), 97–115.

109 *Hamilton Diary*, 9.

110 *Ibid.*

111 *Wentworth Papers*, 120–1: Peter Wentworth to Raby, 30 June 1710; Coxe, Walpole, II, 29: Walpole to Townshend, 16 June 1710; Buck and Davies, 'Letters on Godolphin's Dismissal', 230: James Brydges to Geo. Brydges, 17 June 1710.

112 *Hamilton Diary*, 11.

113 B. W. Hill, 'The Change of Government and the "Loss of the City", 1710–1711', *Economic History Review*, 2nd series, XXIV (1971), 401, n. 3, quoting Harley's memorandum of 3 July 1710.

114 Snyder, *Marlborough–Godolphin Correspondence*, III, 1544: Godolphin to Sarah, 26 June 1710.

115 *Ibid.*, 1549: Godolphin to Marlborough, 29 June 1710.

116 H. L. Snyder, 'The British Diplomatic Service during the Godolphin Ministry', in *Studies in Diplomatic History*, ed. Hatton and Anderson, 65.

117 Blenheim G II 32: queen to Godolphin, Sunday night, 25 June 1710.

118 Felix Salomon, *Geschichte des letzten Ministeriums Königin Annas von England, 1710–1714, und der englischen Thronfolgefrage* (Gotha, 1894), 35; Klopp, *Der Fall des Hauses Stuart*, XIII, 477–9; HMC *Astley*, 202: Joanna Cutts to [?], [August 1710], quoting Cressett.

119 Snyder, *Marlborough–Godolphin Correspondence*, III, 1510: Godolphin to Marlborough, 29 May 1710.

120 HMC *Bath*, I, 198: Shrewsbury to Harley, 22 July 1710.

121 Salomon, *Letzten Ministeriums*, 30;

122 Churchill, *Marlborough*, IV, 249–52; Coxe, *Marlborough*, V, 280; Coxe, *Walpole*, II, 24–9.

123 Salomon, *Letzten Ministeriums*, 64–5; Churchill, *Marlborough*, IV, 253–5; NSA, Hannover 93, 12A, 11–7, ff. 8–9: Bothmer to Townshend, 15 July 1710 NS, The Hague.

124 Klopp, *Der Fall des Hauses Stuart*, XIII, 569 and n. 1.

125 HMC *Portland*, II, 211: Harley to Newcastle, 1 July 1710.

126 *Hamilton Diary*, Blenheim Index, 121; cf. Buck and Davies, 'Letters on Godolphin's Dismissal', 231: Brydges to Stair, 31 July 1710.

127 Dartmouth's cabinet minute for 2 July 1710, quoted in Snyder, *Marlborough–Godolphin Correspondence*, III, 1548, n. 4; cf. Holmes, *British Politics*, 196.

128 For this suspicion, see Snyder, *Marlborough–Godolphin Correspondence*, III, 1577: Godolphin to Marlborough, 24 July 1710; Klopp, *Der Fall des Hauses Stuart*, XIII, 470; Churchill, *Marlborough*, IV, 254; AAE, CP Angleterre, 230, f. 211: Gaultier to Torcy, 18 July 1710 NS, London.

129 Davies and Tinling, 'Letters from James Brydges to Henry St. John', 167: St John to Brydges, 7 July 1710; Coningsby, 13.

130 HMC *Bath*, I, 198: Shrewsbury to Harley, 22 July 1710; cf. Somerville, *King of Hearts*, 273.

131 Salomon, *Letzten Ministeriums*, 33: Bonet's report of 4/15 August 1710; cf. BM, Add. MSS 57,861, ff. 141–2: Maynwaring to Coningsby, 1 August 1710: 'I can only inform you that there seems to be an End of all Treaties here & even of the false Professions.'

132 Snyder, *Marlborough–Godolphin Correspondence*, III, 1572: Godolphin to Marlborough, 18 July 1710.

133 *Ibid.*, 1584: Godolphin to Marlborough, 31 July 1710.

134 BM, Add. MSS 57,861, ff. 141–2: Maynwaring to Coningsby, 1 August 1710.

135 HMC *Portland*, II, 213: Harley to Newcastle, 5 August 1710.

136 *Hamilton Diary*, 9.

137 Holmes, *British Politics*, 462, n. 66, citing Harley to Mansell, 1 August 1710; cf. *The Correspondence of Sir Thomas Hanmer*, ed. Sir Henry Bunbury (London, 1838), 127–8: Shrewsbury to Sir Thomas Hanmer, 2 August 1710.

138 HMC *Portland*, II, 213: Harley to Newcastle, 5 August 1710.

139 Buck and Davies, 'Letters on Godolphin's Dismissal', 232, n. 31, 235: Brydges to John Drummond, 24 August 1710.

140 BM, Loan 29/196, f. 67: Somerset to Harley, 6 August 1710.

141 Brown, *Letters and Diplomatic Instructions*, 305: queen to Godolphin, 7 August 1710, Kensington.

142 *Hamilton Diary*, 66.

143 Herts. R.O., Panshanger D/EP/F 56: Somers to Cowper, Tuesday past 3 a clock [8 August 1710]; *ibid.*, 63, ff. 64–5: Sarah to Cowper, 22 September [1710], Althorp; *Wentworth Papers*, 130–1: Peter Wentworth to Raby, 11 August 1710; *Swift Correspondence*, I, 174: Swift to Archbishop King, 9 September 1710.

144 Printed by Lever, *Godolphin*, 241–2.

145 Wm Salt Library, Dartmouth MSS 1778, I, i, f. 134: Somerset to Dartmouth, Tuesday night [8 August 1710].

146 Blenheim B II 32: queen to Marlborough, 8 August 1710, Kensington.

147 Blenheim G I 4: Sarah's essay on Godolphin's dismissal.

148 Burnet, *History of His Own Time*, VI, 10, 144, Dartmouth's notes.

149 Herts. R.O., Panshanger D/EP/F 54, f. 156: Godolphin to Cowper, 28 September 1710, Althorp.

150 Snyder, *Marlborough–Godolphin Correspondence*, III, 1626: Godolphin to Marlborough, 5 September 1710.

151 Trevelyan, *England under Queen Anne*, III, 328–30: Godolphin to '126' [Sir David Hamilton], 17 December 1710.

152 *Hamilton Diary*, 23, 127: Godolphin to Hamilton [*c.* 28 December 1710].

153 Burnet, *History of His Own Time*, VI, 143–4: Dartmouth's note.

154 Sharp, *Life of John Sharp*, I, 323.

155 Snyder, *Marlborough–Godolphin Correspondence*, III, 1497: Godolphin to Marlborough, 16 May 1710.

156 *Wentworth Papers*, 123–4, 152: Peter Wentworth to Raby, 18 July, 31 October 1710, London.

157 *Bolingbroke Correspondence*, I, 216–17: St John to Orrery, 18 May 1711.

158 *The Prose Works of Jonathan Swift*, VIII:

Political Tracts, 1713–19, ed. Herbert Davis and Irvin Ehrenpreis (Oxford, 1953), 151.

159 Burnet, *History of His Own Time*, VI, 12, Dartmouth's note.

160 *Lord Cowper's Diary*, 43.

161 HMC *Portland*, V, 467: Harley's 'An Account of Public Affairs', 1/12 July 1714; cf. Oxford to Abigail Harley, 29 July 1714.

162 Buck and Davies, 'Letters on Godolphin's Dismissal', 234: Brydges to Morice, 21 August 1710.

163 *Wentworth Papers*, 138–9: Peter Wentworth to Raby, 25 August 1710.

164 HMC *Portland*, II, 219: Harley to Newcastle, 14 September 1710.

165 Herts. R.O., Panshanger D/EP/F 55, f. 180: Halifax to Cowper, Friday [15 September 1710]; cf. HMC *Portland*, II, 219–20: Harley to Newcastle, 16 September 1710.

166 *Hamilton Diary*, 18; cf. *Addison Correspondence*, 240: Addison to Joshua Dawson, 23 September 1710, London; Burnet, *History of His Own Time*, VI, 12; Buck and Davies, 'Letters on Godolphin's Dismissal', 241: Brydges to Cardonnell, 22 September 1710.

167 Burnet, *History of His Own Time*, VI, 12, Dartmouth's note.

168 *Hamilton Diary*, 7, 78, n. 7.

169 *Lord Cowper's Diary*, 46–7.

170 BM, Add. MSS 57,861, f. 149: Maynwaring to Coningsby, 23 September 1710; cf. Leidiard, *John, Duke of Marlborough*, III, 24.

171 Elizabeth Handasyde, *Granville the Polite* (London, 1935), 107.

172 Snyder, *Marlborough–Godolphin Correspondence*, III, 1591–2: Marlborough to Godolphin, 5/16 August 1710.

173 *Bolingbroke Correspondence*, I, 118, 129–67: St John to Marlborough, 20, 27 March, 27 April 1711.

174 Blenheim B II 15: Brydges to Marlborough, 26 March 1711, London.

175 I. F. Burton, 'The Committee of Council at the War Office: An Experiment in Cabinet Government under Anne', *Historical Journal*, VI (1961), 81–4; H. T. Dickinson, 'Henry St. John: A Reappraisal of the Young Bolingbroke', *Journal of British Studies*, VII (1968), 42.

176 Handasyde, *Granville the Polite*, 107; G. W. Cooke, *Memoirs of Lord Bolingbroke*

(London, 1833), I, 118–19; Thomas Macknight, *The Life of Henry St. John, Viscount Bolingbroke* (London, 1863), 149; cf. Campbell, *Lives of the Lord Chancellors*, IV, 453–4; HMC *Portland*, IV, 536: St John to Harley, 8 March 1710.

177 *Bolingbroke Correspondence*, I, 28: St John to John Drummond, 28 November 1710; Klopp, *Der Fall des Hauses Stuart*, XIV, 673: Robethon to Bernstorff, 21 March 1711 NS, The Hague.

178 Coxe, *Marlborough*, V, 338–50; for a summary of Newcastle's career, see S. N. Nulle, *Thomas Pelham-Holes, Duke of Newcastle* (Philadelphia, 1931), 5–8.

179 *Journal to Stella*, 84.

180 Speck, *Tory and Whig*, 123.

181 *Hamilton Diary*, 8.

182 *Ibid.*, xxxvii; cf. *Bolingbroke Correspondence*, I, 27: St John to John Drummond, 28 November 1710.

183 *Hamilton Diary*, 12.

184 *Ibid.*, 23.

185 Blenheim G I 8: Sarah to '260' [Sir David Hamilton], 26 June [1710], Windsor Lodge.

186 Snyder, *Marlborough–Godolphin Correspondence*, III, 1515: Marlborough to Sarah, 1/12 June 1710.

187 *Hamilton Diary*, 15.

188 *Ibid.*, 16.

189 Blenheim G I 8: Sarah to Sir David Hamilton, 28 November 1710.

190 *Hamilton Diary*, 20.

191 *Ibid.*, 21.

192 Ellis, *Poems on Affairs of State*, VII, 309, n. 16: Sarah to Sir David Hamilton, 6 December [1710], Windsor Lodge, from Blenheim G I 8.

193 *Hamilton Diary*, 20–1.

194 Handasyde, *Granville the Polite*, 108; AAE, CP Angleterre, ff. 124–9: James III to Torcy, 2 December 1713; cf. *Private Correspondence*, II, 118.

195 Churchill, *Marlborough*, IV, 285–6.

196 *Hamilton Diary*, 21.

197 Macpherson, *Original Papers*, II, 240–1: Marlborough to the elector, 2 January 1711, The Hague; cf. Salomon, *Letzten Ministeriums*, 84; for Whig and Hanoverian pressure, see *Lord Cowper's Diary*, 49; Blenheim B II 3: Bothmer to Marlborough, 29 October 1710, The Hague.

198 *Hamilton Diary*, 22–3; for Henrietta's

loss of reputation, see Lever, *Godolphin*, 148–50.

199 *Hamilton Diary*, 23; *Swift Correspondence*, I, 201: Swift to Archbishop King, 30 December 1710.

200 *Hamilton Diary*, 23–4.

201 *Ibid.*, 25.

202 *Ibid.*, 25.

203 Burnet, *History of His Own Time*, VI, 35, Dartmouth's note.

204 *Hamilton Diary*, 26–7.

205 R. Pauli, 'Die Aussichten des Hauses Hannover auf den Englischen Thron in Janre 1711', *Aufsatze zur Englischen*

Geschichte (Leipzig, 1883), 353: Bothmer's dispatch of 12/23 January 1711; cf. *Bolingbroke Correspondence*, I, 77: St John to John Drummond, 23 January 1711.

206 Pauli, 'Die Aussichten', 354; Salomon, *Letzten Ministeriums*, 89.

207 *Hamilton Diary*, 29.

208 Burnet, *History of His Own Time*, VI, 34, Dartmouth's note.

209 Snyder, *Marlborough–Godolphin Correspondence*, III, 1668 and n.: Marlborough to Sarah, 14/25 May 1711.

Chapter 13:   The Peace of Utrecht

1 *Journal to Stella*, 328: 1 August 1711.

2 Burnet, *History of His Own Time*, VI, 32, Dartmouth's note.

3 *Ibid.*, 35, Dartmouth's note.

4 *Hamilton Diary*, 49.

5 *Swift Correspondence*, I, 248: Swift to Archbishop King, 26 August 1711.

6 HMC *Portland*, II, 221: Somerset to Newcastle, 27 September 1710.

7 AAE, CP Angleterre 230, f. 413: Gaultier to Torcy, 13 December 1710 NS, London.

8 *Swift Works*, VIII, 146, 167: 'An Enquiry into the Behaviour of the Queen's Last Ministry'.

9 HMC *Portland*, V, 63: Erasmus Lewis to Oxford, 26 July 1711.

10 *Hamilton Diary*, 57.

11 *Journal to Stella*, 658: 10 April 1713.

12 *Verney Letters*, I, 370: Penelope Vickers to Lord Fermanagh, 19 October 1712.

13 *Hamilton Diary*, 47.

14 *Journal to Stella*, 206: 4 March 1711.

15 Blenheim G I 8: Sarah's notes on the Duke of Shrewsbury.

16 HMC *Bath*, I, 216: queen to Oxford, 15 November [1711].

17 *Hamilton Diary*, 29, quoting Cowper.

18 Burnet, *History of His Own Time*, V, 453: Dartmouth's note.

19 AAE, CP Angleterre 272, ff. 377–82: d'Iberville to Torcy, 20 May 1715 NS, London; NSA, Hannover 93, 12 A, II–11, vol. 1, ff. 370–5: Bothmer to the elector, 30 July/10 August 1714, London; *Journal inédit de Jean-Baptiste Colbert, Marquis de Torcy* (hereafter cited as Torcy, *Journal inédit*), ed. Frédéric Masson (Paris, 1884),

400–1; Pauli, 'Die Aussichten', 352–3; Murray, *Marlborough Dispatches*, V, 330–1, 420, 518; Blenheim B II 15: Shrewsbury to Marlborough, 13, 16, 27 March, 3 April, 29 May, 29 June, 3, 22 August, 14 September 1711.

20 AAE, CP Angleterre 246, ff. 68–73: d'Aumont to Louis XIV, 29, 30 July 1713 NS.

21 Torcy, *Journal inédit*, 355; AAE, CP Angleterre 240, ff. 216–18: Gaultier to Torcy, 3 December 1712 NS, London; 246, ff. 89–93: d'Aumont to Louis XIV, 7 August 1713 NS, London; Charles Eves, *Matthew Prior* (New York, 1939), 222; *Wentworth Papers*, 134: Strafford's 'Caracteres de plusieurs Ministres de la Cour d'Angleterre'. I disagree with Holmes' assessment of Shrewsbury's influence: *British Politics*, 192.

22 HMC *Bath*, I, 216: queen to Oxford, 15 November 1711.

23 AAE, CP Angleterre 246, ff. 68–73: d'Aumont to Louis XIV, 29, 30 July 1713 NS, London; ff. 89–93: 7 August 1713 NS; 254, ff. 37–9: d'Iberville to Torcy, 14 February 1714 NS, London; HMC *Portland*, V, 467: Harley's 'Brief Account of Public Affairs'; Somerville, *King of Hearts*, 293, 309–10; Macpherson, *Original Papers*, II, 479–80: Robethon to Galke, 21 March 1713.

24 *Journal to Stella*, 206: 4 March 1711.

25 HMC *Bath*, I, 223–4: queen to Oxford, Thursday night, 27 November [1712], Windsor.

26 *Hamilton Diary*, 56.

27 H. T. Dickinson, 'The October Club', *HLQ*, XXXIII (1970), 155–73.

28 *Hamilton Diary*, 33–4.

29 G. M. Trevelyan, 'The "Jersey Period" of the Negotiations Leading to the Peace of Utrecht', *EHR*, XLIX (1934), 100–5.

30 Frederick W. Head, *The Fallen Stuarts* (Cambridge, 1901), 158–9.

31 Trevelyan, 'Jersey Period', 102: Gaultier to Torcy, 7 October 1710 NS, London.

32 Torcy, *Journal inédit*, 355.

33 HMC *Portland*, V, 49: Jersey to Oxford, 13 July 1711.

34 Feiling, *Tory Party*, 424; Holmes, *British Politics*, 201.

35 HMC *Portland*, V, 69–70: Jersey to Oxford, 4 August 1711.

36 Holmes, *British Politics*, 201–2: Oxford's draft of 21 August 1711, Oxford's italics; cf. Feiling, *Tory Party*, 425; *Swift Correspondence*, I, 259: Swift to Charles Ford, 8 September 1711.

37 Holmes, *British Politics*, 93; Klopp, *Der Falls des Hauses Stuart*, XIV, 673.

38 Macpherson, *Original Papers*, II, 222; Salomon, *Letzten Ministeriums*, 68–9; *Mémoires du Maréchal de Berwick* (hereafter cited as Berwick, *Mémoires*), vol. LXIV in *Collection des Mémoires Relatifs à l'Histoire de France*, ed. A. Petitot et Monmerqué (Paris, 1828), 219–20; AAE, CP Angleterre 243, f. 139: James to Torcy, 12 October 1712 NS, Chalons; cf. Macpherson, *Original Papers*, II, 417: Thomas Carte's memorandum of 3 March 1724.

39 Burnet, *History of His Own Time*, VI, 43–4: Dartmouth's note.

40 Holmes, *British Politics*, 197, citing Kreyenberg's dispatch of 13/24 March 1711.

41 William Salt Library, Dartmouth MSS 1778, V, 188, f. 134: Dartmouth's cabinet minute, 25 March 1711, St James's.

42 *Ibid.*, f. 153: Dartmouth's cabinet minute, 26 April 1711, St James's.

43 Salomon, *Letzten Ministeriums*, 96: Bothmer's report of 8/19 May 1711; cf. Pauli, 'Die Aussichten', 370.

44 HMC *Portland*, V, 665, for Auditor Harley's account that Somers and Newcastle requested Harley to assume this position.

45 *Swift Correspondence*, I, 222: Swift to Argyle, 16 April 1711, London.

46 HMC *Various Collections*, VIII, 252: William Smytson to John Molesworth,

31 May 1711; *Wentworth Papers*, 201: Peter Wentworth to Raby, 29 May 1711, London.

47 *Hamilton Diary*, 31.

48 Pauli, 'Die Aussichten'; 372; Bothmer's dispatches of 23 June, 7 July 1711 NS, London.

49 SP 84/243, f. 18v: Strafford to St John, 1 January 1712 NS, The Hague.

50 Mark A. Thomson, *The Secretaries of State, 1681–1782* (London, 1968), 20, n. 1.

51 AAE, CP Angleterre 256, ff. 45–7: d'Iberville to Torcy, 19 May 1714 NS, London, quoting Bolingbroke.

52 *Journal to Stella*, 388–9: 20 October 1711.

53 *Report of the Committee of Secrecy, 9 June 1715* (London, 1803), 39.

54 AAE, CP Angleterre 246, f. 56: d'Aumont to Torcy, 21 July 1713 NS, London, quoting Bolingbroke.

55 L. G. Wickham Legg, *Matthew Prior: A Study of his Public Career and Correspondence* (Cambridge, 1921), 149.

56 HMC *Bath*, I, 210–11: queen to Oxford, Wensday night, 19 September [1711].

57 *Ibid.*, 211: queen to Oxford, 20 September [1711].

58 *Bolingbroke Correspondence*, I, 333–7: Shrewsbury to St John, 23, 27 August 1711; cf. D. H. Somerville, 'Shrewsbury and the Peace of Utrecht', *EHR*, XLVII (1932), 646–7.

59 AAE, CP Angleterre 234, f. 18: Mesnager to Torcy, 21 September/2 October, 1711, London; *Mémoires du Marquis de Torcy* (hereafter cited as Torcy, *Mémoires*), vol. LXVII in *Collection des Mémoires Relatifs à l'Histoire de France*, ed. A. Petitot et Monmerqué (Paris, 1828), 60–1; Legg, *Prior*, 164–5.

60 HMC *Bath*, I, 212: queen to Oxford, 24 September 1711.

61 The preliminary articles are printed in *Bolingbroke Correspondence*, I, 374–81, 402–4, and II, 5.

62 Klopp, *Der Fall des Hauses Stuart*, XIV, 175: Hoffmann's dispatch of 5/16 October 1711.

63 *Ibid.*, 181–4.

64 *Ibid.*, 177–8; cf. NSA, Cal. Br. 24, England 107 A, ff. 18–19: Kreyenberg to the elector, 16/27 October 1711, London.

65 Horwitz, *Revolution Politicks*, 222–3, 228–9; cf. *Lady Cowper's Diary*, 18–19.

66 HMC *Portland*, V, 101: Nottingham to Oxford, 16 October 1711.

67 *Ibid.*, 119: Poulett to Oxford, [?] November 1711.
68 Macpherson, *Original Papers*, II, 247–51: Marlborough to the elector, 31 August 1711 NS; elector to Marlborough, 14 September 1711 NS.
69 Churchill, *Marlborough*, IV, 376–7; Trevelyan, *England under Queen Anne*, III, 154.
70 Salomon, *Letzten Ministeriums*, 117.
71 HMC *Bath*, I, 212–13: queen to Oxford, Wensday morning [26 September 1711], Windsor.
72 *Journal to Stella*, 324, 328: entries for 31 July, 7 August 1711.
73 HMC *Bath*, I, 212–13: queen to Oxford, Wensday morning [26 September 1711], Windsor.
74 Legrelle, *La Diplomatie française*, VI, 51; Roderick Geikie and Isabel Montgomery, *The Dutch Barrier, 1705–1719* (Cambridge, 1930), 229; J. G. Stork-Penning, 'The Ordeal of the States – Some remarks on Dutch Politics during the War of the Spanish Succession', *Acta Historiae Neerlandica*, II (Leiden, 1967), 137–41.
75 HMC *Bath*, I, 215: queen to Oxford, 3 November [1711].
76 *Ibid.*, 215–16: queen to Oxford, 9 November [1711].
77 Burnet, *History of His Own Time*, VI, 76–7, and n. citing Oldmixon.
78 *Wentworth Papers*, 222: Lady Strafford to Strafford, 11 December 1711.
79 Burnet, *History of His Own Time*, VI, 77–8; *Hamilton Diary*, 50.
80 HMC *10th Report*, pt 1, 143: Henry Watkins to John Drummond, 3 September 1711 NS, camp before Bouchain.
81 HMC *Bath*, I, 216: queen to Oxford, 15 November [1711].
82 *Ibid.*, 216: queen to Oxford, 9 November [1711].
83 *Ibid.*, 217: queen to Oxford, 19 November [1711].
84 *Wentworth Papers*, 208–10: Lady Strafford, Peter Wentworth to Strafford, 23 November 1711.
85 Blenheim G 19: Sarah's 'The Character of Princes' (1715), 196–7.
86 NSA, Cal. Br. 24, England 109, ff. 4–7: Bothmer to the elector, 24 November/4 December 1711; cf. Salomon, *Letzten Ministeriums*, 128.
87 AAE, CP Angleterre 234, ff. 225–30: Gaultier to Torcy, 4 December 1711 NS; cf. Legg, *Prior*, 171, n. 1.
88 Klopp, *Der Fall des Hauses Stuart*, XIV, 210.
89 Printed in Dumont, *Corps Diplomatique*, VIII (Amsterdam, 1731), 285–7.
90 Klopp, *Der Fall des Hauses Stuart*, XIV, 217: Hoffmann's report of 6/17 December 1711; NSA, Cal. Br. 24, England 109, ff. 47–9: Bothmer to the elector, 7/18 December 1711; *ibid.*, 107 A, ff. 41–2: Kreyenberg to the elector, same date.
91 *Bolingbroke Correspondence*, II, 49–50: Oxford to Strafford, 8/19 December 1711.
92 HMC *Portland*, V, 108, 115–16, 120, 125: Halifax to Oxford, 9, 25 November, 3, 6 December 1711; p. 126: John Toland to Oxford, 7 December 1711.
93 *Journal to Stella*, 294.
94 Klopp, *Der Fall des Hauses Stuart*, XIV, 227, n. 2: Bonet's report.
95 BM, Loan 29/10/15: Oxford's memorandum, 30 August 1712.
96 AAE, CP Angleterre 234, f. 252: Gaultier to Torcy, 18 December 1711 NS.
97 Salomon, *Letzten Ministeriums*, 132: Bothmer to the elector, 21 December 1711 OS; Klopp, *Der Fall des Hauses Stuart*, XIV, 234; Coxe, *Marlborough*, VI, 144–5.
98 Salomon, *Letzten Ministeriums*, 129: Bothmer to the elector, 11/22 December 1711.
99 N. Tindall, *Continuation of the History of England by Rapin de Thoyras* (London, 1745–6), XXVI, 167. The Queen's Speech was written by Oxford and circulated to his cabinet colleagues for their comments: HMC *Portland*, V, 120: Buckingham to Oxford, 1 December 1711.
100 Tindall, *Continuation*, XXVI, 171.
101 *Journal to Stella*, 433: 8 December 1711.
102 *Ibid.*, 433, 435: 8, 9 December 1711.
103 Tindall, *Continuation*, XXVI, 174.
104 For this incident, see Geoffrey Holmes, 'The Hamilton Affair of 1711–1712: A Crisis in Anglo-Scottish Relations', *EHR*, LXXVII (1962), 257–82.
105 *Hamilton Diary*, 34.
106 Burnet, *History of His Own Time*, VI, 89, Dartmouth's note.
107 *Hamilton Diary*, 32.

108 BM, Loan 29/10/16: 'Lyst, 10 December 1711', by Oxford.

109 *Ibid.*, 12/1: [queen to Marlborough] Oxford's draft, 29 December 1711.

110 Coxe, *Marlbourgh*, VI, 153–4: Marlborough to the queen, n.d. [30 December 1711].

111 Salomon, *Letzten Ministeriums*, 133: Bothmer to the elector, 1/12 January 1712, London; M&M, 3 F 114, f. 8: Le Beque to Leopold, 19 January 1712, The Hague.

112 *Hamilton Diary*, 37.

113 *Lord Cowper's Diary*, 53.

114 Salomon, *Letzten Ministeriums*, 135: Bothmer to the elector, 1/12 January 1712, London.

115 *The Works of the Late Rt. Honourable Henry St. John, Lord Viscount Bolingbroke* (London, 1809), I, 15; Burnet, *History of His Own Time*, VI, 94–5; Robert Woodrow, *Analecta* (Edinburgh, Maitland Club, 1843), II, 8; M&M, 3 F 114, f. 8: Le Beque to Leopold, 19 January 1712, The Hague.

116 HMC *Bath*, I, 236: queen to Oxford, Tuesday [21 July 1713].

117 Burnet, *History of His Own Time*, VI, 95, Dartmouth's note.

118 BM, Loan 29/10/21: undated memorandum by Oxford [c. 29 December 1711]; my dating of this memorandum disagrees with that of Holmes, *British Politics*, 491, n. 103.

119 Burnet, *History of His Own Time*, VI, 36–7, Dartmouth's note.

120 *Wentworth Papers*, 252: Peter Wentworth to Strafford, 15 January 1712.

121 *Ibid.*, 280, 285: Lady Strafford to Strafford, 21 March, 15 April 1712.

122 HMC *Bath*, I, 225: queen to Oxford, 3 January 1713.

123 Burnet, *History of His Own Time*, VI, 36–7, Dartmouth's note; *Hamilton Diary*, 35, hints that the queen was beset with spies.

124 *Wentworth Papers*, 232–3: Peter Wentworth to Strafford, 28 December 1711, London.

125 *Journal to Stella*, 304–5.

126 Herbert Davis, ed., *Swift Poetical Works* (Oxford, 1967), 97.

127 *Hamilton Diary*, 37: entry for 10 January 1712.

128 *Wentworth Papers*, 235: Peter

Wentworth to Raby, 22 January 1712.

129 *Hamilton Diary*, 37.

130 *Ibid.*, 39.

131 *Ibid.*, 40.

132 *Wentworth Papers*, 280: Lady Strafford to Strafford, 25 March 1712.

133 Philip Roberts, 'Swift, Queen Anne, and *The Windsor Prophecy*', *Philological Quarterly*, XLIX (1970), 254–8.

134 *Hamilton Diary*, 40.

135 *Ibid.*, 41.

136 *Ibid.*, 43.

137 *Ibid.*, 47.

138 *Ibid.*, 54.

139 AAE, CP Angleterre 241, f. 21: Gaultier to Torcy, 19 January 1712 NS; 237, ff. 28–35: Gaultier to Torcy, 27 January 1712 NS; 241, ff. 54–5: Gaultier to [Polignac], 5 February 1712 NS; 237, ff. 97–9: British government's 'Memoire pour le Sieur Gaultier', 4/15 March 1712, London; cf. Salomon, *Letzten Ministeriums*, 140 and n. 2, citing Oxford to Torcy, 17 January 1712 NS; *Bolingbroke Correspondence*, II, 156: St John to Torcy, 12/23 January 1712.

140 *Wentworth Papers*, 247–8: Peter Wentworth to Strafford, 12 February 1712, misdated January by editor.

141 Cobbett, *Parliamentary History*, VI, 1093.

142 NSA, Hannover 93, 12 A, II–11, ff. 35–8: Bothmer to the elector, 25 March 1712 OS, London; cf. ff. 43–6: Bothmer to Bernstorff, 26 April 1712 NS, The Hague.

143 AAE, CP Angleterre 234, ff. 225–30: Gaultier to Torcy, 4 December 1711 NS, quoting Oxford.

144 *Ibid.*, 237, ff. 28–35: Gaultier to Torcy, 27 January 1712 NS; SP 103/98: Louis XIV to plenipotentiaries, 8 February 1712 NS; *ibid.*, Gaultier's memoire, 23 March 1712; Salomon, *Letzten Ministeriums*, 140–2; Weber, *Der Friede*, 223–4.

145 *Bolingbroke Correspondence*, II, 207–9: memoire of 4/15 March 1712; p. 225: 'Reponce au Memoire apporte par le Sieur Gaultier, 23 March 1712' NS.

146 *Ibid.*, 300: St John to Strafford, 29 April/10 May 1712; cf. Salomon, *Letzten Ministeriums*, 145; Geikie and Montgomery, *Dutch Barrier*, 243. Bolingbroke repeated this thirty years later: *Marchmont Papers*, I, 14.

147 AAE, CP Angleterre 239, ff. 124–6:
Gaultier to Torcy, 29 July 1712 NS.

148 Coxe, *Marlborough*, VI, 186: *Mémoires du Maréchal de Villars*, vol. LXIX in *Collection des Mémoires Relatifs à l'Histoire de France*, ed. A. Petitot et Monmerqué (Paris, 1828), 361–3.

149 Burnet, *History of His Own Time*, VI, 119.

150 Instructions printed in *The Conduct of His Grace the Duke of Ormonde in the Campagne of 1712* (London, 1715), 1–3. This pamphlet was based on official dispatches and was written to Oxford's orders during the 1715 impeachments: AAE, CP Angleterre 269, ff. 21–7: d'Iberville to Torcy, 30 June 1715 NS. It is probably the pamphlet referred to by Lord Harley to Abigail Harley, 23 June 1715, HMC *Portland*, V, 512.

151 *Bolingbroke Correspondence*, II, 314–17: Torcy to St John, 13 May 1712 NS.

152 *Ibid.*, 320: St John to Ormonde, 10 May 1712.

153 Trevelyan, *England under Queen Anne*, III, 251: Gaultier to Torcy, 10/21 May 1712, quoting St John.

154 *Bolingbroke Correspondence*, II, 327: St John to Thomas Harley, 17/28 May 1712; Burnet, *History of His Own Time*, VI, 130; *Memoirs of the Life of his Grace, James, late Duke of Ormonde* (London, 1738), 152; Geikie and Montgomery, *Dutch Barrier*, 274.

155 NSA, Hannover 93, 12 A II–11, ff. 35–8: Bothmer to the elector, 25 March/5 April 1712, London.

156 Weber, *Der Friede*, 464.

157 Cobbett, *Parliamentary History*, VI, 1135–8.

158 *Ibid.*, 1141–51, 1165.

159 BM, Add. MSS 40,621, ff. 112–14: Oxford to Thomas Harley, 12/23 August 1712.

160 Trevelyan, *England under Queen Anne*, III, 242.

161 *Ibid.*, 242–3; Churchill, *Marlborough*, IV, 467–8.

162 McInnes, *Harley*, 154; Trevelyan, *England under Queen Anne*, III, 165; Churchill, *Marlborough*, IV, 332; H. T. Dickinson, *Bolingbroke* (London, 1970), 85.

163 HMC *Portland*, V, 194, 198: St John to Oxford, 28 June, 3 July 1712; cf. AAE, CP Angleterre 255, ff. 179–81:

d'Iberville to Torcy, 3 May 1714 NS, quoting Bolingbroke.

164 *Hamilton Diary*, 43.

165 *Journal to Stella*, 542: 17 June 1712; *Wentworth Papers*, 287, 297, 301: Lord Berkeley of Stratton to Strafford, 15 April, 12 August, 30 September 1712.

166 *Wentworth Papers*, 292: Peter Wentworth to Strafford, 25 July 1712, Windsor.

167 *Journal to Stella*, 557: 18 September 1712; cf. Royal College of Surgeons, Hunter-Baillie Collection, vol. 1–A, f. 4: Oxford to Dr Arbuthnot, 18 September 1712.

168 Blenheim E 27: Maynwaring to Sarah, 29 September [1712].

169 NSA, Cal. Br. 24, England 107 A, ff. 334–5: Kreyenberg to the elector, 3/14 October 1712.

170 Salomon, *Letzten Ministeriums*, 204; NSA, Cal. Br. 24, England 107 A, ff. 334–5, 336–7: Kreyenberg to the elector, 3/14, 7/18 October 1712; HMC *Portland*, V, 231–2: Erasmus Lewis to Thomas Hare, 6 October 1712, Windsor; pp. 234–5: Lewis to Oxford, 13, 14 October 1712.

171 HMC *Bath*, I, 222: queen to Oxford, Tuesday [21 October 1712].

172 HMC *Portland*, V, 465: Oxford's 'Account', 15 June 1714.

173 AAE, CP Angleterre 256, ff. 45–7: d'Iberville to Torcy, 19 May 1714 NS, quoting Bolingbroke.

174 HMC *Bath*, I, 223: queen to Oxford, 13 November [1712], Windsor.

175 Macpherson, *Original Papers*, II, 370–1: 'Mrs White' to Middleton [January 1713]; cf. 479–80: Robethon to Gatke, 21 March 1713.

176 HMC *Portland*, V, 467: Oxford's 'Account', 15 June 1714; Boyer, *Queen Anne*, 650.

177 BM, Loan 29/159: Shrewsbury to Oxford, 4 April 1712.

178 *Hamilton Diary*, 44.

179 Edward Gregg, 'Marlborough in Exile, 1712–1714', *Historical Journal*, XV (1972), 593–618.

180 *Wentworth Papers*, 307: Lady Strafford to Strafford, 19 December 1712, London.

181 *Journal to Stella*, 615, 629: 6, 28 February 1713.

182 Trevelyan, *England under Queen Anne*, III, 185–6.

Chapter 14: The Protestant Succession

1 [William Pittis,] *Queen Anne Vindicated from the Base Aspersions of some late Pamphlets Publish'd to screen the Mismanagers of the Four last Years from Publick Justice* (London, 1714–15); for a complete examination of this topic, see Gregg, 'Was Queen Anne a Jacobite?', 358–75.

2 NSA, Cal. Br. 24, England 113, ff. 26–7, 33–4: Kreyenberg to the elector, 28 February, 10 March 1713 NS; BM, Stowe 225, ff. 163–4: L'Hermitage to Robethon, 25 July 1713 NS.

3 BM, Add. MSS 46,495, ff. 21–2, 31–5: James Dempster to Cardinal Gualterio, 17 December 1713, 21 January 1714, St Germain. Oxford was responsible for the pardon of John Stafford, the Pretender's secretary and an active Jacobite agent in England. Bodleian, Carte MSS 231, f. 38: Thomas Carte's memorandum of 10 June 1724.

4 NSA, Cal. Br. 24, England 113 A, ff. 33–4: Kreyenberg to the elector, 10 March 1713 NS, London.

5 *Ibid.*, ff. 20–1: Kreyenberg to the elector, 3/14 February 1713. Dupplin was introduced to the queen on this occasion by Oxford: Macpherson, *Original Papers*, II, 479: Robethon to Gatke, 21 March 1713.

6 NSA, Cal. Br. 24, England 107 A, ff. 370–1: Kreyenberg to the elector, 2/13 December 1713; cf. Macpherson, *Original Papers*, II, 516: Marlborough to Robethon, 30 November 1713 NS, Antwerp. Lowndes did not deny this when accused of it by Walpole in the House of Commons: Cobbett, *Parliamentary History*, VI, 1270–1.

7 BM, Stowe 225, ff. 252–3: Schütz to Robethon, 3 November 1713 NS.

8 NSA, Cal. Br. 24, England 113 A, ff. 199–200: Kreyenberg to the elector, 10 November 1713 NS; J. H. Overton, 'Hilkiah Bedford', *DNB*, II, 110.

9 BM, Stowe 227, ff. 31–2: Gatke to Robethon, 7/18 May 1714.

10 J. M. Rigg, 'George Harbin', *DNB*, VIII, 1200; Overton, *Non-Jurors*, 200–3; for Harbin's friendship with Lord Harley, see C. E. and R. C. Wright, *The Diary of Humfrey Wanley, 1715–1726* (London, 1966), *passim*.

11 See G. E. Gregg, 'The Protestant Succession in International Relations, 1710–1716' (unpublished London PhD thesis, 1972).

12 BM, Stowe 225, ff. 22–7: Robethon to de Grote, 27 January 1713, Hanover, mistranslated in Macpherson, *Original Papers*, II, 468.

13 BM, Stowe 255, ff. 159–65: L'Hermitage to Robethon, 25 July [1713 NS], London.

14 *Ibid.*, ff. 229–30, 219–20: Schütz to Robethon, 13, 6 October 1713 OS, quoting Halifax and Cadogan.

15 AAE, CP Angleterre 241, f. 113: Louis XIV to the queen, 26 April 1712 NS; f. 120: queen to Louis XIV, 1/12 May 1712.

16 *Hamilton Diary*, 42.

17 *Ibid.*, 44.

18 *Ibid.*, 44–5.

19 *Ibid.*, 50.

20 *Ibid.*, 51; Macpherson, *Original Papers*, II, 474: Robethon to de Grote, 28 February 1713 NS; NSA, Cal. Br. 24, England 113 A, ff. 28–9: Kreyenberg to the elector, 3 March 713 NS. For James's nomination of Polignac, see Frederick W. Head, *The Fallen Stuarts* (Cambridge, 1901), 151–2; Marquess de Ruvigny and Raineval, *The Jacobite Peerage, Baronetage, Knightage, and Grants of Honour* (Edinburgh, 1904), 227.

21 *Hamilton Diary*, 52.

22 BM, Stowe 225, ff. 259–60: Schütz to Robethon, 7 November 1713 [NS, London].

23 Gregg, 'Was Queen Anne a Jacobite?', 359–60.

24 *Hamilton Diary*, 42.

25 *Ibid.*, 48.

26 *Journal to Stella*, 653, 657: entries for 3, 7 April 1713.

27 Macpherson, *Original Papers*, II, 488–9: Kreyenberg to Robethon, 14 April 1713.

28 Trevelyan, *England under Queen Anne*, III, 260–3; Cobbett, *Parliamentary History*, VI, 1214–15.

29 Salomon, *Letzten Ministeriums*, 209; M&M, 3 F 209, f. 27: Forstner to Leopold, 10 June 1713 NS, London; 3 F 115, ff. 97–8: Le Beque to Leopold, 14, 16 June 1713, The Hague; BM, Stowe 225, ff. 140–1: L'Hermitage to Robethon, 9 June 1713 NS, London; Macpherson, *Original Papers*, II, 506: Schütz to Robethon, 3 October 1713 NS, London. Feiling, *Tory Party*, 449, and P. W. J. Riley, *The English*

Ministers and Scotland, 1707–1727 (London, 1964), 242, say 'the ministry' opposed the malt tax, but Oxford's role remains unclear.

30 *Hamilton Diary*, 55.

31 M&M, 3 F 209, f. 27: [Forstner to Leopold, draft], 10 June 1713 NS, London.

32 Klopp, *Der Fall des Hauses Stuart*, XIV, 472; Salomon, *Letzten Ministeriums*, 207–9; *Parliamentary History*, VI, 1216–20.

33 *Hamilton Diary*, 55.

34 Cobbett, *Parliamentary History*, VI, 1220–3; for the Anglo-French treaty, see D. A. E. Harkness, 'The Opposition of the 8th and 9th Articles of the Commercial Treaty of Utrecht', *Scottish Historical Review*, XXI (1923), 219–26; Hans Schorer, 'Der englisch-französische Handelsvertrag vom Jahre 1713', *Historisches Jahrbuch*, XXI (1900), 353–87, 715–42.

35 *Bolingbroke Correspondence*, II, 425: Bolingbroke to Strafford, 2 July 1713 NS; Macpherson, *Original Papers*, II, 420–1, for Lansdowne's recollections; Paul Baratier, *Lord Bolingbroke, ses écrits politiques* (Lyon, 1939), 87.

36 HMC *Bath*, I, 235: queen to Oxford, Sunday morning [5 July 1713]; NSA, Cal. Br. 24, England 113 A, ff. 156–7, 160–1: Kreyenberg to the elector, 11, 14 July 1713 NS, London; NSA, Hannover 92, III A, No. 12 III, ff. 41–2: Robethon to Bothmer [July 1713]; M&M, 3 F 115, f. 108: Le Beque to Leopold, 18 July 1713, The Hague.

37 Bolingbroke's orders to Prior were only issued on 6/17 November 1713 (SP 104/27), although Bromley's orders for a similar application to the States of Brabant had been issued three weeks earlier: SP 104/14, ff. 8v–9: Bromley to John Laws, 19/30 October 1713; cf. M&M, F 118 bis, f. 14: Baron de Langen to Leopold, 24 April 1714, The Hague; NSA, Cal. Br. 24, England 113 A, ff. 208–9: Bothmer to the elector, 11 November 1713, The Hague; BM, Stowe 225, f. 273: [Schütz to Robethon] 21 November 1713 NS, London.

38 L. G. Wickham Legg, 'Extracts from Jacobite Correspondence, 1712–1714', *EHR*, XXX (1915), 506: Gaultier to Torcy, 14 December 1713 NS; cf. AAE, CP Lorraine 87, ff. 224–7: d'Audiffret to Louis XIV, 30 November 1713, Nancy; f. 252: Louis XIV to d'Audiffret, 28 December 1713.

39 BM, Loan 29/10/33: Oxford's memorandum of his conversation with the queen, 11 May 1713, St James's.

40 Macpherson, *Original Papers*, II, 552: Schütz to Robethon, 9 February 1714 NS, London; p. 585: Schütz to Bothmer, 6 April 1714 NS; Klopp, *Der Fall des Hauses Stuart*, XIV, 522: Hoffmann's report of 12/23 February 1714; BM, Stowe 226, ff. 266–7, 391–3: Schütz to Robethon, 9/20 March, 9/20 April 1714.

41 Legg, 'Jacobite Correspondence', 506: Gaultier to Torcy, 14 December 1713 NS; cf. Salomon, *Letzten Ministeriums*, 242, n. 3

42 H. W. Wolff, 'The Pretender at Bar-le-Duc', *Blackwood's Magazine*, CLVI (1894), 237; AAE, CP Angleterre 251, ff. 87–8: d'Iberville to Torcy, 23 January 1714 NS, London; 261, ff. 19–21: James to Gaultier, 1 January 1714; cf. NSA, Hannover 92, LXVI, 1B, ff. 31–5: Thomas Wilson to Sophia, 5 April 1714, Paris, printed in *Hanmer Correspondence*, 165–8.

43 SP 104/27: Dartmouth to d'Aumont, 3 July 1713, Whitehall.

44 *Hamilton Diary*, 56.

45 HMC *Bath*, I, 235: queen to Oxford, Sunday morning [5 July 1713].

46 Plumb, *Political Stability*, 192–4.

47 Holmes, *British Politics*, 279; H. N. Fieldhouse, 'Bolingbroke's Share in the Jacobite Intrigue of 1710–1714', *EHR*, LII (1937), 458: d'Iberville to Torcy, 6 March 1714 NS, London.

48 Holmes, *British Politics*, 283.

49 Macpherson, *Original Papers*, II, 558–61: Polwarth to Robethon, 9 February 1714 NS; cf. BM, Stowe 226, ff. 310–12: Schütz to Robethon, 23 February 1714 NS, London.

50 [Daniel Defoe,] *The Secret History of the White-Staff* (London, 1714), II, 15.

51 Plumb, *Political Stability*, 194: a contemporary 1715 list gives Scotland 15 Tory members and 31 Whigs; cf. Macpherson, *Original Papers*, II, 510: Schütz to Robethon, 30 October 1713 NS, estimates that there were 34 or 35 Whigs; Riley, *English Ministers and Scotland*, 251, estimates that court and Tory representation totalled 15, while the opposition had 23 members and the remainder were 'floating'.

52 BM, Stowe 225, ff. 217–18: Schütz to Robethon, 6/17 October 1713, London; cf. ff. 317–20. L'Hermitage to Hop, 12 December 1713 NS, London.

53 *Wentworth Papers*, 274: Lady Strafford to Strafford, [5 March] 1712.

54 Sarah Churchill, *Conduct*, quoted by Green, *Sarah*, 117.

55 *Hamilton Diary*, 65.

56 HMC *Bath*, I, 223: queen to Oxford, 27 November [1712], Windsor.

57 Burnet, *History of His Own Time*, VI, 176; Sykes, 'Queen Anne and the Episcopate', 454–6.

58 Burnet, *History of His Own Time*, VI, 176, Dartmouth's note.

59 *Hamilton Diary*, 57.

60 Hamilton, *Backstairs Dragon*, 240–1; McInnes, *Harley*, 149.

61 HMC *Portland*, V, 466–7: Oxford's 'Account', 15 June 1714; AAE, CP Angleterre 248, ff. 68–73, 88–93: d'Aumont to Louis XIV, 29, 30 July, 7 August 1713 NS, London.

62 HMC *Portland*, V, 467: Oxford's 'Account', 15 June 1714.

63 BM, Add. MSS 40,621, f. 175: Oxford to Thomas Harley, 1/12 March 1714.

64 *Swift Correspondence*, II, 85: Oxford to Swift, 27 July 1714.

65 BM, Loan 29/151: Arthur Moore to Oxford, 25 August 1713.

66 PRO 31/3/201, f. 87: d'Aumont to Louis XIV, 13 September 1713 NS, London.

67 HMC *Bath*, I, 214: queen to Oxford, 26 October [1711].

68 David Nichol Smith, ed., *The Letters of Thomas Burnet to George Duckett, 1712–1722* (Oxford, Roxburghe Club, 1914), 5: Burnet to Duckett, 8 April 1712 [London].

69 *Hamilton Diary*, 56.

70 PRO, SP 34/11, pt 1, f. 1: draft of letters patent from the queen to Sieur de Plessen, 13 July 1709.

71 NSA, Hannover 92, III A, No. 12, III, ff. 76–9: Robethon to Bothmer [end of August 1713].

72 Macpherson, *Original Papers*, II, 589–90: Schütz to Robethon, 6/17 April 1714, London, corrected from the original, BM, Stowe 226, ff. 389–90.

73 *Wentworth Papers*, 349: Peter Wentworth to Lord Strafford, 17 August 1713.

74 BM, Stowe 225, ff. 229–30: Schütz to Robethon, 13/24 October 1713 [London],

quoting von Plessen.

75 HMC *Bath*, I, 237: queen to Oxford, 21 August 1713, Windsor.

76 BM, Loan 29/70: Oxford to Auditor Harley, 13 August 1713.

77 *Hamilton Diary*, 64: entry for 23 July 1714.

78 AAE, CP Angleterre 247, ff. 34–6: Gaultier to Torcy, 18 October 1713 NS, London.

79 *Ibid.*, ff. 167–8: Gaultier to Torcy, 22 December 1713 NS, London.

80 BM, Stowe 225, ff. 321–2, 355–7: Schütz to Robethon, 4, 18 December 1713 NS, London.

81 HMC *Bath*, I, 243: queen to Oxford, 8 December 1713, Windsor.

82 BM, Stowe 225, ff. 169–70: L'Hermitage to Robethon, 11 August 1713 NS; ff. 200–1: Schütz to Bothmer, 18/29 September 1713, London.

83 Holmes, *British Politics*, 193–4.

84 Wolfgang Michael, *Englische Geschichte in achtzehnten Jahrhundert*, I (Hamburg, 1896), 313: Schütz to the elector, 1/12 December 1713, London.

85 BM, Stowe 225, ff. 350–1: Schütz to Robethon, 15/26 December 1713, London.

86 Tindall, *Continuation*, XXV, 99–100: Dr Shadwell's account.

87 BM, Stowe 226, ff. 1–2: Schütz to Robethon, 1/12 January 1714, London.

88 BM, Sloane 4,934, ff. 46–50: Dr Hans Sloane's account of the queen's illness, December 1713 – January 1714.

89 Macpherson, *Original Papers*, II, 569: Strafford to Sophia, 23 February 1714, The Hague; PRO 31/3/202, ff. 31–6: d'Iberville to Louis XIV, 15 January 1714 NS; Trevelyan, *England under Queen Anne*, III, 285; John Kemble, *State Papers and Correspondence Illustrative of the Social and Political State of Europe, from the Revolution to the Accession of the House of Hanover* (London, 1857), 486–7: Steingens to Schulenburg, 16/27 March 1714, London.

90 NSA, Hannover 92, III A, No. 13, ff. 161–2: [Sunderland to Marlborough] 31 December 1713, London; M&M, 3 F 115, ff. 185–6: Le Beque to Leopold, 19 January 1714, The Hague; BM, Stowe 225, ff. 382–3, 384: Schütz to Robethon, 25 December 1713 OS, London; ff. 385–6: Kreyenberg to Bothmer, same date.

91 Strickland, *Lives of the Queens of England*,

VI, 397: Oxford to Dr Arbuthnot [25 December 1713].

92 BM, Stowe 226, ff. 9–10: Ormonde to Sophia, 5 January 1714; cf. NSA, Cal. Br. 24, England 113 A, ff. 240–1: Kreyenberg to the elector, 12/23 January 1714.

93 *Bolingbroke Correspondence*, IV, 455–6: Bolingbroke to the queen, 11 February 1714.

94 AAE, CP Angleterre 261, ff. 160–5: Gaultier to James, 6 February 1714 NS; 253, ff. 268–9: Gaultier to Torcy, 5 February 1714 NS; 261, ff. 14–16: 'Projet de Manifeste du Chevalier de St. Georges', sent with 253, ff. 268–9.

95 One sentence of the manifesto is written in Oxford's hand on a page of notes in English which Gaultier made regarding the 'Projet de Manifeste' (n. 94 above): University of Pennsylvania Library, MSS Fr. 139, f. 196. A French translation of this in Lansdowne's hand confirms his recollection, printed in Macpherson, *Original Papers*, II, 529.

96 AAE, CP Angleterre 261, ff. 270–81: d'Iberville to Louis XIV, 6 March 1714 NS; cf. Fieldhouse, 'Bolingbroke's Share', 457: d'Iberville to Torcy, 18 February 1714 NS, quoting Bolingbroke.

97 See Derek McKay, 'Bolingbroke, Oxford, and the defence of the Utrecht Settlement in Southern Europe', *EHR*, LXXXVI (1971), 264–84.

98 AAE, CP Angleterre 251, f. 126: d'Iberville to Torcy, 18 February 1714 NS, quoting Bolingbroke.

99 H. N. Fieldhouse, 'Oxford, Bolingbroke, and the Pretender's Place of Residence, 1711–1714', *EHR*, LII (1937), 293: James to Torcy, 3 March 1714 NS; cf. HMC *Stuart*, I, 299–300, 310: Berwick to James, 21 February, 28 March 1714 NS.

100 Gregg, 'The Protestant Succession in International Relations, 1710–1716', 114–15.

101 Salomon, *Letzten Ministeriums*, 335–6: James to Torcy [misaddressed 'Gaultier'], 26 February 1714 NS; Legg, 'Jacobite Correspondence', 514.

102 Salomon, *Letzten Ministeriums*, 353: James to Gualterio, 23 April 1714.

103 AAE, CP Angleterre 261, ff. 311–12: James to Gaultier, 2/13 March 1714; an English translation is printed in Macpherson, *Original Papers*, II, 525–6.

104 See Charles Leslie, *A Letter from Mr.*

Leslie to a Member of Parliament in London, dated 23 April 1714.

105 AAE, CP Angleterre 262, ff. 325–8: James to Torcy, 27 July 1714 NS.

106 Klopp, *Der Fall des Hauses Stuart*, XIV, 521: Hoffmann's report of 6 February 1714 NS; Bolingbroke to Arthur Moore, 6 February 1714 NS.

107 Boyer, *Queen Anne*, 660.

108 HMC *Portland*, V, 380–1: Abigail Masham to Oxford, Saturday 8 o'clock [23 January 1714].

109 BM, Stowe 226, ff. 127–9: Schütz to [Bothmer], 9/20 February 1714, London.

110 BM, Stowe 226, ff. 60–1: Schütz to [Robethon], 26 January/6 February 1714, London, quoting von Plessen.

111 BM, Add. MSS 40,621, ff. 175–80: Oxford to Thomas Harley, 1/12 March 1714.

112 Macpherson, *Original Papers*, II, 563: Schütz to Robethon, 16/27 February 1714.

113 *Ibid.*, 575: Schütz to Bothmer, 1/12 March 1714.

114 BM, Stowe 226, ff. 175–7: Schütz to Bothmer, 16/27 February 1714; ff. 266, 281: Schütz to Robethon [early March], 12/23 March 1714.

115 AAE, CP Angleterre 254, ff. 145–51: d'Iberville to Torcy, 8 March 1714 NS, London.

116 PRO 31/3/202, ff. 49–52: d'Iberville to Louis XIV, 31 March 1714 NS.

117 Sykes, 'Queen Anne and the Episcopate', 457–9; Sharp, *Life of John Sharp*, I, 332–3; AAE, CP Angleterre, 255, ff. 49–52, 109–12: d'Iberville to Torcy, 14, 22 April 1714 NS, London; NSA, Cal. Br. 24, England 113 A, ff. 35–6: Kreyenberg to the elector, 3/14 March 1714.

118 PRO 31/3/202, ff. 45–6: d'Iberville to Louis XIV, 15, 16 March 1714 NS.

119 Tindall, *Continuation*, XXV, 116.

120 BM, Stowe 226, ff. 279–80: Schütz to Robethon, 12/23 March 1714; ff. 297–8: Schütz to [Bothmer], 16/27 March 1714; *Wentworth Papers*, 360: Peter Wentworth to Strafford, 12 March 1714.

121 NSA, Cal. Br. 24, England 113 A, ff. 285–8: Kreyenberg to the elector, 3 April 1714 NS.

122 BM, Stowe 226, ff. 358–9: Schütz to Robethon, 30 March/10 April 1714.

123 BM, Add. MSS 40,621, ff. 175–80:

Oxford to Thomas Harley, 31 March/11 April 1714.

124 BM, Add. MSS 31,256, ff. 80–2: Perth to Gualterio, 14 May 1714 NS; 46,495, ff. 113–14: James Dempster to Gualterio, 17 June 1714 NS; AAE, CP Angleterre 255, ff. 59–62: d'Iberville to Torcy, 14 April 1714 NS.

125 BM, Stowe 226, ff. 364–5: Kreyenberg to [Bothmer], 10 April 1714 NS, London.

126 Macpherson, *Original papers*, II, 585: Schütz to [Bothmer], 26 March/6 April 1714, London.

127 BM, Stowe 225, ff. 390–2: Bothmer to Robethon, 6 January 1714, The Hague; cf. AAE, CP Angleterre 256, ff. 45–7: d'Iberville to Torcy, 19 May 1714 NS.

128 *Swift Correspondence*, II, 34: Dr Arbuthnot to Swift, 12 June 1714, St James's.

129 BM, Loan 29/12/1: Oxford to Lady Masham [undated draft].

130 Holmes, *British Politics*, 216.

131 AAE, CP Angleterre 255, ff. 59–62: d'Iberville to Torcy, 14 April 1714 NS.

132 BM, Add. MSS 40,621, ff. 175–80: Oxford to Thomas Harley, 31 March/11 April 1714.

133 Macpherson, *Original Papers*, II, 588: Kreyenberg to Bothmer, 2/13 April 1714.

134 HMC *Portland*, V, 417: Oxford to Thomas Harley, 13/24 April 1714.

135 AAE, CP Angleterre 256, ff. 56–7: Gaultier to Torcy, 21 May 1714.

136 AAE, CP Angleterre 255, ff. 90–2: d'Iberville to Torcy, 19 April 1714 NS.

137 AAE, CP Angleterre 261, ff. 126–7: Gaultier to Torcy, 31 January 1714 NS, quoting Oxford.

138 BM, Stowe 226, ff. 387–8: Schütz to Robethon, 6/17 April 1714; PRO 31/3/202, ff. 60–2: d'Iberville to Louis XIV, 17 April 1714 NS.

139 Klopp, *Der Fall des Hauses Stuart*, XIV, 557: Hoffmann's report of 5/16 April 1714.

140 *Journal, House of Lords*, XIX, 647–8; HMC *House of Lords*, X (new series), 274; Boyer, *Queen Anne*, 684.

141 PRO 31/3/202, ff. 60–2: d'Iberville to Louis XIV, 17 April 1714 NS; BM, Stowe 226, f. 394: Schütz to Robethon, 9/20 April 1714.

142 Cobbett, *Parliamentary History*, VI,

1338; PRO 31/3/202, ff. 63–6: d'Iberville to Louis XIV, 22 April 1714 NS; HMC *House of Lords*, X (new series), 276; NSA, Cal. Br. 24, England 113 A, ff. 289–90: Kreyenberg to the elector, 9/20 April 1714; Klopp, *Der Fall des Hauses Stuart*, XIV, 558: Hoffmann's report of 9/20 April 1714.

143 *The Harcourt Papers*, ed. Edward William Harcourt (Oxford, 1832), II, 51.

144 Tindall, *Continuation*, XXV, 158; Klopp, *Der Fall des Hauses Stuart*, XIV, 559: Hoffmann's report of 9/20 April 1714; Macpherson, *Original Papers*, II, 590: Schütz to Robethon, 20 April 1714 NS.

145 Macpherson, *Original Papers*, II, 590–1: Schütz to Robethon, 13/24 April 1714.

146 Salomon, *Letzten Ministeriums*, 284, n. 1; cf. Dickinson, *Bolingbroke*, 122.

147 Macpherson, *Original Papers*, II, 598–9: [Schütz to Robethon], 16/27 April 1714; HMC *Portland*, V, 417–19: Oxford to Thomas Harley, 13/24 April 1714; Kemble, *State Papers*, 493: Steingens to Schulenburg, 1/12 May 1714; p. 525: Roger Acherley to Leibniz, 12/23 October 1714, London; Michael, *Englische Geschichte*, I, 330: Bonet's report of 1 May 1714 NS.

148 NSA, Hannover 91, Schütz I, ff. 83–4: Schütz to Robethon, 16/27 April 1714.

149 Macpherson, *Original Papers*, II, 595: Schütz to Robethon, 15/26 April 1714.

150 Klopp, *Der Fall des Hauses Stuart*, XIV, 566–9.

151 Percy M. Thornton, 'The Hanover Papers', *EHR*, I (1886), 770: John Chamberlayne to Sophia, 27 April 1714, London; Macpherson, *Original Papers*, II, 612: Kreyenberg to Bothmer, 8 May 1714 NS; Kemble, *State Papers*, 500: Sarah to Comte de Bonneval, 21 May 1714, Antwerp: BM, Stowe 227, f. 9: L'Hermitage to Robethon, 11 May 1714 NS: 226, ff. 509–10: Gatke to Robethon, 11 May 1714 NS, London.

152 AAE, CP Angleterre 255, ff. 154–7, 191–3, 194–5, 203–4: d'Iberville to Torcy, 30 April, 4, 5, 7, 8 May 1714 NS; 256, ff. 14–17, 48–9: same, 17, 21 May 1714 NS; BM, Stowe 226, ff. 500–2: Kreyenberg to Bothmer, 8 May 1714 NS; ff. 509–10: Gatke to Robethon, 11 May 1714 NS; BM, Stowe 227, f. 9: L'Hermitage to Robethon, 11 May 1714; ff. 11–12, 31–2: Gatke to Robethon, 4, 7 May 1714 OS;

Macpherson, *Original Papers*, II, 613: Gatke to Robethon, 8 May 1714 NS.

153 AAE, CP Angleterre 255, ff. 179–81: d'Iberville to Torcy, 3 May 1714 NS; 256, ff. 14–17: same, 17 May 1714 NS.

154 *Ibid.*, 256, ff. 45–7: d'Iberville to Torcy, 19 May 1714 NS; ff. 56–7: Gaultier to Torcy, 21 May 1714 NS.

155 NSA, Hannover 93, 12 A, II–11, vol. 1, ff. 217–18: Kreyenberg to the elector, 18/29 May 1714; cf. Macpherson, *Original Papers*, II, 612: Kreyenberg to Bothmer, 8 May 1714 NS.

156 *Hannibal Not at the Gates*, quoted in Boyer, *Queen Anne*, 687–8; cf. [Bolingbroke,] *Considerations upon the Secret History of the White Staff* (London, 1714), 25.

157 NSA, Hannover 93, 12 A, II–11, vol. I, f. 317: Bothmer to Robethon, 10 July 1714 NS, London.

158 BM, Loan 29/10/8: Oxford's memorandum of his conversation with the queen, 8 June 1714.

159 BM, Loan 29/10/9: Oxford's memorandum, 'Wensday six evening May 5 1714 at York Buildings'; cf. AAE, CP Angleterre 256, ff. 56–7: Gaultier to Torcy, 21 May 1714 NS.

160 Macpherson, *Original Papers*, II, 620: Cadogan to Bothmer, 15 May 1714, London.

161 HMC *Portland*, V, 417–19: Oxford to Thomas Harley, 13/24 April 1714.

162 Klopp, *Der Fall des Hauses Stuart*, XIV, 553; Weber, *Der Friede*, 250–2; AAE, CP Angleterre 246, ff. 54–7: d'Aumont to Torcy, 21 July 1713 NS; 247, ff. 27–30: Gaultier to Torcy, 11 October 1713 NS; 250, ff. 38–9: Gaultier to Torcy, 28 October 1713 NS; 256, ff. 134–8: d'Iberville to Torcy, 7 June 1714 NS.

163 Johann Mathias von der Schulenburg, *Leben und Denkwürdigkeiten Johann Mathias, Reichsgrafen von der Schulenburg* (Leipzig, 1834), I, 533–4: elector to Schulenburg, 7 June 1714 NS.

164 *Hamilton Diary*, 61, entry for 27 May: 'Plimpton', from the context, can only refer to Robethon.

165 Macpherson, *Original Papers*, II, 608–10: Sophia and Georg Ludwig's Memorial, presented to Thomas Harley on 7 May 1714 NS.

166 *Marchmont Papers*, II, 404: Robethon to Polwarth, 8/19 June 1714.

167 Kemble, *State Papers*, 503: Princess

Caroline to Leibniz, 7 June 1714 NS; cf. R. L. Arkell, *Caroline of Ansbach* (Oxford, 1939), 53–4.

168 BM, Loan 29/10/9: Oxford's memorandum, 'Wensday six evening May 5 1714 at York Buildings'; Kreyenberg's name is written in Hebrew.

169 BM, Add. MSS 40,621, ff. 233–4: Stambken to Thomas Harley, 12 May 1714, Hanover.

170 M&M, 3 F 118 bis, f. 23: Baron von Langen to Leopold, 1 June 1714, The Hague; cf. NSA, Hannover 92, 12 A, II–11, vol. 1, ff. 220–1: Kreyenberg to the elector, 1 June 1714 NS.

171 NSA, Hannover 92, 12 A, II–11, vol. 1, ff. 215–16, 220–1: Kreyenberg to the elector, 29 May, 1 June 1714 NS, London; BM, Add. MSS 40,621, f. 125: Thomas Harley to Bromley, 11 May 1714, Hanover.

172 NSA, Hannover 92, 12 A, II–11, vol. 1, ff. 215–16: Kreyenberg to the elector, 18/29 May 1714.

173 *Ibid.*, ff. 220–2: Kreyenberg to the elector, 1 June 1714 NS.

174 The letters are printed in Tindall, *Continuation*, XXV, 184–90, and Macpherson, *Original Papers*, II, 621.

175 BM, Loan 29/12/3: undated drafts, in Oxford's hand, of the queen's letters to Sophia, the elector, and the electoral prince of 19 May 1714, corrected in an unknown clerk's hand.

176 BM, Stowe 227, ff. 27–8: Kreyenberg to Robethon, 7/18 May 1714; cf. ff. 31–2, 40–1: Gatke to Robethon, 7/18, 11/22 May 1714.

177 *Hamilton Diary*, 61.

178 NSA, Hannover 92, 12 A, II–11, vol. 1, f. 265: printed English proclamation of 5 June 1714.

179 Klopp, *Correspondence de Leibniz*, III, 486: elector to the queen, 15 June 1714 NS; Ellis, *Original Letters*, 2nd series, IV (London, 1827), 278–81: elector to Oxford, 15 June 1714 NS.

180 John Kemble, 'Zur Geschichte der Succession des Hauses Hannover in England', *ZHVN* (1852), 125: Steingens to Schulenburg, 12 July [1714 NS], Bath; Kemble, *State Papers*, 115: Steingens to Schulenburg, 24 July 1714 NS, Bath.

181 For the abrupt change in Oxford's position, see BM, Stowe 227, f. 75:

Gatke to Robethon, 1 June 1714 NS; f. 113: Kreyenberg to Bothmer, 1/12 June 1714.

182 BM, Loan 29/151: Peterborough to Oxford, 5 March [1714], Turin.

183 AAE, CP Angleterre, ff. 45–7: d'Iberville to Torcy, 19 May, 4 June 1714 NS; *Hamilton Diary*, 61.

184 Derek McKay, 'Bolingbroke, Oxford', 274; AAE, CP Angleterre 247, ff. 27–30: Gaultier to Torcy, 11 October 1713 NS; 250, ff. 38–9: Gaultier to Torcy, 28 October 1713 NS; 261, ff. 73–4: same, 15 January 1714 NS; Supplement 5, ff. 96–7: same, 14 October 1713 NS. But see BM, Loan 29/155: General Charles Ross to Oxford, 14 [November] 1713, thanking Oxford for his help in Ross's nomination.

185 AAE, CP Angleterre 255, ff. 87–9, 177–8: d'Iberville to Torcy, 18 April, 3 May 1714 NS; ff. 76–7: Gaultier to Torcy, 16 April 1714.

186 AAE, CP Angleterre 256, ff. 134–8, 167–9: d'Iberville to Torcy, 7, 14 June 1714 NS; 262, ff. 197–9: same, 18 June 1714 NS.

187 Kemble, *State Papers*, 493: Steingens to Schulenburg, 1/12 May 1714, London.

188 BM, Stowe 227, f. 9: L'Hermitage to Robethon, 11 May 1714 NS; ff. 23–4: Gatke to Robethon, 7/18 May 1714; ff. 13–14: Kreyenberg to the elector, 4/15 May 1714.

189 HMC *Portland*, V, 446–50: Paget to Oxford, 22, 24, 25 May 1714.

190 AAE, CP Angleterre 256, ff. 164–5: Gaultier to Torcy, 11 June 1714 NS; AAE, CP Hollande 266, ff. 177–81: Chavigny to Torcy, 20 July 1714, The Hague.

191 *Hamilton Diary*, 61; BM, Stowe 227, ff. 117–20; Bothmer to Robethon, 16 June 1714, The Hague; cf. Macpherson, *Original Papers*, II, 625–6; AAE, CP Angleterre 266, ff. 147–9, 151–2: d'Iberville to Torcy, to Louis XIV, 10 June 1714 NS.

192 AAE, CP Angleterre 256, ff. 186–7: Gaultier to Torcy, 18 June 1714 NS. On 4 June, the queen called for £500 equipage and £5 per day for Clarendon's expenditure under the privy seal: *Cal. Treas. Books*, XXVIII, pt 2, 296; on 7 June, a money warrant was issued to Clarendon for £500 equipage

and £455 for one quarter of his ordinary salary.

193 SP 81/164, pt 2: queen's answer to the elector's Memorial [19/30 June 1714], cf. BM, Stowe 242, ff. 145–7.

194 Macpherson, *Original Papers*, II, 629: Bromley to Clarendon [instructions], 22 June 1714, Whitehall; cf. Thornton, 'The Hanover Papers', 71–3.

195 [Defoe,] *Secret History of the White-Staff*, I, 33.

196 AAE, CP Angleterre 256, ff. 193–5, 220–2: d'Iberville to Torcy, 21, 28 June 1714 NS; 257, ff. 25–6: same, 2 July 1714 NS; cf. E. S. Roscoe, *Robert Harley, Earl of Oxford, Prime Minister 1710–14* (London, 1902), 172.

197 AAE, CP Angleterre 257, ff. 76–8: Gaultier to Torcy, 9 July 1714 NS; ff. 91–5: d'Iberville to Torcy, 15 July 1714 NS.

198 BM, Loan 29/10/9: Oxford's memorandum of his conversation with the queen, 16 June 1714.

199 BM, Add. MSS 46,495, ff. 127–9: James Dempster to Cardinal Gualterio, 22 July 1714, St Germain.

200 Macpherson, *Original Papers*, II, 529–30: Lord Mar's recollections.

201 NSA, Cal. Br. 24, England 113 A, ff. 295–6, 297–8: Kreyenberg to the elector, 1, 3 July 1714 NS.

202 *Ibid.*, ff. 312–13: Kreyenberg to the elector, 10 July 1714 NS; AAE, CP Angleterre 262, ff. 242–5: d'Iberville to Torcy, 2 July 1714 NS.

203 BM, Loan 29/151, f. 152: Halifax to Oxford [23 June 1714].

204 AAE, CP Angleterre 256, ff. 29–30: Gaultier to Torcy, 2 July 1714 NS.

205 *Ibid.*, 257, ff. 42–4: Gaultier to Torcy, 6 July 1714 NS; cf. Macpherson, *Original Papers*, II, 530.

206 NSA, Cal. Br. 24, England 113 A, f. 326: Kreyenberg to the elector, 6/17 July 1714.

207 Gregg, 'Marlborough in Exile', 614.

208 Macpherson, *Original Papers*, II, 633–4, 636–7: Bothmer to Robethon, 9/20, 16/27 July 1714, London.

209 NSA, Cal. Br. 24, England 113 A, f. 320: Kreyenberg to the elector, 2/13 July 1714.

210 Macpherson, *Original Papers*, II, 635: Bothmer to Robethon, 13/24 July 1714; NSA, Hannover 93, 12 A, II–11, vol. 1,

ff. 370–5: Bothmer to the elector, 30 July/10 August 1714; cf. Macknight, *Bolingbroke*, 411. For Oxford's attempts to gain the Duchess of Somerset, see Holmes, *British Politics*, 216.

211 BM, Stowe 227, ff. 246–7: Bothmer to Robethon, 30 July/10 August 1714; AAE, CP Angleterre 256, ff. 244–5: newsletter, marked 'Journal extraordinaire' by d'Iberville, 26 July/6 August 1714.

212 AAE, CP Angleterre 262, ff. 186, 197–9: d'Iberville to Torcy, 13, 18 June 1714 NS; cf. H. N. Fieldhouse, 'Bolingbroke and the d'Iberville Correspondence, August 1714 – June 1715', *EHR*, LII (1937), 680; W. R. Ward, *Georgian Oxford: University Politics in the Eighteenth Century* (Oxford, 1958), 50.

213 Riley, *English Ministers and Scotland*, 255.

214 NSA, Cal. Br. 24, England 113 A, ff. 312–13: Kreyenberg to the elector, 10 July 1714 NS.

215 For Poulett and Dartmouth, see AAE, CP Angleterre 257, ff. 233–6: d'Iberville to Torcy, 5 August 1714 NS.

216 Ward, *Georgian Oxford*, 50.

217 AAE, CP Angleterre 254, ff. 37–9: d'Iberville to Torcy, 14 February 1714 NS; f. 79: newsletter, 11/22 February 1714; BM, Stowe 226, ff. 169–70: Schütz to Robethon, 16/27 February 1714.

218 *Bolingbroke Correspondence*, IV, 489–90: Bolingbroke to Shrewsbury, 9/20 March 1714.

219 AAE, CP Angleterre 256, ff. 220–2: d'Iberville to Torcy, 28 June 1714 NS; cf. Cobbett, *Parliamentary History*, VI, 1355.

220 *Swift Correspondence*, II, 51: Charles Ford to Swift, 6 July 1714, London.

221 Macpherson, *Original Papers*, II, 630: Gatke to Robethon, 18 June 1714 NS; cf. 634–5: Bothmer to Robethon, 9–20 July 1714, London.

222 *Swift Correspondence*, II, 69: Dr Arbuthnot to Swift, 17 July 1714.

223 AAE, CP Angleterre 257, ff. 119–22, 146–7: d'Iberville to Torcy, 19, 22 July 1714 NS.

224 *Ibid.*, ff. 244–5: newsletter, marked 'Journal extraordinaire' by d'Iberville,

225 NSA, Hannover 93, 12 A, II–11, vol. 1, ff. 370–5, 366–7: Bothmer to elector, 30 July/10 August 1714, London.

226 *Ibid.*, ff. 370–5 (see n. 225 above).

227 H. L. Snyder, 'The Last Days of Queen Anne: The Account of Sir John Evelyn Examined', *HLQ*, XXXIV (1971), 262–3; *Hamilton Diary*, 66.

228 Gregg, 'Marlborough in Exile', 615.

229 *Ibid.*, 616.

230 *Ibid.*, 612–14.

231 *Hamilton Diary*, 62–3.

232 Campbell, *Lives of the Lord Chancellors*, IV, 477–8: Bolingbroke to Harcourt, 19 July 1714.

233 Aitken, *The Life and Works of John Arbuthnot*, 74–5: Arbuthnot to Swift, 24 July 1714.

234 The remainder of this chapter, except for material specifically cited, is based on Henry Snyder's masterly study, 'The Last Days of Queen Anne: The Account of Sir John Evelyn Examined', 261–76.

235 *Hamilton Diary*, 67.

236 Gregg, 'Was Queen Anne a Jacobite?', 374; *Hamilton Diary*, 66.

237 *Swift Correspondence*, II, 86: Erasmus Lewis to Swift, 27 July 1714.

238 Gregg, 'Marlborough in Exile', 616.

239 Snyder, 'Last Days of Queen Anne', 266–7.

240 Gregg, 'Was Queen Anne a Jacobite?', 375; cf. Snyder, 'Last Days of Queen Anne', 269.

241 SP 104/217: Bromley to Clarendon, 31 July 1714.

242 *Wentworth Papers*, 407–8: Peter Wentworth to Strafford, 30 July 1714, London.

243 Klopp, *Correspondance de Leibniz*, III, 504–5: James Stanhope to Charles VI, 30 July 1714, London.

244 NSA, Hannover 93, 12 A, II–11, vol. 1, ff. 380–1: Privy Council of Great Britain to the elector, Saturday, 31 July 1714, Kensington.

245 *Swift Correspondence*, II, 121: Arbuthnot to Swift, 12 August 1714, London.

246 HMC *Portland*, VII, 198: Dr William Stratford to Edward, Lord Harley, 2 August 1714, Christ Church.

Epilogue

1 PRO, P.C. 112, no. 245: proceedings of the Privy Council, 1–17 August 1714.
2 Burnet, *History of His Own Time*, VI, 35, Dartmouth's note.
3 PRO, P.C. 112, no. 260: draft of the queen's will, unsigned, dating from 1710–1711.
4 HMC *11th Report*, pt IV, 132: Bishop Smallridge of Bristol to Townshend, 1 October 1715.
5 *Cal. Treas. Books*, XXIX (1714–15), 335: Treasury commissioners to George I, 11 January 1715.
6 Royal Archives, Windsor, R.A. 83,164.
7 HMC *11th Report*, pt IV, 221: orders in council, 5, 17 August 1714.
8 PRO, SP 35/1, ff. 70–80: extracts from the Chapter Books of the Heralds.
9 *Swift Correspondence*, II, 101: John Barber to Swift, 3 August 1714.
10 *Wentworth Papers*, 408: Peter Wentworth to Strafford, 3 August 1714, London.
11 *Ibid.*, 416: Peter Wentworth to Strafford, 20 August 1714.
12 *Verney Letters*, I, 297: Ralph Palmer to Ralph Verney, 17 July 1714; *Victoria County History of England, Buckinghamshire*, III (London, 1925), 96, 298.
13 Chevening MSS, 86(6): James Craggs the younger to Lord Stair, 17 July 1718, Whitehall.
14 'High Laver Church', *Essex Archaeological Society*, new series, XI (1911), 182.

Bibliography

Archival sources

Great Britain

The British Library, London: manuscripts in the British Museum (BM) collections, including the Sloane, Egerton, Stowe, and Additional Manuscripts (Add. MSS); also Loan 29 (Robert Harley Papers), Loan 57 (Bathurst Papers), and Loan 58 (Wentworth Papers).

Public Record Office, London: State Papers (Foreign) and PRO 30/24 (Shaftesbury Papers) and 31/3 (Baschet transcripts of French diplomatic reports).

Althorp, Northampton (Earl Spencer): papers of Sarah, Duchess of Marlborough, including many letters from Queen Anne.

Blenheim Palace, Woodstock (Duke of Marlborough): the papers of John and Sarah, Duke and Duchess of Marlborough, Sidney, Lord Godolphin, and Charles, Earl of Sunderland. Blenheim E 17, 18, and 19 contain most of the letters from Queen Anne to the duchess, and B II 32 contains those from the queen to the Duke and to Godolphin. These papers are at present in the British Library, London.

The Bodleian, Oxford: Carte MSS 180–1, 208–11, 238–56, 231, 237; Rawlinson MSS A. 285–6, C. 391–2, 983.

Chevening, Sevenoaks (HRH the Prince of Wales): the papers of General James Stanhope.

Hertfordshire Record Office, Hertford: the Panshanger MSS, containing the papers of the first Earl and Countess Cowper.

Hove Public Library: the Wolseley Papers, containing the privy purse accounts of Sarah, Duchess of Marlborough.

Longleat (Marquess of Bath): the Portland MSS, containing political correspondence of Robert Harley.

National Library of Wales: MSS 18091 D: privy purse accounts for 1705, and one letter from Queen Anne to the Duchess of Marlborough.

National Library of Scotland: the journal of Sir David Nairne.

Royal College of Surgeons, London: Hunter-Baillie Collection, containing the papers of Dr John Arbuthnot.

William Salt Library, Staffordshire Record Office, Stafford: the papers of William, second Earl of Dartmouth.

Windsor, the Royal Archives (HM the Queen): R.A. 83164, records of the master of the wardrobe.

The Continent

Algemeen Rijksarchiv, The Hague: political correspondence of Anthonie Heinsius.

Archives des Affaires Étrangères, Paris: Correspondance politique (CP) Angleterre, Hollande, Espagne, Lorraine.

Archives de Meurthe-et-Moselle, Nancy, Lorraine: correspondence of Leopold, Duke of Lorraine, and his envoys in England, 1713–15.

Niedersächsisches Staatsarchiv, Hanover: correspondence of Sophia, dowager Electress of Hanover, Georg Ludwig, Elector of Hanover, and their envoys in England, Holland, and France.

United States

Folger Library, Washington, DC: V.B. 267: Queen Anne to Godolphin, 1 May 1705.

New York Public Library, Montagu Collection, No. 11: Queen Anne to Godolphin, 5 June 1703.

Pierpont Morgan Library, New York: Rulers of England, Box 11: correspondence of James II, William and Mary, Queen Anne.

University of Kansas, Spencer Library: Spencer MSS 163: letterbook of Sir William Simpson.

University of Pennsylvania: French MSS 139: papers of Abbé François Gaultier.

Frequently cited printed works

Bathurst, Lt-Col. Benjamin, ed., *Letters of Two Queens* (London, 1924).

Baxter, Stephen, *William III* (London, 1966).

Bolingbroke Correspondence: Letters and Correspondence of Henry St. John, Viscount Bolingbroke, ed. Gilbert Parke, 4 vols (London, 1798).

Boyer, Abel, *The Life and Reign of Queen Anne* (London, 1735).

Brown, Beatrice Curtis, ed., *The Letters and Diplomatic Instructions of Queen Anne* (London, 1935, reprinted 1968).

Burnet, Gilbert, *History of His Own Time*, 6 vols (Oxford, 1833).

Churchill, Winston S., *Marlborough, His Life and Times*, 2 vols (London, 1948).

Clarendon Correspondence: The Correspondence of Henry Hyde, Earl of Clarendon, and of his brother, Laurence Hyde, Earl of Rochester, with the Diary of Lord Clarendon from 1687 to 1690, ed. S. W. Singer, 2 vols (London, 1828).

Coxe, William, *Memoirs of John, Duke of Marlborough*, 6 vols (London, 2nd edn, 1820).

Coxe, William, *Memoirs of the Life and Administration of Sir Robert Walpole*, 3 vols (London, 1798).

Dalrymple, Sir John, *Memoirs of Great Britain and Ireland from the Dissolution of the last Parliament of Charles II till the Capture of the French and Spanish Fleets at Vigo*, 3 vols (London, 1790).

Dickinson, H. T., *Bolingbroke* (London, 1970).

Feiling, Keith G., *History of the Tory Party, 1640–1714* (Oxford, 1924).

Green, David, *Sarah, Duchess of Marlborough* (London, 1967).

Grovestins, Baron Charles van, *Histoire des luttes et rivalités politiques entre les puissances maritimes et la France durant la seconde moitié du XVIIᵉ siècle*, 8 vols (Paris, 1851–4).

Haile, Martin, *Mary of Modena* (London, 1905).

Hamilton Diary: The Diary of Sir David Hamilton, 1709–1714, ed. Philip Roberts (Oxford, 1975).

Hatton Correspondence: Correspondence of the Family of Hatton, Being Chiefly Letters addressed to Christopher, First Viscount Hatton, 1601–1704, ed. E. M. Thompson, 2 vols (Camden Society, 1878).

Holmes, Geoffrey, *British Politics in the Age of Queen Anne* (London, 1967).

Horwitz, Henry, *Revolution Politicks: The Career of Daniel Finch, Second Earl of Nottingham, 1647–1730* (Cambridge, 1968).

Kemble, John, *State Papers and Correspondence Illustrative of the Social and Political State of Europe, from the Revolution to the Accession of the House of Hanover* (London, 1857).

Klopp, Onno, *Der Fall des Hauses Stuart und die Sukzession des Hauses Hannover in Gross-Britannien und Irland*, 14 vols (Vienna, 1875–88).

Legrelle, Arsène, *La Diplomatie française et la succession d'Espagne*, 6 vols (2nd edn, Braine-le-Comte, 1899).

Lever, Sir Tresham, *Godolphin, His Life and Times* (London, 1952).

McInnes, Angus, *Robert Harley, Puritan Politician* (London, 1970).

Macpherson, James, *Original Papers containing the Secret History of Great Britain, 1660–1714*, 2 vols (London, 1775).

Marchmont Papers: A Selection from the Papers of the Earls of Marchmont, 1685–1750, ed. G. H. Rose, 3 vols (London, 1831).

Morgan, William Thomas, *English Political Parties and Leaders in the Reign of Queen Anne, 1702–1710* (New Haven, Conn., 1920).

Private Correspondence: Private Correspondence of Sarah, Duchess of Marlborough, ed. Lord John Russell, 2 vols (London, 1838).

Ranke, Leopold von: *A History of England, Principally in the Seventeenth Century*, tr. G. W. Kitchin and others, 6 vols (Oxford, 1875).

Russell Letters: The Letters of Rachel, Lady Russell, ed. Lord John Russell, 2 vols (Campden Society, 1853).

Salomon, Felix, *Geschichte des letzten Ministeriums Königin Annas von England, 1710–1714, und der englischen Thronfolgefrage* (Gotha, 1894).

Sharp, Thomas, *The Life of John Sharp, D.D., Lord Archbishop of York*, ed. Thomas Newcome, 2 vols (London, 1825).

Shrewsbury Correspondence: Private and Original Correspondence of Charles Talbot, Duke of Shrewsbury, ed. William Coxe (London, 1821).

Snyder, Henry L., ed., *The Marlborough–Godolphin Correspondence,* 3 vols (Oxford, 1975).

Strickland, Agnes, *Lives of the Queens of England since the Norman Conquest* (London, 1852).

Swift, Jonathan, *The Journal to Stella,* ed. Herbert Davis (Oxford, 1948).

Swift Correspondence: The Correspondence of Jonathan Swift, ed. Harold Williams, vols I and II (Oxford, 1963).

Tindall, N., *Continuation of the History of England by Rapin de Thoyras,* vols XXIV and XXV (London, 1745–6).

Trevelyan, G. M., *England under Queen Anne,* 3 vols (London, 1930–4).

Turner, F. C., *James II* (London, 1948).

Vernon Correspondence: Letters Illustrative of the Reign of William III from 1696 to 1708 . . . by James Vernon, Secretary of State, ed. G. P. R. James, 3 vols (London, 1841).

Walcott, Robert, *English Politics in the Early Eighteenth Century* (Oxford, 1956).

Weber, Ottocar, *Der Friede von Utrecht* (Gotha, 1891).

Wentworth Papers: The Wentworth Papers, 1705–1739, selected from the Private and Family Correspondence of Thomas Wentworth, Lord Raby, created in 1711 Earl of Strafford, ed. J. J. Cartwright (London, 1883).

Index

INDEX

Anne, Queen of England – *Continued.*
  Marlborough and Godolphin, 170–1; defends
  Tories against Sarah's accusations of Jacobitism,
  173–5; journey to Bath (1703), 176; ambivalent
  towards second Occasional Conformity bill, 177;
  object of Tory wrath, 177–8; dismisses High Tory
  ministers, 178–81; the Hanoverian invitation,
  182–5; forced to sign Scots Act of Security (1704),
  185–6; joyful reception of Blenheim victory, 187–
  8, 194–5; continued disagreements with Sarah,
  188–9; struggle with Godolphin over office of
  lord chancellor, 189–90; 'the Tack', 191–2, 196–7;
  continued disagreements with Sarah, and first
  estrangement from, 193; against third
  Occasional Conformity bill, 194; elections of
  1705, 196–7; reluctance to dismiss Tories, 197,
  200–1; Whig campaign for office for Sunderland,
  199–200, 218–30; struggle over lord chancellor-
  ship, 202–6; election of speaker (1705), 207–8;
  proposed invitation to Sophia, 208–13; 'Church
  in Danger' vote, 214; welcomes victory at
  Ramillies, 215–16; opposes precipitate peace,
  216–17; opposes Sunderland's entry to Cabinet,
  218–30; concessions to Whigs (1706), 230;
  ignores Sarah, 231; estranged from Sarah and
  Godolphin, 233–4; growing importance of
  Abigail, 234–7; growing influence of Harley,
  237–8; bishoprics crisis, 238–53; Act of Union,
  239–40; angered by Sarah's accusations, 244–5;
  quarrels with Sarah over Abigail, 246–53;
  accepts Harley's 'moderate' scheme, 254–7;
  forced to dismiss Harley, 257–61; Jacobite
  invasion (1708), 261–3; resists Whig demands for
  more Cabinet offices, 263–6; demands
  Sunderland's resignation (1708), 267–8;
  increasing disillusionment with Marlborough,
  269–72; Sarah accuses of lesbianism, 272–8;
  death of Prince George, 279–83; gives in to Whig
  demands, 283–4; peace negotiations at The
  Hague (1709), 285–6, 287–9; Marlborough's
  request for captain-generalcy for life, 286–7, 293;
  battle of Malplaquet, 289; 1709 quarrels with
  Sarah, 290–5; the Sacheverell trial, 297–8, 305–7;
  crisis with Marlborough (1710), 300–5;
  appointment of Shrewsbury, 309–11; dismissal
  of Sunderland, 312–14; dismissal of Godolphin,
  315–21; struggles for 'moderation', 321–3;
  dissolution of Parliament and appointment of
  Tory ministry, 322–4; dismissal of Sarah, 324–9;
  preference for Duchess of Somerset over
  Abigail, 330–2; influence of Shrewsbury, 332–4;
  initial peace negotiations, 334–42; parliamentary
  opposition to peace, 342–7; creation of dozen
  peers, 347–50; dismissal of Marlborough, 348–9;
  the Somersets, 351–3; the Utrecht negotiations,
  353–62; the succession question, 363–6; the
  preservation of the Union, 367; growing disillusionment with Oxford, 348–9, 369–70; Cabinet
  crisis (1713), 370–4; Christmas (1713) illness,
  374–5; succession question (1714), 375–8;
  Cabinet crisis (1714), 379; electoral prince's writ,
  380–1; support for Oxford, 381–5; support for
  Bolingbroke, 385–7; Marlborough's return to
  England, 389–90; last days and death, 390–5; last
  will, 397; funeral, 397–8
  assessment of, as monarch, 136–8, 400–5
  bishops, appointment of, 146–6, 200
  character, 7, 11, 43, 68, 212
  children: Mary (1685–7), 38, 47, 51–2; Anne
    Sophia (1686–7), 46, 47, 51–2; William Henry
    (1689–1700), *see* Gloucester, Duke of; Mary (b.
    and d. 1690), 80; George (b. and d. 1692), 90
  class distinctions made by, 140, 146, 167, 231–2
  descriptions of, 5, 35, 182, 231–2, 347, 374
  education, 11–13
  Hanoverian succession, support for, 122–3, 149–
    50, 158, 209–13, 366, 372, 402, 381–2, 390–1
  health: eyes, 6–7; invalidism, due to 'gout', 182,
    343, 361, 368, 374, 379; invalidism, due to
    rheumatism, 106–7; miscarriages, 46–7, 52,
    55, 99, 100, 108, 116, 120; pregnancies, 36–7,
    51, 54–5, 69, 72, 84, 86, 95, 99–100, 107, 116,
    120, 170, pregnancies, hysterical, 55–6, 100–1,
    106; smallpox, 17–18, 47, 101
  Irish independence, opposition to, 130
  Jacobitism, enmity to, 83–4, 93, 96–7, 103, 107–
    8, 121–2, 149, 159, 364–6, 377, 402
  judiciary, head of, 144, 364
  peers, appointment of, 142–3, 348–50, 358–9
  political parties, hostility to, 134–5, 197
  popularity in country, 150
  prerogative, jealous defence of, 134–5, 143, 350
  recreations: gambling, 26, 27, 39, 68; hunting, 12,
    26–7, 343; racing, 12
  religion: devotion to Church of England, 15–16,
    20, 27, 42–3, 159, 164, 178–9, 386, 401; hostility
    to Roman Catholicism, 15–16, 22, 37, 42–3,
    374
  touching for 'King's evil', 148
  union with Scotland, support for, 26–7, 130–1,
    157, 184–5, 201–2, 214–15

Apsley, Sir Allen (1616–83), 8–9, 21
Apsley, Lady Frances, *see* Bathurst, Lady Frances
Arbuthnot, John (1667–1735), MD, 234, 247, 379,
  390, 394
Arbuthnot, Robert, Jacobite agent in Rouen, 234
Argyll, Archibald Campbell (1628–85), Marquess
  of (1663), 40
Argyll, John Campbell (1678–1743), second Duke
  of (1703), 201–2, 214, 299–300, 306, 369, 383, 393
Arlington, Henry Bennett (1618–85), first Earl of
  (1672), 9
Ascot race (1712), 13
Ashley Cooper, Anthony, *see* Shaftesbury, first
  Earl of
Asiento, 341, 361, 387
Assassination Plot (1696), 107–8, 150
Atholl, James Murray (1659–1724), first Duke of
  (1703), 36, 178
Atterbury, Dr Francis (1662–1732), Bishop of
  Rochester (1713), 239, 370
Aumont, Louis, duc d' (1667–1720), French
  ambassador to England (1712–13), 140, 368, 371
Aylesford, Heneage Finch (1647?–1719), first
  Baron Guernsey (1703) and first Earl of (1714),
  172, 306

481